ATLA BIBLIOGRAPHY SERIES
edited by Dr. Kenneth E. Rowe

An Index to
English Periodical Literature
on the Old Testament
and
Ancient Near Eastern Studies

Volume IV

Compiled and Edited by

William G. Hupper

ATLA Bibliography Series, No. 21

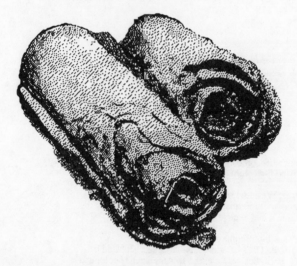

The disclosure of your words is illuminating,
it brings insight to the inexperienced.
... Psalm 119:130

The American Theological Library Association, and
The Scarecrow Press, Inc.
Metuchen, N.J., & London 1990

Illustration of the Copper Scrolls (3QTreasure) from Qumran *in situ*. Used by permission of the Department of Antiquities and Museums, Ministry of Education and Culture, State of Israel

British Library Cataloguing-in-Publication data available

Library of Congress Cataloging-in-Publication Data
(Revised for volume 4)

Hupper, William G
    An index to English periodical literature on the Old
Testament and ancient Near Eastern studies.

    (ATLA bibliography series no. 21)
    1. Bible. O.T.—Periodicals—Indexes. 2. Middle
East—Periodicals—Indexes. I. American Theological
Library Association. II. Title. III. Series.
Z 7772.A1H86 1987 [BS1171.2]   016.221   86-31448
ISBN 0-8108-1984-8 (v. 1)
ISBN 0-8108-2126-5 (v. 2)
ISBN 0-8108-2319-5 (v. 3)
ISBN 0-8108-2393-4 (v. 4)

Table of Contents

iii

Table of Contents

Table of Contents

v

Table of Contents

Table of Contents

Table of Contents

Table of Contents

Table of Contents

Table of Contents

Table of Contents

Table of Contents

xiii

Table of Contents

Table of Contents

Preface

Work on Volume IV has proceeded so well that it was finished only about a month after the publication of Volume III. It is with a great deal of enthusiasm that Volume IV is presented to students and scholars, since it contains the beginnings of Section 3, which is the heart of the material on Old Testament studies, and was the original purpose for producing this index. This volume is devoted entirely to articles on Textual and Literary Criticism and related studies.

The latter sections (§§278-416) in this volume are arranged according to the division of the Hebrew Scriptures (i.e., the Pentateuch, the Prophets, and the Hagiographa). The term "Literary Criticism" should be understood in the broadest sense,[1] since articles included in these sections are those which are not easily classified by chapter and verse. Some articles may actually be exegetical in nature. This format has been used as a matter of convenience, but it should not hinder the users. A later volume primarily on "Exegetical Studies" is in preparation, and most likely will become Volume VI or VII of this series. It will be organized as is the present volume according to the triad of the Hebrew Scriptures, and then subdivided by chapters and verses.

William G. Hupper
Melrose, MA
July 1990

---

1.   See Volume I, p. xxii for details of the editor's approach.

Periodical Abbreviations*

A

A&A	*Art and Archaeology; the arts throughout the ages* (Washington, DC, Baltimore, MD, 1914-1934)
A/R	*Action/Reaction* (San Anselmo, CA, 1967ff.)
A&S	*Antiquity and Survival* (The Hague, 1955-1962)
A(A)	*Anadolu (Anatolia)* (Ankara, 1956ff.) [Subtitle varies; Volume 1-7 as: *Anatolia: Revue Annuelle d'Archeologie*]
AA	*Acta Archaeologica* (Copenhagen, 1930ff.)
AAA	*Annals of Archaeology and Anthropology* (Liverpool, 1908-1948; Suspended, 1916-1920)
AAAS	*Annales archéologiques arabes Syriennes. Revue d'Archéologie et d'Histoire* (Damascus, 1951ff.) [Volumes 1-15 as: *Les Annales archéologiques de Syrie* - Title Varies]
AAASH	*Acta Antiqua Academiae Scientiarum Hungaricae* (Budapest, 1951ff.)
AAB	*Acta Archaeologica* (Budapest, 1951ff.)
AAI	*Anadolu Araştirmalari Istanbul Üniversitesi Edebiyat Fakültesi eski Önasya Dilleri ve Kültürleri Kürsüsü Tarafindan Čikarilir* (Istanbul, 1955ff.) [Supersedes: *Jahrbuch für Kleinasiatische Forschungen*]
AAOJ	*American Antiquarian and Oriental Journal* (Cleveland, Chicago 1878-1914)
AASCS	*Antichthon. The Australian Society for Classical Studies* (Sydney, 1967ff.)
ABBTS	*The Alumni Bulletin [of] Bangor Theological Seminary* (Bangor, ME; 1926ff.)
ABenR	*The American Benedictine Review* (St. Paul, 1950ff.)
ABR	*Australian Biblical Review* (Melbourne, 1951ff.)
Abr-N	*Abr-Nahrain, An Annual Published by the Department of Middle Eastern Studies, University of Melbourne* (Melbourne, 1959ff.)
ACM	*The American Church Monthly* (New York, 1917-1939) [Volumes 43-45 as: *The New American Church Monthly*]

*All the journals indexed are listed in the Periodical Abbreviations even though no specific citation may appear in the present volume. Although the titles of many foreign language journals have been listed, only English Language articles are included in this index (except as noted). Articles from Modern Hebrew Language Journals are referred to by their English summary page.

Periodical Abbreviations

ACQ   *American Church Quarterly* (New York, 1961ff.)
[Volume 7 on as: *Church Theological Review*]

ACQR   *The American Catholic Quarterly Review* (Philadelphia, 1876-1929)

ACR   *The Australasian Catholic Record* (Sydney, 1924ff.)

ACSR   *American Catholic Sociological Review* (Chicago, 1940ff.)
[From Volume 25 on as: *Sociological Analysis*]

ADAJ   *Annual of the Department of Antiquities of Jordan* (Amman, 1957ff.) [Volume 14 not published—destroyed by fire at the publishers]

AE   *Annales d'Ethiopie* (Paris, 1955ff.)

AEE   *Ancient Egypt and the East* (New York, London, Chicago, 1914-1935; Suspended, 1918-1919)

Aeg   *Aegyptus: Rivista Italiana di Egittologia e di Papirologia* (Milan,1920ff.)

AER   *American Ecclesiastical Review* (Philadelphia, New York, Cincinnati, Baltimore, 1889ff.) [Volumes 11-19 as: *Ecclesiastical Review*]

AfER   *African Ecclesiastical Review: A Quarterly for Priests in Africa* (Masaka, Uganda, 1959ff.)

Aff   *Affirmation* (Richmond, VA, 1966ff.) [Volume 1 runs from 1966 to 1980 inclusive]

AfO   *Archiv für Orientforschung; Internationale Zeitschrift für Wissenschaft vom Vorderen Orient* (Berlin, 1923ff.)

AfRW   *Archiv für Religionswissenschaft* (Leipzig, 1898-1941)

AHDO   *Archives d'histoire du droit oriental et Revue internationale des droits de l'antiquité* (Brussels, 1937-38, 1947-1951, N.S., 1952-53)

AIPHOS   *Annuaire de l'institut de philologie et d'histoire orientales et slaves* (Brussels, 1932ff.)

AJ   *The Antiquaries Journal. Being the Journal of the Society of Antiquaries of London* (London, 1921ff.)

AJA   *The American Journal of Archaeology* (Baltimore, 1885ff.) [Original Series, 1885-1896 shown with *O. S; Second Series* shown without notation]

AJBA   *The Australian Journal of Biblical Archaeology* (Sydney, 1968ff.) [Volume 1 runs from 1968 to 1971 inclusive]

AJP   *The American Journal of Philology* (Baltimore, 1880ff.)

AJRPE   *The American Journal of Religious Psychology and Education* (Worcester, MA, 1904-1911)

AJSL   *The American Journal of Semitic Languages and Literatures* (Chicago, 1884-1941) [Volumes 1-11 as: *Hebraica*]

AJT   *American Journal of Theology* (Chicago, 1897-1920)

AL   *Archivum Linguisticum: A Review of Comparative Philology and General Linguistics* (Glasgow, 1949-1962)

ALUOS	*The Annual of the Leeds University Oriental Society* (Leiden,1958ff.)
Amb	*The Ambassador* (Wartburg Theological Seminary, Dubuque, IA, 1952ff.)
AmHR	*American Historical Review* (New York, Lancaster, PA, 1895ff.)
AmSR	*American Sociological Review* (Washington, DC, 1936ff.)
Anat	*Anatolica: Annuaire International pour les Civilisations de l'Asie Anterieure* (Leiden, 1967ff.)
ANQ	*Newton Theological Institute Bulletin* (Newton, MA, 1906ff.) [Title varies as: *Andover-Newton Theological Bulletin; Andover-Newton Quarterly, New Series,* beginning 1960ff.]
Anthro	*Anthropos; ephemeris internationalis ethnologica et linguistica* (Salzburg, Vienna, 1906ff.)
Antiq	*Antiquity: A Quarterly Review of Archaeology* (Gloucester, England, 1927ff.)
Anton	*Antonianum. Periodicum Philosophico-Theologicum Trimestre* (Rome, 1926ff.)
AO	*Acta Orientalia ediderunt Societates Orientales Bœtava Donica, Norvegica* (Lugundi Batavorum, Havniæ, 1922ff.)
AOASH	*Acta Orientalia Academiae Scientiarum Hungaricae* (Budapest, 1950ff.)
AOL	*Annals of Oriental Literature* (London, 1820-21)
APST	*Aberdeen Philosophical Society, Transactions* (Aberdeen, Scotland, 1840-1931)
AQ	*Augustana Quarterly* (Rock Island, IL, 1922-1948)
AQW	*Anthropological Quarterly* (Washington, DC, 1928ff.) [Volumes1-25 as: *Primitive Man*]
AR	*The Andover Review* (Boston, 1884-1893)
Arch	*Archaeology* (Cambridge, MA, 1948ff.)
Archm	*Archaeometry. Bulletin of the Research Laboratory for Archaeology and the History of Art, Oxford University* (Oxford,1958ff.)
ARL	*The Archæological Review* (London, 1888-1890)
ArOr	*Archiv Orientální. Journal of the Czechoslovak Oriental Institute, Prague* (Vlašska, Czechoslovakia, 1929ff.)
AS	*Anatolian Studies: Journal of the British Institute of Archaeology at Ankara* (London, 1951ff.)
ASAE	*Annales du service des antiquités de l'Égypte* (Cairo, 1899ff.)
ASBFE	*Austin Seminary Bulletin. Faculty Edition* (Austin, TX; begins with volume 71*[sic]*, 1955ff.)

ASR	*Augustana Seminary Review* (Rock Island, IL, 1949-1967) [From volume 12 on as: *The Seminary Review*]
ASRB	*Advent Shield and Review* (Boston, 1844-45)
ASRec	*Auburn Seminary Record* (Auburn, NY, 1905-1932)
ASSF	*Acta Societatis Scientiarum Fennicae* (Helsinki, 1842-1926) [Suomen tideseura]
ASTI	*Annual of the Swedish Theological Institute (in Jerusalem)* (Jerusalem, 1962ff.)
ASW	*The Asbury Seminarian* (Wilmore, KY, 1946ff.)
AT	*Ancient Times: A Quarterly Review of Biblical Archaeology* (Melbourne, 1956-1961)
ATB	*Ashland Theological Bulletin* (Ashland, OH, 1968ff.)
ATG	*Advocate for the Testimony of God* (Richmond, VA, 1834-1839)
AThR	*The American Theological Review* (New York, 1859-1868) [*New Series* as: *American Presbyterian and Theological Review,* 1863-1868]
'Atiqot	*'Atiqot: Journal of the Israel Department of Antiquities* (Jerusalem, 1955ff.)
ATJ	*Africa Theological Journal* (Usa River, Tanzania, 1968ff.)
ATR	*Anglican Theological Review* (New York, Lancaster, Pa; 1918ff.)
AubSRev	*Auburn Seminary Review* (Auburn, NY, 1897-1904)
Aug	*Augustinianum* (Rome, 1961ff.)
AugQ	See *AQ*
AULLUÅ	*Acta Universitatis Lundensis. Lunds Universitets Årsskrift. Första Avdelningen. Teologi, Juridik och Humanistika Ämnen* (Lund, 1864-1904; *N. S.,* 1905-1964)
AUSS	*Andrews University Seminary Studies* (Berrien Springs, MI, 1963ff.)
AusTR	*The Australasian Theological Review* (Highgate, South Australia, 1930-1966)

B

B	*Biblica* (Rome, 1920ff.)
BA	*The Biblical Archaeologist* (New Haven; Cambridge, MA; 1938ff.)
Baby	*Babyloniaca Etudes de Philologie Assyro-Babylonienne* (Paris, 1906-1937)
BASOR	*Bulletin of the American Schools of Oriental Research* (So. Hadley, MA; Baltimore, New Haven, Philadelphia, Cambridge, MA; 1919ff.)

BASP	*Bulletin of the American Society of Papyrologists* (New Haven, 1963ff.)
BAVSS	*Beiträge zur Assyriologie und vergleichenden semitischen Sprachwissenschaft* (Leipzig, 1889-1927)
BBC	*Bulletin of the Bezan Club* (Oxford, 1925-1936)
BC	*Bellamire Commentary* (Oxon., England; 1956-1968)
BCQTR	*British Critic, Quarterly Theological Review and Ecclesiastical Record* (London, 1793-1843) [Superseded by: *English Review*]
BCTS	*Bulletin of the Crozer Theological Seminary* (Upland, PA, 1908-1934)
Bery	*Berytus. Archaeological Studies* (Copenhagen, 1934ff.)
BETS	*Bulletin of the Evangelical Theological Society* (Wheaton, IL, 1958ff.)
BFER	*British and Foreign Evangelical Review, and Quarterly Record of Christian Literature* (Edinburgh, London, 1852-1888)
BH	*Buried History. Quarterly Journal of the Australian Institute of Archaeology* (Melbourne, 1964-65; 1967ff.)
BibR	*Biblical Repertory* (Princeton, NJ; New York, 1825-1828)
BibT	*The Bible Today* (Collegeville, MN, 1962ff.)
BIES	*Bulletin of the Israel Exploration Society* (Jerusalem, 1937-1967) [*Yediot*-ידיעות ארץ־ישראל החברה ועאקותיה לחקירת-Begun as: *Bulletin of the Jewish Palestine Exploration Society* through volume 15. English summaries discontinued from volume 27 on as translations published in: *Israel Exploration Journal*]
BIFAO	*Bulletin de l'institut français d'archéologie orientale au Caire* (Cairo, 1901ff.)
BJ	*Biblical Journal* (Boston, 1842-1843)
BJRL	*Bulletin of the John Rylands Library* (Manchester, 1903ff.)
BM	*Bible Magazine* (New York, 1913-1915)
BMB	*Bulletin du Musée de Byrouth* (Paris, 1937ff.)
BN	*Bible Numerics: a Periodical Devoted to the Numerical Study of the Scriptures* (Grafton, MA; 1904)
BO	*Bibliotheca Orientalis* (Leiden, 1944ff.)
BofT	*Banner of Truth* (London, 1955ff.)
BOR	*The Babylonian and Oriental Record: A Monthly Magazine of the Antiquities of the East* (London, 1886-1901)
BQ	*Baptist Quarterly* (Philadelphia, 1867-1877)
BQL	*Baptist Quarterly* (London, 1922ff.)
BQR	*Baptist Quarterly Review* (Cincinnati, New York, Philadelphia, 1879-1892)
BQRL	*The British Quarterly Review* (London, 1845-1886)
BR	*Biblical Review* (New York, 1916-1932)

BRCM   *The Biblical Review and Congregational Magazine* (London, 1846-1850)

BRCR   *The Biblical Repository and Classical Review* (Andover, MA, 1831-1850) [Title varies as: *Biblical Repository; The Biblical Repository and Quarterly Observer; The American Biblical Repository*]

BRec   *Bible Record* (New York, 1903-1912) [Volume 1, #1-4 as: *Bible Teachers Training School, New York City,Bulletin*]

BRes   *Biblical Research: Papers of the Chicago Society of Biblical Research* (Amsterdam, Chicago, 1956ff.)

BS   *Bibliotheca Sacra* (New York, Andover, Oberlin, OH; St. Louis, Dallas, 1843, 1844ff.)

BSAJB   *British School of Archaeology in Jerusalem, Bulletin* (Jerusalem, 1922-1925)

BSOAS   *Bulletin of the School of Oriental and African Studies. University of London* (London, 1917ff.)

BSQ   *Bethel Seminary Quarterly* (St. Paul, MN; 1952ff.) [From Volume 13 on as: *Bethel Seminary Journal*]

BT   *Biblical Theology* (Belfast, 1950ff.)

BTF   *Bangalore Theological Forum* (Bangalore, India, 1967ff.)

BTPT   *Bijdragen Tijdschrift voor philosophie en theologie* (Maastricht,1938ff.) [Title varies as: *Bijdragen. Tijdschrift voor filosofie en theologie*]

BTr   *Bible Translator* (London, 1950ff.)

BUS   *Bucknell University Studies* (Lewisburg, PA; 1941ff.) [From Volume 5 on as: *Bucknell Review*]

BVp   *Biblical Viewpoint* (Greenville, SC, 1967ff.)

BW   *Biblical World* (Chicago, 1893-1920)

BWR   *Bible Witness and Review* (London, 1877-1881)

BWTS   *The Bulletin of the Western Theological Seminary* (Pittsburgh, 1908-1931)

BZ   *Biblische Zeitschrift* (Paderborn, 1903-1939; *New Series,* 1957ff.) [*N.S.* shown without notation]

C

C&C   *Cross and Crown. A Thomistic Quarterly of Spiritual Theology* (St. Louis, 1949ff.)

CAAMA   *Cahiers archéologiques fin de l' antiquité et moyen age* (Paris, 1961ff.)

CAAST   *Connecticut Academy of Arts and Sciences, Transactions* (New Haven, 1866ff.)

Carm   *Carmelus. Commentarii ab instituto carmelitano editi* (Rome, 1954ff.)

CBQ	*Catholic Biblical Quarterly* (Washington, DC; 1939ff.)
CC	*Cross Currents* (West Nyack, NY; 1950ff.)
CCARJ	*Central Conference of American Rabbis Journal* (New York,1953ff.)
CCBQ	*Central Conservative Baptist Quarterly* (Minneapolis, 1958ff.) [From volume 9, #2 on as: *Central Bible Quarterly*]
CCQ	*Crisis Christology Quarterly* (Dubuque, IA; 1943-1949) [Volume 6 as: *Trinitarian Theology*]
CD	*Christian Disciple* (Boston, 1813-1823) [Superseded by: *Christian Examiner*]
CdÉ	*Chronique d'Égypte* (Brussels, 1925ff.)
CE	*Christian Examiner* (Boston, New York, 1824-1869)
Cent	*Centaurus. International Magazine of the History of Science and Medicine* (Copenhagen, 1950ff.)
Center	*The Center* (Atlanta, 1960-1965)
CFL	*Christian Faith and Life* (Columbia, SC, 1897-1939) [Title varies: Original Series as: *The Bible Student and Religious Outlook,* volumes 1 & 2 as: *The Religious Outlook;* New Series as: *The Bible Student;* Third Series as: *The Bible Student and Teacher;* several volumes as: *Bible Champion*]
ChgoS	*Chicago Studies* (Mundelein, IL; 1962ff.)
CJ	*Conservative Judaism* (New York, 1945ff.)
CJL	*Canadian Journal of Linguistics* (Montreal, 1954ff.)
CJRT	*The Canadian Journal of Religious Thought* (Toronto, 1924-1932)
CJT	*Canadian Journal of Theology* (Toronto, 1955ff.)
ClR	*Clergy Review* (London, 1931ff.)
CM	*The Clergyman's Magazine* (London, 1875-1897)
CMR	*Canadian Methodist Review* (Toronto, 1889-1895) [Volumes 1-5 as: *Canadian Methodist Quarterly*]
CNI	*Christian News from Israel* (Jerusalem, 1949ff.)
CO	*Christian Opinion* (New York, 1943-1948)
Coll	*Colloquium. The Australian and New Zealand Theological Review* (Auckland, 1964ff.) [Volume 1 through Volume 2, #1 as: *The New Zealand Theological Review*]
CollBQ	*The College of the Bible Quarterly* (Lexington, KY, 1909-1965) [Break in sequence between 1927 and 1937, resumes in 1938 with volume 15 duplicated in number]
ColTM	*Columbus Theological Magazine* (Columbus, OH; 1881-1910)
CongL	*The Congregationalist* (London, 1872-1886)
CongML	*The Congregational Magazine* (London, 1818-1845)
CongQB	*The Congregational Quarterly* (Boston, 1859-1878)
CongQL	*The Congregational Quarterly* (London, 1923-1958)

CongR	*The Congregational Review* (Boston, Chicago, 1861-1871) [Volumes 1-6 as: *The Boston Review*]
CongRL	*The Congregational Review* (London, 1887-1891)
ConstrQ	*The Constructive Quarterly. A Journal of the Faith, Work, and Thought of Christendom* (New York, London, 1913-1922)
Cont	*Continuum* (St. Paul, 1963-1970)
ContextC	*Context (Journal of the Lutheran School of Theology at Chicago)* (Chicago, 1967-1968)
ContR	*Contemporary Review* (London, New York, 1866ff.)
CovQ	*The Covenant Quarterly* (Chicago, 1941ff.) [Volume 1, #1 as: *Covenant Minister's Quarterly*]
CQ	*Crozer Quarterly* (Chester, PA; 1924-1952)
CQR	*Church Quarterly Review* (London, 1875-1968)
CR	*The Church Review* (New Haven, 1848-1891) [Title varies; Volume 62 not published]
CraneR	*The Crane Review* (Medford, MA; 1958-1968)
CRB	*The Christian Review* (Boston, Rochester; 1836-1863)
CRDSB	*Colgate-Rochester Divinity School Bulletin* (Rochester, NY; 1928-1967)
Crit	*Criterion* (Chicago, 1962ff.)
CRP	*The Christian Review: A Quarterly Magazine* (Philadelphia, 1932-1941)
CS	*The Cumberland Seminarian* (McKenzie, TN; Memphis; 1953-1970)
CSQ	*Chicago Seminary Quarterly* (Chicago, 1901-1907)
CSQC	*The Culver-Stockton Quarterly* (Canton, MO; 1925-1931)
CSSH	*Comparative Studies in Society and History: An International Quarterly* (The Hague, 1958ff.)
CT	*Christian Thought* (New York, 1883-1894)
CTJ	*Calvin Theological Journal* (Grand Rapids, 1966ff.)
CTM	*Concordia Theological Monthly* (St. Louis, 1930ff.)
CTPR	*The Christian Teacher [and Chronicle]* (London, 1835-1838; N.S., 1838-1844 as: *A Theological and Literary Journal*) [Continues as: *The Prospective Review; A Quarterly Journal of Theology and Literature*]
CTSB	*Columbia Theological Seminary Bulletin* (Columbia, SC; Decatur, GA; 1907ff.) [Title varies]
CTSP	*Catholic Theological Society, Proceedings* (Washington, DC; Yonkers, NY; 1948ff.)
CTSQ	*Central Theological Seminary Quarterly* (Dayton, OH; 1923-1931)
CUB	*Catholic University Bulletin* (Washington, DC; 1895-1914) [Volumes 1-20 only]

D

DDSR	*Duke Divinity School Review* (Durham, NC; 1936ff.) [Volumes 1-20 as: *The Duke School of Religion Bulletin;* Volumes 21-29 as: *Duke Divinity School Bulletin*]
DG	*The Drew Gateway* (Madison, NJ; 1930ff.)
DI	*Diné Israel. An Annual of Jewish Law and Israeli Family Law* ישואל שנתון למשפ ט עברי ולדיני משפחה ביראלדיני (Jerusalem, 1969ff.)
DJT	*Dialogue: A Journal of Theology* (Minneapolis, 1962ff.)
DownsR	*Downside Review* (Bath, 1880ff.)
DQR	*Danville Quarterly Review* (Danville, KY; Cincinnati; 1861-1864)
DR	*Dublin Review* (London, 1836-1968) [Between 1961 and 1964 as: *Wiseman Review*]
DS	*Dominican Studies. A Quarterly Review of Theology and Philosophy* (Oxford, 1948-1954)
DSJ	*The Dubuque Seminary Journal* (Dubuque, IA; 1966-1967)
DSQ	*Dubuque Seminary Quarterly* (Dubuque, IA; 1947-1949) [Volume 3, #3 not published]
DTCW	*Dimension: Theology in Church and World* (Princeton, NJ; 1964-1969) [Volumes 1 & 2 as: *Dimension* ; New format beginning in 1966 with full title, beginning again with Volume 1]
DTQ	*Dickinson's Theological Quarterly* (London, 1875-1883) [Superseded by *John Lobb's Theological Quarterly*]
DUJ	*The Durham University Journal* (Durham, 1876ff.; *N.S.,* 1940ff.) [Volume 32 of *O.S.* = Volume 1 of *N.S.*]
DUM	*Dublin University Magazine* (Dublin, London, 1833-1880)
DunR	*The Dunwoodie Review* (Yonkers, NY; 1961ff.)

E

EgR	*Egyptian Religion* (New York, 1933-1936)
EI	*Eretz-Israel. Archaeological, Historical and Geographical Studies* (Jerusalem, 1951ff.) ארץ־ישראל מחקרים בידיעת הארץ ועתיקותיה [English Summaries from Volume 3 on]

EJS	*Archives européennes de Sociologie / European Journal of Sociology / Europäisches Archiv für Soziologie* (Paris, 1960ff.)
EN	*The Everlasting Nation* (London, 1889-1892)
EQ	*Evangelical Quarterly* (London, 1929ff.)
ER	*Evangelical Review* (Gettysburg, PA; 1849-1870) [From Volume 14 on as: *Evangelical Quarterly Review*]
ERCJ	*Edinburgh Review, or Critical Journal* (Edinburgh, London, 1802-1929)
ERG	*The Evangelical Repository: A Quarterly Magazine of Theological Literature* (Glasgow, 1854-1888)
ERL	*The English Review, or Quarterly Journal of Ecclesiastical and General Literature* (London, 1844-1853) [Continues *British Critic*]
ESS	*Ecumenical Study Series* (Indianapolis, 1955-1960)
ET	*The Expository Times* (Aberdeen, Edinburgh, 1889ff.)
ETL	*Ephemerides Theologicae Lovanienses* (Notre Dame, 1924ff.)
Eud	*Eudemus. An International Journal Devoted to the History of Mathematics and Astronomy* (Copenhagen, 1941)
Exp	*The Expositor* (London, 1875-1925)
Exped	*Expedition* (Philadelphia, 1958ff.) [Continues: *The University Museum Bulletin*]

F

F&T	*Faith and Thought* (London, 1958ff.) [Supersedes: *Journal of the Transactions of the Victoria Institute, or Philosophical Society of Great Britain*]
FBQ	*The Freewill Baptist Quarterly* (Providence, London, Dover, 1853-1869)
FDWL	*Friends of Dr. Williams's Library (Lectures)* (Cambridge, Oxford, 1948ff.)
FLB	*Fuller Library Bulletin* (Pasadena, CA; 1949ff.)
FO	*Folia Orientalia* (Kraków, 1960ff.)
Focus	*Focus. A Theological Journal* (Willowdale, Ontario, 1964-1968)
Folk	*Folk-Lore: A Quarterly Review of Myth, Tradition, Institution & Custom being The Transactions of the Folk-Lore Society And Incorporating the Archæological Review and the Folk-Lore Journal* (London, 1890ff.)
Found	*Foundations (A Baptist Journal of History and Theology)* (Rochester, NY; 1958ff.)
FUQ	*Free University Quarterly* (Amsterdam-Centrum, 1950-1965)

G

GBT	*Ghana Bulletin of Theology* (Legon, Ghana; 1957ff.)
GJ	*Grace Journal* (Winona Lake, IN; 1960ff.)
GOTR	*Greek Orthodox Theological Review* (Brookline, MA; 1954ff.)
GR	*Gordon Review* (Boston; Beverly Farms, MA; Wenham, MA; 1955ff.)
GRBS	*Greek, Roman and Byzantine Studies* (San Antonio; Cambridge, MA; University, MS; Durham, NC; 1958ff.) [Volume 1 as: *Greek and Byzantine Studies*]
Greg	*Gregorianum; Commentarii de re theologica et philosophica* (Rome, 1920ff.) [Volume 1 as: *Gregorianum; rivista trimestrale di studi teologici e filosofici*]
GUOST	*Glasgow University Oriental Society, Transactions* (Glasgow, 1901ff.)

H

H&T	*History and Theory: Studies in the Philosophy of History* (The Hague, 1960ff.)
HA	*Hebrew Abstracts* (New York, 1954ff.)
HDSB	*Harvard Divinity School Bulletin* (Cambridge, MA; 1935-1969)
Herm	*Hermathena; a Series of Papers on Literature, Science and Philosophy by Members of Trinity College, Dublin* (Dublin, 1873ff.) [Volumes 1-20; changes to issue number from #46 on]
HeyJ	*The Heythrop Journal* (New York, 1960ff.)
HJ	*Hibbert Journal* (London, Boston, 1902-1968)
HJAH	*Historia. Zeitschrift für alte Geschichte / Revue d'Histoire Ancienne / Journal of Ancient History / Rivista di Storia Antica* (Baden, 1950ff.)
HJud	*Historia Judaica. A Journal of Studies in Jewish History Especially in the Legal and Economic History of the Jews* (New York, 1938-1961)
HQ	*The Hartford Quarterly* (Hartford, CT; 1960-1968)
HR	*Homiletic Review* (New York, 1876-1934) [page numbers may vary greatly since more than one edition was produced!]
HRel	*History of Religions* (Chicago, 1961ff.)
HS	*Ha Sifrut. Quarterly for the Study of Literature* הספרוה רבעון למדע הספרות (Tel-Aviv, 1968ff.)

HSR	*Hartford Seminary Record* (Hartford, CT; 1890-1913)
HT	*History Today* (London, 1951ff.)
HTR	*Harvard Theological Review* (Cambridge, MA; 1908ff.)
HTS	*Hervormde Teologiese Studien* (Pretoria, 1943ff.)
HUCA	*Hebrew Union College Annual* (Cincinnati, 1904, 1924ff.)

I

IA	*Iranica Antiqua* (Leiden, 1961ff.)
IALR	*International Anthropological and Linguistic Review* (Miami, 1953-1957)
IAQR	*Asiatic Quarterly Review* (London, 1886-1966) [1st Series as: *Asiatic Quarterly Review,* (1886-1890); 2nd Series as: *The Imperial and Asiatic Quarterly and Oriental and Colonial Record,* (1891-1895); 3rd Series, (1896-1912); New Series, Volumes 1 & 2 as: *The Asiatic Quarterly Review* (1913); Volumes 3-48 (1914-1952) as: *Asiatic Review, New Series;* Volumes 49-59 (1953-1964) as: *Asian Review, New Series;* continued as: *Asian Review, Incorporating Art and Letters [and] the Asiatic Review, New Series,* Volumes 1-3 (1964-1966)]
ICHR	*Indian Church History Review* (Serampore, West Bengal, 1967ff.)
ICMM	*The Interpreter. A Church Monthly Magazine* (London, 1905-1924)
IEJ	*Israel Exploration Journal* (Jerusalem, 1950ff.)
IER	*Irish Ecclesiastical Record (A Monthly Journal under Episcopal Sanction)* (Dublin, 1864-1968)
IES	*Indian Ecclesiastical Studies* (Bangalore, India, 1962ff.)
IJA	*International Journal of Apocrypha* (London, 1905-1917) [Issues #1-7 as: *Deutero-Canonica,* pages unnumbered]
IJT	*Indian Journal of Theology* (Serampore, West Bengal, 1952ff.)
ILR	*Israel Law Review* (Jerusalem, 1966ff.)
Inter	*Interchange: Papers on Biblical and Current Questions* (Sydney, 1967ff.)
Interp	*Interpretation; a Journal of Bible and Theology* (Richmond, 1947ff.)
IPQ	*International Philosophical Quarterly* (New York, 1961ff.)
IR	*The Iliff Review* (Denver, 1944ff.)
Iran	*Iran: Journal of the British Institute of Persian Studies* (London, 1963ff.)
Iraq	*Iraq. British School of Archaeology in Iraq* (London, 1934ff.)

IRB   *International Reformed Bulletin* (London, 1958ff.)
IRM   *International Review of Missions* (Edinburgh, London, Geneva, 1912ff.)
Isis   *Isis. An International Review devoted to the History of Science and Civilization* (Brussels; Cambridge, MA; 1913ff.)
ITQ   *Irish Theological Quarterly* (Dublin, Maynooth, 1906ff.)

J

JAAR   *Journal of the American Academy of Religion* (Wolcott, NY; Somerville, NJ; Baltimore; Brattleboro, VT) [Volumes 1-4 as: *Journal of the National Association of Biblical Instructors;* Volumes 5-34 as: *Journal of Bible and Religion*]
JANES   *Journal of the Ancient Near Eastern Society of Columbia University* (New York, 1968ff.)
Janus   *Janus; Archives internationales pour l'Histoire de la Médecine et pour la Géographie Médicale* (Amsterdam; Haarlem; Leiden; 1896ff.)
JAOS   *Journal of the American Oriental Society* (Baltimore, New Haven, 1843ff.)
JAOSS   *Journal of the American Oriental Society, Supplements* (Baltimore, New Haven, 1935-1954)
JARCE   *Journal of the American Research Center in Egypt* (Gluckstadt, Germany; Cambridge, MA; 1962ff.)
JASA   *Journal of the American Scientific Affiliation* (Wheaton, IL, 1949ff.)
JBL   *Journal of Biblical Literature* (Middletown, CT; New Haven; Boston; Philadelphia; Missoula, MT; 1881ff.)
JC&S   *The Journal of Church and State* (Fresno, CA; 1965ff.)
JCE   *Journal of Christian Education* (Sydney, 1958ff.)
JCP   *Christian Philosophy Quarterly* (New York, 1881-1884) [From Volume 2 on as: *The Journal of Christian Philosophy*]
JCS   *Journal of Cuneiform Studies* (New Haven; Cambridge, MA;1947ff.)
JCSP   *Journal of Classical and Sacred Philology* (Cambridge, England, 1854-1857)
JEA   *Journal of Egyptian Archaeology* (London, 1914ff.)
JEBH   *Journal of Economic and Business History* (Cambridge, MA;1928-1932)
JEOL   *Jaarbericht van het Vooraziatisch-Egyptisch Gezelschap Ex Oriente Lux* (Leiden, 1933ff.)
JES   *Journal of Ethiopian Studies* (Addis Ababa, 1963ff.)

Periodical Abbreviations

JESHO	*Journal of the Economic and Social History of the Orient* (Leiden, 1958ff.)
JHI	*Journal of the History of Ideas. A Quarterly Devoted to Intellectual History* (Lancaster, PA; New York;1940ff.
JHS	*The Journal of Hebraic Studies* (New York; 1969ff.)
JIQ	*Jewish Institute Quarterly* (New York, 1924-1930)
JJLP	*Journal of Jewish Lore and Philosophy* (Cincinnati, 1919)
JJP	*Rocznik Papirologii Prawniczej-Journal of Juristic Papyrology* (New York, Warsaw, 1946ff.) [Suspended 1947 & 1959-60]
JJS	*Journal of Jewish Studies* (London, 1948ff.)
JKF	*Jahrbuch für Kleinasiatische Forschungen* (Heidelberg, 1950-1953) [Superseded by *Anadolu Araştirmalari Istanbul Üniversitesi Edebiyat Fakültesi eski Önasya Dilleri ve Kültürleri Kürsüsü Tarafindan Čikarilir*]
JLTQ	*John Lobb's Theological Quarterly* (London, 1884)
JMTSO	*Journal of the Methodist Theological School in Ohio* (Delaware, OH; 1962ff.)
JMUEOS	*Journal of the Manchester Egyptian and Oriental Society* (Manchester, 1911-1953) [Issue #1 as: *Journal of the Manchester Oriental Society*]
JNES	*Journal of Near Eastern Studies* (Chicago, 1942ff.)
JP	*The Journal of Philology* (Cambridge, England; 1868-1920)
JPOS	*Journal of the Palestine Oriental Society* (Jerusalem, 1920-1948) [Volume 20 consists of only one fascicle]
JQR	*Jewish Quarterly Review* (London, 1888-1908; *N.S.,* Philadelphia, 1908ff.) [Includes 75th Anniversary Volume as: *JQR, 75th*]
JR	*Journal of Religion* (Chicago, 1921ff.)
JRAI	*Journal of the Royal Anthropological Institute of Great Britain and Ireland* (London, 1872-1965) [Volumes 1-69 as: *Journal of the Anthropological Institute* Continued as: *Man, N.S.*]
JRAS	*Journal of the Royal Asiatic Society of Great Britain and Ireland* (London, 1827ff.) [*Transactions, 1827-1835* as *TRAS; Journal* from 1834 on: (Shown without volume numbers)]
JRelH	*Journal of Religious History* (Sydney, 1960ff.)
JRH	*Journal of Religion and Health* (Richmond, 1961ff.)
JRT	*Journal of Religious Thought* (Washington, DC; 1943ff.)
JSL	*Journal of Sacred Literature and Biblical Record* (London,1848-1868)
JSOR	*Journal of the Society of Oriental Research* (Chicago, 1917-1932)
JSP	*The Journal of Speculative Philosophy* (St. Louis, 1868-1893)

JSS   *Journal of Semitic Studies* (Manchester, 1956ff.)

JTALC   *Journal of Theology of the American Lutheran Conference*
           (Minneapolis, 1936-1943) [Volumes 1-5 as: *American
           Lutheran Conference Journal;* continued from volume
           8, #3 as: *Lutheran Outlook* (not included)]

JTC   *Journal for Theology and the Church* (New York, 1965ff.)

JTLC   *Journal of Theology: Church of the Lutheran Confession*
           (Eau Claire, WI; 1961ff.)

JTS   *Journal of Theological Studies* (Oxford, 1899-1949; *N.S.*,
           1950ff.)

JTVI   *Journal of the Transactions of the Victoria Institute, or
           Philosophical Society of Great Britain* (London,
           1866-1957) [Superseded by *Faith & Thought*]

Jud   *Judaism. A Quarterly Journal of Jewish Life and Thought*
           (New York, 1952ff.)

JWCI   *Journal of the Warburg and Courtauld Institutes*
           (London,1937ff.)

JWH   *Journal of World History-Cahiers d' Histoire Mondiale
           -Cuadernos de Historia Mundial* (Paris, 1953ff.)

K

Kêmi   *Kêmi. Revue de philologie et d' archéologie égyptiennes et
           coptes* (Paris, 1928ff.)

Klio   *Klio. Beiträge zur alten Geschichte* (Leipzig, 1901ff.)

Kobez   *Kobez (Qobeş);* קובץ החברה העברית לחקירת
           ארץ־ישראל ועתיקתיה (Jerusalem, 1921-1945)

KSJA   *Kedem; Studies in Jewish Archaeology* (Jerusalem,
           1942, 1945)

Kuml   *Kuml. Årbog for Jysk Arkæologisk Selskab* (Århus,
           1951ff.)

Kush   *Kush. Journal of the Sudan Antiquities Service*
           (Khartoum, Sudan, 1953-1968)

KZ   *Kirchliche Zeitschrift* (St. Louis; Waverly, IA; Chicago;
           Columbus; 1876-1943)

KZFE   *Kadmos. Zeitschrift für vor-und frühgriechische
           Epigraphik* (Berlin, 1962ff.)

L

L	*Levant (Journal of the British School of Archaeology in Jerusalem)* (London, 1969ff.)
Lang	*Language. Journal of the Linguistic Society of America* (Baltimore, 1925ff.)
LCQ	*Lutheran Church Quarterly* (Gettysburg, PA; 1928-1949)
LCR	*Lutheran Church Review* (Philadelphia, 1882-1927)
Lĕš	*Lĕšonénu. Quarterly for the Study of the Hebrew Language and Cognate Subjects* לשוננו (Jerusalem, 1925ff.) [English Summaries from volume 30 onward]
LIST	*Lown Institute. Studies and Texts* (Brandeis University. Lown School of Near Eastern and Judaic Studies. Cambridge, MA; 1963ff.)
Listen	*Listening* (Dubuque, IA; 1965ff.) [Volume numbers start with "zero"]
LofS	*Life of the Spirit* (London, 1946-1964)
LQ	*The Quarterly Review of the Evangelical Lutheran Church* (Gettysburg, PA; 1871-1927; revived in 1949ff.) [From 1878 on as: *The Lutheran Quarterly*]
LQHR	*London Quarterly and Holborn Review* (London, 1853-1968)
LS	*Louvain Studies* (Louvain, 1966ff.)
LSQ	*Lutheran Synod Quarterly* (Mankato, MN, 1960ff.) [Formerly *Clergy Bulletin* (Volume 1 of *LSQ* as *Clergy Bulletin,* Volume 20, #1 & #2)]
LTJ	*Lutheran Theological Journal* (North Adelaide, South Australia, 1967ff.)
LTP	*Laval Theologique et Philosophique* (Quebec, 1945ff.)
LTQ	*Lexington Theological Quarterly* (Lexington, KY; 1966ff.)
LTR	*Literary and Theological Review* (New York; Boston, 1834-1839)
LTSB	*Lutheran Theological Seminary Bulletin* (Gettysburg, PA; 1921ff.)
LTSR	*Luther Theological Seminary Review* (St. Paul, MN; 1962ff.)
LWR	*The Lutheran World Review* (Philadelphia, 1948-1950)

M

Man	*Man. A Monthly Record of Anthropological Science* (London,1901-1965; *N. S.*, 1966ff.) [Articles in original series referred to by *article* number not by *page* number - New Series subtitled: *The Journal of the Royal Anthropological Institute*]
ManSL	*Manuscripta* (St. Louis, 1957ff.)
MB	*Medelhavsmuseet Bulletin* (Stockholm, 1961ff.)
MC	*The Modern Churchman* (Ludlow, England; 1911ff.)
McQ	*McCormick Quarterly* (Chicago, 1947ff.) [Volumes 1-13 as: *McCormick Speaking*]
MCS	*Manchester Cuneiform Studies* (Manchester, 1951-1964)
MDIÄA	*Mitteilungen des deutsches Instituts für ägyptische Altertumskunde in Kairo* (Cairo, 1930ff.)
Mesop	*Mesopotamia* (Torino, Italy, 1966ff.)
MH	*The Modern Humanist* (Weston, MA; 1944-1962)
MHSB	*The Mission House Seminary Bulletin* (Plymouth, WI; 1954-1962)
MI	*Monthly Interpreter* (Edinburgh, 1884-1886)
MidS	*Midstream (Council on Christian Unity)* (Indianapolis, 1961ff.)
Min	*Ministry. A Quarterly Theological Review for South Africa* (Morija, Basutolan, 1960ff.)
Minos	*Minos. Investigaciones y Materiales Para el Estudio de los Textos Paleocretenses Publicados Bajo la Dirección de Antonio Tovar y Emilio Peruzzi* (Salamanca, 1951ff.) [From Volume 4 on as: *Minos Revista de Filología Egea*]
MIO	*Mitteilungen des Instituts für Orientforschung [Deutsche Akademie der Wissenschaften zu Berlin Institut für Orientforschung]* (Berlin, 1953ff.)
Miz	*Mizraim. Journal of Papyrology, Egyptology, History of Ancient Laws, and their Relations to the Civilizations of Bible Lands* (New York, 1933-1938)
MJ	*The Museum Journal. Pennsylvania University* (Philadelphia,1910-1935)
MMBR	*The Monthly Magazine and British Register* (London, 1796-1843) [*1st Ser.*, 1796-1826, Volumes 1-60; *N.S.*, 1826-1838, Volumes 1-26; *3rd Ser.*, 1839-1843, Volumes 1-9, however, Volumes 7-9 are marked 95-97*[sic]*]

ModR	*The Modern Review* (London, 1880-1884)
Monist	*The Monist. An International Quarterly Journal of General Philosophical Inquiry* (Chicago; La Salle, IL; 1891ff.)
Mosaic	*Mosaic* (Cambridge, MA; 1960ff.)
MQ	*The Minister's Quarterly* (New York, 1945-1966)
MQR	*Methodist Quarterly Review (South)* (Louisville, Nashville, 1847-1861; 1879-1886; 1886-1930) [*3rd Ser.* as: *Southern Methodist Review;* Volume 52 (1926) misnumbered as 53; Volume 53 (1927) misnumbered as 54; and the volume for 1928 is also marked as 54]
MR	*Methodist Review* (New York, 1818-1931) [Volume 100 not published]
MTSB	*Moravian Theological Seminary Bulletin* (Bethlehem, PA; 1959-1970) [Volume for 1969 apparently not published]
MTSQB	*Meadville Theological School Quarterly Bulletin* (Meadville, PA;1906-1933) [From Volume 25 on as: *Meadville Journal*]
Muséon	*Le Muséon. Revue d'Études Orientales* (Louvain, 1882-1915;1930/32ff.)
MUSJ	*Mélanges de l'Université Saint-Joseph. Faculté orientale* (Beirut, 1906ff.) [Title varies]
Mwa-M	*Milla wa-Milla. The Australian Bulletin of Comparative Religion* (Parkville, Victoria, 1961ff.)

N

NB	*Blackfriars. A Monthly Magazine* (Oxford, 1920ff.) [From Volume 46 on as: *New Blackfriars*]
NBR	*North British Review* (Edinburgh, 1844-1871)
NCB	*New College Bulletin* (Edinburgh, 1964ff.)
NEAJT	*Northeast Asia Journal of Theology* (Kyoto, Japan, 1968ff.)
NEST	*The Near East School of Theology Quarterly* (Beirut, 1952ff.)
Nexus	*Nexus* (Boston, 1957ff.)
NGTT	*Nederduitse gereformeerde teologiese tydskrif* (Kaapstad, N.G., Kerk-Uitgewers, 1959ff.)
NOGG	*Nihon Orient Gakkai geppo* (Tokyo, 1955-1959) [Being the *Bulletin of the Society for Near Eastern Studies in Japan*-Continued as: *Oriento*]
NOP	*New Orient* (Prague, 1960-1968)

NPR	*The New Princeton Review* (New York, 1886-1888)
NQR	*Nashotah Quarterly Review* (Nashotah, WI; 1960ff.)
NT	*Novum Testamentum* (Leiden, 1955ff.)
NTS	*New Testament Studies* (Cambridge, England; 1954ff.)
NTT	*Nederlandsch Theologisch Tijdschrift* (Wageningen, 1946ff.)
NTTO	*Norsk Teologisk Tidsskrift* (Oslo, 1900ff.)
Numen	*Numen; International Review for the History of Religions* (Leiden, 1954ff.)
NW	*The New World. A Quarterly Review of Religion, Ethics and Theology* (Boston, 1892-1900)
NYR	*The New York Review. A Journal of The Ancient Faith and Modern Thought (St. John's Seminary)* (New York, 1905-1908)
NZJT	*New Zealand Journal of Theology* (Christchurch, 1931-1935)

O

OA	*Oriens Antiquus* (Rome, 1962ff.)
OBJ	*The Oriental and Biblical Journal* (Chicago, 1880-1881)
OC	*Open Court* (Chicago, 1887-1936)
ONTS	*The Hebrew Student* (Morgan Park, IL; New Haven; Hartford; 1881-1892) [Volumes 3-8 as: *The Old Testament Student;* Volume 9 onwards as: *The Old and New Testament Student*]
OOR	*Oriens: The Oriental Review* (Paris, 1926)
OQR	*The Oberlin Quarterly Review* (Oberlin, OH; 1845-1849)
Or	*Orientalia commentarii de rebus Assyri-Babylonicis, Arabicis, and Aegyptiacis, etc.* (Rome 1920-1930)
Or, N.S.	*Orientalia: commentarii, periodici de rebus orientis antiqui* (Rome, 1932ff.)
Oriens	*Oriens. Journal of the International Society of Oriental Research* (Leiden, 1948ff.)
Orient	*Orient. The Reports of the Society for Near Eastern Studies in Japan* (Tokyo, 1960ff.)
Orita	*Orita. Ibadan Journal of Religious Studies* (Ibadan, Nigeria, 1967ff.)
OrS	*Orientalia Suecana* (Uppsala, 1952ff.)
OSHTP	*Oxford Society of Historical Theology, Abstract of Proceedings* (Oxford, 1891-1968) [Through 1919 as: *Society of Historical Theology, Proceedings*]
Osiris	*Osiris* (Bruges, Belgium; 1936-1968) [Subtitle varies]
OTS	*Oudtestamentische Studiën* (Leiden, 1942ff.)

OTW	*Ou-Testamentiese Werkgemeenskap in Suid-Afrika, Proceedings of die* (Pretoria, 1958ff.) [Volume 1 in Volume 14 of: *Hervormde Teologiese Studies*]

P

P	*Preaching: A Journal of Homiletics* (Dubuque, IA; 1965ff.)
P&P	*Past and Present* (London, 1952ff.) [Subtitle varies]
PA	*Practical Anthropology* (Wheaton, IL; Eugene, OR; Tarrytown, NY; 1954ff.)
PAAJR	*Proceedings of the American Academy for Jewish Research* (Philadelphia, 1928ff.)
PAOS	*Proceedings of the American Oriental Society* (Baltimore, New Haven; 1842, 1846-50, 1852-1860) [After 1860 all proceedings are bound with *Journal*]
PAPA	*American Philological Association, Proceedings* (Hartford, Boston, 1896ff.) [*Transactions* as: *TAPA. Transactions* and *Proceedings* combine page numbers from volume 77 on]
PAPS	*Proceedings of the American Philosophical Society* (Philadelphia, 1838ff.)
PBA	*Proceedings of the British Academy* (London, 1903ff.)
PEFQS	*Palestine Exploration Fund Quarterly Statement* (London, 1869ff.) [From Volume 69 (1937) on as: *Palestine Exploration Quarterly*]
PEQ	*Palestine Exploration Quarterly* [See: *PEFQS*]
PER	*The Protestant Episcopal Review* (Fairfax, Co., VA; 1886-1900) [Volumes 1-5 as: *The Virginia Seminary Magazine*]
Person	*Personalist. An International Review of Philosophy, Religion and Literature* (Los Angeles, 1920ff.)
PF	*Philosophical Forum* (Boston, 1943-1957; *N.S.,* 1968ff.)
PHDS	*Perspectives. Harvard Divinity School* (Cambridge, MA; 1965-1967)
PIASH	*Proceedings of the Israel Academy of Sciences and Humanities* (Jerusalem, 1967ff.)
PIJSL	*Papers of the Institute of Jewish Studies, London* (Jerusalem,1964)
PJT	*Pacific Journal of Theology* (Western Samoa, 1961ff.)
PJTSA	*Jewish Theological Seminary Association, Proceedings* (New York, 1888-1902)

PP   *Perspective* (Pittsburgh, 1960ff.) [Volumes 1-8 as: *Pittsburgh Perspective*]

PQ   *The Presbyterian Quarterly* (New York, 1887-1904)

PQL   *The Preacher's Quarterly* (London, 1954-1969)

PQPR   *The Presbyterian Quarterly and Princeton Review* (New York, 1872-1877)

PQR   *Presbyterian Quarterly Review* (Philadelphia, 1852-1862)

PR   *Presbyterian Review* (New York, 1880-1889)

PRev   *The Biblical Repertory and Princeton Review* (Princeton, Philadelphia, New York, 1829-1884) [Volume 1 as: *The Biblical Repertory, New Series;* Volumes 2-8 as: *The Biblical Repertory and Theological Review*]

PRR   *Presbyterian and Reformed Review* (New York, Philadelphia, 1890-1902)

PSB   *The Princeton Seminary Bulletin* (Princeton, 1907ff.)

PSTJ   *Perkins School of Theology Journal* (Dallas, 1947ff.)

PTR   *Princeton Theological Review* (Princeton, 1903-1929)

PUNTPS   *Proceedings of the University of Newcastle upon Tyne Philosophical Society* (Newcastle upon Tyne, 1964-70)

Q

QCS   *Quarterly Christian Spectator* (New Haven, 1819-1838) *[1st Series* and *New Series* as: *Christian Spectator]*

QDAP   *The Quarterly of the Department of Antiquities in Palestine* (Jerusalem, 1931-1950)

QRL   *Quarterly Review* (London, 1809-1967)

QTMRP   *The Quarterly Theological Magazine, and Religious Repository* (Philadelphia, 1813-1814)

R

R&E   *[Baptist] Review and Expositor* (Louisville, 1904ff.)

R&S   *Religion and Society* (Bangalore, India, 1953ff.)

RAAO   *Revue d'Assyriologie et d'Archéologie Orientale* (Paris, 1886ff.)

RChR   *The Reformed Church Review* (Mercersburg, PA;
Chambersburg, PA; Philadelphia; 1849-1926)
[Volumes 1-25 as: *Mercersburg Review;*
Volumes 26-40 as: *Reformed Quarterly Review;*
4th Series on as: *Reformed Church Review*]

RCM   *Reformed Church Magazine* (Reading, PA; 1893-1896)
[Volume 3 as: *Reformed Church Historical Magazine*]

RdQ   *Revue de Qumran* (Paris, 1958ff.)

RDSO   *Rivista degli Studi Orientali* (Rome, 1907ff.)

RÉ   *Revue Égyptologique* (Paris, 1880-1896; *N.S.,*
1919-1924)

RefmR   *The Reformation Review* (Amsterdam, 1953ff.)

RefR   *The Reformed Review. A Quarterly Journal of the
Seminaries of the Reformed Church in America*
(Holland, MI; New Brunswick, NJ; 1947ff.)
[Volumes 1-9 as: *Western Seminary Bulletin*]

RÉg   *Revue d'Égyptologie* (Paris, 1933ff.)

RelM   *Religion in the Making* (Lakeland, FL; 1940-1943)

Resp   *Response—in worship—Music—The arts* (St. Paul, 1959ff.)

RestQ   *Restoration Quarterly* (Austin, TX; Abilene,TX; 1957ff.)

RFEASB   *The Hebrew University / Jerusalem: Department of
Archaeology. Louis M. Rabinowitz Fund for the
Exploration of Ancient Synagogues, Bulletin*
(Jerusalem, 1949-1960)

RHA   *Revue Hittite et Asianique* (Paris, 1930ff.)

RIDA   *Revue internationale des droits de l'antiquité* (Brussels,
1948ff.)

RJ   *Res Judicatae. The Journal of the Law Students' Society
of Victoria* (Melbourne, 1935-1957)

RL   *Religion in Life* (New York, 1932ff.)

RO   *Rocznik Orjentalistyczny. (Wydaje Polskie towarzystwo
orjentalisyczne)* (Kraków, Warsaw, 1914ff.)

RP   *Records of the Past* (Washington, DC; 1902-1914)

RR   *Review of Religion* (New York, 1936-1958)

RS   *Religious Studies* (London, 1965ff.)

RTP   *Review of Theology and Philosophy* (Edinburgh,
1905-1915)

RTR   *Recueil de travaux relatifs à la philologie et à
l'archéologie egyptiennes et assyriennes* (Paris,
1870-1923)

RTRM   *The Reformed Theological Review* (Melbourne, 1941ff.)

S

SAENJ	*Seminar. An Annual Extraordinary Number of the Jurist* (Washington, DC; 1943-1956)
SBAP	*Society of Biblical Archæology, Proceedings* (London, 1878-1918)
SBAT	*Society of Biblical Archæology, Transactions* (London, 1872-1893)
SBE	*Studia Biblica et Ecclesiastica* (Oxford, 1885-1903) [Volume 1 as: *Studia Biblica*]
SBFLA	*Studii (Studium) Biblici Franciscani. Liber Annuus* (Jerusalem, 1950ff.)
SBLP	*Society of Biblical Literature & Exegesis, Proceedings* (Baltimore, 1880)
SBO	*Studia Biblica et Orientalia* (Rome 1959) [Being Volumes 10-12 respectively of *Analecta Biblica. Investigationes Scientificae in Res Biblicas*]
SBSB	*Society for Biblical Studies Bulletin* (Madras, India, 1964ff.)
SCO	*Studi Classici e Orientali* (Pisa, 1951ff.)
Scotist	*The Scotist* (Teutopolis, IL; 1939-1967)
SCR	*Studies in Comparative Religion* (Bedfont, Middlesex, England, 1967ff.)
Scrip	*Scripture. The Quarterly of the Catholic Biblical Association* (London, 1944-1968)
SE	*Study Encounter* (Geneva, 1965ff.)
SEÅ	*Svensk Exegetisk Årsbok* (Uppsala-Lund, 1936ff.)
SEAJT	*South East Journal of Theology* (Singapore, 1959ff.)
Sefunim	*Sefunim (Bulletin)* [היפה] סינים (Haifa, 1966-1968)
SGEI	*Studies in the Geography of Eretz-Israel* מחקרים בגיאוגרפיה של ארץ־ישראל (Jerusalem, 1959ff.) [English summaries in Volumes 1-3 only; continuing the *Bulletin of the Israel Exploration Society (Yediot)*]
SH	*Scripta Hierosolymitana* (Jerusalem, 1954ff.)
Shekel	*The Shekel* (New York, 1968ff.)
SIR	*Smithsonian Institute Annual Report of the Board of Regents* (Washington, DC; 1846-1964; becomes: *Smithsonian Year* from 1965 on]
SJH	*Seminary Journal* (Hamilton, NY; 1892)
SJT	*Scottish Journal of Theology* (Edinburgh, 1947ff.)
SL	*Studia Liturgica. An International Ecumenical Quarterly for Liturgical Research and Renewal* (Rotterdam, 1962ff.)

SLBR	*Sierra Leone Bulletin of Religion* (Freetown, Sierra Leone; 1959-1966)
SMR	*Studia Montes Regii* (Montreal, 1958-1967)
SMSDR	*Studi e Materiali di Storia Delle Religioni* (Rome, Bologna, 1925ff.)
SO	*Studia Orientalia* (Helsinki, 1925ff.)
SOOG	*Studi Orientalistici in Onore di Giorgio Levi Della Vida* (Rome, 1956)
Sophia	*Sophia. A Journal for Discussion in Philosophical Theology* (Parkville, N.S.W., Australia, 1962ff.)
SP	*Spirit of the Pilgrims* (Boston, 1828-1833)
SPR	*Southern Presbyterian Review* (Columbia, SC; 1847-1885)
SQ/E	*The Shane Quarterly* (Indianapolis, 1940ff.) [From Volume 17 on as: *Encounter*]
SR	*The Seminary Review* (Cincinnati, 1954ff.)
SRL	*The Scottish Review* (London, Edinburgh, 1882-1900; 1914-1920)
SS	*Seminary Studies of the Athenaeum of Ohio* (Cincinnati, 1926-1968) [Volumes 1-15 as: *Seminary Studies*]
SSO	*Studia Semitica et Orientalia* (Glasgow, 1920, 1945)
SSR	*Studi Semitici* (Rome, 1958ff.)
ST	*Studia Theologica* (Lund, 1947ff.)
StEv	*Studia Evangelica* (Berlin, 1959ff.) [Being miscellaneous volumes of: *Text und Untersuchungen zur Geschichte der altchristlichen Literatur,* beginning with Volume 73]
StLJ	*The Saint Luke's Journal* (Sewanee, TN; 1957ff.) [Volume 1, #1 as: *St. Luke's Journal of Theology*]
StMR	*St. Marks Review: An Anglican Quarterly* (Canberra, A.C.T., Australia, 1955ff.)
StP	*Studia Patristica* (Berlin, 1957ff.) [Being miscellaneous volumes of: *Text und Untersuchungen zur Geschichte der altchristlichen Literatur,* beginning with Volume 63]
StVTQ	*St. Vladimir's Theological Quarterly* (Crestwood, NY; 1952ff.) [Volumes 1-4 as: *St. Vladimir's Seminary Quarterly*]
Sumer	*Sumer. A Journal of Archaeology in Iraq* (Bagdad, 1945ff.)
SWJT	*Southwestern Journal of Theology* (Fort Worth, 1917-1924; *N.S.*, 1950ff.)
Syria	*Syria, revue d'art oriental et d'archéologie* (Paris, 1920ff.)

T

T&C	*Theology and the Church* / *SÎN-HÁK kap kàu-Hōe (Tainan Theological College)* (Tainan, Formosa, 1957ff.)
T&L	*Theology and Life* (Lancaster, PA; 1958-1966)
TAD	*Türk tarih, arkeologya ve etnoğrafya dergisi* (Istanbul, 1933-1949); continued as: *Türk arkeoloji Dergisi,* (Ankara, 1956ff.)
TAPA	*American Philological Society, Transactions* (See: *PAPA*)
TAPS	*Transactions of the American Philosophical Society* (Philadelphia, 1789-1804; *N.S.,* 1818ff.)
Tarbiz	*Tarbiz. A quarterly review of the humanities;* תרביץ רעזן למדעי היהדות. שנת (Jerusalem, 1929ff.) [English Summaries from Volume 24 on only]
TB	*Tyndale Bulletin* (London, 1956ff.) [Numbers 1-16 as: *Tyndale House Bulletin*]
TBMDC	*Theological Bulletin: McMaster Divinity College* (Hamilton, Ontario, 1967ff.)
TE	*Theological Education* (Dayton, 1964ff.)
Tem	*Temenos. Studies in Comparative Religion* (Helsinki, 1965ff.)
TEP	*Theologica Evangelica. Journal of the Faculty of Theology, University of South Africa* (Pretoria, 1968ff.)
Text	*Textus. Annual of the Hebrew University Bible Project* (Jerusalem, 1960ff.)
TF	*Theological Forum* (Minneapolis, 1929-1935)
TFUQ	*Thought. A Quarterly of the Sciences and Letters* (New York, 1926ff.) [From Volume 15 on as: *Thought. Fordham University Quarterly*]
ThE	*Theological Eclectic* (Cincinnati; New York, 1864-1871)
Them	*Themelios, International Fellowship of Evangelical Students* (Fresno, CA; 1962ff.)
Theo	*Theology; A Journal of Historic Christianity* (London, 1920ff.)
ThSt	*Theological Studies* (New York; Woodstock, MD; 1940ff.)
TLJ	*Theological and Literary Journal* (New York, 1848-1861)
TM	*Theological Monthly* (St. Louis, 1921-1929)
TML	*The Theological Monthly* (London, 1889-1891)
TPS	*Transactions of the Philological Society* (London, 1842ff.) [Volumes 1-6 as: *Proceedings*]
TQ	*Theological Quarterly* (St. Louis, 1897-1920)
Tr	*Traditio. Studies in Ancient and Medieval History, Thought and Religion* (New York, 1943ff.)

Trad	*Tradition, A Journal of Orthodox Jewish Thought* (New York, 1958ff.)
TRAS	See *JRAS*
TRep	*Theological Repository* (London, 1769-1788)
TRFCCQ	*Theological Review and Free Church College Quarterly* (Edinburgh, 1886-1890)
TRGR	*The Theological Review and General Repository of Religious and Moral Information, Published Quarterly* (Baltimore, 1822)
TRL	*Theological Review: A Quarterly Journal of Religious Thought and Life* (London, 1864-1879)
TT	*Theology Today* (Lansdown, PA; 1944ff.)
TTCA	*Trinity Theological College Annual* (Singapore, 1964-1969) [Volume 5 apparently never published]
TTD	*Teologisk Tidsskrift* (Decorah, IA; 1899-1907)
TTKB	*Türk Tarih Kurumu Belleten* (Ankara, 1937ff.)
TTKF	*Tidskrift för teologi och kyrkiga frågor (The Augustana Theological Quarterly)* (Rock Island, IL; 1899-1917)
TTL	*Theologisch Tijdschrift* (Leiden, 1867-1919) [English articles from Volume 45 on only]
TTM	*Teologisk Tidsskrift* (Minneapolis, 1917-1928)
TUSR	*Trinity University Studies in Religion* (San Antonio, 1950ff.)
TZ	*Theologische Zeitschrift* (Basel, 1945ff.)
TZDES	*Theologische Zeitschrift (Deutsche Evangelische Synode des Westens, North America)* (St. Louis, 1873-1934) [Continued from Volumes 22 through 26 as: *Magazin für Evangel. Theologie und Kirche;* and from Volume 27 on as: *Theological Magazine*]
TZTM	*Theologische Zeitblätter, Theological Magazine* (Columbus, 1911-1919)

U

UC	*The Unitarian Christian* (Boston, 1947ff.) [Volumes 1-4 as: *Our Faith*]
UCPSP	*University of California Publications in Semitic Philology* (Berkeley, 1907ff.)
UF	*Ugarit-Forschungen. Internationales Jahrbuch für die Altertumskunde Syrien-Palästinas* (Neukirchen, West Germany; 1969ff.)
ULBIA	*University of London. Bulletin of the Institute of Archaeology* (London, 1958ff.)

UMB	*The University Museum Bulletin (University of Pennsylvania)* (Philadelphia, 1930-1958)
UMMAAP	*University of Michigan. Museum of Anthropology. Anthropological Papers* (Ann Arbor, 1949ff.)
UnionR	*The Union Review* (New York, 1939-1945)
UPQR	*The United Presbyterian Quarterly Review* (Pittsburgh, 1860-1861)
UQGR	*Universalist Quarterly and General Review* (Boston, 1844-1891)
URRM	*The Unitarian Review and Religious Magazine* (Boston, 1873-1891)
USQR	*Union Seminary Quarterly Review* (New York, 1945ff.)
USR	*Union Seminary Review* (Hampton-Sidney, VA; Richmond; 1890-1946) [Volumes 1-23 as: *Union Seminary Magazine*]
UTSB	*United Theological Seminary Bulletin* (Dayton, 1905ff.) [Including: *The Bulletin of the Evangelical School of Theology; Bulletin of the Union Biblical Seminary,* later, *Bonebrake Theological Bulletin*]
UUÅ	*Uppsala Universitets Årsskrift* (Uppsala, 1861-1960)

V

VC	*Virgiliae Christianae: A Review of Early Christian Life and Language* (Amsterdam, 1947ff.)
VDETF	*Deutsche Vierteljahrsschrift für englisch-theologische Forschung und Kritik / herausgegeben von M. Heidenheim* (Leipzig, Zurich, 1861-1865) [Continued as: *Vierteljahrsschrift für deutsch – englisch- theologische Forschung und Kritik...* 1866-1873]
VDI	*Vestnik Drevnei Istoriĭ. Journal of Ancient History* (Moscow, 1946ff.) [English summaries from 1967 on only]
VDR	*Koinonia* (Nashville, 1957-1968) [Continued as: *Vanderbilt Divinity Review,* 1969-1971]
VE	*Vox Evangelica. Biblical and Historical Essays by the Members of the Faculty of the London Bible College* (London, 1962ff.)
Voice	*The Voice* (St. Paul, 1958-1960) [Subtitle varies]
VR	*Vox Reformata* (Geelong, Victoria, Australia, 1962ff.)
VT	*Vetus Testamentum* (Leiden, 1951ff.)
VTS	*Vetus Testamentum, Supplements* (Leiden, 1953ff.)

W

Way	*The Way. A Quarterly Review of Christian Spirituality* (London, 1961ff.)
WBHDN	*The Wittenberg Bulletin (Hamma Digest Number)* (Springfield, OH; 1903ff.) [Volumes 40-60 (1943-1963) only contain *Hamma Digest Numbers*]
WesTJ	*Wesleyan Theological Journal. Bulletin of the Wesleyan Theological Society* (Lakeville, IN; 1966ff.)
WLQ	*Wisconsin Lutheran Quarterly* (Wauwatosa, WI; Milwaukee;1904ff.) [Also entitled: *Theologische Quartalschrift*]
WO	*Die Welt des Orients . Wissenschaftliche Beiträge zur Kunde des Morgenlandes* (Göttingen, 1947ff.)
Word	*Word: Journal of the Linguistic Circle of New York* (New York, 1945ff.)
WR	*The Westminster Review* (London, New York, 1824-1914)
WSQ	*Wartburg Seminary Quarterly* (Dubuque, IA; 1937-1960) [Volumes 1-9, #1 as: *Quarterly of the Wartburg Seminary Association*]
WSR	*Wesleyan Studies in Religion* (Buckhannon,WV; 1960-1970) [Volumes 53-62 only*[sic]*]
WTJ	*Westminster Theological Journal* (Philadelphia, 1938ff.)
WW	*Western Watch* (Pittsburgh, 1950-1959) [Superseded by: *Pittsburgh Perspective*]
WZKM	*Wiener Zeitschrift für die Kunde des Morgenlandes* (Vienna, 1886ff.)

Y

YCCAR	*Yearbook of the Central Conference of American Rabbis* (Cincinnati, 1890ff.)
YCS	*Yale Classical Studies* (New Haven, 1928ff.)
YDQ	*Yale Divinity Quarterly* (New Haven, 1904ff.) [Volumes 30-62 as: *Yale Divinity News,* continued as: *Reflections*]
YR	*The Yavneh Review. A Religious Jewish Collegiate Magazine* (New York, 1961ff.) [Volume 2 never published]

Z

Z	*Zygon. Journal of Religion and Science* (Chicago, 1966ff.)
ZA	*Zeitschrift für Assyriologie und verwandte Gebiete* [Volumes 45 on as: *Zeitschrift für Assyriologie und vorderasiatische Archäologie*] (Leipzig, Strassburg, Berlin, 1886ff.)
ZÄS	*Zeitschrift für ägyptische Sprache und Altertumskunde* (Leipzig, Berlin, 1863ff.)
ZAW	*Zeitschrift für die alttestamentliche Wissenschaft* (Giessen, Berlin, 1881ff.)
ZDMG	*Zeitschrift der Deutschen Morgenländischen Gesellschaft* (Leipzig, Wiesbaden, 1847ff.)
ZDPV	*Zeitschrift des Deutschen Palästina-Vereins* (Leipzig, Wiesbaden, 1878ff.) [English articles from Volume 82 on only]
Zion	*Zion. A Quarterly for Research in Jewish History, New Series* ציון סדרה חדשה רכעון לחקר תולדוה ישראל (Jerusalem, 1935ff.) [English summaries from Volume 3 on only]
ZK	*Zeitschrift für Keilschriftforschung* (Leipzig, 1884-1885)
ZNW	*Zeitschrift für die neutestamentliche Wissenschaft und die Kunde des Urchristentums (...Kunde der älteren Kirche, 1921—)* (Giessen, Berlin, 1900ff.)
ZS	*Zeitschrift für Semitistik und verwandte Gebiete* (Leipzig, 1922-1935)

(§232) *3. Critical Studies of the Old Testament*

§233 *3.1 Textual Criticism - General Studies [See also: §272*
       Theory, Method, and Practice of Textual Criticism
       (includes Paleography) - For studies on Qumran
       Texts see: Qumran Texts, Relation to other
       Hebrew Manuscripts→]

*William M. Willett, "The History of the Hebrew Text, with Some
Considerations for the Study of the Hebrew," *MR* 21 (1839) 164-176.

(   ) F., "Illustrations of Biblical Literature, exhibiting the History and Fate
of the Sacred Writings, from the earliest Period to the present Century;
including Biographical Notices of Translators, and other eminent
Biblical Scholars," *MR* 25 (1843) 325-350. *(Review)*

Samuel Davidson, "To the Editor of the Journal of Sacred Literature," *JSL,
1st Ser.,* 4 (1849) 153-159. *[Textual Criticism]*

G. R. N., "Porter's Principles of Textual Criticism," *CE* 48 (1850) 26-40.
(Review)

Anonymous, "Biblical Criticism," *FBQ* 1 (1853) 243-68. *(Review) [Pages
251-268 are misnumbered; since it appears that pages 251-259 are
missing. The article is complete; page numbers 266-275 being dupli-
cated. (See page iv of Journal for explanatory note)]*

†Anonymous, "The Text of Scripture," *NBR* 19 (1853) 423-444. *(Review)*

Anonymous, "The Text of the Hebrew Bible," *DUM* 50 (1857) 690-696.
(Review)

*Anonymous, "Smith's Dictionary of the Bible," *BFER* 13 (1864) 696-719.
(Review) [The LXX and MT compared]

Anonymous, "Textual Criticism," *ONTS* 3 (1883-84) 123-124.

H[enry] P. Smith, "Textual Criticism in the Old Testament," *ONTS* 4 (1884-
85) 337-344, 402-408.

*Henry P. Smith, "The Old Testament Text and the Revised Version," *PR* 6
(1885) 623-652. *[Revised of 1881]*

1

*Charles A. Briggs, "The Attitude of the Revised Version Toward the Textual Criticism of the Old Testament," *AJSL* 2 (1885-86) 65-78. *[Revised of 1881]*

Charles Rufus Brown, "Textual Criticism of the Old Testament," *ONTS* 5 (1885-86) 32.

( ) Muhlan, "Have We the Original Text of the Holy Scripture?" *LQ* 16 (1886) 529-548. *(Trans. by B. Pick)*

George H. Schodde, "Old Testament Textual Criticism," *ONTS* 7 (1887-88) 44-48.

*Henry Preserved Smith, "The Value of the Vulgate Old Testament for Textual Criticism," *PRR* 2 (1891) 216-234.

*Ad. Neubauer, "The Introduction of the Square Characters in Biblical MSS., and an Account of the earliest MSS. of the Old Testament," *SBE* 3 (1891) 1-36.

Lewis B. Paton, "Some Recent Works on Textual Criticism of the Old Testament," *PRR* 3 (1892) 123-131. *(Review)*

*E. Davis, "The Siloam and Later Palestinian Inscriptions Considered in Relation to Sacred Textual Criticism," *PEFQS* 26 (1894) 269-277.

*Claude R. Conder, "Notes on Mr. Davis' Paper," *PEFQS* 26 (1894) 301-302.

*H. C. Hatcher, "The language and literature of the Old Testament," *CMR* 7 (1895) 20-29. [IV. The genuineness of the text, pp. 27-28]

F. E. Gigot, "The Hebrew Bible," *AER* 14 (1896) 111-126.

H[enry] A. Redpath, "A Means Towards Arriving at a More Correct Hebrew Text of the Old Testament," *Exp, 5th Ser.,* 3 (1896) 346-348.

*Francis Brown, "Old Testament problems," *JBL* 15 (1896) 63-74. [Textual, pp. 64-66]

William A. Lukyn, "The Text of the Old Testament," *ET* 7 (1895-96) 275-276.

A. G., "Paragraphs on Textual Criticism," *TQ* 1 (1897) 285-287.

*Charles Taylor, "The Genizah of Old Cairo," *ET* 9 (1897-98) 344-346.

*R. Mackintosh, "O.T. Quotations in N.T. Speeches: What Version or What Recension of the O.T. Text do they seem to Presuppose?" *OSHTP* (1898-99) 20-26.

J. A. Selbie, "The Text of the Old Testament," *ET* 10 (1898-99) 118-119.

*T. K. Cheyne, "Textual Criticism in the Service of Archeology," *ET* 10 (1898-99) 238-240.

J. A. Howlett, "Textual Criticism of the Hebrew Text," *DR* 125 (1899) 121-143.

*C. D. Ginsburg, "The Text of the Hebrew Bible in Abbreviations," *JP* 28 (1901-03) 254-270.

*J. H. A. Hart, "Primitive Exegesis as a Factor in the Corruption of the Texts of Scripture Illustrated from the Versions of Ben Sira," *JQR* 15 (1902-03) 627-631.

*F[rederic] G. Kenyon, "The Evidence of Greek Papyri with Regard to Textual Criticism," *PBA* 1 (1903-04) 141-168.

‡Wm. J. Hinke, "Books on Textual Criticism," *ASRec* 3 (1907-08) 423-426.

Harold M. Wiener, "Textual Criticism, History, and Faith," *BS* 67 (1910) 346-351.

Ira Maurice Price, "The Hebrew Text of the Old Testament," *BW* 37 (1911) 247-254.

*Margaret D. Gibson, "The Sources of Our Bible," *USR* 24 (1912-13) 303-309.

*Harold M. Wiener, "The Advent of Textual Criticism," *BS* 70 (1913) 145-174.

*John Skinner, "The Divine Names in Genesis," *Exp, 8th Ser.,* 6 (1913) 23-45, 97-116, 266-288. [IV. The Hebrew Text, 1. Hebrew Manuscripts, 2. The Samaritan Pentateuch; V. The Limits of Textual Uncertainty]

*Johannes Dashe, "Divine Appelations, Textual Criticism and Documentary Theory. My Reply to Dr. Skinner," *Exp, 8th Ser.,* 6 (1913) 481-510.

*A. T. Olmstead, "Source Study and the Biblical Text," *AJSL* 30 (1913-14) 1-35.

*G. Ch. Aalders, "The Wellhausen Theory of the Pentateuch and Textual Criticism," *BS* 71 (1914) 393-405.

D. S. Margoliouth, "The Bible of the Jews," *LQ* 44 (1914) 66-85.

George H. Schodde, The Old Testament Text," *TZTM* 6 (1916) 93-95. *(Editorial)*

Harold M. Wiener, "Some Substitutions in Old Testament Texts," *BS* 74 (1917) 479-482.

Anonymous, "The Text of the Old Testament," *MR* 99 (1917) 965-969. *[The language in which the O.T. was written]*

H. W. Magoun, "The 'Versions'," *CFL, 3rd Ser.,* 24 (1918) 430-433.

*Robert Dick Wilson, "Scientific Biblical Criticism," *PTR* 17 (1919) 190-240, 401-456. [C. The Old Testament Text, pp. 218-240]

*J. F. Springer and A. Yohannan, "A New Branch of Textual Criticism," *AQ* 2 (1923) 11-24. [O.T. refs., 13-14, 14-16]

*T. H. Robinson, "Metre and Textual Criticism," *Exp, 9th Ser.,* 1 (1924) 266-283.

*George B. Michell, "Scientific Criticism as Applied to the Bible," *JTVI* 48 (1926) 10-24, 29-31. (Discussion, pp. 24-29)

*Israel W. Slotki, "Faded Letters in Ancient Texts," *JMUEOS* #13 (1927) 60-64.

*R[obert] D[ick] Wilson, "The Textual Criticism of the Old Testament," *PTR* 27 (1929) 36-59. [I. Preface; II. The Manuscripts; III. Parallel Passages; IV. Versions; V. The Septuagint Version]

Joseph Reider, "The Present State of Textual Criticism of the Old Testament," *HUCA* 7 (1930) 285-315.

H. W. Sheppard, "Orthodox Variants from old Biblical Manuscripts," *JRAS* (1931) 265-296.

Paul Ruben, "A Proposed New Method of Textual Criticism in the Old Testament," *AJSL* 51 (1934-35) 30-45, 177-188.

Paul Ruben, "A Proposed New Method of Textual Criticism in the Old Testament—*Concluded,*" *AJSL* 52 (1935-36) 34-42.

T. W. Rosmarin, "Chaim Heller's Works on the Text of the Old Testament," *JBL* 55 (1936) vii.

Alexander Sperber, "The Bible in Israel and Judah," *JBL* 56 (1937) ii-iii.

L. Waterman, "The Authentication of Theoretical Glosses," *JBL* 56 (1937) iii.

A. R. Siebens, "MSS of 'Bracton's Notebook' and Variations in Bible MSS," *JBL* 57 (1938) xvii.

Kyle M. Yates, "An Investigation of the Principal Sources for the Study of the Text of the Old Testament," *R&E* 38 (1941) 3-19.

*H. L. Ginsberg, "The Ugaritic Texts and Textual Criticism," *JBL* 62 (1943) 109-115.

*C. Wolf Umhau, "A Study in the Transmission of Poetic Text," *LCQ* 18 (1945) 305-312.

*Gillis Gerleman, "Synoptic Studies in the Old Testament," *AULLUÅ, N.S.,* 44 (1948) #5, 1-35.

*G. Douglas Young, "The Significance of the Karatepe Inscriptions for Near Eastern Textual Criticism," *OTS* 8 (1950) 291-299.

*J. L. Teicher, "Method in Hebrew Palaeography," *JJS* 2 (1950-51) 200-202.

Merrill F. Unger, "The Text of the Old Testament," *BS* 108 (1951) 15-43.

*D. N. Freedman, "The Orthography of the Masoretic Text of the Pentateuch," *JBL* 70 (1951) iv.

*M. Wallenstein, "The Piyyut, with Special Reference to the Textual Study of the Old Testament," *BJRL* 34 (1951-52) 469-476.

*Ronald M. Hals, "The Usefulness of the LXX in the Study of the Hebrew Text of the Old Testament," *LQ, N.S.,* 4 (1952) 447-456.

*William A. Irwin, "Textual Criticism and Old Testament Translation," *BTr* 5 (1954) 54-58.

*Edwin M. Good, "Jots and Tittles and the Gospel," *USQR* 11 (1955-56) #1, 39-46. *[Apology for Textual Criticism]*

*Moshe Greenberg, "The Stabilization of the Text of the Hebrew Bible, Reviewed in the Light of the Biblical Materials from the Judean Desert," *JAOS* 76 (1956) 157-167.

*Patrick W. Skehan, "The Period of the Biblical Texts from Khirbet Qumran," *CBQ* 19 (1957) 435-440.

J[acob] Weingreen, "Rabbinic-Type Glosses in the Old Testament," *JSS* 2 (1957) 149-162.

*George W. Frey Jr., "Archaeology and Biblical Manuscripts," *UTSB* 57 (1957-58) #2, 9-13.

Fernando Diaz Esteban, "The Sefer Okalah w' Oklah as a source of not registered Bible textual variants," *ZAW* 70 (1958) 250-253.

*M[itchell] Dahood, "The Value of Ugaritic for Textual Criticism," *B* 40 (1959) 160-170.

*W. D. McHardy, "Philology and Textual Criticism," *LQHR* 184 (1959) 4-9.

*M[itchell] Dahood, "The value of Ugaritic for textual criticism," *SBO* 1 (1959) 26-36.

S[hemaryahu] Talmon, "Double Readings in the Massoretic Text," *Text* 1 (1960) 144-184.

Shemaryahu Talmon, "Synonymous Readings in the Textual Traditions of the Old Testament," *SH* 8 (1961) 335-383.

Moshe Goshen-Gottstein, "The Rise of the Tiberian Bible Text," *LIST* 1 (1963) 79-122.

*M. H. Goshen-Gottstein, "Theory and Practice of Textual Criticism. *The Text-critical Use of the Septuagint*," *Text* 3 (1963) 130-158.

A. Mirsky, "Biblical Variants in Medieval Hebrew Poetry," *Text* 3 (1963) 159-162.

*Frank Moore Cross Jr., "The History of the Biblical Text in the Light of Discoveries in the Judean Desert," *HTR* 57 (1964) 281-299. [1. The Rabbinic Recension of the Bible; 2. Proto-Lucian in Samuel and the Text of Samuel used by the Chronicler and Josephus; 3. (4.) A Theory of Local Texts]

L. Lipschutz, "Kitāb al-Khilaf. The Book of the Hillufim. Mishael ben Uzziel's Treatise on the Differences between ben Asher and ben Naphtali," *Text* 4 (1964) 1-29.

*S[hemaryahu] Talmon, "Aspects of the Textual Transmission of the Bible in the Light of Qumran Manuscripts," *Text* 4 (1964) 95-132.

*P. Wernberg-Moller, "The Contribution of the *Hadayot* to Biblical Textual Criticism," *Text* 4 (1964) 133-175.

J. C. L. Gibson, "On the Linguistic Analysis of Hebrew Writing," *AL* 17 (1965) 131-160.

S. Esh, "Variant Readings in Mediaeval Hebrew Commentaries. R. Samuel Ben Meir (Rashbam)," *Text* 5 (1966) 84-92.

Elmer B. Smick, "A Lesson in Textual Criticism as Learned from a Comparison of Akkadian and Hebrew Textual Variants," *BETS* 10 (1967) 127-134.

*I. O. Lehman, "A Forgotten Principle of Biblical Textual Tradition Rediscovered," *JNES* 26 (1967) 93-101. [I. Extra-Masoretic Texts; II. In Aramaic and Samaritan Tradition; III. The Peshitta; IV. Biblical Greek; V. Biblical Hebrew; VI. When Was the Principle in Use?]

N. H. Tur-Sinai, "By What Means and to What Extent Can We Establish the Original Text of the Hebrew Bible?" *PIASH* 1 (1967) #1, 1-13.

*P. Wernberg-Møller, "Some Scribal and Linguistic Features of the Genesis Part of the Oldest Peshiṭta Manuscript (B.M. Add. 14425)," *JSS* 13 (1968) 136-161.

§234 **3.1.1 The Materials of Textual Criticism: Papyri and Ostraca - General Studies [See also: §273 Text Families →]**

Adolf Deissmann, "The New Biblical Papyri at Heidelberg," *ET* 17 (1905-06) 248-254. *[LXX]*

*E. O. Winstedt, "Some Unpublished Sahidic Fragments of the Old Testament," *JTS* 10 (1908-09) 233-254. {Or. 3579A; Pap. LV (I) [= Crum 46] Cop Pap. XI (I) [= Crum 52]}

Anonymous, "Biblical Papyri," *MR* 88 (1906) 653-656. *[LXX]*

*Hugh Pope, "The Oxyrhynchus Papyri and Pentateuchal Criticism," *ITQ* 6 (1911) 145-157.

*H. A. Sanders, "A Papyrus Manuscript of the Minor Prophets," *HTR* 14 (1921) 181-187.

H. Loewe, "The Petrie-Hirschfeld Papyri," *JTS* 24 (1922-23) 126-141.

F. C. Burkitt, "The Chester Beatty Papyri," *JTS* 34 (1933) 363-368. [O.T. sections, p. 368 *[LXX]*]

F. C. Burkitt, "Daniel, Esther, Ezekiel," *JTS* 35 (1934) 68-69. *[LXX papyri]*

Frederic George Kenyon, "The Chester Beatty Biblical Papyri," *Miz* 2 (1936) 9-12.

C. A. Phillips, "The Oldest Biblical Papyrus, and a Leaf from a Testimony Book," *ET* 48 (1936-37) 168-170. [*Pap. Osloenses, ii II*]

Frank W. Beare, "The Chester Beatty Biblical Papyrus," *CdÉ* 12 (1937) 81-91.

Frank W. Beare, "The Chester Beatty Papyri of the Old Testament in Greek," *CdÉ* 13 (1938) 364-372.

Frederic George Kenyon, "The Chester Beatty Biblical Papyri (Second Article)," *Miz* 7 (1938) 7-10.

J. E. Cousar Jr., "New Meanings from Old Scraps of Paper," *USR* 51 (1939-40) 341-357. *[Papyri]*

*Allen Wikgren, "Two Ostraca Fragments of the Septuagint Psalter," *JNES* 5 (1946) 181-184.

*J. Barton Payne, "The Relationship of the Chester Beatty Papyri of Ezekiel to Codex Vaticanus," *JBL* 68 (1949) 251-265.

George D. Kilpatrick, "The Bodmer and Mississippi Collection of Biblical and Christian Texts," *GRBS* 4 (1963) 33-47.

*Meir Wallenstein, "Genizah Fragments in the Chetham's Library," *BJRL* 50 (1967-68) 159-177. *[Includes fragments of Genesis]*

Bruce E. Donovan, "An Isaiah Fragment in the Library of Congress," *HTR* 61 (1968) 625-628. *[LXX Papyrus Fragment]*

*Robert A. Kraft and Antonia Tripolitis, "Some Uncatalogued Papyri of Theological and Other Interest in the John Rylands Library," *BJRL* 51 (1968-69) 137-163. [1. Psalm XIX. 7-8*LXX;* 2. Prayer - Amulet(?); etc.]

*Lawrence Feinberg, "A Papyrus Text of I Kingdoms (I Samuel)," *HTR* 62 (1969) 349-374.

§235 *3.1.1.1 The Nash Papyrus*

S[tanley] A. Cook, "A Pre-massoretic Hebrew Papyrus," *SBAP* 24 (1902) 272.

Stanley A. Cook, "A Unique Biblical Papyrus," *ET* 14 (1902-03) 200-203.

*F. C. Burkitt, "The Nash Papyrus, A New Photograph, with plate," *JQR* 16 (1903-04) 559-561. *[Text of the Decalogue and the Shema']*

Joseph Offord, "The Newly Discovered Pre-Massoretic Hebrew Papyrus," *AAOJ* 25 (1903) 37-39.

B[enjamin] B. Warfield, "The Papyrus of the Ten Commandments," *CFL, N.S.,* 8 (1903) 119-120.

S[tanley] A. Cook, "A Pre-Massoretic Biblical Papyrus," *SBAP* 25 (1903) 34-56.

Harold M. Wiener, "The Nash Papyrus," *BS* 72 (1915) 510.

Anonymous, "A New Biblical Manuscript," *HR* 104 (1932) 222. *[Nash Papyrus(?)]*

F. A. Baepler, "Fragment of Old Testament Traced Back to Before Christ," *CTM* 8 (1937) 536-537.

W[illiam] F[oxwell] Albright, "A Hebrew Biblical Papyrus from the Maccabean Age," *JBL* 56 (1937) iv.

*W[illiam] F[oxwell] Albright, "A Biblical Fragment from the Maccabaean: The Nash Papyrus," *JBL* 56 (1937) 145-176.

*W[illiam] F[oxwell] Albright, "On the Date of the Scrolls from 'Ain Feshkha and the Nash Papyrus," *BASOR* #115 (1949) 10-19.

§236 *3.1.2 Manuscripts, Scrolls and Codices in General*
      [For Qumran Biblical Manuscripts see:
      Qumran Literature →]

*John W. Barrow, "On a Hebrew MS. of the Pentateuch, from the Jewish Congregation at Kai-fung-fu in China," *JAOS* 9 (1869-71) liii.

J. C. Stockbridge, "Polyglot Bibles in the 'John Carter Brown Library'," *BS* 38 (1881) 578-581.

Bernhard Pick, "Lost Hebrew Manuscripts," *JBL* 2 (1882) 122-127. [Codex Hillelis; Codex Sanbuki; The Jericho Pentateuch; Codex Sinai; Codex Ben-Naphtali]

*Hinckley G. Mitchell, "A Hebrew Manuscript," *JBL* 5 (1885) 20-27.

[William Pope Harrison], "The Codex Vaticanus," *MQR, 3rd Ser.*, 15 (1893-94) 343-371.

Anonymous, "The Hebrew Text of the Old Testament," *MR* 78 (1896) 473-477.

M. Friedländer, "Some Fragments of the Hebrew Bible with Peculiar Abbreviations and Peculiar Signs for Vowels and Accents," *SBAP* 18 (1896) 86-98.

M. Gaster, "Hebrew Illuminated MSS. of the Bible of the IXth and Xth Centuries," *SBAP* 22 (1900) 226-239.

*Christian D. Ginsburg, "The text of the Hebrew Bible in abbreviations," *JP* 28 (1901-03) 254-270.

*Christian D. Ginsburg, "The Hamburg Stadtbibiothek Codex No. I," *JP* 29 (1903-04) 126-138. *[Hebrew MS on the Pentateuch]*

*Harold M. Wiener, "Samaritan Septuagint Massoretic Text," *Exp, 8th Ser.,* 2 (1911) 200-219.

*John Skinner, "The Divine Names in Genesis," *Exp, 8th Ser.,* 6 (1913) 23-45, 97-116, 266-288. [IV. The Hebrew Text, pp. 23-25; 1. Hebrew Manuscripts, pp. 25-45; 2. The Samaritan Pentateuch, pp. 97-116; V. The Limits of Textual Uncertainty, pp. 266-288]

F. W. Schillinger, "A Concise History of the Bible Manuscripts (A Conference Paper.)," *TZTM* 5 (1915) 67-72.

Jacob Z. Lauterbach, "The Three Books Found in the Temple at Jerusalem," *JQR, N.S.,* 8 (1917-18) 385-423.

*B. Halper, "Descriptive Catalogue of Genizah Fragments in Philadelphia," *JQR, N.S.,* 12 (1921-22) 397-433. [Many Biblical Codices; Commentaries, some in Arabic; Some Grammars & Lexicons]

H[enry] P[reserved] Smith, "Biblical Manuscripts in America," *JBL* 42 (1923) 239-250; 44 (1925) 188-189.

*R. D. Wilson, "The Textual Criticism of the Old Testament," *PTR* 27 (1929) 36-59. [II. The Manuscripts, pp. 40-42]

Sheldon H. Blank, "A Hebrew Bible MS. in the Hebrew Union College Library," *HUCA* 8&9 (1931-32) 229-255.

Harold R. Willoughby, "The Reconstruction of Lost Rockefeller McCormick Miniatures," *JBL* 51 (1932) 253-262.

*Michael Wilensky, "About Manuscripts," *HUCA* 12&13 (1937-38) 559-572. [I. A Psalm MS. and its Entries]

C. A. Phillips, "The Codex Sinaiticus and the Codex Alexandrinus," *ET* 51 (1939-40) 299-301.

Michael Wilensky, "Additions and Corrections," *HUCA* 16 (1941) 243-249.

Henry S. Gehman, "Manuscripts of the Old Testament in Hebrew," *BA* 8 (1945) 100-103.

E[dmund] F. Sutcliffe, "St. Jerome's Hebrew Manuscripts," *B* 29 (1948) 195-204.

Edmund F. Sutcliffe, "Notes on St. Jerome's Hebrew Text," *CBQ* 11 (1949) 139-143.

Kenneth W. Clark, "Manuscripts Belonging to Archaeology," *BASOR* #122 (1951) 7-8.

J. C. Trever, "A Report on Some Important Hebrew Manuscripts in England," *JBL* 71 (1952) ix.

*Sergio J. Sierra, "Hebrew Codices with Miniature Belonging to the University of Bologna," *JQR, N.S.*, 63 (1952-53) 229-248.

R. Loewe, "Latin Superscriptio MSS on Portions of the Hebrew Bible other than the Psalter," *JJS* 9 (1958) 63-72.

I. Yeivin, "A Biblical Fragment with Tiberian Non-Masoretic Vocalisation," *Tarbiz* 29 (1959-60) #4, III-IV.

S. Talmon, "The Three Scrolls of the Law that were Found in the Temple Court," *Text* 2 (1962) 14-27.

M. [H.] Goshen-Gottstein, "Biblical Manuscripts in the United States," *Text* 2 (1962) 28-59.

*B. Kedar-Kopfstein, "Divergent Hebrew Readings in Jerome's Isaiah," *Text* 4 (1964) 176-210.

M. H. Goshen-Gottstein, "Hebrew Biblical Manuscripts. Their History and Their Place in the HUBP Edition," *B* 48 (1967) 243-290.

Eleazar Birnbaum, "The Michigan Codex. An Important Hebrew Bible Manuscript Discovered in the University of Michigan Library," *VT* 17 (1967) 373-415.

§237 *3.1.2.1 Pre-Masoretic Texts [For Qumran Biblical Manuscript see: Qumran Literature→]*

Anonymous, "The Hebrew Text Before the Massoretes," *CQR* 28 (1889) 112-133.

*H. Graetz, "Notes and Discussion. Historical Notices. I. Alexander and his gold-lettered Scroll," *JQR* 2 (1889-90) 102-104.

Shelomo Morag, "The Vocalization of Codex Reuchlinianus: Is the 'Pre-Masoretic' Bible Pre-Masoretic?" *JSS* 4 (1959) 216-237.

P. E. Kahle, "Pre-Massoretic Hebrew," *Text* 2 (1962) 1-7.

§238 *3.1.2.2 Masoretic Texts*

*Anonymous, "Smith's Dictionary of the Bible," *BFER* 13 (1864) 696-719. *(Review) [The LXX and MT Compared]*

*Schiller Szinessy, "The Prideaux Pentateuch," *SBAT* 1 (1872) 263-270.

Anonymous, "Manuscripts of the Hebrew Scriptures," *PEFQS* 8 (1876) 55-56. *[Allepo Codex]*

W[illiam] R. Harper, "The True Massoretic Text," *ONTS* 2 (1882-83) 27-28.

*Cyrus Adler, "On a Hebrew Manuscript of the Year 1300," *AJSL* 1 (1884-85) 80-85. *[Masoretic MS on Psalms]*

Howard Crosby, "A Question," *ONTS* 4 (1884-85) 279. *[Defense of the Masoretic Text]*

Anonymous, "The Massoretic Text of the Old Testament," *CQR* 24 (1887) 38-67.

*W. E. Barnes, "The Septuagint and the Massoretic Text, Two Interesting Passages," *ET* 6 (1894-95) 223-225.

I. Abrahams, "Note to *J.Q.R.*, XVI, P. 392, L. 25," *JQR* 16 (1903-04) 602. *[Ben Asher MS]*

Richard Gottheil, "Some Hebrew Manuscripts in Cairo," *JQR* 17 (1904-05) 609-655. *[Ben Asher MS, pp. 639-644]*

W. Bacher, "Notes on *J.Q.R.*," *JQR* 18 (1905-06) 146-148. [II. Notes on No. LXVIII of the *J.Q.R.*] *[Reference previous article]*

N. Porges, "Notes on *J.Q.R.*," *JQR* 18 (1905-06) 149-150. [III. Notes on Gottheil's "Some Hebrew MSS. in Cairo."]

Richard Gottheil, "Notes to *J.Q.R.*," *JQR* 18 (1905-06) 566. [II.]*[Reference Gottheil's article, above]*

Alexander Marx, "Notes to *J.Q.R.*," *JQR* 18 (1905-06) 567-570. [IV.] *[Reference Bacher's and Porges' articles, above]*

*Harold M. Wiener, "Samaritan Septuagint Massoretic Text," *Exp. 8th Ser.*, 2 (1911) 200-219.

Anonymous, "Uncertainty of the Massoretic Text," *BS* 70 (1913) 531.

*James Kennedy, "Plea for a Fuller Criticism of the Massoretic Text, with Illustrations from the First Psalm," *Exp, 8th Ser.*, 5 (1913) 378-384.

Georg Richter, "Concerning the Hebrew Text of the Old Testament and the Masoretic Text Tradition," *BM* 3 (1915) 923-938.

*Harold M. Wiener, "Historical Criticism of the Pentateuch. A Reply to Dr. Koenig (II.)," *BS* 72 (1915) 83-153. [Some Inferior Readings in the Massoretic Text, pp. 105-111]

*M. Gaster, "A Codex of the Bible according to the Massora of Ben Naphtali and the Oriental Tradition," *SBAP* 39 (1917) 73-84, 141-151, 172-183.

Anonymous, "A Newly Discovered Hebrew Codex," *HR* 75 (1918) 113. *[Ben Asher MS]*

J[ames] A. Montgomery , "Notes on Two Syriac MSS.," *JBL* 39 (1920) 113-117. [C. A Lost Torah MS., p. 117]

*James Jeffrey, "The Massoretic Text and the Septuagint Compared, with Special Reference to the Book of Job," *ET* 36 (1924-25) 70-73.

*J. Battersby Harford, "Since Wellhausen," *Exp, 9th Ser.*, 4 (1925) 164-182, 244-265. [Article 3. Textual Criticism. The Massoretic Text and the Septuagint; Part I *The Massoretic Text,* pp. 168-174]

*Herbert W. Magoun, "The Massoretic Text and the Versions," *BS* 85 (1928) 82-94.

P. Kahle, "The Reputed Ancient Hebrew Bible at Cambridge," *JTS* 32 (1930-31) 69-71.

Sheldon H. Blank, "A Hebrew MS. in the Hebrew Union College Library," *HUCA* 8&9 (1931-32) 229-255.

Alexander Sperber, "The Targum Onkelos in its Relation to the Masoretic Hebrew text," *PAAJR* 6 (1934-35) 309-351.

F[rank] Zimmerman*[sic]*, "The Edited Masoretic Text," *JBL* 61 (1942) x.

Edward Robertson, "Points of Interest in the Masoretic Text," *JNES* 2 (1943) 35-39.

*Frank Zimmermann, "The Perpetuation of Variants in the Masoretic Text," *JQR, N.S.*, 34 (1943-44) 459-474.

B. J. Roberts, "The Emergence of the Tiberian Masoretic Text," *JTS* 69 (1948) 8-16.

Bleddyn J. Roberts, "The Divergences in the Pre-Tiberian Masoretic Text," *JJS* 1 (1948-49) 147-155.

J. L. Teicher, "The Ben Asher Bible Manuscripts," *JJS* 2 (1950-51) 17-25. [a. The Cairo Codex of the Earlier and Later Prophets; b. The Aleppo Codex; c. The Leningrad Codex, B.19a; d. The British Museum Codex, Or. 4445]

Paul Kahle, "The Hebrew Ben Asher Bible Manuscripts," *VT* 1 (1951) 161-167. *[Cairo Codex of the Prophets; Aleppo Codex; Leningrad Codex B 19a; British Museum Codex Or. 4445]*

*M. H. Segal, "The Promulgation of the Authoritative Text of the Hebrew Bible," *JBL* 72 (1953) 35-47.

Paul Kahle, "The Ben Asher Text of the Hebrew Bible," *OrS* 4 (1955) 43-52.

*P[aul] Kahle, "The Massoretic Text of the Bible and the Pronunciation of Hebrew," *JJS* 7 (1956) 133-154.

I. L. Seeligmann, "Researches into the Criticism of the Masoretic Text of the Bible," *Tarbiz* 25 (1956-57) #2, I-II.

Abba Ben-David, "The Differences between Ben Asher and Ben Naftali," *Tarbiz* 26 (1956-57) #4, IV-V.

*Robert Gordis, "The Origin of the Masoretic Text in the Light of the Rabbinic Literature and the Dead Sea Scrolls," *Tarbiz* 27 (1957-58) III-IV.

*Patrick W. Skehan, "Qumran and the Present State of the Old Testament Text Studies: The Masoretic Text," *JBL* 78 (1959) 21-25.

Izhak Ben-Zvi, "The Codex of Ben Asher," *CNI* 11 (1960) #4, 10-16.

I[zhak] Ben-Zvi, "The Codex of Ben Asher," *Text* 1 (1960) 1-16.

M. H. Goshen-Gottstein, "The Authenticity of the Aleppo Codex," *Text* 1 (1960) 17-58.

D. S. Loewinger, "The Aleppo Codex and the Ben Asher Tradition," *Text* 1 (1960) 59-111.

G. R. Driver, "Abbreviations in the Massoretic Text," *Text* 1 (1960) 112-131.

Arie Rubinstein, "Singularities in the Massorah of the Leningrad codex (B 19a)," *JJS* 12 (1961) 123-131.

N. H. Snaith, "The Ben Asher Text," *Text* 2 (1962) 8-13.

*D[avid] N[oel] Freedman, "The Massoretic Text and the Qumran Scrolls: A Study in Orthography," *Text* 2 (1962) 87-102.

I. Yeivin, "A Babylonian Fragment of the Bible in the Abbreviated System," *Text* 2 (1962) 120-139.

*Menahem Mansoor, "The Massoretic text in the light of Qumran," *VTS* 9 (1963) 305-321.

M. H. Goshen-Gottstein, "The Aleppo Codex and Ben Būyā'ā the Scribe," *Tarbiz* 33 (1963-64) #2, V.

Aharon Dotan, "Was the Aleppo Codex Actually Vocalized by *Aharon ben Asher*?" *Tarbiz* 34 (1964-65) #2, II-III.

Norman H. Snaith, "The Ben Asher Text," *BTr* 15 (1964) 142-146.

G. R. Driver, "Once Again Abbreviations," *Text* 4 (1964) 76-94.

M. H. Goshen-Gottstein, "A Recovered Part of the Aleppo Codex," *Text* 5 (1966) 53-59.

Y. Ratzabi, "Masoretic Variants to the Five Scrolls from a Babylonian-Yemenite MS," *Text* 5 (1966) 93-113.

E. J. Revell, "A New Biblical Fragment with Palestinian Vocalisation," *Text* 7 (1969) 59-75.

§239 *3.1.2.2.1 Studies concerning the Masora*

*Christian D. Ginsburg, "The Babylonian Codex of Hosea and Joel, also the Book of Jonah, Dated 916 A.D. (*now at St. Petersburg*), compared with the received Massoretic Texts," *SBAT* 5 (1876-77) 129-176, 475-549.

J. B. Courtenay, "The Masora," *BQRL* 73 (1881) 310-341.

*Willis J. Beecher, "Had the Massorites the Critical Instinct?" *ONTS* 2 (1882-83) 1-7.

Anonymous, "'The Massorah'," *LQHR* 63 (1884-85) 74-97. *(Review)*

Benjamin B. Warfield, "The Massora Among the Syrians," *AJSL* 2 (1885-86) 13-23.

Isaac H. Hall, "A Note in Reference to the 'Massora Among the Syrians'," *AJSL* 2 (1885-86) 95-97.

B[ernhard] Pick, "The Masoretic Piska in the Hebrew Bible," *JBL* 6 (1886), Part 1, 135-139.

Henry M. Harman, "Some Observations upon Tikkun Sopherim," *AJSL* 4 (1887-88) 34-42.

I. Harris, "The Rise and Development of the Massorah," *JQR* 1 (1888-89) 128-142, 223-257.

*W. Bacher, "A Contribution to the History of the Term 'Massorah'," *JQR* 3 (1890-91) 785-790.

†Joseph Strauss, "Requests and Replies," *ET* 4 (1892-93) 80. [The *lacuna* or פסקא באמצע פסוק]

L[udwig] Blau, "Massoretic Studies," *JQR* 8 (1895-96) 343-359. [I. Number of Letters in the Bible; II. Number of Words in the Bible]

*Ludwig Blau, "Massoretic Studies, III. The Division into Verses," *JQR* 9 (1896-97) 122-144, 360. [1. Age of the Division into Verses; 2. The Division into Verses in the Talmud and the Midrash; 3. The Division of the Verses of the Massorah]

Ludwig Blau, "Massoretic Studies, IV. The Division into Verses (Continued)," *JQR* 9 (1896-97) 471-490. [3. The Division of Verses of the Massorah; 4. Division into Verses and Stichometry; 5. The Number of Verses of the Pentateuch; 6. The Number of Verses of the Prophets, the Hagiographa, and the whole Bible]

Anonymous, "A Contribution to the Study of the Massorah," *IAQR, 3rd Ser.*, 6 (1898) 110-112.

Romain Butin, "The Extraordinary Points in the Massoretic Text," *NYR* 1 (1905-06) 771-781. *[Vowel Point Study]*

*M. Gaster, "A Codex of the Bible according to the Massora of Ben Naptali and the Oriental Tradition,"*SBAP* 39 (1917) 73-84, 141-151, 172-183.

*Israel W. Slotki, "'Breaks in the Midst of Verses' or פִּסְקָא בְּאֶמְצַע פָּסוּק," *JTS* 22 (1920-21) 263-265.

W. B. Stevenson, "History and Sources of the Jewish Masorah," *GUOST* 6 (1929-33) 22-23.

*Alexander Sperber, "Problems of the Masora," *HUCA* 17 (1942-43) 293-394.

Robert Gordis, "The Date and Origins of Early Masoretic Activity," *JBL* 69 (1950) x.

James Wood, "A Syriac Masora," *GUOST* 14 (1950-52) 35-42.

*Solomon Zeitlin, "The Masora and the Dead Sea Scrolls," *JQR, N.S.*, 49 (1958-59) 161-163.

I. Yeivin, "Fragment of a Massoretic Treatise," *Text* 1 (1960) 185-208.

*I. Yeivin, "Notes and Communications. 1. A Unique Combination of Accents," *Text* 1 (1960) 209-210.

*A. Rubinstein, "The Terms משתבשין and דחי׳. in the Babylonian Massorah," *VT* 10 (1960) 198-212

*M. Gertner, "The Masorah and the Levites. An Essay in the History of a Concept," *VT* 10 (1960) 241-272.

*I. Yeivin, "Two Terms of the Babylonian Masora to the Bible," *Lěš* 30 (1965-66) #1, n.p.n. [בע, דק]

F. Dias Estaban, "References to Ben Asher and Ben Naftali in the *Masora Magna* Written in the Margins of MS Leningrad B19A," *Text* 6 (1968) 62-74.

§240 *3.1.2.2.2 Problems of Kethib-Qere*

*H[arry] M. Orlinsky, "The Septuagint and the Origin of the *Kethib-Qere*," *JBL* 57 (1938) ix.

W[illiam] F[oxwell] Albright, "On Dr. Gordis's Communication," *JBL* 57 (1938) 332-333. *[Reexamination of the Review of: The Biblical Text in the Making: The Study of the Kethib Qere* by Robert Gordis]

Robert Gordis, "A Reply to One of Professor Albright's Reviews," *JBL* 57 (1938) 329-331. *[Rejoinder to above article]*

Harry M. Orlinsky, "Problems of Kethib-Qere," *JAOS* 60 (1940) 30-45.

*H[arry] M. Orlinsky, "Some Biblical Prepositions and Pronouns," *JBL* 59 (1940) x. *[Kethib-Qere]*

*Arie Rubinstein, "A Kethib-Qere Problem in the Light of the Isaiah Scroll," *JSS* 4 (1959) 127-133.

Harry M. Orlinsky, "The origin of the kethib-qere system: a new approach," *VTS* 7 (1960) 184-192.

Israel Yeivin, "The Vocalization of Qere-Kethiv in A," *Text* 2 (1962) 146-149.

*Samuel E. Lowenstamm, "The Nouns צֶעַר, צֵעוּר (Ketīb) צָעִיר (Qeré)," *Tarbiz* 36 (1966-67) #2, I-II.

§241 *3.1.2.2.3 Synagogue Scrolls and Torahs*

John W. Barrow, "On a Hebrew MS. of the Pentateuch, from the Jewish Congregation at Kai-fung-fu in China," *JAOS* 9 (1871) liii-liv.

*John P. Peters, "Miscellaneous Notes," *AJSL* 1 (1884-85) 115-119. [An Aramaean Synagogue Scroll containing Ex. 29:32ff., pp. 116-117]

S. A. Birnbaum, "A Sheet on an Eighth Century Synagogue Scroll," *VT* 9 (1959) 122-129.

*J. Yahalom, "The Palestinian Vocalization in Hedwata's Qedŭštot, and the Language Tradition it Reflects," *Lĕš* 34 (1969-70) #1/2, 3-4. *[English Supplement]*

§242 *3.1.2.2.4 Lectionaries*

D. S. Margoliouth, "Studia Sinaitica, Part vi," *ET* 9 (1897-98) 190-192. *[Palestine Syriac Lectionary] (Review)*

Agnes Smith Lewis, "Palestinian Syriac Lectionaries of the Bible," *LQHR* 91 (1899) 75-86.

F. C. Burkitt, "The Old Lectionary of Jerusalem," *JTS* 24 (1922-23) 415-424.

§243 *3.1.2.3 The Samaritan Pentateuch*

M. Stuart, "Samaritan Pentateuch and Literature," *BRCR* 2 (1832) 681-724.

T. W., "The Samaritan Pentateuch," *CE* 28 (1840) 147-165; 29 (1840-41) 63-83.

W. E. T., "On the Samaritan Pentateuch," *JSL, 2nd Ser.*, 4 (1853) 298-327.

John Mills, "The Samaritan Pentateuch," *JSL, 4th Ser.*, 3 (1863) 131-139.

Anonymous, "Samaritan Manuscripts," *ThE* 4 (1867) 208. *[Samaritan Pentateuch]*

*B. Pick, "Horae Samaritanae; or, a Collection of Various Readings of the Samaritan Pentateuch Compared with the Hebrew and Other Ancient Versions," *BS* 33 (1876) 264-288. *[I.—Genesis]*

*B. Pick, "Horae Samaritanae; or, a Collection of Various Readings of the Samaritan Pentateuch Compared with Hebrew and Other Ancient Versions," *BS* 33 (1876) 533-557. *[II.—Exodus]*

*B. Pick, "Horae Samaritanae; or, a Collection of Various Readings of the Samaritan Pentateuch Compared with the Hebrew and Other Ancient Versions," *BS* 34 (1877) 79-88. *[III.—Leviticus]*

*B. Pick, "Horae Samaritanae; or, a Collection of Various Readings of the Samaritan Pentateuch Compared with the Hebrew and Other Ancient Versions," *BS* 35 (1878) 76-92. *[IV.—Numbers]*

*B. Pick, "Horae Samaritanae; or a Collection of Various Readings of the Samaritan Pentateuch Compared with the Hebrew and Other Ancient Versions," *BS* 35 (1878) 309-325. *[V.—Deuteronomy]*

Albert Lowy, "An account given by a Samaritan A.D. 1713, on the ancient copy of the Pentateuch of Nablus," *SBAP* 2 (1879-80) 13-15.

Kerr B. Tupper, "The Samaritan Pentateuch," *ONTS* 1 (1882) #2, 7-8.

Isaac H. Hall, "On a Manuscript Fragment of the Samaritan Pentateuch," *JAOS* 11 (1885) lxix-lxx.

G. F. Moore, "On a fragment of the Samaritan Pentateuch in the library at Andover Theological Seminary," *JAOS* 14 (1890) xxxv-xxxvii.

W. Scott Watson, "A Critical Copy of the Samaritan Pentateuch Written in A. D. 1232," *AJSL* 9 (1892-93) 216-225.

W. Scott Watson, "A Critical Copy of the Samaritan Pentateuch Written in A. D. 1232," *PRR* 4 (1893) 656-662.

W. Scott Watson, "A Critical Copy of the Samaritan Pentateuch," *AJSL* 10 (1893-94) 122-158.

George G. Cameron, "Requests and Replies," *ET* 5 (1893-94) 539. *[The Samaritan Pentateuch]*

W. Scott Watson, "A Samaritan Manuscript of the Hebrew Pentateuch written in A. H. 35," *JAOS* 20 (1899) 173-179.

M. Gaster, "A Samaritan Scroll of the Hebrew Pentateuch," *SBAP* 22 (1900) 240-269.

*J. Skinner, "Notes on a Newly Acquired Samaritan Manuscript, (with plate)," *JQR* 14 (1901-02) 26-36. *[Gen. 6:22 thru Deut. 31:3]*

A. [E.] Cowley, "Notes on *J.Q.R.*, XIV., pages 26 sqq., 'Notes on a Newly Acquired Samaritan Manuscript'," *JQR* 14 (1901-02) 352-353.

George Margoliouth, "An Early Copy of the Samaritan-Hebrew Pentateuch," *JQR* 15 (1902-03) 632-639.

William E. Barton, "The Samaritan Pentateuch," *BS* 60 (1903) 601-632.

Anonymous, "An Ancient Pentateuch," *MQR, 3rd Ser.*, 29 (1903) 795. *[Samaritan Pentateuch]*

S. Garratt, "The Samaritan Pentateuch," *JTVI* 36 (1904) 197-207. (Discussion, pp. 207-213)

A. E. Cowley, "A Supposed Early Copy of the Samaritan Pentateuch," *PEFQS* 36 (1904) 394-396.

Hans H. Spoer, "Description of the Case of the Roll of a Samaritan Pentateuch," *JAOS* 27 (1906) 105-107.

J. E. H. Thomson, "The Samaritan Pentateuch in Relation to Criticism," *GUOST* 3 (1907-12) 55-57.

William W. Everts, "The Date of the Samaritan Pentateuch," *HR* 56 (1908) 193-196.

*Harold M. Wiener, "Samaritan Septuagint Massoretic Text," *Exp, 8th Ser.*, 2 (1911) 200-219.

*John Skinner, "The Divine Names in Genesis," *Exp, 8th Ser.*, 6 (1913) 23-45, 97-116, 266-288. [IV. The Hebrew Text (continued) 2. The Samaritan Pentateuch, pp. 97-116]

J. Iverach Munro, "The Samaritan Pentateuch and Philological Questions connected Therewith," *JTVI* 45 (1913) 183-199, 205-208. [(Discussion, pp. 199-205) (Communications by A. H. Sayce, p. 208; M. Gaster, pp. 208-209)]

*Harold M. Wiener, "Historical Criticism of the Pentateuch. A Reply to Dr. Koenig (II.)," *BS* 72 (1915) 83-153. [II. The Samaritan Pentateuch, pp. 83-96]

M. Gaster, "A Samaritan MS. of the Second or Third Century: A Palaeographic Study," *JRAS* (1918) 63-83.

*W. Ewing, "The Samaritan Pentateuch and Higher Criticism," *Exp, 8th Ser.,* 18 (1919) 451-469.

Anonymous, "The Samaritan Pentateuch," *MR* 102 (1919) 964-970.

J. E. H. Thomson, "The Pentateuch of the Samaritans: When they Got it, and Whence," *JTVI* 52 (1920) 142-158, 174-176. [(Discussion, pp. 158-165) (Communications by: Harold M. Wiener, pp. 165-167; A. S. Geden, pp. 167-169; H. Langhorne Orchard, p. 169; J. J. Lias, pp. 169-171; A. H. Finn, pp. 171-173)]

J. W. Lightley, "The Samaritans and the Pentateuch," *LQHR* 133 (1920) 250-253.

J. E. H. Thomson, "The Samaritan Pentateuch, Its Date and Origin," *BR* 6 (1921) 72-93.

William E. Barton, "The War and the Samaritan Colony," *BS* 78 (1921) 1-22. *[The Photographing of the Samaritan Pentateuch]*

C. W. Dugmore, "Two Samaritan MSS in the Library of Queen's College, Cambridge," *JTS* 36 (1935) 131-146.

Edward Robertson, "Notes and Extracts from the Semitic MSS in the John Rylands Library, III. Samaritan Pentateuch MSS," *BJRL* 21 (1927) 244-272.

*A. S. Halkin, "The Original Version of the Arabic Translation of the Samaritan Pentateuch," *JBL* 56 (1937) xiii.

*A. S. Halkin, "The Scholia to Numbers and Deuteronomy in the Samaritan-Arabic Pentateuch," *JQR, N.S.,* 34 (1943-44) 41-59.

S. Talmon, "The Samaritan Pentateuch," *JJS* 2 (1950-51) 144-150.

S. Talmon, "Some Unrecorded Fragments of the Hebrew Pentateuch in the Samaritan Version," *Text* 3 (1963) 60-73.

§244 **3.1.3 Versions - General Studies**

Archibald R. S. Kennedy, "Some Ancient Versions of the Scriptures," *ET* 2 (1890-91) 210-211. [(a) The Septuagint; (b) The Targums; (c) The Peshitto; (d) The Vulgate]

*T. H. Darlow, "The Character of the Bible Inferred from Its Versions," *JTVI* 46 (1914) 87-97. (Discussion, pp. 97-101)

*George Farmer, "The Origins of the Septuagint and of Other Old Versions," *Theo* 3 (1921) 212-218.

*Herbert W. Magoun, "The Massoretic Text and the Versions," *BS* 85 (1928) 82-94.

*R. D. Wilson, "The Textual Criticism of the Old Testament," *PTR* 27 (1929) 36-59. [V. The Versions, pp. 47-49]

†Anonymous, "Version of the Scriptures," *DR* 1 (1936) 367-399. *(Review)*

Alice Philena Hubbard, "'The Bible of Vatable'," *JBL* 66 (1947) 197-209.

*C. Rabin, "The Ancient Versions and the Indefinite Subject," *Text* 2 (1962) 60-76.

§245 **3.1.3.1 Septuagint Studies [See also: The Letter of Aristeas →]**

†Anonymous, "Dr. Holmes's Septuagint. Exodus, Leviticus," *BCQTR* 18 (1801) 449-453. *(Review)*

†Anonymous, "Holmes's Collation of the Septuagint, continued," *BCQTR* 36 (1810) 321-323. *(Review) [No previous article under this title]*

Iota, "Remarks on the Septuagint," *QCS* 6 (1824) 404-410.

*H. B. Hackett, "The Greek Version of the Pentateuch," *BS* 4 (1847) 188-196.

W. Fitzgerald, "On the Supposed Samaritan Text of the Septuagint," *JSL, 1st Ser.,* 2 (1848) 324-332.

T. A., "Septuagint," *JSL, 1st Ser.,* 7 (1851) 83-126. *(Review)*

M. N. O., "Tischendorf's Septuagint," *JSL, 1st Ser.*, 7 (1851) 413-419. *(Review)*

†Anonymous, "Grinfield's Apology for the Septuagint," *BFER* 1 (1852) 307-320. *(Review)*

Constantin Tischendorf, "Prolegomena to Tischendorf's New Edition of the Septuagint," *BS* 9 (1852) 581-608; 10 (1853) 82-113. *(Trans. by Charles Short)*

S. P. Tregelles, "Liturgical Origin of the Parts of the LXX., etc., Notes and Queries," *JSL, 2nd Ser.,* 1 (1852) 207-211.

Anonymous, "Tischendorf's Edition of the Septuagint," *ER* 5 (1853-54) 120-125. *(Review)*

G. P., "The Septuagint Version," *JSL, 3rd Ser.*, 1 (1855) 308-323.

G. P., "The Septuagint Version. Part II," *JSL, 3rd Ser.*, 4 (1856-57) 371-387. [I.—Corruptions by the Jews; II.—Corruptions by Christians]

†Anonymous, "The Vatican Greek Testament," *BQRL* 28 (1858) 315-332. *(Review) [Codex Vaticanus]*

G. P., "The Septuagint Version. Part III. *The Quotations in the New Testament Considered ,*" *JSL, 3rd Ser.,* 7 (1858) 35-59.

Anonymous, "The Sinaitic Manuscript," *AThR* 3 (1861) 357-374.

E. W. G., "'Essays and Reviews,' and the Septuagint," *JSL, 3rd Ser.,* 13 (1861) 412-416.

J. Challis, "The Septuagint," *JSL, 4th Ser.,* 1 (1862) 162-165.

†Anonymous, "The Sinaitic Codex," *BQRL* 38 (1863) 343-368. *(Review)*

*Anonymous, "Smith's Dictionary of the Bible," *BFER* 13 (1864) 696-719. *(Review) [The LXX and MT Compared]*

W. E. Manley, "The Septuagint," *UQGR, N.S.,* 7 (1870) 277-286.

Ezra Abbot, "On the Comparative Antiquity of the Sinaitic and Vatican Manuscripts of the Greek Bible," *PAOS, May and October,* (1872) viii.

F. W. Farrar, "The Septuagint Translation," *Exp, 1st Ser.,* 1 (1875) 15-29, 104-119.

Ezra Abbot, "On the Comparative Antiquity of the Sinaitic and Vatican Manuscripts of the Greek Bible," *JAOS* 10 (1880) 189-200.

Anonymous, "Recent Translations of the Septuagint," *CQR* 13 (1881-82) 67-84. *(Review)*

H. P. Smith, "Legarde's Septuagint," *PR* 3 (1882) 764-765. *(Review)*

William J. Deane, "The Septuagint Additions to the Hebrew Text," *Exp, 2nd Ser.*, 8 (1884) 139-157, 223-237, 293-305.

E[dward] Maguire, "The Septuagint," *IER, 3rd Ser.*, 7 (1886) 890-898, 999-1008.

George H. Schodde, "The Septuagint," *BS* 8 (1888-89) 134-140.

J. M. Wright, "The Septuagint—Its Critical Value," *MQR, 3rd Ser.*, 5 (1888-89) 102-119.

Henry A. Redpath, "The Study of the Septuagint," *CM, N.S.*, 4 (1888) 324-330; 5 (1889) 14-18.

*J. Freudenthal, "Are There Any Traces of Greek Philosophy in the Septuagint?" *JQR* 2 (1889-90) 205-222. [1. Ψυχή; 2. Πνοή; 3. Νοῦς; 4. Φρόνησις, φρόνιμος, ἄφρων; 5,6. - Δόξα and λογός; 7. Αἰσθάνομαι, αἴσθησις; 8. 'Αρετή; 9. 'Ανδρεία, ἀνδρεῖος; 10. Μεγαλοπρεπής, μεγαλοπρέπεια; 11. Πρόνοια; 12. Κόσμος]

H. B. Swete, "The Septuagint. Professor Graetz's Theory," *ET* 2 (1890-91) 209.

H. Graetz, "The Septuagint, Professor Graetz's Reply to Professor Swete," *ET* 2 (1890-91) 277-278.

H. Graetz, "The Genesis of the So-Called Septuagint," *JQR* 3 (1890-91) 150-156.

*Fred C. Conybeare, "Upon Philo's Text of the Septuagint," *Exp, 4th Ser.*, 4 (1891) 456-466.

George Farmer, "A Problem in the History of the Septuagint," *ET* 3 (1891-92) 172-173.

H. Carmichael, "The Study of the Septuagint," *PER* 5 (1891-92) 70-79.

*James M. Ludlow, "The Septuagint and Old Testament Quotations in the New Testament," *HR* 24 (1892) 11-15.

(   ) G., "The Septuagint," *ONTS* 14 (1892) 244-245.

*F[red] C. Conybeare, "The Philonean Text of the Septuagint," *JQR* 5 (1892-93) 246-280.

R. B. Woodworth, "The Origin of the Septuagint," *PQ* 7 (1893) 425-432.

*W. E. Barnes, "The Septuagint and the Massoretic Text, Two Interesting Passages," *ET* 6 (1894-95) 223-225. [(A) I Samuel 26:20b; (B) Ezekiel 1:13]

C. van den Biesen, "Origin and History of the Septuagint," *DR* 117 (1895) 41-56.

F. E. Gigot, "The Septuagint," *AER* 15 (1896) 152-169.

Geo. H. Schodde, "The Septuagint," *ColTM* 16 (1896) 177-183.

*A. F. Kirkpatrick, "The Septuagint Version: Its Bearing on the Text and Interpretation of the Old Testament," *Exp, 5th Ser.,* 3 (1896) 263-287.

†Anonymous, "The Septuagint Version of the Old Testament," *QRL* 83 (1896) 473-495. *(Review)*

Henry A. Redpath, "Codex Zittaviensis," *ET* 8 (1896-97) 383.

*T. K. Cheyne, "The Septuagint in 'The Encyclopedia Biblica'," *ET* 11 (1899-1900) 285. [Psa. 22:13(12); Ezek. 38:19]

Clyde W. Votaw, "The Septuagint Greek Version of the Old Testament," *BW* 16 (1900) 186-198.

D. S. Margoliouth, "Lines of Defence of the Biblical Revelation. 1. The Bible of the Gentiles," *Exp, 6th Ser.,* 1 (1900) 32-52.

*W. Emery Barnes, "On the Influence of the Septuagint on the Peshitta," *JTS* 2 (1900-01) 186-197.

*Henry H. Howorth, "Some Unconventional Views on the Text of the Bible. I. *The Apocryphal Book Esdras A and the Septuagint,*" *SBAP* 23 (1901) 147-159.

*Agnes Smith Lewis, "A Remarkable Palimpsest," *ET* 13 (1901-02) 55-57.

James B. Johnston, "The Date of the Septuagint," *ET* 13 (1901-02) 382-383.

A. E. Brooke and N. McLean, "The Forthcoming Cambridge Septuagint," *JTS* 3 (1901-02) 601-621. *[A Critical Analysis]*

Anonymous, "The Vatican Codex," *ColTM* 22 (1902) 58-59.

*C. Taylor, "A New Septuagint Fragment," *JTS* 4 (1902-03) 130. [Psa. 143:1-144:6]

*J. H. A. Hart, "The New Septuagint Fragment," *JTS* 4 (1902-03) 215-217. [Psa. 143:1-144:6]

Henry A. Redpath, "The Present Position of the Study of the Septuagint," *AJT* 7 (1903) 1-19.

*Henry A. Redpath, "The Geography of the Septuagint," *AJT* 7 (1903) 289-307.

Eb. Nestle, "Scotch Editions of the Septuagint," *ET* 15 (1903-04) 427-428.

*Eb. Nestle, "A Forgotten Letter on the English Bible and the Septuagint," *ET* 16 (1904-05) 380-381.

W. O. E. Oesterley, "Codex Taurinensis (Y)," *JTS* 6 (1904-05) 372-380.

H. H. Howorth, "The Coming Cambridge Septuagint: A Plea for a Pure Text," *JTS* 6 (1904-05) 436-438.

Eb. Nestle, "Cambridge Editions of the Septuagint," *JTS* 6 (1904-05) 611-614.

W. O. E. Oesterley, "A Lost Uncial Codex of the Psalms," *ET* 17 (1905-06) 353-358. *[The Turin Psalter - B. vii 30 (MS. Y)]*

Arthur G. Jayne, "The Origin and Value of the Septuagint," *ICMM* 2 (1905-06) 305-310.

W. O. E. Oesterley, "Codex Taurinensis (Y). II.," *JTS* 7 (1905-06) 51-74.

W. O. E. Oesterley, "Codex Taurinensis (Y). III.," *JTS* 7 (1905-06) 228-235.

W. O. E. Oesterley, "Codex Taurinensis (Y). IV.," *JTS* 7 (1905-06) 373-391.

W. O. E. Oesterley, "Codex Taurinensis (Y). V.," *JTS* 7 (1905-06) 518-539.

H[enry] A. Redpath, "The Dates of the Translation of the Various Books of the Septuagint," *JTS* 7 (1905-06) 606-615.

James Hope Moulton, "The Cambridge Septuagint," *LQHR* 106 (1906) 137-138. *(Review)*

W. O. E. Oesterley, "Codex Taurinensis (Y). VI.," *JTS* 8 (1906-07) 49-66.

W. O. E. Oesterley, "Codex Taurinensis (Y). VII.," *JTS* 8 (1906-07) 233-239.

*H. St J. Thackeray, "The Greek Translators of the Four Books of the Kings," *JTS* 8 (1906-07) 262-278.

W. O. E. Oesterley, "Codex Taurinensis (Y). VIII.," *JTS* 8 (1906-07) 366-393.

W. O. E. Oesterley, "Codex Taurinensis (Y). IX.," *JTS* 8 (1906-07) 515-525.

*Adolf Deissmann, "The Philology of the Greek Bible: Its Present and Future. I. The Greek Bible as a Compact Unity. The New Linguistic Records," *Exp, 7th Ser.*, 4 (1907) 289-302.

*Adolf Deissmann, "The Philology of the Greek Bible: Its Present and Future. III. Septuagint Philology," *Exp, 7th Ser.*, 4 (1907) 506-520.

H. St J. Thackeray, "The Bisection of Books in Primitive Septuagint MSS," *JTS* 9 (1907-08) 88-98.

*F. Hugh Pope, "The Historical Geography of the Greek Bible," *NYR* 3 (1907-08) 686-703.

Henry A. Sanders, "New Manuscripts of the Bible from Egypt," *AJA* 12 (1908) 49-55. *[Freer MSS]*

Edgar J. Goodspeed, "The Detroit Manuscripts of the Septuagint and New Testament," *BW* 31 (1908) 218-226.

H. B. Swete, "The Old Testament in Greek. I. Origin, Contents, and Language of the Septuagint; other Greek Versions of the Old Testament," *ICMM* 5 (1908-09) 17-33.

H. B. Swete, "The Old Testament in Greek. II. The Greek Old Testament in the Christian Church," *ICMM* 5 (1908-09) 129-146.

Henry A. Sanders, "Age and Ancient Home of the Biblical Manuscripts in the Freer Collection," *AJA* 13 (1909) 130-141.

*M. Gaster, "The Samaritan Book of Joshua and the Septuagint," *SBAP* 31 (1909) 115-127, 149-153.

Edgar J. Goodspeed, "The Freer Manuscript of Deuteronomy-Joshua," *BW* 36 (1910) 203-208.

*Max L. Margolis, "The Grouping of Codices in the Greek Joshua," *JQR, N.S.,* 1 (1910-11) 259-263.

Edgar J. Goodspeed, "Professor Sanders' Deuteronomy-Joshua," *BW* 37 (1911) 199.

*Harold M. Wiener, "Samaritan Septuagint Massoretic Text," *Exp, 8th Ser.,* 2 (1911) 200-219.

George F. Moore, "The Antiochian Recension of the Septuagint," *AJSL* 29 (1912-13) 37-62.

*Max L. Margolis, "The Mode of Expressing the Hebrew 'ā'id in the Greek Hexateuch," *AJSL* 29 (1912-13) 237-260.

*Harold M. Wiener, "Studies in the Septuagintal Texts of Leviticus," *BS* 70 (1913) 498-527, 669-686; 71 (1914) 80-94.

*John Skinner, "The Divine Names in the Genesis," *Exp, 8th Ser.,* 6 (1913) 289-313, 400-420, 494-514. [III. Recensions in the Septuagint, pp. 494-514.]

J. P. Wilson, "Hebrew Syntax in the Septuagint," *GUOST* 4 (1913-22) 71-72.

Harold M. Wiener, "'Studies in the Septuagintal Text of Leviticus'," *BS* 71 (1914) 483-484.

*Harold M. Wiener, "Historical Criticism of the Pentateuch. A Reply to Dr. Koenig (II.)," *BS* 72 (1915) 83-153. [The Critical Value of the Septuagint, pp. 96-105]

F. G. Vial, "What we owe to Alexandria," *IJA* #44 (1916) 7-9. *[Septuagint]*

*Adam C. Welch, "The Septuagint Version of Leviticus," *ET* 30 (1918-19) 277-278.

J. B. Johnson, "The Dating of the Septuagint," *ET* 30 (1918-19) 525.

*M[ax] L. Margolis, "The Aldina as a Source of the Sixtina," *JBL* 38 (1919) 51-52.

*D. D. Luckenbill, "The Influence of the Greek Bible on the Peshitta," *AJSL* 36 (1919-20) 161-166.

*George Farmer, "The Origins of the Septuagint and of Other Old Versions," *Theo* 3 (1921) 212-218.

*James Jeffrey, "The Massoretic Text and the Septuagint Compared, with Special Reference to the Book of Job," *ET* 36 (1924-25) 70-73.

A. V. Billen, "The Classification of the Greek MSS of the Hexateuch," *JTS* 26 (1924-25) 262.

*J. Battersby Harford, "Since Wellhausen," *Exp, 9th Ser.,* 4 (1925) 164-182, 244-265. [Article 3. Textual Criticism. The Massoretic Text and the Septuagint; Part II. *The Septuagint,* pp. 174-182]

Eduard König, "The Newest Debate on the Septuagint," *CFL, 3rd Ser.,* 32 (1926) 383-385. *(Trans. by E. W. Hammer)*

*A. Lykyn Williams, "The Problem of the Septuagint and Quotations in the New Testament," *JTVI* 58 (1926) 152-161, 174. [(Discussion, pp. 162-170) (Communications by Miss Hamilton Law, p. 170; Miss L. M. Mackinlay, pp. 170-171; J. M. Pollock, p. 171; H. Biddulph, pp. 171-172; William Hoste, pp. 172-173)]

Eduard König, "The Latest Theories Concerning the Septuagint Version," *MR* 109 (1926) 302-306.

R. M. Gwynn, "Notes on the Authorship of some Books of the Greek Old Testament," *Herm* 20 (1926-30) 52-61.

Max L. Margolis, "Textual Criticism of the Greek Old Testament," *PAPS* 67 (1928) 187-197.

C. Theodore Benze, "The Old Testament in Greek," *LCQ* 2 (1929) 459-471.

*R. D. Wilson, "The Textual Criticism of the Old Testament," *PTR* 27 (1929) 36-59. [V. The Septuagint Version, pp. 49-59]

M[ax] L. Margolis, "Corrections in the Apparatus of the Book of Joshua in the larger Cambridge Septuagint," *JBL* 49 (1930) 234-264.

A. Haire Forster, "The Study of the Septuagint," *ATR* 14 (1932) 152-155.

P. L. Hedley, "The Göttingen Investigation and Edition of the Septuagint," *HTR* 26 (1933) 57-72.

*O. J. Baab, "A Theory of Two Translators for the Greek Genesis," *JBL* 52 (1933) 239-243.

*Pinkhos Churgin, "The Targum and the Septuagint," *AJSL* 50 (1933-34) 41-65.

H. Hamann, "A New Edition of the Septuagint of the Old Testament," *AusTR* 6 (1935) 101-102.

E. C. Edwards, "The Septuagint in Criticism," *EQ* 7 (1935) 172-178.

Alexander Sperber, "The Problems of the Septuagint Recensions," *JBL* 54 (1935) 73-92.

W. E. B[arnes], "The Recovery of the Septuagint," *JTS* 36 (1935) 123-131.

H. Hamann, "The Oldest Page of the Bible," *AusTR* 7 (1936) 129.

P. E. Kretzmann, "Are We Using Our Septuagint?" *CTM* 7 (1936) 906-912.

*C. A. Phillips, "The Oldest Biblical Papyrus, and a Leaf from a Testimony Book," *ET* 48 (1936-37) 168-170. [*Pap. Osloenses, ii II*]

Matthew Spinka, "Acquisition of the Codex Alexandrinus by England," *JR* 16 (1936) 10-29.

H. Offermann, "A New Critical Edition of the Septuagint," *LCQ* 9 (1936) 87-89. *(Review)*

*Sherman E. Johnson, "The Septuagint and the New Testament," *JBL* 56 (1937) 331-345.

*H[arry] M. Orlinsky, "The Septuagint and the Origin of the *Kethib-Qere*," *JBL* 57 (1938) ix.

E. H. Daniell, "The Codex Sinaiticus," *BQL* 9 (1938-39) 405-406.

*Alexander Sperber, "New Testament and Septuagint," *JBL* 59 (1940) 193-293. [A. THE PROBLEM; I. The Old Testament and the Christian Mission; II. The Old and New Testament Combined Form the Bible of the Church; III. Old Testament Quotations in the New Testament, a. Quotations in the Gospels, b. Classification of the Differences, c. These Differences are of Theological Importance, d. Jerome was aware of these difficulties; IV. Previous Researches in this Field; V. The Problem; B. ORIGEN'S HEXAPLA; VI. Lagarde's Archetype Theory; VII. The Current View on Origen's Work; VIII. Refutation of the Current View; IX. A New Approach; X. The Septuagint according to the Hexapla, 1. Septuagint Quotations of the *Hexapla*, 2. Hexaplaric Symbols, 3. Asterisk and Obelus Readings Originate in Marginal Notes, a. Asterisk readings, b. Obelus readings; 4. Obelus and O' Quotations, 5. Asterisk and *Alia Exemplaria* Quotations, 6. Origen's Sources, 7. Later confusions Resulting in Doublets, 8. Classification of the Doublets, 9. Results of this Classification, 10. Inner Greek Development of Hexaplaric Septuagint-Quotations; XI. The Hebrew Bible According to the Hexapla; C. THE OLDEST MANUSCRIPTS OF THE BIBLE IN GREEK; XII. Codices B and A on the Pentateuch; XIII. Codices B and A on the Judges; XIV. Codices B and A on the Bible; D. THE CHURCH FATHERS AND VETUS LATINA; XV. The Minor Prophets in Greek; XVI. The LXX in Latin; E. CONCLUSIONS; XVII. The NT and the Two LXX Types; XVIII. The Final Redaction of the Hebrew Bible; INDEX OF PASSAGES FROM THE OT AND NT WHICH ARE QUOTED HERE IN GREEK OR LATIN]

Harry M. Orlinsky, "On the Present State of Proto-Septuagint Studies," *JAOS* 61 (1941) 81-91.

*A. V. Billen, "The Hexaplaric Element in the LXX Version of Judges," *JTS* 43 (1942) 12-19.

Samuel Krauss, "Two Hitherto Unknown Bible Versions in Greek," *BJRL* 27 (1942-43) 97-105. [I. Ben La'ana and Ben Tilga Probably Identified; II. Doublets in Greek Bible Versions; III. The Greek Glosses in Question—Genuine or Spurious?]

F. G. Kenyon, "Greek Manuscripts and Archaeology," *JTVI* 75 (1943) 111-115.

*W. G. Waddell, "The Tetragrammaton in the LXX," *JTS* 45 (1944) 158-161. [P. Fouad 266]

Harry M. Orlinsky, "The Septuagint—Its Use in Textual Criticism," *BA* 9 (1946) 21-34. [The Septuagint as a Jewish Work; The Correct Use of the Septuagint; Other Phases of Septuagint Study]

Floyd V. Filson, "The Septuagint and the New Testament," *BA* 9 (1946) 34-42. [Judaism and Greek Culture; Importance of the Chester Beatty LXX Manuscripts; Character of the LXX Version; The Use of the LXX in the New Testament]

*Allen Wikgren, "Two Ostraca Fragments of the Septuagint Psalter," *JNES* 5 (1946) 181-184.

E. E. Flack, "Values in the Septuagint," *WBHDN* 48 (1951) #8, 17-19.

*Ronald M. Hals, "The Usefulness of the LXX in the Study of the Hebrew Text of the Old Testament," *LQ, N.S.,* 4 (1952) 447-456.

F. F. Bruce, "The Old Testament in Greek," *BTr* 4 (1953) 129-135, 156-162.

H[enry] S. Gehman, "Some Types of Errors of Transmission in the LXX," *JBL* 72 (1953) xiv-xv.

H[enry] S. Gehman, "Some Types of Errors of Transmission in the LXX," *VT* 3 (1953) 397-400.

*P. Peters, "A Missing Link in the History of the Septuagint," *WLQ* 51 (1954) 146.

*Everett F. Harrison, "The Importance of the Septuagint for Biblical Studies," *BS* 112 (1955) 344-355; 113 (1956) 37-45.

*‡Raymond F. Surburg, "Intertestamental Studies 1946—1955," *CTM* 27 (1956) 95-114. [II. Septuagint Studies, pp. 99-101]

Ian A. Moir, "Two Septuagint Palimpsest Fragments," *JTS, N.S.,* 8 (1957) 1-11.

P. Kahle, "Problems of the Septuagint," *StP* 1 (1957) 328-338.

Frederick W. Danker, "Aids to Bible Study. The Septuagint—Its History," *CTM* 30 (1959) 271-284.

*Harry M. Orlinsky, "Qumran and the Present State of the Old Testament Text Studies: The Septuagint Text," *JBL* 78 (1959) 26-33.

*G. Zuntz, "Aristeas Studies II: Aristeas on the Translation of the Torah," *JSS* 4 (1959) 109-126.

Elias J. Bickerman, "The Septuagint as a Translation," *PAAJR* 28 (1959) 1-39.

*P. Kahle, "The Greek Bible and the Gospels. Fragments from the Judaean Desert," *StEv* 1 (1959) 613-621.

*A. S. Tritton, "Some Notes on the Septuagint," *GUOST* 18 (1959-60) 49-52.

*Sidney Jellicoe, "Aristaes, Philo, and the Septuagint *Vorlage*," *JTS, N.S.*, 12 (1961) 261-271.

*Edwin Yamauchi, "The Sapiential Septuagint," *BETS* 5 (1962) 109-115.

*B. Lifshitz, "The Expedition to the Judean Desert, 1961. The Greek Documents from the Cave of Horror," *IEJ* 12 (1962) 201-207. *[Septuagint]*

George Howard, "Introduction to Septuagintal Studies," *RestQ* 7 (1963) 132-142; 8 (1964) 10-25.

*M. H. Goshen-Gottstein, "Theory and Practice of Textual Criticism. *The Text-critical Use of the Septuagint*," *Text* 3 (1963) 130-158.

D. W. Gooding, "Aristes and Septuagint Origins: A Review of Recent Studies," *VT* 13 (1963) 357-379.

Dikran Y. Hadidian, "The Septuagint and Its Place in Theological Education," *ET* 76 (1964-65) 102-103.

*A. F. J. Klijn, "The Letter of Aristeas and the Greek Translation of the Pentateuch in Egypt," *NTS* 11 (1964-65) 154-158.

*John F. X. Sheehan, "The Septuagint and the New Testament," *BibT* #17 (1965) 1133-1136.

S[idney] Jellicoe, "The Septuagint To-day," *ET* 77 (1965-66) 68-74.

*Ernest G. Clarke, "The Hebraic Spirit," *CJT* 12 (1966) 153-163.

*Bruce E. Donovan, "Notes and Observations. An Isaiah Fragment in the Library of Congress," *HTR* 61 (1968) 625-628.

Sidney Jellicoe, "Septuagint Studies in the Current Century," *JBL* 88 (1969) 191-199.

§246 **3.1.3.1.1 Studies in "Translation Greek"**

*Joseph D. Wilson, "The Seventy Weeks of Daniel in the Hands of a Septuagint Translator," *CFL, 3rd Ser.*, 14 (1911-12) 351-352.

*Max L. Margolis, "Transliterations in the Greek Old Testament," *JQR, N.S.*, 16 (1925-26) 117-125.

R[aymond] S. Haupert, "The Transcription Theory of the Septuagint," *JBL* 53(1934) xi.

Raymond S. Haupert, "The Transcription Theory of the Septuagint," *JBL* 53 (1934) 251-255.

*Sherman E. Johnson, "The Septuagint and the New Testament," *JBL* 56 (1937) 331-345.

*Henry Snyder Gehman, "Exegetical Methods Employed by the Greek Translator of I Samuel," *JAOS* 70 (1950) 292-296.

H[enry] S. Gehman, "The Hebraic Character of Septuagint Greek," *JBL* 69 (1950) x.

*R. A. Martin, "Some Syntactical Criteria of Translation Greek," *VT* 10 (1960) 295-310.

C. Rabin, "The Translation Process and the Character of the Septuagint," *Text* 6 (1968) 1-26.

R. A. Kraft, "Jewish Greek Scriptures and Related Topics: Reports on Recent Discussions," *NTS* 16 (1969-70) 384-396.

§247 *3.1.3.1.2 Aquila's Version*

F. C. Burkitt, "Aquila," *JQR* 10 (1897-98) 207-216.

*Eb. Nestle, "Symmachus, Not Aquila," *ET* 22 (1910-11) 377.

Joseph Reider, "Prolegomena to a Greek-Hebrew and Hebrew-Greek Index to Aquila, Introduction," *JQR, N.S.,* 4 (1913-14) 321-356.

Joseph Reider, "Prolegomena to a Greek-Hebrew and Hebrew-Greek Index to Aquila, Chapter II, Aquila's Knowledge of the Hebrew Grammar and Lexicon," *JQR, N.S.,* 4 (1913-14) 577-598.

Joseph Reider, "Prolegomena to a Greek-Hebrew and Hebrew-Greek Index to Aquila, Chapter III, Aquila's Exegesis," *JQR, N.S.,* 4 (1913-14) 599-620.

*Joseph Reider, "Prolegomena to a Greek-Hebrew and Hebrew-Greek Index to Aquila, Chapter IV, The Hebrew Text Underlying Aquila's Version (and Appendices)," *JQR, N.S.,* 7 (1916-17) 287-364. [Appendix I - Aquila's Vocabulary; Appendix II - Aquila Remains in Syriac and Latin; Appendix III - Aquila Readings in Talmud and Midrash; Appendix IV - 3 Kings 14:1-20]

*Peter Katz, "Notes on the Septuagint, II. A Fresh Aquila Fragment recovered from Philo," *JTS* 47 (1946) 31-33.

J[oseph] Reider, "An Index to Aquila. (Greek-Hebrew, Hebrew-Greek, Latin-Hebrew; with the Syriac and Armenian evidence," *VTS* 12 (1966) i-xii, 1-331. *(Completed and Revised by N. Turner)*

Sidney Jellicoe, "Aquila and His Version," *JQR, N.S.,* 59 (1968-69) 326-332.

§248 *3.1.3.1.3 Symmachus*

*Eb. Nestle, "Symmachus, Not Aquila," *ET* 22 (1910-11) 377.

*L. J. Liebreich, "Notes on the Greek Version of Symmachus," *JBL* 63 (1944) 397-403.

§249 *3.1.3.1.4 Theodotion*

*Charles M. Cooper, "Theodotion's Influence on the Alexandrian Text of Judges," *JBL* 67 (1948) 63-68.

John M. Grindel, "Another Characteristic of the *Kaige* Recension: נצ‎ה/ νικρος," *CBQ* 31 (1969) 499-513.

§250 *3.1.3.1.5 Origen (includes Hexapla)*

Max L. Margolis, "Hexapla and Hexaplaric," *AJSL* 32 (1915-16) 126-140.

Harry M. Orlinsky, "The Columnar Order of the Hexapla," *JQR, N.S,* 27 (1936-37) 137-149.

H[arry] M. Orlinsky, "The Priority of the Tetrapla to the Hexapla," *JBL* 56 (1937) x.

W. E. Staples, "The Second Column of Origen's Hexapla," *JAOS* 59 (1939) 71-80.

*Raymond Thornhill, "The Greek Text of the Book of Ruth: A Grouping of Manuscripts According to Origen's Hexapla," *VT* 3 (1953) 236-249.

J. A. Emerton, "The Purpose of the Second Column of the Hexapla," *JTS, N.S.,* 7 (1956) 79-87.

P. E. Kahle, "The Greek Bible Manuscripts Used by Origen," *JBL* 79 (1960) 111-118.

§251 *3.1.3.1.6 Other LXX Texts and Revisions*

*F. C. Conybeare, "Philoean Text of the Septuagint," *JQR* 8 (1895-96) 88-122.

Anonymous, "Lucian's Recension of the Septuagint," *CQR* 51 (1900-01) 379-398.

Robert M. Grant, "The Bible of Theophilus of Antioch," *JBL* 66 (1947) 173-196.

R[obert] M. Grant, "The Septuagint Text of Theophilus of Antioch," *JBL* 68 (1949) xv-xvi.

*Raymond Thornhill, "Six of Seven Nations: A Pointer to the Lucianic Text in the Heptateuch, with Special Reference to the Old Latin Version," *JTS, N.S.*, 10 (1959) 233-246.

§252 *3.1.3.2 Old Latin Versions*

*J. I. Mombert, "Emendations and Corrections," *JBL* 4 (1884) 93-125. *[Hieronymian Version]*

Anonymous, "The Codex Amiatinus, When and Where Written," *CQR* 25 (1887-88) 435-448.

Fred[rick] C. Conybeare, "On Some Fragments of a Pre-Hieronymian Latin Version of the Bible," *Exp, 4th Ser.*, 4 (1891) 63-80, 129-141.

C. H. Turner, "Notes on the Old Latin Version of the Bible," *JTS* 2 (1900-01) 600-610.

Anonymous, "The Old Latin Version of the Old Testament," *CQR* 52 (1901) 103-156.

*W. O. E. Oesterley, "The Old Latin Texts of the Minor Prophets. I.," *JTS* 5 (1903-04) 76-88.

*W. O. E. Oesterley, "The Old Latin Texts of the Minor Prophets. II.," *JTS* 5 (1903-04) 242-253.

*W. O. E. Oesterley, "The Old Latin Texts of the Minor Prophets. III.," *JTS* 5 (1903-04) 378-386.

*W. O. E. Oesterley, "The Old Latin Texts of the Minor Prophets. IV.," *JTS* 5 (1903-04) 570-579.

*W. O. E. Oesterley, "The Old Latin Texts of the Minor Prophets. V.," *JTS* 6 (1904-05) 67-70.

*W. O. E. Oesterley, "The Old Latin Texts of the Minor Prophets Appendix," *JTS* 6 (1904-05) 217-220.

*E. von Dobschütz, "A Collection of Old Latin Bible Quotations: Somnium Neronis," *JTS* 16 (1914-15) 1-27.

F. C. Burkitt, "The Old-Latin Heptateuch," *JTS* 29 (1927-28) 140-146.

*A. V. Billen, "The Old Latin Version of Judges," *JTS* 43 (1942) 140-149.

Louis H. Gray, "Biblical Citations in Latin Lives of Welsh and Breton Saints Differing from the Vulgate," *Tr* 8 (1952) 389-397.

A. W. Adams, "The Old-Latin Version," *BTr* 5 (1954) 101-106.

*Raymond Thornhill, "Six or Seven Nations: A Pointer to the Lucianic Text in the Heptateuch, with Special Reference to the Old Latin Version," *JTS, N.S.,* 10 (1959) 233-246.

## §253	*3.1.3.3 Latin Vulgate (including Jerome's Translation)*

G. E. E., "Biblia Sacra Vulgatæ Editionis. Juxta Exemplar ex Tyographiâ Apostolicâ Vaticanâ Romæ 1592. Correctis corrigendis ex Indicibus correctariis Romæ &c. Edidit Leander Van Ess, S. T. D. Tubingæ, 1824," *CE* 21 (1837) 354-370.

[Edward William Grinfield], "The Vulgate and Old Italic Versions," *BRCM* 6 (1849-50) 669-670.

T[heophilus] Rubinsohn, "The Vulgate," *CRB* 18 (1853) 237-257.

Anonymous, "The Origin of the Latin Vulgate," *CongR* 1 (1861) 184-195.

Rudolph Wahl, "The Vulgate Version and the Catholic Church," *UQGR, N.S.,* 15 (1878) 69-83.

Robert Henderson, "A Bible Reviser of the Fourth Century," *BFER* 31 (1882) 34-47. *[Jerome]*

J. A. Smith, "Alcuin's Bible," *ONTS* 2 (1882-83) 322-324.

*B. Pick, "Jerome as an Old Testament Student," *LCR* 6 (1887) 230-243, 287-295; 7 (1888) 137-149, 272-293.

M. Samuel Berger, "The History of the Vulgate in France," *AR* 9 (1888) 187-196.

Anonymous, "The Vulgate Old Testament," *ONTS* 12 (1891) 376.

*Henry Preserved Smith, "The Value of the Vulgate Old Testament for Textual Criticism," *PRR* 2 (1891) 216-234.

*George F. Moore, "Vulgate Chapters and Numbered Verses in the Hebrew Bible," *JBL* 12 (1893) 73-78.

William Barry, "Our Latin Bible," *DR* 139 (1906) 1-23. *(Review)*

G. M[allows] Youngman, "Hetzenauer's Edition of the Vulgate," *AJT* 12 (1908) 627-636.

Albert Condamin, "The 'Vulgate' of Prof. Henslow, I.," *ET* 21 (1909-10) 330-332.

George Henslow, "The 'Vulgate' of Prof. Henslow, II.," *ET* 21 (1909-10) 332.

G. Mallows Youngman, "Manuscripts of the Vulgate in the British Museum," *AJT* 14 (1910) 608-626.

Edward J. Kissane, "St. Jerome and the Vulgate," *ITQ* 14 (1919) 156-158.

F. C. Burkitt, "The Text of the Vulgate," *JTS* 24 (1922-23) 406-414.

E. Power, "The Lost Ninth Century Bible of Carcassonne," *B* 5 (1924) 197-201.

*E. Power, "Corrections from the Hebrew in the Theodulfian MSS. of the Vulgate," *B* 5 (1924) 233-258.

E. K. Rand, "Dom Quentin's Memoir on the Text of the Vulgate," *HTR* 17 (1925) 197-264.

John H. Chapman, "The Latin Bible (Part I)," *DR* 180 (1927) 1-18.

J[ohn] H. Chapman, "The Latin Bible *(continued)*," *DR* 180 (1927) 161-172.

F. C. Burkitt, "Jerome's Work on the Psalter," *JTS* 30 (1928-29) 395-397.

*J. A. F. Gregg, "Transliteration as Translation: A Study of Certain Features in the Influence of the Vulgate on the Authorized Version," *ET* 42 (1930-31) 8-14.

*Algernon Ward, "Jerome's Work on the Psalter," *ET* 44 (1932-33) 87-92.

William L. Newton, "Influences on St. Jerome's Translation of the Old Testament," *CBQ* 5 (1943) 17-32.

Adrian Weld-Blundell, "The Revision of the Vulgate Bible," *Scrip* 2 (1947) 100-105.

E[dmund] F. Sutcliffe, "The Name 'Vulgate'," *B* 29 (1948) 345-352.

Edmund F. Sutcliffe, "The Council of Trent on the *Authentia* of the Vulgate," *JTS* 49 (1948) 35-42.

*Charles M. Cooper, "Jerome's 'Hebrew Psalter' and the New Latin Version," *JBL* 69 (1950) 233-244.

Boleslaw Szcześniak, "The Laurentian Bible of Marco Polo," *JAOS* 75 (1955) 173-179.

Richard J. Sneed, "The Amazing St. Jerome," *ABenR* 7 (1956) 230-247.

*Sakae Kubo, "The Influence of the Vulgate on the English Translation of the Psalms," *AUSS* 3 (1965) 34-41.

C. M. Kauffmann, "The Bury Bible (Cambridge, Corpus Christi College, MS. 2)," *JWCI* 29 (1966) 60-81.

*Bezalel Narkiss, "Towards a further Study of the Ashburnham Pentateuch (Pentateuque de Tours) Paris Bibliothèque Nationale, Nouv. Acq. Lat 2334," *CAAMA* 19 (1969) 45-60.

§254 *3.1.3.3.1 The Gutenberg Bible*

J. M. Lenhart, "The Gutenberg Bibles," *ACQR* 39 (1914) 593-617.

Edmund Meier, "Interesting Old Bibles," *CTM* 6 (1935) 928-931. *[Gutenberg Bible]*

Otto Maurice Forkert, "The Gutenberg Bible," *CTM* 11 (1940) 788-790.

Francis J. Crump, "The Gutenberg Bible," *CBQ* 14 (1952) 213-218.

§255 *3.1.3.4 Arabic Versions*

†Anonymous, "Eli Smith's Arabic Bible," *BFER* 6 (1857) 119-122. *(Review)*

*A. S. Halkin, "The Original Version of the Arabic Translation of the Samaritan Pentateuch," *JBL* 56 (1937) xiii.

*A. S. Halkin, "The Scholia to Numbers and Deuteronomy in the Samaritan-Arabic Pentateuch," *JQR, N.S.,* 34 (1943-44) 41-59.

John A. Thompson, "The Origin and Nature of the Chief Printed Arabic Bibles," *BTr* 6 (1955) 2-12, 51-55, 98-106, 146-150.

A. S. Tritton, "The Old Testament in Muslim Spain," *BSOAS* 21 (1958) 392-394. *[Arabic Texts]*

Eric F. Bishop, "The Arabic Bible After a Century," *BTr* 15 (1964) 167-172.

§256 *3.1.3.5 Coptic Versions (including Bohairic and Sahidic)*

*A. E. Brooke, "The Bohairic Version of the Pentateuch," *JTS* 3 (1901-02) 258-278.

*J. D. Prince, "Two Versions of the Coptic Psalter," *JBL* 21 (1902) 92-99.

E. O. Winstedt, "Sahidic Biblical Fragments," *SBAP* 25 (1903) 317-325. [Gen. 7:13-20; Ex. 18; I Sam. 16:14-16; Ps. 31:6-7, 10-13, 14-17, 19-23; Ps. 106:15-20]

E. O. Winstedt, "Sahidic Biblical Fragments in the Bodleian Library. II," *SBAP* 26 (1904) 215-221.

A. E. Brooke, "Sahidic Fragments of the Old Testament," *JTS* 8 (1906-07) 67-74. [Bibl. Nat. Copt. 129[1]]

E. O. Winstedt, "Some Unpublished Sahidic Fragments of the Old Testament," *JTS* 10 (1908-09) 233-254. {Or. 3579A; Pap. LV (I) [= Crum 46] Cop Pap. XI (I) [= Crum 52]}

S. Gaselee, "Notes on the Coptic Versions of the LXX," *JTS* 11 (1909-10) 246-257.

Frank N. Hallock, "The Coptic Old Testament," *AJSL* 49 (1932-33) 325-335.

*P. L. Hedley, "Three Graeco-Coptic Biblical Texts," *JTS* 35 (1934) 58-60. [MSS Borgia Copt. 46 (Gen. I-XV); Borgia Copt. 78 - (Gen. and Ex.); Brussels, Musée National #10952 (Psa. CIX 1-4)]

J. Barton Payne, "Characteristics of Coptic Bible Translation," *ASW* 5 (1950) 64-66.

*J. Barton Payne, "The Sahidic Coptic Text of 1 Samuel," *JBL* 72 (1953) 51-61.

§257 *3.1.3.6 Ethiopic Versions*

*George H. Schodde, "A Manuscript of the Ethiopic Psalter," *AJSL* 5 (1888-89) 199-200.

*George A. Barton, "On an Ethiopic MS. of the Octateuch in the Library of Haverford College, Pa.," *JAOS* 15 (1893) cxcix-ccii.

*Edgar J. Goodspeed, "Ethiopic Manuscripts from the Collection of Wilberforce Eames," *AJSL* 20 (1903-04) 235-244. *[Some MSS on the Psalms]*

Samuel A. B. Mercer, "An Expedition to Abyssinia,"*BASOR* #39 (1930) 27-29. *[Ethiopic MSS. of the Asmara Bible]*

§258 *3.1.3.7 Georgian Versions*

A. A. Tsagareli, "Professor Tsagareli's Catalogue of Georgian Manuscripts in the Monastery of the Holy Cross at Jerusalem," *JBL* 12 (1893) 168-179. *(Trans. from the Russian by Oliver Wardrop)*

O[liver] Wardrop, "Georgian Manuscripts at the Iberian Monastery on Mount Athos," *JTS* 12 (1910-11) 593-607.

Robert P. Blake, "Ancient Georgian Versions of the Old Testament," *HTR* 19 (1926) 271-297.

Robert P. Blake, "The Athos Codex of the Georgian Old Testament," *HTR* 22 (1929) 33-56.

Robert P. Blake, "Catalogue of the Georgian Manuscripts in the Cambridge University Library," *HTR* 25 (1932) 207-224.

*P. L. Hedley, "The Georgian Fragments of Jeremiah," *JTS* 34 (1933) 392-395.

§259 *3.1.3.8 Syriac Versions (including Peshiṭta)*

B. H. C., "On the Syriac Language Peshito*[sic]* Version," *JSL, 2nd Ser.*, 5 (1853-54) 455-464.

J. A. Edgren, "The Peshito*[sic]*," *ONTS* 1 (1882) #1, 12-13.

George H. Schodde, "The Peshitto*[sic]*," *ONTS* 9 (1889) 86-90.

*G. Margoliouth, "More Fragments of the Palestinian Syriac Version of the Holy Scriptures," *SBAP* 18 (1896) 223-236, 275-285. [BM Or. 4951] [Gen. 2:4-19; 2 Kgs. 2:19-22; Amos 9:5-14a; Acts 16:16-34]

*G. Margoliouth, "More Fragments of the Palestinian Syriac Version of the Holy Scriptures *[concluded]*," *SBAP* 19 (1897) 39-60. [2 Kgs. 2:19-22; Amos 5:14a]

Eb. Nestle, "The Palestinian Syriac Version of the Holy Scriptures," *ET* 9 (1897-98) 510-511.

W. E[mery] Barnes, "The Printed Editions of the Peshitta of the Old Testament," *ET* 9 (1897-98) 560-562.

G. Margoliouth, "'The Palestinian Syriac Version'," *ET* 9 (1897-98) 562-563.

Eb. Nestle, "'The Palestinian Syriac Version'," *ET* 10 (1898-99) 47.

G. Margoliouth, "'The Palestinian Syriac Version'," *ET* 10 (1898-99) 91.

*W. Emery Barnes, "On the Influence of the Septuagint on the Peshitta," *JTS* 2 (1900-01) 186-197.

*Charles C. Torrey, "Portions of the First Esdras and Nehemiah in the Syro-Hexaplar Version," *AJSL* 23 (1906-07) 65-74.

John Pinkerton, "The Earliest Syriac Version of the Pentateuch," *GUOST* 4 (1913-22) 19-20.

John Pinkerton, "The Origin and the Early History of the Syriac Pentateuch," *JTS* 15 (1913-14) 14-41.

Alphonse Mingana, "Syriac Versions of the Old Testament," *JQR, N.S.,* 6 (1915-16) 385-398.

Joshua Bloch, "The Authorship of the Peshitta," *AJSL* 35 (1918-19) 215-222.

*D. D. Luckenbill, "The Influence of the Greek Bible on the Peshitta," *AJSL* 36 (1919-20) 161-166.

Joshua Bloch, "The Printed Texts of the Peshitta Old Testament," *AJSL* 37 (1920-21) 136-144.

Charles C. Torrey, "The Loss of the Urumia Concordance to the Peshitta," *JAOS* 43 (1923) 128-129.

†Anonymous, "Concordance to the Peshitta Old Testament," *JRAS* (1923) 269-270. *[Announcement]*

*F. Zimmermann, "The Text of the Psalms in the Peshitta," *JTS* 41 (1940) 44-46.

*Harold R. Willoughby, "Stray New Testament-Psalter Leaves Identified," *JBL* 61 (1942) 57-60. [Ex. 15:1b-19; Deut. 32:1-6b]

M. H. Gottstein, "A List of Some Uncatalogued Syriac Biblical Manuscripts," *BJRL* 37 (1954-55) 429-445.

*P. A. H. DeBoer, "A Description of the Sinai Syriac MS. 35," *VT* 9 (1959) 408-412. *[1 and 2 Samuel]*

M. Wilcox, "Some Recent Contributions to the Problem of Peshitta Origins," *Abr-N* 1 (1959-60) 62-67.

*W. Baars, "A Palestinian Syriac Text of the Book of Lamentations," *VT* 10 (1960) 224-227.

M. H. Goshen-Gottstein, "Prolegomena to a Critical Edition of the Peshitta," *SH* 8 (1961) 26-67.

J. A. Emerton, "Unclean Birds and the Origin of the Peshitta," *JSS* 7 (1962) 204-211.

*P. Wernberg-Møller, "Prolegomena to a Re-Examination of the Palestinian Targum Fragments of the Book of Genesis Published by P. Kahle, and Their Relationship to the Peshitta," *JSS* 7 (1962) 253-266.

W. Baars, "The 'Nicene' Creed in the Manuscripts of the Syriac Massora," *JTS, N.S.*, 13 (1962) 336-339.

Anonymous, "Peshiṭta Institute Communications I, First Supplement to the *List of Old Testament Peshiṭta Manuscripts*," *VT* 12 (1962) 127-128.

Anonymous, "Peshiṭta Institute Communications II, Second Supplement to the *List of Old Testament Peshiṭta Manuscripts*," *VT* 12 (1962) 237-239.

Anonymous, "Peshiṭta Institute Communications III, Third Supplement to the *List of Old Testament Peshiṭta Manuscripts*," *VT* 12 (1962) 351.

*P. B. Dirksen, "Peshiṭta Institute Communications IV, A Sixth Century Palimpsest of Judges Reconstructed," *VT* 13 (1963) 349-355.

W. Baars, "Description of Three Syriac Old Testament Manuscripts," *VT* 13 (1963) 260-268.

W. Baars, "Peshiṭta Institute Communications V, On the Order of Books in a Beth Mawtabhe," *VT* 17 (1967) 132-133.

*J. A. Emerton, "The Printed Editions of the Song of Songs in the Peshiṭta Version," *VT* 17 (1967) 416-429.

M. D. Koster, "Peshiṭta Institute Communications VI, A Clue to the Relationship of Some West Peshiṭta Manuscripts," *VT* 17 (1967) 494-496.

P. A. H. de Boer, "Dispersed Leaves," *JSS* 13 (1968) 33-35. *[Peshiṭta]*

*P. Wernberg-Møller, "Some Scribal and Linguistic Features of the Genesis Part of the Oldest Peshiṭta Manuscript (B. M. Add. 14425)," *JSS* 13 (1968) 136-161.

Anonymous, "Peshiṭta Institute Communications VII, Fourth Supplement to the *List of Old Testament Peshiṭta Manuscripts*," *VT* 18 (1968) 128-145.

N. Walker, "The Peshiṭta Puzzle and Its Implications," *VT* 18 (1968) 268-270.

*Leona G. Running, "Peshiṭta Institute Communications VIII, The Problem of the Mixed Syriac MSS of Susanna in the Seventeenth Century," *VT* 19 (1969) 377-383.

§260 *3.1.3.8.1 Tatian's Diatessaron and the Old Testament*

*George F. Moore, "Tatian's Diatessaron and the Analysis of the Pentateuch," *JBL* 9 (1890) 201-215.

*Charles M. Mead, "Tatian's Diatessaron and the analysis of the Pentateuch, A Reply," *JBL* 10 (1891) 44-54.

J. Rendel Harris, "Was the Diatessaron Anti-Judaic?" *HTR* 18 (1925) 103-109.

*Robert P. Casey, "The Armenian Marcionites and the Diatessaron," *JBL* 57 (1938) 185-194.

§261 *3.1.3.9 Other Early Versions - Unclassified*

C. K. Nelson, "The Gothic Bible of Ulfilas," *PAPA* 17 (1885) xxxvii.

Theodore W. Hunt, "The Gothic Bible," *HR* 44 (1902) 206-211.

H. M. Bannister, "Irish Psalters," *JTS* 12 (1910-11) 280-284.

J. W. Bright and R. L. Ramsay, "Notes on the 'Introductions' of the West-Saxon Psalms," *JTS* 13 (1911-12) 520-558.

Edward Kennar Rand, "A Preliminary Study of Alcuin's Bible," *HTR* 24 (1931) 323-396.

*Toyozo W. Nakarai, "Columbus in the Genoa Psalter," *SQ/E* 3 (1942) 171-182.

John M. Lenhart, "Protestant Latin Bibles of the Reformation from 1520-1570," *CBQ* 8 (1946) 416-432.

W[alter] J. Fischel, "The Earliest Persian Bible Manuscripts in European Libraries—as Collected by Giambattista Vechiete (1552-1619)," *JBL* 69 (1950) xiv.

Walter J. Fischel, "The Bible in Persian Translation. A Contribution to the History of Bible Translations in Persia and India," *HTR* 45 (1952) 3-45.

E. Z. Melamed, "On the Tafsir of the Persian Jews," *EI* 4 (1956) XIV.

W. Leonard Grant, "Neo-Latin Verse-Translations of the Bible," *HTR* 52 (1959) 205-211.

*Herbert H. Paper, "The Vatican Judeo-Persian Pentateuch. Genesis," *AO* 28 (1964-65) 263-340.

*M. Altbauer, "Traces of Hebrew Commentaries in the Slavonic Translations of the Bible," *Tarbiẕ* 34 (1964-65) #4, IX-X.

*Herbert H. Paper, "The Vatican Judeo-Persian Pentateuch. Exodus and Leviticus," *AO* 29 (1965-66) 75-181.

*Herbert H. Paper, "The Vatican Judeo-Persian Pentateuch. Numbers," *AO* 29 (1965-66) 253-310.

Herbert H. Paper, "A Note on Judea-Persian Copulas," *JAOS* 87 (1967) 227-230. *[Persian Biblical Texts]*

*Herbert H. Paper, "The Vatican Judeo-Persian Pentateuch. Deuteronomy," *AO* 31 (1968) 56-113.

*Herbert H. Paper, "The Use of *(ha)mē* in Selected Judeo-Persian Texts," *JAOS* 88 (1968) 483-494.

§262 *3.1.4 Early English MSS and Printed Texts*

Anonymous, "A Proposal for correcting the English Translation of the Scriptures," *TRep* 4 (1784) 187-188.

†Anonymous, "Dr. Geddes on the Bible," *BCQTR* 4 (1794) 1-12, 147-158.

†Anonymous, "Mr. Pratt's Prospectus of a new Polyglott Bible," *BCQTR* 11 (1798) 105-117.

†Salopiensis, "Roman Catholic Translation of the Bible," *MMBR* 6 (1798) 347-348. *[Philip Buonamici Translation]*

†Anonymous, "Geddes's Bible.   Vol. II.," *BCQTR* 14 (1799) 577-586. *(Review)*

†Anonymous, "Mr. Reeves's Edition of the Bible," *BCQTR* 19 (1802) 441-448. *(Review)*

†M. Smart, "On the Incorrectness of our printed Bibles," *MMBR* 27 (1809) 37-40.

†D. Copsey, "On the Errata in the Oxford Stereo-type Bible, 8vo.," *MMBR* 34 (1812-13) 298.

†Anonymous, "Hewlett's Bible," *BCQTR, N.S.,* 1 (1813) 337-352. *(Review)*

†S. Collingwood, "Accuracy of Stereotype Editions," *MMBR* 34 (1812-13) 483-484. *[Oxford Stereotype Bible]*

Anonymous, "Varieties, Literary and Philosophical, Including Notices of Works in Hand, Foreign and Domestic," *MMBR* 43 (1817) 57-63. [The Geneva Bible, pp. 59-60]

Anonymous, "Varieties, Literary and Philosophical, Including Notices of Works in Hand, Domestic and Foreign," *MMBR* 44 (1817-18) 160-167. [John Bellamy's Translation of the Hebrew Scriptures, pp. 162-163]

W. O., "The Geneva Bible," *CongML* 1 (1818) 129-133.

W. O., "The Bishop's Bible," *CongML* 1 (1818) 305-308.

†Anonymous, "Critical Notes on New Books," *MMBR* 45 (1818) 343-346. [John Bellamy's Translation of the Hebrew Bible, pp. 344-346]

†J. T. Smith, "The Rev. J. T. Smith on Mr. Bellamy's New Bible," *MMBR* 45 (1818) 481-485.

†Anonymous, "Bellamy's *Translation of the Bible,*" *QRL* 19 (1818) 250-280.

†Anonymous, "Bellamy's *Reply to the Quarterly Review,*" *QRL* 19 (1818) 446-460. *(Review)*

C. Lucas, "Mr. Lucas on the Inaccuracies in the Oxford Bible, &c.," *MMBR* 47 (1819) 130-131.

†Anonymous, "On the New Translation of the Holy Scriptures," *BCQTR, N.S.,* 13 (1820) 337-366, 449-478. *[Bellamy's Translation]*

†Anonymous, *"Translations of the Bible* —Bellamy, Sir J. B. Burges, &c.," *QRL* 23 (1820) 287-325. *(Review)*

†Anonymous, "Todd's Memoirs of Brian Walton," *BCQTR, N.S.,* 18 (1822) 641-652. *(Review) [Bellamy's Translation]*

†Pater-familias, "Editions of the Bible," *MMBR* 54 (1822-23) 212-214. *[Mistakes in printing]*

Anonymous, "Remarks on the Propriety of a New Translation of the Scriptures into English," *BibR* 1 (1825) 307-391, 463-498.

[B. B. Edwards], "Early English Versions of the Bible," *BRCR* 6 (1835) 451-482.

†Anonymous, "Catholic Versions of the Scriptures," *DR* 2 (1836-37) 475-492. *(Review)*

†Anonymous, "Annals of the English Bible," *BQRL* 3 (1846) 438-468. *(Review)*

N. L. F., "Noyes's Proverbs, Ecclesiastes, and Canticles," *CE* 40 (1846) 424-434. *(Review)*

*R. B[abcock], "Hebrew Poetry Made Intelligible to Readers of Our Common Bible. Nourse's Edition of the Bible," *CRB* 12 (1847) 387-396.

(   ) R., "Historical Sketch of Translations of the Scripture into the Languages of Britain," *CRB* 13 (1848) 234-248.

G. L., "John Wycliffe and the First English Bible," *CE* 51 (1851) 53-75. *(Review)*

Anonymous, "Wycliffe's Bible," *JSL, 2nd Ser.,* 1 (1851-52) 116-134. *(Review)*

Anonymous, "English Translations of the Bible," *BS* 15 (1858) 261-288.

[B. F. Hayes], "The English Bible in Manuscript, and its Translators," *FBQ* 10 (1862) 241-260.

Anonymous, "The English Bible: Its Revision and History," *JSL, 4th Ser.,* 1 (1862) 116-127. *(Review)*

Anonymous, "The English Bible: Its Early History and Literary Characteristics," *DUM* 66 (1865) 363-381.

Anonymous, "Tyndale and the English Bible," *BFER* 17 (1868) 89-114. *(Review)*

John Gemmel, "Our English Bible," *BFER* 21 (1872) 347-371.

James A. Corcoran, "Vernacular Versions of the Bible, Old and New," *ACQR* 4 (1879) 344-388.

A. St. John Chambré, "The English Bible, and Revision," *UQGR, N.S.,* 17 (1880) 133-149.

Charles A[ugustus] Briggs, "Tyndale's Pentateuch," *PR* 5 (1884) 131.

Samuel J. Barrows, "John Bellamy's Bible," *URRM* 24 (1885) 289-302.

J.L.Ewell,"Wiclif's*[sic]* Bible Honored by the Revision,"*BS* 44(1887)36-45.

William Levering Devries, "The English Bible," *ONTS* 9 (1889) 152-161.

F. A. Gasquet, "The Pre-Reformation English Bible," *DR* 115 (1894) 122-152.

*James Brown, "The Germ of Astruc's Theory," *ET* 10 (1898-99) 91-92. *[Matthew's Bible]*

*Eb. Nestle, "A Forgotten Letter on the English Bible and the Septuagint," *ET* 16 (1904-05) 380-381.

George Joseph Reid, "The Evolution of Our English Bible," *ACQR* 30 (1905) 563-591.

C. Abbetmeyer, "The Wycliffite Versions of the Bible," *TQ* 9 (1905) 149-169.

W. Aldis Wright, "The Prayer Book Psalter," *JTS* 7 (1905-06) 270-272. (Corrections p. 629) *[Coverdale Bible]*

J. T. Davies, "The Three English Versions of the Scriptures," *MQR, 3rd Ser.,* 32 (1906) 64-83.

E[b]. Nestle, "On Some Early Editions of Tindal's*[sic]* Translations," *JTS* 10 (1908-09) 129-133.

Bede Jarrett, "A Thirteenth Century Revision Committee of the Bible," *ITQ* 5 (1910) 53-63.

John Rothwell Slater, "English Versions before 1611," *BW* 37 (1911) 232-239.

*Henry H. Howorth, "The Bible Canon of the Reformation: Coverdale's Bible," *IJA* #31 (1912) 67-71.

Clyde Weber Votaw, "Martyrs for the English Bible," *BW* 52 (1918) 296-299.

P. E. Kretzmann, "Vernacular Versions of Parts of the Bible in England before Wyclif," *TQ* 24 (1920) 171-178.

Hugh Pope, "The Lollard Bible," *DR* 168 (1921) 60-72.

J. Herbert Willams, "Scripture Versions and Variants,"*DR* 170 (1922) 20-53.

John Alfred Faulkner, "English Bible Translations," *BR* 9 (1924) 199-231.

Ernest Clapton, "Coverdale and the Psalter," *CQR* 107 (1928-29) 288-307.

E[dmund] J. C. Meier, "Old And Curious Editions of the Bible," *CTM* 5 (1934) 717-719.

Henry J. Cowell, "Miles Coverdale and His Bible," *CRP* 4 (1935) 126-132.

T. Wilber Elmore, "Myles*[sic]* Coverdale and the English Bible," *CRP* 4 (1935) 261-267.

John Theodore Mueller, "The First Complete Printed Bible," *CTM* 6 (1935) 721-731. *[Miles Coverdale Bible]*

Edmund [J. C.] Meier, "Interesting Old Bibles," *CTM* 6 (1935) 928-931.

Ismar J. Peritz, "The Coverdale Bible—1535," *RL* 4 (1935) 505-515.

A. D. Mattson, "Four Hundredth Anniversary of Myles Coverdale's Translation of the Bible," *TF* 7 (1935) 181-183.

H[arold] R. Willoughby, "Current Errors Concerning the Coverdale Bible," *JBL* 55 (1936) v.

Harold R. Willoughby, "Current Errors Concerning the Coverdale Bible," *JBL* 55 (1936) 1-16.

W. T. Whitley, "Thomas Matthew's Bible," *CQR* 125 (1937-38) 48-69.

J. H. Morrison, "The Reformation and the English Bible," *ET* 49 (1937-38) 246-248.

Reginald F. Rynd, "A Biblical Anniversary," *HJ* 36 (1937-38) 602-608. *[The Great Bible]*

*Hugh Pope, "Misprints, or Heresies," *ClR* 23 (1943) 114-120.

Hugh Pope, "The MacMahon Bibles, 1783-1810," *IER, 5th Ser.,* 68 (1946) 1-11.

T. Connelly, "The Haydock Bible," *Scrip* 1 (1946) 81-85.

J. F. H. Tregear, "The First English Bible. Part I," *ClR* 27 (1947) 145-162.

J. F. H. Tregear, "The First English Bible. Part II," *ClR* 27 (1947) 325-341.

Joan M. Frayn, "Early English Versions of the Scriptures," *CongQL* 29 (1951) 153-158.

Eric Colledge, "The Lollard Bible," *NB* 33 (1952) 306-310.

‡E. J. Saleska, "Our English Bible," *CTM* 24 (1953) 13-25. *[Extensive Bibliography]*

Daniel G. Kratz, "The Geneva Bible," *T&L* 3 (1960) 23-31.

Ira Jay Martin III, "The Geneva Bible," *ANQ, N.S.,* 1 (1960-61) #4, 46-51.

Bruce M. Metzger, "The Geneva Bible of 1560," *TT* 17 (1960-61) 339-352.

Carle S. Meyer, "The Geneva Bible," *CTM* 32 (1961) 139-145.

Robert Sumner Jackson, "The 'Inspired' Style of the English Bible," *JAAR* 29 (1961) 4-15.

*Robert John Wilson, "1691-1961—A Two Hundred and Seventieth Anniversary. The Burning Bush," *ET* 73 (1961-62) 30.

*George Rust, "The Burning Bush," *ET* 73 (1961-62) 93.

*Sakae Kubo, "The Influence of the Vulgate on the English Translation of the Psalms," *AUSS* 3 (1965) 34-41.

Chaim Wirszubski, "Giovanni Pico's Book of Job," *JWCI* 32 (1969) 171-199.

§263 *3.1.4.1 Authorized Version of 1611*

*Anonymous, "Cornucopia," *MMBR* 42 (1816-17) 231-233. *[Translation of the Bible: names of those employed in translating the KJV and rules for conducting the Translation]*

W. O., "King James's Version of the Bible," *CongML* 1 (1818) 410-412, 468-471.

*†Anonymous, "The Authorized Translation of the Bible," *BCQTR, N.S.*, 6 (1829) 232-240.

†Anonymous, "Mr. Curtis's Misrepresentations of the authorized Versions of the Bible," *BCQTR, 4th Ser.*, 14 (1833) 1-26. *(Review)*

T[homas] C[urtis], "History and State of the Present Received Version of the Bible," *CRB* 3 (1838) 34-53.

Thomas Watts, "On some Philological Peculiarities in the English Authorized Version of the Bible," *TPS* 6 (1852-53) 7-11.

Anonymous, "A New Translation of the Bible," *DUM* 48 (1856) 345-353. *[List of Names of Translators of the KJV, pp. 347-348]*

Edward W. Gilman, "Early Editions of the Authorized Version of the Bible," *BS* 16 (1859) 56-81.

C. P. Krauth, "On the Internal History of the Authorized English Version of the Bible," *JAOS* 7 (1862) lvi.

James A. Corcoran, "How Heresy Deals with the Bible," *ACQR* 4 (1879) 123-137. *[Review of KJV]*

Charles Short, "On the use of the Article: a study in the revision of the King James' version of the Bible," *SBLP* (Dec., 1880) 4-5.

Benjamin Dawson, "Notes on the *N* and *AN,* etc., in the Authorized and Revised Versions of the Bible," *TPS* (1880-81) 347-353.

*Howard Osgood, "Is the Revised Version of the Old Testament Better than the Authorized?" *BS* 44 (1887) 71-90.

*R. W. Thompson, "The King James and Douay Versions of the Bible," *HR* 49 (1905) 193-197.

S. R. Driver, "The Authorized Version of the Bible," *ET* 22 (1910-11) 341-346.

H. C. Hoskier, "The 'Authorized' Version of the 1611," *BS* 68 (1911) 693-704.

John F. Genung, "Why the Authorized Version Became an English Classic," *BW* 37 (1911) 224-231.

Walter R. Betteridge, "The Accuracy of the Authorized Version of the Old Testament," *BW* 37 (1911) 262-270.

Robert G. Armstrong, "The Inheritance of the Authorized Bible of 1611," *BW* 38 (1911) 402-415.

Henry E. Dosker, "The Version of 1611," *HR* 62 (1911) 8-15.

L. Franklin Gruber, "The Version of 1611: Propriety of Calling It 'The Authorized Version' or 'King James's Version'," *BW* 42 (1913) 218-233.

L. Franklin Gruber and Henry E. Dosker, "'The Authorized Version'," *HR* 67 (1914) 425.

L. Franklin Gruber, "The Version of 1611: Propriety of Calling It 'The Authorized Version' or 'King James's Version'," *LCR* 33 (1914) 75-90, 279-286.

*John A. F. Gregg, "Transliteration as Translation: A Study of Certain Features in the Influence of the Vulgate on the Authorized Version," *ET* 42 (1930-31) 8-14.

Charles Short, "On the use of the Article: a study in the revision of the Bible," *JBL* 49 (1931) xl-xli. *[Reprint of the proceedings of the second meeting of the Society of Biblical Literature - May be bound separately]*

Edgar J. Goodspeed, "'The Translators to the Reader'," *RL* 1 (1932) 407-418. *[KJV]*

*Geo. A. W. Vogel, "A Comparison of the King James and the Douay Version," *CTM* 6 (1935) 18-24, 102-113.

Kendrick Grobel, "Death-throes of English Grammatical Gender in the King James Bible," *JBL* 58 (1939) iv.

*T. C. Dunham, "A Layman on King James Versus Moffatt," *JAAR* 14 (1946) 107-110.

C. F. Nesbitt, "On the Authorization of the English Bible," *JBL* 68 (1949) vii.

Charles F. Nesbitt, "The Authorization of the English Bible," *RL* 19 (1950) 70-82.

Anonymous, "The Bible in English. The Three Hundred and Fiftieth Anniversary of the Authorized Version 1611-1961," *RefmR* 8 (1960-61) 200-210.

*F. F. Bruce, "The Authorized Version and Others," *IRM* 50 (1961) 409-416.

Susie I. Tucker, "The Historical and Literary Setting of the Authorized Version," *LQHR* 186 (1961) 89-94.

§264 *3.1.5 Modern English Translations (c. 1850ff.)*

[Matthew(?)] Arnold, "The Translations of the Bible. [From the German of Dr. Arnold]," *MQR* 11 (1857) 414-428. *(Trans. by [John Adam(?) Reubelt])*

Anonymous, "Revision of the English Bible," *WR* 67 (1857) 134-172.

†Anonymous, "Revision of the English Bible," *PQR* 6 (1857-58) 255-284. *(Review)*

Alpha, "The Catholic Church and the Bible," *IER, 1st Ser.,* 1 (1864-65) 253-261, 323-333.

(　) V., "Sharpe's Hebrew Scriptures," *TR* 2 (1865) 574-583. *[O.T. English Translation] (Review)*

T. K. Cheyne, "The Revision of the Authorized Version:—Old Testament," *ContR* 2 (1866) 141-165.

S. D., "English Versions of the Bible and the Necessity for a New One," *TR* 3 (1866) 188-210.

Anonymous, "The English Bible," *CE* 86 (1869) 263-279. *(Review)*

James H. Means, "The Revision of the English Bible," *CongQB* 13 (1871) 514-531.

Russell Martineau, "The Revision of the Authorized Version of the Old Testament," *TRL* 8 (1871) 53-72.

Anonymous, "Bible Revision," *MQR, 2nd Ser.,* 2 (1880) 70-82.

Richard Gee, "The English of the English Bible," *CM* 15 (1882) 129-139, 234-245.

*Francis Bowen, "An Early American Version of the Scriptures, compared with the Revised Version of 1881," *PRev* 59 (1883) Part 1, 19-45. *[Charles Thomson translation]*

†Anonymous, "The Bible in the British Museum," *QRL* 178 (1894) 157-184. *(Review) [Correction slip inserted before p. 289]*

Anonymous, "Haupt's Polychrome Old Testament," *MR* 78 (1896) 644-646. *(Review)*

Geo. H. Schodde, "Biblical Research Notes. Bible Text and Bible Translations," *ColTM* 17 (1897) 371-373. *(Review)*

*Bernhard Pick, "The Text of Jeremiah in the Polychrome Edition of the Old Testament," *HR* 33 (1897) 354-356.

T. P. W., "The New Woman on the Bible," *SRL* 30 (1897) 300-322. *[Woman's Bible]*

[Paul Carus], "The Polychrome Bible," *OC* 12 (1898) 288-292. *(Review)*

C[arl] H[einrich] Cornill, "The Polychrome Bible," *Monist* 10 (1899-1900) 1-21.

W[illiam] Henry Green, "The Polychrome Bible," *Monist* 10 (1899-1900) 22-40.

C[arl] H[einrich] Cornill, "The New Bible and the Old. In Reply to Professor Green," *Monist* 10 (1899-1900) 441-454.

B[ernhard] Pick, "A Century of Biblical Versions," *LQ* 31 (1901) 197-216.

Thos. F. Lockyer, "The Bible in English. Some Recent Versions and Editions," *LQHR* 98 (1902) 119-139. *(Review)*

A. G., "The History of the English Bible," *TQ* 7 (1903) 42-64.

Ivan Panin, "A Letter to the American Baptist Publication Society of 'The Psalms of David'," *CFL, 3rd Ser.,* 13 (1910) 107-110.

Henry Thatcher Fowler, "The Great Modern Versions of the English Bible," *BW* 37 (1911) 278-285.

G. C. Macaulay, "The English Bible," *QRL* 215 (1911) 505-530. *(Review)*

Randolph H. McKim, "A Critical Examination of the 'The Bible of 1911'," *BS* 70 (1913) 123-144. [Errata, p. viii]

F. H. Woods, "The Revision of the Prayer-book Psalter," *ET* 25 (1913-14) 112-116.

Alexander Nairne, "Versions of the Holy Scripture," *CQR* 78 (1914) 406-435. *(Review)*

Anonymous, "New Versions of the Bible," *MR* 96 (1914) 633-637.

David James Burrell, "Wanted: A Bible in the Vernacular," *BR* 3 (1918) 522-529.

E. Herman, "The Need for a New Translation of the Old Testament. *Interview with Professor James Moffatt, D.D., D.Litt., Glasgow, Scotland," HR* 76 (1918) 5-9.

Anonymous, "A New English Translation of the Bible for the Jews," *MR* 101 (1918) 453-459.

[Paul Carus], "A Jewish Translation of the Old Testament," *OC* 32 (1918) 103-105. *[The Holy Scriptures According to the Masoretic Text]*

David Reid, "An Abridged Old Testament for Popular Use," *ET* 30 (1918-19) 200-203.

R. Somervell, "An Abridged Old Testament, I.," *ET* 30 (1918-19) 328.

J. Claire Hudson, "An Abridged Old Testament, II.,"*ET* 30 (1918-19) 328.

E. Herman, "An Abridged Old Testament," *HR* 77 (1919) 366-367.

*David E. Culley, "The Revised Version and Other Recent Translations of the Bible," *BWTS* 13 (1920-21) 28-38.

John Fox, "The Shorter Bible," *KZ* 46 (1922) 201-216. *(Review)*

R. Lechner, "English Bible Translations," *KZ* 46 (1922) 336-348.

Leander S. Keyser, "'The Shorter Bible' and Its Authors," *LQ* 52 (1922) 227-231.

John Fox, "The Shorter Bible—The Old Testament," *PTR* 20 (1922) 118-132. *(Review)*

H. F. B. Compston, "Dr. Moffatt's Translation of the Old Testament," *CQR* 100 (1924-25) 220-241.

Edward Mack, "Dr. Moffatt's New Translation of the Old Testament," *USR* 36 (1924-25) 135-137.

Herbert H. Gowen, "Dr. Moffatt's Translation of the Old Testament," *ACM* 17 (1925) 208-217.

Parke P. Flournoy, "Doctor Moffatt's New Translation of the Bible," *BS* 82 (1925) 462-471. *(Review)*

I. G. Matthews, "Moffatt's Genesis to Esther," *CQ* 2 (1925) 223-231. *(Review)*

E. B. Pollard, "Rhetorical Word-Play in Moffatt's Old Testament," *CQ* 2 (1925) 331-337.

Anonymous, "Doctor Moffatt's New Translation of the Old Testament," *HR* 89 (1925) 112.

Julius A. Bewer, "Translation of the Bible—Dr. Moffatt's Old Testament," *HR* 89 (1925) 471-474.

Oswald T. Allis, "Dr. Moffatt's 'New Translation' of the Old Testament," *PTR* 23 (1925) 267-317.

Parke P. Flournoy, "The Old Testament, A New Translation by Dr. James Moffatt," *BS* 83 (1926) 229-232. *(Review)*

Junius B. Remensynder, "Dr. Moffatt's Translation of the Old Testament," *LQ* 56 (1926) 304-306.

*E. Berrum, "The Difference Between the Protestant and the Catholic Bible," *TTM* 10 (1926-27) 241-256.

*A. Z. Conrad, "One-Man Bible Translations," *CFL, 3rd Ser.,* 33 (1927) 657-658. *[Moffatt's Translation]*

Leander S. Keyser, "A New Translation of the Old Testament," *CFL, 3rd Ser.,* 34 (1928) 685-689. *[Smith and Goodspeed(?)]*

Anonymous, "A New Translation of the Old Testament," *HR* 95 (1928) 108-109. *[University of Chicago Version/Publication]*

H. J. Schick, "Modern Bible Translations and Their Problems," *TZDES* 57 (1929) 105-111.

Oswald T. Allis, "The Short Bible—Its Meaning and Menace," *EQ* 6 (1934) 7-25.

Claud H. Edmunds, "Versions of the Bible," *Theo* 30 (1935) 36. *[Moulton's—The Modern Reader's Bible]*

Evert Mordecai Clark, "Some Stylistic Aspects of the Smith-Goodspeed Bible," *JAAR* 4 (1936) #2, 74-83.

Leroy Waterman, "Spiritual Gains from New Translations of the Bible," *JAAR* 5 (1937) 120-126.

Edgar J. Goodspeed, "A Complete Bible," *JAAR* 9 (1941) 35-38.

Hugh Pope, "Misprints, or Heresies," *ClR* 23 (1943) 114-120.

Henry H. Walker, "A Survey of Short Bibles," *JAAR* 13 (1945) 201-204.

*T. C. Dunham, "A Layman on King James Versus Moffatt," *JAAR* 14 (1946) 107-110.

Fred H. Ilten, "Moffatt's Translation of the Bible (A Conference Essay)," *CTM* 18 (1947) 218-228. [O.T., pp. 220-224]

James A. Montgomery, "A Modern Translation of the Hebrew Bible Compared with the Ancient Versions," *JBL* 66 (1947) 311-314.

Reginald Ginns, "New Biblical Versions," *LofS* 4 (1949-50) 163-169.

W. Rees, "The New Latin Translation of the Psalms," *Scrip* 4 (1949-51) 205-212.

E. C. Blackman, "The Bible in Basic English," *CongQL* 28 (1950) 357-358.

Ovid R. Seller, "English Bibles," *McQ* 5 (1951-52) #4, 3-6.

J. [Barton] Payne, "The Berkeley Version of the OT," *JBL* 71 (1952) xv.

Edward P. Arbez, "Modern Translations of the Old Testament," *CBQ* 16 (1954) 201-209, 343-347, 450-457.

C. Leslie Mitton, "Modern Translations of the Bible," *LQHR* 179 (1954) 113-119.

Edward P. Arbez, "Modern Translations of the Old Testament," *CBQ* 17 (1955) 76-85, 456-485.

*F. F. Bruce, "The Authorized Version and Others," *IRM* 50 (1961) 409-416.

Bernard M. G. Reardon, "The New English Bible," *QRL* 299 (1961) 422-428.

Sidney B. Hoenig, "The New Translation of the Torah—A Preliminary Inquiry," *Trad* 5 (1962-63) 172-205.

Eugene H. Maly, "The English Bible," *BibT* #7 (1963) 444-451.

Dewey M. Beegle, "A New Translation of the Torah," *BTr* 14 (1963) 97-105. *(Review)*

H. L. Ginsberg, "The New Jewish Publication Society Translation of the Torah," *JAAR* 31 (1963) 187-192.

Theophile J. Meek, "A New Bible Translation," *JBL* 82 (1963) 265-271. *[JPS Torah]*

Maurice L. Zigmond, "The New JPS Torah—A Critical Appraisal," *CCARJ* 11 (1963-64) #4, 4-16.

Ralph P. Kingsley, "The Burber-Rosenzweig Translation of the Bible," *CCARJ* 11 (1963-64) #4, 17-22.

David Mowbray, "Tentative Thoughts on the Berkeley Version," *BofT* #65 (1969) 24-28.

Harold A. Guy, "An Eighteenth Century N. E. B.," *ET* 81 (1969-70) 148-159. [*A New and Literal Translation of all the Books of the Old and New Testaments, with Notes Critical and Explanatory,* by Anthony Purver]

E. H. Robertson, "N. E. B. 1970," *ET* 81 (1969-70) 203-204.

T. H. Brown, "The New English Bible—1970," *RefR* 17 (1969-70) 223-236.
[O.T., p. 226]

§265 *3.1.5.1 Catholic Versions*

A. B. Rich, "The Douay or Catholic Bible," *CongR* 7 (1867) 576-619.

L. T[oole], "Catholic Translations of the Bible into English, and Editions of Them," *IER, 3rd Ser.,* 2 (1881) 85-95.

Thomas J. Butler, "The Douay Bible," *IER, 4th Ser.,* 8 (1900) 23-35.

*George L. Robinson, "The Origin and History of (1) The Version of the Bible Authorized by the Roman Catholic Church (2) The Version of the Bible Known as the Revised Version, American Standard Version," *BRec* 2 (1905) 352-374, 391-431.

Hugh Pope, "The Origin of the Douay Bible," *DR* 147 (1910) 97-118.

E. Olive Dutcher, "The Douay Version," *BW* 37 (1911) 240-246.

William L. Newton, "Bishop Challoner's Revision of the Old Testament," *CBQ* 2 (1940) 215-228.

Hugh Pope, "Some Omissions in the Douay-Rheims Version," *ClR* 19 (1940) 112-121.

H. D. Morris, "A New Revision of our English Bible," *ACR* 18 (1941) 162-174. *[Douay-Rheims Challoner]*

Hugh Pope, "Should We Continue to Use the Challoner's Version in Church?" *IER, 5th Ser.,* 59 (1942) 111-127.

*Hugh Pope, "Misprints, or Heresies," *ClR* 23 (1943) 114-120.

Hugh Pope, "The History of the Rheims-Douay Version of the Bible," *DownsR* 62 (1944) 157-171.

Matthew P. Stapleton, "Catholic Bible Translations," *JAAR* 14 (1946) 198-202.

Anonymous, "Bishop Challoner and the Douay Bible," *Scrip* 2 (1947) 8-18.

Charles M. Cooper, "Msgr. Knox's Old Testament in English," *LQ, N.S.,* 3 (1951) 366-382.

Edward P. Arbez, "The New Catholic Translation of the Old Testament," *CBQ* 14 (1952) 237-254.

John M. T. Barton, "Knox Bible: Final Edition," *ClR* 40 (1955) 708-714.

C. Umhau Wolf, "Recent Roman Catholic Bible Study and Translation," *JAAR* 29 (1961) 280-289.

*Frank Pack, "An Evaluation of the Revised Standard Version, Catholic Edition," *RestQ* 9 (1966) 21-30.

Frederick W. Danker, "The Jerusalem Bible: A Critical Examination," *CTM* 38 (1967) 168-180.

James Brennan, "The Jerusalem Bible," *IER, 5th Ser.,* 107 (1967) 319-326.

*James Barr, "Biblical Translation and the Church," *NB* 49 (1967-68) 285-292. *[Jerusalem Bible]*

Marcus A. Ward, "A New Bible Translation," *PQL* 13 (1967) 11-17. *[The Jerusalem Bible]*

Bruce M. Metzger, "New Editions of the Scriptures: The Jerusalem Bible," *PSB* 60 (1967) #2, 45-48. *[English Text Edition]*

Adam Fox, "The Bible," *QRL* 305 (1967) 196-204. *[Jerusalem Bible]*

C. R. Badger, "The Jerusalem Bible," *StMR* #49 (1967) 28-52. *[English Edition]*

§266 *3.1.5.2 Revised Version of 1881*

W. Sanday, "The New Bible," *Exp, 1st Ser.*, 5 (1877) 401-406.

*John DeWitt, "Bible Revision and the Psalms," *PR* 1 (1880) 499-525.

James A. Corcoran, "The Latest of the Revisions," *ACQR* 6 (1881) 481-507

John B. Adger, "Revision of the English Bible," *SPR* 32 (1881) 369-387.

Anonymous, "The Revised Version and Its Critics," *CQR* 15 (1882-83) 343-368.

Anonymous, "The Revised Scriptures," *ONTS* 2 (1882-83) 22.

*Francis Bowen, "An Early American Version of the Scriptures, compared with the Revised Version of 1881," *PRev* 59 (1883) Part 1, 19-45. *[Charles Thomson translation]*

Anonymous, "Shall the Revision be Revised?" *ONTS* 5 (1884-85) 137

Anonymous, "The Revision, Considered Theologically," *ONTS* 5 (1884-85) 137-138.

Edwin Cone Bissell, "The Revised Psalter," *ONTS* 5 (1884-85) 150-157, 245-248, 295-299.

Anonymous, "The New Version of the English Protestant Bible," *ACQR* 10 (1885) 520-531.

Anonymous, "The Revision of the Old Testament, and the Religious Public," *AR* 3 (1885) 472-477.

C. M. Mead, "The Revised Old Testament," *AR* 3 (1885) 493-508.

T. J. Conant, "The Revised Version of the Old Testament," *BQR* 5 (1885) 334-354.

W. Gray Elmslie, "The Revised Old Testament," *BQRL* 82 (1885) 122-136.

Talbot W. Chambers, "Professor Briggs on the Revised Version of the Old Testament," *BS* 42 (1885) 736-765.

Anonymous, "The Revised Version of the Old Testament," *CQR* 20 (1885) 438-461.

Henry Hayman, "The Revised Version of the Old Testament," *CM* 21 (1885) 65-77.

Frederic Gardiner, "The Revision of the Old Testament," *CR* 46 (1885) 448-465.

†Anonymous, "The Revised Version of the Old Testament," *ERCJ* 162 (1885) 448-494.

A. C. Jennings and W. H. Lowe, "The Revised Version of the Old Testament—A Critical Estimate," *Exp, 3rd Ser.,* 2 (1885) 57-70, 119-131, 277-288, 346-356, 425-436.

G. C. M. Douglas, "The Revision of the English Old Testament. No. 1," *MI* 2 (1885) 81-90.

G. C. M. Douglas, "The Revision of the English Old Testament. No. II," *MI* 2 (1885) 254-263.

G. C. M. Douglas, "The Revision of the English Old Testament. No. III," *MI* 2 (1885) 456-469.

Anonymous, "The Revised Old Testament," *MR* 67 (1885) 758-764. *(Editorial)*

Charles A[ugustus] Briggs, "The Revised English Version of the Old Testament," *PR* 6 (1885) 486-533.

*Henry P[reserved] Smith, "The Old Testament Text and the Revised Version," *PR* 6 (1885) 623-652.

†Anonymous, "The Revised Version of the Old Testament," *QRL* 161 (1885) 281-329. *(Review)*

Edward J. Young, "The Revised Version of the Old Testament," *URRM* 24 (1885) 55-64.

*Charles A. Briggs, "The Attitude of the Revised Version Toward the Textual Criticism of the Old Testament," *AJSL* 2 (1885-86) 65-78. *[Revised of 1881]*

Anonymous, "The Revised Version of the Old Testament. Second Article," *CQR* 21 (1885-86) 181-213.

A. Stewart, "The Revised Old Testament," *ERG, 8th Ser.,* 4 (1885-86) 37-46.

Anonymous, "The Revised Bible," *LQHR* 65 (1885-86) 63-87.

Anonymous, "The Old Testament Revision," *ONTS* 5 (1885-86) 39-41.

Henry P[reserved] Smith, "The Revised Version of the Old Testament," *ONTS* 5 (1885-86) 61-67.

Benjamin Dawson, "Notes on the Revised Version of the Old Testament," *TPS* (1885-87) 333-342.

J. A. Corcoran, "A Few Words More on the New Bible," *ACQR* 11 (1886) 154-168.

Talbot W. Chambers, "Professor Briggs on the Revised Version of the Old Testament," *BFER* 35 (1886) 129-154.

Frederic Gardiner, "The Revision of the Old Testament," *BFER* 35 (1886) 705-721.

Samuel Ives Curtiss, "The Revised Version of the Old Testament," *BS* 43 (1886) 547-564.

J. J. Stewart Perowne, "The Quarterly Reviewer and the Old Testament Revision," *ContR* 49 (1886) 535-545, 638-652.

Benjamin B. Warfield, "What Should be the Attitude of the American Clergy Towards the Revised Version of the Scriptures? No. I," *HR* 11 (1886) 106-112.

T. D. Witherspoon, "What Should be the Attitude of the American Clergy Towards the Revised Version of the Scriptures? No. II," *HR* 11 (1886) 195-201.

G. C. M. Douglas, "The Revision of the English Old Testament. No. IV.," *MI* 4 (1886) 253-268.

G. C. M. Douglas, "The Revision of the English Old Testament. No. V.," *MI* 4 (1886) 372-382.

James Strong, "The Revised Old Testament," *MR* 68 (1886) 33-55.

William Caven, "The Revised Version of the Bible as a Whole," *PR* 7 (1886) 45-88.

W[illiam] Henry Green, "The Critics of the Revised Version of the Old Testament," *PR* 7 (1886) 304-354.

C[harles] A[ugustus] Briggs, "The Discussion of the Revised Version of the Old Testament," *PR* 7 (1886) 369-378.

F. A. Gast, "General Character of the Old Testament Revision," *RChR* 33 (1886) 149-180.

*Howard Osgood, "Is the Revised Version of the Old Testament Better than the Authorized?" *BS* 44 (1887) 71-90.

*Philip Schaff, "The German and Anglo-American Revisions of the Bible," *Exp, 3rd Ser.,* 5 (1887) 468-472.

Henry M. Harman, "Old Testament Revision," *MR* 69 (1887) 421-438.

Elias Riggs, "Some Reasons in Favor of Retouching the Revised English Version of the Scriptures," *PR* 9 (1888) 28-36.

*James M. Garnett, "Why the Revised Version Should be 'Appointed to be Read in Churches'," *PER* 5 (1891-92) 321-336, 431-442.

*Edward Abbott, "The Revised Version in Public Worship," *PER* 6 (1892-93) 169-186.

*Edward Abbott, "The Revised Version in Public Worship. II," *PER* 6 (1892-93) 284-295.

*T. K. Cheyne, "The New Versions of the Psalter and the Book of Judges," *Exp, 5th Ser.,* 7 (1898) 259-275.

*George L. Robinson, "The Origin and History of (1) The Version of the Bible Authorized by the Roman Catholic Church (2) The Version of the Bible Known as the Revised Version, American Standard Version," *BRec* 2 (1905) 352-374, 391-431.

§267 *3.1.5.3 American Revised Version (1901)*

Willis J. Beecher, "The Bible of the American Revision Committee," *HR* 42 (1901) 452-454.

Henry M. Whitney, "The Latest Translation of the Bible," *BS* 59 (1902) 217-237, 451-475, 653-681. (Corr. p. viii) *[Parts I-III]*

Henry M. Whitney, "The Latest Translation of the Bible," *BS* 60 (1903) 109-120, 342-357. *[Parts IV-V]*

John C. Granbery, "The American Revised Version," *MQR, 3rd Ser.,* 29 (1903) 68-76.

Henry M. Whitney, "The Latest Translation of the Bible," *BS* 61 (1904) 248-271. *[Part VI]*

*George L. Robinson, "The Origin and History of (1) The Version of the Bible Authorized by the Roman Catholic Church (2) The Version of the Bible Known as the Revised Version, American Standard Version," *BRec* 2 (1905) 352-374, 391-431.

Henry M. Whitney, "The Latest Translation of the Bible (VII)," *BS* 62 (1905) 71-89.

Henry M. Whitney, "The Latest Translation of the Bible (VIII)," *BS* 62 (1905) 245-263.

Henry M. Whitney, "The Latest Translation of the Bible (IX)," *BS* 64 (1907) 464-488.

Henry M. Whitney, "The Latest Translation of the Bible," *BS* 66 (1909) 467-497. *[Part X]*

Henry M. Whitney, "The Latest Translation of the Bible (XI)," *BS* 68 (1911) 405-415.

Anonymous, "The American Standard Bible and Dr. Charles Marsh Mead," *MR* 94 (1912) 769-771. *(Editorial)*

Randolph H. McKim, "A Critical Examination of the Bible of 1911," *BS* 70 (1913) 123-144. (Errata, p. viii)

William M. Langdon, "Some Merits of the American Standard Bible," *BS* 70 (1913) 486-497.

*David E. Culley, "The Revised Version and Other Recent Translations of the Bible," *BWTS* 13 (1920-21) 28-38.

J. A. Selbie, "The American Translation of the Old Testament," *ET* 39 (1927-28) 171-173. *(Review)*

W. E. Barnes, "The Old Testament. An American Translation," *JTS* 29 (1927-28) 219-220. *(Review)*

Oswald T. Allis, "An 'American' Translation of the Old Testament," *PTR* 26 (1928) 109-141. [Philology and Textual Criticism; Metrics—Its Use and Abuse; The "Unintelligibility" of the AV]

P. E. Kretzmann, "Americanizing the Bible," *CTM* 3 (1932) 55-56.

George Dahl, "Revision of the American Standard Version," *JAAR* 9 (1941) 104-106.

§268 *3.1.5.4 Revised Standard Version*

George S. Hendry, "A New Translation of the Bible," *Theo* 52 (1949) 203-208.

Wilbert F. Howard, "Some Thoughts on a New Translation of the Bible," *LQHR* 175 (1950) 103-122.

John K. S. Reid, "Concerning the New Translation of the Bible," *ET* 63 (1951-52) 172-176.

Walter Harrelson, "The Word of Life in Living Language," *ANQ* 45 (1952) #1, 3-12.

Luther A. Weigle, "The Revised Standard Version of the Bible," *CBQ* 14 (1952) 310-318.

William H. Brownlee, "'The New Bible'," *DDSR* 17 (1952) 69-71. *(Review)*

Sebastian Bullough, "The Revised Standard Version," *LofS* 7 (1952-53) 463-466.

Frank M. Cross Jr., "Notes on the Revised Standard Old Testament," *McQ* 6 (1952-53) #2, 7-10.

Lester J. Kuyper, "The Revised Standard Version," *RefR* 6 (1952-53) #3, 4-7.

C. F. Lincoln, "A Critique of the Revised Standard Version," *BS* 110 (1953) 50-66.

Arthur F. Katt, "Thinking Clearly on the RSV," *CTM* 24 (1953) 273-282.

Clyde T. Francisco, "Revised Standard Version of the Old Testament," *R&E* 50 (1953) 30-55.

*A. R. Crabtree, "The Revised Standard Version of the Psalms," *R&E* 50 (1953) 443-452.

E. J. Poole-Connor, "The Revised Standard Version," *RefmR* 1 (1953-54) #4, 33-41.

Gurdon C. Oxtoby, "An Estimate of the Revised Standard Version," *TT* 10 (1953-54) 19-33.

Jean Henkel Johnson, "The Revised Standard Version of the Old Testament," *ATR* 36 (1954) 111-123.

Nelson B. Baker, "The Revised Version in the Light of History," *R&E* 51 (1954) 62-73.

Theophile J. Meek, "The Revised Standard Version of the Old Testament: An Appraisal," *RL* 23 (1954) 70-82.

G. Ch. Aalders, "The New American Revised Standard Version," *RefmR* 2 (1954-55) 143-157.

E. Milner-White, "The New Joint Translation of the Bible," *CQR* 160 (1959) 293-301.

Millar Burrows, "The Revised Standard Version of the Old Testament," *VTS* 7 (1960) 206-221.

Gerald A. Larue, "Another Chapter in the History of Bible Translation," *JAAR* 31 (1963) 301-310. *[Attacks on the RSV]*

*Frank Pack, "An Evaluation of the Revised Standard Version, Catholic Edition," *RestQ* 9 (1966) 21-30.

*Charles M. Cooper, "The Revised Standard Version of Psalms," *JQR, 75th* (1967) 137-148.

§269 *3.1.6 Foreign Language Translations (i.e., other than English)*

*†Theoph. Abauzit, "Mistakes in the French Stereotype Bible," *MMBR* 36 (1813-14) 128-130.

I. H. Y., "Luther and the German Translation of the Bible," *MR* 19 (1837) 46-51.

S. F. Smith, "Biblical Literature," *CRB* 9 (1844) 256-279. *[Translations of the Scriptures into modern languages]*

[John Ludwig] Krapf, "Three Chapters of Genesis translated into the Sooahele Language by the Rev. Dr. Krapf," *JAOS* 1 (1843-49) 259-274. *[Introduction by W. W. Greenough]*

Anonymous, "The British and Foreign Bible Society," *LQHR* 1 (1853) 353-393. *[Translations of the Scriptures, pp. 381-382]*

P. S., "Polyglott Bibles," *JSL, 3rd Ser.,* 3 (1856) 327-336.

E. C. Lord, "Notices of Scripture Translation in the Chinese Language," *CRB* 22 (1857) 81-110.

†Anonymous, "The French Bible," *BQRL* 41 (1865) 412-442. *(Review)*

Gustave Masson, "Biblical Literature in France during the Middle Ages.—Peter Comestor and Guiart Desmoulins," *JSL, 4th Ser.,* 8 (1865-66) 81-106. *[Published Bibles]*

[S. Pr.] Tregelles, "The Breton Bible," *JSL, 5th Ser.,* 1 (1867) 95-114.

J. Hammond Trumbull, "On Some Mistaken Notions of Algonkin Grammar, and on Mistranslations of Words from Eliot's Bible, &c.," *TAPA* 1 (1869-70) 105-123.

J. H[ammond] Trumbull, "Some Mistakes concerning the Grammar, and in Vocabularies of the Algonkin Language," *PAPA* 2 (1870) 13-14. *[Bound with Transactions, but paged separately]*

S. I. J. Schereschewsky, "Account of the Versions of the Scriptures in the Chinese Language, with remarks on a proposed Mongolian Version," *JAOS* 10 (1880) cxvi-cxvii.

Frederic Vinton, "Vernacular Bibles and the Reformation," *PR* 2 (1881) 384-388.

Anonymous, "The Irish Bible," *CM* 18 (1884) 193-205.

Charles W. Wendte, "Martin Luther and the German Bible," *URRM* 21 (1884) 23-43.

George H. Schodde, "The Revised Luther Bible," *HR* 9 (1885) 394-400.

Isaac H. Hall, "The Arabic Bible of Drs. Eli Smith and Cornelius V. A. Van Dyck," *JAOS* 11 (1885) 276-286.

Isaac H. Hall, "An account of the Arabic Bible of Drs. Eli Smith and Cornelius V. A. Van Dyck," *JAOS* 11 (1885) clxxix-clxxxi.

Hermann L. Strack, "The Work of Bible Revision in Germany. I. Historic Part," *Exp. 3rd Ser.,* 5 (1887) 178-187.

Hermann L. Strack, "The Work of Bible Revision in Germany. II. Critical Part," *Exp, 3rd Ser.,* 5 (1887) 193-201.

*Philip Schaff, "The German and the Anglo-American Revisions of the Bible," *Exp, 3rd Ser.,* 5 (1887) 468-472.

Richard Francis Weymouth, "On French Versions of the Scriptures," *TML* 2 (1889) 361-379.

Geo[rge] S. Goodspeed, "The New German Revised Bible," *ONTS* 14 (1892) 326-331.

N. Forsander, "The Earliest Swedish Bible Translations," *TTKF* 2 (1900) 109-114.

Henry M. Woods, "The Mandarin Revision of the Bible in China," *USR* 15 (1903-04) 65-70.

Anonymous, "The Translators of the Welsh Bible," *CQR* 60 (1905) 46-70.

Anonymous, "The Bible in the World," *HR* 56 (1908) 50-54.

W. D. Reynolds, "How We Translated the Bible into Korean," *USR* 22 (1910-11) 292-303.

T. K. Abbott, "On the History of the Irish Bible," *Herm* 17 (1912-13) 29-50.

W. M. Morrison, "Translation of the Bible into the Buluba Language," *USR* 24 (1912-13) 414-422.

*Henry H. Howorth, "The Bible Canon of the Reformation: Some famous French Bibles, &c., X.," *IJA* #33 (1913) 36-40.

M. A. Honline, "The Bible as a Factor in Civilization," *HR* 68 (1914) 143-145. *[Translations]*

Herbert L. Bishop, "The Translation of Holy Scripture into the Bantu Languages," *LQHR* 130 (1918) 189-198.

R. B. Douglas, "The Bible in Mārāthi," *GUOST* 5 (1923-28) 23-24. *[Indian Language]*

Henry S. Gehman, "The Arabic Bible in Spain," *PAPA* 56 (1925) xxxiii-xxxiv.

W. M. Page, "The Bible in Esperanto," *TM* 6 (1926) 328-331. *(Trans. by Th. Hanssen)*

E. J. Quigley, "The Bible and Ireland," *IER, 5th Ser.,* 35 (1930) 465-473, 604-614; 36 (1930) 75-85, 144-155, 245-255, 471-482, 588-600; 37 (1931) 65-74, 275-289.

Samuel A. B. Mercer, "An Expedition to Abyssinia," *JSOR* 15 (1931) 1-6. *[Translation of the O.T. into Ethiopic]*

Matthew Spinka, "Slavic Translations of the Scriptures," *JR* 13 (1933) 415-432.

S. Ralph Harlow, "Sharing the Bible in Strange Tongues," *JAAR* 5 (1937) 3-10.

Hilding Bradeen, "Sources of Swedish Psalms," *AQ* 17 (1938) 146-155, 251-260.

Charles E. Wilson, "The B. M. S. and Bible Translation," *BQL* 10 (1940-41) 97-105, 159-167.

Harry M. Orlinsky, "Yehoash's Yiddish Translation of the Bible," *JBL* 60 (1941) 173-177.

Theodore W. Anderson, "The First Swedish Bible," *CQ* 2 (1942) #1, 12-17.

Eugene A. Nida, "'Every Man...In His Own Language'," *IRM* 31 (1942) 453-457.

(Miss) Margaret Wrong, "The Development of Literature in Negro and Hamitic-Semitic Languages," *Man* 43 (1943) #20 *[Bible Publications]*

Sisto A. Rosso, "A New Catholic Chinese Version of the Bible," *CBQ* 9 (1947) 96-100.

*Joshua Block, "The New Latin Version of the Psalter," *JQR, N.S.,* 38 (1947-48) 267-288.

Walter Fischel, "The Persian Translation as Ordered by Nadir Shah (1740-1741)," *JBL* 68 (1949) viii.

C. Lattey, "The *Cerf* Edition of Scripture," *Scrip* 4 (1949-51) 301-304.

N. Driver, "The Story of the Tibetan Bible," *IRM* 40 (1951) 197-203.

Dewi Morgan, "The British and Foreign Bible Society's Third Jubilee," *QRL* 291 (1953) 503-515.

A. Osipoff, "Publication of the Russian Bible. Part I," *BTr* 7 (1956) 56-65.

A. Osipoff, "More About the Russian Bible," *BTr* 7 (1956) 98-101.

*Johannes A. Gaerter, "The Latin Verse Translation of the Psalms 1500-1620," *HTR* 49 (1956) 271-305.

Herbert M. Zorn, "Notes on Translation of the Malayalam Bible," *CTM* 28 (1957) 110-117.

R. E. W. Maddison, "Robert Boyle and the Irish Bible," *BJRL* 61 (1958-59) 81-101.

George A. Barrois, "Reflections on Two French Bibles," *TT* 15 (1958-59) 211-216.

Masashi Takahashi, "The Colloquial Japanese Bible of 1955. With a Short History of Bible Translation in Japan," *BTr* 10 (1959) 101-106.

J. R. S. Law, "The Translation of the Bible into Mende," *SLBR* 2 (1960) 40-44.

P. P. Saydon, "Philological and Textual Notes on the Maltese Translation of the Old Testament," *CBQ* 23 (1961) 249-257.

J. Bessem, "Scripture Translations in East Africa," *AfER* 4 (1962) 201-211.

B. Enholc-Narzynska, "The Polish Translations of the Bible," *BTr* 14 (1963) 133-138.

J. Vermeulen, "Scripture Translations in Northern Rhodesia," *AfER* 6 (1964) 67-73.

P. P. Saydon, "The Maltese Translation of the Old Testament," *BTr* 14 (1964) 14-21.

Richard Rutt, "Concerning the New Translation of the Korean Bible," *BTr* 14 (1964) 80-82.

Paul H. Nilson, "Western Turkish Version of the Bible," *BTr* 17 (1966) 133-138.

Errol F. Rhodes, "Japanese Bible Translations," *BTr* 18 (1967) 61-70.

S. Billigheimer, "On Jewish Translations of the Bible in Germany," *Abr-N* 7 (1968) 1-34.

Reinhold Wagner, "The Malayalam Bible," *ICHR* 2 (1968) 119-145.

§270 *3.1.7 Hermeneutics*

(   ) G., "On the Principles of Interpretation, particularly of the Bible," *QCS* 2 (1820) 9-12.

Augustus Hahn, "On the Grammatico-Historical Interpretation of the Scriptures," *BRCR* 1 (1831) 111-138. *(Trans. by Edward Robinson)*

M. Stuart, "Remarks on Hahn's definition of Interpretation, and some topics connected with it," *BRCR* 1 (1831) 139-159.

Anonymous, "On the Importance of a Correct Interpretation of the Scriptures," *SP* 4 (1831) 67-75.

M. Stuart, "Are the Same Principles of Interpretation to be Applied to the Bible as to Other Books?" *BRCR* 2 (1832) 124-137.

Parsons Cooke, "Have any passages in the Scriptures a Double sense?" *LTR* 1 (1834) 368-378.

*C. E. Stowe, "On Expository Preaching and the Principles which should guide us in the Exposition of Scripture," *BRCR* 5 (1835) 384-402.

J. A., "Reason a Test of Scriptural Interpretations," *CTPR* 4 (1838) 153-156.

(   ) R., "Biblical Interpretation. Qualifications of an Interpreter," *CRB* 5 (1840) 211-218.

*Joseph Muenscher, "On Types and the Typical Interpretation of Scripture," *BRCR, N.S.,* 5 (1841) 92-113.

*(   ) C., "The Importance of a Knowledge of Hebrew to the Interpreter of the Scriptures," *CongML* 25 (1842) 85-91.

[S. F. Smith], "Davidson's Sacred Hermeneutics," *CRB* 8 (1843) 613-625. *(Review)*

†Anonymous, "Biblical Literature: Allegorical Interpretation," *BQRL* 2 (1845) 173-196. *(Review)*

(   ) L., "Sacred Hermeneutics.—Horne's Introduction," *BRCM* 4 (1847-48) 73-94.

*[David N. Lord], "Analysis of the Principal Figures of the Scriptures and Statement of their Laws," *TLJ* 1 (1848-49) 353-399.

Mason Grosvenor, "The Province of Philosophy in the Interpretation of the Scripture," *BRCR, 3rd Ser.,* 5 (1849) 599-617.

Julius, "Biblical Hermeneutics," *MQR* 3 (1849) 319-327. *(Review)*

*[David N. Lord], "Objections to the Laws of Symbolization," *TLJ* 2 (1849-50) 596-632; 8 (1855-56) 1-50.

W. P. L., "The Figurative Language of the Scriptures," *CE* 48 (1850) 390-411. *(Review)*

*†[David N. Lord], "Prof. McClelland's Rules for the Interpretation of Prophecy," *TLJ* 3 (1850-51) 80-102. *(Review)*

*[David N. Lord], "Objections to the Laws of Figures," *TLJ* 3 (1850-51) 102-113.

†Anonymous, "Modern Systems of Biblical Hermeneutics," *TLJ* 3 (1850-51) 234-262. *(Review)*

*[David N. Lord(?)], "Objections to the Laws of Figurative Language," *TLJ* 3 (1850-51) 613-642.

*H[iram] C[arleton], "Thoughts on the Interpretation of Prophecy," *TLJ* 3 (1850-51) 642-667.

*Anonymous, "The Chief Characteristics and Laws of Prophetic Symbols," *TLJ* 3 (1850-51) 667-695.

Enoch Pond, "The Interpretation of Scripture," *TLJ* 4 (1851-52) 415-425.

Leroy M. Lee, "Pulpit Hermeneutics," *MQR* 6 (1852) 107-133, 401-426.

C. E. Stowe, "The Right Interpretation of the Sacred Scriptures—The Helps and the Hindrances," *BS* 10 (1853) 34-62.

M. B., "Difficulties in Understanding the Holy Scriptures," *UQGR* 10 (1853) 138-147.

*[David N. Lord], "The Truth of the Laws of Symbolization and the Importance of their Results," *TLJ* 7 (1854-55) 177-217. *(Review)*

*Anonymous, "The Reproduction of Biblical Life in its Bearing on Biblical Exposition," *JSL, 3rd Ser.,* 4 (1856-57) 1-16.

*†Anonymous, "Dr. Fairbairn on Prophecy and its Proper Interpretation," *TLJ* 9 (1856-57) 353-396. *(Review)*

James A. Clark, "Diversity of Interpretation," *CRB* 22 (1857) 196-215.

†Anonymous, "Biblical Hermeneutics," *DR* 50 (1861) 312-329. *(Review)*

Joseph Baylee, "On the Nature of Human Language, the Necessities of Scientific Phraseology, and the Application of the Principles of both to the Interpretation of Holy Scripture," *JTVI* 3 (1868-69) 251-269. (Discussion, pp. 269-278)

Rhys Gwesyn Jones, "The Central Idea of the Bible—A Guide to its Interpretation," *ThE* 6 (1869) 282-291.

J. H. Titcomb, "On Certain Magnitudes in Nature, and Their Bearings upon Biblical Interpretation," *JTVI* 9 (1875-76) 110-127. [(Discussion, pp. 127-139) (Remarks by J. Challis, pp. 140-146)]

*A. I. McCaul, "On Biblical Interpretation in connexion with Science," *JTVI* 9 (1875-76) 147-157. [(Discussion pp. 157-172) (Remarks by J. W. Dawson, pp. 173-175)]

Charles Wordsworth, "The Rules laid down in the Holy Scripture for its own Interpretation," *CM* 11 (1880) 1-13, 113-128.

Denis Hallinan, "Modern Erroneous Systems of Biblical Interpretation," *IER, 3rd Ser.,* 3 (1882) 235-243, 345-352, 465-478; 4 (1883) 529-537. [*(No Part I Specifically Titled);* Part II: The Rational and Pietistic Systems; Part III: The Rational and Pietistic Systems—(continued); IV. The System of Accommodation]

[Charles] Elliott and [William Justin] Harsha, "Employment of the Original Texts," *ONTS* 1 (1882) #1, 15-16.

[Charles] Elliott and [William Justin] Hersha*[sic]*, "Importance of Hermeneutics," *ONTS* 2 (1882-83) 88-89.

[Charles] Elliott and [William Justin] Harsha, "Use of the Context in Interpretation," *ONTS* 2 (1882-83) 176.

*Anonymous, "Internal Evidence," *ONTS* 3 (1883-84) 58-60.

Charles A[ugustus] Briggs, "The Use of Proof Texts," *ONTS* 3 (1883-84) 121-122.

Milton S. Terry, "The Historical Standpoint," *ONTS* 3 (1883-84) 160-161.

*( ) C., "The Term Higher Criticism," *ONTS* 3 (1883-84) 310-311.

Robert Crook, "Biblical Hermeneutics," *MR* 66 (1884) 738-756. *(Review)*

*R. P. Stebbins, "The Hebrew Prophets. No. V. Rules to be Observed in Interpreting the Prophets," *URRM* 22 (1884) 240-251.

W. O. Stearns, "Biblical Interpretation as an Ideal," *ONTS* 4 (1884-85) 28-29.

B. Felsenthal, "Bible Interpretation: How and How Not," *ONTS* 4 (1884-85) 114-119.

*Anonymous, "Translation or Interpretation," *ONTS* 4 (1884-85) 186-187.

Anonymous, "The Jewish Attitude," *ONTS* 4 (1884-85) 187. *[Jewish Interpretation of the Old Testament]*

Milton S. Terry, "Studies in Old Testament Hermeneutics," *ONTS* 4 (1884-85) 202-205, 245-251.

Anonymous, "How to Learn to Interpret," *ONTS* 4 (1884-85) 231-233.

*Milton S. Terry, "Hermeneutics and the Higher Criticism," *ONTS* 4 (1884-85) 294-299.

E. R. Pope, "Some Suggestions as to Bible Interpretation," *ONTS* 4 (1884-85) 409-412.

Anonymous, "The Use of Common Sense in Interpretation," *ONTS* 5 (1885-86) 88-89.

Franz Delitzsch, "Must We Follow the New Testament Interpretation of Old Testament Texts?" *ONTS* 6 (1886-87) 77-78.

Joseph M. Clarke, "The Interpretation of the Bible," *CR* 49 (1887) 188-201. *(Review)*

Sylvester Burnham, "False Methods of Interpretation," *ONTS* 7 (1887-88) 37-39, 83-85, 113-115, 144-146.

M. Loy, "Hermeneutical Principles," *ColTM* 8 (1888) 107-122, 192-213, 265-280.

Alvah Hovey, "The New Testament as a Guide to the Interpretation of the Old Testament," *ONTS* 8 (1888-89) 207-213.

Anonymous, "Uses and Abuses of an Important Principle of Interpretation," *BS* 46 (1889) 304-320. *[Context]*

C. H. Waller, "Partial Exegesis," *TML* 1 (1889) 217-230.

*W. Pakenham Walsh, "From 'The Voices of the Psalms'," *CM, N.S.,* 8 (1890) 65-72.

Reginald Walsh, "The Mystical Sense of the Scriptures," *IER, 3rd Ser.,* 11 (1890) 708-717, 1113-1124; 13 (1892) 611-622; 14 (1893) 512-534; 16 (1895) 835-851; 17 (1896) 802-832; *4th Ser.,* 4 (1898) 131-147, 206-219, 318-342.

James Mudge, "Scripture Interpretation," *HR* 22 (1891) 218-224, 317-322.

Albert Temple Swing, "The Importance and Limitations of the Historical Argument," *BS* 52 (1895) 48-68.

*A. F. Kirkpatrick, "The Septuagint Version: Its Bearing on the Text and Interpretation of the Old Testament," *Exp, 5th Ser.,* 3 (1896) 263-287.

*H. L. Wayland, "The Interpretation of Prophecy," *HR* 35 (1898) 261.

A. G., "The Practice of Exegesis," *TQ* 2 (1898) 22-32.

F. A. Gast, "The Euphemistic Principle as Applied to the Old Testament," *RChR, 4th Ser.,* 6 (1902) 453-472.

Thomas K. Davis, "The Interpretation of Scripture," *BS* 60 (1903) 334-341.

W. A. Lambert, "The Science of Hermeneutics," *LCR* 22 (1903) 247-253.

Camden M. Cobern, "The Suggestion of a New Method in Bible Interpretation," *MR* 88 (1906) 703-715.

Geo. H. Trever, "Some Principles of Scientific Biblical Criticism," *MR* 88 (1906) 890-907.

*Kemper Fullerton, "The Reformation Principle of Exegesis and the Interpretation of Prophecy," *AJT* 12 (1908) 422-442.

Ernest DeWitt Burton, "The Scientific Method in Biblical Interpretation,"
  BW 32 (1908) 155-158. *(Editorial)*

John R. Sampey, "The Figure of Exaggerated Contrast," *R&E* 5 (1908) 181-
  186.

W. M. McPheeters, "Grammatical Interpretation: Its Primary Problems and
  Products," *USR* 20 (1908-09) 270-276.

G. A. Cooke, "Some Principles of Biblical Interpretation," *Exp, 7th Ser.,* 7
  (1909) 193-208.

*Willis J. Beecher, "Some Problems Concerning the Bible," *CFL, 3rd Ser.,*
  12 (1910) 417-420. [II. Method of Interpreting the Bible as Literature,
  pp. 418-419]

George H. Schodde, "In How Far is the Bible to be Interpreted Like Other
  Books?" *ColTM* 30 (1910) 197-205.

Edward E. Braithwaite, "Some Principles for Scripture Interpretation," *BW*
  40 (1912) 118-129.

John E. McFadyen, "How to Interpret the Bible," *HR* 64 (1912) 439-444.

*G. Buchanan Gray, "The Forms of Hebrew Poetry. 6. The Bearing of
  Certain Critical Theories on Criticism and Interpretation," *Exp, 8th Ser.,*
  6 (1913) 529-553.

Robert H. Kennett, "Some Principles of Interpretation," *ICMM* 10 (1913-14)
  13-42.

George A. Barton, "The Hermeneutic Canon 'Interpret Historically' in the
  Light of Modern Research," *JBL* 33 (1914) 56-77.

George Smith, "The Value of Familiarity with the Ipsissima Verba of the
  Bible as a Method of Interpretation," *ICMM* 11 (1914-15) 199-205.

Harlan Creelman, "The Place of the Imagination in Biblical Interpretation,"
  ASRec 12 (1916) 424-435.

Ira M. Price, "Some Methods and Problems of the Modern Old Testament
  Exegetes," *BW* 47 (1916) 298-305.

H. N. Probst, "Some Fundamental Principles of Scripture Interpretation,"
  TZTM 6 (1916) 545-571.

*Anonymous, "Old Testament Interpretation. An interview with Dr. J. R. Sampey," *TTM* 2 (1919) 233-235.

Powell H. Norton, "Some Aids to Old Testament Exegesis," *BCTS* 13 (1921) 77-87.

H. Northcote, "The Fact and Idea in Biblical Interpretation," *ICMM* 18 (1921-22) 304-310.

W. K. Lowther Clarke, "In the Study. VI," *Theo* 3 (1922) 353-354. *[Hermeneutics]*

*Israel Eitan, "The Bearing of Ethiopic on Biblical Exegesis and Lexicography," *JPOS* 3 (1923) 136-143.

F. H. Marshall, "Old Testament Interpretation in Mediaeval Greek and Slavonic Literature," *CQR* 97 (1923-24) 71-85.

John E. McFadyen, "Fact and Interpretation," *ET* 35 (1923-24)103-107.

Henry Preserved Smith, "The Commentator's Temptation," *HR* 90 (1925) 44-47.

Anonymous, "On Letting the Bible Alone," *CQ* 3 (1926) 83-87.

Frank Eakin, "The Interpretation of the Scriptures," *JR* 7 (1927) 596-611.

Edward E. Braithwaite, "Sound Biblical Interpretation. The Historic Principle," *CJRT* 5 (1928) 38-43.

Rollin Thomas Chafer, "A Syllabus of Study in Hermeneutics," *BS* 91 (1934) 457-462.

L. Elliott Binns, "Varieties of Biblical Interpretation," *MC* 24 (1934-35) 323-339.

Issac Husik, "Maimonides and Spinoza on the Interpretation of the Bible," *JAOSS* #1 (1935) 22-40.

Joachim Wach, "The Interpretation of Sacred Book," *JBL* 55 (1935) 59-63.

Rollin Thomas Chafer, "A Syllabus of Studies in Hermeneutics," *BS* 93 (1936) 110-118, 201-203, 331-335; 94 (1937) 72-94, 207-217, 470-478; 95 (1938) 91-101.

Herbert W. Magoun, "Words and Their Content," *CFL, 3rd Ser.*, 42 (1936) 26-33.

G. Ernest Wright, "Exegesis and Eisegesis in the Interpretation of Scripture," *ET* 48 (1936-37) 353-357.

*Louise Pettibone Smith, "Light from North Syria on Old Testament Interpretation," *JAAR* 7 (1939) 185-190.

G. T. Thomson, "On the Interpretation of Scripture," *EQ* 12 (1940) 327-334.

Julius A. Bewer, "Progressive Interpretation," *ATR* 24 (1942) 89-100.

*J. Philip Hyatt, "The Ras Shamra Discoveries and the Interpretation of the Old Testament," *JAAR* 10 (1942) 67-75.

*T. H. Robinson, "Hebrew Metre and Old Testament Exegesis," *ET* 54 (1942-43) 246-248.

H. Wheeler Robinson, "The Higher Exegesis," *JTS* 44 (1943) 143-147.

James Wood, "The Interpretation of the Old Testament," *ET* 57 (1943-44) 165-167.

Charles S. Braden, "Hindu Interpretations of the Bible and Jesus," *JAAR* 12 (1944) 42-47.

C[hester] C. McCown, "Symbolic Interpretation," *JBL* 63 (1944) 329-338.

E[mil] G. [H.] Kraeling, "Biblical Interpretation Tomorrow," *RL* 14 (1944-45) 488-498.

Solomon Simonson, "Four Modes of Interpretation," *RR* 9 (1944-45) 339-345.

Ovid R. Sellers, "Limits in Old Testament Interpretation," *JNES* 5 (1946) 83-91.

Richard Kehoe, "The Spiritual Sense of Scripture," *NB* 27 (1946) 246-251.

G. Ernest Wright, "Interpreting the Old Testament," *TT* 3 (1946-47) 176-191.

John Henry Bennetch, "Literal Interpretation," *BS* 104 (1947) 350-358.

Anthony C. Cotter, "The Obscurity of Scripture," *CBQ* 9 (1947) 453-464.

H. H. Rowley, "The Relevance of Biblical Interpretation," *Interp* 1 (1947) 3-19.

[Balmer H.(?) Kelly], "'A' Bible or 'The' Bible? *An Editorial*," *Interp* 1 (1947) 466-470.

Reginald Glanville, "The Symbolic Interpretation of the Bible," *LQHR* 172 (1947) 105-113.

Clyde T. Francisco, "The Importance of Literary Analysis in Old Testament Interpretation," *R&E* 44 (1947) 411-429.

Rudolph Bierberg, "Does Sacred Scripture Have a *Sensus Plenior*?" *CBQ* 10 (1948) 182-195.

M. H. Franzmann, "Essays in Hermeneutics," *CTM* 19 (1948) 595-605, 641-652, 738-746.

*James L. Kelso, "Implements of Interpretation. V. Archaeology," *Interp* 2 (1948) 66-73.

William A. Irwin, "The Interpretation of the Old Testament," *ZAW* 62 (1949-50) 1-10.

R. Tamisier, "The Total Sense of Scripture," *Scrip* 4 (1949-51) 141-143.

R. C. Fuller, "Trends in Biblical Interpretation," *Scrip* 4 (1949-51) 175-180, 244-249.

James Stewart, "Patterns in Scripture," *CongQL* 28 (1950) 134-142.

Floyd V. Filson, "How I Interpret the Bible," *Interp* 4 (1950) 178-188.

Christian Spreus, "The Contemporary Relevance of Hofmann's Hermeneutical Principles," *Interp* 4 (1950) 311-321.

Arthur Gabriel Hebert, "The Interpretation of the Bible," *Interp* 4 (1950) 441-452.

J. Coert Rylaarsdam, "Preface to Hermeneutics," *JR* 30 (1950) 79-89.

*P. W. Stoner, "Fifty Years of Development in Astronomy and Its Impact on Scriptural Interpretation," *JASA* 2 (1950) #3, 7-10.

George A. F. Knight, "The Interpretation of the Old Testament," *RTRM* 9 (1950) #1, 1-16.

Edward A. Cerny, "The Senses of Sacred Scripture," *CTSP* 6 (1951) 146-148. *[Summary of Discussion only]*

Dom Ralph Russell, "'Humani Generis' and the 'Spiritual' Sense of Scripture," *DownsR* 69 (1951) 1-15.

R. B. Y. Scott, "How I Interpret the Bible," *Interp* 5 (1951) 318-328.

*Julian Obermann, "Survival of an Old Canaanite Participle and its Impact on Biblical Exegesis," *JBL* 70 (1951) 199-209.

*Cuthbert Lattey, "Vicarious Solidarity in the Old Testament," *VT* 1 (1951) 1267-274.

Raymond F. Surburg, "The Historical Method in Biblical Interpretation," *CTM* 23 (1952) 81-104.

Carl Gaenssle, "Velikovsky and the Hebrew Bible," *CTM* 23 (1952) 105-114.

Senex., "Practical Scripture Interpretation—Extracts from a 'Meditation'," *Scrip* 5 (1952-53) 122-126.

E[dmund] F. Sutcliffe, "The Plenary Sense as a Principle of Interpretation," *B* 34 (1953) 333-343.

Raymond E. Brown, "The History and Development of the Theory of a Sensus Plenior," *CBQ* 15 (1953) 141-162.

Webb B. Garrison, "The Necessity and Relativity of Biblical Interpretation," *Interp* 7 (1953) 426-441.

*L. Jacobs, "The Talmudic Hermeneutical Rule of 'Binyan 'Abh' and J. S. Mill's 'Method of Agreement'," *JJS* 4 (1953) 59-64.

Joseph Coppens, "The Different Senses of Sacred Scripture," *TD* 1 (1953) 15-20.

A. Bea, "Progress in the Interpretation of Sacred Scripture," *TD* 1 (1953) 67-71.

Severiano del Paramo, "The Biblical Question from Its Origins to Humani Generis," *TD* 1 (1953) 72-78.

*G. W. H. Lampe, "Typological Exegesis," *Theo* 56 (1953) 201-208.

*G. W. H. Lampe, "Typological Exegesis," *Theo* 56 (1953) 201-208.

*E. F. Kevan, "The Covenants and the Interpretation of the Old Testament," *EQ* 26 (1954) 19-28.

John O'Flynn, "The Senses of Scripture," *ITQ* 21 (1954) 181-184; 22 (1955) 57-66.

J. DeFraine, "The Encyclical *Humani Generis* and Sacred Scripture," *TD* 2 (1954) 155-158.

*Morris Sigel Seale, "Arabic and Old Testament Interpretation," *ET* 66 (1954-55) 92-93.

Fred D. Gealy, "Symposium: Contemporary Theological Concern. The Theological Approach to the Interpretation of the Bible," *PSTJ* 8 (1954-55) #3, 15-18.

Paul K. Jewett, "Concerning the Allegorical Interpretation of Scripture," *WTJ* 17 (1954-55) 1-20.

Arthur A. Cohen, "On Scriptural Exegesis," *CC* 5 (1955) 39-50.

*David Weiss, "Halakhic Exegesis," *CJ* 10 (1955-56) #3, 52-58.

Erich Dinkler, "Principles of Biblical Interpretation," *JRT* 13 (1955-56) 20-30.

*G. W. H. Lampe, "Hermeneutics and Typology," *LQHR* 190 (1955) 17-25.

*M. E. Gibbs, "An Examination of Some Presuppositions of Biblical Criticism," *IJT* 5 (1956) #2, 31-37.

*J. Stafford Wright, "The Place of Myth in the Interpretation of the Bible," *JTVI* 88 (1956) 17-30, 151-152. [(Discussion, pp. 145-149) (Communications by H. L. Ellison, p. 149; B. B. Knopp, pp. 149-151)]

*Brevard S. Childs, "Jonah: A Study in Old Testament Interpretation," *MHSB* 3 (1956) #1, 7-14.

William F. Forrester, "The *Sensus Plenior* of Scripture," *BC* 1 (1956-58) 116-117.

Simon Rawidowicz, "On Interpretation," *PAAJR* 26 (1957) 83-126.

Robert H. Krumholtz, "Instrumentality and the 'Sensus Plenior'," *CBQ* 20 (1958) 200-205.

*Carroll Stuhlmueller, "The Influence of Oral Tradition upon Exegesis and the Senses of Scripture," *CBQ* 20 (1958) 299-326.

Brevard S. Childs, "Prophecy and Fulfillment. *A Study of Contemporary Hermeneutics*," *Interp* 12 (1958) 259-271.

*H. W. Wolff, "The Old Testament in Controversy. *Interpretive Principles and Illustration*," *Interp* 12 (1958) 281-290. *(Trans. by James L. Mays)*

Scott McCormick, "The Bible as Record and Medium. *Contemporary Scholarship and the Word of God*," *Interp* 12 (1958) 291-308.

James Muilenberg, "Preface to Hermeneutics," *JBL* 77 (1958) 18-25.

J. Coert Rylaarsdam, "The Problem of Faith and History in Biblical Interpretation," *JBL* 77 (1958) 26-32.

*Krister Stendahl, "Implications of Form-Criticism and Tradition-Criticism for Biblical Interpretation," *JBL* 77 (1958) 33-38.

*Brevard S. Childs, "Jonah: A Study in Old Testament Hermeneutics," *SJT* 11 (1958) 53-61.

*Henry Joel Cadbury, "The Exegetical Conscience," *Nexus* 2 (1958-59) 3-6.

Joseph A. Grispino, "The Liturgical Meaning of Scripture," *AER* 141 (1959) 155-164.

Thomas Barrosse, "The Senses of Scripture and the Liturgical Pericopes," *CBQ* 21 (1959) 1-23.

John J. O'Rourke, "Marginal Notes on the *Sensus Plenior*," *CBQ* 21 (1959) 64-71.

Norman K. Gottwald, "Hermeneutics and Exegesis. (Part I)," *Found* 2 (1959) 171-174.

Norman K. Gottwald, "Hermeneutics and Exegesis. (Part II)," *Found* 2 (1959) 269-272.

Norman K. Gottwald, "Hermeneutics and Exegesis. (Part III)," *Found* 2 (1959) 356-359.

Nels F. S. Ferre, "Notes by a Theologian on Biblical Hermeneutics," *JBL* 78 (1959) 105-114.

Nicholas Ozerov, "On Biblical Interpretation," *StVTQ, N.S.,* 3 (1959) #2, 26-31.

John D. W. Watts, "The Methods and Purpose of Biblical Interpretation," *SWJT, N.S.,* 2 (1959-60) #2, 7-16.

William L. Hendricks, "Biblical Interpretation—the Pastor—and the Contemporary Scene," *SWJT, N.S.,* 2 (1959-60) #2, 17-26.

Samuel S. Schultz, "Today's Critic—Presuppositions, Tools and Methods," *BETS* 3 (1960) 87-88, 92.

J. Barton Payne, "Hermeneutics as a Cloak for the Denial of Scripture," *BETS* 3 (1960) 93-100.

Anonymous, "Guiding Principles for the Interpretation of the Bible," *ESS* 5 (1960-61) 12-15.

Robert Tobias, "An Analysis of Guiding Principles of Interpretation," *ESS* 5 (1960-61) 16-31.

H. H. Rex, "Hermeneutics Today," *RTR* 19 (1960) 11-21.

G. Douglas Young, "The Relevance of Scientific Thought to Scriptural Interpretation," *BETS* 4 (1961) 117-120.

Martin Noth, "The Interpretation of the Old Testament. I. The 'Representation' of the Old Testament in Proclamation," *Interp* 15 (1961) 50-60.

*Gerhard von Rad, "The Interpretation of the Old Testament. II. Typological Interpretation of the Old Testament," *Interp* 15 (1961) 174-192.

Walther Zimmerli, "The Interpretation of the Old Testament. III. Promise and Fulfillment," *Interp* 15 (1961) 310-338. *(Trans by James Wharton)*

Hans Walter Wolff, "The Interpretation of the Old Testament. IV. The Hermeneutics of the Old Testament," *Interp* 15 (1961) 439-472.

G. Douglas Young, "The Relevance of Scientific Thought to Scriptural Interpretation," *JASA* 13 (1961) 74-76.

*Ben Zion Bokser, "The Time-Bound and the Timeless in Rabbinic Thought," *Jud* 10 (1961) 265-270.

Ronald M. Hals, "The Problem of Old Testament Hermeneutics," *LQ, N.S.,* 13 (1961) 97-102.

*John P. McIntyre, "Scriptural Sense and Literary Criticism," *MH* 16 (Spring, 1961) 45-57.

Don H. McGaughey, "The Problem of Biblical Hermeneutics," *RestQ* 5 (1961) 251-256.

Paul W. Jones, "Aesthetics and Biblical Hermeneutics," *RL* 31 (1961-62) 394-408.

George Huttar, "The Use of Language and Biblical Interpretation," *BETS* 5 (1962) 116-120.

*M. Gertner, "Terms of Scriptural Interpretation: A Study in Hebrew Semantics," *BSOAS* 25 (1962) 1-27.

P. J. Murnion, "*Sensus Plenior* and the Progress of Revelation," *DunR* 2 (1962) 117-142.

*Samuel   Sandmel,   "Parallelomania,"   *JBL*   81   (1962)   1-13.

*Claus Westermann, "The Meaning of Hermeneutics in Theology," *DG* 33 (1962-63) 127-141.

Raymond E. Brown, "The *Sensus Plenior* in the Last Ten Years," *CBQ* 25 (1963) 262-285.

Luis Alonso Schokel, "Hermeneutics in the Light of Language and Literature," *CBQ* 25 (1963) 371-386.

*Horace D. Hummel, "Christological Interpretation of the Old Testament," *DJT* 2 (1963) 108-117.

James Barr, "The Interpretation of Scripture. II. Revelation Through History in the Old Testament and Modern Theology," *Interp* 17 (1963) 193-205.

David Noel Freedman, "The Interpretation of Scripture. III. On the Method in Biblical Studies: The Old Testament," *Interp* 17 (1963) 308-318.

Isma'il Ragi al Faruqi, "A Comparison of the Islamic and Christian Approaches to Hebrew Scripture," *JAAR* 31 (1963) 283-293.

*Solomon Zeitlin, "Hillel and the Hermeneutic Rules," *JQR, N.S.*, 54 (1963-64) 161-174.

*Francis Foulkes, "Typology or Allegory?" *Them* 2 (1963-64) #2, 8-15.

Bruce Vawter, "The Fuller Sense: Some Considerations," *CBQ* 26 (1964) 85-96.

*Gary G. Cohen, "Hermeneutical Principles and Creation Theories," *GJ* 5 (1964) #3, 17-29.

*Brevard S. Childs, "Interpretation in Faith. *The Theological Responsibility of an Old Testament Commentary*," *Interp* 18 (1964) 432-449.

Douglas R. Jones, "History and Tradition in Old Testament Studies," *SJT* 17 (1964) 211-225.

*F. Hecht, "The Theological Interpretation of the Old Testament: An Act of Deliberation," *NGTT* 5 (1964) 93-98.

Dallas M. Roark, "Emphases in Hermeneutics," *SWJT, N.S.*, 7 (1964-65) #1, 63-71.

James M. Robinson, "Scripture and Theological Method: A Protestant Study in *Sensus Plenior*," *CBQ* 27 (1965) 6-27.

*Patrick D. Miller Jr., "God the Warrior. *A Problem in Biblical Interpretation and Apologetics*," *Interp* 19 (1965) 39-46.

*James Zink, "The Place of Archaeology in Biblical Interpretation," *RestQ* 8 (1965) 111-118.

Luis Alonso-Schökel, "The Function of Language in the Scriptures," *Cont* 3 (1965-66) 22-32.

*G. Sarfatti, "Semantics of Mishnaic Hebrew and Interpretation of the Bible by the Tanna'i," *Lĕš* 30 (1965-66) n.p.n.

Frank K. Flinn, "Toward a Model of Hermeneutics," *PHDS* 1 (1965-66) #2, 13-17.

John A. Balchin, "An Introduction to Biblical Hermeneutics," *Them* 3 (1965-66) #2, 35-46.

Manfred Hausmann, "Some Thoughts on the Nature of Biblical Language," *BTr* 17 (1966) 114-117.

Richard L. Lucas, "Considerations of Method in Old Testament Hermeneutics," *DunR* 6 (1966) 7-66.

*Robert Murray, "The Inspiration and Interpretation of Scripture," *HeyJ* 7 (1966) 428-434.

*Sh. Yeivin, "On the Use and Misuse of Archaeology in Interpreting the Bible," *PAAJR* 34 (1966) 141-154.

Basil De Pinto, "The Mystery of the Word. *Thoughts on Biblical Language,"* *Scrip* 18 (1966) 10-18.

Simon J. De Vries, "Basic Issues in Old Testament Hermeneutics," *JMTSO* 5 (1966-67) #1, 1-19.

Luis Alonso Schokel, "Hermeneutics in the Light of Language and Literature," *BTr* 18 (1967) 40-48.

Albert E. Glock, "The Study and Interpretation of the Old Testament," *CTM* 38 (1967) 90-108.

R[aymond] E. Brown, "The Problems of *Sensus Plenior,"* *ETL* 43 (1967) 460-469.

Eduard Haller, "On the Interpretive Task," *Interp* 21 (1967) 158-166. *(Trans. by Ruth Grob)*

*Richard N. Soulen, "The *waṣfs* of the Song of Songs and Hermeneutic," *JBL* 86 (1967) 183-190.

Frithjof Schuon, "Keys to the Bible," *SCR* 1 (1967) 2-5.

Norbert Lohfink, "On interpreting the OT," *TD* 15 (1967) 228-229. *(Synopsis)*

*John Van Seters, "History and Myth in Biblical Interpretation," *ANQ, N.S.,* 8 (1967-68) 154-162.

Francis I. Andersen, "The Instrument at Hand: The Problem of the Language of Scripture," *Inter* 1 (1967-68) 67-70.

J. A. Thompson, "Interpreting the Old Testament," *Inter* 1 (1967-68) 140-155.

George A. Turner, "The Interpreter's Task," *ASW* 22 (1968) #2, 3-7.

*George Eldon Ladd, "The Hermeneutics of Prophecy," *ASW* 22 (1968) #2, 14-18.

John E. Hartley, "Hermeneutical Principles Relevant to the Two Testaments," *ASW* 22 (1968) #2, 19-27.

George A. F. Knight, "New Perspectives in Old Testament Interpretation," *BTr* 19 (1968) 50-57.

*Stanley N. Gundry, "Typology as a Means of Interpretation: Past and Present," *BETS* 12 (1969) 233-240.

B. Siertsema, "Language and World View (Semantics for Theologians)," *BTr* 20 (1969) 3-20. (Corr. p. 55-56)

Gene M. Tucker, "Toward an Old Testament Hermeneutic," *DDSR* 34 (1969) 53-66.

*Graeme Goldworthy, "The Old Testament—A Christian Book," *Inter* 2 (1969-70) 24-33. [V. Establishing hermeneutics, pp. 28-31; VI. The application of hermeneutics, pp. 31-32]

§271 *3.1.8 History of Interpretation and Criticism*

Anonymous, "Brief Historical View of the Science of Interpretation," *QCS* 8 (1826) 169-172.

B. B. Edwards, "Remarks on Certain Erroneous Methods and Principles of Biblical Criticism," *BS* 6 (1849) 185-196.

O. Cone, "Biblical Interpretation from the Apostolic Age to the time of Origen," *UQGR, N.S.,* 11 (1874) 36-54.

O. Cone, "Origen's Hermeneutics," *UQGR, N.S.,* 11 (1874) 209-227.

E. P. Evans, "Christian Hermeneutics and Hebrew Literature," *URRM* 23 (1885) 346-359.

O. Cone, "Farrar's History of Interpretation," *UQGR, N.S.,* 24 (1887) 144-160. *(Review)*

*Henry M. Harman, "Some Observations upon Tikkun Sopherim," *AJSL* 4 (1887-88) 34-42.

Henry S. Nash, "Exegesis in the School of Antioch," *JBL* 11 (1892) 22-37.

T. G. Law, "Biblical Studies in the Middle Ages," *SRL* 21 (1893) 1-33.

B. Whitefoord, "Bacon as an Interpreter of Holy Scripture," *Exp, 5th Ser.,* 6 (1897) 349-360.

W. H. Kent, "Jewish and Christian Exegesis," *AER* 29 (1903) 123-136.

*James A. Kelso, "Theodoret and the Law Book of Josiah," *JBL* 22 (1903) 50.

George G. Findlay, "The Interpretation of Holy Scripture, Ancient and Modern," *LQHR* 99 (1903) 1-23. *(Review)*

*G. E. Price, "Allegorical and Literal in the Fathers," *IER, 4th Ser.,* 16 (1904) 201-221. [I. The method of allegorical interpretation applied by pagans to pagan literature, pp. 203-205; II. The method applied by Jewish writers to the Old Testament, pp. 205-208; III. The method applied by Christian writers to both Testaments, pp. 208-213; IV. The reaction to literal interpretation, pp. 213-221]

R. J. H. Bottheil, "Some Early Jewish Bible Criticism," *JBL* 23 (1904) 1-12.

D. S. Margoliouth, "Biblical Criticism in the Eleventh Century," *Exp, 7th Ser.,* 2 (1906) 553-563.

*Kemper Fullerton, "The Reformation Principle of Exegesis and the Interpretation of Prophecy," *AJT* 12 (1908) 422-442.

George A. Barton, "The Astro-Mythological School of Biblical Interpretation," *BW* 31 (1908) 433-444.

J. S. Banks, "Allegory in Scripture," *LQHR* 111 (1909) 316-319.

Jackson Case, "The Scribes' Interpretation of the Old Testament," *BW* 38 (1911) 28-40.

[Henry] Preserved Smith, "The Methods of Reformation Interpreters of the Bible," *BW* 38 (1911) 235-245.

George Jackson, "The Reformation Doctrine of the Bible," *LQHR* 120 (1913) 1-20.

*F. C. Burkitt, "On *Celtis* 'A Chisel': A Study in Textual Tradition," *JTS* 17 (1915-16) 389-397.

Ira M. Price, "Some Methods of Old Testament Exegetes before Modern Times," *BW* 47 (1916) 237-243.

*F. C. Burkitt, "On *Celtis* 'A Chisel': A Further Note," *JTS* 22 (1920-21) 380-381.

*Lewis B. Radford, "Psalm LXXIV. A Study in the History of Biblical Interpretation," *ET* 42 (1930-31) 556-562.

F. G. Bratton, "Precursors of Biblical Criticism," *JBL* 50 (1931) 176-185. [I. Origen, pp. 176-181; II. *Abraham ben Ezra,* pp. 181-185]

D. Tyng, "Theodore of Mopsuestia as an Interpreter of the Old Testament," *JBL* 50 (1931) 298-303.

Montgomery J. Shroyer, "Alexandrian Jewish Literalists," *JBL* 55 (1936) 261-284.

Augustana, "The Principles of Biblical Interpretation of M. Luther," *JTALC* 1 (1936) #3, 9-30.

David Baumgardt, "The Bible Today: A Jewish Viewpoint," *CQ* 18 (1941) 219-224.

Herman Hailperin, "Jewish 'Influence' on Christian Biblical Scholarship in the Middle Ages," *HJud* 4 (1942) 163-174.

M. Reu, "A Short History of Exegesis," *KZ* 66 (1942) 257-288.

Herman Hailperin, "The Hebrew Heritage of Mediaeval Christian Scholarship," *HJud* 5 (1943) 133-154.

*Luitpold Wallach, "The Origin of Testimonia Biblica in Early Christian Literature," *RR* 8 (1943-44) 130-136.

Barnabas Ahern, "Textual Directives of the Encyclical *Divino Afflante Spiritu*," *CBQ* 7 (1945) 340-347. [1. Need of Familiarity with Biblical Languages; 2. Importance of Textual Criticism; 3. Meaning of the Tridentine Decree]

Charles S. Braden, "Some Contemporary Moslem Interpretations of the Bible," *CQ* 22 (1945) 246-259.

*Robert M. Grant, "Historical Criticism in the Ancient Church," *JR* 25 (1945) 183-196. [IV. Greek Criticism of the Old Testament, p. 186; V. Christian Criticism of the Old Testament, pp. 186-188]

G. Ernest Wright, "The Christian Interpreter as Biblical Critic. The Relevance of Valid Criticism," *Interp* 1 (1947) 131-152.

David Daube, "Rabbinic Methods of Interpretation and Hellenistic Rhetoric," *HUCA* 22 (1949) 239-264.

G. Ernest Wright, "The World Council of Churches and Biblical Interpretation," *Interp* 3 (1949) 50-61.

Anonymous, "Guiding Principles for the Interpretation of the Bible as Accepted by the Ecumenical Study Conference, Held in Oxford from June 29th to July 5th, 1949," *Interp* 3 (1949) 457-459.

‡Wolfgang Schweitzer, "Annotated Bibliography on Biblical Interpretation," *Interp* 4 (1950) 342-357.

*J. Bowman, "The Exegesis of the Pentateuch among the Samaritans and among the Rabbis," *OTS* 8 (1950) 220-262.

*Richard C. Mills, "Principles of Interpretation Relative to the Prophets," *SQ/E* 11 (1950) 96-110.

O. S. Rankin, "Old Testament Interpretation. Its History and Development," *HJ* 49 (1950-51) 146-154.

S. B. Gurewicz, "The Mediaeval Jewish Exegetes of the Old Testament," *ABR* 1 (1951) 23-43.

*William H. Brownlee, "Biblical Interpretation Among the Sectaries of the Dead Sea Scrolls," *BA* 14 (1951) 54-76.

*J. Barton Payne, "Biblical Problems and Augustine's Allegorizing," *WTJ* 14 (1951-52) 46-53.

H. F. Thomson, "Old Testament Interpretation Among the Arabic-Speaking Christians of Tenth Century Baghdad," *JBL* 72 (1953) ix-x.

Henry R. Van Til, "The Definition and History of Biblical Hermeneutics," *JASA* 7 (1955) #3, 9-15.

*G. Vermes, "The Symbolical Interpretation of *Lebanon* in the Targums: The Origin and Development of an Exegetical Tradition," *JTS, N.S.,* 9 (1958) 1-12.

*T. Jansma, "Investigations into the Early Syrian Fathers on Genesis. An Approach to the Exegesis of the Nestorian Church and to the Comparison of Nestorian and Jewish Exegesis," *OTS* 12 (1958) 69-181.

*M. Gertner, "The Masorah and the Levites. An Essay in the History of a Concept," *VT* 10 (1960) 241-272.

*W. H. C. Frend, "Notes on Tertullian's Interpretation of Scripture," *JTS, N.S.,* 12 (1961) 273-284.

*I. L. Seeligmann, "Indications of Editorial Alteration and Adaption in the Massoretic Text and the Septuagint," *VT* 11 (1961) 201-221.

*John P. Newport, "Biblical Interpretation and Eschatological-Holy History," *SWJT, N.S.,* 4 (1961-62) #1, 83-110.

*E. E. Hallewy, "Biblical Midrash and Homeric Exegesis," *Tarbiz* 31 (1961-62) #2, III-IV.

*M. Gertner, "Terms of Scriptural Interpretation: A Study in Hebrew Semantics," *BSOAS* 25 (1962) 1-27.

Erwin I. J. Rosenthal, "Medieval Jewish Exegesis: Its Character and Significance," *JSS* 9 (1964) 265-281.

Raphael Loewe, "The 'Plain' Meaning of Scripture in Early Jewish Exegesis," *PIJSL* 1 (1964) 140-185.

Arthur Voobus, "Abraham De-bēt Rabban and His Role in the Hermeneutic Traditions of the School of Nasibis," *HTR* 58 (1965) 203-214.

S. du Toit, "Exegesis and Philosophy," *OTW* 9 (1966) 62-71.

P. D. Pahl, "Baptism in Luther's 'Lectures on Genesis'," *LTJ* 1 (1967-68) 26-35.

David E. Aune, "Early Christian Biblical Interpretation," *EQ* 41 (1969) 89-96.

§272 *3.1.9 Theory, Method, and Practice of Textual Criticism - General Studies (includes Paleography)*

J. R., "Remarks on the Variæ Lectiones of the Hebrew Bible," *JSL, 3rd Ser.*, 3 (1856) 137-152. (Note by P. S., pp. 433-434)

(   ) K., "Miscellanea Theologica. 2. Researches in Hebrew Palæography," *TRL* 1 (1864) 222-224.

*(   ) K., "Jewish Coins and Hebrew Palæography," *TRL* 5 (1868) 244-259. *(Review)*

*Willis J. Beecher, "Had the Massorites the Critical Instinct?" *ONTS* 2 (1882-83) 1-7.

B. Felshenthal, "Inverted Nuns in the Bible," *ONTS* 2 (1882-83) 169-170.

Oliver Turnbull Crane, "Tikkun Sopherim," *AJSL* 3 (1886-87) 233-248.

Hermann L. Strack, "Mr. Crane on Tikkun Sopherim," *AJSL* 4 (1887-88) 54.

*Henry M. Harman, "Some Observations upon Tikkun Sopherim," *AJSL* 4 (1887-88) 34-42.

*Ad. Neubauer, "The Introduction of the Square Characters in Biblical MSS., and an Account of the earliest MSS. of the Old Testament," *SBE* 3 (1891) 1-36.

Francis Brown, "Old Testament Problems," *JBL* 15 (1896) 63-74. [I. Textual, pp. 64-66]

W. Emery Barnes, "Ancient Corrections in the Text of the Old Testament *(Tikkun Sopherim),*" *JTS* 1 (1899-1900) 387-414.

*J. H. A. Hart, "Primitive Exegesis as a Factor in the Corruption of the Texts of Scripture Illustrated from the Versions of Ben Sira," *JQR* 15 (1902-03) 627-631.

A. Souter, "Palaeography and its Uses," *JTS* 4 (1902-03) 506-516.

Richard Gottheil, "The Dating of their Manuscripts by the Samaritans," *JBL* 25 (1906) 29-48.

Eb. Nestle, "The Shortest and Longest Verses of the Bible," *ET* 24 (1912-13) 92.

A. H. Sayce, "The Transmission of Religious Texts in the Ancient Oriental World," *ET* 24 (1912-13) 36-38.

*A. T. Olmstead, "Source Study and the Biblical Text," *AJSL* 30 (1913-14) 1-35.

*Harold M. Wiener, "Historical Criticism of the Pentateuch. A Reply to Dr. Koenig (II.)," *BS* 72 (1915) 83-153. [Rival Views of Textual History, pp. 111-153]

*Arthur A. Dembitz, "Haplophony," *JQR, N.S.,* 22 (1931-32) 153.

Leroy Waterman, "The Authentication of Conjectural Glosses," *JBL* 56 (1937) 253-265.

*Charles C. Torrey, "Some Important Editorial Operations in the Book of Isaiah," *JBL* 57 (1938) 109-140.

*Harry Torczyner, "Abbreviation or Haplography?" *JBL* 64 (1945) 399.

Harry M Orlinsky, "A Rejoinder," *JBL* 64 (1945) 400-402.

*Harry Torczyner, "Yes, Haplography!" *JBL* 64 (1945) 545-546. [Editorial note by Robert H. Pfeiffer, p. 546]

Ernest R. Lacheman, "A Matter of Method in Hebrew Palaeography," *JQR, N.S.,* 40 (1949-50) 15-39.

Ernest R. Lacheman, "Can Hebrew Paleography be Called 'Scientific'?" *JQR, N.S.,* 42 (1951-52) 377-385.

*Robert Gordis, "Was Koheleth a Phoenician? Some Observations on Methods in Research," *JBL* 74 (1955) 103-114.

*Moshe Greenberg, "The Stabilization of the Text of the Hebrew Bible, Reviewed in the Light of the Biblical Materials from the Judean Desert," *JAOS* 76 (1956) 157-167.

Francis S. North, "Textual Variants in the Hebrew Significant for Critical Analysis," *JQR, N.S.,* 47 (1956-57) 77-80.

M. H. Goshen-Gottstein, "The History of the Bible-Text and Comparative Semitics," *VT* 7 (1957) 195-201.

S. Talmon, "The Three Scrolls of the Law that were Found in the Temple Court," *Text* 2 (1962) 14-27.

S[olomon] Zeitlin, "Were there Three Torah-Scrolls in the Azarah?" *JQR, N.S.,* 56 (1965-66) 269-272.

*F. J. Morrow Jr., "Psalm XXI 10—An Example of Haplography," *VT* 18 (1968) 558-559.

§273 *3.1.10 Text Similarities and Families*

*Frank Zimmermann, "The Perpetuation of Variants in the Masoretic Text," *JQR, N.S.,* 34 (1943-44) 459-474.

*W[illiam] F[oxwell] Albright, "New Light on Early Recensions of the Hebrew Bible," *BASOR* #140 (1955) 27-33.

Sidney Jellicoe, "The Hesychian Recension Reconsidered," *JBL* 82 (1963) 409-418.

§274 *3.1.11 Arrangement, Chapter Divisions, and Other Aids for Readers*

H. Rood, "Division of the Bible into Chapters and Verses," *BJ* 2 (1843) 255-262.

Anonymous, "Clausula Libri Geneseos," *ONTS* 2 (1882-83) 22.

Willis J. Beecher, "Italics in our English Bibles," *PR* 7 (1886) 355-356.

J. F. McCurdy, "Popular Uses of the Margin in the Old Testament Revision," *ONTS* 6 (1886-87) 229-234.

*George F. Moore, "Vulgate Chapters and Numbered Verses in the Hebrew Bible," *JBL* 12 (1893) 73-78.

C. Kegan Paul, "Bible Chapter Headings in the 'Authorized Version'," *TR* 6 (1896) 99-111.

*Ludwig Blau, "Massoretic Studies, III. The Division into Verses," *JQR* 9 (1896-97) 122-144, 360. [1. Age of the Division into Verses; 2. The Division into Verses in the Talmud and the Midrash; 3. The Division of the Verses of the Massorah]

E. N. Adler, "An Eleventh Century Introduction to the Hebrew Bible: Being a Fragment from Sepher ha-Ittim of Rabbi Judah ben Barzilai of Barcelona," *JQR* 9 (1896-97) 669-716.

S. J. Halberstam, "Notes to J. Q. R., IX, pp. 669-721*[sic]*," *JQR* 10 (1897-98) 165-167. *[Ref. Previous Article]*

Eb. Nestle, "Leviticum and Deteronomius," *ET* 9 (1897-98) 188-189.

J. Anthony Barnes, "The Evolution of a Reference Bible," *LQHR* 92 (1899) 99-112. *(Review)*

T. H. Stokoe, "The Edition of the Revised Version, with Marginal References, 1898," *Exp, 6th Ser.,* 8 (1903) 1-11.

*W. E. Boulter, "Marginal References to the Apocrypha in the Bible of 1611," *IJA* #6 (1906) 8-9.

Eb. Nestle, "Why are Two Books of Samuel, Kings, Chronicles in Our Bibles?" *ET* 18 (1906-07) 383.

Anonymous, "Italicized Words in the Bible," *R&E* 9 (1912) 404-412. *[O.T. Refs. pp. 407-408]*

W. H. Bennett, "The Arrangement of the Old Testament," *JMUEOS* #7 (1917-18) 43-51.

Anonymous, "Bible Facts," *CFL, 3rd Ser.,* 38 (1932) 539.

*Edgar J. Goodspeed, "'The Translators to the Reader'," *RL* 1 (1932) 407-418. *[KJV]*

E. Lawrence Marwick, "The Order of the Books in Yefet's Bible Codex," *JQR, N.S.,* 33 (1942-43) 445-460.

*A. P. Wikgren, "Translation and Use of Marginal Notes in the English Bible," *JBL* 66 (1947) v.

John R. Richardson, "The Westminister Study Edition of the Holy Bible," *CCQ* 6 (1948-49) #1/2, 25-26.

Johannes Adler, "The Revision of the Reference Sytem in the New Luther Bible," *BTr* 12 (1961) 178-181.

J. Meysing, "The Numbers of the Verses of the Biblical Books," *CNI* 14 (1963) #3/4, 35-40; 15 (1964) #1, 24-30.

Robert P. Markham, "Ancient and Modern Titles of Books of the Bible, Part I," *BTr* 18 (1967) 86-94.

Luther A. Weigle, "New Editions of the Scriptures: An Ecumenical Bible," *PSB* 60 (1967) #2, 43-45. *[Oxford Annotated Bible]*

J. W. Roberts, "Revision of Schofield Bible," *RestQ* 10 (1967) 161-166.

§275 *3.1.12 Printed Hebrew Texts and Their Apparatus*

Henry Burgess, "Suggestions for a Critical Edition of the Hebrew Bible," *JSL, 1st Ser.,* 3 (1849) 152-158.

Christian D. Ginsburg, "Introduction to the Rabbinic Bible: by Jacob ben Chajim," *JSL, 4th Ser.,* 3 (1863) 382-412.

A. W. Thayer, "Critical Theology. A Revised Text of the Hebrew Bible," *URRM* 30 (1888) 58-69.

B. Pick, "History of the Printed Editions of the Old Testament, Together with a Description of the Rabbinic and Polyglot Bibles," *AJSL* 9 (1892-93) 47-116.

Paul Haupt, "On a new critical edition of the Hebrew text of the Old Testament," *JAOS* 16 (1894-96) vii-ix.

Ludwig Blau, "Dr. Ginsburg's Edition of the Hebrew Bible," *JQR* 12 (1899-1900) 217-254.

J. A. Selbie, "The Smallest Hebrew Bible," *ET* 13 (1901-02) 336.

John Taylor, "A Critical Edition of the Hebrew Bible," *ET* 17 (1905-06) 74. *(Review)*

John Taylor, "A Critical Edition of the Hebrew Bible," *ET* 18 (1906-07) 126-127. *(Review) [Corrections to Biblia Hebraica]*

Eberhard Nestle, "The New Hebrew Bible of the British and Foreign Bible Society," *ET* 20 (1908-09) 313-315. *['The Trinitarian Bible']*

Hermann L. Strack, "The New Hebrew Bible of the British and Foreign Bible Society," *ET* 20 (1908-09) 376-377. *['The Trinitarian Bible']*

Rudolf Kittel, "Some Suggestions in Regard to the Use of the Biblia Hebraica," *BWTS* 2 (1909-10) #4, 28-31. *(Trans. by D. E Culley)*

R. Kilgour, "Two Hebrew Bibles of Four Hundred Years Ago," *GUOST* 4 (1913-22) 45-51. [I. The Complutensian Polyglot; II. The First Biblia Rabbinica]

R. Kilgour, "Two Hebrew Bibles of Four Hundred Years Ago," *Exp, 8th Ser.,* 14 (1917) 48-57. [I. The Complutensian Polyglot, pp. 49-51; II. The First Biblia Rabbinica, pp. 51-57]

*W. H. Griffith Thomas, "The Church and the Old Testament," *CFL, 3rd Ser.,* 29 (1923) 217-221.

W. B. Stevenson, "Rabbinical Bibles in the Library of Glasgow University," *GUOST* 5 (1923-28) 44-51.

C[harles] C. Torrey, "The Critical Apparatus of a Hebrew Bible," *JBL* 58 (1939) v.

*Alexander Sperber, "Problems of the Masora," *HUCA* 17 (1942-43) 293-394. [I. The Masoretic Bible, pp. 296-298]

*Alexander Sperber, "Biblical Hebrew," *PAAJR* 18 (1948-49) 301-382. [Textual Criticism of *BHS,* pp. 314-374]

N. N. Snaith, "New Edition of the Hebrew Bible," *VT* 7 (1957) 207-208.

Frederick W. Danker, "Aids·to Bible Study. The Hebrew Old Testament," *CTM* 29 (1958) 902-918.

Anonymous, "A New Edition of the Hebrew Old Testament," *BTr* 10 (1959) 110-112.

Anonymous, "Notes and Communications. 2. A Brief Report on the Hebrew University Bible Project," *Text* 1 (1960) 210-211.

Harry M. Orlinsky, "The New Jewish Version of the Torah," *JBL* 82 (1963) 249-264.

Bleddyn J. Roberts, "The Hebrew Bible Since 1937," *JTS, N.S.,* 15 (1964) 253-264.

Anonymous, "Report on the Hebrew University Bible Project 1960-1964," *Text* 4 (1964) 232.

Harry M. Orlinsky, "Some Recent Jewish Translations of the Bible," *McQ* 19 (1965-66) 293-300.

Anonymous, "Report on the Hebrew University Bible Project 1965-1966," *Text* 5 (1966) 145.

Anonymous, "Report on the Hebrew University Bible Project 1967," *Text* 6 (1968) 134.

B. J. Roberts, "To Welcome the New 'Biblia Hebraica'," *ET* 80 (1968-69) 214-215.

I[srael] Yeivin, "The New Edition of the Biblica Hebraica—its Text and Massorah," *Text* 7 (1969) 114-123.

§276 **3.1.13 Translation Principles - General Studies**

*Anonymous, "Cornucopia," *MMBR* 42 (1816-17) 231-233. *[Translation of the Bible: names of those employed in translating the KJV and rules for conducting the Translation, pp. 232-233]*

Anonymous, "On Translating Scripture," *TRGR* 1 (1822) 91-96.

Gaius, "On the State of the English Translation of the Bible," *CongML* 11 (1828) 302.

J. K. Young, "Translation of the Bible into English," *BJ* 1 (1842) 21-29.

Anonymous, "Chinese Translations of the Word 'God'," *JSL, 2nd Ser.,* 6 (1854) 411-419. *(Review)*

F. P. S., "Biblical Revision," *JSL, 3rd Ser.,* 9 (1859) 326-332.

*Lewis Tayler, "The Emotional Element in Hebrew Translation. [First Article]," *MR* 44 (1862) 85-108.

*Lewis Tayler, "The Emotional Element in Hebrew Translation. [Second Article]," *MR* 45 (1863) 55-74.

*Lewis Tayler, "The Emotional Element in Hebrew Translation. [Third Article]," *MR* 45 (1863) 382-406.

*Lewis Tayler, "The Emotional Element in Hebrew Translation. [Fourth Article]," *MR* 46 (1864) 57-77.

James A. Corcoran, "Beza as a Translator; His Perversions of the Word of God," *ACQR* 4 (1879) 521-550.

*Anonymous, "Internal Evidence," *ONTS* 3 (1883-84) 58-60.

*( ) C., "The Term Higher Criticism," *ONTS* 3 (1883-84) 310-311.

F. J. Gurney, "The Translation of Proper Names," *ONTS* 4 (1884-85) 210-212.

E. Riehm, "Luther as Bible Translator," *MR* 67 (1885) 375-396. *(Adapted from the German by W. W. Davies)*

*Geo. H. Schodde, "Biblical Research Notes," *ColTM* 17 (1897) 371-384. [Bible Text and Bible Translations, pp. 371-373]

J. Shillidy, "Transliteration of Proper Names in the Revised Version of the Bible," *ET* 9 (1897-98) 238-239.

W. Aldis Wright, "The Transliteration of Proper Names in the Revised Version," *ET* 9 (1897-98) 523.

*H. St. J. Thackeray, "The Greek Translators of Jeremiah," *JTS* 4 (1902-03) 245-266.

*H. St. J. Thackeray, "The Greek Translators of Ezekiel," *JTS* 4 (1902-03) 398-411.

*H. St. J. Thackeray, "The Greek Translators of the Prophetical Books," *JTS* 4 (1902-03) 578-585.

[Martin Luther], "Luther on Translation," *OC* 21 (1907) 465-471. *(Trans. by W. H. Carruth)*

A. Kampmeier, "Remarks on 'Luther on Translation'," *OC* 21 (1907) 574.

Anonymous, "The Edinburgh Apocrypha Controversy in Caricature, 1827-8," *IJA* #29 (1912) 29-33; #31 (1912) 76-78.

E. J. Sewell, "The Principles Governing Bible Translation," *JTVI* 48 (1916) 43-59. (Discussion, pp. 59-64)

R. Kilgour, "The Order of First Translations of Scripture in Mission Fields," *IRM* 7 (1918) 456-469.

*W. Emery Barnes, "Bible Translation—Official and Unofficial: A Study of Psalm IV in English," *JTS* 28 (1926-27) 39-48.

Morris O. Evans, "The Bible in Translation," *HR* 106 (1933) 13-15.

*O. J. Baab, "A Theory of Two Translators for the Greek Genesis," *JBL* 52 (1933) 239-243.

George F. Hall, "Luther and Coverdale: Biblical Glossators," *AugQ* 14 (1935) 291-303.

J. F. Mozley, "Tyndale's Knowledge of Hebrew," *JTS* 36 (1935) 392-396.

Beatrice Allard Brooks, "In Defense of the Translator and of New Translations," *JAAR* 5 (1937) 11-17.

O. M. Norlie, "Those Nine Old Verbs," *JTALC* 2 (1937) #5, 29-31. *[Translation principles of the KJV]*

*T[heophile] J. Meek, "Hebrew Poetic Structure as a Translation Guide," *JBL* 57 (1938) viii.

Frederick C. Grant, "Why Change the Bible?" *RL* 7 (1938) 510-524.

Charles H. Pickar, "Biblical News," *CBQ* 1 (1939) 266-270. *[Principles Governing the Revision of the Old Testament]*

*William L. Newton, "The Revison of our Old Testament in English," *CBQ* 2 (1940) 308-319.

*Theophile J. Meek, "Hebrew Poetic Structure as a Translation Guide," *JBL* 59 (1940) 1-9.

Patrick W. Skehan, "The Old Testament Revision Project. Historical Sketch," *CBQ* 5 (1943) 214-219.

Edward P. Arbez, "Translating the Old Testament out of the Original Languages," *CBQ* 7 (1945) 48-75.

*Louis H. Gray, "Man in Anglo-Saxon and Old High German Bible-Texts," *Word* 1 (1945) 19-32.

Patrick A. Sullivan, "Idiom in Scripture Translation (1)," *MH* 2 (1945-46) #1, 11-12.

*Augustine Bea, "The New Psalter: Its Origin and Spirit," *CBQ* 8 (1946) 4-35. *(Trans. by Augustine Wand)*

A. R. Crabtree, "Translating the Bible in Portuguese," *R&E* 43 (1946) 40-49.

*A. P. Wikgren, "Translation and the Use of Marginal Notes in the English Bible," *JBL* 66 (1947) v.

R. A. Knox, "Farewell to Machabees*[sic]*," *ClR* 30 (1948) 217-231.

Edgar J. Goodspeed, "The Present State of Bible Translation," *JAAR* 18 (1950) 99-100.

T. H. Robinson, "Special Features of Old Testament Translation," *BTr* 2 (1951) 113-117.

G. D. Young, "Bible Translations in the Light of Ancient Bilinguals," *JBL* 70 (1951) iv.

*John W. Wevers, "Principles of Interpretation Guiding the Fourth Translator of the Book of the Kingdoms (3 K. 22:1 - 4 K. 25:30)," *CBQ* 14 (1952) 40-56.

G. Ch. Aalders, "Some Aspects of Bible Translation Concerning the Old Testament," *BTr* 4 (1953) 97-102.

*John W. Wevers, "A Study in the Exegetical Principles Underlying the Greek Text of 2 Sm 11,2 - 1 Kings 2,11," *CBQ* 15 (1953) 30-45.

Harry M. Orlinsky, "Jewish Scholarship and Christian Translations of the Hebrew Bible," *YCCAR* 63 (1953) 235-252.

*William A. Irwin, "Textual Criticism and Old Testament Translation," *BTr* 5 (1954) 54-58.

*Ellis E. Pierce, "The Translation of Biblical Poetry," *BTr* 5 (1954) 62-73.

W. Schwarz, "Principles of Biblical Translation," *BTr* 5 (1954) 163-169.

*F. W. Grosheide, "The Translation of Quotations from the Old Testament in the New," *BTr* 6 (1955) 16-20.

*P. Peters, "Luther's Rendition of II Samuel 22:36 and Psalm 18:36: und wenn du mich demuetigest machst du mich gross," *WLQ* 52 (1955) 137-143.

*Nigel Turner, "The Greek Translators of Ezekiel," *JTS, N.S.,* 7 (1956) 12-24.

*William A. Irwin, "Some Principles and Problems in the Translation of the Old Testament," *NTT* 11 (1956-57) 241-248.

*Dewey M. Beegle, "The Meaning of the Qumran Scrolls for Translators of the Bible," *BTr* 8 (1957) 1-8.

Cecil Northcott, "Putting the Bible Into Modern Speech," *RL* 26 (1957) 122-128.

Hugh Ross, "Principles of Bible Translating in the Year 1727," *BTr* 10 (1959) 22-27. *[Editorialized selections from a book by Hugh Ross published in 1727]*

C. H. Dodd, "The Translation of the Bible: Some Questions of Principle," *BTr* 11 (1960) 4-9.

Theophile J. Meek, "Translating the Hebrew Bible," *JBL* 79 (1960) 328-335.

F. W. Ratcliffe, "The Psalm Translation of Heinrich von Mugeln," *BJRL* 43 (1960-61) 426-451.

John J. Kijne and W. R. Hutton, "Bible Translation and the 'Bible Translator'," *IRM* 50 (1961) 328-335.

*Howard McKaughan, "Bible Translation and Linguistics," *JCE* 4 (1961) 7-16.

*Henry R. Moeller, "Biblical Research and Old Testament Translation," *BTr* 13 (1962) 16-22.

Theophile J. Meek, "Old Testament Translation Principles," *JBL* 81 (1962) 143-154.

N. Adriani, "Some Principles of Bible Translation," *BTr* 14 (1963) 9-13.

Joseph E. Grimes, "Measuring 'Naturalness' in a Translation," *BTr* 14 (1963) 49-62.

*Constance Naish and Gillian Story, "'The Lord is my Goat Hunter'," *BTr* 14 (1963) 91-92.

H. L. Ginsberg, "The Story of the New Translation of the Torah," *BTr* 14 (1963) 106-113.

*Anonymous, "Translating the Psalms," *HJ* 62 (1963-64) 78-82.

*Leo Schwartz, "On Translating the 'Song of Songs'," *Jud* 13 (1964) 64-76.

*Eugene B. Borowitz, "Theological Issues in the New Torah Translation," *Jud* 13 (1964) 335-345.

William J. Samarin, "Controlling Elicitation of Equivalents," *BTr* 16 (1965) 36-38.

Theophile J. Meek, "Translating the Hebrew Bible," *BTr* 16 (1965) 141-148.

Geoffrey E. Marrison, "The Art of Translation and the Science of Meaning," *BTr* 16 (1965) 176-184.

*Abraham Cronbach, "Unmeant Meanings of Scripture," *HUCA* 36 (1965) 99-123. [2. Latitude of Translation, pp. 106-113; 3. The Translator's Punctuation, pp. 114-115]

*Judah Stampfer, "On Translating Biblical Poetry. *Isaiah,* Chapters 1 and 2:1-4," *Jud* 14 (1965) 501-510.

W. H. Semple, "St. Jerome as a Biblical Transator," *BJRL* 48 (1965-66) 227-243.

*Edwin Yamauchi, "Slaves of God," *BETS* 9 (1966) 31-50. [The Word "Slave" and The Translators of the King James Version, pp. 40-43]

*Peter R. Ackroyd and Michael A. Knibb, "Translating the Psalms," *BTr* 17 (1966) 1-11.

Geoffrey E. Marrison, "Style in Bible Translation," *BTr* 17 (1966) 129-132.

L. Lengrand, "Vatican II on Bible Translation," *IES* 5 (1966) 237-247.

*Sakae Shibayama, "Notes on *Yārad* and *'Ālāh:* Hints on Translating," *JAAR* 34 (1966) 358-362.

Burton L. Goddard, "Concerns in Bible Translation: Introduction," *BETS* 10 (1967) 85-87.

Earl S. Kalland, "Concerns in Bible Translation: Considerations of Verbal and Idea Rendition," *BETS* 10 (1967) 88-92.

Martin H. Woudstra, "Concerns in Bible Translation: Theological Influence upon Translation," *BETS* 10 (1967) 93-100.

John H. Skilton, "Concerns in Bible Translation: Considerations of English Style," *BETS* 10 (1967) 101-110. [I. Various Influences on the English Style of Translations; II. The Stylistic Aims of Translators; III. Basic Approaches Used by Translators; IV. The Stylistic Accomplishments of Translators; V. Assistance for Future Translators]

William E. Nix, "Theological Presuppositions and Sixteenth Century English Bible Translation," *BS* 124 (1967) 42-50, 117-124.

*F. Charles Fensham, "Ugaritic and the Translation of the Old Testament," *BTr* 18 (1967) 71-74.

*James Barr, "Biblical Translation and the Church," *NB* 49 (1967-68) 285-292. *[Jerusalem Bible]*

*Elmer B. Smick, "Suggested New Translation of Old Testament Poetry," *BETS* 11 (1968) 85-92.

Walter M. Abbott, "The Shape of the Common Bible," *BibT* #37 (1968) 2553-3566.

*Christine Downing, "Theology as Translation," *RL* 37 (1968) 401-416.

*Gareth Lloyd Jones, "Jewish Exegesis and the English Bible," *ASTI* 7 (1968-69) 53-63.

B. Siertsema, "Language and World View (Semantics for Theologians),"
BTr 20 (1969) 3-21.

Eugene A. Nida, "Science of Translation," *Lang* 45 (1969) 483-498.

§277 *3.1.14 Translation Problems - General Studies*

*†Theoph[ilus] Abauzit, "Mistakes in the French Stereotype Bible," *MMBR*
36 (1813-14) 182-130.

†Theophilus Abauzit, "The Rev. T. Abauzit, on the English Bible," *MMBR*
36 (1813-14) 485-486.

†Anonymous, "The Genevese Controversy," *BCQTR, N.S.,* 12 (1819) 1-23.

†Anonymous, "On the Writers who recommend a new Translation,"
BCQTR, N.S., 14 (1820) 611-630. *(Review)*

P. S., "Supposed Errors in the English Bible," *JSL, 3rd Ser.,* 5 (1857) 130-
144.

†A. P. Happer, "On the Word for 'God' in Chinese," *PAOS* (October, 1868)
viii-ix.

[Theodore D.] Woolsey, "On the rendering of the word God in Chinese,"
JAOS 9 (1871) xvi-xvii.

†A. P. Happer, "On the Word for 'God' in Chinese," *JAOS* 9 (1871) xlii-
xliv.

S. Wells Williams, "The Controversy Among the Protestant Missionaries on
the Proper Translation of the Words God and Spirit into Chinese," *BS*
35 (1878) 732-778.

*Anonymous, "Translation or Interpretation," *ONTS* 4 (1884-85) 186-187.

*Erastus Wentworth, "Musical Instruments in the Revision," *MR* 68 (1886)
546-564.

†Anonymous, "The Bible at Home and Abroad," *QRL* 180 (1895) 289-323.
(Review) [History of Translation Problems]

*A. A. B[erle], "Babylonian Palæography and the Old Testament," *BS* 54
(1897) 391-393.

*Robert Kilgour, "Old Testament Names for God: Their Rendering into Hindi and Cognate Languages. *A Plea for the Transliteration of the Sacred Name,*" *GUOST* 2 (1901-07) 50-52.

*Dunlop Moore, "The Significance of the Different Printing of a Letter in Two Versions of the Bible," *CFL, N.S.,* 7 (1903) 354-357.

Edmund B. Fairfield, "Treatment of Idioms—In Translation," *HR* 46 (1903) 449-452.

*Wentworth Webster, "The Language of Early Bible History," *ET* 16 (1904-05) 521-523.

A. L. Kitching, "Capturing a Language," *IRM* 5 (1916) 115-126.

W. H. Bennett, "On the Impossibility of Translating the Old Testament," *Exp, 8th Ser.,* 15 (1918) 339-350.

Anonymous, "Is the Old Testament Translatable," *HR* 76 (1918) 108.

Floyd R. Maynard, "The Bible in the Orient," *MR* 101 (1918) 924-931.

*Allen Howard Godbey, "Ancient Hebrew Science," *MQR, 3rd Ser.,* 49 (1923) 139-163. *[Translation Problems]*

W. G. Jordan, "Problems of Translation," *CJRT* 2 (1925) 111-127.

J. M. Powis Smith, "Some Difficulties of a Translator," *JR* 5 (1925) 163-171.

E. B. Pollard, "Quaint Mistranslations," *CQ* 3 (1926) 222-225.

*A. Z. Conrad, "One-Man Bible Translations," *CFL, 3rd Ser.,* 33 (1927) 657-658. *[Moffat's Translation]*

Theophile James Meek, "The Trials of an Old Testament Translator," *CJRT* 4 (1927) 290-304.

W[illiam] A. Irwin, "Old Testament Translation," *CJRT* 4 (1927) 508-521.

*E. B. Pollard, "Some Traditional Misinterpretations," *CQ* 4 (1927) 92-94.

*E. B. Pollard, "Other Traditional Misinterpretations," *CQ* 4 (1927) 204-206.

*E. B. Pollard, "Further Misinterpretations of Familiar Passages," *CQ* 4 (1927) 323-330. *[The Book of Job]*

*Leo Jung, "Mis-Translations a Source in Jewish and Christian Lore," *PAAJR* 5 (1933-34) 55-67.

Theophile James Meek, "Translation Difficulties in the Old Testament," *RL* 3 (1934) 491-506.

*R. F. Bevan, "A Great Text Mistranslated," *ET* 48 (1936-37) 476-478. [Psalm 65:3]

Theophile James Meek, "Lapses of Old Testament Translation," *JAOS* 58 (1938) 122-129.

Charles Callan, "Some English Idioms in the English Bible," *CBQ* 2 (1940) 44-56, 156-172.

William Newton, "Problems of Bible Revision. The External Form of the Old Testament," *CBQ* 3 (1941) 174-178.

Norman H. Snaith, "The Width and Length of Words," *ET* 55 (1943-44) 265-268.

G. W. Sheppard, "The Problem of Translating 'God' into Chinese," *HJ* 43 (1944-45) 48-54.

John Hackett, "Problems of Translation and the Bible," *IER, 5th Ser.,* 68 (1946) 217-226.

*G. R. Driver, "Mistranslations in the Old Testament," *WO* 1 (1947-52) 29-31.

W. K. Lowther Clarke, "A New Translation of the Bible," *Theo* 51 (1948) 303-306.

Sebastian Bullough, "Translation from the Hebrew," *CIR* 31 (1949) 289-301.

*Henry S. Gehman, "The Theological Approach of the Greek Translator of Job 1-15," *JBL* 68 (1949) 231-240.

G. Ch. Aalders, "Notes on Some Difficulties of Old Testament Translation," *BTr* 1 (1950) 9-15.

E. A. Nida, "The Translator's Problems," *BTr* 1 (1950) 41-50.

E. A. Nida, "The Most Common Errors in Translation," *BTr* 1 (1950) 51-56.

*L. H. Brockington, "The Greek Translator of Isaiah and His Interest in *ΔΟΞΑ*," *VT* 1 (1951) 23-32.

P. Middelkoop, "Problems of the Bible Translator in Connection with the Cultural and Religious Background of the People, Translating the Divine Names (with Discussion)," *BTr* 3 (1952) 171-199.

H. Rosin, "Questionnaire Concerning the Divine Names," *BTr* 3 (1952) 199-204.

H. van der Veen, "The Use of Literary or Poetic Language in Poetic Parts of the Bible (with Discussion)," *BTr* 3 (1952) 212-220.

G. W. Sheppard, "The Problem of Translating 'God' into Chinese," *BTr* 6 (1959) 23-30.

*A. S. Tritton, "Some Notes on the Septuagint," *GUOST* 18 (1959-60) 49-52.

Theophile J. Meek, "Translation Problems in the Old Testament," *JQR, N.S.*, 50 (1959-60) 45-54.

Anonymous, "Old Testament Translation Problems," *BTr* 11 (1960) 40-41.

*J. C. Hindley, "The Translation of the Words for 'Covenant'," *IJT* 10 (1961) 13-24.

William A. Irwin, "The Bible and the Translator," *PSTJ* 15 (1961-62) #3, 17-26.

C. S. Thoburn, "Biblical Names in Hindi," *BTr* 13 (1962) 134-139.

*P. Middelkoop, "A Word Study. The Sense of PAQAD in the second Commandment and its general background in the O. T. in regard to the translation into the Indonesian and Timorese Languages," *SEAJT* 4 (1962-63) #3, 33-47.

*John Eaton, "Problems of Translation in Psalm 23:3f.," *BTr* 16 (1965) 171-175.

Philippa Guillebaud, "Some Points of Interest and Difficulty Experienced in Translating Genesis into Bari," *BTr* 16 (1965) 189-192.

*Abraham Cronbach, "Unmeant Meanings of Scripture," *HUCA* 36 (1965) 99-123. [1. Detachment from the Context, pp. 100-105; 2. Latitude of Translation, pp. 106-113; 3. The Translator's Punctuation, pp. 114-115; 4. Changes of Hebrew Vocalization, pp. 115-117; 5. Consonantal Changes, pp. 117-123]

Daniel E. Pilarczyk, "Jonah's Gourd: Augustine and Jerome on a New Translation of Sacred Scripture," *BibT* #26 (1966) 1848-1852.

*Roland E. Clements, "Divine Titles as a Problem of Old Testament Translation," *BTr* 17 (1966) 81-84.

Eugene H. Maly, "Haggadah," *BTr* 17 (1966) 85-87. *[Problems of Biblical Names and References between "Faiths"]*

*Ernest G. Clarke, "The Hebraic Spirit," *CJT* 12 (1966) 153-163.

*E. Reim, "The Problem of Translation—Ps 71 and 73," *JTLC* 6 (1966) 1-7.

[Stan F. Aranjo(?)], "Language of the People of God," *IES* 7 (1968) 61-68. *(Editorial)*

*James Barr, "Seeing the Wood for the Trees? An Enigmatic Ancient Translation," *JSS* 13 (1968) 11-20.

*Wesley J. Culshaw, "Translating Biblical Poetry," *BTr* 19 (1968) 1-5.

A. Capell, "Names for 'God' in Oceanic Languages," *BTr* 20 (1969) 154-157.

William D. Reyburn, "Cultural Equivalences and Nonequivalences in Translation," *BTr* 20 (1969) 158-167.

*Aelred Baker, "The Strange Case of Job's Chisel," *CBQ* 31 (1969) 370-379. *[Job 19:24]*

*Chr. A. W. Brekelmans, "Some Translation Problems," *OTS* 15 (1969) 170-176.

§278 **3.2 *Literary Criticism of the Old Testament***
    - *General Studies*

*†Anonymous, "Dr. Geddes on the Hebrew Scriptures," *BCQTR* 19 (1802)
    1-15, 134-154, 283-293, 343-355, 524-530, 623-631; 20 (1802) 53-61,
    165-171. *(Review)*

Φ, "Remarks on the criticism of the Bible," *QCS* 3 (1821) 169-179.

†Anonymous, "Carpenter's Introduction to the Study of the Holy
    Scriptures," *BCQTR, 4th Ser.*, 1 (1827) 101-110. *(Review)*

Augustus Tholuck, "Hints on the Importance of the Study of the Old
    Testament," *BibR* 3 (1827) 371-426. *(Trans. by R. B. Patton)*

E. P. Barrows, "The Advancement of Biblical Knowledge," *BRCR* 11 (1838)
    60-74.

†Anonymous, "Biblical Criticism," *ERCJ* 72 (1840-41) 132-158. *(Review)*

*Edward Robinson, "The Bible and its Literature," *BRCR, N.S.*, 5 (1841)
    334-359.

H. Rood, "A Brief History of Biblical Criticism," *BJ* 1 (1842) 154-156.

S. O., "Parker's De Wette on the Old Testament," *CE* 35 (1843-44) 303-311.
    (Review)

†Anonymous, "*DeWitte's* Introduction," *NBR* 7 (1847) 355-367. *(Review)*

O. T. Dobbin, "German Rationalism in Its Early Indications," *JSL, 1st Ser.*,
    1 (1848) 126-154.

O. T. Dobbin, "German Rationalism in Its Recent Developments," *JSL, 1st
    Ser.*, 1 (1848) 257-278.

*Henry Burgess, "Is Biblical Criticism Unfavorable to Piety?" *JSL, 1st Ser.*,
    4 (1849) 111-124.

B. B. Edwards, "Present State of Biblical Science," *BS* 7 (1850) 1-13.

Anonymous, "First Lessons in Biblical Criticism," *JSL, 1st Ser.*, 5 (1850)
    415-422.

Tayler Lewis, "The Spirit of the Old Testament," *BFER* 1 (1852) 115-152.

G. R. N., "Davidson on Biblical Criticism," *CE* 54 (1853) 419-427. *(Review)*

H. B., "Biblical Criticism," *JSL, 2nd Ser.*, 4 (1853) 146-159. *(Review)*

Anonymous, "The Spirit of the Bible," *CTPR, 3rd Ser.*, 10 (1854) 229-260. *(Review)*

*S. P. Tregelles, "Dr. S. Davidson and Horne's Introduction," *JSL, 3rd Ser.*, 4 (1856-57) 424-439.

T. N., "Dr. Davidson and the Rev. Hartwell Horne's Introduction to the Holy Scriptures," *JSL, 3rd Ser.*, 6 (1857-58) 383-403. *(Review)*

†Anonymous, "Dr. Davidson's Rationalistic Views of the Scriptures," *LTJ* 10 (1857-58) 315-347. *(Review)*

Anonymous, "Kurtz on the History of the Old Covenant," *LQHR* 12 (1859) 447-462. *(Review)*

James W. M'Lane, "Speculation and the Bible," *BS* 18 (1861) 338-357.

Anonymous, "Hebrew Men and Times," *CE* 70 (1861) 362-388. *(Review)*

Geo. Howe, "Bunsen on the Bible," *SPR* 14 (1861-62) 96-133. *(Review)*

Anonymous, "*Introduction to the Old Testament.* By Samuel Davidson, D.D. Vol. I.," *LQHR* 19 (1862-63) 285-322. *(Review)*

†Anonymous, "Biblical Criticism—Reformers and Destructives," *BQRL* 38 (1863) 186-220. *(Review)*

Anonymous, "On Current Methods of Biblical Criticism," *JSL, 4th Ser.*, 4 (1863-64) 1-18.

Anonymous, "Davidson's Introduction to the Old Testament," *BFER* 13 (1864) 397-423. *(Review)*

*W. R. Coxwell Rogers, "Upon the Necessity of Cautiousness in Criticism," *JSL, 4th Ser.*, 9 (1866) 193-200.

Anonymous, "A Mahomedan Commentary on the Bible," *BFER* 16 (1867) 556-570. *(Review)*

Anonymous, "A Mahomedan Commentary on the Bible. (Second Notice)," *BFER* 17 (1868) 50-66. *(Review)*

Leroy S. Blake, "The Bible and Its Critics," *CongQB* 11 (1869) 528-542.

†Anonymous, "G. H. Augustus von Ewald," *BQRL* 57 (1873) 151-178. *(Review)*

†Anonymous, "The Bible's Place in a Science of Religion," *BQRL* 61 (1875) 94-125. *(Review)*

W. R[obertson] Smith, "The Progress of Old Testament Studies," *BFER* 25 (1876) 471-493.

J. H. Allen, "The Old Testament and the New Criticism," *URRM* 7 (1877) 135-151.

J. H. Morison, "Biblical Criticism," *URRM* 10 (1878) 651-673.

E. A. Washburn, "The Aim and Influence of Modern Biblical Criticism," *PRev* 55 (1879) Part 2, 27-46.

John W. Chadwick, "'Biblical Criticism': A Reply," *URRM* 11 (1879) 62-79. (Reply by J. H. Morison, pp. 79-82)

†Anonymous, "Colenso's Last Volume and Supernatural Religion," *LQHR* 53 (1879-80) 104-151. *(Review)*

Robert Watts, "Strictures on the Article 'Bible' in the recent edition of the 'Encyclopedia Britannica'," *BFER* 29 (1880) 220-247.

Anonymous, "Spinozism and Old Testament Criticism," *BFER* 29 (1880) 716-734. *[Translated from* Evangelische Kirchenzeitung, *July 24, 1880]*

Talbot W. Chambers, "The Theory of Professor Kuenen," *PR* 1 (1880) 304-320.

*Felix Adler, "On the Exegesis and Criticism of the Old Testament," *JAOS* 10 (1880) lxxxix-xc.

J. E[stlin] C[arpenter], "Some Old Testament Criticism," *ModR* 1 (1880) 446-450.

S. R. Calthrop, "The Old Testament," *URRM* 14 (1880) 289-315. *[Marked as "to be concluded" but never was]*

Edward H. Hall, "The Bible," *URRM* 14 (1880) 421-456.

Edward F. X. McSweeny, "The Scholars and the Bible," *ACQR* 6 (1881) 300-315.

Alfred Cave, "The Old Testament in the Jewish Church," *BFER* 30 (1881) 613-638. *(Review)*

R. B. Girdlestone, "Modern Biblical Criticism, its Bearing on Ministerial Work," *CM* 13 (1881) 65-73, 172-186. [O.T. Refs. pp. 181-186]

O. S. Stearns, "The Old Testament in the Jewish Church," *BQR* 4 (1882) 221-252.

Charles F. Thwing, "Professor W. Robertson Smith and His Theories of Old Testament Criticism," *BS* 39 (1882) 133-158.

John Phelps Taylor, "Prof. W. Robertson Smith from a Conservative Standpoint," *BS* 39 (1882) 291-344.

†Anonymous, "The Newer Criticism on the Old Testament," *LQHR* 58 (1882) 281-305. *(Review)*

Barnard C. Taylor, "Self Contractions in 'The Old Testament in the Jewish Church'," *ONTS* 1 (1882) #3, 45-47.

Barnard C. Taylor, "The Old Testament in the Jewish Church," *ONTS* 1 (1882) #2, 5-6.

Willis J. Beecher, "The Logical Methods of Professor Kuenen," *PR* 3 (1882) 701-731.

Willis J. Beecher, "The Logical Methods of Professor Kuenen," *BFER* 32 (1883) 114-150.

Francis A. Henry, "The Critical Study of the Scriptures," *PR* 12 (1883) 294-320. *(Review)*

*Charles A[ugustus] Briggs, "The Tract Baba Bathra of the Talmud and the Old Testament," *PR* 4 (1883) 417-420.

Francis A. Henry, "The Critical Study of the Scriptures," *PRev* 59 (1883) Part 2, 294-320. *(Review)*

C[yrus] A. Bartol, "The Bible," *URRM* 19 (1883) 30-52.

John Visher, "Kuenen vs. Delitzch," *URRM* 20 (1883) 315-334.

William Norman Irish, "Modern Biblical Criticism," *ONTS* 3 (1883-84) 39-49.

D. G. Lyon, "The Results of Modern Biblical Criticism," *ONTS* 3 (1883-84) 102-110. (Editorial Note, pp. 164-165)

J. A. Smith, "Modern Biblical Criticism: Its Practical Bearings," *ONTS* 3 (1883-84) 177-186.

Geo. H. Schodde, "Old Testament Criticism in the American Church," *ONTS* 3 (1883-84) 376-381.

J. W. Weddell, "The New Critical School," *ONTS* 3 (1883-84) 401-402.

J. W. Weddell, "Difficulties in the New Critical Views," *ONTS* 3 (1883-84) 402-403.

Howard Osgood, "Modern Biblical Criticism: its History and Methods," *BFER* 33 (1884) 125-133.

W. Robertson Smith, "The Attitude of Christians to the Old Testament," *Exp, 2nd Ser.,* 7 (1884) 241-251.

*Hermann L. Strack, "The Higher Criticism, a Witness to the Credibility of the Biblical Narrative," *AJSL* 1 (1884-85) 5-10.

H. G. Tomkins, "Recent Advances in Biblical Criticism and in Historical Discovery in Relation to the Christian Faith," *JTVI* 18 (1884-85) 92-94.

T. K. Cheyne, "Recent Advances in Biblical Criticism in Relation to the Christian Faith," *ONTS* 4 (1884-85) 73-78.

Anonymous, "Questions of Criticism: How and By Whom Shall They Be Settled?" *ONTS* 4 (1884-85) 134-136.

A. A. Pfanstiehl, "Gains and Losses of Modern Biblical Criticism," *ONTS* 4 (1884-85) 157-161

Anonymous, "The Outcome of Higher Criticism," *ONTS* 5 (1884-85) 182-183.

G[eo.] H. Schodde, "The Central Problem of Old Testament Discussion," *ONTS* 4 (1884-85) 241-245.

B. F. Simpson, "The Proper Attitude of the Ministry Towards Biblical Criticism," *ONTS* 5 (1884-85) 250-255.

*M[ilton] S. Terry, "Hermeneutics and the Higher Criticism," *ONTS* 4 (1884-85) 294-299.

G[eorge] H. S[chodde], "The New Theory of the Old Testament," *ColTM* 6 (1886) 168-178.

E. C. Bissell, "'Has Modern Criticism Affected Unfavorably any of the Essential Doctrines of Christianity?' No. III," *HR* 11 (1886) 189-195. *[Parts I & II not applicable to O.T.]*

George H. Schodde, "Problems of Old Testament Discussion," *LQ* 17 (1887) 335-353.

Anonymous, "The Higher Criticism in the Sunday-Schools," *MR* 69 (1887) 447-451.

Edward White, "The Influence of Spiritual States upon Biblical Criticism," *CongRL* 1 (1887-88) 982-1000.

Anonymous, "Works on Biblical Criticism," *CongRL* 2 (1888) 1127-1133. *(Review)*

Marcus Dods, "How Far is the Church Responsible for Present Scepticism?" *Exp, 3rd Ser.,* 8 (1888) 297-306.

Anonymous, "Dr. Briggs on the Higher Criticism and its Results," *BS* 46 (1889) 381-383.

T. K. Cheyne, "Reform in the Teaching of the Old Testament," *ContR* 56 (1889) 216-233.

*J. Rawson Lumby, "Old Testament Criticism in the Light of New Testament Quotations," *Exp, 3rd Ser.,* 9 (1889) 337-351.

George H. Schodde, "Modern Biblical Criticism," *HR* 18 (1889) 10-16.

G[eorge] H. Schodde, "The Biblical Criticism of Our Day," *ColTM* 10 (1890) 81-90.

S. R. Driver, "The Critical Study of the Old Testament," *ContR* 57 (1890) 215-231.

Alfred Cave, "The Old Testament and the Critics," *ContR* 57(1890) 537-551.

Anonymous, "The Critical Study of the Old Testament," *EN* 2 (1890) 427-429.

W. H. Bennett, "The Old Testament and the New Reformation," *Exp, 4th Ser.*, 2 (1890) 401-418.

Anonymous, "Old Testament Criticism," *HR* 20 (1890) 550-551.

Anonymous, "Limitations of Biblical Criticism," *MR* 72 (1890) 109-115.

Anonymous, "The Crime of the Higher Criticism," *MR* 72 (1890) 898-907.

Anonymous, "What Shall we do with the Old Testament," *AR* 15 (1891) 206-210. *(Editorial)*

Anonymous, "A Benefit of the Higher Criticism," *AR* 16 (1891) 279-282.

D[aniel] S. Gregory, "The Divine Authority of the Scriptures *Versus* Rationalistic Criticism," *HR* 21 (1891) 203-213.

*Camden M. Cobern, "The Higher Criticism and the Tombs of Egypt. Egyptology No. VIII," *HR* 22 (1891) 299-306.

Henry E. Jacobs, "A Critique of the Negative Criticism," *LCR* 10 (1891) 98-126.

Anonymous, "The Present State of Old Testament Study," *LQHR* 76 (1891) 291-311. *(Review)*

Edward Cowley, "The Old Testament After the Battle," *MR* 73 (1891) 577-590.

Anonymous, "The Progress of Criticism," *MR* 73 (1891) 945-955.

A. F. Kirkpatrick, "The Old Testament in the Christian Church," *ONTS* 13 (1891) 8-15.

V. M. Olyphant, "Higher Criticism," *ONTS* 12 (1891) 348-350.

N. West, "The Higher Criticism: *An American View*," *TML* 6 (1891) 1-7.

Anonymous, "Bishop Ellicott on Old Testament Criticism," *CQR* 33 (1891-92) 307-323. *(Review)*

A. R. S. Kennedy, "Canon Driver's Introduction to the Old Testament," *ET* 3 (1891-92) 169-172.

A. R. S. Kennedy, "Canon Cheyne's Bampton Lectures," *ET* 3 (1891-92) 245-250.

T. K. Cheyne, "A Friendly Reply to Professor Kennedy," *ET* 3 (1891-92) 319-321.

Edward H. Knight, "Logic in Biblical Criticism," *HSR* 2 (1891-92) 219-226.

*C. R. Brown, "Do the Literary Postulates of Hexateuch Criticism have any Parallels in other Books of the Old Testament?" *AR* 18 (1892) 205-220.

Howard Osgood, "The History and Definition of Higher Criticism," *BS* 49 (1892) 529-545.

W. E. Barton, "Driver on the Literature of the Old Testament," *BS* 49 (1892) 596-614. *(Review)*

A. Colchester, "Professor Driver on the Old Testament," *ContR* 61 (1892) 709-724, 865-879.

†Anonymous, "British Criticism of the Old Testament," *ERCJ* 176 (1892) 453-484. *(Review)*

T. K. Cheyne, "Dr. Driver's Introduction to the Old Testament Literature," *Exp, 4th Ser.,* 5 (1892) 81-114, 210-240, 241-269.

T. K. Cheyne, "On Some Points in Professor Robertson Smith's Lecture on the Old Testament," *Exp, 4th Ser.,* 6 (1892) 155-160. *(Review)*

S. R. Driver, "Professor W. Robertson Smith on the Old Testament," *Exp, 4th Ser.,* 6 (1892) 199-208. *(Review)*

Robert Watts, "The Methodology of the Higher Criticism and Its Allies Demonstrably Unscientific," *HR* 23 (1892) 12-19.

Francis Brown, "Is the Higher Criticism Scientific?" *HR* 23 (1892) 275-296. Anonymous, "A Liberal View of Old Testament Literature," *ONTS* 15 (1892) 167.

Anonymous, "The Twentieth Century View of the Old Testament," *ONTS* 15 (1892) 184.

R. C. Reed, "The Modern Jehu," *PQ* 6 (1892) 539-558.

Talbot W. Chambers, "Driver's Introduction to the Literature of the Old Testament," *PRR* 3 (1892) 518-520. *(Review)*

Charles A. Aiken, "The Bible and Criticism," *PRR* 3 (1892) 687-708.

Anonymous, "The Old Testament and the 'Higher Criticism'," *CQR* 35 (1892-93) 1-33.

Edward C. Ray, "Why Use the Old Testament?" *CT* 10 (1892-93) 371-377.

Joseph Strauss, "Judaism and Higher Criticism," *ET* 4 (1892-93) 168-169. *[Historical Study of the Practice of Higher Criticism by the Jews]*

Edward Lewis Curtis, "The Higher Criticism and Its Application to the Bible," *AR* 19 (1893) 137-154.

Owen H. Gates, "The Development of Old Testament Work in Theological Seminaries," *BS* 50 (1893) 119-130.

B. Pick, "Spinoza and the Old Testament," *BW* 2 (1893) 113-122, 194-203.

*James Ten Broeke, "Biblical Criticism in some of its Theological and Philosophical Relations," *BW* 2 (1893) 330-342, 444-451.

J. Westby Earnshaw, "'The Higher Criticism'," *HR* 26 (1893) 1-10, 123-127.

George H. Schodde, "Modern Biblical Criticism," *HR* 26 (1893) 396-401.

G. F. Spieker, "The Negative Criticism of the Old Testament," *LCR* 12 (1893) 335-348.

S. F. Breckenridge, "The Higher Criticism," *LQ* 23 (1893) 349-364.

E. C. Bissell, "Illogical Methods in Biblical Criticism," *PQ* 7 (1893) 485-504.

Anonymous, "The Old Testament and Modern Criticism," *CQR* 37 (1893-94) 276-300.

Howard Osgood, "The Bible and Higher Criticism," *CT* 11 (1893-94) 83-92.

E. L. Curtis, G. Frederick Wright, H. G. Mitchell, D[aniel] S. Gregory, and W. W. McLane, "Higher Criticism under Review," *CT* 11 (1893-94) 92-106.

W. W. Elwang, "The Higher Criticism. What it is and what it does," *USR* 5 (1893-94) 31-37.

Charles P. Grannan, "Higher Criticism and the Bible," *ACQR* 19 (1894) 562-581.

L. W. Batten, "The Attitude of the Christian Toward the Higher Criticism of the Bible," *BW* 3 (1894) 275-280.

W. Taylor Smith, "Christianity and Old Testament Criticism," *BW* 3 (1894) 345-348.

*Prescott F. Jernegan, "Christological Implications of the Higher Criticism," *BW* 3 (1894) 420-428.

*J.A.Howlet, "The Higher Criticism and Archæology,"*DR* 115 (1894) 71-95.

*Andrew Harper, "Archæology and Criticism," *Exp, 4th Ser.*, 10 (1894) 372-385.

*Alex. Macalister, "The Higher Criticism and the Verdict of the Monuments," *Exp, 4th Ser.*, 9 (1894) 401-416. *(Review)*

Anonymous, "The Burning Question," *MR* 76 (1894) 136-138. *[Higher Criticism of the O.T.]*

John Poucher, "Some Distinctive Features of Old Testament Study," *MR* 76 (1894) 238-251.

†Anonymous, "Old Testament Criticism," *QRL* 178 (1894) 377-413. *(Review)*

Wilbur F. Tillett, "The Higher Criticism," *MQR, 3rd Ser.*, 17 (1894-95) 321-332.

A[ngus] Crawford, "Higher Criticism," *PER* 8 (1894-95) 77-88.

J. J. Quinn, "Biblical Criticism," *AER* 13 (1895) 55-57.

Charles Rufus Brown, "The Interpretation of the Old Testament as Affected by Modern Scholarship," *BW* 5 (1895) 88-105.

*Milton S. Terry, "What Higher Criticism is Not," *BW* 6 (1895) 22-25.

R. B. Denio, "The Questions of Higher Criticism and the Sources Whence the Answers May be Sought," *BW* 6 (1895) 95-96.

Willis J. Beecher, "What Higher Criticism is Not," *BW* 6 (1895) 351-355.

*T. K. Cheyne, "The Archæological Stage of Old Testament Criticism," *ContR* 68 (1895) 89-102.

*A. H. Sayce, "Archæology *v.* Old Testament Criticism," *ContR* 68 (1895) 477-484.

*A. A. Bevan, "Professor Sayce *versus* the Archæologists," *ContR* 68 (1895) 805-814.

*Henry Preserved Smith, "What Has the Higher Criticism Proved?" *HR* 29 (1895) 10-15. [I. The Composite Nature of the Historical Books; II. The Composite Character of Some of the Prophetical Books; III. The Wisdom Literature; IV. The Date of Daniel; V. The Psalms; VI. The Pentateuch]

Alfred W. Benn, "The Higher Criticism and the Supernatural," *NW* 4 (1895) 429-444.

Howard Osgood, "'Philosophers' and 'Higher Critics'," *PRR* 6 (1895) 688-702.

J. M. Wright, "The Higher Criticism: Expository," *MQR, 3rd Ser.,* 19 (1895-96) 384-393.

A. H. Sayce, "Biblical Critics on the War-Path," *ContR* 70 (1896) 728-736.

J. A. Howlett, "Biblical Science and the Bible," *DR* 118 (1896) 282-308.

A. J. F. Behrends, "The Defective Logic of the Rationalistic Critics," *HR* 31 (1896) 9-14.

*A. H. Sayce, "Archaeology Versus Old Testament Literary Criticism," *HR* 31 (1896) 99-104.

*Francis Brown, "Old Testament Problems," *JBL* 15 (1896) 63-74. [I. Literary Criticism, pp. 66-71.]

Henry A. Buttz, "Conditions of Authoritative Biblical Criticism," *MR* 78 (1896) 191-204.

Thomas J. Packard, "The Higher Criticism," *PER* 10 (1896-97) 109-124.

A. J. Maas, "Recent Phases of Bible Study," *ACQR* 22 (1897) 832-849.

*A. A. B[erle], "Archaeology and Biblical Criticism," *BS* 54 (1897) 389-391.

Willis J. Beecher, "The Most Urgent Need in Old Testament Study," *BW* 10 (1897) 117-124.

Jno. M. Mecklin, "The Opponents of the Old Testament Radical Criticism in Germany," *CFL, O.S.,* 1 (1897) 200-202.

Anonymous, "The Old Testament," *CQR* 45 (1897-98) 265-279. *(Review)*

A. B. Davidson, "Notes on Driver's 'Introduction'," *ET* 9 (1897-98) 187-188.

*J. A. Selbie, "Archaeology and Old Testament Criticism," *ET* 9 (1897-98) 448-449.

A. J. F. Behrends, "Criticism and the Old Testament," *HR* 33 (1897) 411-418.

J. H. Eccleston, "Biblical Criticism from a Familiar Standpoint [Sixth Reinicker Lecture for 1897-'98]," *PER* 11 (1897-98) 463-477.

Samuel Colcord Bartlett, "Higher Criticism at High-Water Mark," *BS* 55 (1898) 656-692.

W. M. McPheeters, "'Criticism and the Authority of the Bible'," *CFL, O.S.,* 2 (1898) 99-101.

Geo. H. Schodde, "Biblical Research Notes. Aspects of Modern Biblical Research," *ColTM* 18 (1898) 122-124.

*Geo. H. Schodde, "The Bible of the Old and the Bible of the New Theology," *ColTM* 18 (1898) 321-327.

F. A. Gasquet, "English Biblical Criticism in the Thirteenth Century," *DR* 122 (1898) 1-21.

*D[aniel] S. Gregory, "Philosophy of History and the Old Testament," *HR* 35 (1898) 167-173.

Andrew C. Zenos, "The Accredited Principles of the Higher Criticism," *HR* 36 (1898) 300-306.

H. G. Mitchell, "The New Old Testament," *MR* 80 (1898) 543-558.

C. J. Oehlschlaeger, "The Higher Criticism Betrays the Master with a Kiss," *TQ* 2 (1898) 142-149.

(   ) R., "Higher Criticism Adapted to Children," *CFL, O.S.*, 3 (1899) 131-136.

Wm. Caven, "Our Attitude Towards the Old Testament," *CFL, O.S.*, 3 (1899) 262-266.

Howard Osgood, "Why Seek After a Lie?" *CFL, O.S.*, 3 (1899) 448-451.

E. H. Dewart, "Can any but Expert Linguists Judge the Theories of 'Higher Critics'?" *HR* 37 (1899) 401-405.

J. H. W. Stuckenberg, "Present Theological Tendencies. II. Criticism and Negation," *HR* 37 (1899) 501-505.

W. F. Warren, "Current Biblical Discussions—The Proper Attitude of Theological Faculties with Respect to Them," *MR* 81 (1899) 368-381.

L. A. Sherman, "The Prolegomena of Criticism—I.," *MR* 81 (1899) 749-762.

George C. M. Douglas, "The Bible Stories," *ET* 11 (1899-1900) 93-94.

Henry A. Stimson, "The Bible in the Conditions Created by Modern Scholarship," *BS* 57 (1900) 366-376.

Philip S. Moxom, "The Various Attitudes of Scholars and People Toward the Bible," *BW* 15 (1900) 341-346.

Anonymous, "Advancing Criticism on the Bible," *CQR* 50 (1900) 106-124.

Anonymous, "Wellhausen on the 'Encyclopedia Biblica'," *HR* 39 (1900) 359-360.

Willis J. Beecher, "Recent Developments in Biblical Criticism," *HR* 39 (1900) 501-510.

Joseph Kennard Wilson, "The Scant Service of Negative Criticism," *HR* 40 (1900) 403-408.

George H. Schodde, "Higher Criticism," *LQ* 30 (1900) 453-463.

Anonymous, "The New Criticism," *MR* 82 (1900) 311-315.

L. A. Sherman, "The Prolegomena of Criticism—II.," *MR* 82 (1900) 361-380.

H. Hirschfeld, "Mohammedan Criticism of the Bible," *JQR* 13 (1900-01) 222-240.

*S. Schechter, "Geniza Specimens, The Oldest Collection of Bible Difficulties, by a Jew," *JQR* 13 (1900-01) 345-374.

W. G. Jordan, "The Outlook for Old Testament Interpretation at the Beginning of the Twentieth Century," *BW* 17 (1901) 420-431.

Ed. König, "False Generalizations in Modern Old Testament Criticism," *CFL, N.S.,* 4 (1901) 189-200.

Anonymous, "Old and New Testament Criticism," *CQR* 52 (1901) 261-280.

S. R. Driver, "The Old Testament in the Light of To-day," *Exp, 6th Ser.,* 3 (1901) 27-49.

*D. S. Margoliouth, "Old-Testament Criticism in its Relation to Teaching," *HR* 41 (1901) 8-13.

*Reginald Walsh, "The Rise and Progress of Higher Criticism," *IER, 4th Ser.,* 10 (1901) 498-513; 11 (1902) 16-34, 127-144, 494-523; 13 (1903) 228-245, 532-556; 15 (1904) 27-47.

C. M. Cobern, "The Higher Criticism," *MR* 83 (1901) 92-98.

Anonymous, "Higher Criticism and Kindred Things," *MR* 83 (1901) 304-307.

Paul Carus, "The Old Testament Scriptures as they appear in the light of scientific enquiry," *OC* 15 (1901) 156-175.

B[enjamin] B. Warfield, "The Present State of Old Testament Criticism," *CFL, N.S.,* 6 (1902) 235.

George H. Schodde, "The Lutheran Church and Higher Criticism," *ColTM* 22 (1902) 193-209.

George H. Schodde, "What Have the Critics Made of the Old Testament?" *ColTM* 22 (1902) 257-292.

G. S. Streatfield, "A Parish Clergyman's Thoughts about the Higher Criticism," *Exp, 6th Ser.,* 6 (1902) 401-424.

*E. H. Dewart, "'Modern Criticism and the Preaching of the Old Testament'," *HR* 43 (1902) 118-124.

George H. Schodde, "The Lutheran Church and Biblical Criticism," *LCR* 21 (1902) 323-338.

Anonymous, "Dr. Behrends on Old Testament Criticism," *MR* 84 (1902) 785-802.

John D. Davis, "Current Old Testament Discussions and Princeton Opinion," *PRR* 13 (1902) 177-206.

S. Sale, "The Bible and Modern Thought," *YCCAR* 12 (1902) 153-162. [Discussion by: H. Barnstein, pp. 163-181; G. Deutsch, pp. 181-184; Jacob S. Raisin, p. 184; H. H. Mayer, pp. 184-186]

*A. F. Kirkpatrick, "Modern Criticism and Its Influence on Theology," *ET* 14 (1902-03) 172-175.

J. A. Selbie, "Biblical Criticism," *ET* 14 (1902-03) 362-363.

T. K. Cheyne, "Pressing Needs of the Old Testament Study," *HJ* 1 (1902-03) 747-762.

*E. N. Alder, "Professor Blau on the Bible as a Book," *JQR* 15 (1902-03) 715-728.

F. P. Ramsay, "The Place of Higher Criticism," *USR* 14 (1902-03) 42-48.

C. W. Heisler, "Some Present-day Aspects of Higher Criticism," *LQ* 33 (1903) 478-504.

F. A. Gast, "The Higher Criticism: Its Aim and Method," *RChR, 4th Ser.,* 7 (1903) 355-366.

G. M. Bevan, "The Bible and Modern Criticism," *ET* 15 (1903-04) 92-93.

Geo. W. Gilmore, "The Higher Criticism. An Inaugural," *Monist* 14 (1903-04) 215-252.

R. E. Vinson, "The Old Testament in the Light of Its Own Times," *PQ* 17 (1903-04) 161-188.

F. P. Ramsay, "Old Testament Criticism and the Christian Church," *PQ* 17 (1903-04) 189-206. *(Review)*

Abraham Kuyper, "The Biblical Criticism of the Present Day," *BS* 61 (1904) 409-442, 666-688. *(Trans. by J. Hendrik de Vries)*

Henry A. Buttz, "Conditions of Authoritative Biblical Criticism," *CFL, 3rd Ser.*, 1 (1904) 75-84.

E. Fitch Burr, "To Christian Laymen: Concerning 'The Higher Criticism'," *CFL, 3rd Ser.*, 1 (1904) 140-151.

John Urquhart, "The Bible and Criticism: Is the Battle Ended?" *CFL, 3rd Ser.*, 1 (1904) 203-213.

J. P. Sheraton, "Higher Criticism, and Why it Can Not be Accepted," *CFL, 3rd Ser.*, 1 (1904) 226-234, 305-313, 424-436.

Theodore E. Schmauk, "Some Counts Against the Rationalistic Criticism," *CFL, 3rd Ser.*, 1 (1904) 272-275.

G. Frederick Wright, "'The Unscientific Character of the Prevailing Higher Criticism.' 'Its Unscientific Treatment of the Facts of Scripture; or, Misdirected Scholarship'," *CFL, 3rd Ser.*, 1 (1904) [347] 348-355.

Robert Dick Wilson, "'Groundless Attacks in the Field of Oriental Scholarship'," *CFL, 3rd Ser.*, 1 (1904) 356-360.

Henry C. Thomson, "Manufactured Errors," *CFL, 3rd Ser.*, 1 (1904) 510-511.

Cornelius Walker, "Criticism—Its Distinctions and Value," *CFL, 3rd Ser.*, 1 (1904) 534-538.

W. M. Lisle, "The Passing of the Higher Criticism," *CFL, 3rd Ser.*, 1 (1904) 639-641.

William Henry Burns, "'Considerations and Suggestions' Toward Correct Critical Conclusions," *CFL, 3rd Ser.*, 1 (1904) 744-750.

T. K. Cheyne, "An Appeal for a Higher Exegesis," *Exp, 6th Ser.*, 9 (1904) 1-19.

Jno. Beveridge, "The Norwegians and the Old Testament," *LCR* 23 (1904) 325-335.

Gabrial Oussani, "Is the Bible in Danger? An Appreciation and Criticism," *OC* 18 (1904) 641-660.

Jacob Cooper, "Destructive Criticism," *PTR* 2 (1904) 570-591.

F. A. Gast, "The Higher Criticism: Positive and Constructive," *RChR, 4th Ser.*, 8 (1904) 1-21, 184-204.

Edward L. Curtis, "The Messages of Biblical Criticism to the Preacher," *YDQ* 1 (1904-05) 43-50.

*Theodore G. Soares, "Old Testament Criticism and the Pulpit," *BW* 25 (1905) 267-273.

George F. Moore, "Interview with Old Testament Scholars on Living Problems," *BW* 25 (1905) 436-442.

*William H. Bennett, "The Apologetic Value of Modern Criticism, with Special Reference to the Old Testament," *BW* 25 (1905) 427-435.

Anonymous, "'The Failure of the Higher Criticism': Report of the First Lecture of Dr. Emil Reich," *CFL, 3rd Ser.*, 3 (1905) 237-241. *[Marked as "to be continued" but never was]*

[William M. McPheeters (?)], "'The Bankruptcy of Higher Criticism'—A Review (I)," *CFL, 3rd Ser.*, 2 (1905) 344-355. *(Review)*

[William M. McPheeters (?)], "'The Bankruptcy of Higher Criticism:' Second Article," *CFL, 3rd Ser.*, 2 (1905) 441-442.

Randolph H. McKinn, "Concerning the Higher Criticism—Extravagant Claims," *CFL, 3rd Ser.*, 3 (1905) 429-432.

W. M. Riley, "Higher Criticism and Its Fruits," *CFL, 3rd Ser.*, 3 (1905) 468-473.

T. K. Cheyne, "Shall We Put the Clock Back in Biblical Criticism? A Remonstrance," *ContR* 87 (1905) 359-368.

T. K. Cheyne, "Has the Clock Stopped in Biblical Criticism? A Reply," *ContR* 87 (1905) 657-660.

Emil Reich, "The Bankruptcy of Higher Criticism," *ContR* 87 (1905) 201-213.

Emil Reich, "The Bankruptcy of Higher Criticism—II," *ContR* 87 (1905) 500-515.

S. R. Driver, "The Permanent Religious Value of the Old Testament," *ICMM* 1 (1905) 10-21.

H. D. Lockett, "Modern Criticism of the Old Testament," *ICMM* 1 (1905) 201-218.

P. J. Boyer, "The Value of the Old Testament. A German Estimate," *ICMM* 1 (1905) 258-263.

J. T. Curry, "What is Higher Criticism," *MQR, 3rd Ser.,* 31 (1905) 472-478.

H. C. Sheldon, "The Question of Biblical Criticism in the Roman Catholic Church," *MR* 87 (1905) 376-391.

*Francis Brown, "President Harper and Old Testament Studies," *AJSL* 22 (1905-06) 177-194.

S. R. Driver, "On Dillmann's Critical Position," *ET* 17 (1905-06) 282-285.

Stanley A. Cook, "Critical Notices. Old Testament Literature," *JQR* 18 (1905-06) 151-158. *(Review)*

Stanley A. Cook, "Critical Notices. Tendencies of Old Testament Study," *JQR* 18 (1905-06) 361-382. *(Review)*

Harold M. Wiener, "Notes to *J. Q. R.* III," *JQR* 18 (1905-06) 566-567. *[Reference to Review Article]*

Francis E. Gigot, "The Higher Criticism of the Bible: The Name and the Thing," *NYR* 1 (1905-06) 724-727.

*Matthew Leitch, "Unscientific Criticism of the Bible," *CFL, 3rd Ser.,* 4 (1906) 409-415.

Ernest DeWitt Burton, "A Quarter Century of Old Testament Study," *BW* 28 (1906) 355-359. *(Editorial)*

*Henry B. Master, "The Value of Facts to the Historian," *CFL, 3rd Ser.,* 4 (1906) 111-119.

James Orr, "The Problem of the Old Testament Stated," *CFL, 3rd Ser.,* 4 (1906) 246-258, 329-336.

*Randolph H. McKim, "The Radical Criticism Tested by Amos, Hosea and Ezekiel," *CFL, 3rd Ser.,* 5 (1906) 267-272.

C. J. Ellicott, "The Traditional and Analytical Views—A Contrast," *CFL, 3rd Ser.,* 5 (1906) 337-346, 407-418.

Francis J. Hall, "Presuppositions of Old Testament Biblical Criticism," *CFL, 3rd Ser.*, 5 (1906) 434-439.

Emil Reich, "The Bankruptcy of Higher Criticism—III," *ContR* 89 (1906) 45-58.

*W. H. Bennett, "Archæology and Criticism," *ContR* 89 (1906) 518-527.

D. S. Margoliouth, "Dr. Emil Reich on the Failure of the Higher Criticism," *Exp, 7th Ser.*, 1 (1906) 51-60.

Stanley A. Cook, "A Criticism of the Old Testament," *Exp, 7th Ser.*, 1 (1906) 524-543.

D. S. Margoliouth, "Dr. Orr on the Problem of the Old Testament," *Exp, 7th Ser.*, 2 (1906) 19-28.

Henry Preserved Smith, "The Method of Advance in Biblical Science," *HR* 51 (1906) 129-130.

Lewis Bayles Paton, "Critical Study of the Bible. First Article," *HR* 51 (1906) 209-211.

Lewis Bayles Paton, "Critical Study of the Bible. Second Article," *HR* 51 (1906) 285-286.

Lewis Bayles Paton, "Critical Study of the Bible. Third Article," *HR* 51 (1906) 364-365.

Lewis Bayles Paton, "The Critical Study of the Bible. Fourth Article," *HR* 51 (1906) 442-443.

James Orr, "Some Aspects of Modern Criticism," *HR* 52 (1906) 251-257.

*G. Macloskie, "The Latest on Old Testament Chronology, and Its Bearing on the Negative Criticism," *LCR* 25 (1906) 115-124.

*Ernest G. Loosley, "Jewish Home Teaching and Old Testament Criticism," *LQHR* 106 (1906) 288-298.

D. F. Estes, "Higher Criticism," *R&E* 3 (1906) 501-516. [O. T. Refs, p. 515]

Stanley A. Cook, "Notes on Old Testament History, VII, Literary and Historical Criticism," *JQR* 19 (1906-07) 342-362.

Stanley A. Cook, "Notes on Old Testament History, IX, Conclusion," *JQR* 19 (1906-07) 383-395.

Francis E. Gigot, "The Higher Criticism of the Bible: Nature of Its Problems," *NYR* 2 (1906-07) 66-69. *[Part II]*

Francis E. Gigot, "The Higher Criticism of the Bible: III. Its General Principles," *NYR* 2 (1906-07) 158-161.

Francis E. Gigot, "The Higher Criticism of the Bible: III. *[sic]* Its Constructive Aspect," *NYR* 2 (1906-07) 302-305. *[Table of Contents reads: IV]*

Francis E. Gigot, "The Higher Criticism of the Bible: V. Its Relation to Tradition," *NYR* 2 (1906-07) 442-451.

Francis E. Gigot, "The Higher Criticism of the Bible: VI. Its Objective Aspect," *NYR* 2 (1906-07) 585-589.

*Gabriel Oussani, "Oriental Archaeology and Higher Criticism," *NYR* 2 (1906-07) 719-748.

Henry Preserved Smith, "General Survey of Work on the Old Testament," *BW* 29 (1907) 284-292.

*G. Frederick Wright, "Abstract of Professor Wright's Lectures in New York," *CFL, 3rd Ser.,* 6 (1907) 156-161, 235-238. [Lecture Fourth—Turning of the Tide in Biblical Criticism, pp. 235-237]

James Orr, "Professor Paton's Review of Professor Orr's Book," *CFL, 3rd Ser.,* 6 (1907) 250-254. [cf. *HSR* 17 (1907) pp. 58-63 *(Rebuttal by the author)*]

Daniel S. Gregory, "Criticism According to 'Punch's Rule'," *CFL, 3rd Ser.,* 6 (1907) 255-259. *[Critique on the Review of Orr's Book]*

Melvin Grove Kyle, "Archaeology Department—, 'Light on the Old Testament from Babel'," *CFL, 3rd Ser.,* 6 (1907) 259-261. *(Review)*

B. A. M. Schapiro, "The Higher Critic's Hebrew," *CFL, 3rd Ser.,* 6 (1907) 306-308.

B. A. M. Schapiro, "The Higher Critic's Hebrew—Second Article," *CFL, 3rd Ser.,* 6 (1907) 367-371.

James Orr, "Some Phases of Criticism," *CFL, 3rd Ser.,* 7 (1907) 16-20.

George H. Schodde, "The Present Old Testament Problem in Germany," *CFL, 3rd Ser.,* 7 (1907) 105-109.

Melvin Grove Kyle, "The 'Pan-Orientalists' and the Latest Fad," *CFL, 3rd Ser.,* 7 (1907) 169-170. *(Editorial)*

James Orr, "Old Testament Problem Restated," *CFL, 3rd Ser.,* 7 (1907) 248-250.

James Orr, "'Settled Results' in Criticism," *CFL, 3rd Ser.,* 7 (1907) 355-360.

J. A. Leavitt, "'Old Testament Problems': Dr. Thirtle's New Book," *CFL, 3rd Ser.,* 7 (1907) 402-404. *(Review)*

James Orr, "'Settled Results' in Criticism—Concluded," *CFL, 3rd Ser.,* 7 (1907) 418-422.

George H. Schodde, "The Beginning of the End of 'Higher Criticism'," *ColTM* 27 (1907) 203-211.

G. Buchanan Gray, "The Comparative Criticism of Semitic Literature," *ContR* 92 (1907) 94-101.

*T. H. Weir, "Higher Criticism and the Korán," *ContR* 91 (1907) 388-398.

Arthur S. Peake, "The Problem of the Old Testament," *ContR* 91 (1907) 493-509.

Andrew C. Zenos, "The Established Results of Old-Testament Study," *HR* 53 (1907) 17-20.

Randolph H. McKim, "The Trend of Old-Testament Criticism," *HR* 54 (1907) 286-289.

Andrew C. Zenos, "The Bible Under Trial," *HR* 54 (1907) 328-331.

Arthur S. Peake, "Dr. James Orr on Biblical Criticism," *ICMM* 4 (1907-08) 253-268.

James Orr, "Professor Peake on Biblical Criticism," *ICMM* 4 (1907-08) 364-372.

Theodore E. Schmauk, "The Work of God and Criticism. Is the Danger of the Latter Over-Estimated?" *LCR* 26 (1907) 65-79.

James Orr, "Developments in Criticism and Theology," *PTR* 5 (1907) 177-187.

Anonymous, "Recent Developments in Old Testament Criticism," *QRL* 206 (1907) 173-196. *(Review)*

George H. Schodde, "The Beginning and the End of 'Higher Criticism'," *TTKF* 9 (1907) 247-254.

Willis J. Beecher, "Old Testament Criticism," *ASRec* 3 (1907-08) 421-423.

John Muir, "The Status of the Old Testament," *GUOST* 3 (1907-12) 7-8.

Stanley A. Cook, "Biblical Criticism 'Moderate' and 'Advanced'," *JQR* 20 (1907-08) 145-166.

Anonymous, "The Higher Criticism: Its Rationalistic Type," *USR* 19 (1907-08) 108-119.

Egbert Watson Smith, "Some Impressions of Radical Old Testament Criticism," *USR* 19 (1907-08) 163-172.

Louis Wallis, "Professor Orr and Higher Criticism," *AJT* 12 (1908) 241-249.

F. J. Lamb, "Science and Higher Criticism," *BS* 65 (1908) 57-86.

William Marcellus M'Pheeters, "A Remarkable Claim on Behalf of Radical Criticism," *BS* 65 (1908) 679-693.

Joseph D. Wilson, "Rationalistic Criticism—Is It Sincere? Or, Is It Silly?" *CFL, 3rd Ser.,* 8 (1908) 41-47.

William H. Bates, "The Collapse of the Higher Criticism," *CFL, 3rd Ser.,* 9 (1908) 101-105.

*T. McK. Stuart, "Critical Theories and the Old Testament Sabbath School Lessons," *CFL, 3rd Ser.,* 9 (1908) 164-168.

Dyson Hauge, "The Moderate School of Higher Criticism—An Explanation," *CFL, 3rd Ser.,* 8 (1908) 181-183.

James Orr, "Some Issues in Criticism: 'The Bible Under Trial'. Professor James Orr's Reply to Professor Zenos," *CFL, 3rd Ser.,* 8 (1908) 257-262.

Willis J. Beecher, "Old Testament Criticism: The Present Situation," *CFL, 3rd Ser.,* 8 (1908) 266-268.

Dyson Hauge, "The Story of the Development of the Higher Criticism," *CFL, 3rd Ser.*, 8 (1908) 365-372.

William M. McPheeters, "The Really Assured Results of the Radical Criticism: Or the Changed Conceptions of the Bible and of Religion Necessitated By the Radical Criticism," *CFL, 3rd Ser.*, 9 (1908) 223-235; 36 (1930) 73-81.

H. L. Hastings, "The Two Records: The Bible and the Inscriptions," *CFL, 3rd Ser.*, 9 (1908) 240-244.

Harold M. Wiener, "'On the Present Condition of Biblical Studies'," *CFL, 3rd Ser.*, 9 (1908) 324-334.

Henry Wace, "The Limits of Biblical Criticism," *CFL, 3rd Ser.*, 9 (1908) 388-391.

John E. McFadyen, "A Closing Word," *HR* 55 (1908) 48-50.

B. D. Eerdmans, "A New Development in Old Testament Criticism," *HJ* 7 (1908-09) 813-826.

F. J. Foakes-Jackson, "The Old Testament Before Modern Criticism," *ICMM* 5 (1908-09) 46-55, 157-166.

W. M. McPheeters, "The Determination of Religious Value, the Ultimate Problem of Higher Criticism," *PTR* 6 (1908) 455-478.

*Julian Morgenstern, "The Significance of the Bible for Reform Judaism in the Light of Modern Scientific Research," *YCCAR* 18 (1908) 217-238. [Responses by: N. Krass, pp. 239-242; H. W. Ettelson, pp. 243-248]

James Orr, "'Biblical Criticism and Modern Thought'—A Criticism," *CFL, 3rd Ser.*, 10 (1909) 296-297. *(Review)*

Henry Gracey, "'Biblical Criticism and Modern Thought'—Review of Professor Jordan's Book," *CFL, 3rd Ser.*, 10 (1909) 409-414. *(Review)*

G. Frederick Wright, "The Crisis in Biblical Criticism," *CFL, 3rd Ser.*, 11 (1909) 21-29.

James Orr, "'Biblical Criticism and its Critics'," *CFL, 3rd Ser.*, 11 (1909) 90-94.

W. H. Griffith Thomas, "Modifications of Old Testament Criticism, Especially by the Successor of Kuenen," *CFL, 3rd Ser.,* 11 (1909) 201-203.

Wilbur F. Crafts, "The Old Testament Issue Ultimately a Question of Logic," *CFL, 3rd Ser.,* 11 (1909) 83-90.

Gavin Carlyle, "The 'Higher' Criticism Untenable: Whence it Proceeds and Whither it Leads," *CFL, 3rd Ser.,* 11 (1909) 172-173.

A. W. F. Blunt, "What Have the Critics Given Us?" *HR* 58 (1909) 360-365.

James Orr, "Criticism in Troubled Waters *Prof. B. D. Eerdmans' 'Old Testament Studies',*" *HR* 58 (1909) 370-373. *(Review)*

Lucius Hopkins Miller, "The Bible in the New Light," *BW* 36 (1910) 49-54.

Melvin Grove Kyle, "Have we Come to a New Epoch in Criticism? Professor Clay's Book," *CFL, 3rd Ser.,* 12 (1910) 3-6. *(Review)*

W. H. Griffith Thomas, "The Old Testament and Current Criticism," *CFL, 3rd Ser.,* 12 (1910) 30-32.

*Ellen Adelaide Copp, "Is the Radical Higher Criticism Scientific?—Tested by Briggs on the Psalms," *CFL, 3rd Ser.,* 13 (1910) 17-21.

J. Agar Beet, "The Bible and Modern Research: Loss and Gain," *HR* 59 (1910) 97-102.

Charles Herber Huestis, "Shall We Teach the Bible from the New Viewpoint," *HR* 59 (1910) 305-306.

Hinckley G. Mitchell, "Has Old Testament Criticism Collapsed?" *HTR* 3 (1910) 464-481.

Henry Preserved Smith, "Old Testament Ideals," *JBL* 29 (1910) 1-20.

J. S. Banks, "Old Testament Criticism and Faith," *LQHR* 114 (1910) 304-308.

Anonymous, "The Conservative Tendency of Old Testament Scholarship," *MR* 92 (1910) 142-144.

W. Rogers, "Fifty Years of Old Testament Research," *R&E* 7 (1910) 101-111.

Harold M. Wiener, "The Scientific Study of the Old Testament," *BS* 68 (1911) 249-263.

Harold M. Wiener, "The Higher Critical Quandary: A Correspondence with Drs. Briggs and Driver," *BS* 68 (1911) 510-531.

Albert C. Knudson, "The Evolution of Modern Bible Study," *MR* 93 (1911) 899-910.

James Orr, "Prof. Hinckley G. Mitchell on 'The Problem of the Old Testament'," *CFL, 3rd Ser.,* 14 (1911-12) 36-39.

Anonymous, "W. H. H.*[sic]* Griffith Thomas on What is at Stake in the Old Testament Criticism," *CFL, 3rd Ser.,* 14 (1911-12) 138.

Charles A. Blanchard, "Method in Biblical Criticism," *CFL, 3rd Ser.,* 14 (1911-12) 244-248.

[Geo. G.] Cameron, "'A Progressive Revelation'—Professor Mathew's False Views," *CFL, 3rd Ser.,* 14 (1911-12) 322-327.

Albert C. Knudson, "The Philosophy and Theology of Leading Old Testament Critics," *BS* 69 (1912) 1-21.

W. H. Griffith Thomas, "Reasonable Biblical Criticism," *BS* 69 (1912) 409-420. *(Review)*

Kemper Fullerton, "The Problem of the Old Testament," *BW* 40 (1912) 224-235, 330-337.

William M. McPheeters, "Dr. Willis J. Beecher's Latest Book: 'Reasonable Biblical Criticism'," *CFL, 3rd Ser.,* 15 (1912) 15-17. *(Review)*

A. J. R. Schumaker, "The Cultivation of Sound Criticism," *CFL, 3rd Ser.,* 15 (1912) 34-36.

Howard Osgood, "'Old Wine in Fresh Wine Skins'—A Review of the Introductions of Driver and Cornill," *CFL, 3rd Ser.,* 15 (1912) 77-82, 155-167.

William Day Crockett, "Reasonable Biblical Criticism—An Appreciation," *ASRec* 8 (1912-13) 452-455. *(Review)*

*William H. Bates, "The Society of Biblical Literature and Exegesis," *CFL, 3rd Ser.,* 16 (1913) 147-149.

A[dam] C. Welch, "The Present Position of Old Testament Criticism," *Exp, 8th Ser.,* 6 (1913) 518-529.

Andrew C. Zenos, "Criticism and the Old Testament," *HR* 66 (1913) 31-32.

*George A. Barton, "'Higher' Archaeology and the Verdict of Criticism," *JBL* 32 (1913) 244-260.

William Sinclair, "Methods of Biblical Criticism," *JTVI* 45 (1913) 97-115. [(Discussion, pp. 115-118) (Communication by A. Irving, p. 118)]

H. Wace, "The Position and Principles of the Criticism of the Old Testament," *JTVI* 45 (1913) 233-241, 248 (Discussion, pp. 241-247)

Adam Stump, "Some Harmful Results of Higher Criticism," *LQ* 43 (1913) 95-105.

Anonymous, "Where are We?" *MR* 95 (1913) 967-972.

James A. Montgomery, "Present Tendencies in Old Testament Criticism," *BW* 43 (1914) 310-320.

J. W. Mendenhall, "The Crime of Higher Criticism," *CFL, 3rd Ser.,* 18 (1914) 60-63, 151-155.

D. M. K., "The Value of the Old Testament to the Church," *ConstrQ* 2 (1914) 773-785.

H. Wheeler Robinson, "The Practical Value of Old Testament Literature," *HR* 68 (1914) 316-317.

P[aul] C[arus], "Deussen's Philosophy of the Bible. Editorial Introduction," *Monist* 24 (1914) 460-469. [Deussen on the Bible in Present Thought, pp. 464-469]

C. J. Södergen, "Some Reflections on Present-day Tendencies in the Theological World," *TTKF* 16 (1914) 171-188.

J. A. F. Gregg, "The Use of the Old Testament," *ET* 26 (1914-15) 359-363.

Parke P. Flournoy, "The Present Trend of Old Testament Criticism," *USR* 26 (1914-15) 34-41.

Leroy Waterman, "A Half-Century of Biblical and Semitic Investigation," *AJSL* 32 (1915-16) 219-229.

John B. Kelso, "A History of Radical Biblical Criticism. I.," *BM* 3 (1915) 506-532.

John B. Kelso, "A History of Radical Biblical Criticism. II.," *BM* 3 (1915) 618-652.

W. H. Griffith Thomas, "Old Testament Criticism To-day," *BS* 72 (1915) 298-307.

*G. H. Richardson, "A Plea for Unprejudiced Historical Biblical Study," *BW* 45 (1915) 160-165.

Francis J. Lamb, "Higher Criticism of the Bible. Examined by Scientific Methods," *CFL, 3rd Ser.,* 20 (1915) 3-7.

Parke P. Flournoy, "The Present Trend of Old Testament Criticism," *CFL, 3rd Ser.,* 19 (1915) 107-110.

W. H. Griffith Thomas, "Old Testament Criticism and Christian Work," *CFL, 3rd Ser.,* 20 (1915) 202-204.

Leander S. Keyser, "Some Specimens of Liberal Biblical Criticism," *LCR* 34 (1915) 235-259.

Herbert C. Alleman, "The Present Status of Old Testament Criticism," *LQ* 45 (1915) 27-46.

Anonymous, "The Latest in Old Testament Criticism," *MR* 97 (1915) 805-809.

George H. Schodde, "The Record and Word of Conservative Old Testament Criticism," *BR* 1 (1916) 101-138.

*J. S. Ross, "Methodist Higher Criticism Arm-in-Arm with Infidelity," *CFL, 3rd Ser.,* 21 (1916) 116-118.

*J. S. Ross, "Methodist Higher Criticism Arm-in-Arm with Infidelity. Paper No. II.," *CFL, 3rd Ser.,* 21 (1916) 161-163.

*J. S. Ross, "Methodist Higher Criticism Arm-in-Arm with Infidelity," *CFL, 3rd Ser.,* 21 (1916) 208-211. *[Part III]*

Herbert C. Alleman, "'The Old Testament in the Light of Today'," *LQ* 46 (1916) 517-531.

G. H. Richardson, "The Bible in Modern Light," *OC* 30 (1916) 479-496.

M[orris] Jastrow [Jr.], "Constructive Elements in the Critical Study of the Old Testament," *JBL* 36 (1917) 1-30.

Leander S. Keyser, "A Recent 'History of the Hebrews'," *LQ* 47 (1917) 204-223. *(Review)*

[Horace M. Du Bose], "The Failure of Higher Criticism," *MQR, 3rd Ser.,* 43 (1917) 395-406.

T. H. Weir, "German Critics and the Hebrew Bible," *BS* 75 (1918) 70-79.

Louis Wallis, "The Paradox of Modern Biblical Criticism," *BW* 52 (1918) 41-49.

W. H. Griffith Thomas, "The German Attitude to the Bible," *BS* 76 (1919) 165-175.

W. E. Glanville, "Modern Research and the Old Testament as Related to the Ministry," *BW* 53 (1919) 127-133.

George P. Mains, "Methodist Ministerial Training: Are the Books Vicious?" *CFL, 3rd Ser.,* 25 (1919) 138-140.

[Jay Benson Hamilton], "Modern Methodist Champion," *CFL, 3rd Ser.,* 25 (1919) 141-143.

[Robert Dick Wilson], "Infallibility of the Higher Criticism Disproved," *CFL, 3rd Ser.,* 25 (1919) 418-420.

*W. Ewing, "The Samaritan Pentateuch and Higher Criticism," *Exp, 8th Ser.,* 18 (1919) 451-469.

J. M. Hawley, "What the Higher Critic Must Reckon With," *MQR, 3rd Ser.,* 45 (1919) 484-500.

A[rthur] S. Peake, "The Present Position of Some Biblical Problems," *OSHTP* (1919-20) 3-27.

*Robert Dick Wilson, "Scientific Biblical Criticism," *PTR* 17 (1919) 190-240, 401-456. [A. Examples of Critical Methods, Genesis XIV; B. Laws in the Pentateuch; C. The Old Testament Text; D. The Grammar; E. The Vocabulary; F. The History; G. Religion; Conclusion]

Edward König and W. H. Griffith Thomas, "Germany and Biblical Criticism," *BS* 77 (1920) 102-108.

William Marcellus McPheeters, "Some Strictures on Current Conceptions of Biblical Criticism," *BS* 77 (1920) 125-146.

"U. P. Todate"*[sic]*, "Higher Criticism—A Present Appraisement," *CFL, 3rd Ser.,* 26 (1920) 46-51.

A. H. Finn, "The Silences of Scripture," *JTVI* 52 (1920) 74-90, 98. [(Discussion, pp. 90-97) (Communication by W. E. Leslie, p. 97; Theodore Roberts, p. 98)]

Eduard König, "Present Problems of the Old Testament," *LCR* 39 (1920) 436-455. *(Trans. by C. Theodore Benze)*

G. A. Cooke, "The Christian Use of the Old Testament in the Present Day," *Theo* 1 (1920) 318-327.

[W.] Maurice Pryke, "The Child and Higher Criticism," *MC* 10 (1920-21) 19-30, 147-148.

Vincent McNabb, "St. Thomas Aquinas and Biblical Criticism," *NB* 1 (1920-21) 135-147.

Anonymous, "Higher and Destructive Criticism," *CFL, 3rd Ser.,* 27 (1921) 206-207.

H[erbert] W. M[agoun], "The Work of the Higher Critics," *CFL, 3rd Ser.,* 27 (1921) 351-353. *(Editorial)*

George William Brown, "Interpreting the Old Testament in the Light of Modern Experience," *CollBQ* 11 (1921-22) #1, 12-16.

Walter Lock, "The Constructive Value of the Bible," *ConstrQ* 9 (1921) 267-285.

E. Herman, "The Christian Use of the Old Testament," *HR* 81 (1921) 196-197.

B. W. Barton, "Ultimate Problems of Biblical Science," *JBL* 22 (1921) 1-15.

H. Wace, "The Old Testament and the Present State of Criticism," *JTVI* 53 (1921) 269-281. [Discussion, pp. 281-282]

William M. McPheeters, "Biblical Criticism Proper: The Critical Process," *BS* 79 (1922) 351-362.

B. A. Disney, "Higher Criticism *vs.* Christ and the Bible," *CFL, 3rd Ser.,* 28 (1922) 407-414.

George Holley Gilbert, "Juggling with the Bible," *HR* 84 (1922) 261-266.

W. K. Lowther Clarke, "In the Study VIII.—Old Testament Criticism," *Theo* 4 (1922) 165-166.

William M. McPheeters, "Biblical Criticism Proper: The True Critical Attitude," *BS* 80 (1923) 132-144.

W. H. Griffith Thomas, "Higher Critics and Higher Critics," *CFL, 3rd Ser.,* 29 (1923) 418-420.

Adam C. Welch, "On the Present Position of Old Testament Criticism," *Exp, 8th Ser.,* 25 (1923) 344-370.

T. H. Robinson, "A New Introduction to the Old Testament," *ICMM* 20 (1923-24) 108-116. *(Review)*

Hugo Gressman, "New Paths in the Scientific Study of Old Testament Literature," *MR* 106 (1923) 296-304.

Oswald T. Allis, "The Conflict Over the Old Testament," *PTR* 21 (1923) 79-115.

W. K. Lowther Clarke, "Old Testament Criticism: Some Misgivings," *Theo* 6 (1923) 252-257.

Charles Lynn Pyatt, "The Bible and the Church of the Future," *CollBQ* 13 (1923-24) #1, 13-23.

Arthur S. Peake, "The Alleged Reaction in Old Testament Criticism," *CJRT* 1 (1924) 40-46.

Frank Grant Lewis, "The Bible as History," *CQ* 1 (1924) 422-430.

M[ax] L. Margolis, "Our Own Future," *JBL* 43 (1924) 1-8.

*Edouard Naville, "The Historical Method in the Study of the Old Testament," *PTR* 22 (1924) 353-376.

William Haskell DuBose, "The Old Testament in the Light of Today," *ATR* 7 (1924-25) 290-303.

[W. M.] Flinders Petrie, "History and Criticism," *ET* 36 (1924-25) 533-538.

S[tanley] A. Cook, "Some Tendencies in Old Testament Criticism," *JTS* 26 (1924-25) 156-173.

H. M. Du Bose, "A Constructive Biblical Science," *BR* 10 (1925) 491-512.

J. L. Kelso, "Three Major Themes of the Old Testament," *BS* 82 (1925) 164-168. [Biography, History, and Theology]

William R. Henderson, "The Trial of the 'Old Serpent' Or, *Modernism and the Bible*," *CFL, 3rd Ser.*, 31 (1925) 79-84.

J. Gresham Machen, "The Modern Use of the Bible," *PTR* 23 (1925) 66-81.

Oswald T. Allis, "Old Testament Emphasis and Modern Thought," *PTR* 23 (1925) 432-464, 586-636. [Old Testament Emphases—Their Nature; Old Testament Emphases—Their Intrinsic Value; Old Emphases vs. Higher Critical Theories; The Flood; The Plagues, The Critical Analysis is Based on the Repetitions, The Complexity of the Critical Analysis, Convincing Proof of Critical Analysis is Lacking; The Destructiveness of the Critical Analysis]

Frederick J. Rae, "Changes in Religious Thought During the Last Fifty Years," *ET* 37 (1925-26) 451-457.

J. M. Powis Smith, "The Recent History of Old Testament Interpretation," *JR* 6 (1926) 403-424.

*George B. Michell, "Scientific Criticism as Applied to the Bible," *JTVI* 58 (1926) 10-24, 29-31. [Discussion, pp. 24-29]

A. E. Baker, "The Value of the Old Testament," *Theo* 13 (1926) 2-7.

F. L. Cross, "The Present State of Old Testament Study," *MC* 16 (1926-27) 117-128.

I. O. Nothstein, "Higher Criticism as Old as the Bible," *AQ* 7 (1928) 266-267.

A[rthur] S. Peake, "Recent Developments in Old Testament Criticism," *BJRL* 12 (1928) 47-74.

I. G. Matthews, "The Baptist Attitude to*[sic]* the Old Testament," *CQ* 5 (1928) 424-439.

James H. Snowden, "Modernism in the Bible," *MR* 111 (1928) 487-499.

Joseph B. Matthews, "The Bible and Experience," *MR* 111 (1928) 687-693.

W. O. E. Oesterley, "Old Testament Criticism," *CQR* 107 (1928-29) 308-317.

*John E. McFadyen, "The Historical Method and the Preacher," *ET* 40 (1928-29) 36-40, 77-81.

Edward Mack, "The Present State of Old Testament Criticism," *USR* 40 (1928-29) 12-23.

W. G. Jordan, "Some Recent Discussions on the Old Testament," *CJRT* 6 (1929) 117-126.

J. M. Powis Smith, "The Contribution of the United States of America to Old Testament Scholarship," *ET* 41 (1929-30) 169-171. *[Part I]*

H. Wheeler Robinson, "National Contributions to Biblical Science. II. The Contribution of Great Britain to Old Testament Study," *ET* 41 (1929-30) 246-250.

A. R. Gordon, "National Contributions to Biblical Science. III. The Contribution of Germany to Old Testament Study," *ET* 41 (1929-30) 302-306.

W. M. Mathieson, "'The Cambridge Ancient History' and the Old Testament. I. The Old Testament Records," *ET* 41 (1929-30) 371-376.

W. M. Mathieson, "'The Cambridge Ancient History' and the Old Testament. II. The Old Testament History," *ET* 41 (1929-30) 470-475.

H. S. Turner, "Old Testament Criticism," *USR* 41 (1929-30) 1-15.

W. H. Paech, "Modernism and the Bible," *AusTR* 1 (1930) 2-11, 103-113, 143-156, 184-189.

H. W. Magoun, "Seven Canons Which Higher Criticism Must Ultimately Face," *CFL, 3rd Ser.,* 36 (1930) 368-372, 417-421, 482-487, 586-590, 638-645; 37 (1931) 76-81, 126-131.

C. H. Buchanan, "The Antique in Modernism," *CFL, 3rd Ser.,* 36 (1930) 542-546.

Arthur R. Siebens, "National Contributions to Biblical Science. VII. The Contribution of France to Old Testament Science," *ET* 42 (1930-31) 150-157.

J. P. Robertson, "Professor Foreman on 'The Composition of Scripture'," *USR* 42 (1930-31) 203-210.

James L. Kelso, "Present-Day Views of Old Testament Study," *USR* 42 (1930-31) 391-397.

Dyson Hague, "The Higher Criticism," *CFL, 3rd Ser.,* 38 (1932) 244-251, 298-305.

G. H. Box, "The Liturgical Factor in Some Recent Old Testament Criticism," *CongQL* 10 (1932) 434-448.

A. H. T. Clarke, "The Bible in the Light of the Latest Science," *EQ* 4 (1932) 39-49.

S[tanley] A. Cook, "Salient Problems in Old Testament History," *JBL* 51 (1932) 273-299.

Christopher R. North, "Old Testament Study: A Jubilee Retrospect," *LQHR* 157 (1932) 64-76.

Maurice A. Canney, "The Anthropological Approach to the Old Testament," *MC* 22 (1932-33) 128-133.

Percy Gardner, "Professor Canney on the Old Testament," *MC* 22 (1932-33) 200-205.

*W. A. Maier, "Archaeology—The Nemesis," *CTM* 4 (1933) 95-102, 176-183, 264-274. [I. Refuted Arguments from Literary Criticism, pp. 95-102]

George Dahl, "Symposium: The Bible in Modern Education. The Scientific Approach to the Bible," *JAAR* 1 (1933) #2, 1-4.

*James Muilenburg, "Symposium: The Bible in Modern Education. The Literary Approach—The Old Testament as Hebrew Literature," *JAAR* 1 (1933) #2, 14-22.

J. Howard Howson, "Symposium: The Bible in Modern Education. The Shortcomings of the Scientific Method in the Teaching of the Bible," *JAAR* 1 (1933) #2, 22-25.

*L. P. Smith, "The Prophetic Targum as a Guide and Defence for the Higher Critic," *JBL* 52 (1933) 121-130.

Joh. Hempel, "The Religious Value of the Old Testament," *LCQ* 6 (1933) 225-245.

D. Winton Thomas, "The present day scope of Old Testament Study," *DUJ* 28 (1933-34) 417-431.

‡*Robert H. Pfeiffer, "The History, Religion, and Literature of Israel. Research in the Old Testament, 1914-1925," *HTR* 27 (1934) 241-325.

F. C. Burkitt, "The Religious Value of Biblical Criticism," *MC* 24 (1934-35) 340-350.

George B. Michell, "Criticism: What It Is and What It Is Not," *BS* 92 (1935) 460-471.

M. T. Barton, "The Trend of Biblical Criticism," *CIR* 9 (1935) 177-190.

*S. H. Hooke, "The Cultural Value of the Old Testament," *CQR* 120 (1935) 189-204.

Ed. C. Unmack, "Modern Criticism of the Old Testament," *EQ* 7 (1935) 82-86.

W. Kolfhaus, "The Church of Christ and the Old Testament," *EQ* 7 (1935) 129-139.

W. L. Wardle, "Currents of Old Testament Study," *LQHR* 160 (1935) 434-440.

W. Emery Barnes, "The Old Testament in the Christian Church," *Theo* 30 (1935) 269-275.

*J. W. Jack, "Some Outstanding Old Testament Problems.   VIII. The Bearing of Archæology on Old Testament Criticism," *ET* 47 (1935-36) 440-444.

*Stanley A. Cook, "Biblical Criticism and the Interpretation of History," *MC* 26 (1936-37) 121-129, 183-194.

Henry J. Cadbury, "Motives of Biblical Scholarship," *JBL* 56 (1937) 1-16.

S. H. Hooke, "The Church and Modern Historical Research and Biblical Criticism," *MC* 27 (1937-38) 270-278.

W[illiam] A. Irwin, "The Study of the Old Testament—An Introspective Interval," *AJSL* 55 (1938) 166-182.

O. R. Sellers, "The Old Testament Faces 1938 A.D.," *JAAR* 6 (1938) 67-69.

Trude Weiss Rosmarin, "The New Trend in Biblical Criticism," *JAAR* 6 (1938) 83-86. *(Editorial Note, p. 87)*

A. E. Garvie, "The Study of the Bible as a Liberal Education," *LQHR* 163 (1938) 145-155.

J. N. Schofield, "The Present Position of Old Testament Studies," *BQL* 9 (1938-39) 279-282, 296.

*Ernest Williams Parsons, "The Use of the Bible To-day," *CRDSB* 11 (1938-39) 53-66.

T. Crouther Gordon, "Some Permanent Values in the Old Testament," *GUOST* 9 (1938-39) 16-18.

S[tanley] A. Cook, "Criticism, Scripture and Doctrine," *MC* 29 (1939-40) 298-312.

H. Hamann, "Professor Dick Wilson Hits at the Critics," *AusTR* 11 (1940) 57-59.

A. Noordtzy, "The Old Testament Problem," *BS* 97 (1940) 456-475. *(Trans. by Miner B. Stearns)*

*S[tanley] A. Cook, "Biblical Criticism, Theology, and Philosophy," *JTS* 41 (1940) 225-237.

H. H. Rowley, "The Changing Emphasis of Biblical Studies," *BQL* 10 (1940-41) 185-190. [O.T. Refs., 187-189]

H. F. D. Sparks, "A Christian Estimate of the Value of the Old Testament Today," *DUJ, N.S.,* 2 (1940-41) 1-10.

A. Noordtzy, "The Old Testament Problem," *BS* 98 (1941) 99-120, 218-243. *(Trans. by Miner B. Stearns)*

Theophile James Meek, "The Next Task in Old Testament Studies," *JR* 21 (1941) 398-411.

James Leo Green, "The Value of the Old Testament for Our Day," *R&E* 38 (1941) 347-370.

*Nelson Glueck, "How Archaeology Has Contributed to Our Knowledge of the Bible and the Jew," *YCCAR* 51 (1941) 299-327. {Discussion by: [Samuel B.] Freehof, p. 327; Nelson Glueck, pp. 327-330; [Joshua] Trachtenburg, p. 327; [Israel] Harburg, p. 328; [Ephraim] Frisch, p. 328; [David] Philipson, p. 328; Max Raisin, p. 329; Leo Shubow, p. 329; Clifton Herby Levy, p. 330; [Ahron] Opher, p. 330; W. Gunther Plaut, p. 330}

Stanley [A.] Cook, "Biblical Criticism and Christian Culture," *ET* 53 (1941-42) 96-99.

*Fred Plocher, "Biblical Criticism and Theology," *UnionR* 3 (1941-42) #1, 25-30.

Holt Graham, "An Approach to Biblical Criticism," *UnionR* 3 (1941-42) #3, 23-25.

Robert H[enry] Pfeiffer, "Present Tasks for Old Testament Scholars," *CQ* 19 (1942) 223-231.

William F. Stinespring, "Thoughts on the Future of Biblical Studies," *DDSR* 7 (1942-43) 11-16.

James Muilenburg, "Pfeiffer's Introduction to the Old Testament," *JAAR* 10 (1942) 39-41. *(Review)*

James A. Kelso, "The Old Testament After a Half Century," *RL* 11 (1942) 223-234.

*Toyozo W. Nakarai, "Some Problems in Teaching the Old Testament in Relation to the Critical Approach," *SQ/E* 3 (1942) 288-297.

*L. H. Brockington, "The Christian Approach to the Old Testament," *BQL* 11 (1942-45) 264-269. [1. The Old Testament as the Scripture of the Early Church; 2. The Doctrinal Use of the Old Testament; 3. The Modern Approach]

W. R. Taylor, "Biblical Criticism and Modern Faith," *JR* 23 (1943) 229-239.

J. M. Meyers, "The Old Testament Today," *LCQ* 16 (1943) 363-381.

C. Ryder Smith, "The Bible and Its Challengers," *LQHR* 168 (1943) 1-11.

Francis X. Pierce, "Old Testament Evaluations," *AER* 111 (1944) 23-29.

Edward Robertson, "Old Testament Stories: Their Purpose and Their Art," *BJRL* 38 (1944) 454-476.

George S. Hendry, "The Old Testament in the Christian Church," *CCQ* 3 (1945-46) #1, 3-13.

S. K. Mirsky, "The Logical and Chronological Order of the Bible," *JBL* 65 (1946) ix.

Morton S. Enslin, "The Future of Biblical Studies," *JBL* 65 (1946) 1-12.

George W. Frey Jr., "Trends in Old Testament Study Today," *UTSB* 21 (1946-47) #1, 2-4.

*Charles Lee Feinberg, "The Relation of Archaeology to Biblical Criticism," *BS* 104 (1947) 170-181.

Ira Jay Martin, "Higher Criticism and Biblical Problems," *JAAR* 15 (1947) 148-152.

Leroy Waterman, "Biblical Studies in a New Setting," *JBL* 66 (1947) 1-14.

Emil Brunner, "The Significance of the Old Testament for Our Faith," *LCQ* 20 (1947) 330-344. *(Trans. by C. Umhau Wolf)*

John H. Scammon, "Trends in Old Testament Introductions from 1930 to the Present," *ATR* 30 (1948) 150-155.

R. Tamisier, "New Light on Old Testament Problems. Recent Work in France," *Scrip* 3 (1948) 83-85.

*David Daube, "Concerning Methods of Bible-Criticism. Late Law in Early Narratives," *ArOr* 17 (1949) Part 1, 88-99.

Frederic Kenyon, "Literary Criticism, Common Sense, and the Bible," *FDWL* #2 (1949) 1-18. [O.T. Refs., pp. 7-10]

*Frank North, "The True Rationale for Critical Analysis," *JBL* 68 (1949) x.

James B. Pritchard, "Some Strange Fruit of Old Testament Criticism," *RL* 18 (1949) 34-47.

E. Robertson, "Investigations into the Old Testament Problem: The Results," *BJRL* 32 (1949-50) 18-43.

M. Noth, "History and the Word of God in the Old Testament," *BJRL* 32 (1949-50) 194-206.

*G. W. Anderson, "Some Aspects of the Uppsala School of Old Testament Study," *HTR* 43 (1950) 239-256. [I. Oral Tradition and Literary Criticism, pp. 240-249]

Allan A. McRae, "New Light on the Old Testament," *JASA* 2 (1950) #2, 4-12.

Frederic G[eorge] Kenyon, "The Institute and Biblical Criticism Today," *JTVI* 82 (1950) 223-231. [Discussion, pp. 231-232]

*Aage Bentzen, "Biblical Criticism, History of Israel, and Old Testament Theology," *EQ* 23 (1951) 85-88.

*J. Weingreen, "The Rabbinical Approach to the Study of the Old Testament," *BJRL* 34 (1951-52) 166-190.

Sebastian Bullough, "The Bible in Recent Centuries," *LofS* 6 (1951-52) 327-337.

Carl Gaenssle, "Velikovsky and the Hebrew Bible," *CTM* 23 (1952) 105-114.

G. Ch. Aalders, "Old Testament Study To-Day," *EQ* 24 (1952) 3-13.

S. G. F. Brandon, "The Present State of Biblical Studies," *MC* 42 (1952) 200-211.

Hugh Mckay, "The Approach to the Old Testament," *Scrip* 5 (1952-53) 91-97.

Walter C. Klein, "Old Testament Studies Today," *ATR* 35 (1953) 121-131. *(Review)*

T. W. Manson, "The Bible in the Contemporary Situation," *CongQL* 31 (1953) 338-343.

William A. Irwin, "The Modern Approach to the Old Testament," *JAAR* 21 (1953) 9-14.

Anonymous, "A Treatise on Biblical Criticism," *ER* 5 (1953-54) 365-375. *(Review)*

B. F. Price, "Recent Scandinavian Contributions to Old Testament Studies," *IJT* 3 (1954) #2, 1-6.

Robert H[enry] Pfeiffer, "Current Issues in Old Testament Studies," *HDSB* 20 (1954-55) 53-66.

Bernhard W. Anderson, "Changing Emphases in Biblical Scholarship," *JAAR* 23 (1955) 81-88.

Augustine Bea, "Biblical Studies Today," *TD* 3 (1955) 51-54.

G. Henton Davies, "Contemporary Religious Trends: The Old Testament," *ET* 67 (1955-56) 3-7.

W. Montgomery Watt, "The Early Development of the Muslim Attitude to the Bible," *GUOST* 16 (1955-56) 50-62.

*Joseph P. Free, "Archaeology and Biblical Criticism," *BS* 113 (1956) 123-129, 214-226, 322-338; 114 (1957) 23-39, 123-132, 213-224. [Is Rationalistic Biblical Criticism Dead? Archaeology and the Historical Accuracy of Scripture; Archaeology and Liberalism; Archaeology and Higher Criticism; Archaeology and Neo-Orthodoxy]

*M. E. Gibbs, "An Examination of Some Presuppositions of Biblical Criticism," *IJT* 5 (1956) #2, 31-37.

*Amos N. Wilder, "Scholars, Theologians, and Ancient Rhetoric," *JBL* 75 (1956) 1-11.

C[hester] C. McCown, "The Current Plight of Biblical Scholarship," *JBL* 75 (1956) 12-18.

H. L. Ellison, "Some Major Modern Trends in Old Testament Study," *JTVI* 88 (1956) 31-46, 159-160. [(Discussion, pp. 153-155) (Communications by H. H. Rowley, pp. 155-156; B. B. Knopp, pp. 156-157; F. F. Bruce, pp.157-158; D. J. Wiseman, pp. 158-159)]

S. G. F. Brandon, "Present Trends in Old Testament Studies," *MC* 46 (1956) 71-80.

G. R. Driver, "Presidential Address," *VTS* 4 (1957) 1-7.

Harrell Frederick Beck, "The Old Testament in Recent Research," *Nexus* 1 (1957-58) 3-9.

H. D. Beeby, "Tendencies in Recent Writings on the Old Testament," *T&C* 1 (1957-59) #1, 144-158.

J. Barton Payne, "The Uneasy Conscience of Modern Liberal Exegesis," *BETS* 1 (1958) #1, 14-18.

D. M. M., "The Bible as Problem and Answer," *CJT* 5 (1959) 6.

Eugene R. Fairweather, "Scripture in Tradition," *CJT* 5 (1959) 7-14.

William A. Irwin, "A Still Small Voice...Said, What are You Doing Here?" *JBL* 78 (1959) 1-12.

Merton A. Christensen, "Taylor of Norwich and Higher Criticism," *JHI* 20 (1959) 179-194.

Norman H. Snaith, "The State of Old Testament Studies Today," *LQHR* 184 (1959) 1-3. *(Editorial)*

*A. S. Herbert, "Literary Criticism and Oral Tradition," *LQHR* 184 (1959) 9-12.

Roland de Vaux, "Approaches to Old Testament study," *TD* 7 (1959) 88-89. *(Synop.)*

Anonymous, "*Criticism and the Bible:* Some Telling Comments," *AT* 4 (1959-60) #4, 20, cont. on p. 5.

Christoph Barth, "Recent Trends in Old Testament Interpretation," *SEAJT* 1 (1959-60) #1, 18-26.

Michael Novak, "The Philosophy Impact in Biblical Studies," *CBQ* 22 (1960) 306-314. [A Response, by John L. Mckenzie, pp. 315-316]

James Muilenburg, "Old Testament Scholarship. *Fifty Years in Retrospect,*" *JAAR* 28 (1960) 173-181.

G. Ernest Wright, "Old Testament Scholarship in Prospect," *JAAR* 28 (1960) 182-193.

Cyrus H. Gordon, "New Horizons in Old Testament Literature," *SQ/E* 21 (1960) 131-160.

*J. Philip Hyatt, "The Place of the Old Testament in the Christian Faith," *SQ/E* 21 (1960) 181-193.

*Ivan Engnell, "Methodological aspects of Old Testament Study," *VTS* 7 (1960) 13-30.

Horace Hummel, "Toward Greater Use And Understanding of the Old Testament," *WSQ* 23 (1960) #1, 3-17.

Norman K. Gottwald, "Whither Old Testament Studies?" *ANQ, N.S.,* 1 (1960-61) #1, 17-27.

George A. F. Knight, "New Perspectives in Old Testament Interpretation," *McQ* 14 (1960-61) #1, 3-14.

Max Kapustin, "Biblical Criticism," *Trad* 3 (1960-61) 25-33.

*R. B. Y. Scott, "Priesthood, Prophecy, Wisdom and the Knowledge of God," *JBL* 80 (1961) 1-15.

*John P. McIntyre, "Scriptural Sense and Literary Criticism," *MH* 16 (Spring, 1961) 45-57.

Joseph Bourke, "A Survey of Old Testament Studies," *NB* 42 (1961) 261-270.

Joseph Bourke, "A Catholic Approach to the Bible," *LofS* 16 (1961-62) 502-508.

J. A. Emerton, "Old Testament Scholarship and the Church—A Century after Colenso," *MC, N.S.,* 5 (1961-62) 266-271. *(Sermon)*

H. Neil Richardson, "Reflections on Old Testament Studies," *Nexus* 5 (1961-62) #3, 7-10, 22.

J. R. Brown, "Old Testament Studies Today," *ACQ* 2 (1962) 227-234.

Carmino de Cantanzaro, "Some Trends and Issues in Old Testament Studies," *ATR* 44 (1962) 251-263.

*Henry R. Moeller, "Biblical Research and Old Testament Translation," *BTr* 13 (1962) 16-22.

Simon Ulrich, "The Bible and Modern Historical Methods," *CQR* 163 (1962) 4-13.

Elmer Prout, "Alexander Campbell and the Old Testament," *RestQ* 6 (1962) 131-143.

*Harold Forshey, "Apologetics and Historical Criticism," *RestQ* 6 (1962) 217-228. [I. Julius Wellhausen and Israel's History; II. Gunkel and Tradition History; III. Albright and Archaeology; IV. Conclusions]

L. Johnston, "The Christian Reading of the Old Testament," *ClR* 48 (1963) 549-556.

William F[oxwell] Albright and David N[oel] Freedman, "The Continuing Revolution in Biblical Research," *JAAR* 31 (1963) 110-113.

Lou H. Silberman, "Problems and Trends in Biblical Scholarship," *Jud* 12 (1963) 92-97.

Peter R. Ackroyd, "The Old Testament in the Christian Church," *Theo* 66 (1963) 46-52.

William [Lee] Pitts, "The Use of the Old Testament in the Light of the Critical Method,"*VDR* 7 (1963) #3, 5-8.

Joseph Rhymer, "Exploring the Old Testament," *LofS* 18 (1963-64) 500-510.

Frederick Sontag, "The Philosopher and The Bible," *USQR* 19 (1963-64) 213-219.

R. Davidson, "The Old Testament in the Catholic Church," *BT* 14 (1964) #2, 1-13.

*Brevard S. Childs, "The Interpretation in Faith. *The Theological Responsibility of an Old Testament Commentary*," *Interp* 18 (1964) 432-449.

Carl McIntire, "Destroying the Bible," *RefmR* 12 (1964-65) 78-86. *(Review)*

Richard A. Henshaw, "What is New in the Study of the Old Testament?" *ATR* 47 (1965) 59-65.

Barnabas Aherne, "The Bible and the People. The Book of the People of God,"*ClR* 50 (1965) 39-44.

*Martin Noth, "God, King, People in the Old Testament: A Methodological Debate with a Contemporary School of Thought," *JTC* 1 (1965) 20-48. *(Trans. by Alice F. Carse)*

Th. C. Vriezen, "Twenty-five Years of Old Testament Study in the Netherlands," *OTS* 1 (1965) 397-416.

*David Berger, "St. Peter Damian. His Attitude Toward the Jews and the Old Testament," *YR* 4 (1965) 80-112.

James Alvin Sanders, "The Vitality of the Old Testament: Three Theses," *USQR* 21 (1965-66) 161-184. [I. The Old Testament is Vital to any historically or theologically vital understanding of the New Testament; II. The Old Testament is vital to the ecumenical conversations which in their next phase must center in the Jewish-Christian Dialogue; III. The Old Testament is vital to the current theological crisis heralded by the so-called death-of-God movement]

Robert North, "Old Testament Horizon of 1966," *AER* 154 (1966) 361-383. [Shrine-Games-Defense Pattern in the Bible? Exodus-Wonders Reexamined; Genesis Themes Ever Ancient, Ever New; Prophets' Spiritually Practical; Psalms-Research Focuses Qumran; Congress Themes Varied, with Favor for Archaeology]

Bastiaan Van Elderen, "New Perspectives in Biblical Research," *CTJ* 1 (1966) 165-181.

Jack P. Lewis, "Old Testament Studies in the Past Fifty Years," *RestQ* 9 (1966) 201-215.

Anthony L. Ash, "Old Testament Studies in the Restoration Movement," *RestQ* 9 (1966) 216-228. *[Part I]*

Thomas H. Olbricht, "The American Albright School," *RestQ* 9 (1966) 241-248.

James K. Zink, "The Scandinavian Oral Tradition School," *RestQ* 9 (1966) 249-256.

Richard Batey, "The Continental *Heilsgeschichte* School," *RestQ* 9 (1966) 257-260.

Norman Young, "Bultmann's View of the Old Testament," *SJT* 19 (1966) 269-279.

K. A. Kitchen, "Historical Method and Early Hebrew Traditions," *TB* #17 (1966) 63-98.

A. S. Kapelrud, "Sigmund Mowinckel and Old Testament Study," *ASTI* 5 (1966-67) 4-29.

Dennis F. Kinlaw, "Some Observations on Current Old Testament Studies," *ASW* 21 (1967) #2, 7-13.

John H. Stek, "The Modern Problem of the Old Testament in the Light of Reformation Perspective," *CTJ* 2 (1967) 202-225.

Anthony Ash, "Old Testament Studies in the Restoration Movement: Part II: From 1887-1891," *RestQ* 10 (1967) 25-39.

Tony*[sic]* Ash, "Old Testament Studies in the Restoration Movement," *RestQ* 10 (1967) 89-98. *[Part III]*

Anthony L. Ash, "Old Testament Studies in the Restoration Movement—No. IV," *RestQ* 10 (1967) 149-160.

John J. Mitchell, "'Yea, Hath God Said...?'" *Them* 4 (1967) #3, 19-26.

Stanley A. Hardwick, "Why Study the Old Testament?" *BSQ* 16 (1967-68) 3-12.

P. M. K. Morris and Edward James, "Computers and the Old Testament: A Progress Report," *ET* 79 (1967-68) 211-214.

Henry Wansbrough, "Change and Revaluation in The Bible," *NB* 49 (1967-68) 174-179.

*J. A. Motyer, "Dead Prey or Living Oracles?" *Them* 5 (1968) #1, 44-47.

Steven Shaw, "Orthodox Reactions to the Challenge of Biblical Criticism," *Trad* 10 (1968-69) #3, 61-85.

*J[acob] Weingreen, "The pattern theory in Old Testament Studies," *Herm* #108 (1969) 5-13.

Morton Smith, "The Present State of Old Testament Studies," *JBL* 88 (1969) 19-35.

Gustaf A. Danell, "Certain Axioms of Old Testament Criticism Critically Examined," *Them* 6 (1969) #1, 3-10.

§279 *3.2.1 Studies concerning Date, Authorship, Authenticity,*
Inerrancy, and Language of the Old Testament
[See also: §292 The Old Testament in the Canon
of Scripture →]

†Anonymous, "Bryant's Observations on Scripture," *BCQTR* 24 (1804) 665-
679; 25 (1805) 46-58. *(Review) [Authenticity]*

John Raby, "To the Editor of the Methodist Magazine," *MR* 4 (1821) 247-
248. *[Authenticity]*

†Anonymous, "Dissertations on some Parts of the Old and New Testaments,
which have been supposed Unsuitable to the Divine Attributes,"
BCQTR, N.S., 22 (1824) 637-643. *(Review) [Authenticity]*

Anonymous, "On the Antiquity of the different Parts of the Old Testament,"
MMBR 60 (1825-26) 387-390.

Ephraim N. Hidden, "Hebrew Literature," *BJ* 2 (1843) 28-33.

H. Rood, "Explanation of the Names applied to the Scriptures, and the
Places where the Several Books were written," *BJ* 2 (1843) 34-41.

J. F., "Biblical Truth Tested and Justified. No. I.," *JSL, 1st Ser.,* 5 (1850)
215-221. *[Authenticity]*

K. L., "On the Relative Authority of the Hebrew and Greek Scriptures of the
Old Testament," *JSL, 2nd Ser.,* 1 (1851-52) 251-282.

G. L., "The Meaning of Scripture Silence, or, the Negative Internal
Evidence," *JSL, 2nd Ser.,* 4 (1853) 398-406. *[Authenticity]*

*†Anonymous, "Types of Mankind—Ethnology and Revelation," *BQRL* 22
(1855) 1-45. *(Review) [Authenticity]*

*Thomas Laurie, "Testimony of Assyrian Inscriptions to the Truth of
Scripture," *BS* 14 (1857) 147-165.

†Anonymous, "Biblical Infallibility—'Evangelical' Defenders of the Faith,"
WR 75 (1861) 89-114. *(Review)*

T. B. Thayer, "Ancient and Modern Unbelief," *UQGR, N.S.,* 1 (1864) 149-
162. [II. The alleged Contradictions of Scripture, pp. 153-157]

Anonymous, "The Structure of the Old Testament," *PRev* 37 (1865) 161-187.

John W. Haley, "Discrepancies of the Bible," *DTQ* 1 (1875) 259-274. *[Authenticity]*

Frederic Gardiner, "'Errors' of the Scriptures," *BS* 36 (1879) 496-534. *[Authenticity]*

Frederic Gardiner, "'Errors' of the Scriptures," *DTQ* 5 (1879) 601-622. *[Authenticity]*

Anonymous, "Credibility of the Scriptures. A Review of the Historico-Critical Arguments, reprinted from an article on inspiration in the July number (1880) of the 'British Quarterly'," *LQ* 10 (1880) 592-604.

*Reginald Stuart Poole, "Hebrew Ethics in Evidence of the Date of Hebrew Documents," *ContR* 39 (1881) 629-636.

Francis Brown, "New Testament witness to the authorship of Old Testament books," *JBL* 2 (1882) 95-121.

R. E. Bartlett, "M. Renan and Scripture Infallibility," *Exp, 2nd Ser.*, 6 (1883) 416-429.

Wilbur F. Crafts, "The Old Testament Tested," *JCP* 3 (1883-84) 552-53.

G. Anderson, "The Bible," *ONTS* 3 (1883-84) 154-156.

J. Andrews Harris, "Matters in Dispute Concerning 'The Old Testament'," *CR* 44 (1884) 136-146. *[Authenticity]*

John W. Burgon, "Dr. Burgon to Canon Fremantle," *MQR, 3rd Ser.*, 4 (1888) 3-18. *[Authenticity]*

George B. Stevens, "The Bearing of New Testament Statements upon the Authorship of Old Testament Books," *ONTS* 8 (1888-89) 164-170.

C. L. E., "Errors in the Bible," *ONTS* 9 (1889) 117. *[Authenticity]*

Anonymous, "Modern Science in Bible Lands," *WR* 131 (1889) 474-484. *(Review)*

Herbert E. Ryle, "The Study of the Old Testament, with Special Reference to the Element of Compilation in the Structure of the Books," *Exp, 4th Ser.*, 1 (1890) 321-339.

Richard Travers Smith, "The Old Testament and Our Lord's Authority," *Exp, 4th Ser.,* 2 (1890) 81-101.

B. R. Rawlins, "Antiquity of Sacred Writings," *MR* 72 (1890) 764-765.

Franz Delitzsch, "Notes of Delitzsch on True and False Defence of the Bible, Introduction and Translation by Professor H. M. Scott," *BS* 48 (1891) 310-321.

*James H. Fairchild, "Authenticity and Inspiration of the Scriptures," *BS* 49 (1892) 1-29.

Henry P[reserved] Smith, "The Evidence of Complication," *ONTS* 14 (1892) 77-83. *[Authorship]*

Anonymous, "The Effect of Errors in the Bible," *ONTS* 15 (1892) 77-78.

D. W. C. Huntington, "The Human Element in the Bible," *CT* 10 (1892-93) 451-458. *[Authenticity]*

*Anonymous, "The Case of Professor Briggs before the General Assembly," *AR* 19 (1893) 464-477. [The Genesis of the Old Testament, pp. 473-475] *(Editorial) [Authorship]*

Leonhard Staehlin, "Christianity and Holy Scripture," *LQ* 23 (1893) 9-39. *(Trans. by J. W. Richard) [Authenticity]*

D. G. W. Ellis, "Inerrancy of the Sacred Scriptures," *MQR, 3rd Ser.,* 16 (1894) 234-243.

J. Elder Cumming, "Is the Old Testament Authentic?" *ET* 6 (1894-95) 61-63, 166-169, 308-310, 421-424.

*H. C. Hatcher, "The language and literature of the Old Testament," *CMR* 7 (1895) 20-29. [II. The authenticity of the Old Testament writers, pp. 25-26; III. The genuineness of the Old Testament literature, pp. 26-27]

J. Elder Cumming, "Is the Old Testament Authentic?" *ET* 7 (1895-96) 38-39.

John D. Davis, "The Chief Literary Productions in Israel Before the Division of the Kingdom," *BW* 7 (1896) 497-509.

H. F. Mallory, "The Chief Literary Productions in Israel Before the Division of the Kingdom," *BW* 7 (1896) 510-519.

*Samuel Ives Curtiss, "Style as an Element in Determining the Authorship of the Old Testament Documents," *AJT* 1 (1897) 312-327.

Charles P. Grannan, "The Twofold Authorship of Sacred Scripture," *CUB* 3 (1897) 131-160.

E. König, "The Linguistic History of the Old Testament, and Maurice Vernes' Dating of the Documents," *Exp, 5th Ser.,* 5 (1897) 59-68.

John D. Davis, "The Literary Productions of Israel from Josiah to Ezra," *BW* 11 (1898) 422-435.

Edward L. Curtis," The Literary Productions of Israel from Josiah to Ezra," *BW* 11 (1898) 435-446.

Charles P. Grannan, "The Human Element in Scripture," *CUB* 4 (1898) 167-182.

Arthur Carr, "The Exclusion of Chance from the Bible," *Exp, 5th Ser.,* 8 (1898) 181-190.

*†Ed. König, "Requests and Replies. The Massoretical note at the end of the Minor Prophets," *ET* 10 (1898-99) 255-257. [Answer to a question posed by Eb. Nestle regarding §70 of the *Dikdûkê ha-ṭe'amîm*]

Ed. König, "§70 of the Dikdûkê ha-ṭe'amîm," *ET* 10 (1898-99) 333-335.

J. M. P[owis] Smith, "The Chief Literary Productions in Israel from Ezra to the Maccabees," *BW* 13 (1899) 389-398. [Translated and Condensed from Wildeboer's *Die Litteratur des Alten Testaments*]

Ed. König, "Requests and Replies," *ET* 11 (1899-1900) 229-230. [§70 of Dikdûkê ha-tĕ'amîm]

Samuel Ives Curtiss, "The Book, the Land, the People; or, Divine Revelations Through Ancient Israel," *BS* 58 (1901) 103-135

John Tuckwell, "Modern Theories Concerning the Composition of Holy Scripture," *JTVI* 35 (1903) 167-188. [Discussion, pp. 188-197]

William M. McPheeters, "The Question of the Authorship of the Books of Scripture: A Criticism of Current Views," *PTR* 1 (1903) 362-383.

William M. McPheeters, "The Question of Authorship: Practice *vs.* Theory," *PTR* 1 (1903) 579-596.

*Ivan Panin, "The Old Testament Writers Named in the Bible," *BN* 1 (1904) #8, 273-275.

*John Urquhart, "Roger's Reasons," *CFL, 3rd Ser.,* 1 (1904) 553-561. *[Authenticity and Historical Accuracy]*

W. McDonald, "Father von Hummelauer on the Errors in the Bible," *IER, 4th Ser.,* 17 (1905) 335-346. *(Review)*

W. Sanday, "The Still Small Voice of the Scriptures," *ICMM* 2 (1905-06) 9-14.

*Milton S. Terry, "The Old Testament and the Christ," *AJT* 10 (1906) 233-250.

Grainger Tandy, "Elementary Studies in Biblical Criticism. II. The Question of Authorship," *ICMM* 3 (1906-07) 162-175. *[Part I not applicable to "Authorship"]*

W. E. C. Wright, "Alleged Discrepancies of the Bible," *BS* 64 (1907) 767-769.

A. Kampmeier, "'Pious Fraud'," *OC* 21 (1907) 53-58.

C. B. Wilmer, "In Extenuation of Pious Fraud. Comments on Rev. A. Kampmeier's Article. A Protest," *OC* 21 (1907) 179-181. [The Use of Pseudonyms in the Bible by Joseph C. Allen, pp. 182-185; Editorial Comment, pp. 185-187]

Anonymous, "Editorial Notes. Old Testament Problems," *ICMM* 4 (1907-08) 1-4.

*S. A. P. Kermode, "The Influence of Nature on the Literature of the Bible," *ICMM* 4 (1907-08) 315-329.

*A. H. Sayce, "The Language and Script of the Earlier Old Testament Books," *HR* 60 (1910) 100-104.

Bompas, "Theses on Scripture," *IJA* #23 (1910) 71-72.

Alvin Sylvester Zerbe, "Were the Early Old Testament Books Written in the Babylonian-Assyrian Language and the Cuneiform Script?" *RChR, 4th Ser.,* 15 (1911) 141-152.

Stanley A. Cook, "A Study of the Composite Writings of the Old Testament," *JTS* 13 (1911-12) 84-93.

*J. S. Ross, "Archaeology's Contribution Towards the Grave of Higher Criticism," *CFL, 3rd Ser.*, 18 (1914) 25-28, 64-67, 116-119.

Langhorne Orchard, "The Testimony of Science to the Word of God," *CFL, 3rd Ser.*, 17 (1914) 150-151. *[Authenticity]*

D. M. Kay, "Was the Old Testament written in Hebrew?" *IJA* #37 (1914) 37-39. *(Review)*

*T. H. Darlow, "The Character of the Bible Inferred from Its Versions," *JTVI* 46 (1914) 87-97. [Discussion, pp. 97-101]

*J. Iverach Munro, "The Witness of Philology to the Truth of the Old Testament," *JTVI* 49 (1917) 199-216. [Discussion, pp. 216-220]

Arthur Wright, "Contradictions in the Holy Scripture," *ICMM* 14 (1917-18) 116-120.

J. C. Hardwick, "Three Bible Story-Books," *ICMM* 16 (1919-20) 147-154. *[Authenticity of Ruth, Esther, and Jonah]*

Walter Drum, "Biblical Inerrancy," *ACQR* 45 (1920) 501-507.

*Francis B. Denio, "Bible Authors and the Imagination," *BS* 77 (1920) 83-101.

Anonymous, "Who Wrote the Bible?" *CFL, 3rd Ser.*, 26 (1920) 248-250.

George H. McCrea, "Who Wrote the Bible?" *MR* 103 (1920) 805-806.

John A. Maynard, "Hebrew or Akkadian? A Critique of Naville's Hypothesis of a Cuneiform Text of the Old Testament," *ATR* 3 (1920-21) 284-299.

E. Herman, "The Fetish of Biblical Infallibility," *HR* 81 (1921) 27-28.

John A. Maynard, "Hebrew or Aramaic? A Critique of Naville's Hypothesis of an Aramaic Text of the Old Testament," *ATR* 4 (1921-22) 29-45.

*(Miss) A. M. Hodgkin, "The Witness of Archaeology to the Bible," *JTVI* 54 (1922) 200-220. [Discussion, pp. 220-222]

*A. H. Godbey, "'Moses' and Other Titles," *OC* 36 (1922) 490-496.

George McCready Price, "The Bible Triumphant," *CFL, 3rd Ser.*, 29 (1923) 507-510.

W. Leonard, "Biblical Inerrancy and the *Manuel Biblique*," *ACR* 1 (1924) #3, 8-16.

W. Leonard, "More About the Condemnation of the *Manuel Biblique*," *ACR* 1 (1924) #4, 16-24.

S. G. Craig, "The Testimony of the Scriptures to Their Own Trustworthiness," *PTR* 22 (1924) 303-325.

William H. Bates, "Alleged Discrepancies of the Bible," *CFL, 3rd Ser.*, 31 (1925) 145-146, 207-210, 265-267, 303-308, 341-345, 445-447, 553-555; 32 (1926) 88-91, 151-156, 213-216, 338-343, 438-441, 525-528, 646-647; 33 (1927) 42-45, 94-98, 160-162, 220-224, 283-285, 366-369.

*Darwin A. Leavitt, "Some Aspects of History-Writing in the Old Testament," *MTSQB* 20 (1925-26) #3, 16-28.

S. D. Chown, "The Authority of Biblical Truth," *BR* 12 (1927) 189-198.

George Johnson, "Holy Scriptures and Imaginal Contexts," *PTR* 25 (1927) 59-82.

R[obert] D[ick] Wilson, "Evidence in Hebrew Diction for the Dates of Documents," *PTR* 25 (1927) 353-388.

P[hilip] M[auro], "The Credibility of the Bible," *CFL, 3rd Ser.*, 34 (1928) 6-7. *(Editorial)*

D[avid] S. K[ennedy], "In what Sense are the Scriptures Inerrant?" *CFL, 3rd Ser.*, 34 (1928) 361.

*W. G. Jordan, "Early Historical Writing," *CJRT* 5 (1928) 270-278.

*R[obert] D[ick] Wilson, "Foreign Words in the Old Testament as an Evidence of Historicity," *PTR* 26 (1928) 177-247. [Foreign Words in Biblical Aramaic; Foreign Words in Biblical Hebrew; Excursus on the Name "Cyrus"]

Kenneth J. Foreman, "The Composition of Scripture," *USR* 41 (1929-30) 279-292.

J. P. Robertson, "Professor Foreman on 'the Composition of Scripture'," *USR* 42 (1930-31) 203-210.

Leander S. Keyser, "Were the Biblical Writers Borrowers?" *BS* 89 (1932) 470-479.

*Charles Marston, "New Bible Evidence," *JTVI* 66 (1934) 124-132, 138. [Discussion and Communications, pp. 132-138]

Frank E. Gaebelein, "A Modernist Tragedy," *BS* 92 (1935) 219-225. *[Authenticity]*

L[eander] S. K[eyser], "Explaining Bible Difficulties," *CFL, 3rd Ser.,* 41 (1935) 1-5. *(Editorial)*

J. M. Stanfield, "God, the Author of the Old Testament," *CFL, 3rd Ser.,* 42 (1936) 301-302.

Herbert C. Alleman, "The Bible and the Word of God," *LCQ* 9 (1936) 233-243. *[Authenticity]*

Robert E. Keighton, "Reality in the Bible," *CQ* 14 (1937) 207-212.

*Charles Marston, "How the Old Testament Stands To-day. The Lachish Discoveries," *JTVI* 71 (1939) 156-165. [Discussion, pp. 165-169] *[Authenticity]*

H. Hamann, "Bible Difficulties," *AusTR* 11 (1940) 24-25. *[Authenticity]*

T. W. Fawthrop, "The Stones Cry out: Scriptural Confirmation often Overlooked," *JTVI* 72 (1940) 137-148, 154-155. [(Discussion, pp. 148-152) (Communication by H. S. Curr, pp. 152-153)]

Paul E. Huffman, "The Christian's Use of the Old Testament," *LCQ* 14 (1941) 76-84.

Henry S. Curr, "The Inerrancy of the Bible," *BS* 99 (1942) 221-230.

Herbert C. Alleman, "The Bible as the Word of God," *LCQ* 17 (1944) 215-225. [In the Old Testament, pp. 217-220]

B. F. C. Atkinson, "The Historicity and Accuracy of Scripture," *EQ* 19 (1947) 81-92.

*Felix V. Hanson, "The Word of God," *AQ* 27 (1948) 276-279.

Robert Rendall, "The Note of Progression in Old Testament History," *EQ* 20 (1948) 84-96.

Anonymous, "The Foundation of the Apostles and Prophets," *Interp* 2 (1948) 180-185. *[Authenticity]*

John McConnachie, "The Uniqueness of the Word of God," *SJT* 1 (1948) 113-135.

L. H. Brockington, "The Problem of Pseudonymity," *JTS, N.S.,* 4 (1953) 15-22.

Immanuel Lewy, "The Feminine Element in Biblical Judaism," *Jud* 2 (1953) 339-344. *[Authorship]*

John P. Weisengoff, "Inerrancy of the Old Testament in Religious Matters," *CBQ* 17 (1955) 248-257.

*Pierre Lobez, "Literary genres in the Bible," *TD* 4 (1956) 67-71.

Elizabeth [Rice] Achtemeier, "The Old Testament in the Church," *USQR* 12 (1956-57) #3, 45-49.

*Richard L. Twomey, "Human Authorship in the Bible—The Book of Judith," *MH* 13 (1957-58) #1, 1-10.

*J. T. Forestell, "The Limitation of Inerrancy," *CBQ* 20 (1958) 9-18.

*Francis Ian Andersen, "Doublets and Contamination," *RTR* 19 (1960) 48-57, 73-81.

John S. Marshall, "The Impregnable Rock of Holy Scripture," *ATR* 44 (1962) 131-144.

*David Noel Freedman, "The Law and the Prophets," *VTS* 9 (1962) 250-265.

Gordon R. Lewis, "What Does Biblical Infallibility Mean?" *BETS* 6 (1963) 18-27.

R. H. Altus, "Human Factors in Holy Scripture," *AusTR* 35 (1964) 55-61.

*Edward J. Young, "The Bible and Error," *BS* 121 (1964) 303-310.

Walter G. Williams, "The Making of Biblical Literature," *IR* 21 (1964) #2, 3-20.

Robert Preus, "Notes on the Inerrancy of Scripture," *BETS* 8 (1965) 127-138.

Arthur Carl Piepkorn, "What Does 'Inerrancy' Mean?" *CTM* 36 (1965) 577-593.

*Norbert Lohfink, "The inerrancy and unity of the Scripture," *TD* 13 (1965) 185-192.

Anonymous, "The Witness of Jesus and Old Testament Authorship," *CTM* 38 (1967) 117-126.

Norbert Lohfink, "The truth of the Bible and Historicity,"*TD* 15 (1967) 26-29.

Anonymous, "A Comment on Bible Accuracy and Apparent Inaccuracies," *BH* 4 (1968) 81-85.

*Otto W. Heick, "Biblical Inerrancy and the Hebrew Mode of Speech," *LQ, N.S.,* 20 (1968) 7-19.

§280 *3.2.2 Unity of the Old Testament*

*C. C. Hersman, "The Bible Divine in Its Unity of Plan—In Its Evidences Cumulative," *USR* 8 (1896-97) 176-185.

G. F. Spieker, The Organic Unity of the Old Testament," *LCR* 20 (1901) 446-458.

A. Troelstra, "The Organic Unity of the Old Testament," *BS* 49 (1912) 377-408. *(Trans. by John H. deVries)*

*O[swald] T. Allis, "Modern Dispensationalism and the Doctrine of the Unity of Scripture," *EQ* 8 (1936) 22-35.

H[arold] H. Rowley, "The Unity of the Old Testament," *BJRL* 29 (1945-46) 326-358.

Robert Rendall, "Old Testament History: Its Nature and Unity," *EQ* 18 (1946) 251-261.

A. J. B. Higgins, "Some Recent Trends in Biblical Scholarship," *CongQL* 27 (1949) 122-133. [The Unity of the Old Testament, pp. 126-128]

Robert C. Dentan, "The Unity of the Old Testament," *Interp* 5 (1951) 153-173.

Raymond Abba, "The Unity of the Old Testament," *RTRM* 10 (1951) #3, 73-83.

Joseph Bourke, "The Unity of the Old Testament," *NB* 40 (1959) 299-312.

§281 *3.2.3 Relation of the Old Testament to the New Testament (Unity of the Bible)*

[August Detlev Christian] Twesten, "Connection of the Old and New Testament," *BRCR* 11 (1838) 232-245. *(Trans. by B. B. Edwards)*

S. O., "Relation Between the Old and New Testaments," *CE* 39 (1845) 116-129. *(Review)*

Anonymous, "The Relation of the Old to the New Dispensation," *PRev* 23 (1851) 635-649.

†Anonymous, "Kurtz on the Old Covenant," *BFER* 2 (1853) 129-159. *(Review)*

Anonymous, "The Arrow-Headed Inscriptions," *PQR* 9 (1860-61) 623-663. *(Review)*

Henry Harbaugh, "Relation of the Old Testament to the New," *AThR, N.S.,* 4 (1866) 33-50.

J. M. Titzel, "The Relation of the Old Testament to the New," *RChR* 16 (1869) 48-61.

Anonymous, "The Two Testaments in their Relation to each Other," *BFER* 19 (1870) 661-681.

Anonymous, "The Two Testaments in their Relation to each other," *ThE* 7 (1871) 286-309.

W. F. Bainbridge, "The Unity of the Bible," *BQ* 10 (1876) 83-98.

W. F. Bainbridge, "The Unity of the Bible," *DTQ* 2 (1876) 590-600.

Alfred Nevin, "The Unity of the Bible," *DTQ* 6 (1880) 634-639.

Eustace R. Conder, "The Unity of the Bible," *CongL* 11 (1882) 391-398.

F. A. Gast, "The Relationship of the Old Testament to the New," *ONTS* 2 (1882-83) 234-239.

*William Burnett, "The Relation of the Old Testament to the New," *ONTS* 3 (1883-84) 115-119.

Clark Smith Beardslee, "The Unity of the Bible," *HSR* 5 (1894-95) 135-157.

J. A. Selbie, "The Unity of the Bible," *ET* 7 (1895-96) 471.

Hermann Gunkel, "The Religio-Historical Interpretation of the New Testament," *Monist* 13 (1902-03) 398-455. [Relation of Old Testament to New, pp. 448-450]

George H. Schodde, "The Unity of the Scriptures," *ColTM* 24 (1904) 351-359.

George H. Schodde, "The Unity of the Scriptures," *LCR* 24 (1905) 468-476.

Robert Stuart MacArthur, "The Unity of the Bible—The First Three and the Last Three Chapters," *CFL, 3rd Ser.,* 11 (1909) 136-137.

F. N. Peloubet, "Unity of the Bible," *CFL, 3rd Ser.,* 26 (1920) 285.

William H. Bates, "The Relation of the Old Testament to the New," *CFL, 3rd Ser.,* 27 (1921) 72-76.

John Moore, "The Structural Unity of the Bible," *CFL, 3rd Ser.,* 32 (1926) 321-325.

H. Hamann, "The Miraculous Unity of the Bible," *AusTR* 9 (1938) 93-94.

H[enry] S. Curr, "The Two Testaments," *EQ* 12 (1940) 354-361.

H. W. Robinson, "The Old Testament in Relation to the Gospel," *BQL* 11 (1942-45) 197-206.

Mary Ely Lyman, "The Unity of the Bible," *JAAR* 14 (1946) 5-12.

Aage Bentzen, "The Old Testament and the New Covenant," *HTS* 7 (1950-51) 1-15.

G. Ernest Wright, "Unity of the Bible," *Interp* 5 (1951) 131-133.

‡Floyd V. Filson, "The Unity of the Old and New Testaments. *A Biographical Survey,*" *Interp* 5 (1951) 134-152.

G. Ernest Wright, "The Unity of the Bible. A Summary," *Interp* 5 (1951) 304-317.

G. Ernest Wright, "Wherein Lies the Unity of the Bible?" *JAAR* 20 (1952) 194-198.

Virginia Corwin, "Wherein Does the Unity Lie?" *JAAR* 20 (1952) 199.

John A. Hutchison, "Can It Be Communicated on the Undergraduate Level?" *JAAR* 20 (1952) 199-200.

S. Vernon McCasland, "A Comment on Dr. Wright's Paper," *JAAR* 20 (1952) 200-201.

Robert H[enry] Pfeiffer, "A Note on Wright's Views on the Unity of the Bible," *JAAR* 20 (1952) 201.

G. Ernest Wright, "A Brief Rejoinder," *JAAR* 20 (1952) 201-202.

Chester Warren Quimby, "The Unity of the Biblical Message," *JAAR* 21 (1953) 30-32.

S. Vernon McCasland, "The Unity of the Scriptures," *JBL* 73 (1954) 1-10.

G. Ernest Wright, "The Unity of the Bible," *SJT* 8 (1955) 337-352.

G. Ernest Wright, "The Unity of the Bible," *JRT* 13 (1955-56) 5-19.

E. H. Burgmann, "The Unity and Message of the Bible," *StMR* #1 (1955) 6-14.

David N[oel] Freedman, "The Unity of the Bible," *WW* 7 (1956) #4, 7-14.

Walter R. Roehrs, "The Unity of Scripture," *CTM* 31 (1960) 277-302.

*Lionel A. Whiston Jr., "The Unity of Scripture and the Post-Exilic Literature," *JAAR* 29 (1961) 290-298.

Eamonn O'Doherty, "The Unity of the Bible," *BibT* #1 (1962) 53-57.

*A. G. Errey, "The Book about God," *PQL* 8 (1962) 320-326. [The Unity of the Bible, pp. 320-321]

Jay A. Wilcoxen, "An Interpretative View of G. Ernest Wright. *What is the basic unity in the Biblical writings?*" *Crit* 2 (1963-64) #3, 25-31.

Roland E. Murphy, "The Relationship Between the Testaments," *CBQ* 26 (1964) 349-359.

Roy L. Honeycutt Jr., "The Unity and Witness of Scripture," *Found* 8 (1965) 292-310.

*Norbert Lohfink, "The inerrancy and the unity of Scripture," *TD* 13 (1965) 185-192.

*Henri Cazelle, "The Unity of the Bible and the People of God," *Scrip* 18 (1966) 1-10.

F. N. Jasper, "The Relation of the Old Testament to the New: Part I," *ET* 78 (1966-67) 228-232.

F. N. Jasper, "The Relation of the Old Testament to the New: Part II," *ET* 78 (1966-67) 267-270.

John P. Milton, "The Relationship Between the Two Testaments," *LTSR* 7 (1968) #1, 15-29.

§282 *3.2.4 Origin, Sources and Transmission of the Old Testament (includes Studies on Oral Tradition)*

*†Anonymous, "The Connection between the Sacred Writings and the Literature of Jewish and Heathen Authors," *BCQTR, N.S.,* 12 (1819) 638-652; 13 (1820) 309-316. *(Review)*

H. Rood, "Oral Tradition," *BJ* 1 (1842) 109-115.

*Charles Morris, "Characteristics of Hebrew Literature," *URRM* 12 (1879) 412-422.

George W. Henning, "The Old Bibles. The Hebrew Bible Distinguished among Them," *MR* 63 (1881) 231-246.

*[S. R. Calthrop], "Traditional Records of Early Israel," *URRM* 25 (1886) 530-539.

*Karl Budde, "The Folk-Song of Israel in the Mouth of the Prophets," *NW* 2 (1893) 28-51.

Karl Budde, "The Song of the Well," *NW* 4 (1895) 136-144.

Gotthard Deutsch, "The Theory of Oral Tradition," *YCCAR* 7 (1896-97) 129-171.

Willis J. Beecher, "The Book of the Old Testament versus Their Sources," *BS* 56 (1899) 209-222.

*P[arke] P. Flournoy, "'The Books of the Old Testament Versus Their Sources'," *CFL, O.S.*, 3 (1899) 345-348.

Sarah A. Emerson, "The Study of Early Old Testament Traditions," *BW* 21 (1903) 291-296.

Cornelius Walker, "Tradition, Oral and Written," *CFL, 3rd Ser.*, 1 (1904) 406-410.

*Ernest Cushing Richardson, "Oral Tradition, Libraries and the Hexateuch," *LCR* 24 (1905) 511-521.

*Ernest Cushing Richardson, "Oral Tradition, Libraries and the Hexateuch," *PTR* 3 (1905) 191-215.

*Ernest Cushing Richardson, "Oral Tradition, Libraries and the Hexateuch. Part II," *LCR* 24 (1905) 718-725.

*Ernest Cushing Richardson, "Oral Tradition, Libraries and the Hexateuch. Part III," *LCR* 25 (1906) 148-155.

Frank K. Sanders, "The Sources of Early Hebrew History," *BW* 28 (1906) 388-399.

*Ira Maurice Price, "Ancient Monuments in the Louvre Museum Illustrative of Biblical History," *BW* 30 (1907) 429-437.

George A. Barton, "Recent German Theories of Foreign Influences in the Bible," *BW* 31 (1908) 336-347.

Arthur Metcalf, "The Literary Evolution of the Old Testament," *BW* 34 (1909) 173-179.

I. F. Wood, "Folk-Tales in Old Testament Narrative," *JBL* 28 (1909) 314-41.

J[ohn] P. Peters, "The Earliest Hebrew Writings," *JBL* 28 (1909) 169-181.

*W. F. Lofthouse, "Kernel and Husk in Old Testament Stories," *Exp, 8th Ser.*, 1 (1911) 97-117.

*E[duard] König, "A Modern Expert's Judgment on the Old Testament Historical Writings," *Exp, 8th Ser.*, 1 (1911) 308-319.

*Margaret D. Gibson, "The Sources of Our Bible," *USR* 24 (1912-13) 303-309.

James A. Kelso, "Were the Early Books of the Old Testament Written in Cuneiform?" *BWTS* 9 (1916-17) 24-38.

*Herbert H. Gowen, "The Folk Lore of the Old Testament," *ATR* 3 (1920-21) 310-327.

R. Winterbotham, "The Old Testament and the Jews," *Exp, 8th Ser.*, 22 (1921) 161-184.

G[eorge] A. Barton, "Were the Biblical Foundations of Christian Theology derived from Babylonia?" *JBL* 40 (1921) 87-103.

*A. H. Godbey, "'Moses' and Other Titles," *OC* 36 (1922) 490-496.

W. R. Arnold, "Observations on the Origins of Holy Scripture," *JBL* 42 (1923) 1-21.

Eduard König, "The Sources of the Old Testament Historical Books," *LQ* 55 (1925) 425-439. *(Trans. by John Hauptmann)*

Adam C. Welch, "On the Religious Literature of Northern Israel," *AfO* 3 (1926) 162-164.

*W. G. Jordan, "Early Historical Writing," *CJRT* 5 (1928) 270-278.

*J. M. P[owis] Smith, "The Indebtedness of Israel to Its Neighbors," *AJSL* 49 (1932-33) 172-184.

*Solomon Gandz, "The Rōbeh רוֹבֶה or The Official Memorizer of the Palestinian Schools," *PAAJR* 7 (1935-36) 5-12.

*Solomon Gandz, "The dawn of literature. Prolegomena to a history of unwritten literature," *Osiris* 7 (1939) 261-522. [Chapter. XVI.—*The Hebrews. Oral Tradition and the Bible*, pp. 415-438]

*Patrick Cummins, "A Test Case in Text Transmission. Jeremias 33:14-26," *CBQ* 2 (1940) 15-27.

Gutav Carlberg, "The Bible Speaks for Itself," *AQ* 20 (1941) 240-256.

*C. J. Mullo Weir, "Some Problems of Hebrew Literary Origins," *GUOST* 11 (1942-44) 1-4.

*C. Umhau Wolf, "A Study in the Transmission of Poetic Text," *LCQ* 18 (1945) 305-312.

*Geo Widengren, "Literary and Psychological Aspects of the Hebrew Prophets," *UUÅ* (1948) #10, 1-138. [Chapter III. Oral and Written Transmission among the Israelites, Especially in Prophetic Circles, pp. 57-93]

H. Ringgren, "Oral and Written Transmission in the O.T., Some observations," *ST* 3 (1949) 34-59.

C. R. North, "Living Issues in Biblical Scholarship. The Place of Oral Tradition in the Growth of the Old Testament," *ET* 61 (1949-50) 292-296.

*G. W. Anderson, "Some Aspects of the Uppsala School of Old Testament Study," *HTR* 43 (1950) 239-256. [I. Oral Tradition and Literary Criticism, pp. 240-249]

W[illiam] F[oxwell] Albright, "Oral Transmission of Old Testament Literature," *JBL* 72 (1953) xvi-xvii.

*Carroll Suthlmueller, "The Influence of Oral Tradition upon Exegesis and the Senses of Scripture," *CBQ* 20 (1958) 299-326.

*Geo Widengren, "Oral Tradition and Written Language among the Hebrews in the Light of Arabic Evidence, with Special Regard to Prose Narratives," *AO* 23 (1958-59) 201-262.

*A. S. Herbert, "Literary Criticism and Oral Tradition," *LQHR* 184 (1959) 9-12.

Joseph A. Hill, "The Bible and Non-Inspired Sources," *BETS* 3 (1960) 78-81, 92.

Lawrence E. Toombs, "History and Writing in the Old Testament," *DG* 31 (1960-61) 135-146.

Patrick Fannon, "The Formation of the Old Testament," *CIR* 46 (1961) 332-344.

P. R. Ackroyd, "The Vitality of the Word of God in the Old Testament. A Contribution to the Study of the Transmission and Exposition of Old Testament Material," *ASTI* 1 (1962) 7-23.

Shammai Feldman, "Biblical Motives and Sources," *JNES* 22 (1963) 73-103. [Parable in Pentateuch; Sources in Pentateuch; Parable in Joshua and Judges; Bible as History]

Geo Widengren, "Tradition and Literature in Early Judaism and the Early Church," *Num* 10 (1963) 42-86.

R. C. Culley, "An Approach to the Problem of Oral Tradition," *VT* 13 (1963) 113-125.

P. Joseph Cahill, "Scripture, Tradition and Unity," *CBQ* 27 (1965) 315-335. [a. The Old Testament, pp. 317-319]

G. W. Ahlstrom, "Oral and Written Transmission: Some Considerations," *HTR* 59 (1966) 69-81.

*Hyacinthe M. Dion, "The Patriarchal Traditions and the Literary Form of the 'Oracle of Salvation'," *CBQ* 29 (1967) 198-206.

*J. L. Crenshaw, "Method in Determining Wisdom Influence upon 'Historical' Literature," *JBL* 88 (1969) 129-142.

§283 *3.2.4.1 Studies on the so-called "Lost Books" of the Old Testament*

*H. Rood, "The Lost Books of Scriptures," *BJ* 2 (1843) 43-48. [Jasher; Wars of the Lord; Book of Days]

James Macfarlane, "The Lost Books mentioned in the Old Testament," *ER* 17 (1866) 417-425.

Ira M. Price, "The Lost Writings, Quoted and Referred to, in the Old Testament," *BS* 46 (1889) 351-368.

A. S. Zerbe, "Lost Books and Records Quoted in the Old Testament," *RChR, 4th Ser.,* 12 (1908) 145-179.

*A. H. Godbey, "'Moses' and Other Titles," *OC* 36 (1922) 490-496.

*C. J. Mullo Weir, "Some Problems of Hebrew Literary Origins," *GUOST* 11 (1942-44) 1-4.

Anthony C. Cotter, "Lost Books of the Bible?" *ThSt* 6 (1945) 206-228.

*N. H. Tur-Sinai, "Was There an Ancient 'Book of the Wars of the Lord'?" *BIES* 24 (1959-60) #2/3, III-IV.

*J. Liver, "The Book of the Acts of Solomon," *B* 48 (1967) 75-101.

§284 *3.2.4.2 The Book of Jasher*

†Anonymous, "The Book of Jasher," *BCQTR, 4th Ser.,* 15 (1834) 127-153. *(Review)*

†Anonymous, "Bibliographical Notes on the Book of Jasher," *CongML* 17 (1834) 82-89.

*H. Rood, "The Lost Books of Scriptures," *BJ* 2 (1843) 43-48. *[Jasher]*

Anonymous, "The Book of Jasher," *JSL, 3rd Ser.,* 1 (1855) 229-244.

†Anonymous, "Donaldson's Book of Jashar*[sic]*," *LQHR* 5 (1855-56) 455-463. *(Review)*

Albert A. Isaacs, "The Book of Jasher," *EN* 1 (1889) 49-56.

*Anonymous, "Music in the Old Testament," *ONTS* 11 (1890) 114. *[The Book of Jasher]*

H. St. J. Thackeray, "New Light on the Book of Jashar[sic]* (A Study of 3 Regn. VIII 53^b LXX)," *JTS* 11 (1909-10) 518-532.

§285 *3.2.5 Backgrounds of the Old Testament - General Studies*

J. S. Lee, "The Oriental Features of the Bible," *UQGR, N.S.,* 14 (1877) 39-59.

Thomas Laurie, "Bible Illustrations from Bible Lands," *BS* 36 (1879) 534-560, 647-664.

Revere F. Weidner, "The Wonders of Oriental Studies," *LCR* 1 (1882) 54-57. *(Review)*

Edward Herbruck, "Fresh Light from Bible Lands," *RCM* 1 (1893-94) #2, 1-4, #6, 1-4.

*Morris Jastrow Jr., "The Excavations at Sendschirli and Some of Their Bearings on the Old Testament," *BW* 3 (1894) 406-416.

E. Hull, "Holy Scripture Illustrated and Confirmed by Recent Discoveries in Palestine and the East," *JTVI* 28 (1894-95) 129-142. [(Discussion, pp. 142-150) (Remarks by C. R. Conder, pp. 150-152)]

Anonymous, "Lessons from the Monuments," *LQHR* 85 (1895-96) 119-141. *(Review)*

Emil G. Hirsch, "From the Rising to the Setting Sun," *BW* 8 (1896) 111-123.

A. H. Sayce, "Freshest Light from the Ancient Monuments," *HR* 42 (1901) 392-397.

Henry W. McLaughlin, "Scripture Passages Illuminated by Modern Palestine," *USR* 14 (1902-03) 289-296.

A. H. Sayce, "The Latest Light on the Bible from Palestine," *HR* 47 (1904) 83-88.

J. V. Prášek, "The Old Testament in the Light of the Ancient East," *ET* 16 (1904-05) 68-70.

George St. Clair, "Early Background of Scripture Thought," *HR* 50 (1905) 117-119, 200-202.

*C. H. W. Johns, "Ancient Monuments in the British Museum: Illustrative of Biblical History," *BW* 27 (1906) 7-22.

*Andrew Craig Robinson, "The Bearing of Recent Oriental Discoveries on Old Testament History," *JTVI* 38 (1906) 154-176. [Discussion, pp. 176-181]

Ira M. Price, "Some Phases of the Literature of the Old Testament and the Literature of the Ancient Orient," *R&E* 3 (1906) 248-263.

Fayette L. Thompson, "Some Bible Stories Re-Told on the Monuments," *CFL, 3rd Ser.,* 6 (1907) 448-452.

E. W. G. Masterman, "Recent Discoveries in Palestine in Relation to the Bible," *JTVI* 39 (1907) 218-249. [Discussion, pp. 250-254]

Wm. J. Hinke, "The Old Testament in the Light of Recent Excavations," *ASRec* 3 (1907-08) 373-386.

*A. R. S. Kennedy, "Recent Excavations in Palestine and Their Bearing on the Old Testament," *GUOST* 3 (1907-12) 5-6.

T. H. Weir, "Some Fresh Bible Parallels," *Exp, 7th Ser.,* 10 (1910) 81-89.

William J. Hinke, "The Old Testament and Recent Discoveries," *ASRec* 6 (1910-11) 252-273.

Anonymous, "Importance of Studying Palestinian Folklore at Once," *BASOR* #4 (1921) 4.

Herbert C. Alleman, "The Origins of Biblical Traditions," *LQ* 54 (1924) 89-103.

William W. Everts, "Coincidences between the Old Hebrew and Other Literatures," *BS* 83 (1926) 463-475.

*G. B. Michell, "The Comparative Chronology of Ancient Nations in its Bearing on Holy Scripture," *JTVI* 59 (1927) 65-81, 91-95. [(Discussion, pp. 81-90) (Communication by H. Biddulph, pp. 90-91)]

Theophile J. Meek, "The Interpenetration of Cultures as Illustrated by the Character of the Old Testament Literature," *JR* 7 (1927) 244-262.

P. Park Flournoy, "New Light Upon the Bible," *USR* 40 (1928-29) 98-105. [The Creation and the Flood; Nimrod and His Prehistoric Cities, Identified; The Excavations at Bethshan, and Israel's First Three Kings; Ahab and Jezebel; the Scene of Belshazzar's Feast; A Marvelous Discovery, *Earth Gives up Lost Capital of Cyrus the Great, The Tomb of Cyrus*]

*John Garstang, "'The Archaeology of Palestine and the Bible'," *PEFQS* 64 (1932) 221-230. *(Review)*

*James B. Pritchard, "The Hebrew Theologian and His Foreign Colleagues," *CQ* 23 (1946) 21-33.

Norman H. Snaith, "Recent Discoveries and the Bible," *LQHR* 179 (1954) 109-112.

*Sabatino Moscati, "*Israel's Predecessors*. A Re-Examination of Certain Current Theories," *JAAR* 24 (1956) 245-254.

*Lester J. Kuyper, "Israel and Her Neighbors," *RefR* 10 (1956-57) #3, 11-20.

*H. D. Beeby, "The Old Testament and the Redemption of Culture," *SEAJT* 8 (1966-67) #4, 17-28.

§286 *3.2.5.1 Assyrian and Babylonian Backgrounds*

†*Anonymous, "Nineveh and the Bible," *BQRL* 9 (1849) 399-442. *(Review)*

†Anonymous, "Cuneiform Evidences," *LQHR* 16 (1861) 1-33. *(Review)*

(   ) K., "The Cuneiform Inscriptions in Relation to Biblical History," *TRL* 8 (1871) 495-511. *(Review)*

Wm. Henry Green, "Assyrian Monuments and the Bible," *PQPR* 3 (1874) 389-413.

Anonymous, "A New 'Testimony of the Rocks;' or the Cuneiform Inscriptions and Biblical History in the Old Testament," *SPR* 28 (1877) 310-339; 29 (1878) 490-522. *(Review)*

[Wilhelm] Nowack, "The Assyrian-Babylonish Inscriptions and the Old Testament," *BFER* 28 (1879) 178-204.

S. J. Barrows, "Assyriology and the Bible," *URRM* 12 (1879) 21-47.

*G. E. Leeson, "Testimony of the Mesopotamian Monuments to the Reliability of the Sacred Scriptures," *BQR* 3 (1881) 137-165.

*E. H. Plumptre, "Assyrian and Babylonian Inscriptions in their Bearing on Old Testament History," *Exp, 2nd Ser.,* 1 (1881) 113-125, 223-236, 275-291, 443-457. [1. History of the Creation and Fall; 2. The Fall of Angels; 3. The Deluge; 4. The Tower of Babel; 5. Nimrod; 6. Ur of the Chaldees; 7. The Four Kings; 8. The Destruction of Sodom and Gomorrah; 9. Balaam the Son of Beor; 10. Achan and Chusan Rishatham]

*E. H. Plumptre, "Assyrian and Babylonian Inscriptions Bearing on Old Testament History," *Exp, 2nd Ser.,* 2 (1881) 48-64, 230-240, 316-320, 437-458. [11. Solomon and the Kings of the Hittites; 12. Hosea, Shalman, and King Jareb; 13. Menahem and Pul; 14. Israel, Judah, Syria, and Tiglath-Pileser; 15. Hoshea, Shalmanezer, and Sargon; 16. Sennacherib and Hezekiah]

*E. H. Plumptre, "Assyrian Inscriptions in their Bearing on Old Testament History. XVII. Esarhaddon," *Exp, 2nd Ser.,* 4 (1882) 448-461.

George Rawlinson, "The Biblical Notices of Babylon Illustrated from Profane Sources, Ancient and Modern," *CM* 16 (1883) 31-38, 105-113, 162-169, 228-236, 293-301, 347-356; 17 (1883) 34-42, 95-105, 163-171, 233-240, 294-302, 352-359.

S. Burnham, "The Assyrian Literature and the Old Testament," *ONTS* 3 (1883-84) 74-76.

F. A. Gast, "Assyrian Research and the Old Testament," *RChR* 31 (1884) 178-199.

( ) E., "Schrader's 'Cuneiform Inscriptions' and the Old Testament," *Exp, 3rd Ser.,* 2 (1885) 237-240. *(Review)*

*W. St. Chad Boscawen, "Gleanings from Clay Commentaries—No. I.," *BOR* 1 (1886-87) 23-25.

*D. G. Lyon, "Assyriology and the Old Testament," *URRM* 28 (1887) 543-551.

Theo[philus] G. Pinches, "The Old Testament in the Light of the Literature of Assyria and Babylonia," *ET* 4 (1892-93) 123-125, 347-351.

J. F. McCurdy, "Light on Scriptural Texts from Recent Discoveries. Assyriology in its Relations to the Old Testament," *HR* 31 (1896) 204-218.

*A. A. B[erle], "Babylonian Palæography and the Old Testament," *BS* 54 (1897) 391-393.

J. F. McCurdy, "Light on Scriptural Texts from Recent Discoveries. Oriental Discoveries and the Contents of the Bible," *HR* 35 (1898) 313-316.

J. F. McCurdy, "Light on Scriptural Texts from Recent Discoveries," *HR* 35 (1898) 409-412. [Assyriology and Bible Lands]

J. F. McCurdy, "Light on Scriptural Texts from Recent Discoveries," *HR* 35 (1898) 501-504. [Assyriology and Bible Personages]

Karl Budde, "The Old Testament and the Excavations," *AJT* 6 (1902) 685-708.

*Joseph Offord, "The Myths and Laws of Babylon and the Bible," *AAOJ* 25 (1903) 258-261.

Ed[uard] König, "The Literatures of the Hebrews and Babylonians," *HR* 46 (1903) 20-24.

Robert Dick Wilson, "Babylon and Israel: A Comparison of Their Leading Ideas," *PTR* 1 (1903) 239-255.

A. H. Sayce, "The Latest Light on the Bible from the Euphrates Valley," *HR* 47 (1904) 171-175.

*Frederic Blass, "Science and Sophistry," *ET* 16 (1904-05) 8-15. [Assyriology and the Old Testament, p. 12] *(Trans. by Mrs. Gibson)*

Henry T. Hooper, "The Old Testament and Babylon," *LQHR* 104 (1905) 301-320.

*C. H. W. Johns, "Assyriology and the Old Testament," *ICMM* 3 (1906-07) 70-78.

Fayette L. Thompson, "Hammurabi and the 'Creation' and 'Flood' Tablets," *CFL, 3rd Ser.,* 7 (1907) 46-50.

*P. Boylan, "Evolution and Assyriology," *ITQ* 2 (1907) 35-54.

Anonymous, "'Babylon and the Monuments' in Agreement," *CFL, 3rd Ser.,* 9 (1908) 360-361. *(Editorial Note)*

Eduard König, "The Relations of Babylonian and Old-Testament Culture," *HR* 55 (1908) 262-266 *(or pp. 330-334)*[1]

Eduard König, "Relations of Babylonian and Old-Testament Culture," *HR* 56 (1908) 9-12. *(or pp. 92-96)* [II. Differences between Babylonian and Old-Testament Culture][1]

*Eduard König, "Relations of Babylonian and Old-Testament Culture," *HR* 57 (1909) 186-189. *(or pp. 180-183)* [III. The controvertible connection between Babylon and the Bible with regard to primitive history (Gen. 1-2.)][1]

*Eduard König, "Relations of Babylonian and Old-Testament Culture," *HR* 57 (1909) 443-447. *(or Vol. 58 (1909) pp. 176-180)* [IV. The Legislation of the Old Testament and Its Relations to that of Babylon][1]

A. H. Sayce, "The Babylonian Background of the Old Testament," *OSHTP* (1909-10) 5-22.

[1] Page numbers in this journal vary as more than one edition was apparently issued!

*A. H. Sayce, The Language and Script of the Earlier Old Testament Books," *HR* 60 (1910) 100-104. *[Assyrian Background]*

*Ed[uard] König, "Canaan and the Babylonian Civilization," *ET* 24 (1912-13) 546-550.

Ed[uard] König, "Old Testament and Babylonian Language," *Exp, 8th Ser.,* 8 (1914) 97-115, 193-211.

Joseph Offord, "Coincidences of Hebrew and Cuneiform Literature," *PEFQS* 46 (1914) 140-146.

Leonard W. King, "Recent Babylonian Research and Its Relation to Hebrew Studies," *CQR* 81 (1915-16) 271-289. *(Review)*

*G. Buchanan Gray, "Job, Ecclesiastes, and a New Babylonian Literary Fragment," *ET* 31 (1919-20) 440-443.

Stanley A. Cook, "New Babylonian Light upon the Old Testament," *ET* 36 (1924-25) 44-45.

*P. A. Mattson, "Sidelights on the Scriptures from the law of Hammurabi," *AQ* 6 (1927) 23-38.

Mary I. Hussey, "Recent Excavations in Mesopotamia as Related to the Teaching of the Bible," *JAAR* 1 (1933) #1, 19-21.

Cyrus [H.] Gordon, "The Nuzi Tablets and the Old Testament," *JBL* 56 (1937) xiii-xiv.

*J. W. Jack, "Recent Biblical Archaeology," *ET* 49 (1937-38) 272-275.

*George T. Wolz, "Pan-Sumerianism and the Veil Motif," *CBQ* 5 (1943) 275-292, 408-430.

S[amuel] N[oah] Kramer, "Sumerian Literature and the Bible," *SBO* 3 (1959) 185-204.

*W. W. Hallo, "New Viewpoints on Cuneiform Literature," *IEJ* 12 (1962) 13-26. *[Babylonian/Assyrian Background]*

Ronald Youngblood, "Cuneiform Contributions to Old Testament Interpretation," *BSQ* 11 (1962-63) 4-15, 28-43.

§287 *3.2.5.1.1 Babel-Bible Controversy*

J. A. Selbie, "The Babel-Bibel Controversy," *ET* 14 (1902-03) 268, 362, 546-547.

D[aniel] S. Gregory, "'Babel and Bible' or 'Science Falsely So-Called'," *HR* 44 (1903) 377-384.

Anonymous, "Babel and Bible," *MR* 85 (1903) 470-474.

Friedrich Delitzsch, "Babel and Bible. A Lecture Delivered in Berlin Before the German Emperor," *OC* 16 (1903) 209-233, 263-290. *(Trans. by T[homas] J. McCormick)*

Thomas J. McCormick, "The Struggle for Babel and Bible," *OC* 17 (1903) 1-145.

Friedrich Delitzsch, "Reply to Critics of the First Lecture," *OC* 17 (1903) 418-427.

Friedrich Delitzsch, "Second Lecture on Babel and Bible," *OC* 17 (1903) 325-341, 393-408.

Friedrich Delitzsch, "Reply to Critics of the Second Lecture,"*OC* 17 (1903) 428-431.

[Friedrich Viktor Albert] Wilhelm, "Kaiser Wilhelm on 'Babel and Bible'," *OC* 17 (1903) 432-436.

[Adolf von] Harnack, "Professor Harnack on the Emperor's Attitude Toward 'Babel and Bible'," *OC* 17 (1903) 444-447.

Robert W. Rogers, "The Bible and the New Assyriology," *BRec* 1 (1903-04) 247-261.

J. A. Selbie, "The Babel-Bibel Controversy," *ET* 15 (1903-04) 254-255, 500.

Ed[uard] König, "Unscientific Points of View in the Babel-Bibel Controversy," *ET* 15 (1903-04) 479-480.

T. K. Cheyne, "Babylon and the Bible," *HJ* 2 (1903-04) 65-82.

Paul Carus, "Gunkel Versus Delitzsch," *OC* 18 (1904) 226-241.

George W. Richards, "'Babel und Bibel'," *RChR, 4th Ser.,* 8 (1904) 110-121.

*Grey Hubert Skipwith, "The Origins of the Religion of Israel," *JQR* 17 (1904-05) 57-64. *[Babel - Bible]*

Ed[uard] König, "The Latest Phase of the Controversy over Babylon and the Bible," *AJT* 9 (1905) 405-420.

John P. Peters, "The Bible and Babylonia," *HR* 50 (1905) 172-177.

Anonymous, "Theological Reaction in Germany," *MR* 88 (1906) 139-143. *[Babel - Bible]*

Friedrich Delitzsch, "Babel and Bible: Third and Last Lecture," *OC* 20 (1906) 134-155, 266-288. *(Trans. by Lydia Gillingham Robinson)*

William Notz, "The Babel-Bible Controversy," *BS* 68 (1911) 641-657.

Anonymous, "Fresh Examination of the Pan-Babylonian Theory," *HR* 91 (1926) 24.

§288 *3.2.5.2 Canaanite Backgrounds, including Ugaritic*

*A. H. Sayce, "The Latest Discoveries in Palestine: Canaan Before the Israelites," *BW* 25 (1905) 125-133.

*George A. Barton, "Palestine Before the Coming of Israel," *BW* 28 (1906) 360-373.

*Ed[uard] König, "Canaan and the Babylonian Civilization," *ET* 24 (1912-13) 546-550.

*Lewis Bayles Paton, "Canaanite Influence on the Religion of Israel," *AJT* 18 (1914) 205-224.

*Joseph Offord, "Archaeological Notes on Jewish Antiquities. XXVI. *Phoenician and the Old Testament,*" *PEFQS* 49 (1917) 94-96.

*Theodore Harzl Gaster, "The Ras Shamra Texts and the Old Testament," *PEFQS* 66 (1934) 141-146.

*Henry Schaeffer, "The Latest Discoveries in the Old Testament Field," *KZ* 62 (1938) 86-102. 147-165. [7. Biblical Literary Problems in the Light of the Ras Shamra Texts, pp. 163-165]

*Louise Pettibone Smith, "Light from North Syria on Old Testament Interpretation," *JAAR* 7 (1939) 185-190.

*Frederic G. Kenyon, "Ras Shamra and Mari: Recent Archaeological Discoveries Affecting the Bible," *JTVI* 73 (1941) 81-92, 96. [(Discussion, p. 92) (Communications by H. S. Curr, pp. 92-94; P. J. Wiseman, pp. 94-95; Norman S. Denham, pp. 95-96)]

*H. Philip Hyatt, "The Ras Shamra Discoveries and the Interpretation of the Old Testament," *JAAR* 10 (1942) 67-75.

*John Stensvaag, "The Ugaritic Texts and the Bible," *JTALC* 7 (1942) 801-819.

*G. Ernest Wright, "How Did Early Israel Differ from Her Neighbors?" *BA* 6 (1943) 1-10, 13-20. [What Civilization Owes to the Canaanites; Israel's Debt to Canaan, pp. 2-6]

*H. L. Ginsberg, "The Ugaritic Texts and Textual Criticism," *JBL* 62 (1943) 109-115.

*H. L. Ginsberg, "Ugaritic Studies and the Bible," *BA* 8 (1945) 41-58. [I. Geographical and Chronological Definition of Ugarit; II. Writing in Western Asia in General and at Ugarit in Particular; III. Materials for Comparative Biblical and Ugaritic Studies; IV. The Ugaritic Writings and the Bible, 1. Ideas and Ideals, 2. Form and Quality of Canaanite Poetry]

*William Foxwell Albright, "The Old Testament and Canaanite Language and Literature," *CBQ* 7 (1945) 5-31. [I. Introductory Remarks; II. The Discovery and Excavation of Ras Shamra; III. Decipherment and Interpretation of the Tablets; IV. The Ugaritic Dialect and Biblical Hebrew; V. Ugaritic and Biblical Poetry; VI. Canaanite Light on Hebrew Grammar and Lexicography; VII. Canaanite and Biblical Literature]

*W. H. Morton, "Ras Shamra-Ugarit and Old Testament Exegesis," *R&E* 45 (1948) 63-80.

*John Gray, "Canaanite Mythology and Hebrew Traditions," *GUOST* 14 (1950-52) 47-57.

H. Neil Richardson, "Some Literary Parallels Between Ugaritic and the Old Testament," *JAAR* 20 (1952) 172-175.

*John Gray, "Canaanite Kingship in Theory and Practice," *VT* 2 (1952) 193-220.

T. Worden, "The Literary Influence of the Ugaritic Fertility Myth on the Old Testament," *VT* 3 (1953) 273-297.

Cyrus H. Gordon, "Ugarit as a Link between Greek and Hebrew literatures," *RDSO* 29 (1954) 161-169.

*H. St. J. Hart, "The face of Baal: the interest of ancient coin types and legends for biblical studies," *OSHTP* (1955-56) 35-36.

*Dennis Dickman, "The Ugaritic Language and the Old Testament," *Amb* 10 (1960-61) #5, 15, 18-27.

Mitchell Dahood, "Ugaritic studies and the Bible," *Greg* 43 (1962) 55-79.

Mitchell Dahood, "Ugarit Studies and the Old Testament," *BibT* #12 (1964) 780-786.

John H. Hayes, "Ugaritic Studies and the Old Testament," *TUSR* 8 (1964-67) 1-17.

*J. Gray, "The legacy of Canaan. The Ras Shamra texts and their relevance to the Old Testament," *VTS* 5 (1965) i-x, 1-348. (2nd edition)

*F. Charles Fensham, "Ugaritic and the Translation of the Old Testament," *BTr* 18 (1967) 71-74.

Paul Watson, "The Ras Shamra Discoveries and Their Impact on Old Testament Studies," *RestQ* 11 (1968) 144-152.

*S. E. Loewenstamm, "The Ugaritic Myth of the Sea and its Biblical Counterparts," *EI* 9 (1969) 136. *[English Summary]*

*T. L. Fenton, "Ugaritica—Biblica," *UF* 1 (1969) 65-70. [Amos 5:11; Psa. 55:4; 2 Sam. 1:21; Sackcloth and Ashes; Jer. 48:37]

§289 **3.2.5.3 Egyptian Backgrounds**

†E. C., "Biblical Illustrations from Egyptian Anaglyphs," *WR* 37 (1842) 197-206. *(Review)*

W. H. S., "Egypt; Her Testimony to the Truth," *BRCM* 4 (1847-48) 203-211. *(Review)*

Anonymous, "Egypt and the Bible," *DUM* 32 (1848) 371-388. *(Review)*

*B. W. Savile, On the Harmony between the Chronology of Egypt and the Bible," *JTVI* 9 (1875-76) 38-72. [(Discussion, pp. 72-79) (Remarks by S. Birch, pp. 80-83)]

*J. E. Howard, "Egypt and the Bible," *JTVI* 10 (1876-77) 340-377. [(Appendices; pp. 377-379) (Discussion, pp. 379-385)]

Cunningham Geikie, "Ancient Egypt and the Bible," *CR* 33 (1881) 1-10.

Cunningham Geikie, "Ancient Egypt and the Bible," *CR* 36 (1881) 13-24. *[Volume actually listed as No. 135]*

*George Rawlinson, "The Biblical Notices of Egypt Illustrated from Profane Sources," *CM* 18 (1884) 37-46, 98-106, 159-167, 288-296, 359-367; 19 (1884) 41-48, 105-113, 158-166, 223-231, 297-305, 347-354.

Gustavus Seyffarth, "Light on Biblical History from Egyptian Antiquities," *LQ* 16 (1886) 345-368.

*Camden M. Cobern, "Egyptology. No. VII—An Ancient Bible Commentary," *HR* 21 (1891) 402-409.

A. H. Sayce, "The Witness of the Egyptian Monuments to the Old Testament," *HR* 38 (1899) 1-9.

Henry Van Dyke, "Egypt in the Bible," *PER* 13 (1899-1900) 432-447, 488-504, 527-542.

M. G. Kyle, "Biblical Gains from Egyptian Exploration. No. I.," *CFL, N.S.,* 4 (1901) 268-278.

*F. Ll. Griffith, "Chronological Value of Egyptian Words found in the Bible," *SBAP* 23 (1901) 72-77.

W. H. Kent, "Hieroglyphic Records and the Bible," *AER* 27 (1902) 517-520. [I. Modern Biblical Science; II. The Gradual Growth of Modern Criticism; III. The New Light from the Ancient Monuments; IV. The Rosetta Stone and Egyptology; V. First Clue to the Characters: Help Afforded by Coptic; VI. The Cuneiform Hieroglyphics: Grotefend's Centenary; VII. The Persian Inscription at Behistun Deciphered by Rawlinson; VIII. The Cuneiform Hieroglyphics at Babylon and Assyria; IX. How to Regard the Evidence of the Ancient Monuments]

M. G. Kyle, "Biblical Gains from Egyptian Explorations. No. II.," *CFL, N.S.,* 5 (1902) 29-40.

A. H. Sayce, "Freshest Light from Egypt," *HR* 43 (1902) 483-488.

M. G. Kyle, "'Some Gems Recovered from an Old Egyptian Lapidist's Workshop'," *CFL, 3rd Ser.,* 3 (1905) 83-90. [Egyptian Testimony to the Historical Trustworthiness of the Old Testament]

[W. M.] Flinders Petrie, "The Old Testament and Egyptian Monuments," *AAOJ* 28 (1906) 368-370.

J. H. Sammis, "'Judgment'—Do the Critics Score?" *CFL, 3rd Ser.,* 8 (1908) 97-100. *(Editorial Note) [Elephantine Papyri]*

A. B. Mace, "The Influence of Egypt on Hebrew Literature," *AAA* 9 (1922) 3-26.

George W. Gilmore, "Egyptian Literature and the Bible," *HR* 94 (1927) 305.

I. O. Nothstein, "The Wisdom of Egypt and the Old Testament," *AQ* 7 (1928) 48-51.

George McCready Price, "Digging the Bible out of Egypt's Sands," *CLF, 3rd Ser.,* 34 (1928) 256-258.

*Thomas O. Lamdin, "Egyptian Loanwords in the Old Testament," *JAOS* 73 (1953) 145-155.

K. A. Kitchen, "Egypt and the Bible: Some Recent Advances," *F&T* 91 (1959-60) 177-197.

K. A. Kitchen, "Some Egyptian Background to the Old Testament," *TB* #5&6 (1960) 4-18.

§290 *3.2.5.4 Other Backgrounds - Unclassified*

Anonymous, "Antir. Illustrations of Scripture from Ancient Bedouin Romance of that Name," *JSL, 1st Ser.*, 5 (1850) 1-35.

*W. Wright, "The Hittites and the Bible," *BQRL* 76 (1882) 53-78.

*Julia Wedgwood, "Greek Mythology and the Bible," *ContR* 61 (1892) 368-381.

*J. F. McCurdy, "Light on Scriptural Texts from Recent Discoveries. Arabia in the Old Testament," *HR* 33 (1897) 124-126.

*Fritz Hommel, "Miscellanea," *ET* 9 (1897-98) 524-256. [2. Arabisms in the Old Testament, p. 525]

R. E. Conder, "Results of Syrian Stone Lore," *HR* 41 (1901) 104-108.

A. H. Sayce, "The Newest Light from the Ancient Monuments," *HR* 41 (1901) 195-199.

*Fritz Hommel, "Bearing of Arabian Archaeology on Bible and History," *HR* 41 (1901) 291-298.

Joseph Offord and E. J. Pilcher, "Some Punic Analogues," *SBAP* 24 (1902) 283-284.

T. H. Weir, "Some Fresh Bible Parallels from the History of Morocco," *Exp, 6th Ser.*, 7 (1903) 426-433.

*Hugo Winckler, "North Arabia and the Bible: A Defence," *HJ* 2 (1903-04) 571-590.

*John E. McFadyen, "Hellenism and Hebrewism," *AJT* 8 (1904) 30-47.

Samuel Ives Curtiss, "Some Religious Usages of Dhîâb and Ruala Arabs and their Old Testament Parallels," *Exp, 6th Ser.*, 9 (1904) 275-285.

*Henry Proctor, "The Bible and Syrian Archæology," *AAOJ* 27 (1905) 197-199.

*James A. Kelso, "The Significance of the Elephantine Papyri for Old Testament Criticism," *BWTS* 2 (1909-10) #1, 21-32.

*E. G. Harmer, "The Bible and the Latest Research in the Hittite Lands," *CFL, 3rd Ser.*, 13 (1910) 159-161.

*C. F. Burney, "New Aramaic Papyri and the Old Testament History," *CQR* 74 (1912) 392-409.

*Stanley A. Cook, "The Elephantine Papyri and the Old Testament," *Exp, 8th Ser.*, 3 (1912) 193-207.

C. J. Lyall, "The Relation of the Old Arabian Poetry to the Hebrew Literature of the Old Testament," *JRAS* (1914) 253-266.

Marc F. Vallette, "American Mythology as Related to Asiatic and Hebrew Tradition," *ACQR* 40 (1915) 584-601.

*Anonymous, "The Elephantine Papyri and the Old Testament," *HR* 69 (1915) 368.

*Joseph Offord, "The Elephantine Papyri as Illustrative of the Old Testament," *PEFQS* 47 (1915) 72-80, 144-151.

W. Fairweather, "The ποίημα νουθετικόν the Pseudo-Phocylides," *ET* 28 (1916-17) 327.

*Joseph Offord, "Archaeological Notes on Jewish Antiquities. L. *Coptic Terms and the Old Testament*," *PEFQS* 50 (1918) 137-138.

*William Wallace Everts, "The Bible and the Amarna Documents," *R&E* 15 (1918) 311-318.

*William W[allace] Everts, "Statements Concerning the Hittites Affirmed by the Scriptures Confirmed by the Monuments," *BS* 81 (1924) 18-27.

Edward Chiera, "The Bible and Sumerian Research," *CQ* 1 (1924) 85-92.

*Albert T. Clay, "The Early Civilization of Amurru—The Land of the Amorites—Showing Amorite Influence on Biblical Literature," *JTVI* 57 (1925) 88-104. [Discussion and Communications, pp. 104-111]

A. H. Sayce, "Hittite and Mitannian Elements in the Old Testament," *JTS* 29 (1927-28) 401-406.

G. R. Driver, "Supposed Arabism in the Old Testament," *JBL* 55 (1936) 101-120.

*Frederic G. Kenyon, "Ras Shamra and Mari: Recent Archaeological Discoveries Affecting the Bible," *JTVI* 73 (1941) 81-92, 96. [(Discussion, p. 92) (Communications by, H. S. Curr, pp. 92-94; P. J. Wiseman, pp. 94-95; Norman S. Denham, pp. 95-96)]

*H. F. D. Sparks, "The Lachish Excavations and Their Bearing upon Old Testament Study," *Theo* 43 (1941) 17-27.

Hazel E. Foster, "Contributions of India to Bible Knowledge and Understanding," *JAAR* 10 (1942) 211-216.

Edward P. Arbez, "Some Parallels from Arabic Literature to Problems of the Old Testament," *CBQ* 8 (1946) 58-71.

*Raymond A. Bowman, "Arameans, Aramaic, and the Bible," *JNES* 7 (1948) 65-90.

*Cyrus H. Gordon, "Homer and the Bible. The Origin and Character of East Mediterranean Literature," *HUCA* 26 (1955) 43-108.

*A. Malamat, "Doctrines of Causality in Hittite and Biblical Historiography: A Parallel," *VT* 5 (1955) 1-12.

*Jacob J. Rabinowitz, "The Susa Tablets, the Bible and the Aramaic Papyri," *VT* 11 (1961) 55-76.

*Benjamin Mazar, "The Aramean Empire and Its Relations with Israel," *BA* 25 (1962) 98-120.

*David Winston, "The Iranian Component in the Bible, Apocrypha, and Qumran: A Review of the Evidence," *HRel* 5 (1965-66) 183-216.

J. R. Porter, "Pre-Islamic Arabic Historical Traditions and the Early Historical Narratives of the Old Testament," *JBL* 87 (1968) 17-26.

*Harry A. Hoffner Jr., "Some Contributions of Hittitology to Old Testament Study," *TB* #20 (1969) 27-55. [A. Who were the 'Hittites' of the Old Testament? B. Hittite law and the Old Testament; C. Hittite religion and the Old Testament; D. Hittite mythology and the Old Testament]

§291 **3.2.6 The Historical Reliability of the Old Testament -
      General Studies (includes studies on Authority)**

(   ) Amicus, "On the Importance of Placing Biblical Literature and
Antiquities on an Equality, at Least, with the Heathen Classics," *MQR* 1
(1847) 475-477.

W. H. R., "Egypt, Assyria, and the Bible," *UQGR* 10 (1853) 329-360.
(Review)

*Anonymous, "Geographical Accuracy of the Bible," *CRB* 20 (1855) 451-
469.

*B. W. Savile, "Confirmation of Bible History," *JSL, 3rd Ser.,* 10 (1859-60)
388-391.

*†Anonymous, "The Geography of Palestine, in Relation to the Historical
Truth of the Bible," *BFER* 9 (1860) 153-185. *(Review)*

T. H. Beveridge, "Verity of the Old Testament History," *UPQR* 1 (1860)
256-277. *(Review)*

Anonymous, "Rawlinson's Bampton Lectures on the Truth of the Scripture
Records," *TLJ* 13 (1860-61) 177-204. *(Review)*

A. R. Abbott, "The Bible's Worth in History, the Pledge of its Divine
Authority," *UQGR, N.S.,* 6 (1869) 261-275.

W. Thomson, "The Testimony of Ancient Monuments to the Historic Truth
of Scripture," *BFER* 23 (1874) 151-173.

William Henry Green, "The Perpetual Authority of the Old Testament,"
PQPR 6 (1877) 221-255.

Anonymous, "The Question and the Crisis," *BWR* 1 (1877) 399-408.
[Historicity and Authenticity]

J. W. K., "The Difficulties of the Bible," *ERG, 7th Ser.,* 1 (1878-79) 103-
111.

J. S. Lee, "The Realistic Features of the Bible," *UQGR, N.S.,* 16 (1879) 272-
286. *[Accuracy and Authenticity]*

*G. E. Leeson, "Testimony of the Mesopotamian Monuments to the Reliability of the Sacred Scriptures," *BQR* 3 (1881) 137-165.

Addison P. Foster, "Is the Bible Free from Historic and Scientific Errors?" *JCP* 3 (1883-84) 511-526.

J. A. Smith, "Ancient Scripture," *ONTS* 3 (1883-84) 202-204.

Hermann L. Strack, "The Higher Criticism, a Witness to the Credibility of the Biblical Narrative," *AJSL* 1 (1884-85) 5-10.

Anonymous, "Minute Accuracy of the Old Testament," *ONTS* 4 (1884-85) 36-37.

Anonymous, "Light on the Old Testament," *ONTS* 4 (1884-85) 283-284.

George F. Herrick, "A Study in Biblical History," *BS* 42 (1885) 601-628.

C[laude] R. Conder, "The Old Testament: Ancient Monuments and Modern Critics," *ContR* 51 (1887) 376-393.

W. Robertson Smith, "Captain Conder and Modern Critics," *ContR* 51 (1887) 561-569.

George G. Cameron, "Old Testament History," *ET* 4 (1892-93) 296-299.

*George Douglas, "The Historical Difficulties in Kings, Jeremiah, and Daniel," *ET* 4 (1892-93) 549-554.

†Anonymous, "The Verdict of the Monuments," *ERCJ* 180 (1894) 80-107. *(Review)*

*Francis Brown, "Old Testament Problems," *JBL* 15 (1896) 63-74. [Historical, pp. 71-73]

A. E. Thomson, "'The Historical Attitude'," *BS* 55 (1898) 739-742.

R. Somervell, "The Historical Character of the Old Testament Narratives," *ET* 13 (1901-02) 298-302.

Samuel M. Smith, "Historicity of the Scriptures," *CFL, 3rd Ser.,* 6 (1902) 61-68.

Geo. Finke, "The Verdict of the Monuments," *ColTM* 22 (1902) 102-128, 136-159, 223-242. [I. Discovery and Decipherment of Inscriptions in Egypt, Babylonia and Assyria; II. Hieroglyphics, Cuneiform Inscriptions and the Bible]

*John Urquhart, "Roger's Reasons," *CFL, 3rd Ser.*, 1 (1904) 553-561. *[Authenticity and Historical Accuracy]*

George Macloskie, "New Light on the Old Testament," *PTR* 3 (1905) 595-618.

G. Frederick Wright, "Credibility of the Early Bible History in the Light of Recent Explorations," *CFL, 3rd Ser.*, 4 (1906) 168-173.

George Frederick Wright, "Scientific Confirmations of Old Testament History," *CFL, 3rd Ser.*, 5 (1906) 444-452.

*Matthew Leitch, "Unscientific Criticism of the Bible," *CFL, 3rd Ser.*, 4 (1906) 409-415. [I. Unscientific Criticism of the Bible as History]

*Charles Henry Hitchcock, "The Bible and Recent Science," *BS* 64 (1907) 299-313. *(Review)*

W. B. Riley, "Are the Scriptures Unscientific," *CFL, 3rd Ser.*, 7 (1907) 458-466.

*D. Gath Whitley, "Science and Scripture," *LQHR* 108 (1907) 315-317. *(Review)*

*James Wallace, "'History' Manufactured from 'Bogus' Etymology," *CFL, 3rd Ser.*, 10 (1909) 295-296. *(Editorial)*

Anonymous, "The Scientific Accuracy of Scripture," *CFL, 3rd Ser.*, 13 (1910) 6-7.

*E[duard] König, "A Modern Expert's Judgment on the Old Testament Historical Writings," *Exp, 8th Ser.*, 1 (1911) 308-319.

William H. Bates, "The Integrity of the Old Testament Historically and Critically Considered," *CFL, 3rd Ser.*, 18 (1914) 51-59.

Henry T. Hooper, "Exaggeration in Numbers," *LQHR* 121 (1914) 126-128.

G. Frederick Wright, "Scientific Confirmation of Bible History," *CFL, 3rd Ser.*, 19 (1915) 33-35.

L. D. Watson, "The Bible Historical," *CFL, 3rd Ser.,* 20 (1915) 14-17, 64-67, 103-106.

Francis J. Lamb, "The Historical Bible and Jural Science," *CFL, 3rd Ser.,* 20 (1915) 147-151.

[Jay Benson Hamilton], "The Historical Jokesmiths," *CFL, 3rd Ser.,* 20 (1915) 195-199; 21 (1916) 51-55.

*Robert Dick Wilson, "The Title 'King of Persia' in the Scriptures," *PTR* 17 (1915) 90-145.

George H. Schodde, "The Reliability of Old Testament History," *TZTM* 6 (1916) 479-480. *(Editorial)*

J. M. Creed, "History and the Old Testament," *MC* 10 (1920-21) 346-354.

E[duard] König, "The Ideal of Historical Writing and Israel's Relation to it," *MR* 105 (1922) 643-653.

Robert H. Pfeiffer, "The Historicity of the Books of the Old Testament," *MR* 105 (1922) 968-972.

Anonymous, "Is the Bible Scientific?" *CFL, 3rd Ser.,* 30 (1924) 41-43.

*A. B. Miller, "The Relation of the Ancient Amorites to the Historicity of the Old Testament," *SWJT* 8 (1924) 36-44.

*Frank R. Buckalew, "The Science of the Bible," *CFL, 3rd Ser.,* 33 (1927) 278-280.

D. J. Whitney, "Mistaken Ideas about Bible Science," *CFL, 3rd Ser.,* 33 (1927) 416-417.

*R[obert] D[ick] Wilson, "Foreign Words in the Old Testament as an Evidence of Historicity," *PTR* 26 (1928) 177-247. [Foreign Words in Biblical Aramaic; Foreign Words in Biblical Hebrew; Excursus on the Name "Cyrus"]

Frederick Erdman, "Is the Bible Scientifically Correct?" *CFL, 3rd Ser.,* 35 (1929) 74-79, 134-139.

*Kenneth J. Foreman, "The Composition of Scripture," *USR* 41 (1929-30) 279-292.

S. Baron, "The Authenticity of the Numbers in the Historical Books of the O.T.," *JBL* 49 (1930) 287-291.

*Elmer Ellsworth Helms, "Is the Bible Unscientific?" *CFL, 3rd Ser.,* 37 (1931) 92-95.

W. Bell Dawson, "The Bible Confirmed by Science," *CFL, 3rd Ser.,* 37 (1931) 293-299, 349-355, 407-412, 579-584, 638-644; 38 (1932) 27-32, 82-86.

A. H. T. Clarke, "The Historic Accuracy of the Old Testament," *EQ* 3 (1931) 156-167.

*W. A. Maier, "Archaeology—The Nemesis," *CTM* 4 (1933) 95-102, 176-183, 264-274. [II. Refuted Claims of Historical Inaccuracy, pp. 176-183]

*Charles Marston, "New Bible Evidences," *JTVI* 66 (1934) 124-132, 138. [Discussion and Communications, pp. 132-138]

James McKee Adams, "The Integrity of the Scriptures in Historical Detail," *R&E* 33 (1936) 370-390; 34 (1937) 29-43.

*W[illiam] B. R[iley], "Are the Scriptures Scientific?" *CFL, 3rd Ser.,* 43 (1937) 255-262.

*Clive A. Thomson, "Certain Bible Difficulties," *BS* 96 (1939) 459-478. [I. The age of King Saul; II. The age of Abraham; III. The Date of the Founding of the Temple; IV. Certain Genealogies]

*Judah Rosenthal, "Ḥiwi al-Balkhi: A Comparative Study," *JQR, N.S.,* 38 (1947-48) 317-342, 418-430; 39 (1948-49) 79-94.

*M. T. Brackbill, "Modern Physical Science in the Bible," *JASA* 3 (1951) #1, 23-27.

Robert H. Pfeiffer, "Facts and Faith in Biblical History," *JBL* 70 (1951) 1-14.

*J. A. Thompson, "Archaeology and the historicity of the Biblical records," *RTRM* 11 (1952) #1, 15-29.

D. J. Wiseman, "Secular Records in Confirmation of the Scriptures," *JTVI* 87 (1955) 26-36, 122-124. [(Discussion, pp. 119-120) (Communications by F. F. Bruce, pp. 120-121; A. L. Perry, p. 121; J. K. Mickelsen, pp. 121-122)]

*Frank M. Cross Jr., "A Footnote to Biblical History," *McQ* 9 (1955-56) #2, 7-10. *[Unsolved problems of Biblical History and Archaeology]*

*Joseph P. Free, "Archaeology and Biblical Criticism," *BS* 113 (1956) 123-129, 214-226, 322-338; 114 (1957) 23-39, 123-132, 213-224. [Is Rationalistic Biblical Criticism Dead? Archaeology and the Historical Accuracy of Scripture; Archaeology and Liberalism; Archaeology and Higher Criticism; Archaeology and Neo-Orthodoxy]

Walter J. Beasley, "Modern Scientific Research and the Bible," *AT* 1 (1956-57) #1, 2.

Allan A. MacRae, "The Historic Reliability of the Old Testament," *RefmR* 7 (1959-60) 80-91.

*J. Alberto Soggin, "Ancient Biblical Traditions and Modern Archaeological Discoveries," *BA* 23 (1960) 95-100. *[Archaeological Apologetics]*

*G. Van Gronigen, "Old Testament Historicity and Divine Revelation," *VR* #1 (1962) 3-23.

*Edward F. Campbell Jr. and James F. Ross, "The Excavation of Shechem and the Biblical Tradition," *BA* 26 (1963) 2-27.

*Paul Conners, "Haggadic History," *BC* 3 (1963-64) 162-167.

John S. Morris, "Biblical Event-Narratives and Historical Truth," *USQR* 19 (1963-64) 221-230.

[Clifford A. Wilson], "Your Questions Answered. Must the large numbers of the Old Testament be taken literally?" *BH* 4 (1968) 59-61.

§292 *3.2.7 The Old Testament in the Canon of Scripture*

*Anonymous, "Storr's Biblical Theology," *CRB* 1 (1836) 69-82. *(Review)* [§14 Proof that the Jewish canon, in the days of Jesus, contained the same books which now constitute our Old Testament, pp. 79-81]

Anonymous, "On the Canon of the Old Testament," *QCS, 3rd Ser.,* 10 (1838) 69-89. *(Review)*

(   ) *Δ.,* "The Integrity of the Canon of the Holy Scripture Maintained Against Unitarian Objections," *CTPR, N.S.,* 2 (1840) 82-87. *(Review)*

G. R. N., "Stuart on the Old Testament," *CE* 40 (1846) 69-77. *(Review)*

†Anonymous, "Vincenzi's Vindication of the Tridentine Canon of Scripture," *DR* 21 (1846-47) 131-163. *(Review)*

†Anonymous, "The Canon of Sacred Scripture," *DR* 23 (1847) 104-123. *(Review)*

F. W. G., "First Lessons in Biblical Criticism. No. II   Canon of the Scriptures," *JSL, 1st Ser.,* 7 (1851) 174-189.

*C. E. Stowe, "The Apocryphal Books of the Old Testament, and the Reasons for their Exclusion from the Canon of Scripture," *BS* 11 (1854) 278-305.

[John Adam(?)] Reubelt, "The Canon of the Old Testament," *MQR* 12 (1858) 265-274.

Anonymous, "The Biblical Canon," *JSL, 4th Ser.,* 2 (1862-63) 102-113. *(Review)*

Anonymous, "Christ's Testimony to Our Canonical Scripture," *CongR* 3 (1863) 274-286. *(Review)*

Anonymous, "The Canon of Scripture," *CR* 17 (1865-66) 583-600.

*J. L., "Inspiration," *BFER* 16 (1867) 537-556. *(Review)* [O.T. Canon, pp. 553-556]

*B. Gildersleeve, "Canonicity and Inspiration of the Sacred Scriptures," *SPR* 19 (1868) 370-394. *(Review)*

*Bernard Pick, "Philo's Canon of the Old Testament and His Mode of Quoting the Alexandrian Version," *JBL* 4 (1884) 126-143.

E. Reuss, "Luther and the Old Testament Canon," *ONTS* 4 (1884-85) 376-377.

Edwin C. Bissell, "The Canon of the Old Testament," *BFER* 35 (1886) 509-531.

Edwin C. Bissell, "The Canon of the Old Testament," *BS* 43 (1886) 73-99, 264-286.

J. A. Paine, "A Canonical Formula Introducing Certain Historical Books of the Old Testament," *BS* 48 (1891) 652-669.

*W. Sanday, "The Cheltenham List of Canonical Books of the Old and New Testament and the Writings of Cyprian," *SBE* 3 (1891) 217-303. [Appendix by C. H. Turner, pp. 304-325]

[Albert A. Isaacs], "'The Testimony of Our Lord Jesus Christ to the Old Testament Scriptures'," *EN* 4 (1892) 529-537.

A. B. Davidson, "The Canon of the Old Testament," *Exp, 4th Ser.,* 5 (1892) 317-320. *(Review)*

*Anonymous, "The Case of Professor Briggs before the General Assembly," *AR* 19 (1893) 464-477. [The Old Testament Canon, pp. 472-473] *(Editorial)*

J. B. Shearer, "The Canon of Scripture—Its Authentication," *PQ* 7 (1893) 187-197.

Joseph V. Tracy, "Popular Names of the Inspired Books," *AER* 11 (1894) 17-26.

J. A. Howlett, "The Formation of the Palestinian Canon," *IER, 3rd Ser.,* 15 (1894) 144-162.

Willis J. Beecher, "The alleged triple canon of the Old Testament," *JBL* 15 (1896) 118-128.

*G. Buchanan Gray, "Two Notes on the Hebrew Ecclesiasticus," *OSHTP* (1896-97) 36-40. [I. The Reference to Job and the Canon in Eccles. XLIX. 8-10, pp. 36-39]

*Geo[rge] H. Schodde, "Biblical Research Notes," *ColTM* 17 (1897) 371-384. [Research on O.T. Canon, pp. 382-383]

William W. Elwang, "The Old Testament Canon," *PQ* 11 (1897) 125-141.

C. H. Turner, "Latin Lists of the Canonical Books. 1. The Roman Council under Damasus, A.D. 382," *JTS* 1 (1899-1900) 554-560.

*D. S. Margoliouth, "Lines of Defence of the Biblical Revelation. 4. The Argument from Silence," *Exp, 6th Ser.*, 2 (1900) 129-154.

C. H. Turner, "Latin Lists of the Canonical Books. 2. An Unpublished Stichometrical List from the Freisingen MS of Canons," *JTS* 2 (1900-01) 236-253.

C. H. Turner, "Additional Note on the Stichometry of the Barberini MS.," *JTS* 2 (1900-01) 577.

Dunlop Moore, "The Canon of the Old Testament in the Russian Church," *CFL, N.S.*, 5 (1902) 121-122.

C. K. Crawford, "The Canon in the Time of Samuel. Was There One?" *CFL, N..S*, 8 (1903) 339-345.

William M. McPheeters, "The Latest Criticism and the Canon of the Old Testament," *HR* 45 (1903) 23-28, 114-120.

*Henry H. Howorth, "The Modern Roman Canon and the Book of Esdras A," *JTS* 7 (1905-06) 343-354.

Henry H. Howorth, "The Origin and Authority of the Biblical Canon in the Anglican Church," *JTS* 8 (1906-07) 1-40.

Henry H. Howorth, "The Origin and Authority of the Biblical Canon According to the Continental Reformers: I. Luther and Karlstadt," *JTS* 8 (1906-07) 321-365.

*H. Pope, "The Third Book of Esdras and the Tridentine Canon," *JTS* 8 (1906-07) 218-232.

Henry H. Howorth. "The Origin and Authority of the Biblical Canon According to the Reformers. II. Luther, Zwingli, Lefevre, and Calvin," *JTS* 9 (1907-08) 188-230.

Henry H. Howorth, "The Bible Canon of the Reformation. I.," *IJA* #14 (1908) 6-9.

Henry H. Howorth, "The Bible Canon of the Reformation. II.," *IJA* #15 (1908) 8-12.

Henry H. Howorth, "The Canon of the Bible Among the Reformers," *JTS* 10 (1908-09) 183-232.

Henry H. Howorth, "The Influence of St. Jerome on the Canon of the Western Church," *JTS* 10 (1908-09) 481-496.

Henry H. Howorth, "The Bible Canon of the Reformation. III.," *IJA* #18 (1909) 49-53.

Henry H. Howorth, "The Influence of St. Jerome on the Canon of the Western Church. II," *JTS* 11 (1909-10) 321-347.

Henry H. Howorth, "The Bible Canon of the Reformation. IV.," *IJA* #20 (1910) 7-15.

Gerald Birney Smith, "Can the Distinction between Canonical and Non-Canonical Writings be Maintained?" *BW* 37 (1911) 19-29.

William Frederic Bade, "The Canonization of the Old Testament," *BW* 37 (1911) 151-162.

Henry H. Howorth, "The Bible Canon of the Reformation. V," *IJA* #24 (1911) 4-8.

*Archbishop of Milwaukee, "The Deutero-Canonical Books and the Tridentine Decree," *IJA* #25 (1911) 23-24.

Henry H. Howorth, "The Bible Canon of the Reformation. VI," *IJA* #25 (1911) 24-28.

Henry H. Howorth, "The Bible Canon of the Reformation. VII," *IJA* #27 (1911) 61-68.

Henry H. Howorth, "The Influence of St. Jerome on the Canon of the Western Church. III," *JTS* 13 (1911-12) 1-18.

C. H. Turner, "Latin Lists of Canonical Books. III.," *JTS* 13 (1911-12) 77-82.

C. H. Turner, "Latin Lists of Canonical Books. IV.," *JTS* 13 (1911-12) 511-514.

Henry Gracey, "Luther and the Canon of Scripture: Review of Principle Marcus Dods' Book," *CFL, 3rd Ser.,* 15 (1912) 82-87. *(Review)*

Henry H. Howorth, "The Bible Canon of the Reformation. VIII," *IJA* #30 (1912) 56-59.

*Henry H. Howorth, "The Bible Canon of the Reformation: Coverdale's Bible," *IJA* #31 (1912) 67-71.

*T. Witten Davies, "Some Notes on Hebrew Matters, Literary and Otherwise. The Small Kethubim or Hagiography," *R&E* 9 (1912) 555-556.

*Henry H. Howorth, "The Bible Canon of the Reformation: Some famous French Bibles, &c.," *IJA* #33 (1913) 36-40.

Henry H. Howorth, "The Bible Canon of the Reformation. XI," *IJA* #35 (1913) 66-70.

*Robert Dick Wilson, "The Book of Daniel and the Canon," *PTR* 13 (1915) 352-408.

Henry H. Howorth, "The Bible Canon of the Reformation. XII," *IJA* #51 (1917) 59-64.

William James Mutch, "An Open Word," *HR* 81 (1921) 185-190.

*L. Ginzberg, "Some Observations on the Attitude of the Synagogue Towards the Apocalyptic-Eschatological Writings," *JBL* 41 (1922) 115-136.

*T. Herbert Bindley, "Canon and Apocrypha," *ICMM* 19 (1922-23) 252-260.

R[obert] D[ick] Wilson, "The Rule of Faith and Life," *PTR* 26 (1928) 423-480.

Solomon Zeitlin, "An Historical Study of the Canonization of the Hebrew Scriptures," *PAAJR* 3 (1931-32) 121-158.

R. N. Smith, "The Canon of the Old Testament," *EQ* 3 (1932) 50-60.

R. E. Wolfe, "Two Modifications of the Generally Accepted Theory Regarding the Canonization of the Prophets," *JBL* 53 (1934) iii-iv.

*H. Wheeler Robinson, "Some Outstanding Old Testament Problems. II. Canonicity and Inspiration," *ET* 47 (1935-36) 119-123.

Lewis Sperry Chafer, "Bibliology. III. Canonicity and Authority," *BS* 95 (1938) 137-156.

E. Denef, "The Fixing of the Old Testament Canon," *JTALC* 6 (1941) 352-365.

James Wood, "Is the Old Testament Christian Scripture?" *ET* 53 (1941-42) 238-240.

Nahum Levison, "The Canon of the Old Testament," *GUOST* 11 (1942-44) 25-26.

E. C. Blackman, "The Authority of the Old Testament: Is it Christian Scripture?" *CongQL* 24 (1946) 13-24.

Rudolph Gehle, "Outline for a History of the Old Testament Canon," *CTM* 17 (1946) 801-828, 881-904.

J. Stafford Wright, "The Canon of Scripture," *EQ* 19 (1947) 93-109.

Frank Zimmermann, "The Canonization of the Hebrew Scriptures," *JBL* 68 (1949) vii.

J. H. Crehan, "Who Guarantees the Bible?" *Scrip* 4 (1949-51) 231-236.

Jean-Paul Audet, "A Hebrew-Aramaic List of Books of the Old Testament in Greek Transcription," *JTS, N.S.,* 1 (1950) 135-154.

Gunnar Östborn, "Cult and Canon. A Study in the Canonization of the Old Testament," *UUÅ* (1950) #10, 1-117.

Peter G. Duncker, "The Canon of the Old Testament at the Council of Trent," *CBQ* 15 (1953) 277-299.

M. H. Segal, "The Promulgation of the Authoritative Text of the Hebrew Bible," *JBL* 72 (1953) 35-47.

*A. Murtonen, "The Fixation in Writing of Various Parts of the Pentateuch," *VT* 3 (1953) 46-53.

Samuel J. Schultz, "Augustine and the Old Testament," *BS* 112 (1955) 225-234.

*R. Laird Harris, "The Evidence for the Canon from the Dead Sea Scrolls," *RefmR* 3 (1955-56) 139-153.

Samuel J. Schultz, "Augustine and the Old Testament Canon," *EQ* 28 (1956) 93-100.

J. R. Macphail and others, "The Authority of the Bible," *SJT* 9 (1956) 14-30. [O.T. Canon, p. 19]

Peter Katz, "The Old Testament Canon in Palestine and Alexandria," *ZNW* 47 (1956) 191-217.

*Menahem Haran, "Problems of the Canonization of Scripture," *Tarbiz* 25 (1956-57) #3, I-III. [I. The Place of *Ben Sira* in the History of the Canonization of the Bible; II. The Scriptures as "Defiling the Hands"; III. The Holiness of Books and Their Consignment to Storage in *Genizoth*]

*William Schneirla, "The Orthodox Old Testament Canon and the So-Called Apocrypha," *StVTQ, N.S.,* 1 (1957) #3, 40-46.

*Francis I. Andersen, "The Dead Sea Scrolls and the Formation of the Canon," *BETS* 1 (1958) #3, 1-7.

*Walter G. Williams, "Text, Canon and Qumran," *IR* 18 (1961) #1, 23-28.

*I. H. Eybers, "Some Light on the Canon of the Qumran Sect," *OTW* 5 (1962) 1-14.

*David Noel Freedman, "The Law and the Prophets," *VTS* 9 (1962) 250-265.

J. C. O'Neill, "Varieties of Biblical Witness—Theological Comment," *ABR* 10 (1962) 1-9.

Bleddyn J. Roberts, "The Old Testament Canon: A Suggestion," *BJRL* 46 (1963-64) 164-178.

W. W. Simpson, "The Bible Jesus Knew," *PQL* 10 (1964) 252-256, 340-345; 11 (1965) 24-30, 105-110.

R. Laird Harris, "Was the Law and the Prophets Two-Thirds of the Old Testament Canon?" *BETS* 9 (1966) 163-171.

Roland E. Murphy, Albert C. Sundberg Jr., and Samuel Sandmel, "A Symposium on the Canon of Scripture," *CBQ* 28 (1966) 189-207. [1. The Old Testament in the Catholic Church, by Roland E. Murphy, pp. 189-193; 2. The Protestant Old Testament Canon: Should It Be Reexamined? by Albert C. Sundberg Jr., pp. 194-203; 3. On Canon, by Samuel Sandmel, pp. 203-207]

*M. H. Goshen-Gottstein, "The Psalms Scroll (11QPs[a]). A Problem of Canon and Text," *Text* 5 (1966) 22-33.

S[amuel] Yosef Agnon, "Sacred Letters," *HA* 11 (1966-67) 9-12.

‡John M. Zinkand, "The Canon of the Bible: Some Reasons for Contemporary Interest," *BETS* 10 (1967) 15-19. [Bibliography, p. 20]

R. Laird Harris, "The Canon of the Bible. Factors Promoting the Formation of the Old Testament Canon," *BETS* 10 (1967) 21-27.

Robert B. Laurin, "The Problem of the Canon in the Contemporary Church," *Found* 10 (1967) 314-330. [I. The Validity of Canonical Formation; II. The Formation of the Old Testament Canon; III. The Question of the Apocrypha; IV. The Formation of the New Testament Canon; V. The Problem of the Canon]

C. F. Evans, "Tradition and Scripture," *RS* 3 (1967-68) 323-337.

*James A. Sanders, "Cave 11 Surprises and the Question of Canon," *McQ* 21 (1967-68) 284-298.

Albert C. Sundberg Jr., "The 'Old Testament': A Christian Canon," *CBQ* 30 (1968) 143-155.

*Marvin E. Tate, "The Old Testament Apocrypha and the Old Testament Canon," *R&E* 65 (1968) 339-356.

*Peter R. Ackroyd, "The Open Canon," *Coll* 3 (1968-70) 279-292.

*Meredith G. Kline, "Canon and Covenant," *WTJ* 32 (1969-70) 49-67, 179-200.

§293 *3.2.7.1 The Great Synagogue; The Council of Jamnia*
[See also: Mishna - Pirke Aboth →]

Willis J. Beecher, "The Men of the Great Synagogue," *ONTS* 2 (1882-83) 200-207.

George S. Goodspeed, "The Successors of Ezra the Scribe," *BW* 2 (1893) 97-105.

S. Krauss, "The Great Synod," *JQR* 10 (1897-98) 347-377, 725-726.

Joseph Bullen, "The Men of the Great Synagogue," *ACQR* 32 (1907) 298-312.

(   ) Dowling, "Jamnia During the Presidency of Gamaliel II, *c.* A.D. 80-117," *PEFQS* 46 (1914) 84-88.

Henry Englander, "The Men of the Great Synagogue," *HUCA, Jubilee Volume* (1925) 145-170.

*Shalom Spiegel, "Toward Certainty in Ezekiel," *JBL* 54 (1935) 145-171. [Baba Bathra 15a, pp. 159-163]

Louis Finkelstein, "The Maxim of the *Anshe Keneset* Ha-Gedolah," *JBL* 59 (1940) 455-469. *[The Great Assembly]*

Jack P. Lewis, "What Do We Mean By Jabneh?" *JAAR* 32 (1964) 125-132.

Hugo Mantel, "The Nature of the Great Synagogue," *HTR* 60 (1967) 69-91.

§294   *3.2.8 Archaeology and the Bible - General Studies [See also: Archaeological Expeditions, etc., §181ff. ←]*

Samuel Birch, "Progress of Biblical Archaeology," *BFER* 20 (1871) 506-515.

Samuel Birch, "The Progress of Biblical Archaeology: An Address *Read before the Society of Biblical Archaeology on the 21st of March, 1871*," *SBAT* 1 (1872) 1-12.

H. B. Tristram, "Oriental Researches: Their Bearing on the History and Language of Scripture," *CM* 4 (1877) 321-335.

*J. L. Porter, "Exploration as Verifying Scripture," *PRev* 54 (1878) Part 2, 1-32.

*Josiah Miller, "The Talmud in Relation to Biblical Archaeology," *SBAP* 1 (1878-79) 38-39. (Remarks by A. Lowy, 39-40) *[Pages misnumbered as 36-38]*

*J. L. Porter, "Exploration as Verifying Revelation," *DTQ* 5 (1879) 1-19.

Anonymous, "On Some of the Gains to Biblical Archaeology due to the New Survey," *PEFQS* 13 (1881) 34-49.

Alex. Somerville, "Modern Discoveries in Relation to the Bible," *ERG, 8th Ser.,* 1 (1882-83) 254-262.

*[Trelawney Saunders], "The Recent Survey of Western Palestine and its Bearing upon the Bible," *JTVI* 17 (1883-84) 15-28. [Remarks by H. A. Stern, p. 29; H. D. Grant, p. 30; A. S. Ayrton, pp. 30-31; S. A. Crowther, p. 31; The Earl of Shaftesbury, pp. 31-32]

‡E. C. Mitchell, "The Bibliography of Exploration. A List of American Writers Upon Biblical Archaeology and the Work of Exploration in Bible Lands, with the Subjects They Have Discussed, Including Review and Magazine Articles as well as Separate Books," *ONTS* 6 (1886-87) 303-315.

George H. Schodde, "Recent Research in Bible Lands," *ColTM* 8 (1888) 157-168.

Joseph Jacobs, "Recent Research in Biblical Archeology," *ARL* 3 (1889) 1-19.

C[laude] R. Conder, "Biblical Archæology," *ARL* 3 (1889) 215.

[H. B.] Tristram, "Recent Exploration," *EN* 2 (1890) 481-485.

G[eorge] H. Schodde, "New Light from the East," *ColTM* 11 (1891) 28-36.

H. B. Tristram, "Digging up the Bible," *EN* 3 (1891) 403-406.

A. H. Sayce, "Biblical Archaeology and the Higher Criticism," *ET* 3 (1891-92) 15-17, 114-118, 266.

G[eorge] H. Schodde, "Recent Discoveries in Bible Lands," *ColTM* 12 (1892) 32-44.

S. R. Driver, "Archæology and the Old Testament," *ContR* 65 (1894) 408-426.

*J. A. Howlett, "The Higher Criticism and Archæology," *DR* 115 (1894) 71-95.

Andrew Harper, "Archaeology and Criticism," *Exp, 4th Ser.,* 10 (1894) 372-385.

*T. K. Cheyne, "The Archæology Stage of Old Testament Criticism," *ContR* 68 (1895) 89-102.

*A. H. Sayce, "Archæology *v.* Old Testament Criticism," *ContR* 68 (1895) 477-484.

*A. A. Bevan, "Professor Sayce *versus* the Archæologists," *ContR* 68 (1895) 805-814.

W. H. Bennett, "Scope and Significance of Old Testament Archaeology," *Exp, 5th Ser.,* 2 (1895) 422-434.

*A. H. Sayce, "Archaeology versus Old Testament Literary Criticism," *HR* 31 (1896) 99-104.

Anonymous, "Archæology and Old Testament Criticism," *MR* 78 (1896) 136-139.

*A. A. Berle, "Archaeology and Literary Criticism," *BS* 54 (1897) 389-391.

*A. H. Sayce, "The Limitations of Archaeology as a Substitute for Old-Testament History," *HR* 34 (1897) 195-199.

*J. A. Selbie, "Archaeology and Old Testament Criticism," *ET* 9 (1897-98) 448-449.

M. B. Chapman, "The Scriptures in the Light of Archæological Discoveries," *MQR, 3rd Ser.,* 23 (1897-98) 194-204.

Anonymous, "Archaeology vs. Radical Criticism," *CFL, O.S.,* 2 (1898) 22-24.

A. H. Sayce, "The Present Relation of Archaeology to the Higher Criticism," *HR* 35 (1898) 291-296.

Anonymous, "Archaeology and Criticism," *MR* 80 (1898) 312-314.

A. H. Sayce, "Recent Biblical Archaeology, Studies in Ancient Oriental History," *ET* 10 (1898-99) 203-204. *(Review)*

*T. K. Cheyne, "Textual Criticism in the Service of Archeology," *ET* 10 (1898-99) 238-240.

John P. Peters, "Archæology and the Higher Criticism," *NW* 8 (1899) 22-43.

Anonymous, "The Archaeologists and the Bible," *RChR, 4th Ser.,* 3 (1899) 111-119.

*C[laude] R. Conder, "Discoveries in Western Asia," *SRL* 34 (1899) 236-259.

A. H. Sayce, "Recent Biblical Archaeology," *ET* 11 (1899-1900) 12-13, 269-270, 516-517.

A. H. Sayce, "Recent Biblical Archaeology," *ET* 12 (1900-01) 28-29, 86-87, 155-156, 232-233, 276-277, 563-565.

P. A. Gordon Clark, "Recent Biblical Archaeology, 2.," *ET* 12 (1900-01) 156-157.

George S. Duncan, "Archaeology and the Old Testament," *CFL, N.S.,* 4 (1901) 80-87.

J. H. Stevenson, "Archæology and the Bible: With Especial Reference to the Flood Story, the Moabite Stone, and the Siloam Inscription," *MQR, 3rd Ser.,* 27 (1901) 672-683.

A. H. Sayce, "Recent Biblical Archaeology," *ET* 13 (1901-02) 465-467.

A. H. Sayce, "Recent Biblical and Oriental Archaeology," *ET* 14 (1902-03) 219-222, 328-330.

A. H. Sayce, "Recent Biblical and Oriental Archaeology," *ET* 14 (1902-03) 471-472. *(Review)*

Wilbur F. Tillett, "Modern Archaeology and the Old Testament," *PQ* 16 (1902-03) 303-317.

George S. Duncan, "Archaeology in the Old Testament," *BW* 22 (1903) 116-128.

*Charles L. Candee, "'Assyrian and Babylonian Archaeology and the Old Testament'," *CFL, N.S.,* 8 (1903) 169-176.

A. H. Sayce, "Recent Biblical and Oriental Archaeology," *ET* 15 (1903-04) 75-77.

A. H. Sayce, "Recent Biblical and Oriental Archaeology," *ET* 15 (1903-04) 231-233. *(Review)*

J. A. Selbie, "The Old Testament and Archaeology," *ET* 15 (1903-04) 445-446.

Joseph Dunn Burrell, "Recent Archaeological Finds and Their Biblical Significance," *HR* 47 (1904) 357-358, 438-440.

S. G. Dornblaser, "The Bible and Recent Archaeological Discoveries," *LQ* 34 (1904) 577-586.

A. H. Sayce, "Recent Biblical and Oriental Archaeology," *ET* 16 (1904-05) 285-286.

Henry W. Wyman, "Archaeology and the Bible," *AER* 32 (1905) 363-366.

M[elvin] G[rove] Kyle, "Use and Misuse of Archaeological Data in Biblical Criticism," *CFL, 3rd Ser.,* 2 (1905) 107-116.

A. H. Sayce, "The Archaeological Condemnation of the Critical Method," *CFL, 3rd Ser.,* 2 (1905) 341-344.

John Easter, "Archaeological Discoveries as Related to the Bible," *CFL, 3rd Ser.,* 3 (1905) 403-412.

Chauncey J. Hawkins, "Excavations and the Bible," *OC* 19 (1905) 1-7.

John Easter, "Archaeological Discoveries as Related to the Bible," *RP* 4 (1905) 234-242.

A. H. Sayce, "Recent Biblical and Oriental Archaeology," *ET* 17 (1905-06) 29-31.

J. V. Prasek, "Recent Biblical Archaeology," *ET* 17 (1905-06) 182-184.

A. F. Shauffler, "The Excavator's Spade and the Bible," *AAOJ* 28 (1906) 171-172.

Henry Bullard, "The Witness of Archaeology," *CFL, 3rd Ser.,* 4 (1906) 23-33.

*W. H. Bennett, "Archæology and Criticism," *ContR* 89 (1906) 518-527.

Hugo Radan, "The Latest Biblical Archaeology," *HR* 55 (1906) 100-104.

A.H.Sayce, "Recent Biblical and Oriental Archaeology,"*ET* 18 (1906-07) 26.

Gabriel Oussani, "The Bible and the Ancient East," *NYR* 2 (1906-07) 322-334.

*Gabriel Oussani, "Oriental Archeology and Higher Criticism," *NYR* 2 (1906-07) 719-748.

George H. Schodde, "Recent Finds in Biblical Archaeology," *ColTM* 27 (1907) 178-191.

Henry T. Hooper, "Archaeology and Biblical Criticism," *LQHR* 108 (1907) 312-315.

*A. R. S. Kennedy, "Recent Excavations in Palestine and Their Bearing on the Old Testament," *GUOST* 3 (1907-12) 5-6.

A. H. Sayce, "Recent Biblical and Oriental Archaeology," *ET* 20 (1908-09) 88-90, 541-543. *(Review)*

*James Orr, "Archeology as Searchlight," *CFL, 3rd Ser.,* 10 (1909) 31-40. [I. Light from Archeology on the Larger Aspects of the Subject; II. Light from Archeology on the Antiquity of Writing; III. Light from Archeology on Resolving Facts into Myths; IV. Light from Archeology on the Mosaic Period; V. Light from Archeology on Israel and the Nations; VI. Light from Archeology on the Book of Daniel]

A. H. Sayce, "Recent Oriental Archaeology," *ET* 21 (1909-10) 471-473. *(Review)*

Melvin Grove Kyle, "The Recent Testimony of Archaeology to the Scriptures," *BS* 67 (1910) 373-390.

A. H. Sayce, "Recent Biblical and Oriental Archaeology," *ET* 23 (1911-12) 547-548.

John Tuckwell, "Archaeology and Modern Biblical Scholarship," *JTVI* 44 (1912) 219-239. [Discussion, p. 239-246]

A. H. Sayce, "Recent Biblical and Oriental Archaeology," *ET* 24 (1912-13) 54-56, 139-140.

Melvin Grove Kyle, "Critical Theories Discredited by Archeology," *CFL, 3rd Ser.,* 16 (1913) 129-131.

*George A. Barton, "'Higher' Archaeology and the Verdict of Criticism," *JBL* 32 (1913) 244-260.

A. H. Sayce, "Recent Biblical Archaeology," *ET* 25 (1913-14) 15-17, 447-448.

*J. S. Ross, "Archaeology's Contribution Towards the Grave of Higher Criticism," *CFL, 3rd Ser.,* 18 (1914) 25-28, 64-67, 116-119. [*A List of Recent Archæological Discoveries Bearing on the Truthfullness of the Bible, Chronologically Arranged.* 1843. Isaiah and King Sargon; 1854. Did Belshazzar Ever Exist? 1869. Did Mesha, King of Moab, Revolt Against the Bondage of Israel? 1880. Has Hezekiah's Tunnel Been Found? 1881. Discovery of the Tombs of Egyptian Kings; 1884. Finding Egyptian Cities of Brick Without Straw; 1887. The Great Find at Tel El Amarna; 1890. Did Sennacherib Besiege Lachish in Hezekiah's Time? 1901. Wellhausen's Mainstay Broken Down. Also Explanation of Greek Words Found in Daniel; 1902. Discovery of the Wonderful Code of Hammurabi; Application of Hammurabi's Code; Is the Fourteenth Chapter of Genesis Myth? 1902. De Morgan's Discovery; Is Hammurabi Identical with Amraphel? 1906. Discovery of the Great Empire of the Hittites; Archæologists Renouncing Higher Criticism]

Archeo Logicus, "Archaeology and Biblical Criticism," *HR* 68 (1914) 258-259.

A. H. Sayce, "Recent Biblical and Oriental Archaeology," *ET* 26 (1914-15) 128-129.

G. H. Richardson, "The Abuse of Biblical Archaeology," *BW* 46 (1915) 98-109; 47 (1916) 94-99, 174-182.

G. H. Richardson, "The Value of Biblical Archaeology," *BW* 47 (1916) 381-387; 48 (1917) 17-25.

G[eorge] W. Gilmore, "Archaeology and the Bible," *HR* 72 (1916) 398-399. *(Review)*

*Oswald T. Allis, "The Bearing of Archaeology on the Higher Criticism of the Psalms," *PSB* 10 (1916) #3, 12-14.

Melvin Grove Kyle, "The Bible in the Light of Archaeological Discoveries," *BS* 74 (1917) 1-19.

*Oswald T. Allis, "The Bearing of Archaeology upon the Higher Criticism of the Psalms," *PTR* 15 (1917) 277-324.

*Camden M. Cobern, "Archeological Discoveries and the Old Testament," *BR* 3 (1918) 9-38. [I. New Light Upon the Times of Abraham and Moses; II. New Light on Persons and Places Mentioned in the Early Narratives of the Bible; III. New Light on Some of the Symbolical Language and Literary Forms Used in the Old Testament; Palestine; Countries Bordering on Palestine; Babylonia and Assyria; General Conclusions]

‡Samuel A. B. Mercer, "An Old Testament Archaeological Bibliography for 1914 to 1917 Inclusive," *JSOR* 3 (1919) 19-35.

Anonymous, "Driver 'Salting' an Archaeological Mine," *CFL, 3rd Ser.,* 26 (1920) 17-19.

*Julian Morganstern, "The Historical Reconstruction of Hebrew Religion and Archaeology," *JR* 1 (1921) 233-254.

A. H. Sayce, "The Latest Results of Old Testament Archaeology," *ET* 33 (1921-22) 37-39.

Edouard Naville, "The Outlook for Bible Studies in Bible Lands," *BS* 79 (1922) 113-130.

‡Samuel A. B. Mercer, "An Old Testament Archaeological Bibliography for 1918 to 1921 inclusive," *JSOR* 6 (1922) 134-152.

*(Miss) A. M. Hodgkin, "The Witness of Archaeology to the Bible," *JTVI* 54 (1922) 200-220. [Discussion, pp. 220-222]

Parke P. Flournoy, "'Bible and Spade'. *A Review of 'Bible and Spade,' John P. Peters, Ph.D., Sc.D., D.D.*," *USR* 34 (1922-23) 185-199. *(Review)*

*W[illiam] F[oxwell] Albright, "Contributions of Biblical Archaeology and Philology," *JBL* 43 (1924) 363-393.

*J. Walter Johnshoy, "Studies in Biblical Archaeology," *TTM* 9 (1925-26) 116-135. [Egypt (Tell-el-Amarna), pp. 117-121; Palestine, pp. 121-127; *Archæological Light on the History of Palestine*, pp. 127-130; *Cities and Houses*, pp. 130-135]

J. M. Powis Smith, "Archaeology and the Old Testament During the First Quarter of the Twentieth Century," *JR* 6 (1926) 284-301.

J. Magnus Rohne, "Some Recent Testimony of Archaeology to the Truth of the Scriptures," *TTM* 10 (1926-27) 83-106.

Melvin Grove Kyle, "The Bible in its Setting: The Value of the Spade," *BS* 86 (1929) 173-196.

Willard L. Jones, "Old Testament Archaeology," *CFL, 3rd Ser.*, 35 (1929) 362-365.

Theophile James Meek, "Old Testament Problems in the Light of Recent Archaeological Discoveries," *CJRT* 6 (1929) 374-381.

I. G. Matthews, "Archaeology and the Bible," *CQ* 6 (1929) 325-356.

A. H. Sayce, "Archaeology and the Old Testament," *EQ* 1 (1929) 337-344.

J. W. Jack, "Biblical Archaeology," *ET* 41 (1929-30) 475-476.

Raymond P. Dougherty, "The Scope of Biblical Archaeology," *JR* 10 (1930) 333-348.

William F[oxwell] Albright, "A Millennium of Biblical History in the Light of Recent Excavations," *PAPS* 69 (1930) 441-461.

J. W. Jack, "Recent Biblical Archaeology," *ET* 42 (1930-31) 74-76, 231-233, 357-359, 522-525.

T. Fish, "Digging Up Bible Lands," *CIR* 1 (1931) 393-403.

J. W. Jack, "Recent Biblical Archaeology," *ET* 43 (1931-32) 91-95, 233-235, 370-372, 519-522.

*John Garstang, "'The Archaeology of Palestine and the Bible'," *PEFQS* 64 (1932) 221-230. *(Review)*

Ovid R. Sellers, "Recent Excavations and Bible Study," *RL* 1 (1932) 90-101.

J. W. Jack, "Recent Biblical Archaeology," *ET* 44 (1932-33) 71-74, 230-233, 376-379, 519-522.

*W. A. Maier, "Archaeology—The Nemesis," *CTM* 4 (1933) 95-102, 176-183, 264-274. [I. Refuted Arguments from Literary Criticism; II. Refuted Claims of Historical Inaccuracy; III. Refuted Theories of Comparative Religion]

J. W. Jack, "Recent Biblical Archaeology," *ET* 45 (1933-34) 139-141, 222-224, 374-376, 500-503.

J. W. Jack, "Recent Biblical Archaeology," *ET* 46 (1934-35) 90-93, 218-221, 375-378, 544-547.

*D. E. Hart-Davies, "Biblical History in the Light of Archaeological Discovery Since A.D. *1900*," *JTVI* 67 (1935) 65-101, 104-105. (Discussion, pp. 101-104) [I. The Cradle of Civilization and Religion; II. The Genesis Story of the Flood; III. Abraham and the Patriarchal Records; IV. The Destruction of the Cities of the Plain; V. The Conquest of Jericho; VI. The Date of the Exodus; VII. The Antiquity and Authenticity of the Pentateuch; VIII. The Book of Daniel; IX. Gezer, Gaza, and Jerusalem; X. The New Testament: Language and History]

George A. Barton, "Archæology and the Bible," *RL* 4 (1935) 276-283.

J. W. Jack, "Recent Biblical Archaeology," *ET* 47 (1935-36) 139-141, 281-283, 412-415, 548-551.

J. W. Jack, "Some Outstanding Old Testament Problems. VIII. The Bearing of Archaeology on Old Testament Criticism," *ET* 47 (1935-36) 440-444.

James L. Kelso, "The Older and Newer Phases of Biblical Archaeology," *BS* 93 (1936) 181-186.

A. E. Ikin, "Archæology and the Bible in the Twentieth Century," *ContR* 150 (1936) 93-100.

J[ames] L. Kelso, "A Digest of Archaeological History of Palestine in Bible Times," *JAAR* 4 (1936) #2, 86-88.

C[hristopher] R. North, "Archaeology and Criticism," *LQHR* 161 (1936) 52-63.

J. W. Jack, "Recent Biblical Archaeology," *ET* 48 (1936-37) 135-138, 261-264, 408-411, 549-551.

*James L. Kelso, "Archaeology's Influence on Old Testament Exegesis," *BS* 94 (1937) 31-36.

*William F. Stinespring, "Remarks on Biblical Archaeology," *DDSR* 2 (1937) 1-10.

J. W. Flight, "Archaeology and the Bible—(Introduction)," *JAAR* 5 (1937) 30-32.

J. W. Jack, "Recent Biblical Archaeology," *ET* 49 (1937-38) 122-125, 272-275, 422-424, 556-558.

P. E. Kretzmann, "The Lure of Biblical and Christian Archaeology," *CTM* 9 (1938) 828-834.

George Ricker Berry, "Biblical Criticism and Archaeology," *JAAR* 6 (1938) 131-132, 170-171.

‡J. Philip Hyatt, "A Bibliography of Important Books and Articles on Biblical Archaeology," *JAAR* 6 (1938) 144-145, 172-174.

*‡Henry Schaeffer, "The Latest Discoveries in the Old Testament Field," *KZ* 62 (1938) 86-102, 147-165. [1. Practical Value of Biblical Archaeology; 2. The Best Literature for the study of the Most Recent Excavations; 3. Lachish Discoveries. J. L. Starkey, 1932—; 4. Megiddo Excavations. Oriental Institute, Chicago. 1925, 1927—; 5. Ur Excavations. C. L. Woolley. 1923-1929; 6. Ras Shamra Discoveries. F. Schaeffer, 1929—; 7. Biblical Literary Problems in the Light of the Ras Shamra Texts]

J. W. Jack, "Recent Biblical Archaeology," *ET* 50 (1938-39) 135-138, 277-279, 405-408, 533-536.

Miner Brodhead Stearns, "Biblical Archaeology and the Higher Criticism," *BS* 96 (1939) 307-318.

*William F. Stinespring, "Old Testament Criticism, Archaeology, and Religion," *DDSR* 4 (1939) 61-69.

J. Philip Hyatt, "Biblical Archaeology in the College," *JAAR* 7 (1939) 79-83, 112.

J. W. Jack, "Recent Biblical Archaeology," *ET* 51 (1939-40) 118-121, 291-294.

*J. W. Jack, "Recent Biblical Archaeology," *ET* 51 (1939-40) 420-423. [Houses, Streets, Gates; Ras Shamra (Ugarit), Europe and Palestine connected, *c.* 1900 B.C., Deadly Power of Ancient Arrows, The Arsenal and Official Archives; The Rephaim; The Nuzi Tablets, Marriage Customs, Shoes as Legal Symbols; Mummy of Solomon's Father-in-Law]

*J. W. Jack, "Recent Biblical Archaeology," *ET* 51 (1939-40) 544-548. [Cities and Villages, Cities; Beth-Shemesh ('City of the Sun'), The Hyksos City, The Egyptian City, The Philistine City, The Israelite City; Value of Tablets; Tablets from Chagar Bazar (Syria), Barley Food, The Name Jacob; Neo-Babylonian Tablets]

Vernon S. Broyles, "Palestinian Archaeology and the Old Testament," *USR* 51 (1939-40) 137-147.

Millar Burrows, "How Archaeology Helps the Student of the Bible," *BA* 3 (1940) 13-17.

*J. W. Jack, "Recent Biblical Archaeology," *ET* 52 (1940-41) 112-117. [Windows, Doors, Locks; Beth-Shemesh (1 S [6]), Industries, Jewellery; Megiddo, Palatial Houses, Ablution, Altar; Cush and Cushan-Rishathaim]

*J. W. Jack, "Recent Biblical Archaeology," *ET* 52 (1940-41) 229-233. [Dress and Apparel, 1. Loin-cloth and Plaid, 2. Tunic or Sleeved Garment, 3. Outer Garments; Transjordan; Lachish; The Present North Wall of Jerusalem; Jehoiachin, King of Judah]

*J. W. Jack, "Recent Biblical Archaeology," *ET* 52 (1940-41) 353-357. [Agriculture; Ezion-Geber *(Tell el-Kheleifeh);* Guilds of Workmen]

*J. W. Jack, "Recent Biblical Archaeology," *ET* 52 (1940-41) 454-458. [After the Harvest; Shipping at Ugarit (Ras Shamra); Old Testament Mythology]

*J. W. Jack, "Recent Biblical Archaeology," *ET* 53 (1941-42) 113-117. [Israelite Baking Methods; Israelite Warfare; The Jewish Diaspora]

*J. W. Jack, "Recent Biblical Archaeology," *ET* 53 (1941-42) 208-212. [The Moabite Occupation of Jericho; Patriarchal Palestine; Ships of Tarshish; Israelite Horticulture]

*J. W. Jack, "Recent Biblical Archaeology," *ET* 53 (1941-42) 276-280. [Springs, Wells; Canaanite Tomb at *Yazur* (Azor); Ancient Catacombs in Palestine]

*J. W. Jack, "Recent Biblical Archaeology," *ET* 53 (1941-42) 367-370. [1. Pools, 2. Cisterns; Archaeology And the Biblical Text: 1. Incense Altars, 2. Birds Fluttering, 3. Thy Servant a Dog, 4. The Land of Kue, 6. Solomon's Copper Platform, 7. Binding the Springs, 8. Riding the Clouds, 9. Going down to the Pit, 10. Great King, 11. The 'Herdsman' Amos; Children's Games]

James Sprunt, "The Preacher's Use of Archæology," *USR* 53 (1941-42) 34-50.

Albert A. Jagnow, "Recent Excavations In Their Bearing On the Old Testament," *KZ* 66 (1942) 641-664. [I. Glimpses of Very Early Times; II. Abraham and Patriarchal Times; III. The Age of the Exodus; IV. The Period of the Monarchy; V. The General Result of Archaeological Discovery]

*J. W. Jack, "Recent Biblical Archaeology," *ET* 54 (1942-43) 78-82. [1. Gezer, 2. Megiddo, 3. Jerusalem; The Israelite Deportations]

Charles Marston, "Recent Biblical Archaeology," *JTVI* 75 (1943) 93-103.

F. J. Hollinbeck, "Archaeology's Contributions to Bible Knowledge," *CovQ* 4 (1944) #2, 38-43.

Charles Marston, "Positive Conclusions of Biblical Archaeology," *JTVI* 76 (1944) 174-183.

Walter G. Williams, "The Significance of Archaeology for Biblical Studies," *IR* 2 (1945) 170-175.

P.[sic]* J. Wiseman, "Archaeology and Literary Criticism of the Old Testament," *JTVI* 77 (1945) 101-111, 114-115. [(Discussion, pp. 111-114) (Communication by Charles Marston, p. 114)]

Roland Potter, "Note on Biblical Archaeology," *NB* 27 (1946) 257-263.

Robert S. Kinsey, "Recent Developments in Old Testament Archaeology," *WBHDN* 43 (1946) #7, 45-49.

G. Ernest Wright, "Biblical Archaeology Today," *BA* 10 (1947) 7-24.

*Charles Lee Feinberg, "The Relation of Archaeology to Biblical Criticism," *BS* 104 (1947) 170-181.

Merrill F. Unger, "The Use and Abuse of Biblical Archaeology," *BS* 105 (1948) 297-306.

D. J. Wiseman, "Some Recent Trends in Biblical Archaeology," *JTVI* 82 (1950) 1-13, 16-17. (Discussion, pp. 13-16)

Henry Voogd, "Archaeology in the Bible," *RefR* 4 (1950-51) #2, 8-11.

C. Umhau Wolf, "Fifty Years of Biblical Archaeology," *LQ, N.S.,* 3 (1951) 289-307, 402-411.

P. W. Miller, "The Bible and the last Half-Century of Archaeology," *EQ* 24 (1952) 14-23.

William Foxwell Albright, "The Bible After Twenty Years of Archeology (1932-1952)," *RL* 21 (1952) 537-550.

*J. A. Thompson, "Archaeology and the historicity of the Biblical records," *RTRM* 11 (1952) #1, 15-29.

*E. R. Lacheman, "The Use of Comparative Religion, Literature and Archaeology in O.T. Studies," *JBL* 72 (1953) xvii.

Merrill F. Unger, "Great Archaeological Discoveries and Their Bearing Upon the Old Testament," *BS* 112 (1955) 55-61, 137-142.

*Joseph P. Free, "Archaeology and Biblical Criticism," *BS* 113 (1956) 123-129, 214-226, 322-338; 114 (1957) 23-39, 123-132, 213-224. [Is Rationalistic Biblical Criticism Dead? Archaeology and the Historical Accuracy of Scripture; Archaeology and Liberalism; Archaeology and Higher Criticism; Archaeology and Neo-Orthodoxy]

Norman Bentwich, "The Romance of Biblical Archaeology," *ContR* 189 (1956) 270-274.

D. J. Wiseman, "The Place and Progress of Biblical Archaeology," *JTVI* 88 (1956) 118-128.

J. A. Thompson, "Archaeology and Bible Kings: The Days of King Saul," *AT* 1 (1956-57) #1, 7-9.

J. A. Thompson, "The Days of the Kings: Part 2. King David," *AT* 1 (1956-57) #2, 3-5.

J. A. Thompson, "The Days of the Kings: Part 3. King Solomon," *AT* 1 (1956-57) #3, 11-13.

John A. Scott, "The Old Testament and Archaeology," *RestQ* 1 (1957) 41-45, 124-129.

G. Ernest Wright, "Archaeology and Old Testament Studies," *JBL* 77 (1958) 39-51.

Othmar Schilling, "The Bible and archaeology," *TD* 6 (1958) 33-37.

G. Ernest Wright, "The Achievement of Nelson Glueck," *BA* 22 (1959) 98-100.

G. Ernest Wright, "Is Glueck's Aim to Prove the Bible is True?" *BA* 22 (1959) 101-108.

*John Gray, "Archaeology and the History of Israel," *LQHR* 184 (1959) 13-21.

Anonymous, "Why Biblical Archaeology?" *AT* 4 (1959-60) #1, 2.

K. Morgan, "Why Biblical Archaeology? A Personal Experience of Its Value," *AT* 4 (1959) #4, 2.

*J. Alberto Soggin, "Ancient Biblical Traditions and Modern Archaeological Discoveries," *BA* 23 (1960) 95-100. *[Archaeological Apologetics]*

Lawrence A. Sinclair, "Two Basic Principles of Biblical Archaeology," *JAAR* 28 (1960) 437-443.

G. Ernest Wright, "Is Biblical Archaeology Trustworthy?" *AT* 5 (1960-61) #1, 20.

Joseph A. Callaway, "Biblical Archaeology," *R&E* 58 (1961) 155-172.

Horace D. Hummel, "The Role of Archaeology in Biblical Studies," *Amb* 10 (1961-62) #5, 1-3.

*John Gray, "Towards a Theology of the Old Testament: The Contribution of Archaeology," *ET* 74 (1962-63) 347-351.

Thomas Aquinas Collins, "Archaeology and the Bible," *BibT* #6 (1963) 344-351.

G. Ernest Wright, "Archaeology, History, and Theology," *HDSB* 28 (1963-64) #3, 85-96.

Norman Bentwich, "More Biblical Archaeology," *ContR* 205 (1964) 406-408.

*John L. McKenzie, "Archaeology and Genesis 1-11," *BibT* #16 (1965) 1035-1041.

Robert North, "Keeping Up-to-date on Biblical Excavations," *BibT* #16 (1965) 1061-1066.

*James Zink, "The Place of Archaeology in Biblical Interpretation," *RestQ* 8 (1965) 111-118.

*Sh. Yeivin, "On the Use and Misuse of Archaeology in Interpreting the Bible," *PAAJR* 34 (1966) 141-154.

Joseph A. Callaway, "The Emerging Role of Biblical Archaeology," *R&E* 63 (1966) 200-209.

*H. D. Beeby, "The Old Testament and the Redemption of Culture," *SEAJT* 8 (1966-67) #4, 17-28.

Clifford Wilson, "The Value of Archæology to the Bible Student," *BH* 3 (1967) #2, 13-25.

Anonymous, "The Exciting Future of Biblical Archaeology," *BH* 4 (1968) 102-112.

A. D. Tushingham, "How Biblical is Biblical Archaeology?" *AJBA* 1 (1968-71) #1, 5-8.

J. A. Thompson, "Fifty Years of Biblical Archaeology," *Interp* 2 (1969-70) 176-188.

§295 *3.2.9 Literary Criticism of the Pentateuch - General Studies*

†M. R., "Genesis and Exodus compared," *MMBR* 6 (1798) 10.

†S. E., "Attempt to reconcile Genesis and Exodus," *MMBR* 6 (1798) 93.

†Joseph Wise, "Mr. Wise's Reconciliation of Genesis and Exodus," *MMBR* 6 (1798) 189.

†Anonymous, "Grave's Lectures on the Pentateuch," *BCQTR* 33 (1809) 375-382. *(Review)*

*Anonymous, "An Attempt to Explain the Discrepancies Between the Book of Ecclesiastes and the Pentateuch," *CongML* 5 (1822) 686-689.

[Johann] Jahn, "On the Jewish Pentateuch," *BibR* 2 (1826) 549-578. *(Trans. by R. B. Patton)*

J. W., "Academical Lectures on the Jewish Scriptures and Antiquities. By John Gorham Palfrey, D.D., Professor of Biblical Literature in the University of Cambridge. Vol. I. The Last four Books of the Pentateuch," *CE* 25 (1838) 106-128. *(Review)*

*H. B. Hackett, "The Greek Version of the Pentateuch," *BS* 4 (1847) 188-196.

Anonymous, "The Poetry of the Pentateuch," *SPR* 1 (1847-48) 117-132.

(Mrs.) [Marianne Young] Postans, "Recollections of the East, Illustrative of the Pentatuech," *JSL, 1st Ser.,* 2 (1848) 101-115.

Anonymous, "Colenso and the Pentateuch: a criticism of arithmetic," *JSL, 4th Ser.,* 2 (1862-63) 257-281.

Daniel R. Goodwin, "Bishop Colenso on the Pentateuch," *AThR, N.S.,* 1 (1863) 308-343, 444-458. *(Review)*

(   ) D., "Recent Attacks on the Pentateuch—Davidson and Colenso," *BFER* 12 (1863) 377-409. *(Review)*

†Anonymous, "Bishop Colenso on the Pentateuch," *BQRL* 37 (1863) 147-190. *(Review)*

*Anonymous, "Colenso upon Moses and Joshua," *CongR* 3 (1863) 190-193. *(Review)*

†Anonymous, "English Rationalism," *LQHR* 20 (1863) 193-225. *(Review)* *[Studies on the Pentateuch]*

James Strong, "Colenso on the Pentateuch," *MR* 45 (1863) 286-311. *(Review)*

Anonymous, "Recent Attaches on the Pentateuch," *NBR* 38 (1863) 36-74. *(Review)*

*†Anonymous, "Biblical Criticism—Colenso and Davidson," *QRL* 113 (1863) 422-447. *(Review)*

†Anonymous, "The Pentateuch and 'Higher Criticism'," *BQRL* 40 (1864) 1-28. *(Review)*

Isaac Taylor, "Considerations on the Pentateuch," *ThE* 2 (1865) 1-46.

E[rnst] W[ilhelm] Hengstenberg, "Moses and Colenso," *ThE* 2 (1865) 47-71.

(   ) C., "Bishop Colenso on the Pentateuch: Part Fifth," *TR* 2 (1865) 583-588. *(Review)*

*P. H. Gosse, "On the High Numbers in the Pentateuch: Are they Trustworthy?" *JTVI* 5 (1870-71) 349-377.

Anonymous, "Colenso on the Pentateuch. Part VI.," *TR* 9 (1872) 197-206.

*Russell Martineau, "The Legislation of the Pentateuch," *TR* 9 (1872) 474-487. *(Review)*

*J. H. Titcomb, "Ethnic Testimonies to the Pentateuch," *JTVI* 6 (1872-73) 234-258. [(Paper by P. H. Gosse, pp. 258-259) (Discussion, pp.259-271)]

Samuel Hopkins, "Science in the Pentateuch," *DTQ* 4 (1878) 188-198.

*†Anonymous, "Colenso's Last Volume and Supernatural Religion," *LQHR* 53 (1879-80) 104-151. *(Review)*

Alfred Cave, "Professor Robertson Smith and the Pentateuch," *BFER* 29 (1880) 593-621.

W[illiam] Henry Green, "Professor Robertson Smith on the Pentateuch," *BFER* 31 (1882) 313-369.

Samuel Ives Curtiss, "Delitzsch on the Pentateuch," *ONTS* 1 (1882) #1, 1-5; #2, 1-4; #3, 41-45; #4, 61-65.

Franz Delitzsch, "Theses on the Truth of Pentateuchal History," *ONTS* 1 (1882) #3, 49.

William Henry Green, "Prof. Robertson Smith on the Pentateuch," *PR* 3 (1882) 108-156.

F. A. Gast, "Pentateuch-Criticism: Its History and Present State," *RChR* 29 (1882) 179-202, 374-418.

A. H. Newman, "Professor Strack on the Pentateuch," *ONTS* 2 (1882-83) 151-154. *(Review)*

Charles Elliott, "The Unity of the Pentateuch," *ONTS* 2 (1882-83) 304-308.

*H[enry] P[reserved] Smith, "The Law and the Prophets," *ONTS* 2 (1882-83) 315-319.

Francis L. Patton, "The Dogmatic Aspect of Pentateuchal Criticism," *BFER* 32 (1883) 450-531.

G[eorge] H. S[chodde], "The Pentateuchal Problem," *ColTM* 3 (1883) 177-186.

Anonymous, "Biblical Notes. Mosaic Words in the Pentateuch," *DTQ, N.S.,* 2 (1883) 118-123.

Charles A[ugustus] Briggs, "A Critical Study of the History of the Higher Criticism, with Special Reference to the Pentateuch," *PR* 4 (1883) 69-130.

Francis L. Patton, "The Dogmatic Aspect of Pentateuchal Criticism," *PR* 4 (1883) 341-410.

[Charles] A[ugustus] Briggs, "Editorial Statement," *PR* 4 (1883) 425-428. *[Ref. above article]*

I. E. Graeff, "Central Issues of Modern Criticism," *RChR* 30 (1883) 65-81. [Pentateuchal Criticism, pp. 66-69]

*Newell Woolsey Wells, "The Ante-Nicene Fathers and the Mosaic Origin of the Pentateuch," *ONTS* 3 (1883-84) 186-191.

Samuel Ives Curtiss, "Sketches of Pentateuch Criticism," *BS* 41 (1884) 1-23, 660-697; 42 (1885) 291-326.

Milton S. Terry, "The Higher Criticism of the Pentateuch," *MR* 66 (1884) 405-419, 605-623.

*J. M. Stifler, "The Relation of the Gospels and the Pentateuch," *BFER* 34 (1885) 305-319.

George H. Schodde, "The Historical Argument in the Pentateuch Problem," *ONTS* 5 (1885-86) 8-12.

Wm. W. Olssen, "The Origin and Structure of the Pentateuch," *CR* 47 (1886) 370-399. *(Review)*

*Franz Delitzsch, "Dancing and Pentateuch Criticism in Correlation," *Exp, 3rd Ser.,* 4 (1886) 81-95.

C. H. Toy, "The Present Position of Pentateuch Criticism," *URRM* 25 (1886) 47-68.

Anonymous, "The Pentateuchal Criticism," *ONTS* 7 (1887-88) 150-152.

Frederic Gardiner and E. C. Bissell, "Professors Gardiner and Bissell on the Pentateuch Question," *ONTS* 7 (1887-88) 255-259.

Owen C. Whitehouse, "Franz Delitzsch and August Dillmann on the Pentateuch," *Exp, 3rd Ser.,* 7 (1888) 132-145. *(Review)*

*G. Lansing, "The Pentateuch—Egypticity and Authenticity," *Exp, 3rd Ser.,* 8 (1888) 219-231, 307-317.

William Rupp, "The Higher Criticism in Its Theological Bearings, with Special Reference to the Pentateuch Question," *RChR* 35 (1888) 344-377.

Anonymous, "The Pentateuchal Question," *MR* 71 (1889) 742-749.

*George F. Moore, "Tatian's Diatessaron and the Analysis of the Pentateuch," *JBL* 9 (1890) 201-215.

*Henry M. Harman, "The Character of the Book of Joshua, and its Relation and Testimony to the Pentateuch," *MR* 72 (1890) 9-26.

Henry A. Rogers, "Alleged Pentateuchal Anachronisms," *ONTS* 10 (1890) 141-148.

Edwin C[one] Bissell, "The Pentateuchal Discussion—Present Outlook," *HR* 22 (1891) 195-202.

*Charles M. Mead, "Tatian's Diatessaron and the Analysis of the Pentateuch," *JBL* 10 (1891) 44-54.

Edwin C[one] Bissell, "The Pentateuchal Analysis and Inspiration," *HSR* 2 (1891-92) 5-20.

*Henry Hayman, "Prophetic Testimony to the Pentateuch," *BS* 49 (1892) 109-128, 177-198.

S. R. Driver, "Klostermann on the Pentateuch," *Exp, 4th Ser.,* 5 (1892) 321-342.

William Henry Green, "The Anti-biblical Higher Criticism," *PQ* 6 (1892) 341-359.

William Henry Green, "Klostermann on the Pentateuch," *PRR* 5 (1894) 261-286. *(Review)*

Henry Hayman, "Harmony of the Pentateuch Respecting Priestly Dues," *BS* 52 (1895) 18-28.

*Thomas Stoughton Potwin, "Ideas of the Future Life in the Pentateuch," *BS* 52 (1895) 423-438.

William Henry Green, "Fallacies of Higher Criticism," *HR* 29 (1895) 99-106.

*W. Scott Watson, "The References in the Pentateuch to Jair and Havvoth Jair," *PPR* 6 (1895) 323-330.

*W. Bacher, "Contributions to Biblical Exegesis by Rudolph von Ihering," *JQR* 8 (1895-96) 185-188.

Henry Hayman, "The Great Pentateuchal Difficulty Met," *BS* 53 (1896) 645-667.

E[duard] König, "The History and Method of Pentateuchal Criticism," *Exp, 5th Ser.,* 4 (1896) 81-99.

G. Finke, "A Short History of the Higher Criticism of the Pentateuch," *ColTM* 17 (1897) 84-93.

J. A. Selbie, "The Roman Catholic Church and Pentateuchal Criticism," *ET* 9 (1897-98) 405-407.

Joseph Bruneau, "Biblical Research. II. Pentateuch Criticism," *AER* 18 (1898) 274-279.

W[illiam] Henry Green, "Elohim and Jehovah in the Pentateuch," *HR* 36 (1898) 166-171, 257-262.

Anonymous, "The Criticism of the Pentateuch," *CQR* 47 (1898-99) 50-89. *(Review)*

Dunlop Moore, "Dr. W. H. Green of Princeton," *ET* 10 (1898-99) 426-429. *[Higher Criticism of the Pentateuch]*

C. Steuernagel, "Dr W. H. Green of Princeton. I., A Reply to Dr. Dunlop Moore," *ET* 10 (1898-99) 476-480.

J. A. Selbie, "Dr W. H. Green of Princeton. II., A Reply to Dr. Dunlop Moore," *ET* 10 (1898-99) 480.

*A[ngus] C[rawford], "Notes on the Pentateuch," *PER* 12 (1898-99) 346-348. [Notes on the Pentateuch, pp. 347-348]

Samuel Colcord Bartlett, "Rupprecht on the Pentateuch," *BS* 56 (1899) 639-656. *(Review)*

C[laude] R. Conder, "Notes on Antiquities of the Pentateuch," *PEFQS* 31 (1899) 58-62. [Cush; Midian, Ismael, Moab; The Asshurim; The Hyksos; Goren Atad; The Mixed Multitude; The Spies; The Amorites; The Assyrians; Sinai, Sin, Zin; Egyptian Names; Avims; Idolatry; Gad, Reuben; Geshur; Shenir; The Utmost Sea; The Escaped Slave; Captivity]

E. Rupprecht, "Criticism: True and False," *ColTM* 20 (1900) 102-114, 146-167. *(Trans. by Walter E. Tressel)*

George H. Schodde, "Some Seeming Contradictions in the Scriptures," *ColTM* 22 (1902) 330-338; 23 (1903) 1-24. [I. Genesis I and II; The Pentateuch and the History of Israel; III. The Historical Character of the Pentateuch]

F. A. Gast, "The Higher Criticism as Applied to the Pentateuch," *RChR, 4th Ser.*, 7 (1903) 457-477.

Henry A. Redpath, "A New Theory as to the Use of the Divine Names in the Pentateuch," *AJT* 8 (1904) 286-301.

T. H. Weir, "The Koran and the 'Books of Moses'," *Exp, 6th Ser.*, 9 (1904) 349-358.

George Macloskie, "The Core of the Pentateuch," *USR* 16 (1904-05) 205-214.

Camden M. Cobern, "Early Bible Narratives Reinterpreted," *HR* 50 (1905) 343-347. [I. The New Light and the New Interpretation]

*William Henry Green, "The Use of 'Elohim' and 'Jehovah' in the Pentateuch," *CFL, 3rd Ser.*, 4 (1906) 258-265, 337-343.

James Orr, "A Few Words on My Critics," *CFL, 3rd Ser.*, 5 (1906) 355-363.

H. D. L., "Dialogues on Scriptural Subjects: The Pentateuch," *IER, 4th Ser.*, 20 (1906) 300-308, 442-453; 21 (1907) 35-45, 344-354; 22 (1907) 15-29, 576-586; 23 (1908) 152-160; 24 (1908) 191-200.

Fulcranus Vigouroux and P. Laurentius Janssens, "The Roman Church and Biblical Criticism," *MR* 88 (1906) 816-817.

Anonymous, "The Battle of the Critics," *MR* 88 (1906) 827-830.

Anonymous, "The Vatican and the Pentateuch," *MR* 88 (1906) 991-992.

G. B. M. Coore, "The Papal Commission and the Pentateuch," *ET* 18 (1906-07) 285-286.

Anonymous, "Editorial Notes. The Papal Commission and the Pentateuch," *ICMM* 3 (1906-07) 227-229.

Wm. M. McPheeters, "The Middle Books of the Pentateuch (Exodus, Leviticus, Numbers). An Attempt to Determine the Theme and to Outline the Course of the Thought," *CFL, 3rd Ser.*, 6 (1907) 11-16.

Alexander Patterson, "The Historical Evidence for the Pentateuch," *CFL, 3rd Ser.*, 7 (1907) 12-14. *(Editorial Note)*

Anonymous, "Dr. McKim's Book, 'The Problem of the Pentateuch'," *CFL, 3rd Ser.*, 6 (1907) 55-58. *(Review)*

Joseph D. Wilson, "Professor McFadyen's Untenable Criticism of the Pentateuch," *CFL, 3rd Ser.,* 7 (1907) 74-77.

Anonymous, "False Estimates of 'Leviticus and Numbers'," *CFL, 3rd Ser.,* 7 (1907) 176-178. *(Editorial Note)*

J. L. Campbell, "One of the Recent Books: Mr. Wiener's 'Essays in Pentateuchal Criticism'," *CFL, 3rd Ser.,* 13 (1910) 115-116. *(Review)*

Harold M. Wiener, "The Legal Study of the Pentateuch," *R&E* 7 (1910) 214-228.

Harold M. Wiener, "Some Aspects in the Conservative Task in Pentateuchal Criticism," *BS* 68 (1911) 1-12.

*Hugh Pope, "The Oxyrhynchus Papyri and Pentateuchal Criticism," *ITQ* 6 (1911) 145-157.

Anonymous, "The Latest in Pentateuchal Criticism," *MR* 93 (1911) 473-476.

*Hugh Pope, "The Temple of Jahu in Syene and Pentateuchal Criticism," *AER* 47 (1912) 291-303.

J. S. Griffiths, "Moderate Criticism," *BS* 69 (1912) 88-99. *(Review)*

Harold M. Wiener, "Some Aspects of the Conservative Task in Pentateuchal Criticism (II.)," *BS* 69 (1912) 310-328.

Johannes Dahse, "New Methods of Inquiry Concerning the Pentateuch," *BS* 69 (1912) 657-663. *(Trans. by Karl Fredrick Geiser)*

Harold M. Wiener, "The Recensional Criticism of the Pentateuch," *BS* 70 (1913) 278-290.

Hugh Pope, "Where are we in Pentateuchal Criticism?" *ITQ* 8 (1913) 375-398; 10 (1915) 20-37.

*Morris Jastrow Jr., "Wine in the Pentateuchal Code," *JAOS* 33 (1913) 180-192.

W. H. Bennett, "Pentateuchal Criticism. A Review," *JMUEOS* #3 (1913-14) 83-85. *(Review)*

Harold M. Wiener, "Dr. Driver on the Names of God in the Pentateuch," *BS* 71 (1914) 478-483.

Harold M. Wiener, "Historical Criticism of the Pentateuch. A Reply to Dr. Koenig," *BS* 71 (1914) 593-664. *[Part I]*

E[duard] König, "A Statement Concerning My Participation in the Present Discussion of Modern Pentateuchal Criticism," *BS* 71 (1914) 678-679.

*Harold M. Wiener, "Historical Criticism of the Pentateuch. A Reply to Dr. Koenig (II.)," *BS* 72 (1915) 83-153. [II. The Samaritan Pentateuch, pp. 83-96; The Critical Value of the Septuagint, pp. 96-105; Some Inferior Readings in the Massoretic Text, pp. 105-111; Rival Views of Textual History, pp. 111-153]

Harold M. Wiener, "Professor Lofthouse and the Criticism of the Pentateuch," *BS* 72 (1915) 475-500.

Harold M. Wiener, "First Step's in the Study of Glossing," *BS* 72 (1915) 602-617.

M[ilton] S. Terry, "The Pentateuch," *CFL, 3rd Ser.,* 19 (1915) 24-25.

W. F. Lofthouse, "The Criticism of the Pentateuch: A Reply to H. M. Wiener," *BS* 73 (1916) 90-113.

Harold M. Wiener, "Professor Lofthouse and the Criticism of the Pentateuch (II.)," *BS* 73 (1916) 114-136.

Harold M. Wiener, "Professor Lofthouse and the Criticism of the Pentateuch (III.)," *BS* 73 (1916) 214-260.

Frederic Perry Noble, "Negative Criticism of Destructive Critics," *BS* 73 (1916) 396-421.

Harold M. Wiener, "Professor Eiselen on the Books of the Pentateuch," *BS* 74 (1917) 312-320. *(Review)*

M[elvin] G[rove] Kyle, "A New Solution of the Pentateuch Problem," *JBL* 36 (1917) 31-47.

Melvin Grove Kyle, "A New Solution of the Pentateuchal Problem," *BS* 75 (1918) 31-69, 195-212.

W. H. Griffith Thomas, "The Unity of the Pentateuch," *BS* 75 (1918) 150-157. *(Review)*

Harold M. Wiener, "Contributions to a New Theory of the Composition of the Pentateuch," *BS* 75 (1918) 80-103, 237-266. *[Parts I and II]*

Harold M. Wiener, "Observations on Dr. Kyle's Solution of the Pentateuchal Problem," *BS* 75 (1918) 451-456.

Henry Preserved Smith, "Moses and Muhammad," *AJT* 23 (1919) 519-524.

Harold M. Wiener, "Contributions to a New Theory of the Composition of the Pentateuch (III.)," *BS* 76 (1919) 193-220.

*Cuthbert Lattey, "The Chronology of the Pentateuch," *IER, 5th Ser.,* 13 (1919) 1-13.

*Gilbert Binns, "The Religion of the Pentateuch," *IER, 5th Ser.,* 14 (1919) 101-114.

A. Marx, "Number of Letters in the Pentateuch," *JBL* 38 (1919) 24-29.

Robert Dick Wilson, "The Use of 'God' and 'Lord' in the Koran," *PTR* 17 (1919) 644-650.

Harold M. Wiener, "Contributions to a New Theory of the Composition of the Pentateuch (IV.)," *BS* 77 (1920) 305-328.

Harold M. Wiener, "Contributions to a New Theory of the Composition of the Pentateuch (V.)," *BS* 77 (1920) 369-403.

G. F[rederick] W[right], "The Mistakes of Driver," *CFL, 3rd Ser.,* 26 (1920) 452.

Leander S. Keyser, "Dr. Kyle's 'The Problem of the Pentateuch'," *BS* 78 (1921) 103-109. *(Review)*

*W. H. Griffith Thomas, "The Church and the Old Testament," *CFL, 3rd Ser.,* 29 (1923) 217-221.

Christopher R. North, "The Higher Criticism and the Pentateuch," *LQHR* 140 (1923) 253-255.

Melvin Grove Kyle, "The Problem of the Pentateuch from the Standpoint of the Archaeologist," *JTVI* 56 (1924) 21-34. [(Discussion, pp. 34-37) (Communications by A. T. Schofield, p.37; David Anderson-Berry, p. 37; A. H. Finn, pp. 38-39)]

*A. T. Richardson, "Time-Measures of the Pentateuch," *ET* 39 (1927-28) 515-519.

*A. T. Richardson, "'Time-Measures of the Pentateuch'," *ET* 41 (1929-30) 45-46.

G. Ch. Aalders, "The Turn of the Tide in Pentateuchal Criticism," *EQ* 2 (1930) 3-13.

*A. McCaig, "The Use of the Divine Names in the Pentateuch," *EQ* 2 (1930) 14-31.

A. L. Lumb, "The Higher Criticism of the Pentateuch—Re-examined," *EQ* 3 (1931) 139-156, 297-306; 4 (1932) 79-112.

Walter A. Maier, "A Typical Instance of Exaggeration in the Modern Literary Criticism of the Pentateuch," *CTM* 3 (1932) 258-262.

Joseph Rauch, "Torah," *YCCAR* 45 (1935) 246-259.

J. Battersby Harford, "Some Outstanding Old Testament Problems. IX. Problems of the Pentateuch," *ET* 47 (1935-36) 488-494.

Jacob Mann, "A Commentary to the Pentateuch a La Rashi's," *HUCA* 15 (1940) 497-527.

*C. T. Fritsch, "Anti-Anthropomorphisms in the First Five Books of the Septuagint," *JBL* 61 (1942) ix.

Edward Robertson, "The Riddle of the Torah: Suggesting a Solution," *BJRL* 27 (1942-43) 359-383.

John Mauchline, "Singular and Plural Forms of Address in the Legal Sections of the Pentateuch," *GUOST* 11 (1942-44) 20-25.

*Hyman Klein, "Mekilta on the Pentateuch," *JQR, N.S.*, 35 (1944-45) 421-434.

Edward Robinson, "The Pentateuch Problem: Some New Aspects," *BJRL* 29 (1945-46) 121-142.

*J. K. Mikliszanski, "The Law of Retaliation and the Pentateuch," *JBL* 66 (1947) 295-303.

Charles M. Cooper, "The Relevance of Recent Pentateuch Criticism," *LCQ* 21 (1948) 369-382.

*John Bowman, "Prophets and Prophecy in Talmud and Midrash," *EQ* 22 (1950) 107-114, 205-220, 255-275. [III. The Prophets and the Law, pp. 255-275]

*G. W. Anderson, "Some Aspects of the Uppsala School of Old Testament Study," *HTR* 43 (1950) 239-256. [III. The Problem of the Pentateuch, pp. 253-256]

G. Ernest Wright, "Recent European Study in the Pentateuch," *JAAR* 18 (1950) 216-225.

*J. Bowman, "The Exegesis of the Pentateuch among the Samaritans and among the Rabbis," *OTS* 8 (1950) 220-262.

D. R. Ap-Thomas, "Living Issues in Biblical Scholarship. Pentateuchal Criticism: Some Recent Trends," *ET* 62 (1950-51) 67-71.

Ovid R. Sellers, "A Half-Century of Pentateuchal Study," *McQ* 7 (1953-54) #6, 6-9.

*G. R. Driver, "Technical Terms in the Pentateuch," *WO* 2 (1954-59) 254-263. [I. גַּבְלוּת 'welding'; II. חֹשֵׁב 'embroiderer'; חֵשֶׁב 'band'; III. כָּלִיל 'woven in one piece'; IV. מָר־דְּרוֹר; V. קִדָּה 'cassia in strips' and קְצִיעָה 'powdered cassia'; VI. שָׁבֵץ 'lined, quilted']

*D. W. Watts, "The People of God. A Study of the Doctrine in the Pentateuch," *ET* 67 (1955-56) 232-237.

M. H. Segal, "The Unitary Character of the Pentateuch," *Tarbiz* 25 (1955-56) #1, I-III.

*Eugene H. Maly, "Genesis 12, 10-20; 20, 1-18; 26, 7-11 and the Pentateuchal Question," *CBQ* 18 (1956) 255-262.

Arthur Soffer, "'The House of God/Lord' in the Septuagint of the Pentateuch," *JBL* 75 (1956) 144-145.

*G. R. Driver, "Three Technical Terms in the Pentateuch," *JSS* 2 (1956) 97-105. [I. מַזְאֵל 'Jagged Rocks, Precipice'; II. אזכרה 'Token'; III. תנופה 'Special Contribution']

*G. G. Garner, "Writing in the Ancient World: Writing and the Books of Moses," *AT* 1 (1956-57) #1, 14-16.

*Solomon Zeitlin, "The Book of 'Jubilees' and the Pentateuch," *JQR, N.S,* 48 (1957-58) 218-235.

*John C. L. Gibson, "Observations on Some Important Ethnic Terms in the Pentateuch," *JNES* 20 (1961) 217-238. [Canaanites, pp. 217-220; Amonites, pp. 220-224; Hittites, pp. 224-227; Hurrians, pp. 227-229; Arameans, pp. 229-234; Hebrews, pp. 234-237; Conclusion, pp. 237-238]

*Ezra Shereshevsky, "The Significance of Rashi's Commentary on the Pentateuch," *JQR, N.S.,* 54 (1963-64) 58-79.

R. J. Coggins, "A Century of Pentateuchal Criticism," *CQR* 166 (1965) 149-161.

R. J. Coggins, "A Century of Pentateuchal Criticism, II," *CQR* 166 (1965) 413-425.

E. Schaller, "The Pentateuch and Its Critics," *JTLC* 6 (1966) #4, 2-11; #5, 6-16; 7 (1967) #1, 12-19, #2, 14-22, #3, 13-19.

Norman E. Wagner, "Pentateuchal Criticism: No Clear Future," *CJT* 13 (1967) 225-232.

*Basil De Pinto, "The Torah and the Psalms," *JBL* 86 (1967) 154-174.

*B. J. van der Merwe, "Judah in the Pentateuch," *TEP* 1 (1968) 37-52.

*R. N. Whybray, "The Joseph Story and Pentateuchal Criticism," *VT* 18 (1968) 522-528.

D. D. Leslie, "The Judaeo-Persian Colophons to the Pentateuch of the K'ai-Feng Jews," *Abr-N* 8 (1968-69) 1-35.

*C. D. Jathanna, "The Covenant and Covenant Making in Pentateuch," *BTF* 3 (1969-71) #1, 27-54.

§296 **3.2.9.1 *Studies Concerning Date, Authorship, Language,***
       and Authenticity [See also: The Documentary
       Hypothesis §302→]

Pamphilus, "Observations relating to the Inspiration of Moses," *TRep* 4 (1784) 27-38.

†H. A., "Longevity of the Patriarchs proved," *MMBR* 34 (1812-13) 121-123. *[Authorship]*

Anonymous, "Wolf's Anti-Homeric Theory, as applied to the Pentateuch," *PRev* 6 (1834) 490-504.

C. E. Stowe, "Authenticity of the Pentateuch," *LTR* 2 (1835) 171-193.

[Ernst Wilhelm] Hengstenberg, "Causes of the Denial of the Mosaic Origin of the Pentateuch," *BRCR* 11 (1838) 416-448; 12 (1838) 458-491.

B. B. Edwards, "Remarks on the Authenticity and Genuineness of the Pentateuch," *BS* 2 (1845) 356-398, 668-682.

Anonymous, "The Genuineness of the Pentateuch," *SPR* 4 (1850-51) 256-294. *(Review)*

Anonymous, "The Authenticity and Genuineness of the Pentateuch," *BFER* 2 (1853) 57-95.

S[amuel] C. Bartlett, "Authorship of the Pentateuch," *BS* 20 (1863) 799-855; 21 (1864) 495-550, 725-751.

Samuel C. Bartlett, "Authorship of the Pentateuch," *BFER* 13 (1864) 803-846.

W. E. Manley, "The Genuineness and Authenticity of the Books of Moses," *UQGR, N.S.,* 2 (1865) 336-349. *(Review)*

W. Lindsay Alexander, "Age and Authorship of the Pentateuch," *ThE* 6 (1869) 215-235.

James Macgregor, "Age of the Pentateuch, with special reference to Revelation and Inspiration," *BFER* 26 (1877) 254-274.

Wm. Henry Green, "Genuineness of the Pentateuch," *PR, 4th Ser.,* 1 (1878) 143-149.

R. P. Stebbins, "A Study of the Pentateuch," *URRM* 11 (1879) 128-160, 254-279; 12 (1879) 244-267, 515-545. [Introduction; Part I. The External Evidence Concluded; II. The Internal Evidence of its Age; II. Internal Evidence Concluded]

A. M. Wilson, "The Authorship of the Pentateuch—Examination of Robertson Smith's Theory," *ERG, 7th Ser.,* 4 (1881-82) 24-39, 73-85.

R. P. Stebbins, "The Mosaic Origin of the Pentateuch," *ONTS* 2 (1882-83) 88.

George H. Schodde, "Christ's Testimony of Moses," *LQ* 13 (1883) 337-346.

*R. P. Stebbins, "Did Ezra Write or Amend any Portion of the Pentateuch?" *URRM* 20 (1883) 221-229.

R. Payne-Smith, "The Mosaic Authorship of the Pentateuch," *JCP* 3 (1883-84) 75-104.

*R. P. Stebbins, "Did Ezra Write or Amend any Portion of the Pentateuch?" *ONTS* 3 (1883-84) 234-240.

*R. P. Stebbins, "Did the Prophet Ezekiel Write or Edit or Remodel any Portion of the Pentateuch?" *ONTS* 3 (1883-84) 289-295.

*Newell Woolsey Wells, "Ante-Nicene Fathers and the Mosaic Origin of the Pentateuch," *JLTQ* 1 (1884) 467-472.

Charles R. Hemphill, "Christ's Testimony to the Mosaic Authorship of the Pentateuch," *SPR* 35 (1884) 120-136.

*William Henry Green, "Hosea viii. 12 and Its Testimony to the Pentateuch," *PR* 7 (1886) 585-608.

Reginald Stuart Poole, "The Date of the Pentateuch: Theory and Facts," *ContR* 52 (1887) 350-369.

W. Robertson Smith, "Archæology and the Date of the Pentateuch," *ContR* 52 (1887) 490-503.

J. Hellmuth, "The Authenticity and Genuineness of the Pentateuch," *EN* 1 (1889) 193-199.

Henry P[reserved] Smith, "Christ and the Pentateuch," *ONTS* 10 (1890) 327-333.

*Alfred H. Kellogg, "The Egypticity of the Pentateuch, an Argument for its Traditional Authorship," *PRR* 1 (1890) 533-555.

C. G. Montefiore, "Recent Criticism on Moses and the Pentateuchal Narratives of the Decalogue," *JQR* 3 (1890-91) 251-291.

John Burton, "Mosaic and Mosaic," *CMR* 3 (1891) 35-44. *[Authorship of the Pentateuch]*

Owen H. Gates, "Klostermann's 'Contributions to the History of the Origin of the Pentateuch'," *ONTS* 12 (1891) 163-169. *(Review)*

*C. H. Waller, "The Order of the Law and the History of the Exodus, and its Bearing on the Authorship of the Pentateuch," *TML* 5 (1891) 1-13.

*C. H. Waller, "Is Genesis a Compilation After All? *and What is its Real Relation to the Remainder of the Pentateuch?*" *TML* 5 (1891) 289-300.

J. Aidan Howlett, "The Mosaic Authorship of the Pentateuch," *DR* 110 (1892) 264-281.

Joseph M'Rory *(MacRory)*, "Did Moses Write the Pentateuch?" *IER, 3rd Ser.*, 13 (1892) 481-489, 978-989; 14 (1893) 45-58, 289-306.

W. P. McKee, "Did Jesus Intend to Teach that Moses Wrote the Pentateuch?" *ONTS* 14 (1892) 151-153.

F. W. C. Meyer, "Altered View of a Biblical Text-Book," *ONTS* 15 (1892) 76.

*H.   Osgood,   "Jean   Astruc,"   *PRR*   3   (1892)   83-102.

*J. William Dawson, "Physical and Historical Probabilities Respecting the Authorship and Authority of the Mosaic Books," *Exp, 4th Ser.*, 9 (1894) 16-33, 109-123, 276-288, 362-375, 440-451. [*(I. untitled)* II. The Book of Genesis; III. Early Man and Eden; IV. Antediluvians and the Deluge; V. The Dispersion and Abraham]

J. W. Dawson, "Physical and Historical Probabilities Respecting the Authorship and Authority of the Mosaic Books: 6. The Exodus," *Exp, 4th Ser.*, 10 (1894) 161-179.

David Benjamin, "The Authenticity of the Pentateuch," *IER, 3rd Ser.*, 15 (1894) 682-693, 769-787.

*Edward Mack, "The Theology of Hosea and Amos, as a Witness to the Age of the Pentateuch," *PQ* 8 (1894) 512-530.

*E. P. Boys-Smith, "Apostolic and Critical Teaching on the Position of the Pentateuch," *ET* 7 (1895-96) 295-303.

Geo[rge] H. Schodde, "Biblical Research Notes. A Defense of Moses," *ColTM* 17 (1897) 373-374.

Geo[rge] H. Schodde, "Biblical Research Notes. Defender of Moses," *ColTM* 18 (1898) 63-64.

Anonymous, "Historicity and Mosaic Origin of the Pentateuch," *HR* 40 (1900) 162-164.

S. G. Youngert, "Who wrote the Pentateuch? An historical Review and biblical Answer," *TTKF* 4 (1902) 42-52.

S. L. Bowman, "Attack upon the Mosaic Authorship of the Pentateuch," *CFL, 3rd Ser.,* 1 (1904) 277-282.

A. J. Maas, "The Mosaic Authorship of the Pentateuch and the Biblical Commission," *AER* 35 (1906) 379-388.

Anonymous, "Determining Literary Authorship," *CFL, 3rd Ser.,* 5 (1906) 157-158. *[Authorship of the Pentateuch]*

William Henry Green, "The Pentateuchal Codes and Their Mosaic Origin," *CFL, 3rd Ser.,* 7 (1907) 155-156.

*James Oscar Boyd, "Ezekiel and the Modern Dating of the Pentateuch," *PTR* 6 (1908) 29-51.

*E. C. Richardson, "Documents of the Exodus, Contemporary, Original, and Written," *PTR* 10 (1912) 581-605.

W. R. W. Gardner, "Did Moses Write the Pentateuch in Babylonian Cuneiform?" *ET* 25 (1913-14) 526-527.

John H. Raven, "The Mosaic Authorship of the Pentateuch," *CFL, 3rd Ser.,* 18 (1914) 200-205; 19 (1915) 3-7.

Harold M. Wiener, "Pentateuchal Legislation. *Evidence of Mosaic Authenticity,*" *CFL, 3rd Ser.,* 19 (1915) 22-23.

Milton S. Terry, "The Pentateuch. *Positive Evidences of Mosaic Origin,*" *CFL, 3rd Ser.,* 19 (1915) 126-127.

Anonymous, "Was the Pentateuch Written in Hebrew?" *MR* 97 (1915) 642-646.

*J. S. Ross, "Methodist Higher Criticism Arm-in-Arm with Infidelity," *CFL, 3rd Ser.,* 21 (1916) 116-118. [II. Did Moses Write the Pentateuch? p. 117]

*W. F. Lofthouse, "The Mosaic Codes and Popular Hebrew Religion," *Exp, 8th Ser.,* 11 (1916) 66-80.

A. H. Finn, "The Mosaic Origin of the Pentateuch," *JTVI* 50 (1918) 32-50, 54-55. [(Letters by A. F. Kirkpatrick, pp. 50-51; Moses Gaster, pp. 51-53) (Discussion, pp. 53-54) (Communications by R. B. Gridlestone, p. 55; J. J. Lias, pp. 55-57)]

D. J. Satterfield, "Who Wrote the Pentateuch?" *CFL, 3rd Ser.,* 26 (1920) 241-243.

G. F[rederick] W[right], "Moses and the Monuments," *CFL, 3rd Ser.,* 26 (1920) 297-298. *(Review)*

E[dward] J. K[issane], "M. Touzard on Moses and Joshua," *ITQ* 15 (1920) 67-70, 271-272. *(Review)*

H. W. Congdon, "The Hand of Moses," *CFL, 3rd Ser.,* 27 (1921) 254-256.

H. M. DuBose, "The Mosaic Authorship of the Pentateuch," *AQ* 4 (1925) 372.

H. M. DuBose, "A Constructive Bible Science," *BR* 10 (1925) 491-512.

*John E. McFadyen, "The Language of the Pentateuch in its Relation to Egyptian," *ET* 41 (1929-30) 54-58.

*James B. Johnston, "The Chariot and the Pentateuch," *EQ* 3 (1931) 168-171.

James M. Vosté, "Papal Biblical Commission," *ACR* 25 (1948) 180-183. *[Authorship of the Pentateuch]*

*James (Jacques) M. Voste, "A Response of the Biblical Commission," *CBQ* 10 (1948) 318-323. *[Authorship of the Pentateuch]*

Richard T. Murphy, "Moses and the Pentateuch," *CBQ* 11 (1949) 165-178.

W. M: Valk, "Moses and the Pentateuch. A New Approach to an Old Problem," *Scrip* 5 (1952-53) 60-67.

J. Stafford Wright, "Some Thoughts on the Composition of the Pentateuch," *EQ* 25 (1953) 2-16.

*A. Murtonen, "The Fixation in Writings of Various Parts of the Pentateuch," *VT* 3 (1953) 46-53.

Jakob J. Petchowski, "The Supposed Dogma of Mosaic Authorship of the Pentateuch," *HJ* 57 (1958-59) 356-360.

*David Noel Freedman, "The Law and the Prophets," *VTS* 9 (1963) 250-265.

G. Van Groningen, "An Apologetic Approach to Mosaic Authorship," *VR* #11 (1968) 9-21.

§297 *3.2.9.2 Origins and Sources of the Pentateuch* *- General Studies*

Samuel Ives Curtis, "Delitzsch on the Origin and Composition of the Pentateuch," *PR* 3 (1882) 553-588.

Lewis B[ayles] Paton, "Klostermann on the Origin of the Pentateuch," *PRR* 2 (1891) 318-322.

*W. St. Chad Boscawen, "The Hebrew Legend of Civilisation in the Light of Recent Discovery," *ET* 5 (1893-94) 351-356.

Paul Haupt, "The Origin of the Pentateuch," *JAOS* 16 (1896) cii-ciii.

[A. A. Berle], "Cuneiform Originals of the Pentateuch," *BS* 53 (1896) 163-164.

William F. Warren, "The Origin of the Pentateuch," *BW* 18 (1901) 194-196.

F. P. Ramsay, "Concerning the Origin of the Pentateuch," *USR* 16 (1904-05) 129-133.

Anonymous, "'The Origin of the Pentateuch'," *CFL, 3rd Ser.,* 14 (1911-12) 205-207. *(Review)*

Th. Graebner, "Little Journey in the Higher Anticriticism. I The Myth Hypothesis," *TM* 1 (1921) 297-303, 321-329, 359-365.

E. Herman, "A New Theory of the Origin of the Pentateuch: M. Naville's Hypothesis Untenable," *HR* 87 (1924) 28.

*Menahem Haran, "The Nature of the ' 'Ohel Mo'edh' in Pentateuchal Sources," *JSS* 5 (1960) 50-65.

Michael M. Winter, "Reflections on the Sources of the Pentateuch," *Scrip* 12 (1960) 78-89.

§298 *3.2.9.3 Backgrounds of the Pentateuch - General Studies*

*Anonymous, "The Historical Geography of Arabia; or the Patriarchal Evidence of Revealed Religion: a Memoir, with illustrative Maps," *QRL* 74 (1844) 325-358. *(Review)*

†Anonymous, "Forster's Historical Geography of Arabia; or the Patriarchal Evidences of Revealed Religion," *ERL* 3 (1845) 36-68. *(Review)*

C[laude] R. Conder, "Archæology of the Pentateuch," *SRL* 26 (1895) 63-92.

A. H. Sayce, "An Archaeologist on the Pentateuch," *ET* 16 (1904-05) 138-140.

*Anonymous, "The Masai and Higher Criticism," *MR* 87 (1905) 810-815.

Stanley A. Cook, "Notes on Old Testament History, VI, The Calebite Tradition," *JQR* 19 (1906-07) 168-184.

C[yrus] H. Gordon, "Homer, Caphtor and Canaan, *AAI* 1 (1955) 139-146.

*John C. L. Gibson, "Observations on Some Important Ethnic Terms in the Pentateuch," *JNES* 20 (1961) 217-238. [Canaanites; Amorites; Hittites; Hurrians; Arameans; Hebrews; Conclusion]

*H. D. Beeby, "The Old Testament and the Redemption of Culture," *SEAJT* 8 (1966-67) #4, 17-28.

§299 *3.2.9.3.1 Assyrian and Babylonian Backgrounds to the Pentateuch*

Wm. Henry Green, "Assyrian Monuments and the Bible," *PQPR* 3 (1874) 389-413.

J. L. Porter, "Exploration as Verifying Revelation," *PR, 4th Ser.*, 2 (1878) 1-32. *[Babylonian Background to the Pentateuch]*

*C. J. Ball, "Israel and Babylon," *SBAP* 16 (1893-94) 188-200.

*W. W. Moore, "The Cuneiform Corroborations of the Early Narratives of Genesis," *USR* 6 (1894-95) 38-48.

John D. Davis, "Archaeology and the Sabbath School Lessons," *CFL, N.S.*, 4 (1901) 46-56. [The Assyro-Babylonian Story of Creation; The Six Days of Creation; Assyrian Tradition of the Deluge and Pentateuchal Criticism]

John Tuckwell, "'Cuneiform Versions of Bible Stories'," *CFL, 3rd Ser.*, 9 (1908) 250.

*A. H. Sayce, "Adam and Sargon in the Land of the Hittites," *SBAP* 37 (1915) 227-245.

I. O Northstein, "Israel and Babylon," *AQ* 7 (1928) 271-273.

*Michael C. Astour, "Political and Cosmic Symbolism in Genesis 14 and in its Babylonian Sources," *LIST* 3 (1966) 65-112. [1. When and By Whom Was Genesis 14 Written? pp. 65-74; 2. The Personal and Geographical Names in Genesis 14, pp. 74-81; 3. The Characters and Historical References in the "Chedorlaomer Texts", pp. 81-100; 4. Religious Philosophy of History and Cosmic Symbolism, pp. 100-109]

§300 *3.2.9.3.2 Egyptian Backgrounds to the Pentateuch*

[William] Jowett, "Biblical Illustrations," *MR* 7 (1824) 20-23. *[Egyptian Background]*

†Anonymous, "Egypt and the Books of Moses," *ERL* 3 (1845) 387-407. *(Review)*

A. Sutherland, "Egypt and the Pentateuch," *MR* 57 (1875) 221-240.

A. Sutherland, "Egypt and the Pentateuch," *DTQ* 2 (1876) 161-173.

*G. Lansing, "The Pentateuch—Egypticity and Authenticity," *Exp, 3rd Ser.,* 8 (1888) 219-231, 307-317.

A. H. Sayce, "Light on the Pentateuch from Egyptology," *HR* 32 (1896) 195-200.

Anonymous, "Israel and the Egyptian Monuments," *MR* 78 (1896) 976-979.

M. G. Kyle, "Egyptiological Notes," *RP* 4 (1905) 32. *[The Flood Story in Egypt]*

Anonymous, "The Accurate Use of Egyptian Terms in the Pentateuch," *CFL, 3rd Ser.,* 6 (1907) 51-52.

Fayette L. Thompson, "The Egypticity of the Pentateuch," *CFL, 3rd Ser.,* 6 (1907) 364-367.

*A. M. Skelly, "The Inscriptions of Sinai and Their Relation to Certain Facts of Scripture," *ACQR* 37 (1912) 678-692.

*Anonymous, "Archaeological Notes," *HR* 65 (1913) 464-465. [Egypt and the Bible, p. 464]

Anonymous, "New Light on the Pentateuch," *HR* 82 (1921) 111. *[Egyptian Background]*

*G. A. Frank Knight, "The Identification of the Pharaohs of the Pentateuch," *JTVI* 59 (1927) 96-112, 119-120. [(Discussion, pp. 112-117) (Communications by J. A. Fleming, 117-118; G. B. Michell, pp. 118-119)]

*John E. McFadyen, "The Language of the Pentateuch in Its Relation to Egyptian," *ET* 41 (1929-30) 54-58.

§301 *3.2.9.4 Historical Reliability of the Pentateuch*

*B. B. Edwards, "Remarks on the Authenticity and Genuineness of the Pentateuch," *BS* 2 (1845) 356-398, 668-682.

Anonymous, "Historical Value of the Pentateuch," *PRev* 30 (1858) 420-435.

S. C. Bartlett, "The Historic Character of the Pentateuch," *BS* 20 (1863) 381-431.

William Henry Green, "The Genuineness of the Pentateuch," *PRev* 54 (1878) Part 1, 143-149.

G. Frederick Wright, "The Genuineness of the Pentateuch Re-established," *CFL, 3rd Ser.*, 24 (1918) 433-434.

§302 *3.2.9.5 The Documentary Hypothesis (JEDP); Graf-Wellhausen Theory; The Hexateuch - General Studies*

*Anonymous, "Remarks on Some of the Peculiarities which Distinguish the Elohim and Jehovah Documents in Genesis from Each Other," *CTPR, N.S.*, 1 (1838-39) 534-541.

H. M. Harman, "Hengstenberg on the Pentateuch," *MR* 35 (1853) 75-102. *(Review)*

*†Anonymous, "Biblical Criticism—Colenso and Davidson," *QRL* 113 (1863) 422-447. *(Review)*

Anonymous, "Dr. Colenso and the Old Testament," *IER, 1st Ser.*, 1 (1864-65) 271-283, 363-375, 513-524, 553-563. *(Review)*

Alfred Cave, "The Latest Phase of the Pentateuch Question," *BFER* 29 (1880) 248-267. *(Review)*

Archibald Duff, "The History of Research Concerning the Structure of the O.T. Historical Books," *BS* 37 (1880) 729-751.

*Alfred Cave, "Evolution and the Hebrews: A Review of Herbert Spencer's 'Hebrews and Phœnicians'," *BFER* 30 (1881) 17-39. *(Review)*

*John Urquhart, "Jehovistic and Elohistic Theories," *BFER* 31 (1882) 205-238.

Archibald Duff, "The History of Research Concerning the Structure of the O.T. Historical Books, No. II," *BS* 39 (1882) 498-519.

Henry P[reserved] Smith, "The Critical Theories of Julius Wellhausen," *DTQ, N.S.*, 1 (1882) 327-355.

S. R. Driver, "On some alleged linguistic affinities of the Elohist," *JP* 11 (1882) 201-236.

Henry P[reserved] Smith, "The Critical Theories of Julius Wellhausen," *PR* 3 (1882) 357-388.

E. Benj. Andrews, "On the New Pentateuch-Criticism," *ONTS* 2 (1882-83) 97-104.

Edwin C. Bissell, "Proposed Reconstruction of the Pentateuch," *BS* 40 (1883) 1-35, 225-245, 593-630; 41 (1884) 67-94.

Edwin C. Bissell, "Proposed Reconstruction of the Pentateuch," *DTQ, N.S.,* 2 (1883) 288-314, 523-538.

Philip H. Wicksteed, "The Literature of Israel," *ModR* 4 (1883) 1-23. *(Review)*

Edward S. Prout, "Recent Theories on the Pentateuch," *BQRL* 79 (1884) 115-143.

*Edwin C. Bissell, "The Use of עבר and its Compounds in the Hexateuch," *AJSL* 2 (1885-86) 9-12.

W. J. Deane, "The Difficulties of Scripture. No. I.," *MI* 3 (1885-86) 161-184.

W. J. Deane, "The Difficulties of Scripture. No. II.," *MI* 3 (1885-86) 346-366.

W. J. Deane, "The Difficulties of Scripture. No. III.," *MI* 3 (1885-86) 456-461.

Wm. Henry Green, "The Wellhausen Hypothesis, A Question of Vital Consequence," *ONTS* 5 (1885-86) 85-86.

S. Ives Curtiss, "Professor Julius Wellhausen and His Theory of the Pentateuch," *Exp, 3rd Ser.,* 3 (1886) 81-98.

W. J. Deane, "The Difficulties of Scripture. No. IV.," *MI* 4 (1886) 112-131.

*W[illiam] Henry Green, "The Alleged Composite Character of Exodus I., II.," *AJSL* 3 (1886-87) 1-12.

Henry P[reserved] Smith, "The Pentateuch Question,—Recent Phases," *ONTS* 6 (1886-87) 268-270.

William Henry Green, "Is the Current Critical Division of the Pentateuch Inimical to the Christian Faith?" *ONTS* 6 (1886-87) 315-318.

[N. P. Gilman], "Critical Theology. Kuenen on the Hexateuch," *URRM* 27 (1887) 261-272. *(Review)*

Benjamin Wisner Bacon, "Pentateuchal Analysis," *AJSL* 4 (1887-88) 216-243.

J. J. Stewart Perowne, "The Age of the Pentateuch," *ContR* 53 (1888) 129-144, 242-261.

Benjamin Wisner Bacon, "Pentateuchal Analysis. II.," *AJSL* 5 (1888-89) 7-17.

*William R. Harper, "The Pentateuchal Question. I. Gen. 1:1—12:5," *AJSL* 5 (1888-89) 18-73.

W[illiam] Henry Green, "The Pentateuchal Question," *AJSL* 5 (1888-89) 137-189.

*William R. Harper, "The Pentateuchal Question II. Gen. 12:6—37:1," *AJSL* 5 (1888-89) 243-291.

W[illiam] Henry Green, The Pentateuchal Question II. Gen. 12:6—37:1," *AJSL* 6 (1889-90) 109-138, 161-211.

G. A. Chadwick, "Wellhausen's *History of Israel*," *Exp, 3rd Ser.*, 10 (1889) 341-360. *(Review)*

*William R. Harper, "The Pentateuchal Question. III. Gen. 37:2—Ex. 12:51," *AJSL* 6 (1889-90) 1-48.

*William R. Harper, "The Pentateuchal Question. IV.-Historical Matter of Ex. 13—Deut. 34," *AJSL* 6 (1889-90) 241-295.

Anonymous, "The Pentateuch Controversy," *LQHR* 73 (1889-90) 261-288. *(Review)*

James Strachan, "Some Recent Hexateuch Literature," *TRFCCQ* 4 (1889-90) 203-226. *(Review)*

*Benjamin W. Bacon, "JE in the Middle Books of the Pentateuch. Analysis of Ex. 7-12," *JBL* 9 (1890) 161-200; 10 (1891) 107-130.

Anonymous, "Pentateuchal Criticism," *LQHR* 74 (1890) 289-315. *(Review)*

J. J. Lias, "Wellhausen on the Pentateuch," *TML* 3 (1890) 361-374.

J. J. Lias, "Wellhausen on the Pentateuch. Part II," *TML* 4 (1890) 145-161.

J. J. Lias, "Wellhausen on the Pentateuch. Part III," *TML* 4 (1890) 267-279.

J. J. Lias, "Wellhausen on the Pentateuch. Part IV," *TML* 4 (1890) 308-321.

W[illiam] Henry Green, "The Pentateuchal Question. III. Gen. 37:2—Ex. 12:51," *AJSL* 7 (1890-91) 1-38, 104-142.

*Benjamin W. Bacon, "Notes on the Analysis of Gen. XV," *AJSL* 7 (1890-91) 75-76.

*Benjamin W. Bacon, "The Blessing of Isaac, Gen. XXVII.—A Study in Pentateuchal Analysis," *AJSL* 7 (1890-91) 143-148.

Benjamin W. Bacon, "Notes on the Analysis of Genesis I.—XXXI," *AJSL* 7 (1890-91) 222-231.

Benjamin W. Bacon, "Notes on the Analysis of Genesis XXXII.—L," *AJSL* 7 (1890-91) 278-288.

*Alfred Cave, "Canon Driver on the Book of the Law," *ContR* 60 (1891) 892-910. *(Review)*

William Henry Green, "The Pentateuchal Question. IV. Exodus 13—Deuteronomy 34," *AJSL* 8 (1891-92) 15-64, 174-243.

*Benjamin Wisner Bacon, "Chronology of the Account of the Flood in P.—A Contribution to the History of the Jewish Calendar," *AJSL* 8 (1891-92) 79-88.

A. R. S. Kennedy, "Canon Driver and the Pentateuch," *ET* 3 (1891-92) 72-75.

N. L. Walker, "Professor Green on the Pentateuch," *ET* 3 (1891-92) 316-318.

*J. S. Bryan, "Murphy's Genesis and the Documentary Hypothesis," *MQR, 3rd Ser.,* 11 (1891-92) 95-103.

*C. R. Brown, "Do the Literary Postulates of Hexateuch Criticism have any Parallels in other Books of the Old Testament?" *AR* 18 (1892) 205-220.

S. R. Driver, "Principal Cave on the Hexateuch," *ContR* 61 (1892) 262-278.

†Anonymous, "Wellhausen on the History of Israel," *ERCJ* 176 (1892) 58-80. *(Review)*

C. van den Biesen, "The Authorship and Composition of the Hexateuch," *DR* 111 (1892) 245-267; 112 (1893) 40-65.

*Benjamin W. Bacon, "JE in the Middle Books of the Pentateuch. Analysis of Ex. 12:37-17:16," *JBL* 11 (1892) 177-200.

*Benjamin W. Bacon, "JE in the Middle Books of the Pentateuch. Sinai-Horeb: Analysis of Ex. 18-34," *JBL* 12 (1893) 23-46.

William Henry Green, "Dr. Briggs' Higher Criticism of the Hexateuch," *PRR* 4 (1893) 529-561. *(Review)*

H. A. White, "The Original Manuscript of the Pentateuch," *PQ* 8 (1894) 392-403.

*Thomas Whitelaw, "Ezekiel and the Priests' Code," *PRR* 5 (1894) 434-453.

Anonymous, "The Present State of the Pentateuch Controversy," *LQHR* 84 (1895) 31-54. *(Review)*

W[illiam] M. McPheeters, "Dr. Briggs' Higher Criticism of the Hexateuch," *PQ* 9 (1895) 505-528.

*Edwin Cone Bissell, "Origin and Composition of Genesis. History of the Criticism to the Rise of the Grafian Hypothesis," *PRR* 6 (1895) 1-25.

Arthur S. Peake, "Wellhausen and Dr. Baxter," *ET* 7 (1895-96) 400-405.

W. L. Baxter, "Professor Peake on the Reply to Wellhausen," *ET* 7 (1895-96) 505-512.

A[rthur] S. Peake, "A Reply to Dr. Baxter," *ET* 7 (1895-96) 559-564.

F. W. Farrar, "Professor Sayce and the Higher Criticism," *Exp, 5th Ser.,* 3 (1896) 30-48.

*Henry Preserved Smith, "Sources E and J in the Books of Samuel," *JBL* 15 (1896) 1-8.

Wm. L. Baxter, "Professor Peake and Wellhausen," *ET* 8 (1896-97) 47.

G. Harford-Battersby*[sic]*, [J. Battersby Harford(?)] "Professor Sayce on Pentateuchal Criticism," *ET* 8 (1896-97) 91.

Arthur S. Peake, "Dr. Baxter and Wellhausen," *ET* 8 (1896-97) 93-94.

G. Buchanan Gray, "The Character of the Proper Names in the Priestly Code: A Reply to Professor Hommel," *Exp, 5th Ser.,* 6 (1897) 173-190.

Anonymous, "Composition of the Pentateuch," *MR* 79 (1897) 137-140.

Amos Kidder Fiske, "The Unknown Homer of the Hebrews," *NW* 6 (1897) 32-38. *[The Yahwist]*

J. A. Selbie, "The 'Higher Criticism'," *ET* 9 (1897-98) 273-274.

*W. H. Bennett, "The Book of Joshua and the Pentateuch," *JQR* 10 (1897-98) 649-653.

Joseph Bruneau, "Biblical Criticism. 1-6," *AER* 19 (1898) 383-390.

G. Frederick Wright, "Dr. Driver's Proof-Texts," *BS* 55 (1898) 515-525; 56 (1899) 140-147.

Henry Hayman, "The Higher Criticism Applied to a 'Modern Instance'," *BS* 55 (1898) 557-561.

G. Finke, "Documents in the Pentateuch," *ColTM* 18 (1898) 233-235.

Samuel Colcord Bartlett, "The Scientific Results of the Analysis of the Hexateuch," *HR* 36 (1898) 395-402.

T. McK. Stuart, "The Hypothetical Old Testament," *MR* 80 (1898) 534-542.

*James Brown, "The Germ of Astruc's Theory," *ET* 10 (1898-99) 91-92.

J. A. Selbie, "Critics and Apologists," *ET* 10 (1898-99) 221-222.

William R. Harper, "The Priestly Element in the Old Testament as Seen in the Laws," *BW* 14 (1899) 258-266.

*Willis J. Beecher, "The Books of the Old Testament versus Their Sources," *BS* 56 (1899) 209-222.

*P[arke] P. Flournoy, "'The Books of the Old Testament Versus Their Sources'," *CFL, O.S.,* 3 (1899) 345-348.

J. A. Selbie, "The Oxford Hexateuch," *ET* 11 (1899-1900) 526-528. *(Review)*

W[illiam] W. Everts, "The Polychrome Bible Tested by the Assyrian Flood-Tablet," *HR* 40 (1900) 124-130.

William R. Harper, "Constructive Studies in the Priestly Element in the Old Testament. I: Its General Scope," *BW* 17 (1901) 46-54.

*William R. Harper, "Constructive Studies in the Priestly Element in the Old Testament. II: The History of Worship in the Earlier Old Testament Period," *BW* 17 (1901) 121-134.

*William R. Harper, "Constructive Studies in the Priestly Element in the Old Testament. III: The History of Worship in the Middle Old Testament Period," *BW* 17 (1901) 206-220.

*William R. Harper, "Constructive Studies in the Priestly Element in the Old Testament. IV: The History of Worship in the Later Old Testament Period," *BW* 17 (1901) 366-381.

*William R. Harper, "Constructive Studies in the Priestly Element in the Old Testament. V: The Laws and Usages Concerning the Priest, Considered Comparatively," *BW* 17 (1901) 450-462.

*William R. Harper, "Constructive Studies in the Priestly Element in the Old Testament. VI: The Laws and Usages Concerning the Place of Worship, Considered Comparatively," *BW* 18 (1901) 56-63.

*William R. Harper, "Constructive Studies in the Priestly Element in the Old Testament. VII: The Laws and Usages Concerning Sacrifice, Considered Comparatively," *BW* 18 (1901) 120-130.

*William R. Harper, "Constructive Studies in the Priestly Element in the Old Testament. VIII: The Laws and Usages Concerning Feasts, Considered Comparatively," *BW* 18 (1901) 204-217.

*William R. Harper, "Constructive Studies in the Priestly Element in the Old Testament. IX: Laws and Usages Concerning the Sabbath and Kindred Institutions, Considered Comparatively," *BW* 18 (1901) 297-307.

*William R. Harper, "Constructive Studies in the Priestly Element in the Old Testament. X: The Laws and Usages Concerning Clean and Unclean, Considered Comparatively," *BW* 18 (1901) 368-379.

*Reginald Walsh, "The Rise and Progress of Higher Criticism," *IER, 4th Ser.,* 10 (1901) 498-513; 11 (1902) 16-34, 127-144, 494-523; 13 (1903) 228-245, 532-556; 15 (1904) 27-47.

W. F. Lofthouse, "The Hexateuch and the Gospels: A Parallel," *ET* 13 (1901-02) 565-567.

William R. Harper, "Constructive Studies in the Literature of Worship in the Old Testament. III. The Legal Literature—The Priestly Code," *BW* 19 (1902) 300-310.

William R. Harper, "Constructive Studies in the Literature of Worship in the Old Testament. IV. The Historical Writings of the Priestly School," *BW* 19 (1902) 443-455.

William R. Harper, "Constructive Studies in the Literature of Worship in the Old Testament. IV. The Historical Writings of the Priestly School (Continued)," *BW* 20 (1902) 48-57, 134-146.

*William Wallace Martin, "The Fall as a Composite Narrative," *BS* 60 (1903) 84-91.

George Frederick Wright, "Dr. Driver's Rope of Sand," *CFL, 3rd Ser.,* 1 (1904) 151-157.

Samuel Schwarm, "The History of the Hexateuch," *CFL, 3rd Ser.,* 1 (1904) 441.

W[illiam] W. Everts, "The Meyer-Wellhausen Controversy," *CFL, 3rd Ser.,* 1 (1904) 646-648.

*Arthur Babbitt Fairchild, "Jacob or Israel," *BS* 62 (1905) 698-712.

Jesse B. Thomas, "Misapplication of the Canons of Historical Inquiry," *CFL, 3rd Ser.,* 2 (1905) 116-120.

*Ernest Cushing Richardson, "Oral Tradition, Libraries and the Hexateuch," *LCR* 24 (1905) 511-521.

*Ernest Cushing Richardson, "Oral Tradition, Libraries and the Hexateuch. Part II," *LCR* 24 (1905) 718-725.

*Ernest Cushing Richardson, "Oral Tradition, Libraries and the Hexateuch," *PTR* 3 (1905) 191-215.

Ernest Cushing Richardson, "Oral Traditions[sic]*, Libraries and the Hexateuch. Part III," *LCR* 25 (1906) 148-155.

A. C. Dixon, "Modern Myths of Unbelief," *CFL, 3rd Ser.*, 4 (1906) 279-281.

Harold M. Wiener, "Some Fatal Weaknesses of the Wellhausen School," *BS* 64 (1907) 1-18. *(Erratum, p. viii)*

Harold M. Wiener, "Hebrew Monotheism," *BS* 64 (1907) 609-637.

George H. Schodde, "Survey of Current Critical Thought in Germany. The Beginning of the End of the Wellhausen School," *CFL, 3rd Ser.*, 6 (1907) 118-121.

Anonymous, "False 'Induction' and the Pentateuchal 'Codes'," *CFL, 3rd Ser.*, 7 (1907) 95-96. *(Editorial Note)*

James Orr, "The Problem of the Old Testament Restated," *ContR* 92 (1907) 200-212.

*T. H. Weir, "Arab and Hebrew Prose Writers," *ContR* 92 (1907) 375-380. *[Comparative Literature and Pentateuchal Criticism]*

A. H. Sayce, "The Documentary Theory of the Pentateuch. A Test Case," *HR* 54 (1907) 8-12.

*Adolf Hult, "Ezekiel and the Levitic Code," *LCR* 26 (1907) 7-19.

*Adolf Hult, "Ezekiel and the Levitic Code. Part II," *LCR* 26 (1907) 302-314.

J. F. C. Fuller, "Elohim and the Number π," *Monist* 17 (1907) 110-111.

W. F. Lofthouse, "The Old Testament Books and Their Redactors," *ET* 19 (1907-08) 63-67.

*Andrew Craig Robinson, "Lord of Hosts," *ET* 19 (1907-08) 188-189. *[JEPD]*

†*T. Witton Davies, "Traditions and Beliefs of Ancient Israel," *RTP* 3 (1907-08) 689-706. [*Subtitle:* †"The Early Traditions of Genesis", pp. 697-706]

R. C. Thomson, "Wiener's Criticism of the Wellhausen School," *GUOST* 3 (1907-12) 57.

Harold M. Wiener, "Essays in Pentateuchal Criticism," *BS* 65 (1908) 481-509, 723-754; 66 (1909) 119-170, 291-331, 411-430.

T. McK. Stuart, "'The Hexateuch'?—Is the Term Admissible?" *CFL, 3rd Ser.,* 8 (1908) 179-181.

Anonymous, "Some of the Latest German Biblical Criticism," *MR* 90 (1908) 645-649.

Anonymous, "Wellhausenism on the Wane," *MR* 90 (1908) 974-975.

Harold M. Wiener, "First Three Chapters of Wellhausen's Prolegomena," *BS* 66 (1909) 692-743.

*A[lbert] C. Knudson, "The So-called J Decalogue," *JBL* 28 (1909) 82-99.

Anonymous, "'Wellhausenism on the Wane'," *MR* 91 (1909) 646-650.

J. J. Lias, "Is the So-Called 'Priestly Code' Post-Exilic?" *BS* 67 (1910) 20-46, 299-334. *(Errata p. ii)*

Harold M. Wiener, "Priests and Levites: The Fourth Chapter of Wellhausen's Prolegomena," *BS* 67 (1910) 486-539.

Harold M. Wiener, "The Swan-song of the Wellhausen School," *BS* 67 (1910) 654-658.

Henry Gracey, "The Date of J and E, According to Professor Driver," *CFL, 3rd Ser.,* 12 (1910) 365-369.

B. D. Eerdmans, "Ezra and the Priestly Code," *Exp, 7th Ser.,* 10 (1910) 306-326. 2nd Card?

Harold M. Wiener, "Has Dr. Skinner Vindicated the Graf-Wellhausen Theory?" *Exp, 7th Ser.,* 10 (1910) 407-416.

*Harold M. Wiener, "The High Priest," *BS* 68 (1911) 159-161. *[Ref. Wellhausen's Prolegomena]*

Harold M. Wiener, "The Fifth Chapter of Wellhausen's Prolegomena," *BS* 68 (1911) 658-673.

*W. F. Lofthouse, "Kernel and Husk in Old Testament Stories," *Exp, 8th Ser.*, 1 (1911) 97-117.

William H. Bates, "A Revelation or an Evolution—Which?" *CFL, 3rd Ser.*, 14 (1911-12) 153-156.

*C. F. Burney, "The Priestly Code and the New Aramaic Papyri from Elephantine," *Exp, 8th Ser.*, 3 (1912) 97-108.

Herbert W. Magoun, "A Layman's View of the Critical Theory," *BS* 70 (1913) 56-79, 202-227, 382-407.

*Harold M. Wiener, "The Advent of Textual Criticism," *BS* 70 (1913) 145-174.

*Herbert W. Magoun, "Experiences with the Critical Theory," *CFL, 3rd Ser.*, 16 (1913) 200-201.

*John Skinner, "The Divine Names in the Genesis," *Exp, 8th Ser.*, 6 (1913) 289-313, 400-420, 494-514.

*Johannes Dahse, "Divine Appelations, Textual Criticism and Documentary Theory. My Reply to Dr. Skinner," *Exp, 8th Ser.*, 6 (1913) 481-510.

Lewis B[ayles] Paton, "A Harmony of the Hexateuch," *HSR* 23 (1913) 28-53.

H[arold] M. Wiener, "Is the Graf-Wellhausen hypothesis tenable?" *TTL* 47 (1913) 195-207.

Johannes Dahse, "Is the Documentary Theory Tenable?" *BS* 71 (1914) 95-104, 331-342.

Harold M. Wiener, "The Pentateuchal Text, the Divine Appelations, and the Documentary Theory: A Reply to Dr. Skinner," *BS* 71 (1914) 218-268.

J. J. Lias, "Is the So-Called 'Priestly Code' of Post Exilic Date?" *JTVI* 46 (1914) 63-79. (Discussion, pp. 79-86)

*G. Ch. Aalders, "The Wellhausen Theory of the Pentateuch and Textual Criticism," *BS* 71 (1914) 393-405.

W. F. Lofthouse, "Dahse vs. Wellhausen," *LQHR* (1914) 333-338.

Harold M. Wiener, "Has Professor Lofthouse Vindicated the Documentary Theory?" *LQHR* 123 (1915) 128-131. (Reply by W. F. Lofthouse, pp. 131-132)

*Harold M. Wiener, "The Mosaic Authenticity of the Pentateuchal Legislation," *LQHR* 123 (1915) 264-277. (Reply by W. F. Lofthouse, pp. 277-278)

Frederic Perry Noble, "Negative Criticism of Destructive Critics," *BS* 73 (1916) 396-421.

G. Frederick Wright, "J. E. P. R. Imposture," *CFL, 3rd Ser.,* 21 (1916) 14-17.

*H. W. Magoun, "A Lacuna in Scholarship," *BS* 74 (1917) 71-100, 284-311, 425-445, 553-580.

*T. Witton Davies, "The Priestly Code in the Historical Writings of the Old Testament and also in the Apocrypha and Pseudepigrapha," *IJA* #49 (1917) 18-25.

Harold M. Wiener, "'The Sources of the Hexateuch'," *BS* 75 (1918) 594-598. *(Review)*

G. Frederick Wright, "The Documentary Theory an Imposture," *CFL, 3rd Ser.,* 24 (1918) 26. *[Summary]*

H. W. Magoun, "'The Canons of Validity'," *CFL, 3rd Ser.,* 24 (1918) 341-344.

J. J. Lias, "Germanism," *JTVI* 50 (1918) 137-156. (Discussion, pp. 156-158) [Documentary Hypothesis, pp. 147-155]

H[erbert] W[illiam] Magoun, "The Canons of Validity," *MQR, 3rd Ser.,* 44 (1918) 191-208.

Harold M. Wiener, "The Greek Genesis, the Graf-Wellhausen Theory, and the Conservative Position," *BS* 76 (1919) 41-60.

[J. Paterson Smyth], "The Bible in the Making ('Made in Germany')," *CFL, 3rd Ser.,* 25 (1919) 85-86. [The Bible of Northern Israel; The Bible of the Priests]

[J. Paterson] Smyth, "The Romance of the Jahvist," *CFL, 3rd Ser.,* 25 (1919) 172-173.

[Jay Benson Hamilton], "The Well-known Unknown," *CFL, 3rd Ser.,* 25 (1919) 309-310.

[Jay Benson Hamilton], "The Wellhausen Swan Song," *CFL, 3rd Ser.,* 25 (1919) 347-348.

Harold M. Wiener, "The Sources of the Hexateuch," *CFL, 3rd Ser.,* 25 (1919) 393-394.

[Jay Benson Hamilton], "Hun Plot Against the Bible," *CFL, 3rd Ser.,* 25 (1919) 395-396.

[Jay Benson Hamilton], "The Hexateuch Hoax," *CFL, 3rd Ser.,* 25 (1919) 364-367, 410-412, 451-454, 504-505.

Francis J. Lamb, "Higher Criticism of the Bible Examined by Scientific Methods," *CFL, 3rd Ser.,* 25 (1919) 407-410.

Anonymous, "The Incredible Fable," *CFL, 3rd Ser.,* 25 (1919) 417-418.

Anonymous, "Critic or Critique," *CFL, 3rd Ser.,* 25 (1919) 483.

[Frank J. Boyer], "The German Hexateuch—A Hun Fabrication," *CFL, 3rd Ser.,* 26 (1920) 9-11.

[Frank J. Boyer], "False Doctrine—Lying," *CFL, 3rd Ser.,* 26 (1920) 63-64.

*W. W. Canon, "Passover and Priests Code," *Exp, 8th Ser.,* 19 (1920) 226-235.

*Julian Morgenstern, "The Elohist Narrative in Exodus 3:1-15," *AJSL* 37 (1920-21) 242-262.

*William L. Baxter, "'Smooth Stone Out of the Brook'," *PTR* 19 (1921) 177-224.

L[eander] S. Keyser, "Critical Notes on the 'Shorter Bible'," *CFL, 3rd Ser.,* 28 (1922) 102-111.

A. C. Dixon, "Myths and Moths of Criticism. An Examination of the Moths and their Doings. The Origin of the Myths," *CFL, 3rd Ser.,* 28 (1922) 259-262.

L[eander] S. Keyser, "As to Literary Style: A Little Chapter on Biblical Criticism," *CFL, 3rd Ser.,* 28 (1922) 313-314.

* C. M. Mackay, "Ezekiel's Sanctuary and Wellhausen's Theory," *PTR* 20 (1922) 661-665.

Th. Graebner, "Little Journey in the Higher Anticriticism. II The Documentary Hypothesis," *TM* 2 (1922) 9-18. Part I?

W. H. G[riffith] T[homas], "The Latest Phase of Hexateuchal Criticism," *CFL, 3rd Ser.*, 29 (1923) 389-390.

Andrew Craig Robinson, "Three Peculiarities of the Pentateuch which show that the Higher Critical Theories of its Late Composition Cannot be Reasonably Held," *JTVI* 55 (1923) 56-68. (Discussion, pp. 68-74) [(1) The Absence of the Name 'Jerusalem' from the Pentateuch; (2) The Absence of any mention of Sacred Song from the Ritual of the Pentateuch; (3) The Absence of the Divine Title 'Lord of Hosts' from the Pentateuch]

W. F. Lofthouse, "A New Work on the Hexateuch," *LQHR* 140 (1923) 100-102. *(Review)*

John A. Maynard, "The Element of Controversy in the Documents of the Pentateuch," *ATR* 7 (1924-25) 145-151.

*J. Battersby Harford, "Since Wellhausen," *Exp, 9th Ser.*, 4 (1925) 4-26. [Article 1. The Problem and its Solution; Supplementary Note. On the Use of Elohim in the Pentateuch, pp. 20-26]

*J. Battersby Harford, "Since Wellhausen," *Exp, 9th Ser.*, 4 (1925) 83-102. [Article 2. Recent Criticism, with Special Reference to Exodus 6:2-3]

*J. Battersby Harford, "Since Wellhausen," *Exp, 9th Ser.*, 4 (1925) 164-182, 244-265. [Article 3. Textual Criticism. The Massoretic Text and the Septuagint]

*J. Battersby Harford, "Since Wellhausen," *Exp, 9th Ser.*, 4 (1925) 323-349. [Article 4. Deuteronomy]

J. Battersby Harford, "Since Wellhausen," *Exp, 9th Ser.*, 4 (1925) 403-429. [Article 5. The Problem of the Priestly Code]

L[eander] S. K[eyser], "The 'Source' Hypothesis of the Pentateuch," *CFL, 3rd Ser.*, 33 (1927) 306-308.

Julian Morgenstern, "The Oldest Document of the Hexateuch," *HUCA* 4 (1927) 1-138.

Paul R. Stevick, "Notes on the Conceptions of Human Nature in the J and E Sections of the Hexateuch," *MR* 111 (1928) 771-774.

*Th[eophile] J. Meek, "The Translation of *Gêr* in the Hexateuch and its Bearing on the Documentary Hypothesis," *JBL* 49 (1930) 172-180.

D. M. McIntyre, "The Synagogue *versus* Wellhausen," *EQ* 5 (1933) 175-179.

*Beatrice L. Goff, "The Lost Jahwistic Account of the Conquest of Canaan," *JBL* 53 (1934) 241-249.

*G. B[uchanan] Gray, "Passover and Unleavened Bread: The Laws of J, E, and D," *JTS* 37 (1936) 241-253.

E. Kriewaldt, "The 'Documentary Hypothesis' in Court," *AusTR* 9 (1938) 3-10.

*Sigmund Mowinckel, "The Babylonian Matter in the Predeuteronomic Primeval History (JE) in Gen 1-11," *JBL* 58 (1939) 87-91.

*William F[oxwell] Albright, "The Babylonian Matter in the Predeuteronomic Primeval History (JE) in Gen 1-11, II," *JBL* 58 (1939) 91-103.

*A. C. Graham, "Hebronite Tradition Behind P in Genesis," *JTS* 41 (1940) 104-152.

*Leroy Waterman, "Some Repercussions from Late Levitical Genealogical Accretions in P and the Chronicler," *AJSL* 58 (1941) 49-56.

E. Robertson, "Temple and Torah: Suggesting an Alternative to the Graf-Wellhausen Hypothesis," *BJRL* 26 (1941-42) 182-205.

E. Robertson, "The Priestly Code: The Legislation of the Old Testament and Graf-Wellhausen," *BJRL* 26 (1941-42) 369-392.

William A. Irwin, "The Significance of Julius Wellhausen," *JAAR* 12 (1944) 160-173.

*H. F. D. Sparks, "The Witness of the Prophets to Hebrew Tradition," *JTS* 50 (1949) 129-141.

*Manfred Cassirer, "The Date of the Elohist in the Light of Genesis XXXVII. 9," *JTS* 50 (1949) 173-174.

*Cuthbert Lattey, "The Tribe of Levi," *CBQ* 12 (1950) 277-291. *[Graf-Wellhausen Theory]*

*Julian Morgenstern, "The Final Redaction of the J Code," *JBL* 69 (1950) iv.

G. E[rnest] Wright, "The Considerations Favoring the Tenth-Century Date for the Yahwist Writer," *JBL* 70 (1951) iii.

Immanuel Lewy, "Nationalist and Humanist Sections within J of Gen-Num," *JBL* 71 (1952) xv.

J. Coert Rylaarsdam, "The Present Status of Pentateuchal Criticism," *JAAR* 22 (1954) 242-247.

*Morris Sigel Seale, "The Glosses in the Book of Genesis and the J E Theory. An Attempt at a New Solution," *ET* 67 (1955-56) 333-335.

James A. Schwarz, "Practical Use of the Documentary Hypothesis," *Amb* 9 (1960-61) 101-106.

Horace D. Hummel, "'How Do I Teach This to Laymen?'" *Amb* 9 (1960-61) #4, 107-115.

Samuel Sandmel, "The Haggada within Scripture," *JBL* 80 (1961) 105-122. *[Opposition to the Graf-Wellhausen Theory]*

M. H. Segal, "The Composition of the Pentateuch—A Fresh Examination," *SH* 8 (1961) 68-114.

*Menaḥem Haran, "Shiloh and Jerusalem," *Tarbiz* 31 (1961-62) #4, I.

*Menahem Haran, "Shiloh and Jerusalem: The Origin of the Priestly Tradition in the Pentateuch," *JBL* 81 (1962) 14-24.

William Foxwell Albright, "Jethro, Hobab and Ruel in Early Hebrew Tradition (with Some Comments on the Origin of 'JE')," *CBQ* 25 (1963) 1-11.

Simon J. DeVries, "The Hexateuchal Criticism of Abraham Kuenen," *JBL* 82 (1963) 31-57.

Arvid S. Kapelrud, "The Date of the Priestly Code," *ASTI* 3 (1964) 58-64.

C. J. de Catanzaro, "The Primeval History—A Reconsideration of Source Criticism," *ACQ* 5 (1965) 51-56.

Hans Walter Wolff, "The Kerygma of the Yahwist," *Interp* 20 (1966) 131-158. *(Trans. by Wilbur A. Benware)*

Paul L. Watson, "The Deuteronomic Historian," *RestQ* 9 (1966) 281-284.

John A. Scott, "The Priestly Tabernacle," *RestQ* 9 (1966) 295-299.

*J. M. Grintz, "'Ye Shall not Eat *on* the Blood'," *Zion* 31 (1966) #1/2 I-II. *[Priestly Code]*

Ignatius Hunt, "The Yahwist," *BibT* #29 (1967) 2043-2047.

*Avi Hurvitz, "The Usage of שׁשׁ and בוּץ in the Bible and Its Implication for the Date of P," *HTR* 60 (1967) 117-121.

T. E. Fretheim, "The Priestly Document: Anti-Temple?" *VT* 18 (1968) 313-329.

Chayim Cohen, "Was the P Document Secret?" *JANES* 1 (1968-69) #2, 39-44.

*Murray Lichtenstein, "Dream-Theophany and the E Document," *JANES* 1 (1968-69) #2, 45-54.

Allan A. MacRae, "The Higher Critical Assault Upon the Scriptures," *RefmR* 16 (1968-69) 80-90.

Burke O. Long, "Etymological Etiology and the Dt Historian," *CBQ* 31 (1969) 35-41.

J. G. Vink, "The Date and Origin of the Priestly Code in the Old Testament," *OTS* 15 (1969) 1-144.

*J. N. M. Wijngaards, "The Dramatization of Salvific History in the Deuteronomic Schools," *OTS* 16 (1969) 1-127.

§303 *3.2.9.5.1 The Holiness Code*

*Lewis Bayles Paton, "The Holiness Code and Ezekiel," *PRR* 7 (1896) 98-115.

L . E. Elliott-Binns, "Some problems of the holiness code," *ZAW* 67 (1955) 26-40.

§304 *3.2.9.6 Literary Criticism of Genesis - General Studies*

*†Anonymous, "Chronological Remark on Genesis," *MMBR* 2 (1796) 686-687.

†E. T. Pilgrim, "The Word 'Day' in Genesis,"*MMBR* 34 (1812-13) 17.

†Anonymous, "On the Book of Genesis," *MMBR* 35 (1813) 214-217.

Philologus, "Vindication of the Book of Genesis," *CongML* 2 (1819) 154-157.

*Anonymous, "The Mosaic History Accordant with the Existing State of Things," *PRev* 1 (1829) 189-209.

*Anonymous, "Remarks on Some of the Peculiarities which Distinguish the Elohim and Jehovah Documents in Genesis from Each Other," *CTPR, N.S.,* 1 (1838-39) 534-541.

Anonymous, "A Companion to the Book of Genesis," *MR* 27 (1845) 391-402. *(Review)*

†Anonymous, "The Book of Genesis," *BFER* 9 (1860) 497-539. *(Review)*

†Geo. Howe, "Delitzsch on Genesis," *SPR* 15 (1862-63) 161-198. *(Review)*

*C. McCausland, "On some Uses of Sacred Primeval History," *JTVI* 3 (1868-69) 447-458. (Discussion, pp. 458-471)

J. C. H., "The Book of Genesis in Relation to Modern Science," *DUM* 75 (1870) 550-558.

*Anonymous, "Genesis and Geology," *CR* 23 (1871) 343-358. *(Review)*

Alex. Mackenzie Cameron, "Illustrations from Borneo of Passages in the Book of Genesis," *SBAT* 2 (1873) 264-266.

*A. H. Sayce, "The Date of the Ethnological Table of Genesis," *TRL* 11 (1874) 59-69.

Anonymous, "Genesis," *BWR* 1 (1877) 343-345.

†Anonymous, "The Book of Genesis and Science," *LQHR* 48 (1877) 52-66. *(Review)*

*William Aikman, "The Word Elohim and Jehovah in Genesis," *MR* 59 (1877) 610-626.

Frederic Gardiner, "Are the Early Narratives of Genesis to be Literally Understood?" *DTQ* 4 (1878) 501-509.

*J. L. Porter, "Exploration as Verifying Revelation," *DTQ* 5 (1879) 1-19.

*W[illiam] Aikman, "The Word Elohim and Jehovah in Genesis," *DTQ* 5 (1879) 292-302.

*John Urquhart, "The Divine Names in Genesis," *BFER* 30 (1881) 227-242.

Anonymous, "Commentators and the Book of Genesis," *SRL* 1 (1882-83) 126-144. *(Review)*

*Edgar C. S. Gibson, "Some Names in Genesis," *Exp, 2nd Ser.,* 6 (1883) 259-272, 350-362.

*Talbot W. Chambers, "The Occurrence of the Divine Names in Genesis," *ONTS* 3 (1883-84) 91-92.

Jesse B. Thomas, "Genesis—Scriptural and Extra-Scriptural," *CT* 2 (1884-85) 401-423.

G. F. McKibben, "The Significance and Richness of Genesis," *ONTS* 4 (1884-85) 86-87.

*H. P. Laird, "The Ancient Oracle," *RChR* 33 (1886) 301-320. *(Creation/Evolution)*

*A. Crawford, "Genesis and Geology," *PER* 2 (1888-89) 118-127.

William J. Dawson, "Genesis and Some of its Critics," *ContR* 55 (1889) 900-909.

J. Rawson Lumby, "The Study of the Early Chapters of Genesis," *ET* 2 (1890-91) 62.

*Anonymous, "Dana on Genesis and Science," *BS* 48 (1891) 171-174.

T. K. Cheyne, "Brevia: Klostermann *versus* Kautzsch and Socin," *Exp, 4th Ser.,* 4 (1891) 157-158, 397-398.

Henry Colman, "Pre-Adamites," *MR* 73 (1891) 891-902.

*C. H. Waller, "Is Genesis a Compilation After All? *and What is its Real Relation to the Remainder of the Pentateuch?" TML* 5 (1891) 289-300.

*J. S. Bryan, "Murphy's Genesis and the Documentary Hypothesis," *MQR, 3rd Ser.,* 11 (1891-92) 95-103.

*I[srael] Abrahams, "Tobit and Genesis," *JQR* 5 (1892-93) 348-350.

*Thos. Stoughton Potwin, "The Divine Names in the Book of Genesis, in the Light of Recent Discoveries," *BS* 50 (1893) 348-357.

*James Henry Breasted, "Some Egyptian Names in Genesis—A New Inscription of the Oldest Period, etc.," *BW* 2 (1893) 285-288.

Anonymous, "The Book of Genesis a True History," *CQR* 36 (1893) 1-34.

William R. Harper, "The Human Element in the Early Stories of Genesis," *BW* 4 (1894) 266-278.

William R. Harper, "The Divine Element in the Early Stories of Genesis," *BW* 4 (1894) 349-358.

*J. William Dawson, "Physical and Historical Probabilities Respecting the Authorship and Authority of the Mosaic Books," *Exp, 4th Ser.,* 9 (1894) 16-33, 109-123, 276-288, 362-375, 440-451. [II. The Book of Genesis, pp. 109-123]

*P. A. Peters, "The Sabbath in Genesis and Exodus," *ColTM* 16 (1896) 153-169.

*J. William Dawson, "The Historical Relation of the Book of Genesis to the Exodus from Egypt," *HR* 33 (1897) 9-19.

T. R. English, "The Plan and Ruling Thought of the Book of Genesis," *CFL, N.S.,* 4 (1901) 76-80.

Willis J. Beecher, "The International Lessons in Their Literary Setting," *CFL, N.S.,* 4 (1901) 9-15, 71-76, 141-148, 201-207. *[Genesis]*

W[illiam] M. McP[heeters], "Editorial Notes," *CFL, N.S.,* 4 (1901) 121-131. *[The Genesis Narratives]*

H[ermann] Gunkel, "The Legends of Genesis," *OC* 15 (1901) 261-283, 385-398, 450-463, 526-539, 582-595, 650-673. *(Trans. by W. H. Carruth)*

William M. McPheeters, "God Securing the Study of His Word. Attention Centered on Genesis," *CFL, 3rd Ser.*, 6 (1902) 1-8.

*A. J. Maas, "The Chronology of Genesis," *ACQR* 29 (1904) 417-433.

W. W. Everts, "Are There Myths in Genesis?" *CFL, 3rd Ser.*, 1 (1904) 505-509.

J. J. Lias, "'Genesis'—Recent Criticism of," *CFL, 3rd Ser.*, 1 (1904) 678-685.

W[illiam] W. Everts, "The Book of Genesis Unfolded," *CFL, 3rd Ser.*, 2 (1905) 72-82. [Genesis, the Origin of the Divine Law and the Chosen People]

W[illiam] W. Everts, "The Book of Genesis Unfolded—Part First," *CFL, 3rd Ser.*, 2 (1905) 232-240.

Alex. R. Gordon, "The Religious Value of the Narratives in Genesis," *HA* 4 (1905-06) 163-179.

*Edward E. Nourse, "The Book of Genesis and the Religious Development of Israel," *HSR* 16 (1905-06) 91-113.

G. L. Young, "The Book of Genesis—Its Unity," *CFL, 3rd Ser.*, 5 (1906) 254-259.

Anonymous, "An Unexpected Light," *MQR, 3rd Ser.*, 32 (1906) 385. *[Genesis written on Tablets?]*

John McDowell Leavitt, "Science a Key to Genesis," *CFL, 3rd Ser.*, 6 (1907) 3-11.

Anonymous, "'Genesis and Science'—from Dr. Wright's New Book," *CFL, 3rd Ser.*, 6 (1907) 52-55. *(Review)*

*William M. McPheeters, "The Meaning of 'Bara' in Genesis," *CFL, 3rd Ser.*, 7 (1907) 367-372.

S. M. Godbey, "The Sociological Lessons of Genesis," *MQR, 3rd Ser.*, 33 (1907) 525-535.

Henry Gracey, "Driver's 'The Book of Genesis'," *CFL, 3rd Ser.*, 8 (1908) 372-378. *(Review)*

*Harold M. Wiener, "The Name of God in Genesis," *ET* 20 (1908-09) 473-475.

*A. P. Cox, "The Name of God in Genesis. I.," *ET* 20 (1908-09) 378.

*John Skinner, "The Name of God in Genesis. II.," *ET* 20 (1908-09) 378-379.

*Nivard Johann Schlögl, "The Name of God in Genesis,"*ET* 20(1908-09) 563.

C. F. Burney, "The Religious Value of the Early Narratives of Genesis," *ICMM* 6 (1909-10) 278-288.

J. S. Ross, "The Early Narratives of Genesis, Myth or History? A Review of Rev. George Jackson's Lecture," *CFL, 3rd Ser.*, 12 (1910) 358-365.

Alex R. Gordon, "Skinner's 'Genesis'," *Exp, 7th Ser.*, 10 (1910) 242-254. *(Review)*

H. T. F. Duckworth, "The Book of Genesis. *A Review of Dr. John Skinner's Recent Commentary*," *HR* 60 (1910) 352-359. *(Review)*

*Harold M. Wiener, "The Post-Mosaica of Genesis," *BS* 68 (1911) 154-156.

Henry Gracey, "Dr. Driver's Method of Getting Rid of the History in Genesis," *CFL, 3rd Ser.*, 14 (1911-12) 221-228.

Alexander Macdonald, "Is Genesis Expurgated Myth or History?" *AER* 46 (1912) 65-70.

Alex R. Gordon and Harold M. Wiener, "A Correspondence with Dr. Gordon," *BS* 69 (1912) 349-359. *[Concerning Skinner's 'Genesis']*

Harold M. Wiener, "The Only Way: A Correspondence," *BS* 69 (1912) 723-726. *[Concerning Skinner's 'Genesis']*

*Kemper Fullerton, "The International Critical Commentary on Genesis, Chronicles, and the Psalms," *HTR* 5 (1912) 20-109. *(Review)*

*L. S. A. Wells, "The Book of Jubilees: the earliest Commentary on Genesis," *IJA* #28 (1912) 13-17.

*Royden K. Yerkes, "Some Notes on the use of אל in Genesis," *JBL* 31 (1912) 59-62.

*Eb. Nestle, "Three Notes on Skinner's 'Genesis'," *ET* 24 (1912-13) 91-92.

*J[ohn] Skinner, "The Divine Names in Genesis," *Exp, 8th Ser.,* 5 (1913) 289-313, 400-420, 494-514; 6 (1913) 23-45, 97-116, 266-288. [I. Exodus VI. 2, 3; II. The Pericope-Hypothesis; III. Recensions in the Septuagint; IV. The Hebrew Text, 1 Hebrew Manuscripts, 2. The Samaritan Pentateuch; V. The Limits of Textual Uncertainty]

*Johannes Dashe, "Divine Appelations, Textual Criticism and Documentary Theory. My Reply to Dr. Skinner," *Exp, 8th Ser.,* 6 (1913) 481-510.

*Robert C. Thomson, "The Names of God in Genesis," *GUOST* 4 (1913-22) 7-9.

*Robert F. Chisholm, "The Pre-Abrahamic Stories of Genesis as Wisdom Literature," *GUOST* 4 (1913-22) 80-82.

George [H.] Schodde, "The Historical Character of Genesis," *TZTM* 4 (1914) 364-372.

Lewis Bayles Paton, "Archaeology and the Book of Genesis," *BW* 45 (1915) 10-17, 135-145, 202-210, 288-298, 353-361; 46 (1915) 25-32, 82-89, 173-180.

H. Edouard Naville, "The Unity of Genesis," *JTVI* 47 (1915) 329-356. (Discussion, pp. 357-362)

*Theophilus G. Pinches, "Early Babylonian Chronology and the Book of Genesis," *ET* 27 (1915-16) 517-521.

*J. S. Ross, "Methodist Higher Criticism Arm-in-Arm with Infidelity," *CFL, 3rd Ser.,* 21 (1916) 116-118. [III. The Book of Genesis, p. 118]

*J. S. Ross, "Methodist Higher Criticism Arm-in-Arm with Infidelity. Paper No. II.," *CFL, 3rd Ser.,* 21 (1916) 161-163. [IV. The Fall of Man, p. 161; V. the Flood, p. 161-162; VI. The Tower of Babel, p. 162; VII. Abraham, p. 162]

*Alphonse Mingana, "Remarks on the Hebrew of Genesis," *Exp, 8th Ser.,* 11 (1916) 303-310.

*J. P. Robertson, "Genesis a Miracle in Morals," *USR* 28 (1916-17) 187-200.

Harold M. Wiener, "Historical Observations on Some Chapters of Genesis," *BS* 74 (1917) 101-113.

W. W. Martin, "Light Upon the Earliest History of Genesis. From the Telloh Inscriptions," *MQR, 3rd Ser.*, 43 (1917) 576-587.

A. T. Olmstead, "The Greek Genesis," *AJSL* 34 (1917-18) 145-169.

[Jay Benson Hamilton], "International Sunday School Lessons: Book of the Beginning: History or Fable?" *CFL, 3rd Ser.*, 25 (1919) 208-209.

*Thomas J. Agius, "Genesis and Evolution," *IER, 5th Ser.*, 13 (1919) 441-453.

L. Franklin Gruber, "Dr. Eduoard Konig on 'Genesis'," *BS* 77 (1920) 460-464. *(Review)*

William H. Bates, "The Book of Genesis," *CFL, 3rd Ser.*, 26 (1920) 269-272.

H. W. Mengedoht, "Genesis and the Cuneiform Inscriptions," *OC* 34 (1920) 340-345.

*Duncan Black Macdonald, "The Pre-Abrahamic Stories of Genesis, as a Part of the Wisdom Literature," *SSO* 1 (1920) 115-125.

P. H. Ditchfield, "History and Folklore in Genesis," *Theo* 1 (1920) 257-264.

James Cooper, "Old Testament Preparations for the Catholic Church. The Book of Genesis," *ConstrQ* 9 (1921) 558-577.

N. G. Lawson, "The Early Chapters of Genesis," *Theo* 5 (1922) 297-303.

A. J. Westlake, "Genesis and Progress," *ET* 36 (1924-25) 188-190.

William S. Bishop, "Genesis—The Book of Beginnings," *BS* 82 (1925) 185-202.

D[avid] J[ames] B[urrell], "The Book of Origins," *CFL, 3rd Ser.*, 31 (1925) 325-328.

L[eander] S. K[eyser], "A Scientist's View of Genesis," *CFL, 3rd Ser.*, 34 (1928) 191-192. *(Editorial)*

P[hilip] M[auro], "Genesis and Modern Scientific Opinion," *CFL, 3rd Ser.*, 34 (1928) 586-587. *(Editorial)*

*Dudley Joseph Whitney, "The Chronology of Genesis," *CFL, 3rd Ser.*, 36 (1930) 478-482.

S. F. Hunter, "The Babylonian Background of Genesis," *NZJT* 1 (1931-32) 129-137.

*Paul E. Kretzmann, "The word 'year' in the Book of Genesis," *CTM* 4 (1933) 216.

Leander S. Keyser, "Permanent Values in Genesis," *CFL, 3rd Ser.,* 40 (1934) 164-165.

James B. Tannehill, "Have the Defenders of Genesis Met Their Waterloo?" *CFL, 3rd Ser.,* 41 (1935) 278-283; 42 (1936) 41-49.

(   )   A.,   "Genesis   Upheld,"   *CTM*   7   (1936)   862.

*Robert P. Casey, "The Armenian Marcionites and the Diatessaron," *JBL* 57 (1938) 185-194.

*R[obert] H. Pfeiffer, "The Ages of Mankind in Genesis and Hesiod," *JBL* 58 (1939) iv.

*A. C. Graham, "Hebronite Tradition Behind P in Genesis," *JTS* 41 (1940) 140-152.

*Edward McCrady, "Genesis and Pagan Cosmogonies," *JTVI* 72 (1940) 44-64, 68-71. (Communications by E. J. G. Titterington, p. 64; H. S. Curr, pp. 64-66; L. M. Davies, pp. 66-68)

E. J. G. Titterington, "Genesis and the Gospel," *JTVI* 73 (1941) 63-74, 78-80. (Communications by H. S. Curr, 74-75; A. H. van Straubenzee, 75-77, and R. E. D. Clark, 77-78)

S. Pearce Carey, "The Earliest Chapters of Genesis and the Modern Mind," *BQL* 11 (1942-45) 92-94.

*Oscar E. Olson, "The Book of Genesis and Modern Science," *CQ* 5 (1945) #3, 131-137.

John Henry Bennetch, "Genesis: An Apologetic," *BS* 103 (1946) 106-114.

‡Donald G. Miller, "Studia Biblica. I. Genesis," *Interp* 2 (1948) 76-89. *[Extensive Bibliography]*

E. F. Sutcliffe, "Genesis Reconsidered," *Scrip* 4 (1949-51) 49-55.

Roderick A. F. MacKenzie, "'Before Abraham Was...'," *CBQ* 15 (1953) 131-140.

*Martin J. Wyngaarden, "Some Problems of Chronology in Genesis," *JASA* 7 (1955) #3, 43-46.

*Morris Sigel Seale, "The Glosses in the Book of Genesis and the J E Theory. An attempt at a New Solution," *ET* 67 (1955-56) 333-335.

*Meredith G. Kline, "Because It Had Not Rained,"*WJT* 20 (1957-58) 146-157.

*B. Gemser, "God in Genesis," *OTS* 12 (1958) 1-21.

*A. van Selms, "The Canaanites in the Book of Genesis," *OTS* 12 (1958) 182-213.

A. M. Dubarle, "History and Myth in Genesis," *TD* 6 (1958) 95-99.

Victor E. Reichert, "A New Look at Genesis," *CCARJ* #24 (1959) 28-35.

Saul Leeman, "Genesis Retranslated—Some Observations," *CJ* 14 (1959-60) #4, 22-34.

*Charles C. Forman, "Koheleth's Use of Genesis," *JSS* 5 (1960) 256-263.

*E[phraim] A. Speiser, "The Verb *SHR* in Genesis and Early Hebrew Movements," *BASOR* #164 (1961) 23-28.

Robert Sharp, "The Meaning of Genesis: A New Commentary," *LofS* 16 (1961-62) 244-249. *(Review)*

*Milton H. Polin, "Genesis as a Source of Law," *Trad* 4 (1961-62) 36-43.

G. W. Anderson, "Old Testament Books," *PQL* 7 (1961) 283-288. [I. Genesis]

*W[illiam] F[oxwell] Albright, "Some Remarks on the Meaning of the Verb *SHR* in Genesis," *BASOR* #164 (1961) 28.

D. Dias, "Genesis and Modern Science," *IES* 1 (1962) 205-220.

D. Dias, "Genesis and Modern Science. II," *IES* 1 (1962) 257-276.

G. W. Anderson, "Old Testament Books," *PQL* 8 (1962) 44-50. [II. Genesis (cont.)]

E[phraim] A. Speiser, "Mesopotamian Motifs in the Early Chapters of Genesis," *Exped* 5 (1962-63) #1, 18-19, 43.

*Søren Giversen, "The Apocryphon of John and Genesis," *ST* 17 (1963) 60-76.

*Rem Edwards, "Is There a Metaphysics of Genesis?" *Cont* 1 (1963-64) 368-372.

*James Quigley, "A Catholic Response," *Cont* 1 (1963-64) 373-384. *[A Metaphysics of Genesis]*

J. M. Clark, "Genesis and Its Underlying Realities," *F&T* 93 (1963-64) 146-158; 94 (1965-66) 139-141. [Survey of Genesis ii-xi; The Place of Adam in Scripture; Summary of New Testament References; The Role of Adam in Theology; The Spiritual Status of Man; The Typology of Eden] (Correspondence by H. L. Ellison, *F&T* 94 (1965-66) 135-136; Alan Willigale, p. 136)

*Dennis J. McCarthy, "Three Covenants in Genesis," *CBQ* 26 (1964) 179-189.

*Frederick V. Winnett, "Re-Examining the Foundations," *JBL* 84 (1965) 1-19. [The Primeval History; The Patriarchal Narratives; The Joseph Story]

W. G. Lambert, "A New Look at the Babylonian background of Genesis," *JTS, N.S.*, 16 (1965) 287-300.

*James Quigley, "Is There a Metaphysics of Genesis? II," *Cont* 2 (1966) 105-118.

Anonymous, "Introduction to Genesis," *BVp* 2 (1968) 91-93.

Edward M. Panosian, "Genesis: 'This is the Beginning of Miracles...'," *BVp* 2 (1968) 94-97.

*Marshall Neal, "The Messianic Hope in Genesis," *BVp* 2 (1968) 131-136.

*F. G. Smith, "Observations on the Greek Use of the Names and Titles of God in Genesis," *EQ* 40 (1968) 103-110.

*James Barr, "The Image of God in the Book of Genesis—A Study of Terminology," *BJRL* 51 (1968-69) 11-26.

Benjamin Mazar, "The Historical Background of the Book of Genesis," *JNES* 28 (1969) 73-83.

§305 **3.2.9.6.1 Studies on Creation [See also: Doctrine of Creation, → and Science and the Bible, §169 ←]**

*†Anonymous, "On the Meaning of the Word 'Created' in Genesis," *MMBR* 21 (1806) 221-224.

†W. Singleton, "Coincidences in Genesis and Ovid's Metamorphoses," *MMBR* 27 (1809) 243-244.

†J. A. DeLuc, "Mr. DeLuc's Geological Principles," *MMBR* 37 (1814) 11-12.

†J. A. DeLuc, "Mr. DeLuc in Proof of the Verity of the Mosaic Account of Creation," *MMBR* 37 (1814) 206-208.

†Geo. Cumberland, "Mr. Cumberland in Defence*[sic]* of the Mosaic System," *MMBR* 40 (1815-16) 18-20.

†Anonymous, "Brown and Sumner's Essays," *BCQTR, N.S.,* 6 (1816) 333-344, 465-481. *(Review)*

*Anonymous, "A Glance at the History of Opinions Concerning the Creation and Fall of Man," *CD, N.S.,* 1 (1819) 102-108, 169-179.

Anonymous, "Spirit of the Hebrew Scriptures.—No. I. The Creation," *CE* 16 (1834) 174-202.

*Edward Hitchcock, "The Connection between Geology and the Mosaic History of the Creation," *BRCR* 5 (1835) 439-451; 6 (1835) 261-332.

Anonymous, "Creation," *BRCM* 1 (1846) 89-97.

William M'Combie, "The 'Days' of Creation," *JSL, 1st Ser.,* 3 (1849) 159-161.

Anonymous, "On the Mosaic Account of Creation," *JSL, 1st Ser.,* 5 (1850) 186-194.

*M. N., "Genesis and Geology; or an Investigation into the Reconciliation of the Modern Doctrines of Geology with the Declarations of Scripture," *JSL, 1st Ser.,* 6 (1850) 261-291.

*[David N. Lord], "Genesis, and the Geological Theory of the Age of the Earth," *TLJ* 4 (1851-52) 529-614.

S. H. Thompson, "The Mosaic Account of Creation," *MR* 34 (1852) 497-520.

Anonymous, "The Primitive State, Character and Happiness of Man," *SPR* 7 (1853-54) 365-374.

R. S. P and J. W., "The Genesis of the Earth and of Man," *JSL, 2nd Ser.*, 7 (1854-55) 433-451. *(Review)*

*†[David N. Lord], "Hugh Miller's Lecture on Genesis and Geology," *TLJ* 7 (1854-55) 119-144. *(Review)*

John O. Means, "The Narrative of the Creation of Genesis," *BS* 12 (1855) 83-130, 323-338.

B. Harris Cowper, "The Genesis of the Earth and of Man," *JSL, 3rd Ser.*, 1 (1855) 329-334; 2 (1855-56) 403-409.

H. H. B., "On the Genesis of the Earth and of Man," *JSL, 3rd Ser.*, 1 (1855) 417-421.

R. S. P., "The Genesis of the Earth and of Man," *JSL, 3rd Ser.*, 2 (1855-56) 196-201.

†Anonymous, "Professor Lewis' View on the 'Days' of Creation," *PQR* 4 (1855-56) 469-494. *(Review)*

†Anonymous, "Professor Lewis's Scriptural Cosmology—The Six Days of Creation," *TLJ* 8 (1855-56) 271-342.

[David N. Lord(?)], "Professor Lewis's Response in the New York Observer in Reference to his Six Days of Creation," *TLJ* 8 (1855-56) 445-512.

[David N. Lord(?)], "Professor Lewis's Response in Reference to his Six Days of Creation," *TLJ* 8 (1855-56) 529-585.

*E. P. Barrows, "The Mosaic Narrative of the Creation Considered Grammatically and in its Relations to Science," *BS* 13 (1856) 743-789.

W. N. Pendleton, "The Chronology of Creation," *MQR* 10 (1856) 161-185.

R. F., "The Mosaic Account of the Creation," *JSL, 3rd Ser.*, 4 (1856-57) 122-130.

(   ) M., "Mosaic Account of the Creation," *JSL, 3rd Ser.*, 4 (1856-57) 466-469.

*E. P. Barrows, "The Mosaic Six Days and Geology," *BS* 14 (1857) 61-98.

Anonymous, "The Mosaic Account of Creation, Scientific," *PQR* 7 (1858-59) 129-141.

*D. C. M'Laren, "The Facts of Geology consistent with the Revealed History of Creation," *TLJ* 12 (1859-60) 133-151. *(Errata, p. 352)*

B. Harris Cowper, "The Genesis of the Earth and of Man," *JSL, 3rd Ser.,* 12 (1860-61) 123-133. *(Review)*

*[R. B. Jenness], "The Two Histories of Creation—How Reconciled," *FBQ* 9 (1861) 121-145.

Francis Barham, "Dislocation of the Days of Creation," *JSL, 4th Ser.,* 5 (1864) 432-433.

*Anonymous, "Bishop Colenso on the Creation and the Flood," *TRL* 1 (1864) 161-180. *(Review)*

Edward Biley, "The Days of Creation," *JSL, 4th Ser.,* 8 (1865-66) 462-463.

*John Kirk, "On the Doctrine of Creation according to Darwin, Agassiz, and Moses," *JTVI* 4 (1869-70) 45-66. (Discussion, pp. 66-85)

*W. MacDonald, "On Man's Place in Creation; Geologically, Chronologically, Zoologically, Ethnologically, and Historically Considered," *JTVI* 4 (1869-70) 199-214, 230. (Discussion, pp. 214-229)

Russell Martineau, "Note on the Seventh Day of the Creation," *TRL* 10 (1873) 175-177.

*Otto Zöckler, "The Biblical Account of Creation and Natural Science," *DTQ* 1 (1875) 1-17.

*A. I. McCaul, "On Biblical Interpretation in connexion with Science," *JTVI* 9 (1875-76) 147-157. [(Discussion, pp. 157-172) (Remarks by J. W. Dawson, pp. 173-175)]

*J. L. Porter, "Exploration as Verifying Scripture," *PRev* 54 (1878) Part 2, 1-32.

Aug. R. Grote, "The Philosophy of the Biblical Account of Creation," *PAPS* 18 (1878-80) 316-323.

Charles B. Warring, "The Firmament," *BS* 36 (1879) 459-470.

*J. W. Dawson, "Points of Contact Between Science and Revelation," *PRev* 55 (1879) Part 2, 579-606. [Creative Days and the Sabbath, pp. 588-590]

*J. E. Kerschner, "A Review of an Article of the Numbers of Genesis," *RChR* 26 (1879) 434-444. *[Cf. Theologische Jahrbucher, 1878]*

William Clifford, "The Days of the Week, and the Works of Creation," *DR, 3rd Ser.*, 5 (1881) 311-332. *[Original numbering as Vol. 88]*

William Clifford, "The Days of Creation. A Reply" *DR, 3rd Ser.*, 6 (1881) 498-507. *[Original numbering as Vol. 89]*

*John Eliot Howard, "The Early Destinies of Mankind," *JTVI* 15 (1881-82) 159-190. (Discussion, p. 190)

John S. Vaughan, "Bishop Clifford's Theory of the Days of Creation," *DR, 3rd Ser.*, 9 (1883) 32-47. *[Original numbering as Vol. 92]*

William Clifford, "The Days of Creation. Some Further Observations," *DR, 3rd Ser.*, 9 (1883) 397-417. *[Original numbering as Vol. 92]*

Max Moll, "Light from the Post-Biblical Literature of the Jews. No. I," *HR* 8 (1883-84) 107-108. *[Creation of Light]*

*Max Moll, "Light from the Post-Biblical Literature of the Jews. No. II," *HR* 8 (1883-84) 161-162. *[Creation of Man]*

Charles A[ugustus] Briggs, "The Hebrew Poem of the Creation," *ONTS* 3 (1883-84) 273-288.

T[homas] Whitelaw, "The Patriarchal Times. I.—The Creation of the World," *MI* 1 (1884-85) 436-450.

Thomas Whitelaw, "The Patriarchal Times. II.—The Appearing of Man," *MI* 2 (1885) 131-143.

John Miller, "'The Six Days'," *SPR* 36 (1885) 108-116.

Andrew Taylor, "The Chaos of Genesis," *BFER* 35 (1886) 667-681.

*S. R. Driver, "The Cosmogony of Genesis," *Exp, 3rd Ser.*, 3 (1886) 23-45.

*J. M. Hawley, "The Image of God," *MQR, 2nd Ser.*, 8 (1886) 17-40.

*S. R. Driver, "The Cosmogony of Genesis. A Defense and a Critique," *AR* 8 (1887) 639-649.

W. A. Raikes, "The Days of Creation," *CM, N.S.,* 2 (1887) 184-188.

Charles S. Robinson, "The Creation of the World," *HR* 14 (1887) 33-37.

*E. A. Davies, "Bible Account of Creation in the Light of Modern Science," *CT* 5 (1887-88) 296-305.

*James D. Dana, "On the Cosmogony of Genesis," *AR* 9 (1888) 197-200.

Charles S. Robinson, "Was Adam the First Man?" *HR* 15 (1888) 220-225.

Chas. S. Robinson, "Were All Mankind from One Pair?" *HR* 15 (1888) 505-511.

Chas. S. Robinson, "Was Adam Created by Process of Evolution?" *HR* 16 (1888) 323-327.

George D. Armstrong, "The Pentateuchal Story of Creation," *PQ* 2 (1888) 345-368.

D. E. Frierson, "The Famous Six Days," *PQ* 4 (1890) 48-55.

*R. Abbey, "The Three Theories of Human Origin," *CT* 8 (1890-91) [Garden of Eden Theory; Evolution; God Created Man]

*Herbert E. Ryle, "The Early Narratives of Genesis, II. The Assyrian Cosmogony and the Days of Creation," *ET* 2 (1890-91) 197-201. [2. The Days of Creation, pp. 199-201]

M. Friedmann, "Sabbath Light," *JQR* 3 (1890-91) 707-721.

J. J. Perowne, "Genesis and Science," *Exp, 4th Ser.,* 3 (1891) 42.

G. G. Stokes, "Genesis and Science," *Exp, 4th Ser.,* 3 (1891) 42-47, 50-52.

C. Pricthard, "Genesis and Science," *Exp, 4th Ser.,* 3 (1891) 48-50, 52-53.

T. G. Bonney, "Appendix to Dr. Perowne's 'Notes on Genesis.' The Mosaic and Geologic History," *Exp, 4th Ser.,* 3 (1891) 104-109.

*T[heophilus] G. Pinches, "A New Version of the Creation-Story," *JRAS* (1891) 393-408.

*A. H. Huizinga, "Babylonian *versus* Hebrew Account of Creation," *PQ* 6 (1892) 385-398.

*Moncure D. Conway, "Mothers and Sons of God," *OC* 7 (1893) 3671-3672, 3687-3688, 3703-3705. *[Creation of Adam and Eve]*

*John Robson, "The Holy Spirit in Creation," *ET* 5 (1893-94) 467-470.

*J. A. Zahm, "The Mosaic Hexaemeron in the Light of Exegesis and Modern Science," *AER* 10 (1894) 161-227. [I. Moses and Science; II. Allegorism and Literalism; III. St. Gregory of Nyssa and the Nebular Hypothesis; IV. St. Augustine and Evolution (exegesis old and new); V. Modern Theories of Cosmogony]

William R. Harper, "The First Hebrew Story of the Creation," *BW* 3 (1894) 6-16.

Anonymous, "The First Things. I. The Creation of Woman," *CM, 3rd Ser.,* 7 (1894) 46-53.

Anonymous, "The Time-Period of Creation," *HR* 29 (1895) 481-482.

Henry Morton, "The Cosmogony of Genesis and its Reconcilers," *BS* 54 (1897) 264-292, 436-468

G. Frederick Wright, "Editorial Note on Genesis and Geology," *BS* 54 (1897) 570-572.

J. F. McCurdy, "Light on Scriptural Texts from Recent Discoveries," *HR* 33 (1897) 502-504. [The Story of Creation]

*J. F. McCurdy, "Light on Scriptural Texts from Recent Discoveries," *HR* 34 (1897) 24-27, 121-124, 218-221. [The Story of Creation Continued; The Creation Story—Its Origin; Origin of the Creation Story Concluded]

*Fritz Hommel, "A Second Ancient Egyptian Parallel to the Creation Narrative," *ET* 9 (1897-98) 480.

*Fritz Hommel, "Miscellanea," *ET* 9 (1897-98) 524-526. [1. (Ref.: Egyptian Creation Narrative), pp. 524-525]

Friedrich Loofs, "Requests and Replies," *ET* 11 (1899-1900) 153-155. *[Creation]*

Alexander Brown, "The Ethics of Creation," *LQHR* 93 (1900) 38-51. *(Review)*

*Morris Jastrow Jr., "The Hebrew and Babylonian Accounts of Creation," *JQR* 13 (1900-01) 620-654.

Wm. Hohberger, "The Mosaic Account of Creation," *ColTM* 21 (1901) 304-313, 350-370; 22 (1902) 9-31, 73-98.

Alexander Brown, "The Making of Man," *LQHR* 96 (1901) 45-60. *(Review)*

William Wallace Martin, "The Account of Creation According to Reconstructive Higher Criticism," *MQR, 3rd Ser.,* 27 (1901) 323-337.

Cyrus Thomas, "The Genesis or Creation of Man," *RChR, 4th Ser.,* 5 (1901) 487-508.

*Peter Coffey, "The Hexahemeron and Science," *IER, 4th Ser.,* 12 (1902) 141-162, 249-271.

*Fritz Hommel, "The Logos in the Chaldean Story of Creation," *ET* 14 (1902-03) 103-109.

*A. H. Sayce, "Recent Biblical and Oriental Archaeology. The Sumerian Origin of the First Account of the Creation in Genesis," *ET* 14 (1902-03) 124-125.

Samuel W. Howland, "The Story of Eve's Creation," *BS* 60 (1903) 121-128.

B[enjamin] B. Warfield, "Pervasive Bible Witness to Man's Origin in God's Creative Act," *CFL, N.S.,* 8 (1903) 241-251. *(Editorial)*

George Macloskie, "The Making of Man," *HR* 45 (1903) 291-297.

*W. W. Everts, "Are There Myths in Genesis?" *CFL, 3rd Ser.,* 1 (1904) 505-509.

*G[eorge] Macloskie, "Mosaism and Darwinism," *PTR* 2 (1904) 425-441.

A. H. M'Neile, "The Spiritual Value of the Creation Story," *ET* 16 (1904-05) 537-543.

*A. H. Sayce, "The Babylonian and Biblical Accounts of Creation," *AJT* 9 (1905) 1-9.

S. Lawrence Brown, "The Biblical Story of Creation," *ICMM* 1 (1905) 160-163, 342-351.

John J. Young, "The Origin of Woman," *LQ* 35 (1905) 357-369.

*George Macloskie, "The Creation of Man. (Sequel to Article on Creation as Illustrated by Evolution)," *USR* 17 (1905-06) 235-246.

A. C. Dixon, "The Origin of Things as Revealed in Genesis," *CFL, 3rd Ser.,* 5 (1906) 182-190.

*Anonymous, "Professor Driver's 'Assured Results' and His 'Scientific' Method," *CFL, 3rd Ser.,* 5 (1906) 371-374. *[Critique on "The Cosmogony of Genesis"]*

Camden M. Cobern, "Early Narratives Re-Interpreted. II. The Creation," *HR* 51 (1906) 92-99.

A. Irving, "Evolutionary Law in the Creation Story of Genesis," *JTVI* 38 (1906) 69-86, 92. [(Discussion, pp. 86-90) (Communications by John Rate, pp. 90-91; G. F. Whidbone, p. 91; Henry Proctor, pp. 91-92)]

G. Frederick Wright, "The Two Accounts of Creation in Genesis," *CFL, 3rd Ser.,* 6 (1907) 140-141.

*G. Frederick Wright, "Abstract of Professor Wright's Lectures in New York," *CFL, 3rd Ser.,* 6 (1907) 156-161, 235-238 [Lecture Third— "The Genesis Account of Creation," pp. 160-161]

Charles Bartlett Warring, "The Bible: Its Supernaturalism?" *CFL, 3rd Ser.,* 7 (1907) 149-154. *[Creation Story]*

John E. McFadyen, "Are There Two Creation Stories?" *HR* 53 (1907) 48-49.

Leander S. Keyser, "The Bible Narrative of Man's Creation," *LCR* 26 (1907) 466-478.

H[erbert] W. Magoun, "The 'Fourth Day' in Genesis," *BS* 65 (1908) 169-170.

Anonymous, "Dr. Driver on 'Genesis and Science' Again," *CFL, 3rd Ser.,* 8 (1908) 16-19. *(Editorial Note)*

*W. M. Patton, "Cosmogonies in the Apocrypha and in Genesis," *IJA* #17 (1909) 33-37.

A. Irving, "Light, Luminaries and Life; in Connection with the Genesis Account of Creation," *JTVI* 42 (1910) 177-203, 210-221. (Discussion, pp. 203-210)

A. O. Swinebart, "Creation According to the Bible and According to Modern Text-books," *TZTM* 2 (1912) 247-264.

A. O. Swinebart, "Creation According to Genesis and According to the School books in Kansas," *TZTM* 2 (1912) 362-375, 449-460.

Francis Swiney, "The Creation of Woman: or, A Counterblast to 'Man's Sovereign Power'," *WR* 178 (1912) 509-520.

Anonymous, "'Create' and 'Day' in Genesis," *HR* 66 (1913) 512.

[Paul Carus], "The Origin of Woman," *OC* 29 (1915) 656-673.

William H. Bates, "Man—Woman: A Study in Creative Method," *CFL, 3rd Ser.,* 22 (1916) 77-79.

Leo O'Hea, "The Days of Genesis," *IER, 5th Ser.,* 9 (1917) 196-205.

C. Ryder Smith, "The Religious Value of the Bible Story of Creation," *ET* 29 (1917-18) 120-122.

L. Franklin Gruber, "The Creative Days," *BS* 76 (1919) 391-414.

D. Gath Whitley, "The Book of Genesis in the Light of Modern Discovery," *CFL, 3rd Ser.,* 25 (1919) 102-103.

*Luther T. Townsend, "Origin of the First Man; through Chance or by Jehovah—Which?" *CFL, 3rd Ser.,* 25 (1919) 221-225, 265-269.

*Luther T. Townsend, "The Origin of the First Man; his Creation by Jehovah," *CFL, 3rd Ser.,* 25 (1919) 354-359, 397-403.

*Luther T. Townsend, "The Origin of the First Man; Christ the Creator," *CFL, 3rd Ser.,* 25 (1919) 441-445, 499-504; 26 (1920) 4-8.

J. K. Carrington, "The Creation-Story in Genesis," *HR* 78 (1919) 446-452.

Ismar J. Peritz, "The Biblical Conception of the Function of the 'Firmament'," *MR* 104 (1921) 299-307.

*Ismar J. Peritz, "The Biblical Account of Creation and Evolution," *MR* 105 (1922) 960-968.

Edward Mack, "The Bible Story of Creation," *USR* 35 (1923-24) 228-241.

*G. R. Driver, "Some Recent Discoveries in Babylonian Literature. I.—The Epic of Creation," *Theo* 8 (1924) 2-13.

Paul [E.] Kretzmann, "The Length of a Creation Day," *TM* 4 (1924) 37-43.

Nahum Wesley Grover, "The Mosaic Account of Creation: An Exegetical Study," *CFL, 3rd Ser.,* 31 (1925) 493-496, 548-551, 621-623.

F. P. Dunnington, "The 'Days' of Creation," *CFL, 3rd Ser.,* 31 (1925) 559-560.

M[elvin] G[rove] Kyle, "The Antiquity of Man According to the Genesis Account," *JTVI* 57 (1925) 125-138, 145. (Discussion and Communications, pp. 138-145)

C. Cullen Roberts, "The Story of the Creation," *CFL, 3rd Ser.,* 32 (1926) 423-432.

John Moncure, "The Meaning of the Creative Day in Genesis," *CQ* 3 (1926) 84-86.

*Dudley Joseph Whitney, "Pre-Adamic Ruin of the Deluge—Which?" *CFL, 3rd Ser.,* 34 (1928) 331-333.

Dudley Joseph Whitney, "Does Genesis Teach Creation?" *CFL, 3rd Ser.,* 34 (1928) 624-625.

George McCready Price, "Science and the Days of Creation," *CFL, 3rd Ser.,* 35 (1929) 365-368.

*Alan Stuart, "Genesis and Geology," *EQ* 1 (1929) 345-360.

Theophil L. Hass, "The Creation Story and Our Christian Faith," *TZDES* 57 (1929) 161-167, 241-248.

Francis A. Tondorf, "Genesis and the Creation of the World," *TFUQ* 4 (1929-30) 598-623.

Herbert W. Magoun, "The Creative 'Days'," *CFL, 3rd Ser.,* 36 (1930) 537-541.

*Herbert W. Magoun, "Are Geological Ages Irreconcilable with Genesis?" *BS* 88 (1931) 347-357.

E[dmund] F. Sutcliffe, "The Interpretation of the Hexaemeron," *CIR* 4 (1932) 31-40, 123-129.

*George McCready Price, "Some Scientific Aspects of Apologetics," *EQ* 4 (1932) 234-243.

G. Louis Tufts, "Breath of Lives and the Name of Adam," *CFL, 3rd Ser.*, 39 (1933) 198-199.

J. Oliver Buswell, "The Length of the Creative Days," *CFL, 3rd Ser.*, 41 (1935) 117-124.

L[eander] S. K[eyser], "Day and Night in Genesis," *CFL, 3rd Ser.*, 42 (1936) 188-190.

John R. Sampey Jr., "The Six Days of Creation," *R&E* 34 (1937) 470-475.

*Hugh Miller, James D. Dana, J. William Dawson, and Harold Jeffries, "The Relation of Geology to the Days of Creation and the Sabbath Rest," *JTVI* 72 (1940) 202-211. *(Compiled by William Bell Dawson)*

*Dom Ralph Russell, "The Bible and Human Origins," *DownsR* 62 (1944) 77-83.

*Thomas Dann Heald, "The Earlier Form of the Genesis Stories of the Beginning," *Folk* 55&56 (1944-45) 87-103.

F. R. Hoare, "The Work of the Six Days: A Suggestion," *IER, 5th Ser.*, 65 (1945) 246-253.

*Russell L. Mixter, "Genesis and Geology," *CO* 3 (1945-46) 119-121.

Arthur Geddes, "Creation. A Study of the Contrasted Accounts in Genesis," *HJ* 44 (1945-46) 22-25.

C. J. Södergren, "The Story of Creation," *AQ* 25 (1946) 16-24.

Felix V. Hanson, "The Book of Genesis and Science. *A Reply to Dr. Södegeren's Article, 'The Story of Creation,' in the* Augustana Quarterly, *January, 1946*," *AQ* 25 (1946) 158-161.

Otto J. Eckert, "A Brief Summary of an Exegetical Study of the Length of the Days of Creation," *WLQ* 43 (1946) 206-209.

*Frederick Moriarty and William G. Guindon, "Genesis and Scientific Studies on the Origin of the World," *CBQ* 12 (1950) 428-438.

William J. Tinkle, "Why God Called His Creation Good," *JASA* 2 (1950) #4, 20-22. (Discussion, pp. 22-25)

*Merrill F. Unger, "The Babylonian and Biblical Accounts of Creation," *BS* 109 (1952) 304-317.

J. Oliver Buswell Jr., "Creation Days," *JASA* 4 (1952) #1, 10-15.

August C. Renwaldt, "Some Phases of 'After His Kind' in the Light of Modern Science," *CTM* 24 (1953) 330-349.

*R. J. Wilson, "Wilhelm Vischer on 'God Created' בָּרָא," *ET* 65 (1953-54) 94-95.

Peter W. Stoner, "The Reconstruction of Cataclysmic Theory," *JASA* 6 (1954) #3, 9-13.

I. Engnell, "'Knowledge' and 'life' in the creation story," *VTS* 3 (1955) 103-119.

*H. J. Richards, "The Creation and Fall," *Scrip* 8 (1956) 109-115.

John C. Sinclair, "Creation," *JASA* 8 (1956) #1, 16-18.

*Leonard Woolley, "Stories of the Creation and Flood," *PEQ* 88 (1956) 14-21.

George S. Walton, "A Geologist Looks at Genesis," *UTSB* 56 (1956-57) #2, 11-14.

E. C. V. Mackenzie, "The Hexaemeron: Natural Days or Longer Periods?" *AusTR* 29 (1958) 1-17.

Merrill F. Unger, "Rethinking the Genesis Creation Account," *BS* 115 (1958) 27-35.

Ulrich Simon, "Old Testament Problems: The Beginning," *CQR* 159 (1958) 162-178.

T. Worden, "Questions and Answers. The Creation of Woman. Is it correct to say that woman, having received human nature only mediately through man, and to be a helpmate to man, is not an image of God in the full sense as man?" *Scrip* 10 (1958) 60-61.

A. M. Dubarle, "History and Myth in Genesis," *TD* 6 (1958) 95-99.

*Gordon E. Barnes, "Some Reflections on the Evolution Controversy," *F&T* 91 (1959-60) 158-176. [*Evolution and the Concept of Creation*, pp. 159-160, *Evolution and Genesis*, pp. 160-163]

Albert H. Jenemann, "The Formation of Eve," *MH* 15 (1960) #2, 45-50.

S. G. F. Brandon, "'In the beginning': The Hebrew Story of Creation in its Contemporary Setting," *HT* 11 (1961) 380-387.

Colum Devine, "Creation and Restoration," *AER* 146 (1962) 121-131.

Carroll Stuhlmueller, "Genesis and the Secret of Creation," *BibT* #1 (1962) 7-12.

Thomas J. Motherway, "Adam and the Theologians," *ChgoS* 1 (1962) 115-132.

Edward J. Young, "The Days of Genesis—I," *WJT* 25 (1962-63) 1-34.

Edward J. Young, "The Days of Genesis—II," *WJT* 25 (1962-63) 143-172.

*S. B. Gurewicz, "Some Examples of Modern Hebrew Exegeses of the OT," *ABR* 11 (1963) 15-23. [1. The Creation Narratives, pp. 15-18]

*Lucien Legrand, "Creation as cosmic victory of Yahweh," *TD* 11 (1963) 154-158.

William F. Tanner, "Geology and the Days of Genesis," *JASA* 16 (1964) 28-85.

*M. P. John, "Three Bible Studies," *R&S* 11 (1964) #4, 5-12. [I. Creation, pp. 5-8; II. Fall, pp. 8-10; III. New Creation, pp. 10-12]

Gene Rice, "'Let Us Make Man'," *JRT* 21 (1964-65) 109-114.

Walter R. Roehrs, "The Creation Account of Genesis: Guidelines for an Interpretation," *CTM* 36 (1965) 301-321.

*Frederick V. Winnett, "Re-Examining the Foundations," *JBL* 84 (1965) 1-19. [The Primeval History, pp. 1-5]

*John H. Giltner, "Genesis and Geology: The Stuart—Silliman—Hitchcock Debate," *JRT* 23 (1966-67) 3-13.

H. W. Huppenbauer, "In the Beginning God Created the World....," *GBT* 3 (1966-71) #1, 19-24.

*John C. Whitcomb Jr., "The Creation of the Heavens and the Earth," *GJ* 8 (1967) #2, 27-32.

*A. R. Millard, "A New Babylonian 'Genesis' Story," *TB* #18 (1967) 3-28. [Comparison with the Hebrew Genesis, pp. 6-14; Observations on the Babylonian and the Hebrew Accounts Compared, pp. 14-18]

*Efraim Gottlieb, "The Significance of the Story of Creation in the Interpretations of the Early Cabbalists," *Tarbiz̲* 37 (1967-68) #3, IV-V.

W. M. Clark, "The Animal Series in the Primeval History," *VT* 18 (1968) 433-449.

Joseph E. Duncan, "Paradise as the Whole Earth," *JHI* 30 (1969) 171-186.

*Robert C. Neville, "Creation and the Trinity," *ThSt* 30 (1969) 3-26.

§306 *3.2.9.6.2 Eden and the Fall*

Anonymous, "Adam and Eve," *MMBR* 26 (1808-09) 554.

( ) S., "The Reasonableness of Appointing the Fruit of the Tree of Knowledge of Good and Evil, to Our First Parents as a Test of Their Obedience," *QTMRP* 2 (1813) 287-291.

Anonymous, "On the Forbidden Fruit," *QTMRP* 4 (1814) 388-393.

*Anonymous, "A Glance at the History of Opinions Concerning the Creation and Fall of Man," *CD, N.S.,* 1 (1819) 102-108, 169-179.

†Anonymous, "Holden's Dissertation on the Fall of Man," *BCQTR, N.S.,* 22 (1824) 337-345. *(Review)*

Anonymous, "Spirit of the Hebrew Scriptures.—No. II. Temptation, Sin, and Punishment," *CE* 16 (1834) 305-320.

P. T., "On the Test of Adam's Obedience," *CongML* 17 (1834) 89-93.

[A. Bams], "The Law of Paradise," *BRCR* 9 (1837) 180-198.

J. C., "The Serpent and Eve," *CongML* 23 (1840) 92-94.

C. K., "The Serpent and Eve," *CongML* 23 (1840) 213-215.

*J. Pye Smith, "On Death as Connected with the Fall," *JSL, 1st Ser.,* 1 (1848) 167-171.

*John Kitto, "On Sacred Trees," *JSL, 1st Ser.,* 1 (1848) 290-295. *[Tree of Life and the Tree of Knowledge of Good and Evil]*

J. S., "Thoughts on the Primeval Condition of Man," *MQR* 2 (1848) 21-51.

A. Gordon, "Who was the Serpent that Beguiled Eve," *JSL, 1st Ser.,* 4 (1849) 143-145.

G. S. D., "On the Serpent that Beguiled Eve," *JSL, 1st Ser.,* 4 (1849) 392-394.

T. T., "The Serpent," *JSL, 2nd Ser.,* 1 (1851-52) 351-362.

G. L., "The Serpent," *JSL, 2nd Ser.,* 2 (1852) 217-219.

[W. Friedrick] Rinck, "The Origin of Evil and the Fall," *MR* 35 (1853) 568-575. *(Trans. by B. H. Nadal)*

Anonymous, "The Fall: Who was the Tempter?" *JSL, 2nd Ser.,* 5 (1853-54) 450-454.

Anonymous, "The Primitive State, Character and Happiness of Man," *SPR* 7 (1853-54) 365-374.

P. S., "The State of Innocence," *JSL, 3rd Ser.,* 2 (1855-56) 56-65.

E. F., "Geology and the Fall," *UQGR* 14 (1857) 373-389. *(Review)*

H. C. Barlow, "The Tree of Life," *JSL, 4th Ser.,* 2 (1862-63) 64-74.

*John Duns, "The Serpent of Eden, from the Point of View of Advanced Science," *BS* 21 (1864) 163-179.

Anonymous, "The Serpent in Eden and the Fall," *CongR* 4 (1864) 282-292.

R. F. Weymouth, "On the Names Hiddekel, Euphrates, and Tubal (Tver)," *JSL, 4th Ser.,* 5 (1864) 418-421.

(   ) Piper, "The Tree of Life," *JSL, 4th Ser.,* 4 (1863-64) 376-393; 6 (1864-65) 27-50; 8 (1865-66) 57-74.

[Enoch Pond], "The Garden of Eden," *FBQ* 13 (1865) 175-185.

Anonymous, "The Expulsion from the Garden," *JSL, 5th Ser.,* 1 (1867) 331-337.

Anonymous, "The Site and Rivers of Eden," *JSL, 5th Ser.,* 1 (1867) 363-368.

Varnum Lincoln, "The Scenes in Eden not a Fall of Man," *UQGR, N.S.,* 4 (1867) 75-84.

Anonymous, "The Two Trees in Eden," *SPR* 18 (1867-68) 17-30.

*R. C. G., "The Cherubim of Eden," *ERG, 4th Ser.,* 3 (1868-69) 35-43.

Luther Lee, "Literality of the Account of the Garden of Eden," *MR* 51 (1869) 338-346.

D. F. Brendle, "The Fall and Its Import," *RChR* 20 (1873) 376-390.

A. S. A., "Eden: Its Garden and Rivers," *ERG, 6th Ser.,* 3 (1876-77) 48-59.

Lewis J. Dudley, "The Serpent in Genesis," *URRM* 10 (1878) 24-42.

François Lenormant, "The First Sin, as Recorded in the Bible and in Ancient Oriental Tradition," *ContR* 36 (1879) 148-163.

*J. W. Dawson, "Points of Contact Between Science and Revelation," *PRev* 55 (1879) Part 2, 579-606. [Eden, pp. 582-584]

O. D. Miller, "The Gan-Eden of Genesis," *OBJ* 1 (1880) 134-146.

S. H. Trowbridge, "Does the Bible Teach that Adam was the First Man?" *OBJ* 1 (1880) 185-192.

Alexander MacWhorther, "The Edenic Period of Man," *PRev* 56 (1880) Part 2, 62-91.

O. D. Miller, "The Gan-Eden in Genesis," *AAOJ* 3 (1880-81) 39-51.

*M. C. Read, "The Symbolism of the Garden of Eden," *AAOJ* 3 (1880-81) 131-134.

*William Hayes Ward, "The Serpent Tempter in Oriental Mythology," *BS* 38 (1881) 209-230.

Joseph Henry Barker, "Adam's Land; or, the Extent of the Mosaic Creation," *CM* 14 (1881) 227-237, 304-311.

*François Lenormant, "Ararat and 'Eden. A Biblical Study," *ContR* 40 (1881) 453-478. *[Marked as "continued" but was not]*

*F. D. Hoskins, "Evolution and the Christian Doctrine of the Fall," *CR* 36 (1881) 25-40. *[Volume actually listed as No. 135]*

Alexander Brown, "The Place and Function of the Serpent in the Fall," *ERG, 7th Ser.,* 4 (1881-82) 51-65.

[M.] L[oy], "The Original State of Man," *ColTM* 2 (1882) 129-150.

[M.] L[oy], "The Fall of Man," *ColTM* 2 (1882) 193-217.

J. A. Smith, "The Language of Primitive Man," *ONTS* 2 (1882-83) 193-199.

T. Stenhouse, "The Site of Paradise," *BFER* 32 (1883) 89-96. *(Review)*

H. Walter Featherstun, "The Tree of Life," *MQR, 2nd Ser.,* 5 (1883) 120-130.

*G[eorge] Rawlinson, "Biblical Topography. No. I.—The Site of Paradise," *MI* 1 (1884-85) 401-410.

Francis Brown, "A Recent Theory of the Garden of Eden," *ONTS* 4 (1884-85) 1-12.

[Edward] White, "Noble Thoughts in the Edenic Story," *ONTS* 4 (1884-85) 175-177.

*C. H. Toy, "Notice of F. Delitzch's views as to the alleged site of Eden," *JAOS* 11 (1885) lxxii-lxxiii.

Thomas Whitelaw, "The Patriarchal Times. III.—The Cradle of the Race," *MI* 2 (1885) 210-226. *[Paradise]*

Thomas Whitelaw, "The Patriarchal Times. IV.—The Story of the Fall," *MI* 2 (1885) 439-455.

*J. Grape Jr., "The Temptation and Fall, according to the Targums," *UQGR, N.S.,* 23 (1886) 84-98.

E. W. Claypole, "Paradise Found," *UQGR, N.S.,* 24 (1887) 14-25. *[Garden of Eden]*

Terrien de Lacouperie, "The tree of Life and the calendar Plant of Babylonia and China," *BOR* 2 (1887-88) 149-159.

William M. Bryant, "Eden and Paradise: A Meditation," *URRM* 33 (1889) 306-312.

H. E. Ryle, "The Early Narratives of Genesis, III. The Story of Paradise," *ET* 2 (1890-91) 269-273.

*Alexander Kohut, "Parsic and Jewish Literature of the First Man," *JQR* 3 (1890-91) 231-250.

H. E. Ryle, "The Early Narratives of Genesis, IV. The Story of Paradise, continued," *ET* 3 (1891-92) 122-125.

Hormuzd Rassam, "The Garden of Eden and Biblical Sages," *JTVI* 25 (1891-92) 83-123, 129-130. [(Discussion, pp. 123-126) (Remarks by C. R. Conder, pp. 126-127; J. W. Dawson, pp. 127-128; A. H. Sayce, pp. 128-129)]

*John Thomas Gulick, "Evolution and the Fall of Man," *BS* 49 (1892) 516-519.

A. J. Maas, "Adam's Rib—Allegory or History?" *AER* 9 (1893) 88-102.

*J. William Dawson, "Physical and Historical Probabilities Respecting the Authorship and Authority of the Mosaic Books," *Exp, 4th Ser.,* 9 (1894) 16-33, 109-123, 276-288, 362-375, 440-451. [III. Early Man and Eden, pp. 276-288]

William Hayes Ward, "Light on Scriptural Texts from Recent Discoveries. The Tree of Life," *HR* 27 (1894) 117-119.

D. Flynn, "Adam and Eve Before the Fall," *IER, 3rd Ser.,* 15 (1894) 1076-1088.

William Hayes Ward, "Light on Scriptural Texts from Recent Discoveries. The Rivers of Paradise," *HR* 28 (1894) 500-502.

Paul Haupt, "The Rivers of Paradise," *JAOS* 16 (1896) ciii-cv.

J. William Dawson, "The 'Cursing of the Ground,' and the 'Revealing of the Sons of God,' in Relation to Natural Facts: I. Man before the Fall," *Exp, 5th Ser.,* 1 (1895) 411-423.

J. William Dawson, "The 'Cursing of the Ground,' and the 'Revealing of the Sons of God,' in Relation to Natural Facts: II. The Fall and its Consequences," *Exp, 5th Ser.,* 2 (1895) 54-68.

J. William Dawson, "The 'Cursing of the Ground,' and the 'Revealing of the Sons of God,' in Relation to Natural Facts: III. The Restoration," *Exp, 5th Ser.*, 2 (1895) 93-103.

William Alexander Holliday, "The Effect of the Fall of Man upon Nature," *PRR* 7 (1896) 611-621.

*D. W. Simon, "Evolution and the Fall of Man," *BS* 54 (1897) 1-20.

*G. H. Skipwith, "The Burning Bush and the Garden of Eden: A Study in Comparative Mythology," *JQR* 10 (1897-98) 489-502.

W[illiam] H[ayes] Ward, "The Story of the Serpent and Tree," *AAOJ* 20 (1898) 211-227. [Introduction and Notes by Stephen D. Peet]

Paul Carus, "The Food of Life and the Sacrament. Biblical Accounts and Pagan Parallels," *Monist* 10 (1899-1900) 246-279, 343-382. *[The Tree of Life]*

Thomas Nixon Carver, "The Economic Interpretation of the Fall of Man," *BS* 57 (1900) 483-493.

Daniel Seeley Gregory, "The Fall and Modern Thought," *CFL, N.S.*, 4 (1901) 22-33.

Stephen D. Peet, "The Serpent and the Tree," *AAOJ* 23 (1901) 179-198.

Fritz Hommel, "The Four Rivers of Paradise," *ET* 13 (1901-02) 38-40.

Alexander Brown, "The Coming of Sin," *LQHR* 98 (1902) 291-307. *(Review) [The Fall]*

*William Wallace Martin, "The Fall as a Composite Narrative," *BS* 60 (1903) 84-91.

Stephen D. Peet, "The Tree of Life Among All Nations," *AAOJ* 26 (1904) 1-16.

*Wentworth Webster, "The Language of Early Bible History," *ET* 16 (1904-05) 521-523. [The Fall of Man, pp. 522-523]

Stephen D. Peet, "The Story of the Temptation; or, the Contest Between Good and Evil," *AAOJ* 27 (1905) 139-152.

A. H. Sayce, "The Rivers of Paradise," *ET* 17 (1905-06) 469-471.

George Barlow, "The Fall of Woman," *ContR* 90 (1906) 95-106.

Camden M. Cobern, "Early Bible Narratives Reinterpreted. III.—Adam and Eve," *HR* 51 (1906) 173-179.

Camden M. Cobern, "Early Bible Narratives Reinterpreted. IV.—The Garden of Eden," *HR* 51 (1906) 417-421.

Camden M. Cobern, "Early Bible Narratives Reinterpreted. V—The Apple and the Serpent," *HR* 52 (1906) 103-107.

Stephen D. Peet, "The Garden of Eden," *AAOJ* 29 (1907) 283-298.

T. McK. Stuart, "The Story of Eden—History or a Myth?" *CFL, 3rd Ser.,* 6 (1907) 106-111.

Leander S. Keyser, "The First Temptation. Is the Biblical Story Fact or Fiction?" *LCR* 26 (1907) 731-739.

Francesco Mari, "Assyro-Babylonian Elements in the Biblical Account of the Fall," *NYR* 3 (1907-08) 163-180.

Henry Proctor, "The Tree of Life," *AAOJ* 30 (1908) 25-27.

A. H. Sayce, "The Serpent in Genesis," *ET* 20 (1908-09) 562.

J. C. Gregory, "The Garden of Eden and the Fall of the Serpent," *WR* 172 (1909) 540-546.

*C. H. Parez, "Short Studies and Correspondence. Men of Science and Genesis," *ICMM* 6 (1909-10) 105-106.

*Arthur E. Whatham, "Are Adam and Eve Historical Characters?" *AAOJ* 32 (1910) 85-93.

Frederick Carl Eieselen, "'The Tree of the Knowledge of Good and Evil'," *BW* 36 (1910) 101-112.

Anonymous, "Is the Story of Eve's Creation an Allegory?" *CFL, 3rd Ser.,* 12 (1910) 85-86. *(Editorial Note)*

A. W. F. Blunt, "The Fall," *HR* 61 (1911) 12-16.

*Paul Haupt, "An Ancient Protest Against the Curse of Eve," *PAPS* 50 (1911) 505-517.

Edward Robertson, "Where was Eden?" *AJSL* 28 (1911-12) 254-273.

Alfred Roebuck, "The Garden of Eden: Its Location and Restoration," *LQHR* 120 (1913) 147-150.

A. S. Peake, "The Story of Eden," *HR* 71 (1916) 433-437.

Anonymous, "A Northern Paradise," *HR* 71 (1916) 487-488.

Paul Haupt, "The Curse of the Serpent," *JBL* 35 (1916) 155-162.

A. Van Hoonacker, "Is the Narrative of the Fall a Myth?" *Exp, 8th Ser.,* 16 (1918) 373-400.

Robert H. Kennet, "The Story of Eden," *ICMM* 15 (1918-19) 201-205.

Julian Morgenstern, "The Sources of the Paradise Story," *JJLP* 1 (1919) 105-123, 225-240.

Anonymous, "Current Notes and News. The Vindication of Eve," *A&A* 9 (1920) 146-147.

James A. Burrow, "The Serpent," *MQR, 3rd Ser.,* 47 (1921) 720-727.

*W[illiam] F[oxwell] Albright, "The Location of the Garden of Eden," *AJSL* 39 (1922-23) 15-31.

A. E. J. Rawlinson, "The Garden of Eden," *ICMM* 19 (1922-23) 214-218.

*William Hallock Johnson, "Evolution and the Fall," *BR* 9 (1924) 371-386.

Frederick S. Arnold, "The Fall of Man," *ACM* 16 (1924-25) 444-450.

Alexander Haggerty Krappe, "The Story of the Fall," *AJSL* 43 (1926-27) 236-239.

H. Th. Obbink, "The Tree of Life in Eden," *ZAW* 46 (1928) 105-112.

K. L. Stevenson, "The Rivers of Eden," *ET* 40 (1928-29) 330-332.

J. Opie Urmson, "The Four Rivers of Eden," *ET* 40 (1928-29) 526.

*George S. Duncan, "Notes and Comments. The Location of Eden," *A&A* 27 (1929) 92.

*George S. Duncan, "The Biblical and Archaeological Location of Eden," *AJA* 33 (1929) 103-104.

Sara A. Emerson, "An Inquiry concerning the Origin and Basis of Fact of the Story of the Fall of Man," *MR* 112 (1929) 294-297.

M[elvin] G[rove] Kyle, "The Fall and Its Consequences," *BS* 87 (1930) 227-235.

Edwin Deacon, "Was Adam's Fall a Blessing?" *CFL, 3rd Ser.,* 36 (1930) 304-305.

H. Th. Obbink, "The Tree of Life in Eden," *ET* 44 (1932-33) 475; 45 (1933-34) 236-237.

*Edward Ulback, "The Serpent in Myth and Scripture," *BS* 90 (1933) 449-455.

C. W. Browning, "The Tree of Life in Eden," *ET* 45 (1933-34) 44.

*W. Leonard, "Our First Parents," *ACR* 11 (1934) 195-212, 306-319; 12 (1935) 121-131.

Robert Gordis, "The Significance of the Paradise Story," *JBL* 53 (1934) iii.

Robert Gordis, "The Significance of the Paradise Myth," *AJSL* 52 (1935-36) 86-94.

*Bernard Lewis, "An Ismaili Interpretation of the Fall of Adam," *BSOAS* 9 (1937-39) 691-704.

*Ralph Marcus, "The Tree of Life in Proverbs," *JBL* 62 (1943) 117-120.

*Alexander Altmann, "The Gnostic Background of the Rabbinic Adam Legends," *JQR, N.S.,* 35 (1944-45) 371-391.

Robert Eisler, "Man into Wolf. An Anthropological Account of the Fall," *HJ* 44 (1945-46) 159-165.

Arthur Geddes, "The Origin of Sin in Genesis, and a Missing Legend," *HJ* 44 (1945-46) 248-253.

*Raphael Patai, "Note to the Gnostic Background of the Rabbinic Adam Legends," *JQR, N.S.,* 36 (1945-46) 416-417.

James B. Pritchard, "Man's Predicament in Eden," *RR* 13 (1948-49) 5-23.

*Arvid S. Kapelrud, "The Gates of Hell and the Guardian Angels of Paradise," *JAOS* 70 (1950) 151-156.

Brian P. Sutherland, "The Fall and its Relation to Present Conditions in Nature," *JASA* 2 (1950) #4, 14-19.

Humphrey J. T. Johnson, "The Bible, the Church and the Formation of Eve," *DownsR* 69 (1951) 16-30.

*Geo Widengren, "The King and the Tree of Life in Ancient Near Eastern Religion. (King and Saviour IV)," *UUÅ* (1951) #4 , 1-79.

R. E. Wolfe, "The Garden of Eden and the River of God," *JBL* 71 (1952) viii-ix.

Irwin A. Wills, "Genetic Evidence As to the Color of Adam and Eve," *JASA* 6 (1954) #2, 13-14.

Eleanor Simmons Greenhill, "The Child in the Tree: A Study of the Cosmological Tree in Christian Tradition,"*Tr* 10 (1954) 323-371. [O. T. Refs., pp. 335-338]

*Ralph Marcus, "'Tree of Life' in Essene(?) Tradition," *JBL* 74 (1955) 274.

Johs. Pedersen, "The Fall of Man," *NTTO* 56 (1955) 162-172.

Bernard J. LeFrois, "The Forbidden Fruit," *AER* 136 (1956) 175-183.

Immanuel Lewy, "The Two Strata in the Eden Story," *HUCA* 27 (1956) 93-99.

Bo. Reicke, "The Knowledge Hidden in the Tree of Paradise," *JSS* 1 (1956) 193-201.

*H. J. Richards, "The Creation and Fall," *Scrip* 8 (1956) 109-115.

Carmino J. de Catanzaro, "Man in Revolt: A Study in the Primaeval History of the Book of Genesis," *CJT* 4 (1958) 285-292.

A. M. Dubarle, "Original Sin in Genesis," *DownsR* 76 (1958) 223-250. *(Trans. by John Higgins)*

*J. Edgar Bruns, "Depth-Psychology and the Fall," *CBQ* 21 (1959) 78-82.

H. J. Richards, "The Forbidden Fruit," *ClR* 44 (1959) 264-270.

Walter J. Beasley, "The Garden of Eden: Is It History or Legend?" *AT* 4 (1959-60) #3, 15-19.

John Wren-Lewis, "Christian Morality and the Idea of a Cosmic Fall," *ET* 71 (1959-60) 204-206.

John M. Steadman, "'Man's First Disobedience': The Causal Structure of the Fall," *JHI* 21 (1960) 180-197.

*Paul Ramsey, "The Marriage of Adam and Eve," *MTSB, Fall* (1960) 35-56.

John Wren-Lewis, "When Did the Fall Occur?" *ET* 72 (1960-61) 4-7.

*John Wren-Lewis, "What was the Original Sin?"*ET* 72 (1960-61) 177-180.

Harris H. Hirschberg, "The Story of the 'Fall'—Myth or Message?" *CCARJ* 9 (1961-62) #4, 22-27.

*Ray L. Cleveland, "Cherubs and the 'Tree of Life' in Ancient South Arabia," *BASOR* #172 (1963) 55-60.

*M. P. John, "Three Bible Studies,"*R&S* 11(1964)#4,5-12. [II. Fall, pp. 8-10]

Serge Verkhovskoy, "Creation of Man and the Establishment of the Family in the Light of the Book of Genesis," *StVSQ, N.S.,* 8 (1964) 5-30.

*V. Keisch, "The Antiocheans and the Temptation Story," *StP* 7 (1966) 496-502.

*Norman C. Habel, "Ezekiel 28 and the Fall of the First Man," *CTM* 38 (1967) 516-524.

James O. Buswell III, "Genesis, the Neolithic Age, and the Antiquity of Adam," *F&T* 96 (1967) #1, 3-23.

Mark Pontifex, "The Problem of the Fall," *DownsR* 86 (1968) 395-404.

E. O. James, "The Tree of Life," *Folk* 79 (1968) 241-249.

E[dward] J. Young, "What Shall We Believe About The Serpent and the Trees of the Garden of Eden?" *IRB* 32&33 (1968) 42-48.

*D. Neiman, "Eden, the Garden of God," *AAASH* 17 (1969) 109-124.

*R. Vande Walle, "The Sin in the Garden and the Sinfulness of the World," *IJT* 18 (1969) 124-164. [I. The Sin in the Garden, pp. 124-140]

O. Hobart Mowrer, "The Problem of Good and Evil Empirically Considered, with Reference to Psychological and Social Adjustment," *Z* 4 (1969) 301-314. [I. The "Fall of Man" and the Problems of Evil, pp. 302-303]

§307 *3.2.9.6.3 The Antediluvian Period*

Anglo-Scotus, "An Attempt to prove that the fallen Angels were the Sons of Seth," *TRep* 5 (1786) 166-181.

*†J. Woodhouse, "The Antediluvian Year," *MMBR* 3 (1797) 343-344.

*(   ) Hewlett, "On the Longevity of the Antediluvians," *MR* 4 (1821) 412-413.

*Luther Halsey, "The Populousness of the Antediluvian World Considered," *BibR* 4 (1828) 563-590.

H. Rood, "No Wars Before the Flood," *BJ* 2 (1843) 276-280.

*Ernest Bertheau, "On the Different Computations of the First Two Periods in the Book of Genesis, and the Chronological Assumptions on which they are Based," *JSL, 1st Ser.,* 2 (1848)115-128. *(Trans. by John Nicholson)*

*Anonymous, "The Mark of Cain and the Curse of Ham," *SPR* 3 (1849-50) 415-426.

T. T., "The Antediluvian Theocracy," *JSL, 2nd Ser.,* 5 (1853-54)382-406.

*Anonymous, "Queries in Regard to Dr. Seyffarth's Lectures on Egyptian Antiquities," *ER* 8 (1856-57) 415-436. [V. The death of Methuselah and Lamech, pp. 428-430]

*W. R. French, "Longevity of the Antediluvians," *UQGR, N.S.,* 4 (1867)227-235.

*Victor Rydberg, "Key to the Genealogical Table of the First Patriarchs of Genesis, *and the Chronology of the Septuagint. From L. L. H. Combertigue's French MS. Translation of the Original Swedish Brochure and Notes. By S. M. Drach,"* *SBAT* 5(1876-77) 65-87.

*J. W. Dawson, "Points of Contact Between Science and Revelation," *PRev* 55 (1879) Part 2, 579-606. [Antediluvians, pp. 591-596]

François Lenormant, "The First Murder and the Founding of the First City. A Biblical Study," *ContR* 37 (1880) 263-274.

*François Lenormant, "The Genealogies between Adam and the Deluge. A Biblical Study," *ContR* 37 (1880) 565-589.

Samuel Ives Curtiss, "A Symposium on the Antediluvian Narratives.—Lenormant, Delitzsch, Haupt, Dillmann," *BS* 40 (1883) 501-533.

Thomas Whitelaw, "The Patriarchal Times. V.—The First Age of History," *MI* 3 (1885-86) 102-120. *[The Fall to the Flood]*

*H. T. B., "The Names of the Antediluvian Patriarchs Translated," *EN* 3 (1891) 141.

*H. E. Ryle, "The Early Narratives of Genesis," *ET* 3 (1891-92) 209-214. [V. The Story of Cain and Abel, pp. 209-213]

*Anonymous, "The Longevity of the Patriarchs," *ONTS* 15 (1892) 78.

*Fritz Hommel, "The Ten Patriarchs of Berosus," *SBAP* 15 (1892-93)243-246.

*J. William Dawson, "Physical and Historical Probabilities Respecting the Authorship and Authority of the Mosaic Books," *Exp, 4th Ser.,* 9 (1894) 16-33, 109-123, 276-288, 362-375, 440-451. [IV. Antediluvians and the Deluge, pp. 362-375]

William Henry Green, "The Sons of God and the Daughters of Men," *PRR* 5 (1894) 654-660.

J. William Dawson, "Sons of God and Daughters of Men," *Exp, 5th Ser.,* 4 (1896) 201-211.

A. H. Sayce, "The Antediluvian Patriarchs," *ET* 10 (1898-99) 352-353.

Stephen D. Peet, "The History of the Ante-Diluvian World," *AAOJ* 28 (1906) 17-32.

Charles Hallock, "'The World Before the Flood'," *AAOJ* 33 (1911) #2, 12-14, 144-147.

*Charles Caverno, "The Rule in Cain's Case: A Study in Ethics," *BS* 72(1915) 235-245.

*G. Buchanan Gray, "The Sacrifice of Cain and Abel," *Exp, 8th Ser.*, 10 (1915) 1-23.

Archy O. Logist[sic]*, "The Antediluvian 'Span of Life'," *HR* 73 (1917) 83.

M. Milman[sic]*, "Noah and His Family," *Monist* 29 (1919) 259-292. *[Index shows author's name as Max Müller!]*

*E. E. Kellett, "'The Prodigiously Long Ages of the Patriarchs'," *ET* 33(1921-22) 167-169.

*A. Achtermann, "The Great Age of the Antediluvians," *CFL, 3rd Ser.*, 32 (1926) 114-115.

*Dudley Joseph Whitney, "The Antediluvian Earth and its Inhabitants," *CFL, 3rd Ser.*, 34 (1928) 440-445.

C. E. Smith, "The Development of Cain's Posterity: Civilization without Religion," *BS* 86 (1929) 285-289.

*Melvin Grove Kyle, "Antediluvian Regulations," *BS* 87 (1930) 344-351.

*John Lowell Butler, "Causes of Antediluvian Longevity," *BS* 90 (1933) 49-69.

T. E. Bird, "'And the Lord Set a Mark Upon Cain'," *ClR* 8 (1934) 104-112.

E[arl] B[ennett] Cross, "An Answer to J. G. Frazer Anent Cain and Abel," *JBL* 54 (1935) xii.

H. Hamann, "'The Days Before the Flood'," *AusTR* 10 (1939) 120-124.

S. H. Hooke, "Cain and Abel," *Folk* 50 (1939) 58-65.

*G. D. Hornblower, "Cain and Abel: The Choice of Kind of Sacrifice," *Man* 44 (1944) #31.

S. H. Hooke, "Cain and Abel," *Man* 44 (1944) #67.

I. Schapera, "The Sin of Cain," *JRAI* 85 (1955) 33-43.

A. Scheiber, "A Remark on the Legend of the Sacrificial Smoke of Cain and Abel," *VC* 10 (1956) 194-195.

*Robert North, "The Cain Music," *JBL* 83 (1964) 373-389.

*Frank N. Egerton III, "The Longevity of the Patriarchs: A Topic in the History of Demography," *JHI* 27 (1966) 575-584.

§308 *3.2.9.6.4 The Flood*

†G. Cumberland, "Mr. Cumberland on the Deluge," *MMBR* 40 (1815-16) 209-210.

S. N., "The Mosaic History of the Deluge," *CongML* 15 (1832) 18-21, 77-80.

Edward Hitchcock, "The Historical and Geological Deluges Compared," *BRCR* 9 (1837) 78-139; 10 (1837) 328-374; 11 (1838) 1-27.

H. Rood, "Noah's Flood," *BJ* 1 (1842) 287-293.

Anonymous, "The Extent and Character of the Noachian Deluge," *CRB* 20 (1855) 108-117.

J. V. Turner, "Thoughts on the Internal Structure of the Earth, and on the Natural Causes by which the Deluge was Produced," *MQR* 10 (1856) 582-588.

*Anonymous, "Queries in Regard to Dr. Seyffarth's Lectures on Egyptian Antiquities," *ER* 8 (1856-57) 415-436. [VI. The Universality of the Deluge, pp. 430-435]

*Gust. Seyffarth, "To the Author of the 'Queries in regard to Dr. Seyffarth's Lectures on Egyptian Antiquities,' in the Ev. Review, January 1857, p. 415," *ER* 9 (1857-58) 58-75. *[The Flood]*

Charles W. Shields, "Religious Lessons of the Deluge," *TLJ* 11 (1858-59) 440-453.

D. C. M'Laren, "The Deluge a Cause of Geological Change," *TLJ* 12 (1859-60) 263-293.

*Anonymous, "Bishop Colenso on the Creation and the Flood," *TRL* 1 (1864) 161-180. *(Review)*

M. Davison, "On the Noachian Deluge," *JTVI* 4 (1869-70) 121-149. (Discussion, pp. 149-162)

H. Moule, "More than One Universal Deluge recorded in the Scriptures," *JTVI* 4 (1869-70) 231-247, 261. (Discussion, pp. 247-260)

M. Stewart, "The Deluge, and Archæology," *BFER* 22 (1873) 159-168.

*A. H. Sayce, "The Chaldean Account of the Deluge, and Its Relation to the Old Testament," *TRL* 10 (1873) 364-377.

J. Challis, "The Relation of the Scripture Account of the Deluge to Physical Science," *JTVI* 10 (1876-77) 66-92, 101-102. (Discussion, pp. 93-101)

François Lenormant, "The Deluge: Its Traditions in Ancient Nations," *ContR* 36 (1879) 465-500.

*Paul Haupt, "The Cuneiform Account of the Flood," *ONTS* 3 (1883-84) 77-85.

Thomas Whitelaw, "The Patriarchal Times. VI.—The Judgment of the Flood," *MI* 3 (1885-86) 367-384.

Claude R. Conder, "Notes. *Flood Stories in Palestine,*" *PEFQS* 18 (1886) 15.

*†Anonymous, "The Mammoth and the Flood," *QRL* 166 (1888) 112-129. *(Review)*

Anonymous, "The Great Flood," *CQR* 27 (1888-89) 85-101. *(Review)*

*G. Frederick Wright, "The Glacial Period and Noah's Deluge," *BS* 46 (1889) 466-474.

J. William Dawson, "The Deluge—Biblical and Geological," *ContR* 56 (1889) 884-900.

*Maximilian Lindsay Kellner, "The Deluge in the Izdubar Epic and in the Old Testament," *CR* 53 (1889) 40-66.

F. Cane, "The Physics of the Flood," *IER, 3rd Ser.,* 10 (1889) 901-906.

*John D. Davis, "The Babylonian Flood-Legend and the Hebrew Record of the Deluge," *PR* 10 (1889) 415-431.

J. S. Stuart-Glennie, "The Traditional Deluge and its Geological Identification," *BOR* 4 (1889-90) 209-212.

F. B. Denio, "The Rainbow in Genesis," *ONTS* 10 (1890) 274-279.

George D. Armstrong, "The Deluge," *PQ* 5 (1891) 209-228.

*Benjamin Wisner Bacon, "Chronology of the Account of the Flood in P.—A Contribution to the History of the Jewish Calendar," *AJSL* 8 (1891-92) 79-88.

H. E. Ryle, "The Early Narratives of Genesis, VI. The Genealogy of the Sethites," *ET* 3 (1891-92) 353-358. [The Story of the Flood. Chapters vi. 9 - ix. 17]

H. E. Ryle, "The Early Narratives of Genesis, VII. The Story of the Flood continued," *ET* 3 (1891-92) 446-450.

F. H. Woods, "The Noachian Deluge and Its Analogues," *ET* 4 (1892-93) 69-72.

J. A. Zahm, "The Noachian Deluge," *AER* 8 (1893) 14-34, 84-99.

†Anonymous, "Sir H. Howorth on the Great Flood," *ERCJ* 178 (1893) 354-374. *(Review)*

J. Prestwich, "A Possible Cause for the Origin of the Tradition of the Flood," *JTVI* 27 (1893-94) 263-284, 302-305. [(Communication by J. W. Dawson, pp. 285-286) (Discussion, pp. 285-295) (Remarks by R. Ashington Bullen, pp. 295-298; H. D. Grant, pp. 298-299; J. M. Mello, pp. 299-300; Warren Upham, pp. 300-302; (Note, p. 305)]

William R. Harper, "The Deluge in Other Literatures and History," *BW* 4 (1894) 114-123.

G. Frederick Wright, "Professor Prestwich on Some Supposed New Evidence of the Deluge," *BS* 52 (1895) 724-740.

Robert Balgarnie, "Was the Deluge Universal?" *HR* 30 (1895) 65-67.

J. William Dawson, "Natural Facts Illustrative of the Biblical Account of the Deluge," *HR* 31 (1896) 387-393, 483-489; 32 (1896) 3-7, 99-103.

J. A. Selbie, "A New Theory of the Deluge," *ET* 8 (1896-97) 271-272.

J. F. McCurdy, "Light on Scriptural Texts from Recent Discoveries. The Story of the Flood," *HR* 34 (1897) 408-411.

J. F. McCurdy, "Light on Scriptural Texts from Recent Discoveries. How Far is the Flood Story Babylonian?" *HR* 35 (1898) 22-25.

Anonymous, "The Biblical and Other Deluge Stories," *ColTM* 20 (1900) 189-191.

G. Frederick Wright, "Geological Confirmations of the Noachian Deluge," *BS* 59 (1902) 282-293, 537-556, 695-716.

G. A. Adams, "Where was the Flood?" *BS* 59 (1902) 579-583.

Willis J. Beecher, "A Letter with Some Common Problems," *HR* 43 (1902) 352-355. *[The Flood]*

William Cowper Conant, "'Geological Confirmation of the Flood'," *CFL, 3rd Ser.,* 1 (1903) 762-766.

T. G. Bonney, "Science and the Flood," *Exp, 6th Ser.,* 7 (1903) 456-472.

Willis J. Beecher, "Is the Deluge Story in Genesis Self-Contradictory?" *HR* 46 (1903) 258-262.

G. Frederick Wright, "Geological Confirmation of the Flood," *HR* 47 (1904) 256-262.

E[douard] Naville, "The Mention of a Flood in the Book of the Dead," *SBAP* 26 (1904) 251-257, 287-294.

Stephen D. Peet, "The Story of the Deluge," *AAOJ* 27 (1905) 201-216.

G. Frederick Wright, "Contributions of Geology to the Credibility of the Flood," *CFL, 3rd Ser.,* 3 (1905) 11-15. *[Marked as "to be continued" but was not]*

G. L. Young, "The Smelling of the Sweet Savor of Noah's Sacrifice," *CFL, 3rd Ser.,* 3 (1905) 64-67.

*Stephen D. Peet, "The Bow in the Cloud; The Token of a Covenant," *AAOJ* 28 (1906) 65-80.

S. E. Bishop, "Have We Noah's Log-Book?" *BS* 63 (1906) 510-517.

Stephen D. Peet, "The Inheritance of Noah," *AAOJ* 29 (1907) 1-16. *[The Flood Tradition]*

William Restelle, "Traditions of the Deluge," *BS* 64 (1907) 148-167.

*Charles Henry Hitchcock, "The Bible and Recent Science," *BS* 64 (1907) 299-313. [The Noachian Deluge, pp. 306-313] *(Review)*

D. Gath Whitley, "Noah's Flood in the Light of Modern Science," *BS* 64 (1907) 519-551.

*G. Frederick Wright, "Abstract of Professor Wright's Lectures in New York," *CFL, 3rd Ser.,* 6 (1907) 156-161, 235-238. [Lecture Second— "Geology and the Flood," pp. 158-160; The Flood from the Ethical Point of View, pp. 237-238]

Anonymous, "The Universality of the Deluge," *CFL, 3rd Ser.,* 6 (1907) 334. *(Editorial Note)*

Anonymous, "Does Archaeology Contradict the Biblical Date of the Flood?" *CFL, 3rd Ser.,* 6 (1907) 334-336. *(Editorial Note)*

G. L. Young, "The Intrinsic Value of the Deluge Story," *CFL, 3rd Ser.,* 7 (1907) 32-37.

John E. McFadyen, "Are There Two Flood Stories?" *HR* 53 (1907) 128-129.

L[uther] T. Townsend, "'Introductory' to 'The Deluge History or Myth'," *CFL, 3rd Ser.,* 8 (1908) 7-9. *(Editorial Note)*

Henry C. Thomson, "'The Assured Results of Modern Criticism' Tested by the Flood Narrative," *CFL, 3rd Ser.,* 10 (1909) 178-183, 245-254.

*Herbert William Magoun, "The Glacial Epoch and the Noachian Deluge," *BS* 66 (1909) 217-242, 432-457; 67 (1910) 105-119, 204-229.

Anonymous, "The Story of the Deluge. Professor Hilprecht's Remarkable Discovery," *AAOJ* 32 (1910) 118-122.

J. M. P. Smith, "Fresh Light on the Story of the Deluge," *BW* 35 (1910) 282-283.

W. H. Porter, "Genesis and the Flood," *HR* 65 (1913) 512.

Cuthbert Baillon, "The Flood," *IER, 5th Ser.,* 7 (1916) 209-223.

James George Frazer, "Ancient Stories of a Great Flood. *The Huxley Memorial Lecture for* 1916," *JRAI* 46 (1916) 231-283.

*A. H. Sayce, "Assyriological Notes," *SBAP* 39 (1917) 207-212. [Gopherwood, p. 210]

[Jay Benson Hamilton], "The Story of the Deluge," *CFL, 3rd Ser.,* 25 (1919) 509-511.

H[erbert] W[illiam] Magoun, "Creation's Beginnings," *CFL, 3rd Ser.,* 27 (1921) 47-53. *(Part I) [The Flood]*

H[erbert] W[illiam] Magoun, "Creation's Fourth Day," *CFL, 3rd Ser.,* 27 (1921) 90-97. *(Part II) [The Flood]*

H[erbert] W[illiam] Magoun, "Mesozoic and Cenozoic Times," *CFL, 3rd Ser.,* 27 (1921) 140-146. *(Part III) [The Flood]*

H[erbert] W[illiam] Magoun, "Causes and Effects of the Ice Cap," *CFL, 3rd Ser.,* 27 (1921) 181-186. *(Part IV) [The Flood]*

H[erbert] W[illiam] Magoun, "Flood Legends and Traditions," *CFL, 3rd Ser.,* 27 (1921) 239-243. *(Part V)*

H[erbert] W[illiam] Magoun, "Evidences of a Flood in Europe," *CFL, 3rd Ser.,* 27 (1921) 269-274. *(Part VI)*

Herbert W[illiam] Magoun, "Evidences of a Flood in Asia and on other Continents," *CFL, 3rd Ser.,* 27 (1921) 307-313. *(Part VII)*

H[erbert] W[illiam] Magoun, "The Testimony of the Oceanic Islands," *CFL, 3rd Ser.,* 27 (1921) 364-369. *(Part VIII)*

H[erbert] W[illiam] Magoun, "Putting Two and Two Together," *CFL, 3rd Ser.,* 27 (1921) 409-416. *(Part IX)*

H[erbert] W[illiam] Magoun, "The Flood and its Survivors," *CFL, 3rd Ser.,* 27 (1921) 456-463. *(Part X)*

Herbert W[illiam] Magoun, "The Probable Date of the Flood," *CFL, 3rd Ser.,* 28 (1922) 16-23. *(Part XI)*

H[erbert] W[illiam] Magoun, "Other Considerations Bearing on the Flood," *CFL, 3rd Ser.,* 28 (1922) 70-77. *(Part XII)*

Herbert C. Alleman, "A Hebrew Deluge Story," *LQ* 52 (1922) 464-473. *(Review)*

Leroy Waterman, "The Date of the Deluge," *AJSL* 39 (1922-23) 233-247.

Samuel Mercer, "Fresh Light on the History of the Flood," *ATR* 5 (1922-23) 299-307.

Anonymous, "A New Theory of the Flood," *HR* 90 (1925) 110.

J. Martin, "A Famine Element in the Flood Story," *JBL* 45 (1926) 129-133.

A.H.Godbey, "Further Light on the Flood Story," *AJSL* 43 (1926-27) 239-240.

George McCready Price, "Misinformation about the Flood," *CFL, 3rd Ser.*, 33 (1927) 519-520.

Dudley Joseph Whitney, "Geology and the Deluge," *CFL, 3rd Ser.*, 34 (1928) 104-108.

Byron C. Nelson, "What was in the Ark?" *CFL, 3rd Ser.*, 34 (1928) 229-231.

*Dudley Joseph Whitney, "Pre-Adamic Ruin or the Deluge—Which?" *CFL, 3rd Ser.*, 34 (1928) 331-333.

Dudley Joseph Whitney, "Problems of the Deluge," *CFL, 3rd Ser.*, 34 (1928) 377-379. *[A Sequel to "Geology and the Deluge"]*

James Bowron, "Another View of the Deluge," *CFL, 3rd Ser.*, 34 (1928) 542.

Dudley Joseph Whitney, "The Glacial Nightmare of the Deluge?" *CFL, 3rd Ser.*, 34 (1928) 666-668.

Dudley Joseph Whitney, "Puzzles of the Deluge," *CFL, 3rd Ser.*, 34 (1928) 495-499.

Dudley Joseph Whitney, "The Continental Shelf and the Deluge," *CFL, 3rd Ser.*, 34 (1928) 673-674.

Philip J. Le Riche, "Scientific Proofs of a Universal Deluge," *JTVI* 61 (1929) 86-102, 113-117. [(Discussion, pp. 102-108) (Communications by W. M. H. Milner, pp. 108-110; A. T. Schofield, pp. 110-111; W. R. Rowlatt Jones, p. 111; G. Wilson Heath, pp. 111-112; F. C. Wood, pp. 112-113)]

T. C. Skinner, "The Ice Age: Its Astronomical Case, and the Bearing of Drayson's Discovery on the Biblical Account of the Deluge," *JTVI* 61 (1929) 118-132, 138-140. (Discussion, pp. 132-138)

George H. Richardson, "Recent Archaeology and the Noachian Deluge," *ATR* 12 (1929-30) 48-50.

Melvin Grove Kyle, "The Deluge and the World Before and After," *BS* 87 (1930) 453-464.

George McCready Price, "Some Thoughts on Geology and Creation," *CFL, 3rd Ser.,* 36 (1930) 590-594.

George McCready Price, "Facts the Flood Explains," *CFL, 3rd Ser.,* 36 (1930) 206-207.

L. M. Davies, "Scientific Discoveries and Their Bearing on the Biblical Account of the Noachian Deluge," *JTVI* 62 (1930) 62-85, 94-95. [(Discussion, pp. 86-91) (Communications by A. G. Shortt, pp. 92-93; James Knight, pp. 93-94)]

Margaret F. Malim, "Noah's Flood," *Antiq* 5 (1931) 213-220.

Paul Romanoff, "A Third Version of the Flood Narrative," *JBL* 50 (1931) 304-307.

*Chaim Kaplan, "The Flood in the Book of Enoch and Rabbinics," *JSOR* 15 (1931) 22-24.

H. Osborne, "Recent Light on the Flood," *Theo* 22 (1931) 9-16.

George McCready Price, "A History of the Flood Theory of Geology," *CFL, 3rd Ser.,* 38 (1932) 75-77.

W. Bell Dawson, "The Flood and Geology," *CFL, 3rd Ser.,* 38 (1932) 269-272.

George McCready Price, "The Flood Theory Again," *CFL, 3rd Ser.,* 38 (1932) 350-354.

E. T. Brewster, "Genesis and Flood Theories," *BS* 90 (1933) 220-227.

Joseph Dudley Whitney, "The Problem of the Flood," *BS* 90 (1933) 469-478.

*G. Ch. Aalders, "The Biblical Deluge and the Inundation by the Nile," *EQ* 6 (1934) 127-136.

*F. A. Molony, "The Noachian Deluge and its Probable Connection with Lake Van," *JTVI* 68 (1936) 43-53. 64-65. (Discussion and Communications, pp. 54-64)

Byron C. Nelson, "The Biblical Necessity of the Flood Theory for Geology," *JTALC* 3 (1938) #6, 3-14.

Arthur C. Custance, "The Flood Traditions and Their Relation to the Bible," *BS* 96 (1939) 412-427.

John Bright, "Has Archaeology Found Evidence of the Flood?" *BA* 5 (1942) 55-62 [Has Archaeology Found Traces of the Flood; Archaeology and the Antecedents of the Israelite Flood Story]

Donat Poulet, "The Moral Causes of the Flood," *CBQ* 4 (1942) 293-303.

Edmund F. Sutcliffe, "The Ethnographical Restriction of the Flood," *ClR* 22 (1942) 442-454.

†P. Morris, "The Rainbow after the Flood," *Scrip* 1 (1946) 33-34.

C. J. Sodergren, "The Flood," *AQ* 26 (1947) 248-257.

Felix V. Hanson, "The Flood. *An Answer to Dr. Sodergren*," *AQ* 26 (1947) 341-346.

Emil G. Kraeling, "The Earliest Hebrew Flood Story," *JBL* 66 (1947) 279-293.

W. F. Beck, "The 'Window' in the Ark," *CTM* 21 (1950) 520-522.

Edward Ullendorff, "The Construction of Noah's Ark," *VT* 4 (1954) 95-96.

*Leonard Woolley, "Stories of the Creation and Flood," *PEQ* 88 (1956) 14-21.

Walter J. Beasley, "*The Flood Story:* Noah's Flood—Fact or Fiction?" *AT* 1 (1956-57) #1, 10-13. [No. 1]

Walter J. Beasley, "The Flood Story: Noah's Flood—Fact or Fiction?" *AT* 1 (1956-57) #2, 7-10. [No.2]

Walter J. Beasley, "The Flood Story: Part III. Noah's Flood—Fact or Fiction?" *AT* 1 (1956-57) #3, 3-5.

Walter J. Beasley, "The Flood Story: No. 4. Noah's Flood—Fact or Fiction?" *AT* 1 (1956-57) #4, 5-9.

William Dalton, "The Background and Meaning of the Biblical Flood Narrative, I.," *ACR* 34 (1957) 292-303.

W[alter] J. Beasley, "*The Flood Story:* Noah's Flood—Fact or Fiction?" *AT* 2 (1957-58) #1, 5-8. *[Part 5]*

W[alter] J. Beasley, "*The Flood Story:* No. 6, Noah's Flood—Fact or Fiction?" *AT* 2 (1957-58) #2, 5-9.

W[alter] J. Beasley, "*The Flood Story:* Noah's Flood—Fact or Fiction? No. 7.," *AT* 2 (1957-58) #3, 5-8.

William Dalton, "The Background and Meaning of the Biblical Flood Narrative, II," *ACR* 35 (1958) 23-39.

W[alter] J. Beasley, "*The Flood Story:* Noah's Flood—Fact or Fiction? No. 8.," *AT* 3 (1958-59) #1, 6-10.

*W[alter] J. Beasley, "That Noah Story: How did the various races of Mankind originate?" *AT* 4 (1959-60) #4, 6-9.

Henry M. Morris and John C. Whitcomb Jr., "The Genesis Flood—Its Nature and Significance," *BS* 117 (1960) 155-163, 204-213.

William F. Tanner, "Geology and the Great Flood," *JASA* 13 (1961) 117-119.

T. Worden, "Question and Answer: The Story of the Flood," *Scrip* 13 (1961) 57-60.

M. F. L. Mallowan, "Noah's Flood Reconsidered," *Iraq* 26 (1964) 62-82.

R. L. Raikes, "The Physical Evidence for Noah's Flood," *Iraq* 28 (1966) 52-63.

John N. Moore, "Letters to the Editor. The Genesis Flood," *JASA* 18 (1966) 32, continued on page 18.

John C. Whitcomb Jr., "The Supernaturalism of the Flood," *GJ* 8 (1967) #1, 32-38.

Walter S. Olson, "Has Science Dated the Biblical Flood?" *Z* 2 (1967) 272-278.

*Daniel Hammerly-Dupuy, "Some Observations on the Assyro-Babylonian and Sumerian Flood Stories," *AUSS* 6 (1968) 1-18.

[Clifford A. Wilson], "Your Questions Answered. Has any evidence of Noah's Ark been found?" *BH* 4 (1968) 15.

Joseph Sittler, "The Nimbus and the Rainbow," *BTSAB* 43 (1968) #2, 12-14.

J. R. van de Fliert, "Fundamentalism and Fundamentals of Geology (A geologist's response to revived Diluvianism)," *IRB* #32&33 (1968) 5-27. *(Review)*

Merle Meeter, "Geology in the Dark or in Bible Light?" *IRB* #38 (1969) 27-29.

Wm. White Jr., "The Fundamentals of Fundamentalism and Geology," *IRB* #38 (1969) 30-33.

J. R. van de Fliert, "Bible, Man and Science: A Reply," *IRB* #38 (1969) 34-39.

§309 *3.2.9.6.5 The Post-Diluvian Period to "Babel"*

*Ernest Bertheua, "On the Different Computations of the First Two Periods in the Book of Genesis, and the Chronological Assumptions on which they are Based," *JSL, 1st Ser.,* 2 (1848) 115-128. *(Trans. by John Nicholson)*

*Anonymous, "The Mark of Cain and the Curse of Ham," *SPR* 3 (1849-50) 415-426.

W. T., "The History of the World, as Foretold in the Book of Genesis," *JSL, 3rd Ser.,* 13 (1861) 313-336. [I. Promise to Shem, with curse on Canaan; II. Promise to Japheth, with curse on Canaan]

François Lenormant, "Ararat and 'Eden. A Biblical Study," *ContR* 40 (1881) 453-478. *[Marked as "continued" but was not]*

Thomas Whitelaw, "The Patriarchal Times. VII.—The Second Age of History," *MI* 4 (1886) 81-94. *[After the Flood to Babel]*

*Anonymous, "The Longevity of the Patriarchs," *ONTS* 15 (1892) 78.

*Joseph Offord, "The Vicissitudes of the Population of Palestine as Foretold in the Prophecy of Noah," *PEFQS* 50 (1918) 186-188.

E. E. Kellett, "The Ages of the Patriarchs," *ET* 33 (1921-22) 231-232.

Henry Heras, "The Curse of Noe," *CBQ* 12 (1950) 64-67.

J. Hoftijzer, "Some Remarks to the Tale of Noah's Drunkenness," *OTS* 12 (1958) 22-27.

David Neiman, "The Date and Circumstances of the Cursing of Canaan," *LIST* 3 (1966) 113-134.

§310 *3.2.9.6.6 "Babel" and the Division of the Nations*

Z. J., "Dispersion of Mankind at Babel," *CRB* 13 (1848) 510-519.

[Robert] Forsyth, "Confusion of Tongues," *JSL, 1st Ser.,* 7 (1851) 455-456. *[The Tower of Babel]*

A. B. Hyde, "The Problem of Babel," *MR* 53 (1871) 79-98.

W. St. Chad Boscawen, "The Legend of the Tower of Babel," *SBAT* 5 (1876-77) 303-312.

W. S. Hawks, "Notes on the Confusion of Tongues in the Light of Modern Learning," *OBJ* 1 (1880) 111-115.

Anonymous, "The Confusion of Languages," *ERG, 7th Ser.,* 4 (1881-82) 105-111.

*William Simpson, "The Tower of Babel and the Birs-Nimroud —Suggestions as to the Origin of Mesopotamian Tower Temples," *SBAP* 8 (1885-86) 83-86.

Thomas Whitelaw, "The Patriarchal Times. VIII.—The Table of Nations," *MI* 4 (1886) 174-192.

Thomas Whitelaw, "The Patriarchal Times. IX.—The Tower of Babel," *MI* 4 (1886) 306-320.

*William Simpson, "The Tower of Babel and the Birs Nimroud. *Suggestions as to the origin of Mesopotamian Tower-Temples*," *SBAT* 9 (1886-93) 307-332.

Anonymous, "The Tower of Babel," *ONTS* 15 (1892) 268.

A. Lowy, "The Tower of Babel," *SBAP* 15 (1892-93) 229-230.

John F. Cannon, "Babel and its Lessons," *PQ* 10 (1896) 131-137.

Anonymous, "The Tower of Babel," *MQR, 3rd Ser.,* 29 (1903) 386.

Stephen D. Peet, "The Tower of Babel and the Confusion of Tongues," *AAOJ* 29 (1907) 219-234.

Solomon S. Hilcher, "Language and Apostasy; Or the Renaissance of the Babel Scheme," *CFL, 3rd Ser.*, 12 (1910) 141-145. [I. The History and Facts of the Ancient Babel Scheme, pp. 141-143]

Daniel Gurden Stevens, "The Tower of Babel: History in Picture," *BW* 41 (1913) 185-199.

E. G. H. Kraeling, "The Tower of Babel," *JAOS* 40 (1920) 276-281.

John P. Peters, "The Tower of Babel at Borsippa," *JAOS* 41 (1921) 157-159.

Dudley Joseph Whitney, "An Hypothesis for the Confusion of Tongues," *CFL, 3rd Ser.*, 36 (1930) 135-139.

Paul Ramsey, "Beyond the confusion of Tongues," *TT* 3 (1946-47) 446-458.

Paul K. Jewett, "Bruner's Doctrine of the Origin and Unity of the Race," *JASA* 4 (1952) #2, 7-11. (Discussion p. 11)

*E[phraim] A. Speiser, "Word Plays on the Creation Epoch's Version of the Founding of Babylon," *Or, N.S.*, 25 (1956) 317-323.

*Walter J. Beasley, "Boomerangs, Babel and Blood Relations," *AT* 5 (1960-61) #1, 13-19. *[Artifacts and the Dispersion at Babel]*

*Walter J. Beasley, "Boomerangs, Babel and Blood Relations. No. 2.," *AT* 5 (1960-61) #2, 7-8, 13-14. *[Artifacts and the Dispersion at Babel]*

Anonymous, "The Confusion of Tongues," *BH* 5 (1969) 3-5.

§311 *3.2.9.6.7 The Patriarchal Period*

†Anonymous, "Miss O'Keffe's Patriarchal Times," *BCQTR* 38 (1811) 372-373. *(Review)*

Αγρακυλος, "Patriarchal Life, Illustrated from the Iliad of Homer," *CongML* 18 (1835) 467-476.

Φιλοξενος, "Patriarchal Life, Illustrated from the Iliad of Homer," *CongML* 18 (1835) 744-752; 19 (1836) 343-352.

H. M. Harmah, "The Patriarchal Age," *MR* 33 (1851) 601-614. *(Review)*

Anonymous, "The Plan and Purpose of the Patriarchal History," *PRev* 27 (1855) 24-39.

J. K. Plitt, "Isaac Blessing Jacob," *ER* 13 (1861-62) 375-385.

Anonymous, "Studies on the Bible, No. I. *The Sins of the Patriarchs,*" *DQR* 2 (1862) 197-220.

J. W. Blake, "Judah's Grandsons," *JSL, 4th Ser.,* 3 (1863) 178-180.

Δ., "Jacob's Flight," *TRL* 2 (1865) 297-305. *(Review)*

*Philip Mules, "Was the Idolatry of Terah Sabaïsm?" *JSL, 4th Ser.,* 10 (1866-67) 182-183.

*Charles W. Wilson, "On the Site of Ai and the Position of the Altar which Abram Built between Bethel and Ai," *PEFQS* 1 (1869) 123-126.

*Anonymous, "A Bird's Eye View of the Church Under the Patriarchs and Moses," *SPR* 28 (1877) 415-436.

H. G. Tomkins, "On the History in the Time of Abraham, Illustrated by Recent Researches," *JTVI* 12 (1878-79) 110-142. [(Discussion pp. 142-149) (Notes by D. H. Haigh, A. H. Sayce, S. Birch, and W. S. Chad Boscawen, pp. 149-153)]

*[Stephen D. Peet], "The Journey of Jacob," *AAOJ* 3 (1880-81) 151-152. *(Editorial)*

*L. Lund, "The Epoch of Joseph: Amehotep IV as the Pharaoh of the Famine," *SBAP* 4 (1881-82) 96-102. [Remarks by H. Villiers Stuart, pp. 95-96; St. Vincent Beechey, p. 102; Samuel Birch, p. 102]

Clericus, "The Bodies of the Patriarchs," *PEFQS* 14 (1882) 177, 258-259.

T. Forster, "The Bodies of the Patriarchs," *PEFQS* 14 (1882) 257-258.

H. B. S. W., "The Bodies of the Patriarchs," *PEFQS* 14 (1882) 259-260.

W. H. S., "The Bodies of the Patriarchs. I," *PEFQS* 15 (1883) 108-109.

Charles Druitt, "The Bodies of the Patriarchs. II," *PEFQS* 15 (1883) 109-110.

Franz Delitzsch, "The Character of Patriarchal History," *ONTS* 3 (1883-84) 346-352.

J. N. Fradenburg, "Abraham's Offering of Isaac," *AAOJ* 6 (1884) 29-31.

*[Heinrich] Brugsch, "An Inscription from a Tomb in el-Kab," *ONTS* 4 (1884-85) 226-227. *[Ref. to the Famine in Egypt]*

*J. W. Dawson, "The Probable Physical Causes of the Destruction of the Cities of the Plain," *Exp, 3rd Ser.,* 3 (1886) 69-77.

Thomas Whitelaw, "The Patriarchal Times.   XI.—The Pilgrimage of Abraham," *MI* 4 (1886) 464-480.

Thomas Whitelaw, "The Patriarchal Times. X.—The Case of Abram," *MI* 4 (1886) 345-358.

*Joseph Jacobs, "The Junior-Right in Genesis," *ARL* 1 (1888) 331-342.

*T. K. Cheyne, "The Origin and Meaning of the Story of Sodom," *NW* 1 (1892) 236-245.

Lewis B[ayles] Paton, "The Historical Character of the Narratives of the Patriarchs," *BW* 2 (1893) 343-352, 421-429.

*J. William Dawson, "Physical and Historical Probabilities Respecting the Authorship and Authority of the Mosaic Books," *Exp, 4th Ser.,* 9 (1894) 16-33, 109-123, 276-288, 362-375, 440-451. [V. The Dispersion and Abraham, pp. 440-451]

William Hayes Ward, "Light on Scriptural Texts from Recent Discoveries. Chedorlaomer and Abraham," *HR* 28 (1894) 29-31.

H. Gollancz, "The Sacrifice of Isaac," *IAQR, 2nd Ser.,* 9 (1895) 139-143.

R. W. Dale, "The Sacrifice of Isaac," *Exp, 5th Ser.,* 4 (1896) 16-26.

*A. H. Sayce, "Palestine in the Time of Abraham as Seen in the Light of Archaeology," *HR* 33 (1897) 200-205.

William Lower Carter, "Pharaoh's Butler and the Cup," *ET* 10 (1898-99) 379.

*W. O. E. Oesterley, "The Sacrifice of Isaac," *SBAP* 24 (1902) 253-260.

*Ed[uard] König, "The Latest Mythological Theory of the Patriarchs," *ET* 14 (1902-03) 217-219.

A. H. Sayce, "The Historicity of the Hebrew Patriarchs in the Light of Recent Archaeology," *HR* 45 (1903) 195-199.

R. A. Stewart Macalister, "The Scene of the Sacrifice of Isaac," *ET* 15 (1903-04) 141.

E[duard] König, "Latest Mythological Theories Concerning the Patriarchs," *HR* 48 (1904) 117-120.

A. H. Sayce, "The Age of Abraham," *BW* 26 (1905) 248-257.

A. H. Godbey, "Shylock in the Old Testament. The Story of Laban Viewed in the Light of the Code of Hammurabi," *Monist* 15 (1905) 353-360.

Daniel S. Gregory and W[illiam] W. Everts, "The Book of Genesis Unfolded—The Career of Abraham," *CFL, 3rd Ser.,* 5 (1906) 277-288.

*Andrew Craig Robinson, "The Bearing of Recent Oriental Discoveries on Old Testament History," *JTVI* 38 (1906) 154-176. (Discussion, pp. 176-181) [*Abraham,* pp. 156-158; The Incident of Sarai and Hagar, pp. 158-160]

*A. H. Sayce, "The Archaeological Analysis of the Book of Genesis," *ET* 18 (1906-07) 232-234. [The Genealogy of Abraham, pp. 232-234; The Dilmun *[Tilmum/Tilwm]* of the Cuneiform Inscriptions, p. 234]

Daniel S. Gregory and W[illiam] W. Everts, "The Book of Genesis Unfolded—The Career of Isaac," *CFL, 3rd Ser.,* 6 (1907) 64-77.

Daniel S. Gregory and W[illiam] W. Everts, "The Book of Genesis Unfolded—The Career of Jacob," *CFL, 3rd Ser.,* 6 (1907) 217-228.

Anonymous, "Joseph's 'Coat of Many Colors'—What Was It?" *CFL, 3rd Ser.,* 6 (1907) 340. *(Editorial Note)*

John E. McFadyen, "Miracle in the Story of Joseph," *HR* 53 (1907) 290-291.

Anonymous, "The Seven Years of Famine," *RP* 7 (1908) 259.

P. A. Gordon Clark, "The Site of the Sacrifice of Isaac," *ET* 20 (1908-09) 392-397.

Stephen D. Peet, "The Patriarchal Age," *AAOJ* 30 (1908) 330-338; 31 (1909) 80-91.

A. H. Sayce, "What was the Scene of Abraham's Sacrifice?" *ET* 21 (1909-10) 86-88.

W. Emery Barnes, "The Sacrifice of Isaac," *ICMM* 6 (1909-10) 120-127.

Harold M. Wiener, "The Answer of Textual Criticism to the Higher Criticism of the Story of Joseph," *BS* 67 (1910) 59-69, 274-283.

*E[duard] König, "The Significance of the Patriarchs in the History of Religion," *Exp, 7th Ser.,* 10 (1910) 193-207.

*Eduard König, "Alleged Mythological Character of the Patriarchs and Kings," *HR* 62 (1911) 30-32.

Henry Proctor, "The Patriarchs," *AAOJ* 35 (1913) 90-91.

*M[elvin] G[rove] Kyle, "Hammurabi, Abraham, and the Reviewers," *BS* 70 (1913) 528-531.

George A. Barton, "The Historical Value of the Patriarchal Narratives," *PAPS* 52 (1913) 184-200.

*A. H. Sayce, "What We Now Know About the Hittites, and Its Bearing on the Hittites of Genesis," *ET* 26 (1914-15) 89-91.

L[uther] T. Townsend, "The Lean Years in Pharaoh's Dream," *CFL, 3rd Ser.,* 20 (1915) 106.

[Jay Benson Hamilton], "International Sunday School Lessons," *CFL, 3rd Ser.,* 24 (1918) 402-405. [Abraham Leaving Home; Abraham Helping Lot; Abraham Giving Isaac to God; Isaac and Rebekah]

[Jay Benson Hamilton], "International Sunday School Lessons," *CFL, 3rd Ser.*, 24 (1918) 445-447. [Appetite and Greed (Gen. 25:27-34); Jacob Deceives his Father; Jacob Fleeing from his Brother; Jacob Wins Esau]

[Jay Benson Hamilton], "International Sunday School Lessons," *CFL, 3rd Ser.*, 24 (1918) 491-493. [Joseph Sold by His Brethren; Joseph Made Ruler Over Egypt; Joseph Forgives His Brethren; Joseph Cares for His Kindred]

W[illiam] F[oxwell] Albright, "Historical and Mythical Elements in the Joseph Story," *JBL* 37 (1918) 111-143.

H[erbert] W. Magoun, "The Sanity of Abraham's Proposed Sacrifice," *CFL, 3rd Ser.*, 26 (1920) 273-276.

A. H. Godbey, "Shylock in the Old Testament. The Story of Laban in the Light of the Code Hammurabi*[sic]*," *MQR, 3rd Ser.*, 48 (1922) 599-617.

W. E. Denham, "Lectures on Genesis. Lecture V. God's New Plan for Human Redemption," *SWJT* 6 (1922) #4, 28-44.

A. T. Fryer, "The Sacrifice of Isaac," *ET* 34 (1922-23) 138-140.

R. Parkes, "The Sacrifice of Isaac," *ET* 34 (1922-23) 280-281.

*J. P. Wilson, "The Story of Joseph in the Septuagint," *GUOST* 5 (1923-28) 16-17.

*Edward Chiera, "The Length of the Lives of the Patriarchs," *CQ* 1 (1924) 199-201.

W[illiam] F[oxwell] Albright, "Contributions of Biblical Archaeology and Philology," *JBL* 43 (1924) 363-393. [4. The Role of Post-Diluvian Patriarchs in Hebrew History, pp. 385-393]

Ibn Sabil, "Genesis: The Book of the Bedouin," *CQR* 100 (1925-26) 81-95.

*J. Garrow Duncan, "Notes on the Sites of Succoth and Penuel as bearing upon the Routes of Gideon and Jacob," *PEFQS* 59 (1927) 89-95, 188-191.

Dudley Joseph Whitney, "The Age of the Patriarchs," *CFL, 3rd Ser.*, 35 (1929) 543-544.

Roland H. Bainton, "The Immoralities of the Patriarchs According to the Exegesis of the Late Middle Ages and of the Reformation," *HTR* 23 (1930) 39-49.

H[erbert] G[ordon] May, "The Evolution of the Joseph Story," *AJSL* 47 (1930-31) 83-93.

John Steele, "The Patriarchal Narratives," *ET* 45 (1933-34) 523-524.

Walter F. McMillin, "Jacob at Penuel," *BS* 91 (1934) 290-302.

Leander S. Keyser, "Yahuda's Studies and the Bible," *CFL, 3rd Ser.,* 40 (1934) 74-76. *[Joseph Stories in Genesis]*

Leander S. Keyser, "Confirming Bible History," *CFL, 3rd Ser.,* 40 (1934) 165-166. *[Joseph Stories in Genesis]*

*Cyrus H. Gordon, "Biblical Customs and the Nuzu Tablets," *BA* 3 (1940) 1-12. [The Patriarchal Age, pp. 2-9]

W[illiam] F[oxwell] Albright, "New Egyptian Data on Palestine in Patriarchal Age," *BASOR* #81 (1941) 16-21.

Otha L. Clark, "The Patriarchal Narratives in the Light of Today," *JAAR* 9 (1941) 94-97.

Charles Marston, "Archaeological Discovery from the Time of Abraham," *JTVI* 75 (1943) 106-110.

Robert T. O'Callahan, "Historical Parallels to Patriarchal Social Custom," *CBQ* 6 (1944) 391-405.

*Parray Marshall, "Life from the Dead Sea," *ContR* 169 (1946) 296-299.

R. E. Wolfe, "With Whom did Jacob Wrestle?" *JBL* 66 (1947) vi.

*George E. Mendenhall, "Mari," *BA* 11 (1948) 1-19. [Mari and the Patriarchs, pp. 15-19]

J.J. Dougherty, "The World of the Hebrew Patriarchs," *Scrip* 3 (1948) 98-102.

Harold H. Rowley, "Recent Discovery and the Patriarchal Age," *BJRL* 32 (1949-50) 44-79.

*W[illiam] F[oxwell] Albright, "Some Important Recent Discoveries: Alphabetic Origins and the Idrimi Statue," *BASOR* #118 (1950) 11-20. [The Joseph Story, p. 20]

*Cyrus H. Gordon, "Marginal Notes on the Ancient Middle East," *JKF* 2 (1952-53) 50-61. [II. The Interrelation of the Dates of the Patriarchal Age and of the Exodus, pp. 51-53]

*Manfred R. Lehmann, "Abraham's Purchase of Machpelah and Hittite Law," *BASOR* #129 (1953) 15-18.

Merrill F. Unger, "The Patriarchs and Contemporary History," *BS* 110 (1953) 121-129, 227-333.

Merrill F. Unger, "Archaeology and the Age of Abraham," *BS* 110 (1953) 299-308.

*Cyrus H. Gordon, "The Patriarchal Age," *JAAR* 21 (1953) 238-243.

C[yrus] H. Gordon, "A Social and Literary Analysis of the Patriarchal Period," *JBL* 72 (1953) xvii.

*B[enjamin] Maisler (Mazar), "Canaan on the Threshold of the Age of the Patriarchs," *EI* 3 (1954) I-II.

Cyrus H. Gordon, "The Patriarchal Narratives," *JNES* 13 (1954) 56-59.

*E. Shochat, "Political Motives in the Stories of the Patriarchs," *Tarbiẕ* 24 (1954-55) #3, I-II.

*Nelson Glueck, "The Age of Abraham in the Negeb," *BA* 18 (1955) 2-9.

Jozef M. A. Janssen, "Egyptological Remarks on *The Story of Joseph in Genesis*," *JEOL* #14 (1955-56) 63-72.

David Daube and Reuven Yaron, "Jacob's Reception by Laban," *JSS* 1 (1956) 60-62.

*K[enneth] A. Kitchen, "A Recently Published Egyptian Papyrus and Its Bearing on the Joseph Story," *TB* #2 (1956-57) 1-2.

R. H. Altus, "Abraham Lived in the Kingdom of Mari," *AusTR* 28 (1957) 92-98.

*Samson Kardimon, "Adoption as a Remedy for Infertility in the Period of the Patriarchs," *JSS* 3 (1958) 123-126.

*G. Ernest Wright, "Modern Issues on Biblical Studies: History and the Patriarchs," *ET* 71 (1959-60) 292-296.

*G[erhard] von Rad, "History and the Patriarchs," *ET* 72 (1960-61) 213-216.

*W[illiam] F[oxwell] Albright, "Abram the Hebrew: A New Archaeological Interpretation," *BASOR* #163 (1961) 36-54. [I. The Negeb and Sinai in the Middle Bronze I; II. The Caravan Trade of the Early Second Millennium; III. Abraham and the Caravan Trade]

*Moshe Gan, "The Book of Esther in the Light of the Story of Joseph in Egypt," *Tarbiz* 31 (1961-62) #2, I-II.

*James Meysing, "The Biblical Chronologies of the Patriarchs," *CNI* 13 (1962) #3/4, 26-30; 14 (1963) #1, 22-26.

Cameron Mackay, "From Luz to Bethel," *EQ* 34 (1962) 8-15.

J. C. L. Gibson, "Light from Mari on the Patriarchs," *JSS* 7 (1962) 44-62.

John J. Navone, "The Patriarchs of Faith, Hope, Love," *BibT* #6 (1963) 378-384.

*Anson F. Rainey, "Merchants at Ugarit and the Patriarchal Narratives," *CNI* 14 (1963) #2, 17-26.

E[phraim] A. Speiser, "The Wife-Sister Motif in the Patriarchal Narratives," *LIST* 1 (1963) 15-28.

*Shemuel Yeiven, "The Age of the Patriarchs," *RDSO* 38 (1963) 277-302. [I.—*The Patriarchs and the Ḥab\piru;* II.—*The God of Abraham;* III.—*The Three Phases of the Age of the Patriarchs*]

Roland de Vaux, "The Hebrew patriarchs and history," *TD* 12 (1964) 227-240.

Ignatius Hunt, "The Hebrew Patriarchs and Modern Research," *BibT* #16 (1965) 1075-1081.

*Frederick V. Winnett, "Re-Examining the Foundations," *JBL* 84 (1965) 1-19. [The Patriarchal Narratives, pp. 5-15; The Joseph Story, pp. 15-19]

*R. Alan Cole, "Wandering Arameans. How far were the Patriarchs truly nomadic, when in Mesopotamia?" *TTCA* 2 (1965) 10-15. [A Contribution towards a Social History of Israel]

William Etkin, "Jacob's Cattle and Modern Genetics. A Scientific Midrash," *Trad* 8 (1965-66) #1, 5-14.

*L. H. Muntingh, "Some aspects of West-Semitic kingship in the period of the Hebrew patriarchs," *OTW* 9 (1966) 106-115.

*A. Levene, "The Blessings of Jacob in Syriac and Rabbinic Exegesis," *StP* 7 (1966) 524-530.

*Shnayer Z. Leiman, "The Camel in the Patriarchal Narratives," *YR* 6 (1967) 16-26.

C. J. Mullo Weir, "The Alleged Hurrian Wife-Sister Motif in Genesis," *GUOST* 22 (1967-68) 14-25.

Robert L. Reymond, "Practical Principles from the Patriarchs," *BVp* 2 (1968) 122-130.

*Warren Kliewer, "The Daughters of Lot: Legend and Fablaiu," *IR* 25 (1968) #1, 13-28.

*John Van Seters, "The Problem of Childlessness in Near Eastern Law and the Patriarchs of Israel," *JBL* 87 (1968) 401-408.

*R. N. Whybray, "The Joseph Story and Pentateuchal Criticism," *VT* 18 (1968) 522-528.

Anonymous, "Yet Another Theory as to the Joseph Story," *BH* 5 (1969) 36-43.

W. Gunther Plaut, "Notes on the Akedah," *CCARJ* 16 (1969) #1, 45-47. *[Abraham's Testing]*

*R. Laird Harris, "Problem Periods in Old Testament History," *SR* 16 (1969-70) 3-26. [I. The Patriarchal Age, pp. 3-9]

§312 *3.2.9.6.8 Studies concerning Date, Authorship, Sources, and Authenticity*

†E. T. Pilgrim, "Mr. Pilgrim on Moses and Ezra," *MMBR* 37 (1814) 9.

†E. T. Pilgrim, "Mr. E. T. Pilgrim on Genesis," *MMBR* 38 (1814-15) 412-413.

Anonymous, "The Antiquity of the Book of Genesis," *PRev* 33 (1861) 37-58.

Enoch Pond, "The Author of Genesis," *MR* 45 (1863) 601-612.

James Strong, "Documentary Origin of Genesis," *MR* 64 (1882) 28-37.

Geo. H. Whittemore, "On the Origin of the Primitive Historical Traditions of the Hebrews," *BS* 40 (1883) 433-449. *(Trans. by August Dillmann)*

*William Hayes Ward, "Asserted Sevenfold Division of the Sacred Tree," *JBL* 8 (1888) 151-55. *[Sources]*

*Robert Dick Wilson, "The Date of Genesis X," *PRR* 1 (1890) 252-281.

J. J. Quinn, "Is the Book of Genesis Genuine and Authentic?" *AER* 5 (1891) 356-362.

C. M. Cobern, "Exploration and Discovery: Zaphenath-Paneah and the Date of Genesis," *BW* 2 (1893) 454-455.

Lewis B[ayles] Paton, "The Earliest Hebrew Literature," *HSR* 5 (1894-95) 87-102.

*Edwin Cone Bissell, "Origin and Composition of Genesis," *PPR* 6 (1895) 1-25, 262-294, 414-439, 614-642. [History of the Criticism to the Rise of the Grafian Hypothesis; Current Theory of the Origin and Structure of Genesis; The Unity and Continuity of Genesis; The Situation Presupposed in Genesis]

Lewis Bayles Paton, "The Oral Sources of the Patriarchal Narratives," *AJT* 8 (1904) 658-682.

E[duard] König, "Has a New Proof of the Unity of Genesis Been Discovered?" *ET* 16 (1904-05) 524-527.

G. L. Young, "The Historicity of Genesis Corroborated," *CFL, 3rd Ser.,* 5 (1906) 332-337.

*Harold M. Wiener, "The Dating of Genesis XXII," *BS* 67 (1910) 351-353.

*Harold M. Wiener, "The Post-Mosaica of Genesis," *BS* 68 (1911) 154-156.

William H. Bates, "The Age of Genesis," *CFL, 3rd Ser.,* 14 (1911-12) 15-18.

*George A. Barton, "A Sumerian Source of the Fourth and Fifth Chapters of Genesis," *JBL* 34 (1915) 1-16.

John Wilson, "Who Wrote Genesis?" *CFL, 3rd Ser.,* 22 (1916) 35-36.

*Cuthbert Lattey, "Alleged Sources of Genesis I-III," *IER, 5th Ser.,* 10 (1917) 278-288.

John Roaf Wightman, "Naville on the Composition and Sources of Genesis," *BS* 76 (1919) 234-243.

*W. Emery Barnes, "Who Wrote the First Chapter of Genesis," *Exp, 8th Ser.,* 22 (1921) 401-411.

H. M. Du Bose, "Amurru and the Genesis Stories," *BR* 11 (1926) 508-522.

R[obert] H. Pfeiffer, "A Non-Israelic Source of the Book of Genesis," *ZAW* 48 (1930) 66-73.

*Sigmund Mowinckel, "The Babylonian Matter in the Pre-deuteronomic Primeval History (JE) in Gen 1-11," *JBL* 58 (1939) 87-91.

*William F[oxwell] Albright, "The Babylonian Matter in the Pre-deuteronomic Primeval History (JE) in Gen 1-11. II," *JBL* 58 (1939) 91-104.

*J. J. Crowley, "The Indus and the Pentateuch: A Study of the Indus Civilization," *NB* 27 (1946) 264-269.

C. J. de Catanzaro, "The Primeval History—A Reconsideration of Source Criticism," *ACQ* 5 (1965) 51-56.

*Michael C. Astour, "Political and Cosmic Symbolism in Genesis 14 and in its Babylonian Sources," *LIST* 3 (1966) 65-112. [1. When and By Whom Was Genesis 14 Written? pp. 65-74]

Claus Westermann, "Primeval man," *TD* 17 (1969) 30-36.

§313 *3.2.9.7 Literary Criticism of Exodus - General Studies*

†Anonymous, "Bryant on the Plagues of Egypt," *BCQTR* 4 (1794) 33-41.

( ) K., "Reply to the Queries of M. on the Plagues of Egypt," *CongML* 2 (1819) 545-547.

I. C., "Remarks on a Recent Denial of the Destruction of Pharaoh," *CongML* 21 (1838) 340-343. [Additional Note, p. 785]

W. S., "On the Pharaoh of the Exodus," *CongML* 21 (1838) 678-685.

Anonymous, "On the Manna of the Israelites," *SPR* 2 (1848-49) 413-426.

*B. S., "The Voice of Israel from the Rocks of Sinai," *JSL, 2nd Ser.,* 1 (1851-52) 339-350.

James Napier, "The Golden Calf," *JSL, 3rd Ser.,* 6 (1857-58) 161-163.

Anonymous, "Israel and Sinai," *DQR* 2 (1862) 496-513.

Anonymous, "Studies on the Bible, No. III. *The Wonders in Egypt,*" *DQR* 2 (1862) 640-669.

Anonymous, "Studies on the Bible, No. IV. *The Exodus; Passover; Priesthood; Borrowing the Jewels,*" *DQR* 3 (1863) 181-205.

Anonymous, "Studies on the Bible, No. V. *Israel in the Wilderness,*" *DQR* 3 (1863) 453-483.

*Anonymous, "The Borrowing of Jewels from the Egyptians," *DQR* 4 (1864) 362-384.

B. W. Savile, "A Voice from Egypt," *JSL, 4th Ser.,* 7 (1865) 273-280.

Anonymous, "Commentary on the Book of Exodus," *BFER* 16 (1867) 43-60. *(Review)*

R. A. Fink, "Strange Fire Worshippers," *LQ* 1 (1871) 343-346.

John Wilson, "An Argument about the Manna. By a Farmer," *BFER* 24 (1875) 481-487.

Dunbar J.*[sic]* Heath, "Biblical Research. Jannes and Jambres withstanding Moses," *PEFQS* 13 (1881) 311-317.

G. F. S. Stooke Vaughan, "Remarks on 'Jam Suph'," *PEFQS* 13 (1881) 322-323.

[Ernest Wilhelm] Hengstenberg, "The Arrogance of the Pharaohs," *ONTS* 1 (1882) #1, 16.

Martyn Summerbell, "Hardening Pharaoh's Heart," *ONTS* 1 (1882) #2, 8-9.

(   ) Bartlett, "The Manna of the Biblical Narrative as Compared with Modern Manna," *ONTS* 2 (1882-83) 177.

F. B. Denio, "The Revision of the Book of Exodus," *ONTS* 5 (1884-85) 207-212.

*S. T. Anderson, "'I am That I am'," *ONTS* 4 (1884-85) 310-313.

Joseph Parker, "The Second Book of Moses," *Exp, 3rd Ser.*, 1 (1885) 305-312.

*Howard Crowby, "Interpretation of Some Difficult Texts," *HR* 13 (1887) 217-218. *[Hardening of Pharaoh's heart]*

A. J. Lyman, "The Miraculous Element in the Egyptian Plagues," *HR* 13 (1887) 373-382.

Max Muller, "A contribution to the Exodus geography," *SBAP* 10 (1887-88) 467-477.

*W. Bacher, "Seventy-two Modes of Exposition," *JQR* 4 (1891-92) 509. *[The Giving of the Law at Sinai]*

W. W. Moore, "The Oppression in Egypt," *USR* 3 (1891-92) 46-52.

W. W. Moore, "The Ten Plagues," *USR* 3 (1891-92) 106-121.

†P. le Page Renouf, "Summary of Remarks, November 1. Part I. The Pharaoh of the Exodus," *SBAP* 15 (1892-93) 60-62.

A. L. Lewis, "Note on the Pharaoh of the Exodus," *SBAP* 15 (1892-93) 423-424.

Hugh Macmillan, "The Budding Rod," *Exp, 4th Ser.*, 8 (1893) 362-373.

*P. A. Peter, "The Sabbath in Genesis and Exodus," *ColTM* 16 (1896) 153-169.

H. Clay Trumbull, "God's Ensign at Rephidim," *Exp, 5th Ser.*, 5 (1897) 297-300.

*William J. Dawson, "The Historical Relation of the Book of Genesis to the Exodus from Egypt," *HR* 33 (1897) 9-19.

*G. H. Skipwith, "The Burning Bush and the Garden of Eden: A Study in Comparative Mythology," *JQR* 10 (1897-98) 489-502.

A. H. Sayce, "Who was the Pharaoh of the Exodus?" *HR* 38 (1899) 483-487.

Jerome Pollard-Urquhart, "The Manna," *IER, 4th Ser.*, 6 (1899) 205-225.

Willis J. Beecher, "The International Lessons in Their Literary Setting," *CFL, N.S.*, 4 (1901) 347-352; 5 (1902) 40-46. *[Exodus]*

*Joseph Jacobs, "Earliest Representation of the Ark of the Law," *JQR* 14 (1901-02) 737-739.

G. Frederick Wright, "The Years of Plenty and the Years of Famine in Egypt," *BS* 59 (1902) 169-174.

W. W. Moore, "Ruling Ideas of Exodus," *CFL, N.S.*, 6 (1902) 10-16.

Wm. Hoge Marquess, "Manna in the Old Testament and the New," *CFL, N.S.*, 6 (1902) 39-42.

*John D. Davis, "The Ark and the Cloud During the March," *CFL, N.S.*, 6 (1902) 78-83.

Goshn el Howie, "The Manna in the Wilderness," *HR* 47 (1904) 282.

J. C. K. Milligan, "The Hardening of Pharaoh's Heart," *CFL, 3rd Ser.*, 3 (1905) 157-158.

John Urquhart, "The Book of Exodus—'The Messages of Israel's Lawgivers' Reviewed," *CFL, 3rd Ser.*, 5 (1906) 260-267.

John Urquhart, "The Divisions and the Plan of Exodus," *CFL, 3rd Ser.*, 5 (1906) 418-425.

W. O. E. Oesterley, "The Burning Bush," *ET* 18 (1906-07) 510-512.

Parke P. Flournoy, "The Sinaicity of the Pentateuch," *CFL, 3rd Ser.*, 7 (1907) 253-256.

*Edward M. Merrins, "The Plagues of Egypt," *BS* 65 (1908) 401-429, 611-635.

Harold M. Wiener, "Mr. McNeile on the Book of Exodus," *CFL, 3rd Ser.*, 10 (1909) 113-119. *(Review)*

*Francis J. Lamb, "'Exodus' An 'Ancient Document', Proof of Jehovah's Existence and Character 'Once and for All'," *CFL, 3rd Ser.*, 11 (1909) 157-167.

Alfred Martin Haggard, "A Chapter of Romance in Archaeology: On the Pharaoh of the Exodus," *CFL, 3rd Ser.,* 14 (1911-12) 29-36.

John Urquhart, "The Pharaoh of the Exodus and Dean Haggard's View," *CFL, 3rd Ser.,* 14 (1911-12) 262-264.

Harold M. Wiener, "Dr. Driver on Exodus," *BS* 69 (1912) 151-157. *(Review)* [Reply by Dr. S. R. Driver, p. 157]

Harold M. Wiener, "The Negeb in Exodus," *BS* 69 (1912) 345-348.

*Joseph Offord, "The Localities of the Exodus: and a New Egyptian Papyrus," *PEFQS* 44 (1912) 202-205.

S. H. Wainright, "'The Mount of God'," *ET* 25 (1913-14) 90-91. *[Comparative illustration of Sinai]*

*A. H. Finn, "The Tabernacle Chapters," *JTS* 16 (1914-15) 449-482.

W. E. Glanville, "The Pillar of Cloud: The Pillar of Fire," *BW* 48 (1916) 360-361.

*W. T. Pilter, "The Manna of the Israelites," *SBAP* 39 (1917) 155-167, 187-206.

William H. Bates, "The Book of Exodus," *CFL, 3rd Ser.,* 26 (1920) 301-305.

William H. Bates, "Hardening Pharaoh's Heart," *CFL, 3rd Ser.,* 26 (1920) 311-312.

*Paul Haupt, "Biblical Studies," *AJP* 43 (1922) 238-249. [1. The Sixth Egyptian Plague, pp. 238-239]

*Oswald T. Allis, "Old Testament Emphases and Modern Thought, Old Testament Emphases vs. Higher Critical Theories," *PTR* 24 (1926) 252-307. [The Crossing of the Red Sea; The Repetitions in Exodus XIV, Drivers Analysis of Exodus XIV: Based on Repetitions; The Uncertainty of the Critical Analysis; Conclusion]

H. S. Darlington, "Was the Biblical Manna an Animal Product?" *OC* 42 (1928) 372-381.

Arthur S. Langley, "Manna," *ET* 41 (1929-30) 477-478.

James Feather, "The Princess who rescued Moses: Who was she? With a Note on Heb. XI. 24-26," *ET* 43 (1931-32) 423-425.

Edward L. Kessel, "The Plagues of Egypt: A Biological Sequence," *TFUQ* 7 (1932-33) 434-447.

W. J. Phythian-Adams, "Mirage in the Wilderness," *PEFQS* 67 (1935) 69-78, 114-127. [I. The Settlement in Canaan; II. Horeb and Kadesh-barnea]

H[arry] R[immer], "Modern Science and the Ten Plagues of Egypt," *CFL, 3rd Ser.,* 43 (1937) 89-101.

C. S. Jarvis, "The Forty Years' Wanderings of the Israelites," *PEQ* 70 (1938) 25-36. (Discussion, pp. 36-40)

Antonine De Guglielmo, "What was the Manna?" *CBQ* 2 (1940) 112-129.

Julian Obermann, "Koran and Agada: The Events at Mount Sinai," *AJSL* 58 (1941) 23-48.

Peter G. Gordon, "The Burning Bush," *ET* 53 (1941-42) 270.

*G. Ernest Wright, "Two Misunderstood Items in the Exodus-Conquest Cycle," *BASOR* #86 (1942) 32-35. [2. The "Store-City" of Raamses, pp. 34-35]

H. H. Rowley, "Two Observations," *BASOR* #87 (1942) 40. *[Ref. previous article]*

*J. R. Porter, "The Role of Kadesh-Barnea in the Narrative of the Exodus," *JTS* 44 (1943) 139-143.

J. Gwyn Griffiths, "The 'Golden Calf'," *ET* 56 (1944-45) 110-111.

Wilfrid L. Hannam, "The Bones of Joseph: A Study in Exodus," *LQHR* 170 (1945) 18-21.

*Harold Garner, "Exodus, Prophet and West Africa," *ET* 58 (1946-47) 278-279. [Moses, the Prophet; Aaron his "mouthpiece"]

E. E. Flack, "Studia Biblica. V. The Book of Exodus," *Interp* 3 (1949) 78-95.

Julian Morgenstern, "The Despoiling of the Egyptians," *JBL* 68 (1949) 1-28.

†C. Lattey, "Some Old Testament Phenomena," *Scrip* 4 (1949-51) 56-57. *[The Pillar of the Cloud]*

*M. David, "The Codex of Hammurabi and its Relation to the Provisions of the Law in Exodus," *OTS* 7 (1950) 149-178.

Bede Griffiths, "The Cloud on the Tabernacle," *LofS* 7 (1952-53) 478-486.

John Gray, "The Desert Sojourn of the Hebrews and the Sinai-Horeb Tradition," *VT* 4 (1954) 148-154.

Frank M. Cross Jr. and David Noel Freedman, "The Song of Miriam," *JNES* 14 (1955) 237-250.

W. M. Valk, "Pentateuchal Criticism in *La Bible de Jérusalem*," *Scrip* 7 (1955) 14-18. *[Exodus]*

*C. R. A. Cunliffe, "'I am who I am'," *TD* 4 (1956) 23. *[Synopsis]*

Greta Hort, "The Plagues of Egypt," *ZAW* 69 (1957) 84-103; 70 (1958) 48-59.

Immanuel Lewy, "The Story of the Golden Calf Reanalyzed," *VT* 9 (1959) 318-322.

*F. C. Fensham, "The Possibility of the Presence of Casuistic Legal Material at the Making of the Covenant at Sinai," *PEQ* 93 (1961) 143-146.

W. Gunther Plaut, "Pharaoh's Hardened Heart—A Commentary," *CCARJ* 10 (1962-63) #3, 18-23.

*William Foxwell Albright, "Jethro, Hobab and Ruel in Early Hebrew Tradition (with Some Comments on the Origin of 'JE')," *CBQ* 25 (1963) 1-11.

William Holladay, "Preaching the God of Exodus," *NEST* 12 (1964-65) #2, 9-26.

*J. Swetnam, "*Diathēkē* in the Septuagint Account of Sinai: A Suggestion," *B* 47 (1966) 438-444.

Edward L. Bode, "The Death of the Firstborn in Egypt," *BibT* #23 (1966) 1511-1514.

*Philip B. Harner, "Exodus, Sinai and the Hittite Prologues," *JBL* 85 (1966) 233-236.

*S. E. Lowenstamm, "The Making and Destruction of the Golden Calf," *B* 48 (1967) 481-490.

Clifford Wilson, "The Plagues of Egypt," *BH* 3 (1967) #3, 17-25.

*Moses Aberbach and Leivy Smolar, "Aaron, Jeroboam, and the Golden Calves," *JBL* 86 (1967) 129-140.

Leivy Smolar and Moshe Aberbach, "The Golden Calf Episode in Postbiblical Literature," *HUCA* 39 (1968) 91-116.

G. W. Coats, "Despoiling the Egyptians," *VT* 18 (1968) 450-457.

Harold W. Hoehner, "The Duration of the Egyptian Bondage," *BS* 125&126 (1969) 306-316.

§314 *3.2.9.7.1 The Exodus from Egypt*

Anonymous, "The Credibility of the Jewish Exodus, defended against some Remarks of Edward Gibbon, Esq. and the Edinburgh Reviewers," *QRL* 1 (1809) 92-96. *(Review)*

[Edward Robinson], "On the Exodus of the Israelites out of Egypt, and their Wanderings in the Desert," *BRCR* 2 (1832) 743-797.

*Edward Robinson, "The Land of Goshen, and the Exodus of the Israelites,"*BRCR, N.S.,* 3 (1840) 306-324.

*Edward Robinson, "Notes on Biblical Geography," *BS* (1843) 563-566. [The Exodus, pp. 564-565]

*(   ) L., "Sacred Geography. Passage of the Red Sea.—Position of Mount Sinai," *BRCM* 5 (1848-49) 38-54.

H. M. G., "On the Romanish Church and the Passage of the Red Sea," *JSL, 2nd Ser.,* (1854-55) 460-467.

Fanny Corbaux, "On the Miracle of the Passage of the Red Sea," *JSL, 3rd Ser.,* 1 (1855) 108-120.

H. M. G., "The Passage of the Red Sea," *JSL, 3rd Ser.,* 1 (1855) 401-406.

S. C. Malan, "The Passage of the Red Sea," *JSL, 3rd Ser.,* 2 (1855-56) 409-414.

†*Anonymous, "Egyptology and the two Exodes*[sic]*," *BQRL* 32 (1860) 440-479. *(Review)*

H. C., "Sinai, Kadesh, and Mount Hor; or a Critical Enquiry into the Route of the Exodus," *JSL, 3rd Ser.,* 11 (1860) 1-60.

W. Osburn, "The Exodus: the Traces thereof Discoverable on the Monuments of Egypt," *JSL, 3rd Ser.,* 11 (1860) 257-268.

M. R. E., "The Route of the Exodus," *JSL, 3rd Ser.,* 14 (1861-62) 465-470.

B. W. Savile, "Revelation and Science," *JSL, 4th Ser.,* 2 (1862-63) 181-188. *[The Exodus]*

*Thomas John Buckton, "Israelite Population at the Exodus," *JSL, 4th Ser.,* 3 (1863) 444-445.

T. A., "Remarks on the Statistics of Exodus," *JSL, 4th Ser.,* 5 (1864) 426-429.

J. P., "The East Wind and the Passage of the Red Sea," *JSL, 4th Ser.,* 7 (1865) 433-437.

*H. Moule, "Israel in Egypt: The Period of their Sojourn and their numbers at the Exodus and in the Wilderness," *JTVI* 5 (1870-71) 378-393. (Discussion, pp. 394-441)

Joseph P. Thompson, "Dr. Brugsch's Theory of the Exodus," *ZÄS* 12 (1874) 150-156.

Joseph P. Thompson, "Notes on Egyptology.—New Theory of the Exodus by Pasha Brugsch," *BS* 32 (1875) 185-197.

Stephen M. Vail, "Passage of Israel Through Red Sea," *MR* 57 (1875) 306-317.

*J. Estlin Carpenter, "Art and Literature in Egypt at the Time of the Exodus," *URRM* 4 (1875) 441-470.

James Strong, "The Passage of the Red Sea," *MR* 58 (1876) 223-243.

*Philip Schaff, "Disputed Scripture Localities," *PRev* 54 (1878) Part 1, 851-884. [The Locality of the Exodus of the Israelites, pp. 856-861]

*J. W. Dawson, "Points of Contact Between Science and Revelation," *PRev* 55 (1879) Part 2, 579-606. [The Exodus, pp. 599-602]

Claude R. Conder, "Topography of the Exodus," *PEFQS* 12 (1880) 231-234.

*J. P. Lesley, "Notes on an Egyptian element in the Names of the Hebrew kings, and its bearing on the History of the Exodus," *PAPS* 19 (1880-81) 409-435.

Greville J. Chester, "Notes on the Topography of the Exodus," *PEFQS* 13 (1881) 104-110.

Dunbar J.*[sic]* Heath, "Egyptian View of the Exodus," *PEFQS* 13 (1881) 229-232.

John Scarth, "A Few Thoughts upon the Route of the Exodus," *PEFQS* 14 (1882) 235-246.

(Miss) Agnes Grace Weld, "The Route of the Exodus," *Exp, 2nd Ser.,* 5 (1883) 281-296; 6 (1883) 232-240.

Owen C. Whitehouse, "Canon Scarth's Theory of the Exodus," *Exp, 2nd Ser.,* 5 (1883) 442-449.

C[laude] R. Conder, "C. Pickering Clarke, F. Gell, and C. M. W., "The Exodus," *PEFQS* 15 (1883) 79-100.

[(Miss)] A[gnes] G[race] Weld, "The Route of the Exodus," *PEFQS* 15 (1883) 139-142.

Dunbar I. Heath, "The Exodus," *PEFQS* 15 (1883) 149.

Adam Clarke Smith, John Cyprian Rust, and C. Pickering Clarke, "The Route of the Exodus," *PEFQS* 15 (1883) 223-236.

*Alfred H. Kellogg, "The Discovery of Pithom-Succoth and the Exodus Route," *PR* 4 (1883) 838-845.

J. Boyce, "The Exodus of the Children of Israel from Egypt and Their Sojourn in the Wilderness Forty Years," *SPR* 36 (1885) 681-694.

Alexander W. Thayer, "The Route of the Exodus," *CR* 47 (1886) 468-485. *(Review)*

*Anonymous, "Pithom and the Route of the Exodus," *NPR* 1 (1886) 142-143.

R. F. Hutchinson, "The Exode," *PEFQS* 19 (1887) 239-250. [Note by C. R. Condor, *PEFQS* 20 (1888) pp. 40-41]

Anonymous, "Route of the Exodus," *PEFQS* 20 (1888) *Map, facing page* 110.

*Jacob Schwartz, "The Pharaoh and Date of the Exodus: *A Study in Comparative Chronology*," *TML* 1 (1889) 145-166.

Jacob Schwartz, "The Day of the Hebrew Exodus from Egypt Determined by the Egyptian Calendar," *TML* 2 (1889) 35-41.

*Jacob Schwartz, "Synopsis of the Argument on the 'Pharaoh and Date of the Exodus'," *TML* 2 (1889) 129-132.

A. L. Lewis, "Some suggestions respecting the Exodus," *SBAP* 12 (1889-90) 167-179.

*C[laude] R. Conder, "Monumental Notice of Hebrew Victories," *PEFQS* 22 (1890) 326-329. *[Background to the Exodus]*

*A[lexander] W. Thayer, "Critical Theology. The Hebrews in Egypt and the Exodus," *URRM* 33 (1890) 253-268. *(Review)*

†A. L. Lewis, "Theories on the Exodus," *SBAP* 13 (1890-91) 439-440.

Tyron Edwards, "The Israelites in the Desert," *HR* 22 (1891) 71-73.

*C. H. Waller, "The Order of the Law and the History of the Exodus, and its Bearing on the Authorship of the Pentateuch," *TML* 5 (1891) 1-13.

Camden M. Cobern, "Have the Monuments and Papyri Anything to Say of the Hebrews and the Exodus? Egyptology, No. IX," *HR* 23 (1892) 26-30.

Camden M. Cobern, "Have the Monuments and Papyri Anything to Say of the Hebrews and the Exodus? (Positively Considered.) Egyptology, No. X," *HR* 23 (1892) 411-416.

Edouard Naville, "The Route of the Exodus," *JTVI* 26 (1892-93) 12-30. (Discussion, pp. 30-33)

Nathaniel Schmidt, "The External Evidence of the Exodus," *AJSL* 10 (1893-94) 159-174.

A. B. Tulloch, "The Passage of the Red Sea by the Israelites," *JTVI* 28 (1894-95) 267-276. (Discussion, pp. 276-280)

Anonymous, "The Passage of the Red Sea," *MR* 77 (1895) 968.

A. E. Haynes, "The Route of the Exodus," *PEFQS* 28 (1896) 175-185.

A. E. Haynes, "The Date of the Exodus. I.," *PEFQS* 28 (1896) 245-255. (Notes by C. R. Conder, p. 341)

C[laude] R. Conder, "The Date of the Exodus, II.," *PEFQS* 28 (1896) 255-258.

W. M. Flinders Petrie, "The Date of the Exodus," *PEFQS* 28 (1896) 335-337. [Note by C. R. Conder, *PEFQS* 29 (1897) p. 83]

C[laude] R. Conder, "The Date of the Exodus," *ET* 8 (1896-97) 90.

*W. W. Moore, "The Latest Light from Egypt," *USR* 8 (1896-97) 30-38. *[The Exodus]*

*James Orr, "Israel in Egypt and the Exodus. With Reference to Prof. Flinders Petrie's Recent Discovery," *Exp, 5th Ser.,* 5 (1897) 161-177.

Anonymous, "The Time of the Exodus," *MR* 79 (1897) 479.

J. V. Prášek, "On the Question of the Exodus," *ET* 11 (1899-1900) 205-208, 251-254, 319-322, 400-403, 503-507.

G. Frederick Wright, "The Crossing of the Red Sea," *BS* 58 (1901) 570-579.

George L. Robinson, "The Route of the Exodus from Egypt," *BW* 18 (1901) 410-423.

Ira M. Price, "The 'Exodus' Material, and the Use Made of it in the Scriptures. (According to the Text of the American Standard Revised Version)," *BW* 18 (1901) 451-465.

Edward Mahler, "The Exodus," *JRAS* (1901) 33-67.

J. V. Prášek, "The Sojourn in Goshen and the Exodus," *ET* 16 (1904-05) 223-225.

*G. Frederick Wright, "Geological Confirmations of the Biblical History of Israel from Abraham to the Exodus," *CFL, 3rd Ser.,* 2 (1905) 423-430. [Crossing the Red Sea, pp. 423-426]

*E. Mahler, "The *Ḥodeš Ha'bib* הדש האביב in which the Exodus took place: and its identification with the Epiphi of the Egyptian 'Nature-year'," *SBAP* 27 (1905) 255-259.

Geo[rge] W. Shaw, "The Period of the Exodus," *Monist* 16 (1906) 200-218.

George Frederick Wright, "Light from Geology upon the Crossing of the Red Sea by the Children of Israel," *RP* 5 (1906) 295-302.

*K. T. Frost, "The Siege of Jericho and the Strategy of the Exodus," *ET* 18 (1906-07) 464-467.

F. Hugh Pope, "The Date of the Exodus," *NYR* 2 (1906-07) 566-584.

*Geo. St. Clair, "Israel in Camp: A Study," *JTS* 8 (1906-07) 185-217. [The Date of the Exodus, pp. 207-210]

Melvin Grove Kyle, "Archaeology Department: The Exodus Problem Anew—Review of Prof. Tofsteen's Book," *CFL, 3rd Ser.,* 7 (1907) 14-16. *(Review)*

Joseph D. Wilson, "The Narrative of the Crossing of the Red Sea: A Professor's Argument for its Composite Character and Late Date," *CFL, 3rd Ser.,* 7 (1907) 125-128.

Charles Warren Currier, "When Did Israel Go Out of Egypt?" *ACQR* 32 (1907) 82-94.

John E. McFadyen, "At the Red Sea," *HR* 53 (1907) 445-447.

J. Lieblein, "The Exodus of the Hebrews," *SBAP* 29 (1907) 214-218.

D. R. Fotheringham, "The Date of the Exodus," *Exp, 7th Ser.,* 6 (1908) 438-445.

*D. R. Fotheringham, "Merenptah and the Exodus. I.," *ET* 20 (1908-09) 141.

Wm. Fisher, "Merenptah and the Exodus. II.," *ET* 20 (1908-09) 141-142.

M. O. Smith, "Res Gestae Exitus Israel," *BS* 67 (1910) 625-636.

*Anonymous, "The Pharaoh of the Exodus Identified with Menephtah," *CFL, 3rd Ser.,* 13 (1910) 222-223. *(Editorial Note)*

*E. W. Hollingworth, "The Book of Judges and the Date of the Exodus," *SBAP* 33 (1911) 46-50.

*E. C. Richardson, "Documents of the Exodus, Contemporary, Original, and Written," *PTR* 10 (1912) 581-605.

Sartell Prentice Jr., "The Route of Israel in the Desert," *BW* 41 (1913) 238-244.

Sartell Prentice Jr., "Discussion. Naoum Beg Shuquair on the Derb el Hagg," *BW* 41 (1913) 394-409.

*Arthur W. Sutton, "From Suez to Sinai," *JTVI* 45 (1913) 249-264. [The Exodus of the Children of Israel. Notes on the Census Numbers, pp. 265-268]

J. H. Phillipson, "Manna," *ET* 25 (1913-14) 429.

C. M. Cobern, "Notes and Queries. *New light upon incidents in the Exodus," PEFQS* 46 (1914) 156.

W. S. Auchincloss, "Israel of the Exodus," *CFL, 3rd Ser.,* 20 (1915) 152-153. *[Concerning the number who left Egypt]*

Victor L. Trumper, "The Route of the Exodus: From Pithom to Marah," *PEFQS* 47 (1915) 22-29.

J. D. Crace, "The Route of the Exodus," *PEFQS* 47 (1915) 64-66.

Victor L. Trumper, "Notes and Queries. *The Route of the Exodus," PEFQS* 47 (1915) 152-153.

Harold M. Wiener, "The Date of the Exodus," *BS* 73 (1916) 454-480.

*Hanbury Brown, "The Exodus Mentioned on the Stele of Menephtah," *JEA* 4 (1916) 16-20.

W. Shaw Caldecott, "New Light on the Exodus," *LQHR* 125 (1916) 268-273.

*Harold M. Wiener, "The Date of the Exodus and the Chronology of Judges," *BS* 74 (1917) 581-609.

A. E. Whatham, "The Exodus in the Light of Archaeology," *BS* 75 (1918) 543-560.

Harold M. Wiener, "The Exodus in the Light of Archaeology," *BS* 75 (1918) 561-580.

Harold M. Wiener, "The Exodus in Egyptian History," *MQR, 3rd Ser.,* 44 (1918) 644-656.

*Joseph Offord, "Archaeological Notes on Jewish Antiquities. XL. *The Route of the Exodus Wanderings in the Desert,*" *PEFQS* 50 (1918) 35-36.

*Harold M. Wiener, "The Exodus and the Conquest of the Negeb," *BS* 76 (1919) 468-474.

Harold M. Wiener, "Notes on the Exodus," *BS* 76 (1919) 474-483.

Melvin Grove Kyle, "Archaeology's Searchlight on the Exodus: When Omnipotent Providence Crushed Egypt's Magic and Military," *CFL, 3rd Ser.,* 26 (1920) 60-62.

H[erbert] W. Magoun, "The Crossing of the Red Sea," *CFL, 3rd Ser.,* 26 (1920) 151-155.

Samuel A. B. Mercer, "Merneptah's Israel and the Exodus," *ATR* 5 (1922-23) 96-107.

W. B. Stevenson, "Recent Views Regarding the Date of the Exodus," *GUOST* 5 (1923-29) 17-19.

S[tanley] A. Cook, "The Exodus in the Light of Archaeology," *JTS* 25 (1923-24) 437-439.

Edouard Naville, "The Geography of the Exodus," *JEA* 10 (1924) 18-39.

Alan H. Gardiner, "The Geography of the Exodus: an answer to Professor Naville and others," *JEA* 10 (1924) 87-96.

*Oswald T. Allis, "Old Testament Emphases and Modern Thought. Old Testament Emphases vs. Higher Critical Theories," *PTR* 24 (1926) 252-307. [The Crossing of the Red Sea, 254-259]

Harold M. Wiener, "The Historical Character of the Exodus," *AEE* 11 (1926) 104-115.

Frederick Erdman, "Similarities between the Exodus and the Apocalypse," *CFL, 3rd Ser.*, 33 (1927) 510-512.

(   ) E., "Was Moses Weak in Arithmetic?"*TM* 8 (1928) 299-301. *[The Number of Israelites that left Egypt]*

*Howard H. Scullard, "The Passage of the Red Sea," *ET* 42 (1930-31) 55-61.

D. Cunllo Davies, "The Passage of the Red Sea," *ET* 42 (1930-31) 192.

Howard H. Scullard, "The Passage of the Red Sea. I.,"*ET* 42 (1930-31) 286-287.

Algernon Ward, "The Passage of the Red Sea. II.,"*ET* 42 (1930-31) 287.

Joseph J. Egan, "The Contest between Yahweh and the Gods of Egypt," *SS* 5 (1931) 36-45.

C. S. Jarvis, "The Israelites in Sinai," *Antiq* 6 (1932) 434-444.

*W. J. Phythian-Adams, "The Volcanic Phenomena of the Exodus," *JPOS* 12 (1932) 86-103.

*T. H. Robinson, "The Exodus and the Conquest of Palestine," *Theo* 25 (1932) 267-275.

*George B. Michell, "The Land of Goshen and the Exodus," *JTVI* 67 (1935) 231-241, 244-246. (Discussion, pp. 241-244)

C. C. Robertson, "On the Track of the Exodus," *JTVI* 68 (1936) 124-138, 142-145. (Discussion, pp. 138-142)

*B. Weitzel, "The Year of the Exodus in the Talmud," *Miz* 8 (1938) 15-19.

H. H. Rowley, "The Eisodus and the Exodus," *ET* 50 (1938-39) 503-508.

*William Ross, "Jericho and the Date of the Exodus," *HJ* 39 (1940-41) 299-308.

*H. F. D. Sparks, "Lachish and the Date of the Exodus," *JTS* 42 (1941) 178-179.

A. Lucas,   "The Date of the Exodus,"   *PEQ* 73 (1941) 110-121.

H. H. Rowley, "The Date of the Exodus," *PEQ* 73 (1941) 152-157.

*H. H. Rowley, "Jericho and the Date of the Exodus: A Rejoinder," *HJ* 40 (1941-42) 207-208.

H. H. Rowley, "The Exodus and the Settlement in Canaan," *BASOR* #85 (1942) 27-31.

*G. Ernest Wright, "Two Misunderstood Items in the Exodus-Conquest Cycle," *BASOR* #86 (1942) 32-35.

Millar Burrows, "A Comment on Professor Rowley's Paper in the February Bulletin," *BASOR* #86 (1942) 35-36.

A. Lucas, "The Number of Israelites at the Exodus," *PEQ* 76 (1944) 164-168.

Ralph M. Earle Jr., "The Date of the Exodus," *ASW* 1 (1946) 96-104.

Stella Ben-Dor, "The Route of the Exodus. The First Stage. Ramses to Etham," *PEQ* 80 (1948) 48-58.

*George Ogg, "The Year of the Exodus in the Pseudo-Cyprianic de Pascha Computus," *ET* 60 (1948-49) 226.

*Cyrus H. Gordon, "Marginal Notes on the Ancient Middle East," *JKF* 2 (1952-53) 50-61. [II. The Interrelation of the Dates of the Patriarchal Age and of the Exodus, pp. 51-53]

M. B. Rowton, "The Problem of the Exodus," *PEQ* 85 (1953) 46-60.

*R. E. D. Clark, "The Large Numbers of the Old Testament—Especially in Connexion with the Exodus," *JTVI* 87 (1955) 82-93, 151-152. [(Discussion, pp. 145-149) (Communications by F. F. Bruce, pp. 149-150; J. W. Wenham, pp. 150-151; D. C. Mandeville, p. 151)]

H. H. Rowley, "A Recent Theory on the Exodus," *OrS* 4 (1955) 77-86.

Robert North, "Date and Unicity of the Exodus," *AER* 134 (1956) 161-182.

F. Blaess, "The Date of the Exodus," *AusTR* 28 (1957) 99-106.

Mary Neely, "*The Days of Moses:* The Exodus from Egypt," *AT* 2 (1957-58) #2, 13-15.

*S. E. Loewenstamm, "The Bearing of Psalm 81 upon the Problem of the Exodus," *EI* 5 (1958) 88*.

J. H[oward] W. Rhys, "God's Action in the Exodus," *StLJ* 3 (1959-60) #3, 12-19.

*John Rea, "The Time of the Oppression and the Exodus," *BETS* 3 (1960) 58-66.

S. Yeivin, "The Exodus," *Tarbiz̲* 30 (1960-61) #1, I.

*John Rea, "The Time of the Oppression and the Exodus," *GJ* 2 (1961) #1, 5-14.

James K. Solari, "The Exodus in the Life of Israel," *BibT* #5 (1963) 294-301.

Lewis S. Hay, "What Really Happened at the Sea of Reeds?" *JBL* 83 (1964) 397-403.

*R. North, "Some Links between the Hurrians and the Language of the Exodus," *AAI* 2 (1965) 343-357.

*Herbert B. Huffmon, "The Exodus, Sinai and the Credo," *CBQ* 27 (1965) 101-113.

*J. Wijngaards, "הוצא and העלה, a Twofold Approach to the Exodus," *VT* 15 (1965) 91-102.

*Elaine Marie Prevallet, "The Use of the Exodus in Interpreting History," *CTM* 37 (1966) 131-145.

*Henry Wansbrough, "Event and Interpretation. II. Desert Encounter," *ClR* 52 (1967) 929-937. [The Sea of Reeds, pp. 933-935]

*Frank E. Eakin Jr., "The Reed Sea and Baalism," *JBL* 86 (1967) 378-384.

*Michael Walzer, "The Exodus and Revolution: An Exercise in Comparative History," *Mosaic* 8 (1967) #1, 6-21.

G[eorge] W. Coats, "The Traditio-Historical Character of the Reed Sea Motif," *VT* 17 (1967) 253-265.

*Jack M. Sasson, "Bovine Symbolism in the Exodus Narrative," *VT* 18 (1968) 380-387.

Irwin W. Reist, "The Theological Significance of the Exodus," *BETS* 12 (1969) 223-232.

George W. Coats, "History and Revelation: The Reed Sea Event," *LTQ* 4 (1969) 22-32.

§315 *3.2.9.7.2 The Book of the Covenant*

Charles A[ugustus] Briggs, "The Little Book of the Covenant," *ONTS* 2 (1882-83) 264-272.

Charles A[ugustus] Briggs, "The Greater Book of the Covenant," *ONTS* 2 (1882-83) 289-303.

Lewis B[ayles] Paton, "The Original Form of the Book of the Covenant," *JBL* 12 (1893) 79-93.

*James A. Kelso, "The Code of Hammurabi and the Book of the Covenant," *PTR* 3 (1905) 399-412.

*A. S. Zerbe, "The Code of Hammurabi and the Mosaic Book of the Covenant. (First Paper)," *RChR, 4th Ser.,* 9 (1905) 17-38.

*A. S. Zerbe, "The Code of Hammurabi and the Mosaic Book of the Covenant. (Second Paper)," *RChR, 4th Ser.,* 9 (1905) 165-181.

*B. D. Eerdmans, "The Book of the Covenant and the Decalogue," *Exp, 7th Ser.,* 8 (1909) 21-33, 158-167, 223-230.

*Leroy Waterman, "Pre-Israelite Laws in the Book of the Covenant," *AJSL* 38 (1921-22) 36-54.

Julian Morgenstern, "The Book of the Covenant," *HUCA* 5 (1928) 1-154.

Julian Morgenstern, "The Book of the Covenant, Part II," *HUCA* 7 (1930) 19-258.

Robert H. Pfeiffer, "The Transmission of the Book of the Covenant," *HTR* 24 (1931) 99-109. [Ex. 20:22—23:19 (23:20-33)]

Julian Morgenstern, "The Book of the Covenant, Part II. The Ḥuqqim," *HUCA* 8&9 (1931-32) 1-150. (Addenda, pp. 741-746)

J. A. Thompson, "The Book of the Covenant Ex 21-23, in the Light of
Modern Archaeological Research," *ABR* 2 (1952) 97-107. [I. Recently
Discovered Law Codes of Mesopotamia; II. Some Observations; III.
Hurrian Customs; IV. Striking Parallels Between Mesopotamian Law
Codes and Ex. 21-23; V. Law Codes of Post Patriarchal Times; VI. The
Book of the Covenant. Some Conclusions]

Immanuel Lewy, "Dating of Covenant Code Sections and Humaneness and
Righteousness (Ex. 22:20-26; 23:1-9)," *VT* 7 (1957) 322-326.

Julian Morgenstern, "The Book of the Covenant," *HUCA* 33 (1962) 59-105.
[Part IV]

*Edward E. Erpelding, "An Investigation of the Israelite Concept of Law
Expressed in the Covenant Code," *SS* 17 (1965) #2, 41-67.

§316 *3.2.9.7.3 Studies concerning Date, Authorship, Sources, and Authenticity*

†Anonymous, "Date of the extant Redaction of Exodus," *MMBR* 38 (1814-
15) 34-35.

*W. Henry Green, "The Alleged Composite Character of Exodus I., II.,"
AJSL 3 (1886-87) 1-12.

Samuel A. B. Mercer, "The Date of Exodus," *ATR* 10 (1927-28) 211-222.

Robert Moore, "The Date of Exodus," *EQ* 1 (1929) 225-232.

Theodore H. Robinson, "Some Outstanding Old Testament Problems. I. The
Date of Exodus," *ET* 47 (1935-36) 53-55.

§317 *3.2.9.8 Literary Criticism of Leviticus - General Studies*

†Anonymous, "The Mosaic Legislation," *BFER* 1 (1852) 354-380. *(Review)*
[Leviticus]

†Anonymous, "Kalisch on Leviticus," *LQHR* 38 (1872) 194-214. *(Review)*

Lewis B[ayles] Paton, "Notes on Driver's Leviticus," *JBL* 14 (1895) 48-56.

Ph. J. Hoedemaker, "The Structure of Leviticus. I.," *CFL, N.S.,* 6 (1902) 134-139.

Ph. J. Hoedemaker, "The Structure of Leviticus. II.," *CFL, N.S.,* 6 (1902) 189-197.

Henry Nelson Bullard, "The Gospel in Leviticus," *BS* 64 (1907) 76-96.

Anonymous, "Bird's Eye View of the Book of Leviticus," *CFL, 3rd Ser.,* 7 (1907) 61-63.

*Harold M. Wiener, "Studies in the Septuagintal Texts of Leviticus," *BS* 70 (1913) 498-527, 669-686.

William H. Bates, "The Book of Leviticus—An Introduction and an Analysis," *CFL, 3rd Ser.,* 26 (1920) 337-340.

Corwin C. Roach, "Studia Biblica. XII. The Book of Leviticus," *Interp* 4 (1950) 458-469.

§318 *3.2.9.8.1 The Scapegoat*

John Robertson, "The Scape-Goat," *JSL, 1st Ser.,* 1 (1848) 379-380.

*Anonymous, "On the Meaning of 'Azazel' or 'Scape-Goat'," *DTQ* 1 (1875) 140-142.

Claude R. Conder, "On the Mountain of the Scape-Goat," *PEFQS* 8 (1876) 164-167.

Anonymous, "The Scapegoat," *PEFQS* 10 (1878) 118.

*C[laude] R. Conder, "Lieutenant Conder's Reports. The Mountain of the Scape Goat," *PEFQS* 13 (1881) 205-208.

C. Pickering Clarke, "The Mountain of the Scape Goat," *PEFQS* 14 (1882) 135.

*Paul Carus, "Azazel and Satan," *OC* 9 (1895) #44, 4692-4693.

T. K. Cheyne, "The Date and Origin of the 'Scapegoat'," *ZAW* 15 (1895) 153-156.

C. Johnston, "The Scape-Goat," *AAOJ* 20 (1898) 140-143.

*A. H. Sayce, "The Scapegoat Among the Hittites," *ET* 31 (1919-20) 283-284.

*L. W. Barnard, "Some Folklore Elements in an Early Christian Epistle," *Folk* 70 (1959) 433-439. *[The Scapegoat]*

Roger de Verteuil, "The Scapegoat Archetype," *JRH* 5 (1966) 209-225. [O.T. refs.,pp. 210-219]

§319 **3.2.9.8.2 Studies concerning Date, Authorship, Sources and Authenticity**

*John P. Peters, "The Date of Leviticus 1," *JBL* 8 (1888) 128-130.

*Lewis B[ayles] Paton, "The Original Form of Lev. xvii-xix," *JBL* 16 (1897) 31-77.

*Lewis B[ayles] Paton, "The Original Form of Lev. xxi, xxii," *JBL* 17 (1898) 149-175.

*Lewis B[ayles] Paton, "The Original Form of Lev. xxiii, xxv," *JBL* 18 (1899) 35-60.

§320 **3.2.9.9 Literary Criticism of Numbers - General Studies**

†T. P., "Chronology of the Book of Numbers," *MMBR* 3 (1797) 20-21.

Milton S. Terry, "History and Oracles of Balaam," *MR* 50 (1868) 553-580.

F. W. Farrar, "Balaam's Ass," *Exp, 1st Ser.,* 1 (1875) 366-379.

R. P. Stebbins, "The Story of Balaam," *ONTS* 4 (1884-85) 385-395.

Anonymous, "Dr. Stebbins' Interpretation of the Balaam Narrative," *ONTS* 4 (1884-85) 425.

B. F. Simpson, "The Story of Balaam Reconsidered," *ONTS* 5 (1884-85) 125-128.

Edward White, "The Meaning of the Brazen Serpent," *CongL* 15 (1886) 777-784.

Lewis B[ayles] Paton, "The Prophecies of Balaam," *PRR* 2 (1891) 624-646. [I. Composition of the Prophecies; II. Age of the Prophecies; III. Poetic Character of the Prophecies; IV. Interpretation of the Prophecies]

W. W. Martin, "Balaam's Prophecies—their Form and Import," *MR* 74 (1892) 699-711.

Philip A. Nordell, "The Story of the Spies.—A Study in Biblical Criticism," *BW* 1 (1893) 168-183.

W[illia]m Henry Green, "'The Story of the Spies' Once More," *BW* 1 (1893) 328-344.

A. B. Hyde, "Balaam and His Day," *MR* 75 (1893) 206-214.

J. E. Walker, "Two Suggestions as to the 'Story of the Spies'," *BS* 51 (1894) 517-519.

*J. A. Seiss, "Balaam and His Prophecy," *LCR* 14 (1895) 213-225.

*Henry Hayman, "Gilead and Bashan: or, the Prae-Mosaic Manassite Conquest," *BS* 55 (1898) 29-52.

J. E. H. Thompson, "The Book of Numbers," *CFL, N.S.,* 6 (1902) 215-222.

J. A. Selbie, "The International Critical Commentary on 'Numbers'," *ET* 15 (1903-04) 42-44. *(Review)*

*W. M. Flinders Petrie, "The Census of the Israelites," *Exp, 6th Ser.,* 12 (1905) 148-152, 240.

Anonymous, "Outline View of the Book of Numbers," *CFL, 3rd Ser.,* 7 (1907) 129-142. [Parts I & II]

Anonymous, "Outline View of Numbers—Part Third," *CFL, 3rd Ser.,* 7 (1907) 227-232.

Henry Preserved Smith, "The Red Heifer," *AJT* 13 (1909) 207-228.

Thomas T. Eaton, "Moses and the Brazen Serpent," *CFL, 3rd Ser.,* 10 (1909) 56-57.

*G. A. Smith, "The Experience of Balaam as Symbolic of the Origins of Prophecy," *Exp, 8th Ser.,* 5 (1913) 1-11.

Milton S. Terry, "The Traditions of Balak and Balaam," *MR* 95 (1913) 507-523.

George A. Griswold, "The Traditions of Balak and Balaam,"*MR* 95 (1913) 793-794.

J. Gray McAllister, "The Book of Numbers: Disobedience and Discipline," *USR* 28 (1916-17) 201-214.

William H. Bates, "The Book of Numbers—An Introduction and Analysis," *CFL, 3rd Ser.*, 26 (1920) 365-370.

Alexander Haggerty Krappe, "The Story of Eriphyle in Arabic Legend," *AJSL* 41 (1924-25) 194-197. *[Arabic Story of Balaam]*

L[eander] S. K[eyser], "The Biblical Story of the Quails," *CFL, 3rd Ser.*, 38 (1932) 229-230.

Joshua Finkel, "The Phenomenon of Inversion in the Balaam Prophecies," *JBL* 56 (1937) xiii.

A. S. Yahuda, "Remarks on Balaam's Oracles," *JBL* 64 (1945) ix.

John Mauchline, "The Balaam-Balak Songs and Saga," *SSO* 2 (1945) 73-94.

B. D. Eerdmans, "The Composition of Numbers," *OTS* 6 (1949) 101-216.

Allan A. MacRae, "The Book Called 'Numbers'," *BS* 111 (1954) 47-53.

*Ephraim E. Urbach, "Homilies of the Rabbis on the Prophets of the Nations and the Balaam Stories," *Tarbiz* 25 (1956-57) #3, III-VII.

*J. Bowman, "Did the Qumran Sect Burn the Red Heifer?" *RdQ* 1 (1958-59) 73-84.

Elmer E. Flack, "Flashes of New Knowledge. *Recent Study and the Book of Numbers*," *Interp* 13 (1959) 3-23.

*Joseph L. Blau, "The red heifer: a Biblical purification rite in Rabbinic literature," *Numen* 14 (1967) 70-78.

§321 *3.2.9.9.1 Studies concerning Date, Authorship,*
Sources, and Authenticity

M. H. Segal, "The Composition of the Book of Numbers, Part One," *EI* 3 (1954) III. *[No Part II]*

*S. McEvenue, "A Source-Critical Problem in Nm 14, 26-38," *B* 50 (1969) 453-465.

§322 *3.2.9.10 Literary Criticism of Deuteronomy*
- General Studies

*George R. Entler, "A Comparative View of the Language of Deuteronomy and Jeremiah," *PAPA* 7 (1875) 9-10. *[Bound with Transactions, but paged separately]*

Anonymous, "The Book of Deuteronomy and Its Critics," *CQR* 5 (1877-78) 142-163. *(Review)*

James G. Murphy, "The Book of Deuteronomy," *BFER* 27 (1878) 105-126.

J. Estlin Carpenter, "The Book of Deuteronomy," *ModR* 4 (1883) 252-281.

*H. Graetz, "Biblical Studies II—The Central Sanctuary of Deuteronomy," *JQR* 3 (1890-91) 219-230.

*Alfred Cave, "Canon Driver on the Book of the Law," *ContR* 60 (1891) 892-910. *(Review)*

Anonymous, "Truth or Pious Fraud," *BS* 52 (1895) 741-747. *[Critical examination of Driver's "Deuteronomy" in the ICC]*

C[arl] H[einrich] Cornill, "Deuteronomy," *OC* 9 (1895) 4521-4524.

Anonymous, "Deuteronomy and the 'Higher Criticism'," *CQR* 41 (1895-96) 334-358. *(Review) [Driver's "Deuteronomy" in the ICC]*

*G. G. Cameron, "Dr. Driver's 'Deuteronomy.' The Use of the Name of Moses," *ET* 7 (1895-96) 62-67.

*W. Scott Watson, "The Final Chapters of Deuteronomy," *BS* 53 (1896) 681-690.

*George Cormack, "The Holy City of Deuteronomy," *ET* 9 (1897-98) 439-442.

*L. W. Batten, "The Origin and Character of Deuteronomy," *BW* 11 (1898) 246-254.

William Parker McKee, "Transient and Permanent Elements in Deuteronomy," *BW* 13 (1899) 249-251.

Hinckley G. Mitchell, "The Use of the Second Person in Deuteronomy," *JBL* 18 (1899) 61-109.

J. Taylor, "Bertholet's 'Deuteronomium'," *ET* 11 (1899-1900) 180-182. *(Review)*

*G. A. Smith, "Composition of *Deuteronomy* in the Light of the Use of the Singular and Plural Forms of Address both in that Book and in the Discourses of Jeremiah," *OSHTP* (1899-1900) 50-52.

Henry Hayman, "The Blessing of Moses: Its Genesis and Structure," *AJSL* 17 (1900-01) 96-106.

*William R. Harper, "Constructive Studies in the Literature of Worship in the Old Testament. I. The Legal Literature—The Deuteronomic Code of Laws," *BW* 19 (1902) 132-146.

Joseph L. Lampe, "The Structure and Ruling Ideas of the Book of Deuteronomy," *CFL, N.S.*, 6 (1902) 255-263.

George G. Cameron, "The Laws Peculiar to Deuteronomy," *PTR* 1 (1903) 434-456.

*S. Schechter, "The Mechilta to Deuteronomy," *JQR* 16 (1903-04) 695-701. *[Cf. pp. 443-452]*

*A. H. Godbey, "Deuteronomy and the Hammurabi Code," *RChR, 4th Ser.*, 8 (1904) 469-494.

Matthew Leitch, "Deuteronomy and the Higher Criticism," *CFL, 3rd Ser.*, 3 (1905) 16-28.

*G. A. Smith, "Jerusalem and Deuteronomy. Circa 638-608 B.C.," *Exp, 6th Ser.*, 12 (1905) 336-350.

Harold M. Wiener, "The Laws of Deuteronomy and the Arguments from Silence," *PTR* 5 (1907) 188-209.

*W. F. Bade, "Not Monotheism, but Mono-Jahwism Asserted in Deuteronomy," *PAPA* 40 (1908) lii.

Edgar M. Wilson, "'Deuteronomy' in 'A Standard Bible Dictionary'," *CFL, 3rd Ser.*, 11 (1909) 152-156. *(Review)*

G. E. White, "Deuteronomy in Eastern Light—By a Missionary to the Orient," *CFL, 3rd Ser.*, 12 (1910) 47-52.

Harold M. Wiener, "Deuteronomy: Its Place in Revelation," *BS* 69 (1912) 642-656. *(Review)*

*George Aaron Barton, "The Evolution of the Religion of Israel. IV. Deuteronomy and Jeremiah," *BW* 39 (1912) 268-281.

E. Guy Talbott, "The Question of Deuteronomy," *CFL, 3rd Ser.*, 15 (1912) 39-41. [I. The Status of the Question Set Forth; II. The Conclusions of the Destructive Critics from These Assumptions]

E. Guy Talbott, "The Question of Deuteronomy—Concluded," *CFL, 3rd Ser.*, 15 (1912) 169-173. [III. The Critics Answered by 'Higher Critics']

Harold M. Wiener, "Stray Notes on Deuteronomy," *BS* 71 (1914) 466-473.

G. G. Warren, "The Orations of Moses in Deuteronomy," *BM* 3 (1915) 12-36.

Harold M. Wiener, "The Main Problem of Deuteronomy," *BS* 77 (1920) 46-82.

William H. Bates, "The Book of Deuteronomy: An Introduction and an Analysis," *CFL, 3rd Ser.*, 26 (1920) 418-421.

A. Troelstra, "Deuteronomy," *BS* 81 (1924) 393-409. *(Trans. by John H. De Vries)*

George C. Stibitz, "The Deuteronomy Question," *CTSQ* 2 (1924-25) #3, 1-2ι

*Adam C. Welch, "The Sanctuary in Deuteronomy," *ET* 36 (1924-25) 568.

*J. Battersby Harford, "Since Wellhausen. Article 4. Deuteronomy," *Exp, 9th Ser.*, 4 (1925) 323-349.

*Adam C. Welch, "The Two Descriptions of the Sanctuary in Deuteronomy," *ET* 37 (1925-26) 215-219, 442-444.

*F. A. Farley, "Jeremiah and Deuteronomy," *ET* 37 (1925-26) 316-318.

*J. Rendel Harris, "Irenaeus and the Song of Moses," *ET* 37 (1925-26) 333-334.

William Creighton Graham, "The Modern Controversy About Deuteronomy," *JR* 7 (1927) 396-418.

A. P. Gold-Levin, "Deuteronomy Whence and Why? A Study in Scripture Criticism and Hebrew Psychology," *EQ* 1 (1929) 33-40.

A[dam] C. Welch, "The Problem of Deuteronomy," *JBL* 48 (1929) 219-306.

H. M. DuBose, "The Integrity of Deuteronomy," *MR* 112 (1929) 515-526.

F. C. Burkitt, "On the Blessing of Moses," *JTS* 35 (1934) 68.

J[ulius] Morgenstern, "The Stratification and Historical Import of the Sacrificial Legislation of Deuteronomy," *JBL* 56 (1937) ix.

R[obert] H. Pfeiffer, "Successive Editions of the Deuteronomic Code," *JBL* 57 (1938) viii.

*J[ulius] Morgenstern, "The Calendar of Deuteronomy," *JBL* 57 (1938) viii.

*J. H. Hertz, "Deuteronomy: Its Antiquity and Mosaic Authorship," *JTVI* 72 (1940) 86-95, 103. [(Discussion, pp. 96-98) (Communications by H. S. Curr, pp. 99-100, and A. H. van Straubenzee, pp. 100-103)]

*J. Philip Hyatt, "Jeremiah and Deuteronomy," *JNES* 1 (1942) 156-173.

G. T. Manley, "The Moabite Background of Deuteronomy," *EQ* 21 (1949) 81-92.

L. Johnston, "Recent Views on Deuteronomy and the Unity of Sanctuary," *Scrip* 4 (1949-51) 356-362.

Patrick W. Skehan, "The Structure of the Song of Moses in Deuteronomy," *CBQ* 13 (1951) 153-163.

*Kuyper Lester J. Cooper, "Studia Biblica. XIX. The Book of Deuteronomy," *Interp* 6 (1952) 321-340.

L. Johnston, "Reflections on Some Recent Views on Deuteronomy," *Scrip* 5 (1952-53) 12-20.

*G. Ernest Wright, "The Levites in Deuteronomy," *VT* 4 (1954) 325-330.

John Bowman, "The Samaritans and the Book of Deuteronomy," *GUOST* 17 (1957-58) 9-18.

M. H. Segal, "The Book of Deuteronomy," *JQR, N.S.,* 48 (1957-58) 315-351. [I. Deuteronomy and the Pseudepigrapha; II. The Programme of Deuteronomy; III. Deuteronomy and the Preceding Books of the Pentateuch; IV. Deuteronomy and the Centralization of the Sacrifices; V. Parallel Narratives; VI. Later Additions; VII. The Song of Moses; VIII. The Blessing of Moses]

*Robert Dobbie, "Deuteronomy and the Prophetic Attitude to Sacrifice," *SJT* 12 (1959) 68-82.

J. N. Schofield, "Reunion in Ancient Israel. Studies in the Book of Deuteronomy," *MC, N.S.,* 4 (1960-61) 104-111.

Moshe Weinfeld, "The Source of the Idea of Reward in Deuteronomy," *Tarbiz* 30 (1960-61) #1, I-II.

*Gerhard von Rad, "Ancient Word and Living Word. *The Preaching of Deuteronomy and Our Preaching," Interp* 15 (1961) 3-13.

Edward P. Blair, "An Appeal to Remembrance. *The Memory Motif in Deuteronomy," Interp* 15 (1961) 41-47.

M[oshe] Weinfeld, "The Origin of the Humanism in Deuteronomy," *JBL* 80 (1961) 241-247.

*Moshe Weinfeld, "The Change in the Conception of Religion in Deuteronomy," *Tarbiz* 31 (1961-62) #1, I-III.

G. W. Anderson, "Old Testament Books," *PQL* 8 (1962) 128-134. [III. Deuteronomy]

*William L. Moran, "The Ancient Near Eastern Background of the Love of God in Deuteronomy," *CBQ* 25 (1963) 77-87.

E. Nicholson, "The Centralization of the Cult in Deuteronomy," *VT* 13 (1963) 380-389.

Donald L. Williams, "Deuteronomy and Modern Study," *R&E* 61 (1964) 265-273.

John Joseph Owens, "Law and Love in Deuteronomy," *R&E* 61 (1964) 274-283.

Norman K. Gottwald, "'Holy War' in Deuteronomy: Analysis and Critique," *R&E* 61 (1964) 294-310. *(Review)*

*Marvin E. Tate, "The Deuteronomic Philosophy of History," *R&E* 61 (1964) 311-319.

Clyde T. Francisco, "Deuteronomy for Today," *R&E* 61 (1964) 320-329.

*R. Davidson, "Orthodoxy and the Prophetic Word. A Study in the Relationship between Jeremiah and Deuteronomy," *VT* 14 (1964) 407-416.

Derward Deere, "An Introduction to Deuteronomy," *SWJT, N.S.,* 7 (1964-65) #1, 7-16.

*C. W. Scudder, "Ethics in Deuteronomy," *SWJT, N..S,* 7 (1964-65) #1, 33-40.

*M[oshe] Weinfeld, "Traces of Assyrian Treaty Formulae in Deuteronomy," *B* 46 (1965) 417-427.

*Dennis J. McCarthy, "Notes on the Love of God in Deuteronomy and the Father-Son Relationship between Yahweh and Israel," *CBQ* 27 (1965) 144-147.

*Lawrence E. Toombs, "Love and Justice in Deuteronomy. *A Third Approach to the Law,*" *Interp* 19 (1965) 399-411.

*Dennis J. McCarthy, "II Samuel 7 and the Structure of Deuteronomic History," *JBL* 84 (1965) 131-138.

*Arthur E. Cundall, "Sanctuaries (Central and Local) in Pre-exilic Israel, with particular reference to the Book of Deuteronomy," *VE* 4 (1965) 4-27.

*R. E. Clements, "Deuteronomy and the Jerusalem Cult-Tradition," *VT* 15 (1965) 300-312.

*Joseph Blenkinsopp, "Are there Traces of the Gibeonite Covenant in Deuteronomy?" *CBQ* 28 (1966) 207-219.

Moshe Weinfeld, "Deuteronomy—The Present State of Inquiry," *JBL* 86 (1967) 249-262.

*Terence E. Fretheim, "The Ark in Deuteronomy," *CBQ* 30 (1968) 1-14.

Carl Graesser Jr., "The Message of the Deuteronomic Historian," *CTM* 39 (1968) 542-551.

*W. A. Sumner, "Israel's Encounters with Edom, Moab, Ammon, Sihon, and Og According to the Deuteronomist," *VT* 18 (1968) 216-228.

*S. E. Loewenstamm, "The Formula בעת ההיא in Deuteronomy," *Tarbiz* 38 (1968-69) #2, I.

D. Patrick, "The Gift of God. *The Deuteronomic Theology of the Land,*" *Interp* 23 (1969) 451-465.

*David Daube, "The Culture of Deuteronomy," *Orita* 3 (1969) 27-52.

C. Carmichael, "A new view of the origin of the Deuteronomic credo," *VT* 19 (1969) 273-289.

§323 *3.2.9.10.1 Studies Concerning Date, Authorship, Sources, and Authenticity*

C. S. C., "Deuteronomy, as the Production of Moses," *JSL, 3rd Ser.,* 6 (1857-58) 313-325.

Anonymous, "Deuteronomy Written by Moses; Proved from the Book Itself," *ERG, 7th Ser.,* 2 (1879-80) 45-46. *(Review)*

A. F. Simpson, "The Authorship of Deuteronomy," *DTQ* 6 (1880) 161-181.

Anonymous, "The Mosaic Authorship of Deuteronomy," *BWR* 3 (1881) 280-303.

E. C. Bissell, "The Independent Legislation of Deuteronomy," *JBL* 3 (1883) 67-89.

O. M., "The Date of Deuteronomy," *ONTS* 4 (1884-85) 317-319.

C. H. Toy, "The Date of Deuteronomy,"*URRM* 23 (1885) 97-118.

T. S. Potwin, "The Composition and Date of Deuteronomy," *BS* 51 (1894) 1-19, 231-245.

*W. Scott Watson Jr., "Note on the Bearing of Deut. 34:1 upon the Question of the Authorship of Deuteronomy," *BW* 6 (1895) 356-357.

*W. Scott Watson [Jr.], "The Final Chapters of Deuteronomy," *BS* 53 (1896) 618-690. [Author, pp. 687-690]

*L. W. Batten, "The Origin and Character of Deuteronomy," *BW* 11 (1898) 246-254.

George L. Robinson, "The Genesis of Deuteronomy," *Exp, 5th Ser.,* 8 (1898) 241-261, 351-369; 9 (1899) 151-160, 271-295, 356-371.

Ed. König, "The Unity of Deuteronomy," *ET* 10 (1898-99) 16-18, 124-126, 227-230.

*G. A. Smith, "Composition of *Deuteronomy* in the Light of the Use of the Singular and Plural Forms of Address both in that Book and in the Discourses of Jeremiah," *OSHTP* (1899-1900) 50-52.

H. Pereira Mendes, "The Date of Deuteronomy," *OC* 15 (1901) 438. (Editorial reply by Paul Carus, pp. 438-440)

R. H. Kennett, "The Date of Deuteronomy," *JTS* 7 (1905-06) 481-500.

John E. McFadyen, "Who Wrote Deuteronomy?" *HR* 54 (1907) 213-215.

*E[douard] Naville, "Egyptian Writing in Foundation Walls and the Age of the Book of Deuteronomy," *SBAP* 29 (1907) 232-242.

John T. McFarland, "'Moses and Deuteronomy'," *CFL, 3rd Ser.,* 8 (1908) 10-11. *(Editorial Note) [Authorship]*

Francis E. Gigot, "The Mosaic Authorship of Deuteronomy," *ITQ* 4 (1909) 411-426.

H. H. B. Ayles, "The Date of Deuteronomy," *CQR* 69 (1909-10) 282-300.

A. H. Sayce, "The Latest Light from Oriental Archaeology: The Date of Deuteronomy," *ET* 21 (1909-10) 45-46.

Harold M. Wiener, "Dr. Puukko on Deuteronomy—A Review," *CFL, 3rd Ser.,* 13 (1910) 279-283. [I. Deuteronomy xviii. 6-8 No Basis for the Exilic or Post-Exilic Origin of the Book; II. The Other Signs Indicated Do Not Point to the Post-Exilic Origin of P] *(Review)*

Hugh Pope, "The Mosaic Authorship of Deuteronomy," *ITQ* 5 (1910) 159-165.

G. A. Cooke, "Was Deuteronomy Written in Cuneiform?" *ICMM* 8 (1911-12) 380-385.

Edward Day, "The Promulgation of Deuteronomy," *JBL* 21 (1920) 197-213.

W. H. Griffith Thomas, "The Date of Deuteronomy," *CFL, 3rd Ser.*, 29 (1923) 140-142.

C. Ryder Smith, "The Priest-Preachers of Jerusalem," *Exp, 8th Ser.*, 26 (1923) 255-258. *[Authorship of Deuteronomy]*

E. J. Harris, "Deuteronomy: The Post-Exilic Theory," *GUOST* 5 (1923-28) 29-30.

Anonymous, "The Date of Deuteronomy," *Exp, 9th Ser.*, 1 (1924) 230.

Edouard Naville, "Deuteronomy as a Mosaic Book," *JTVI* 56 (1924) 207-220, 229-231. (Discussion and Communications, pp. 220-229)

J. A. Bewer, "The Problem of Deuteronomy: A Symposium. A.The Case for the Early Date of Deuteronomy," *JBL* 47 (1928) 305-321.

L. B. Paton, "The Problem of Deuteronomy: A Symposium. B. The Case for the Post-Exilic Origin of Deuteronomy," *JBL* 47 (1928) 322-357.

G. Dahl, "The Problem of Deuteronomy: A Symposium. C. The Case for the Currently Accepted Date of Deuteronomy," *JBL* 47 (1928) 358-379.

W. W. Cannon, "A Source of Deuteronomy," *Theo* 19 (1929) 196-204.

George Jeshurun, "Who Wrote Deuteronomy?" *BS* 90 (1933) 303-330, 412-437.

W. D. Monro, "Must We Relegate Deuteronomy to the Reign of Josiah?" *EQ* 8 (1936) 3-21.

W. J. Phythian-Adams, "The Origin and Evolution of Deuteronomy," *CQR* 123 (1936-37) 215-247.

Joseph Reider, "The Origin of Deuteronomy," *JQR, N.S.*, 27 (1936-37) 349-371.

W. A. Irwin, "An Objective Criterion for the Dating of Deuteronomy," *AJSL* 46 (1939) 337-349.

A. S. Siebens, "Hiatus in the Regnant Hypothesis of Origin of Deuteronomy," *JBL* 58 (1939) xii.

G[eorge] R[icker] Berry, "The Date of Deuteronomy," *JBL* 59 (1940) vii.

George Ricker Berry, "The Date of Deuteronomy," *JBL* 59 (1940) 133-139.

*J. H. Hertz, "Deuteronomy: Its Antiquity and Mosaic Authorship," *JTVI* 72 (1940) 86-95, 103. [(Discussion, pp. 96-98) (Communications by H. S. Curr, pp. 99-100, and A. H. van Straubenzee, pp. 100-103)]

*Kuyper Lester J. Cooper, "Studia Biblica.   XIX.   The Book of Deuteronomy," *Interp* 6 (1952) 321-340. [Authorship and Date, pp. 322-324]

I. Lewy, "Deuteronomic Code: Dating of Its Two Strata," *JBL* 72 (1953) xviii.

Norman Walker, "The Date of Deuteronomy," *VT* 3 (1953) 413-414.

*Andrew C. Tunyogi, "The Book of the Conquest," *JBL* 84 (1965) 347-380. *[Deuteronomy and Joshua 1-11 originally as one book]*

*R. Frankena, "The Vassal-Treaties of Esarhaddon and the Dating of Deuteronomy," *OTS* 14 (1965) 122-154.

*C. M. Carmichael, "Deuteronomic Laws, Wisdom, and Historical Traditions," *JSS* 12 (1967) 198-206.

§324 *3.2.10 Literary Criticism of the Prophets [Former and Latter] - General Studies*

Alexander Robb, "The Prophetic Writings and Modern Criticism," *DTQ* 3 (1877) 367-373.

C. W. Gallagher, "The Prophetic Writings," *MR* 76 (1894) 597-608.

*H. St. J. Thackeray, "The Greek Translators of the Prophetical Books," *JTS* 4 (1902-03) 578-585.

*D. F. Roberts, "The Usage in Samuel, Kings, Amos, and Hosea," *GUOST* 3 (1907-12) 52-53. *[Use of the Name 'Israel']*

*Louis Finkelstein, "The Beginnings of the Prophetic Doctrine of Peace," *JBL* 55 (1936) xviii-xix.

Vincent McNabb, "The Hebrew Prophets and National Crises," *NB* 21 (1940) 142-150.

*Paul S. Minear, "The Conception of History in the Prophets and Jesus," *JAAR* 11 (1943) 156-161.

Francis W. Boelter, "The Use of History in Selected Pre-Exilic and Post-Exilic Prophets,"*IR* 12 (1955) #3, 33-44.

Lionel du Toit, "The Relevance of the Prophets to Our Own Day," *ET* 70 (1958-59) 179-183.

*J. A. Sanders, "The Grace of God in the Prophets," *Found* 4 (1961) 262-265.

*J. A. Sanders, "The Grace of God in the Prophets. (Part II)," *Found* 4 (1961) 363-365.

Georg Fohrer, "Remarks on Modern Interpretation of the Prophets," *JBL* 80 (1961) 309-319.

*J. A. Sanders, "The Grace of God in the Prophets. (Part III)," *Found* 5 (1962) 74-77.

*E. C. John, "Forgiveness in the Prophecy of Judgment," *IJT* 18 (1969) 206-218.

*James Limburg, "The Root רִיב and the Prophetic Lawsuit Speeches," *JBL* 88 (1969) 291-304.

§325 *3.2.10.1 Literary Criticism of the Former Prophets*
          - General Studies

*(Mrs.) [Marianne Young] Postans, "Recollections of the East, Illustrative of Certain Passages in the Historical Books of the Old Testament," *JSL, 1st Ser.,* 4 (1849) 46-58.

*Anonymous, "Topography of Books of Joshua and Samuel," *CongL* 5 (1876) 109-115.

*A. Kleber, "The chronology of 3 and 4 Kings and 2 Paralipomenon," *B* 2 (1921) 3-29, 170-205.

*Harold M. Wiener, "The Conquest Narrative," *JPOS* 9 (1929) 1-26.

G. Ernest Wright, "Archaeological Observations on the Period of the Judges and the Early Monarchy," *JBL* 60 (1941) 27-42.

*G. Ernest Wright, "The Literary and Historical Problem of Joshua 10 and Judges 1," *JNES* 5 (1946) 105-114.

*Morton Smith, "The So-Called 'Biography of David' in the Books of Samuel and Kings," *HTR* 44 (1951) 167-169.

*J. P. U. Lilley, "The Altar in Joshua and Judges," *TB* #5&6 (1960) 32-33.

John Briggs Curtis, "'East is East....'," *JBL* 80 (1961) 355-363. *[The Crucial significance of the Transjordan area of Israel in the Period of the Monarchy]*

Menaḥem Haran, "Problems in the Composition of the Former Prophets," *Tarbiz* 37 (1967-68) #1, I- II.

*Walter Brueggemann, "David and His Theologian," *CBQ* 30 (1968) 156-181. *[J narrative of Gen 2-11 and 2 Sam. 9-20, 1 Kgs. 1-2]*

T. C. G. Thornton, "Solomonic Apologetics in Samuel and Kings," *CQR* 169 (1968) 159-166.

G. Van Gronigen, "Joshua-II Kings: Deuteronomistic? Priestly? or Prophetic Writings?" *BETS* 12 (1969) 3-26.

§326 *3.2.10.2 Studies concerning Date, Authorship, Sources, and Authenticity*

*Edward Day, "The Search for the Prophets," *Monist* 15 (1905) 386-397.

*David Noel Freedman, "The Law and the Prophets," *VTS* 9 (1963) 250-265.

*M[oshe] Weinfeld, "The Period of the Conquest and of the Judges as seen by the earlier and later sources," *VT* 17 (1967) 93-113.

§327 *3.2.10.3 Studies concerning the Harmony and/or Parallels of Samuel, Kings and Chronicles [See also: Biblical (and Hebrew) Chronology §145 ↩]*

*Anonymous, "Expository Items. 2 Samuel XXIV. 24—1 Chronicles XXI. 25," *MQR, 2nd Ser.,* 2 (1880) 566.

†W. H. Summers, "Communication from W. H. Summers," *SBAP* 7 (1884-85) 179. *[1 Kgs. 10:29; 1 Chron. 1:17]*

Lewis B[ayles] Paton, "Some Alleged Discrepancies Between the Books of Chronicles and Kings," *PQ* 5 (1891) 587-610.

*Thomas Whiteland, "Hilkiah's Book of the Law. *A Study in Modern Criticism.* 2 Kings xxii.8; 2 Chron. xxiv.15," *TML* 6 (1891) 420-430.

*Willis J. Beecher, "The International Lessons in Their Literary Setting. III," *CFL., N.S.,* 8 (1903) 128-133. [Variant Delimitations of the Historical Narratives; The Narrative of Saul's Last Battle; Duplications of Samuel in Chronicles; The Credibility of Chronicles; The Narrative of the Accession of David in Hebron; The Narrative of the Kingdoms of David and Ishbosheth; The Narrative of David's Becoming King of Israel]

John R. Miller, "A Question in Old-Testament Chronology," *HR* 47 (1904) 441-442. *[1 Chron. 11:16, 17 // 2 Sam. 23:13-16 & 2 Sam. 5:17-21]*

J. Oscar Boyd, "Critical Note. An Undesigned Coincidence," *PTR* 3 (1905) 299-303.

*W. O. E. Oesterley, "Dioscurism in the Old Testament," *ET* 17 (1905-06) 477. *[2 Sam. 5:17-25 // 1 Chron. 14:8-17]*

Granger W. Smith, "Parallel Passages in the History of the Hebrew Kings," *CFL, 3rd Ser.,* 9 (1908) 366-368. *[2 Sam. 24:18-25 // 1 Chron. 21:18-22:1]*

John Urquhart, "'A Huge Bible Difficulty'," *CFL, 3rd Ser.,* 11 (1909) 15-17. *[2 Kgs. 9:27, 28 // 2 Chron. 22:8,9]*

*Claude R. Conder, "Notes on New Discoveries," *PEFQS* 41 (1909) 266-275. [Almug or Algum trees (1 Kgs. 10:11; 2 Chron. 9:10) p. 274]

Daniel S. Gregory, "Introductory View to the Subsequent Lessons," *CFL, 3rd Ser.,* 14 (1911-12) 283-289. [I. The Analytic Inspection of the Materials of Kings and Chronicles; II. The Constructive Study of Kings and Chronicles; III. The Study of the Historic Aim of the Prophet-Scribes]

*A. T. Olmstead, "Source Study and the Biblical Text," *AJSL* 30 (1913-14) 1-35.

*L. T. Townsend, "King David and the Rabbahites," *CFL, 3rd Ser.,* 19 (1915) 205-206 *[2. Sam. 12:31; 1 Chron. 20:3; 1 Kgs. 15:5; 1 Chron. 22:14,15]*

David Yellin, "Emek ha-bakha: Bekhaim," *JPOS* 3 (1923) 191-192. *[2 Sam. 5:23, 24; 1 Chron. 14:14,15]*

*A[dam] C. Welch, "The Significance for Old Testament History of a New Tablet," *ET* 35 (1923-24) 170-172. [B. M. 21,901] *[2 Kgs. 23:29ff. // 2 Chron. 35:22ff.*

*W. F. Lofthouse, "Tablet B. M. No. 21,901 and Politics in Jerusalem," *ET* 35 (1923-24) 454-456. *[2 Kgs. 23:29ff. // 2 Chron. 35:22ff.]*

William H. Bates, "The Kingdom Books—Samuel, Kings, Chronicles," *CFL, 3rd Ser.,* 31 (1925) 437-442.

G. R. Driver, "On Some Passages in the Books of Kings and Chronicles," *JTS* 27 (1925-26) 158-160; *JTS* 32 (1930-31) 257 *[2 Kgs. 4:13; 1 Kgs. 18:26; 1 Kgs. 6:29, 32, 35; (6:18 and 7:31); 2 Chron. 22:10 // 2 Kgs. 11:1]* [Corrections, *JTS* 31 (1929-30) pp. 283-284]

J. A. Montgomery, "A Study in Comparison of the Texts of Kings and Chronicles," *JBL* 50 (1931) 115-116.

*Herbert Parzen, "Aspects of the Problems of Chronology of the Two Kingdoms as Treated by Rabbinic Exegesis," *JQR, N.S.*, 18 (1937-38) 305-331.

*S. Yeivin, "Abijam, Asa and Maachah the Daughter of Abishalom," *BIES* 10 (1942-44) #4, III. *[2 Chron. 3:18-22 // 1 Kgs. 15:2]*

D. R. Ap-Thomas, "A Numerical Poser," *JNES* 2 (1943) 198-200. *[2 Sam. 8:4; 10:18; 1 Chron. 19:18; Josephus, Antiq. VII, 6, 3]*

M. D. Goldman, "Lexicographical Notes on Exegesis (2) From Whom Did David Buy the Temple Area?" *ABR* 1 (1951) 138-139. *[2 Sam. 24 and 1 Chron. 21]*

*Zane C. Hodges, "Conflicts in the Biblical Account of the Ammonite-Syrian War," *BS* 119 (1962) 238-243.

*Werner E. Lemke, "The Synoptic Problem in the Chronicler's History," *HTR* 58 (1965) 349-363.

*Ralph W. Klein, "New Evidence for an Old Recension of Reigns," *HTR* 60 (1967) 93-105.

*Leslie C. Allen, "Further Thoughts on an Old Recension of Reigns in Paralipomena," *HTR* 61 (1968) 483-491.

*Ralph W. Klein, "Supplements in the Paralipomena: A Rejoinder," *HTR* 61 (1968) 492-495.

Donald James Shenkel, "A Comparative Study of the Synoptic Parallels in I Paraleipomena[sic]* and I-II Reigns," *HTR* 62 (1969) 63-85.

J. Maxwell Miller, "Geshur and Aram," *JNES* 28 (1969) 60-61. *[1 Chron. 2:23; 1 Kgs. 20:23-24; 22:3; 15:16-22]*

§328 *3.2.10.3.1 Literary Criticism of Joshua - General Studies*

*†Anonymous, "The Law of Moses Viewed in connexion with the History and Character of the Jews, with a Defense of the Book of Joshua against Professor Leo of Berlin; being the Hulsean Lecture for 1833," *BCQTR, 4th Ser.*, 17 (1835) 310-332. *(Review)*

Karl F. Keil, "An Introduction to the Book of Joshua," *JSL, 1st Ser.*, 4 (1849) 217-241. *(Trans. by Benjamin Davis)*

Karl F. Keil, "An Introduction to the Book of Joshua. Part II.," *JSL, 1st Ser.,* 5 (1850) 96-117.

†Anonymous, "Keil on Joshua," *BFER* 1 (1852) 380-404. *(Review)*

*Anonymous, "Colenson upon Moses and Joshua," *CongR* 3 (1863) 190-193. *(Review)*

*Henry M. Harman, "The Character of the Book of Joshua, and its Relation and Testimony to the Pentateuch," *MR* 72 (1890) 9-26.

A. E. Haynes, "The Season of Caleb's Reconnaissance," *PEFQS* 28 (1896) 186-187.

*W. H. Bennett, "The Book of Joshua and the Pentateuch," *JQR* 10 (1897-98) 649-653.

*C[laude] R. Conder, "Notes on the Antiquities of the Book of Joshua," *PEFQS* 31 (1899) 161-162. [Gilgal; Ai; The Battle of Gibeon; The Hivites]

*George C. M. Douglas, "The Higher Criticism. Doublets in the Book of Joshua," *CFL, N.S.,* 5 (1902) 114-119.

Barnard C. Taylor, "Structure and Ruling Ideas of Joshua," *CFL, N.S.,* 6 (1902) 263-268.

*George A. Barton, "The Levitical Cities of Israel in the Light of the Excavation at Gezer," *BW* 24 (1904) 167-179.

John E. McFadyen, "The Capture of Jericho," *HR* 54 (1907) 283-285.

*Claude R. Conder, "Notes on New Discoveries," *PEFQS* 41 (1909) 266-275. [Book of Joshua, p. 272]

H[erbert] W. Magoun, "The Fall of Jericho," *CFL, 3rd Ser.,* 23 (1917) 304-307.

William H. Bates, "The Book of Joshua: An Introduction and an Analysis," *CFL, 3rd Ser.,* 27 (1921) 11-13.

John Garstang, "The Date of the Destruction of Jericho," *PEFQS* 59 (1927) 96-100, 168.

A. T. Richardson, "The Battle of Gibeon," *ET* 40 (1928-29) 426-431. *[map]*

J[ohn] Garstang, "Joshua and the Higher Critics," *JTVI* 62 (1930) 234-238. (Discussion, pp. 238-240)

John Robert Towers, "Correspondence," *PEFQS* 67 (1935) 144. (Reply by W. John Phythian-Adams, p. 207) *[Joshua]*

*George A. Barton, "The Possible Mention of Joshua's Conquest in the El-Amarna Letters," *ET* 47 (1935-36) 380.

*W. J. Phythian-Adams, "Jericho, Ai and the Occupation of Mount Ephraim," *PEFQS* 68 (1936) 141-149.

John Garstang, "The Story of Jericho: Further Light on the Biblical Narrative," *AJSL* 58 (1941) 368-372.

J[ohn] Garstang, "The Story of Jericho: Further Light on the Biblical Narrative," *PEQ* 73 (1941) 168-171.

*H. L. Ginsberg, "The Date of the Town-lists in Joshua," *JBL* 67 (1948) v.

*Oscar J. F. Seitz, "What Do These Stones Mean?" *JBL* 79 (1960) 247-254.

*Murray B. Nicol, "Archaeology and the Fall of Jericho," *R&E* 58 (1961) 173-180.

*I. M. Grintz, "The Treaty with the Gibeonites," *Zion* 26 (1961) #2, I.

P. Giffin, "The Epic of Joshua," *Scrip* 14 (1962) 75-81.

St. Gevirtz, "Jericho and Shechem: A Religio-Literary Aspect of City Destruction," *VT* 13 (1963) 52-62.

*F. Charles Fensham, "The Treaty Between Israel and the Gibeonites," *BA* 27 (1964) 96-100.

*Jehoshua M. Grintz, "The Treaty of Joshua with the Gibeonites," *JAOS* 86 (1966) 113-126.

*A. D. Crown, "Some Traces of the Heterodox Theology in the Samaritan Book of Joshua," *BJRL* 50 (1967-68) 178-198.

*Sh. Yeivin, "Philological Notes 10," *Lěš* 32 (1967-68) #1/2, I-II. [1. Joshua's defeat of the Jerusalemite Confederation]

Henry Wansbrough, "Event and Interpretation: III. Israel at the Walls of Jericho," *ClR* 53 (1968) 434-441.

*E. D. Stockton, "The Fortress Temple of Shechem and Joshua's Covenant," *AJBA* 1 (1968-71) #1, 24-28.

Adrian Jeffers, "Ideal versus Real History in the Book of Joshua," *BETS* 12 (1969) 183-187.

§329 *3.2.10.3.1.1 Joshua's "Long Day"*

†Virgilius, "An Attempt to prove, from Scripture, that the Sun did not stand still in the Time of Joshua," *TRep* 1 (1769) 103-120.

H. T., "Joshua's Miracle," *MR* 11 (1828) 334-338.

J. von Gumpach, "On the Miracle of Joshua," *JSL, 1st Ser.*, 3 (1849) 136-151; 5 (1850) 225-231; 6 (1850) 459-483

William Taylor, "On the Miracle of Joshua," *JSL, 1st Ser.*, 4 (1849) 148-153.

Daniel Katterns, "On the Miracle of Joshua," *JSL, 1st Ser.*, 6 (1850) 208-222. (Note by William Taylor, pp. 222-223)

W. T. Lynn, "The Joshua Miracle," *ET* 2 (1890-91) 273.

M. Brokenshire, "The Joshua Miracle," *ET* 3 (1891-92) 113.

Howard Crosby, "New Exegesis Required by New Discoveries. The Sun and the Moon Standing Still," *HR* 21 (1891) 267-268.

R. Balgarnie, "The Miracle at Gibeon in the Light of Later Scripture," *HR* 25 (1893) 209-214.

A. Smyth Palmer, "Did the Sun and Moon Stand Still?" *ET* 9 (1897-98) 235.

John Reid, "Did the Sun and the Moon Stand Still? In Reply to Dr. Palmer," *ET* 9 (1897-98) 284-285.

*C[laude] R. Conder, "Notes on the Antiquities of the Book of Joshua," *PEFQS* 31 (1899) 161-162. [The Battle of Gibeon]

W. Collins Badger, "The Standing Still of the Sun upon Gibeon," *PEFQS* 31 (1899) 270-273. (Note by C. R. Conder, p. 354)

W. F. Birch, "The Standing Still of the Sun Upon Gibeon," *PEFQS* 32 (1900) 165-166.

W. Collins Badger, "The Sun Standing Still on Gibeon, by the Rev. W. F. Birch, M. A.," *PEFQS* 32 (1900) 283-285.

C[laude] R. Conder, "Notes on Bible Geography. III. The Battle of Gibeon," *PEFQS* 37 (1905) 72-74.

John C. Young, "The Sun and the Moon Standing Still," *ET* 20 (1908-09) 279.

Anonymous, "In the Study. Sun, Stand Thou Still," *ET* 20 (1908-09) 450.

Robert Kelly, "The Sun Standing Still," *ET* 20 (1908-09) 566.

E. W. Maunder, "A Misinterpreted Miracle," *Exp, 7th Ser.,* 10 (1910) 359-372. *[The sun standing still]*

D. E. Spair, "The Cosmic Miracle and Joshua," *HR* 76 (1918) 82.

Robert Dick Wilson, "What Does 'The Sun Stood Still' Mean?" *PTR* 16 (1918) 46-54.

George P. Wallace, "Joshua and the Miracle of the Sun," *ET* 33 (1921-22) 187-189.

C. J. Ritchie, "Joshua and the Miracle of the Sun," *ET* 33 (1921-22) 521.

Robert Eisler, "Joshua and the Sun," *AJSL* 42 (1925-26) 73-85.

A. Lincoln Shute, "The Battle of Beth-Horon. When Sun and Hail Fought for Joshua," *BS* 84 (1927) 411-431.

Herbert W. Magoun, "Joshua's Command to the Sun and Moon," *CFL, 3rd Ser.,* 34 (1928) 94-98.

C. Stanley Thoburn, "Joshua's Long Day," *ET* 47 (1935-36) 373-377.

W. J. Phythian-Adams, "A Meteorite of the Fourteenth Century B.C.," *PEQ* 78 (1946) 116-124. *[Joshua's Long Day]*

*Michael J. Gruenthaner, "Two Sun Miracles of the Old Testament," *CBQ* 10 (1948) 217-290. [I. The Miracle of Joshe, pp. 272-287]

§330 *3.2.10.3.1.2 Studies concerning Date, Authorship, Sources, and Authenticity*

*Claude R. Conder, "Samaritan Topography," *PEFQS* 8 (1876) 182-197. [I. The Samaritan Book of Joshua, pp. 187-190]

Stilton Henning, "Is there a Deuteronomist in Joshua? *Results Claimed by the Disintegrationists,*" *TML* 6 (1891) 385-395.

W. J. Phythian-Adams, "Israelite Tradition and the Date of Joshua," *PEFQS* 59 (1927) 34-46.

M. Gaster, "The Samaritan Hebrew Sources of the Arabic Book of Joshua," *JRAS* (1930) 567-599.

E[dward] J. Young, "The Alleged Secondary Deuteronomic Passages in the Book of Joshua," *EQ* 25 (1953) 142-157.

*A. D. Crown, "The Date and Authenticity of the Samaritan Hebrew Book of Joshua as seen in its Territorial Allotments," *PEQ* 96 (1964) 79-100.

*Andrew C. Tunyogi, "The Book of the Conquest," *JBL* 84 (1965) 374-380. *[Deuteronomy and Joshua 1-11 originally as one book]*

§331 *3.2.10.3.2 Literary Criticism of Judges - General Studies*

O. E., "Remarks Introductory to the Book of Judges," *SP* 6 (1833) 607-622.

Enoch Pond, "The Book of Judges," *TLJ* 12 (1859-60) 463-477.

*H. C., "Chronology of the Book of Judges," *JSL, 4th Ser.,* 9 (1866) 217.

Horatio B. Hackett, "Biblical Notes. Renderings of the Authorized Version in the Book of Judges," *BS* 26 (1869) 203-208.

Stanley Leathes, "Gideon's Fleece," *Exp, 1st Ser.,* 3 (1876) 295-307.

Anonymous, "The Death of Sisera," *PEFQS* 10 (1878) 115-116.

W. F. Birch, "Hiding Places in Canaan. II. Gideon's Wine-press at Ophrah," *PEFQS* 13 (1881) 235-237.

W. F. Birch, "Hiding Places in Canaan. III. Sampson and the Rock Etam," *PEFQS* 13 (1881) 323-324.

J. Estlin Carpenter, "The Book of Judges," *ModR* 4 (1883) 441-463.

*Willis J. Beecher, "The Chronology of the Period of the Judges," *ONTS* 3 (1883-84) 129-141.

Edward L. Curtis, "The Blessing of Jael," *ONTS* 4 (1884-85) 12-18.

Joseph Agar Beet, "Sisera and Jael," *Exp, 3rd Ser.*, 6 (1887) 471-472.

*William J. Deane, "The Chronology of the Book of Judges," *BFER* 37 (1888) 100-113.

*J. Blunt Chesire Jr., "Jael, the Wife of Heber the Kenite," *PER* 2 (1888-89) 277-284.

*Anonymous, "Judges and Ruth," *CongRL* 4 (1890) 301-303. *(Review)*

Howard Crosby, "The Time of the Judges," *HR* 20 (1890) 259-261.

Anonymous, "Professor Moore's Commentary on the Book of Judges," *BS* 53 (1896) 250-265. *[ICC Commentary] (Review)*

A. A. Berle, "The Period of the Judges," *BS* 54 (1897) 387-389.

Anonymous, "The Chronology of Judges," *CFL, O.S.*, 1 (1897) 142-143.

*T. K. Cheyne, "The New Versions of the Psalter and the Book of Judges," *Exp, 5th Ser.*, 7 (1898) 259-275.

George F. Moore, "Shamgar and Sisera," *JAOS* 19 (1898) 159-160.

*C[laude] R. Conder, "Notes on Antiquities of the Book of Judges," *PEFQS* 31 (1899) 162. *[Bochim; The Levites]*

Wm. B. McPherson, "Gideon's Water-lappers," *JAOS* 22 (1901) 70-75.

George H. Schodde, "The Leading Ideas of Judges," *CFL, N.S.*, 6 (1902) 269-271.

*Willis J. Beecher, "The International Lessons in Their Setting. I.," *CFL, N.S.*, 8 (1903) 17-25. [Judges and Ruth and Samuel Form one Book, p. 17]

George H. Schodde, "The Leading Ideas of Judges," *ColTM* 25 (1905) 58-61.

*George S. Goodspeed, "The Men Who Made Israel," *BW* 30 (1907) 266-274. [The Judges and the Preparation for the Kingdom]

Anonymous, "The Book of Judges—Its Place and Plan," *CFL, 3rd Ser.,* 7 (1907) 292-299. [A. The Place and Scope of the Book; B. Outline View and Plans of the Book of Judges]

John E. McFadyen, "The Story of Gideon," *HR* 54 (1907) 365-368.

*[Paul Carus], "Mythical Elements in the Samson Story," *Monist* 17 (1907) 33-83.

*Otto Pfleiderer, "Dr. Pfleiderer on the Samson Story," *Monist* 17 (1907) 626-627.

*John Hendrick de Vries, "Higher Criticism and the Sunday School," *CFL, 3rd Ser.,* 8 (1908) 209-212. *[Deborah and Jael]*

S. R. Driver, "The Book of Judges," *Exp, 8th Ser.,* 2 (1911) 385-404, 518-530.

*E. W. Hollingworth, "The Book of Judges and the Date of the Exodus," *SBAP* 33 (1911) 46-50.

( ) B., "The Book of Judges. Notes from a Pastor's Study," *CFL, 3rd Ser.,* 19 (1915) 70-73.

C. F. Burney, "The Mythological Element in the Story of Samson," *OSHTP* (1915-16) 42-51.

*Harold M. Wiener, "The Date of the Exodus and the Chronology of Judges," *BS* 74 (1917) 581-609.

G. H. Box, "The Book of Judges," *CQR* 89 (1919-20) 90-96. *(Review)*

William H. Bates, "The Book of Judges," *CFL, 3rd Ser.,* 30 (1924) 405-408.

*John C. Montgomery, "The Sin and Salvation of Israel: A Study of Judges and Ruth," *MQR, 3rd Ser.,* 51 (1925) 119-127.

Harry Pirie-Gordon, "The Reduction of Gideon's Army," *ET* 38 (1926-27) 284.

*J. Garrow Duncan, "Notes on the Sites of Succoth and Penuel as bearing upon the Routes of Gideon and Jacob," *PEFQS* 59 (1927) 89-95, 188-191.

L[eander] S. K[eyser], "Samson Agonistes Again," *CFL, 3rd Ser.,* 39 (1933) 317-318.

Bernard G. Hall, "Jaw-Bone of an Ass," *ET* 45 (1933-34) 43.

Algernon Ward, "Jaw-Bone of an Ass," *ET* 45 (1933-34) 184-185.

*H. H. Rowley, "The Danite Migration to Laish," *ET* 51 (1939-40) 466-471.

*A. V. Billen, "The Hexaplaric Element in the LXX Version of Judges," *JTS* 43 (1942) 12-19.

*J. Simons, "Topographical and Archaeological Elements in the Story of Abimelech," *OTS* 2 (1943) 35-78.

*Edward Robertson, "The Period of the Judges: A Mystery Period in the History of Israel," *BJRL* 30 (1946-47) 91-114.

J. R. Porter, "Some Considerations on the Structure of the Book of Judges," *OSHTP* (1950-51) 25-29.

*G. Mendenhall, "Israelite Law in the Period of the Judges," *JBL* 71 (1952) vi.

*A[braham] Malamat, "The War of Gideon and Midian. A Military Approach," *PEQ* 85 (1953) 61-65.

*A[braham] Malamat, "Cushan Rishathaim and the Decline of the Near East Around 1200 B.C.," *JNES* 13 (1954) 231-242.

*C. F. Whitley, "The Sources of the Gideon Stories," *VT* 7 (1957) 157-164.

*F. C. Fensham, "The Judges and Ancient Israelite Jurisprudence," *OTW* 2 (1959) 15-22.

J. P. Oberholzer, "Geografiese Terme in die Rigtersboek en hulle Vertaling (with a Summary in English)," *OTW* 2 (1959) 35-40. *[Geographical Terms in the Book of Judges and their translation (A Summary)]* [English Summary, p. 40]

*A. H. van Zyl, "The Relationship of the Israelite Tribes to the Indigenous Population of Canaan according to the Book of Judges," *OTW* 2 (1959) 51-60.

*A. H. van Zyl, "The Message Formula in the Book of Judges," *OTW* 2 (1959) 61-64.

Yehezkel Kaufmann, "The Gideon Stories," *Tarbiz* 30 (1960-61) #2, IV-V.

*H. C. Thomson, "*Shophet* and *Mishpat* in the Book of Judges," *GUOST* 19 (1961-62) 74-85.

*M[oshe] Weinfeld, "The Period of the Conquest and of the Judges as seen by the earlier and later sources," *VT* 17 (1967) 93-113.

*Donald A. McKenzie, "The Judge of Israel," *VT* 17 (1967) 118-121.

A. D. H. Mayes, "The historical context of the battle against Sisera," *VT* 19 (1969) 353-360.

A. E. Cundall, "Judges—An Apology for the Monarchy?" *ET* 81 (1969-70) 178-181.

§332 *3.2.10.3.2.1 Deborah's "Song"*

*Thomas H. Rich, "Paraphrase of Song of Deborah," *JBL* 1 (1881) 56-58.

Thomas H. Rich, "A Paraphrase of the Song of Deborah," *DTQ, N.S.,* 2 (1883) 408-410.

Anonymous, "The Old Testament and Nature," *ONTS* 11 (1890) 379. *[The Song of Deborah]*

Paul Ruben, "The Song of Deborah," *JQR* 10 (1897-98) 541-558.

James Kennedy, "The Song of Deborah," *JQR* 10 (1897-98) 726-727.

David Heinrich Muller, "The Structure of the Song of Deborah," *AJT* 2 (1898) 110-115.

*L[ewis] B[ayles] Paton, "Deborah's Conception of Yahweh," *BW* 19 (1902) 197-198.

*S. R. Driver, "The Book of Judges. III. Deborah and Barak," *Exp, 8th Ser.,* 3 (1912) 24-38.

*S. R. Driver, "The Book of Judges. IV. Deborah and Barak *(continued),*" *Exp, 8th Ser.,* 3 (1912) 120-136.

Elihu Grant, "Deborah's Oracle," *AJSL* 36 (1919-20) 295-301.

*William F[oxwell] Albright, "The Earliest Form of Hebrew Verse," *JPOS* 2 (1922) 69-86. *[The Song of Deborah]*

William F[oxwell] Albright, "Some Additional Notes on the Song of Deborah," *JPOS* 2 (1922) 284-285.

I. W. Slotki, "The Song of Deborah," *JTS* 33 (1931-32) 341-354.

William F[oxwell] Albright, "The Song of Deborah in the Light of Archaeology," *BASOR* #62 (1936) 26-31.

*Robert M. Engberg, "Historical Analysis of Archaeological Evidence: Megiddo and the Song of Deborah," *BASOR* #78 (1940) 4-7. (Reply by W. F. Albright, pp. 7-9)

*Burton L. Goddard, "The Critic and Deborah's Song," *WTJ* 3 (1940-41) 93-112.

F[rank] M[oore] Cross, "Some Canaanite Stylistic Devices in the Song of Deborah," *JBL* 70 (1951) xiv-xv.

*Peter R. Ackroyd, "The Composition of the Song of Deborah," *VT* 2 (1952) 160-162.

*J. Blenkinsopp, "Ballad Style and Psalm Style in the Song of Deborah: a Discussion," *B* 42 (1961) 61-76.

J. Shunary, "An Arabic *Tafsir* of the Song of Deborah," *Text* 2 (1962) 77-86.

Y. Ratzahbi, "The Arabic *Tafsir* to the Song of Deborah," *Text* 4 (1964) 211-219.

*P. C. Craigie, "The Song of Deborah and the Epic of Tukulti-Ninurta," *JBL* 88 (1969) 253-265.

§333 *3.2.10.3.2.2 Jephthah's Vow*

H. T., "Jephthah's Daughter," *MR* 11 (1828) 30-32.

J. H. Kurtz, "Jephthah's Offering," *ER* 6 (1854-55) 386-411.

S. Comfort, "Jephthah's Vow," *MR* 37 (1855) 558-565.

Anonymous, "Jephthah's Vow," *BFER* 5 (1856) 73-81.

S. Talbot, "The Vow and Sacrifice of Jephthah," *CRB* 27 (1862) 377-394.

Milton S. Terry, "Jephthah's Vow," *MR* 55 (1873) 266-291.

George Patterson, "Jephthah's Vow," *BFER* 24 (1875) 709-736.

Charles W. Currier, "The Story of Jephthah's Daughter," *BQR* 4 (1882) 102-112.

Moncrure D. Conway, "Jephthah's Daughter in Honolulu," *OC* 1 (1887) 86-88.

*J. F. Hogan, "The Sacrifice of Iphigenia," *IER, 3rd Ser.*, 12 (1891) 1070-1086. *[cf. Jephthah's Daughter]*

William Cowper Conant, "The Fate of Jephthah's Daughter," *HR* 41 (1901) 66-68.

*I. Mendelsohn, "The Disinheritance of Jephthah in the Light of Paragraph 27 of the Lipit-Ishtar Code," *IEJ* 4 (1954) 116-119.

A. Penna, "The Vow of Jephthah in the Interpretation of St. Jerome," *StP* 4 (1961) 162-170.

§334 *3.2.10.3.2.3 Studies concerning Date, Authorship, Sources, and Authenticity*

Anonymous, "On the Time when the Book of Judges was Written," *JSL, 3rd Ser.*, 14 (1861-62) 78-85.

J. H. N., "The Book of Judges—When Written?" *JSL, 3rd Ser.*, 14 (1861-62) 431-432.

S. R. Driver, "The Origin and Structure of the Book of Judges," *JQR* 1 (1888-89) 258-270.

*Peter R. Ackroyd, "The Composition of the Song of Deborah," *VT* 2 (1952) 160-162.

*C. F. Whitley, "The Sources of the Gideon Stories," *VT* 7 (1957) 157-164.

*S. B. Gurewicz, "The Bearing of Judges i-ii. 5, on the Authorship of the Book of Judges," *ABR* 7 (1959) 37-40.

G. T. Manley, "The Deuteronomic Redactor in the Book of Judges," *EQ* 31 (1959) 32-36.

§335 *3.2.10.3.3 Literary Criticism of the Books of Samuel - General Studies*

*Francis Brown, "The Books of Chronicles, with especial reference to the Books of Samuel," *AR* 1 (1884) 405-426.

F. H. Woods, "The Light thrown by the Septuagint Version on the Books of Samuel," *SBE* 1 (1885) 21-38.

*Henry Preserved Smith, "Sources E and J in the Books of Samuel," *JBL* 15 (1896) 1-8.

C[laude] R. Conder, "Notes on the Antiquities of the Books of Samuel," *PEFQS* 31 (1899) 343-352. [Ramathaim Zophim; Ahimelech, or Ahiah; Stone Ezel; Cherethites; Ammah and Giah; The Bamoth; Nob; Simeon and Levi; The Tsinnor; Baal Perazim and the Valley of Rephaim; Goren Nachon, Goren Chidon; The Tent; Names and Titles; Bathsheba; Rabbath Ammon; Bahurim; Nahash and Jesse; The Berites; Abel; The Sons of the Giant; The Jebusites]

*W. H. Bennett, "Two Important Works on the Old Testament," *Exp, 6th Ser.*, 2 (1900) 312-320. *[ICC Commentary on Samuel] (Review)*

J. W. Beardslee, "The Spirit of God in the Books of Samuel," *CFL, N.S.*, 8 (1903) 31-36.

George Ricker Berry, "The Ethics of the Books of Samuel," *CFL, N.S.*, 8 (1903) 41-46.

W. D. Kerswill, "Religious Ideas Reflected in the Book of Samuel," *CFL, N.S.*, 8 (1903) 51-58.

John D. Davis, "The Books of Samuel," *CFL, N.S.*, 8 (1903) 65-68. [The Fascination of the Narrative; The Source of Information; The Historical Trustworthiness] *(Editorial)*

James A. Kelso, "The Religious Value of the Books of Samuel," *CFL, N.S.*, 8 (1903) 74-78.

Thomas R. English, "Structure and Purposes of the Books of Samuel," *CFL, N.S.,* 8 (1903) 98-102.

*Willis J. Beecher, "The International Lessons in Their Setting. I.," *CFL, N.S.,* 8 (1903) 17-25. [Judges and Ruth and Samuel Form one Book; Kinds of Materials; Inspiration; Date and Authorship; The Modern View; Narrative of the accession and Rule of Samuel; The Account of the Setting up of the Monarchy; Narrative of the Demand for a King; Narrative of the Election of Saul; Narrative of the Beginnings of Saul's Reign; Two Narratives and a Summary; Narrative of the Final Parting of Samuel and Saul]

*Willis J. Beecher, "The International Lessons in Their Literary Setting. III.," *CFL., N.S.,* 8 (1903) 128-133. [Variant Delimitations of the Historical Narratives; The Narrative of Saul's Last Battle; Duplications of Samuel in Chronicles; The Credibility of Chronicles; The Narrative of the Accession of David in Hebron; The Narrative of the Kingdoms of David and Ishbosheth; The Narrative of David's Becoming King of Israel]

*H. St. J. Thackery, "The Greek Translators of the Four Books of the Kings," *JTS* 8 (1906-07) 262-278. *[1 and 2 Samuel]*

Andrew C. Zenos, "From Theocracy to Monarchy," *HR* 56 (1908) 47-50, 131-133.

Andrew C. Zenos, "The Downfall of Saul and Accession of David," *HR* 56 (1908) 219-220.

Ellis Davies, "The Death of Saul: A Study in Criticism," *ICMM* 6 (1909-10) 177-185. *[1 and 2 Samuel]*

S. R. Driver, "'Notes on Samuel'," *ET* 25 (1913-14) 179-180.

R[obert] H. Pfeiffer, "Midrash in the Books of Samuel," *JBL* 55 (1936) vi-vii.

E[phraim] A. Speiser, "The Nuzi Tablets Solve a Puzzle in the Books of Samuel," *BASOR* #72 (1938) 15-17.

Charles Keeley, "An Approach to the Books of Samuel," *CBQ* 10 (1948) 254-270.

John Bright, "Studia Biblica. XVI. I and II Samuel," *Interp* 5 (1951) 450-461.

*F. C. Fensham, "A Few Aspects of legal practices in Samuel in Comparison with legal material from the Ancient Near East," *OTW* 3 (1960) 18-27.

*A. H. van Zyl, "Israel and the Indigenous Population of Canaan according to the Books of Samuel," *OTW* 3 (1960) 67-80.

John L. McKenzie, "The Four Samuels," *BRes* 7 (1962) 3-18.

*Matitahu Tsevat, "Studies in the Book of Samuel," *HUCA* 36 (1965) 49-58. [IV. Yahweh Ṣeba'ot]

*T. C. G. Thornton, "Studies in Samuel," *CQR* 168 (1967) 413-423. [I. Davidic Propaganda in the Books of Samuel pp. 413-416; II. The so-called 'anti-monarchial' passages of I Samuel, pp. 416-423]

§336 *3.2.10.3.4 Studies concerning Date, Authorship, Sources, and Authenticity*

Stanley A. Cook, "Notes on the Composition of 2 Samuel," *AJSL* 16 (1899-1900) 145-177.

M. H. Segal, "The Composition of the Books of Samuel," *JQR, N.S.,* 55 (1964-65) 318-339; 56 (1965-66) 32-50, 137-157.

*Stephen S. Yonick, "The Rejection of Saul: A Study of Sources," *AJBA* 1 (1968-71) #4, 29-50.

§337 *3.2.10.3.4.1 Literary Criticism of 1 Samuel*

[Patrick] Delany, "An Extract from Dr. Delany's Life of David, concerning Saul's Consulting the Witch of Endor," *MR* 2 (1819) 57-62.

M. F., "On the Difficulties in the History of David's Introduction to Saul," *CongML* 21 (1838) 608-611.

*Claude R. Conder, "The scenery of David's Outlaw Life," *PEFQS* 7 (1875) 41-48.

A. L. Gotwald, "The Apparition at Endor," *LQ* 8 (1878) 321-333.

George Salmon, "The Witch of Endor," *Exp, 2nd Ser.,* 3 (1882) 424-433.

Israel Abrahams, "The Witch of Endor," *Exp, 2nd Ser.,* 4 (1882) 111-120.

[James] Sime, "David's Fight with Goliath," *ONTS* 4 (1884-85) 81.

H. R. Rae, "Ghosts in the Bible; and the Witch of Endor," *HR* 35 (1898) 448-453.

*S. M. Zwemer, "The Bubonic Plague at Ashdod," *HR* 47 (1904) 281-282.

Louis Matthews Sweet, "The Unity of the Narratives in First Samuel. Article I.," *BRec* 5 (1908) 245-250.

Louis Matthews Sweet, "The Unity of the Narratives in First Samuel. Second Article," *BRec* 5 (1908) 286-294.

Henry Gracey, "The Book of Samuel: Professor Kennedy's Commentary," *CFL, 3rd Ser.,* 10 (1909) 119-125. *(Review)*

*B. K. Ratty, "Samuel and the Monarchy," *ICMM* 8 (1911-12) 428-435.

*H. St. J. Thackery, "The Song of Hannah and Other Lessons and Psalms for the Jewish New Year's Day," *JTS* 16 (1914-15) 177-203.

L. W. Batten, "David and Goliath," *AJSL* 35 (1918-19) 61-64.

*Norvelle Wallace Sharpe, "David, Elhanan, and the Literary Digest," *BS* 86 (1929) 319-329. *[David and Goliath]*

*Charles Roads, "The Witch of Endor," *MR* 112 (1929) 454-456.

*D. Winton Thomas, "En-Dor: A Sacred Spring?" *PEFQS* 65 (1933) 205-206.

*M. Kiddle, "Saul and David: A Study of the Conflict Between Northern Prophecy and Southern Priesthood," *Theo* 28 (1934) 95-101.

C. J. Cadoux, "Saul and Samuel," *HJ* 37 (1938-39) 322-326.

*Martin Buber, "Samuel and the Evolution of Authority in Israel," *Zion* 4 (1938-39) #1, I-II.

*W. A. Irwin, "Samuel and the Rise of the Monarchy," *AJSL* 58 (1941) 113-134.

H. A. Rigg Jr., "Saul and the Witch of Endor," *JBL* 72 (1953) ix.

*Joseph Bourke, "Samuel and the Ark, a Study in Contrasts," *DS* 7 (1954) 73-103.

*Mordecai Roshwald, "Ancient Hebrews and Government," *Jud* 4 (1955) 167-174.

*Yagael Yadin, "Goliath's Javelin and the מנור ארגים," *PEQ* 87 (1955) 58-69.

*J. P. Oberholzer, "The 'ibrim in I Samuel," *OTW* 3 (1960) 54. *[Habriu]*

*G. Coleman Luck, "Israel's Demand for a King," *BS* 120 (1963) 56-64.

G. Coleman Luck, "The First Meeting of Saul and Samuel," *BS* 124 (1967) 254-261.

*T. C. G. Thornton, "Studies in Samuel," *CQR* 168 (1967) 413-423. [II. The so-called 'anti-monarchial' passages of I Samuel, pp. 416-423]

*Harry A. Hoffner Jr., "A Hittite Analogue to the David and Goliath Contest of Champions?" *CBQ* 30 (1968) 220-225.

Christian E. Hauer Jr., "The Shape of Saulite Strategy," *CBQ* 31 (1969) 153-167. *The Battle of Mt. Gilboa]*

§338 *3.2.10.3.4.2 Literary Criticism of 2 Samuel*

*W. F. Birch, "Zion, the City of David. Where was it? How did Joab make his way into it? and who helped him?" *PEFQS* 10 (1878) 129-132, 178-189.

Anonymous, "David's Route in Flight," *DTQ, N.S.,* 2 (1883) 411.

*A. F. Kirkpatrick, "The Messianic Interpretation of Nathan's Prophecy to David," *ONTS* 5 (1884-85) 276-277.

R. Payne Smith, "Introduction to the Second Book of Samuel," *MI* 4 (1886) 1-16.

Willis J. Beecher, "The International Lessons in Their Literary Setting. IV.," *CFL, N.S.,* 8 (1903) 188-195. [Parts of 2 Samuel not in Chronological Order; Josephus a Blind Guide; Events Before the Bringing up of the Ark; The Narrative of the Bringing up of the Ark; The Levitical Laws and the Psalms at that Date; Narrative of the Great Promise (2 Sam. 7); Other Narratives and Summarizing Section]

John D. Davis, "Transfer of the Ark to Jerusalem," *CFL, N.S.,* 8 (1903) 203-204.

*William H. Bates, "David's Purchase of the Temple Site from Araunah," *CFL, 3rd Ser.,* 9 (1908) 159-161.

*M.H.Segal, "David's War Against the Philistines,"*PEFQS* 54 (1922) 74-78.

*Norvelle Wallace Sharpe, "David, Elhanan, and the Literary Digest," *BS* 86 (1929) 319-329. *[David and Goliath]*

James Feather, "How Joab Took Jerusalem.   An Unwritten Chapter in Israel's Military History," *ET* 41 (1929-30) 140-141.

*H. S. Gehman, "A Jonah and a David-Uriah Parallel in Buddhist Literature," *JBL* 57 (1938) ix.

*U. Simon, "The Poor Man's Ewe-Lamb.   An Example of Juridical Parable," *B* 48 (1967) 207-242.

*Menakhem Perry and Meir Sternberg, "The King Through Ironic Eyes: The Narrator's Devices in the Biblical Story of David and Batsheba and Two Excursuses on the Theory of the Narrative Text," *HS* 1 (1968-69) 452-449.*[sic] [English Summary]*

*Boaz Arpali, "Bible and Literary Criticism. 1. Caution: A Biblical Story! Comments on the Story of David and Bathsheba and on the Problems of the Biblical Narrative," *HS* 2 (1969-71) 686-684.*[sic] [English Summary]*

*Uriel Simon, "Bible and Literary Criticism. 2. An Ironic Approach to a Biblical Story: On the Interpretation of the Story of David and Bathsheba," *HS* 2 (1969-71) 684-683.*[sic] [English Summary]*

*Menakhem Perry and Meir Sternberg, "Biblical and Literary Criticism, 3. Caution. A Literary Text! Problems in the Poetics and the Interpretation of Biblical Narrative," *HS* 2 (1969-71) 682-679.*[sic] [English Summary]*

§339 **3.2.10.3.5 Literary Criticism of the Books of Kings
      - General Studies**

*W. Robertson Smith, "The chronology of the Books of Kings," *JP* 10
    (1881-82) 209-213.

George H. Schodde, "The Book of Kings in Modern Criticism," *ONTS* 5
    (1884-85) 369-372.

Nicholas M. Steffens, "The Structure and the Purpose of the Books of
    Kings," *CFL, N.S.,* 8 (1903) 153-160.

J. F. Riggs, "The Books of Kings for Edification," *CFL, N.S.,* 8 (1903) 195-
    203.

Willis J. Beecher, "The International Lessons in Their Literary Setting.
    VI.," *CFL, N.S.,* 8 (1903) 312-319. [The Books of Kings; Sources and
    Original Writers; First Topic in Kings. The Adonijah Affair; Second
    Topic in 1 Kings. Solomon's Wisdom; Third Topic. Building the
    Temple and the Palaces; Fourth Topic. The Dedication of the Temple;
    Fifth Topic. Solomon's Later Achievements]

*Daniel S. Gregory, "International Lessons in Their Historical Setting,"*CFL,
    N.S.,* 1 (1904) 412-424. *[Kings]*

*Daniel S. Gregory, "International Lessons in Their Literary and Historical
    Setting. The Close of Elijah's Career, and a Lesson from the Prophet
    Amos,"*CFL, N.S.,* 1 (1904) 538-546.

*H. St. J. Thackeray, "The Greek Translators of the Four Books of the
    Kings," *JTS* 8 (1906-07) 262-278.

W. M. McPheeters, "The Book of Kings: Its Occasion, Theme and
    Purpose," *USR* 19 (1907-08) 263-272.

*E. Day, "The Deuteronomic Judgments of the Kings of Judah," *JTS* 11
    (1909-10) 74-83.

*Daniel S. Gregory, "The International Lessons in Their Historical and
    Literary Setting. Lessons from the Conflict with Idolatry and Baalism,"
    CFL, 3rd Ser., 14 (1911-12) 51-65. [Dr. Beecher's View of the
    Conditions Under the Dynasty of Omri, pp. 58-60]

*A. T. Olmstead, "The Earliest Book of Kings," *AJSL* 31 (1914-15) 169-214.

Robert Burnet Pattie, "The Synchronisms of the Hebrew Book of Kings," *SSO* 1 (1920) 49-56.

J[ames] A. Montgomery, "Archival Data in the Book of Kings," *JBL* 53 (1934) ix-x.

James A. Montgomery, "Archival Data in the Book of Kings," *JBL* 53 (1934) 46-52.

Robert Gordis, "Sectional Rivalry in the Kingdom of Judah," *JQR, N.S.,* 25 (1934-35) 237-259.

John W. Wevers, "Double Readings in the Books of Kings," *JBL* 65 (1946) vi.

*Maurice Blanchard, "Uniqueness of the Hebrew Concept of History as Seen in the Books of Kings," *IJT* 6 (1957) 122-130.

*Maurice Blanchard, "The Uniqueness of Hebrew History," *IJT* 7 (1958) 24-32.

John C. Walker, "The Axiology of the Books of Kings," *JAAR* 27 (1959) 218-222.

J. Maxwell Miller, "The Elisha Cycle and the Accounts of the Omride Wars," *JBL* 85 (1966) 441-454.

Ralph W. Klein, "New Evidence for an Old Recension of Reigns," *HTR* 60 (1967) 93-105.

*Leslie C. Allen, "Further Thoughts on an Old Recension of Reigns in Paralipomena," *HTR* 61 (1968) 483-491.

Ralph W. Klein, "Supplements in the Paralipomena: A Rejoinder," *HTR* 61 (1968) 492-495.

James Donald Shenkel, "A Comparative Study in the Synoptic Parallels in I Paraleipomena[sic]* and I-II Reigns," *HTR* 62 (1969) 63-85.

§340 *3.2.10.3.6 Studies concerning Date, Authorship, Sources, and Authenticity*

*William T. Sabine, "The Witness of the Moabite Stone," *HR* 39 (1900) 419-424.

Andrew C. Zenos, "The Books of Kings as History," *HR* 56 (1908) 388.

*A. C. Welch, "The Significance for Old Testament History of a New Tablet," *ET* 35 (1923-24) 170-172. [B.M. 21,901]

Shoshana R. Bin-Nun, "Formulas From the Royal Records of Israel and Judah," *VT* 18 (1968) 414-432.

§341 *3.2.10.3.6.1 Literary Criticism of 1 Kings*

(   ) G., "Elijah at the Brook Cherith, and at Zarephath," *JSL, 3rd Ser.,* 12 (1860-61) 1-15.

Henry Brass, "The Place of Elijah's Sacrifices," *PEFQS* 22 (1890) 182.

Cunningham Geikie, "Elijah and the Prophets of Baal," *HR* 41 (1901) 307-314.

Ed. König, "Elijah the Tishbite on Mount Horeb," *HR* 50 (1905) 37-39.

*S. Prentice, "Elijah and the Tyrian Alliance," *JBL* 42 (1923) 33-38.

A. S. Peake, "Elijah and Jezebel. A Conflict with the Tyrian Baal," *BJRL* 11 (1927) 296-321.

A. Marmorstein, "The contest between Elijah and the Prophets of Baal," *SMSDR* 9 (1933) 29-37.

J. M. Myers, "Elijah and the Yahweh-Baal Conflict," *LCQ* 19 (1946) 393-402.

C. F. Whitely, "The Deuteronomic Presentation of the House of Omri," *VT* 2 (1952) 137-152.

*G. B. Sarfatti, "Pious Men, Men of Deeds, and the Early Prophets," *Tarbiz* 26 (1956-57) #2, II-IV. (Corrections, #3, p. X)

D. R. Ap-Thomas, "Elijah on Mount Carmel," *PEQ* 92 (1960) 146-155.

H. H. Rowley, "Elijah on Mount Carmel," *BJRL* 43 (1960-61) 190-219.

A.-M. Dubarle, "Biblical authors on Jeroboam's schism," *TD* 12 (1964) 153-158.

*D. W. Gooding, "The Septuagint's version of Solomon's misconduct," *VT* 15 (1965) 325-335.

*J. Liver, "The Book of the Acts of Solomon," *B* 48 (1967) 75-101.

Jon Ruthven, "A Note on Elijah's 'Fire from Yahweh'," *BETS* 12 (1969) 111-116.

D. W. Gooding, "Problems of Text and Midrash in the Third Book of Reigns," *Text* 7 (1969) 1-29.

§342 *3.2.10.3.6.2 Literary Criticism of 2 Kings*

Joseph Horner, "The Baptism of Naaman," *MR* 56 (1874) 60-70. [Supplementary Note, *MR* 57 (1875) p. 67]

*John D. Davis, "The Moabite Stone and the Hebrew Records," *AJSL* 7 (1890-91) 178-182.

*John D. Davis, "The Moabite Stone and the Hebrew Records," *JAOS* 15 (1893) lxvi-lxvii.

*Daniel S. Gregory, "International Lessons in Their Literary and Historical Setting,"*CFL, N.S.,* 1 (1904) 538-546. [The Close of Elijah's Career, pp. 538-543]

John Adams, "Elisha and the Translation of Elijah," *HR* 66 (1913) 369-372.

*A. C. Welch, "The Significance for Old Testament History of a New Tablet," *ET* 35 (1923-24) 170-172. [B.M. 21,901]

*Robert H. Pfeiffer, "Three Assyriological Footnotes to the Old Testament," *JBL* 47 (1928) 184-187. [2. *Judah's tribute to Assyria,* (2 Kings), pp. 185-186]

*P. E. Kretzmann, "Josiah and the Battle of Megiddo," *CTM* 2 (1931) 38-45.

Annie S. D. Maunder, "The Shadow Returning on the Dial of Ahaz," *JTVI* 64 (1932) 83-92, 100-101. [(Discussion, pp. 92-95) (Communications by J. J. B. Coles, pp. 95-96; A. G. Shortt, p. 96; Miss Edith D. James, pp. 96-97; James Knight, p. 97; G. B. Michell, pp. 97-99)]

*Frank E. Allen, "The Destruction of Sennacherib's Army: Was it a Miracle?" *CFL, 3rd Ser.,* 40 (1934) 205-208.

H. S. Darlington, "Elisha and the Two She-Bears," *OC* 50 (1936) 107-114.

*Harry M. Orlinsky, "The Kings-Isaiah Recensions of the Hezekiah Story," *JQR, N.S.,* 30 (1939-40) 33-49.

*W[illiam] F[oxwell] Albright, "The Original Account of the Fall of Samaria in II Kings," *BASOR* #174 (1964) 66-67.

*Siegfried H. Horn, "Did Sennacherib Campaign Once or Twice Against Hezekiah?" *AUSS* 4 (1966) 1-28.

D. W. Gooding, "The Septuagint's Rival Version of Jeroboam's Rise and Power," *VT* 17 (1967) 173-189.

§343 *3.2.10.3.6.2.1 The Deuteronomic Reformation*

*Thomas Whiteland, "Hilkiah's Book of the Law. *A Study in Modern Criticism.* 2 Kings xxii. 8; 2 Chron. xxxiv. 15," *TML* 6 (1891) 420-430.

A. Duff, "Certain Notable Features in the Deuteronomic Reformation," *OSHTP* (1896-97) 22-23.

*Max L. Margolis, "Jeremiah a Protesting Witness of the Act of 621," *PAPA* 34 (1902) cvi-cviii.

*James A. Kelso, "Theodoret and the Law of Josiah," *JBL* 22 (1903) 50.

Melvin Grove Kyle, "Archaeological Notes: The Finding of the Law by Hilkiah," *CFL, 3rd Ser.,* 7 (1907) 327-329.

T. K. Cheyne, "The Finding of the Book in the Temple and Josiah's Reformation," *OSHTP* (1907-08) 68-70.

Edouard Montet, "The Discovery of the Deuteronomic Law," *BW* 36 (1910) 316-322.

*George Aaron Barton, "The Evolution of the Religion of Israel. IV. Deuteronomy and Jeremiah," *BW* 39 (1912) 268-281.

William H. Bates, "Finding the Book of the Law in Josiah's Day," *CFL, 3rd Ser.,* 15 (1912) 217-219.

*A. T. Olmstead, "Notes and Suggestions. The Reform of Josiah and its Secular Aspects," *AmHR* 20 (1914-15) 566-570.

[Jay Benson Hamilton], "The Historical Jokesmiths," *CFL, 3rd Ser.,* 25 (1919) 135-138. ["Found in the Charter Oak"; "Found in the Temple"] *[The Finding of the Book of the Law in the Temple]*

G. R. Berry, "The Code Found in the Temple," *JBL* 39 (1920) 44-51.

Alexander Freed, "The Code Spoken of in II Kings 22-23," *JBL* 40 (1921) 76-80.

F. C. Burkitt, "The Code found in the Temple," *JBL* 40 (1921) 166-167.

J. O. Leath, "The Deuteronomic Reform," *MQR, 3rd Ser.,* 49 (1923) 506-516.

*F. A. Farley, "Jeremiah and Deuteronomy," *ET* 37 (1925-26) 316-318.

*Shalom Spiegel, "Josiah and Jeremiah," *JBL* 61 (1942) iv.

E. W. Nicholson, "Josiah's Reformation and Deuteronomy," *GUOST* 20 (1963-64) 77-84.

Thomas E. Crane, "Israel's Deuteronomic Theologians," *BibT* #26 (1966) 1828-1836.

§344 *3.2.10.4 Literary Criticism of the Latter Prophets - General Studies*

A. P. P., "A new Translation of the Hebrew Prophets, arranged in chronological order. By George R. Noyes, Vols. II & III," *CE* 23 (1837) 375-384. *(Review)*

Heinrich von Ewald, "Ewald on the Prophets: being a Translation of the First Two Sections of the General Introduction to Professor Heinrich von Ewald's Work 'Die Propheten des Alten Bundes Erklart'," *JSL, 2nd Ser.*, 3 (1852-53) 329-382.

B. Harris Cowper, "Dr. Roland Williams and the Prophets," *JSL, 4th Ser.*, 10 (1866-67) 70-86. *(Review)*

Anonymous, "Dr. Williams's New Translation of the Hebrew Prophets," *BFER* 16 (1867) 153-172. *(Review)*

Anonymous, "Noyes's Hebrew Prophets," *CE* 88 (1867) 15-31. *(Review)*

William Henry Green, "The Prophets and Prophecy in Israel," *PR, 4th Ser.*, 2 (1878) 281-328. *(Review)*

*C. J. Bredenkamp, "The Covenant and the Early Prophets," *ONTS* 4 (1884-85) 123-127. *(Trans. by George H. Schodde)*

*C. J. Bredenkamp, "God's Covenant in the Prophets," *ONTS* 4 (1884-85) 353-357. *(Trans. by H. M. Douglas)*

E. C. Bissell, "The Principle of Development and the Work of the Pre-Exilic Prophets," *ONTS* 5 (1884-85) 178-179.

*Barnard C. Taylor, "The Divine Names as they Occur in the Prophets," *AJSL* 2 (1885-86) 109-110.

*Henry Hayman, "Prophetic Testimony to the Pentateuch," *BS* 49 (1892) 109-128, 177-198.

Alfred W. Benn, "The Alleged Socialism of the Prophets," *NW* 2 (1893) 60-88.

C[arl] H[einrich] Cornill, "The Latter Prophets," *OC* 9 (1895) 4608-4609.

*Talbot W. Chambers, "The Messianic Idea in the Prophets," *PRR* 6 (1895) 224-238.

*William R. Harper, "Outline Topics in the History of Old Testament Prophecy. II. Prophetic Situations: Amos, Isaiah, Zephaniah, Deutero-Isaiah.—Principles of Prophecy," *BW* 7 (1896) 120-129.

D[aniel] S. Gregory, "School of Bible Study. Prophets of the Assyrian Period.—*Continued,*" *HR* 32 (1896) 60-65.

D[aniel] S. Gregory, "School of Bible Study. Prophets of the Babylonian Period," *HR* 32 (1896) 154-160.

D[aniel] S. Gregory, "School of Bible Study. The Prophets of the Exile," *HR* 32 (1896) 249-254.

D[aniel] S. Gregory, "School of Bible Study. The Prophets of the Restoration," *HR* 32 (1896) 348-351.

*William C. Conant, "The Prophetic Scope of Sacred History," *HR* 34 (1897) 353-355.

Geerhardus Vos, "The Modern Hypothesis of Recent Criticism of the Early Prophets," *PRR* 9 (1898) 214-238, 411-437, 610-636; 10 (1899) 70-97, 237-266. [I. Amos; II. Hosea; III. Isaiah; IV. Micah]

Lewis B[ayles] Paton, "The Dependence of the Prophets upon History," *BW* 13 (1899) 231-243.

W[illiam] M. McPheeters, "'Recent Criticism of the Early Prophets'," *CFL, O.S.,* 3 (1899) 344-345.

*Edward Day, "The Search for the Prophets," *Monist* 15 (1905) 386-397.

*John Taylor, "The Attitude of the Prophets Towards Social Problems," *ET* 17 (1905-06) 303-305.

*Randolph H. McKim, "The Radical Criticism Tested by Amos, Hosea and Ezekiel," *CFL, 3rd Ser.,* 5 (1906) 267-272.

*[W. B.] Stevenson, "The Use of the Name 'Israel' in Old Testament Times. *In Isaiah and Micah,*" *GUOST* 3 (1907-12) 51-52.

J. A. Selbie, "The Latest Issues of the 'International Critical Commentary'," *ET* 24 (1912-13) 22-24. *(Review) [Isaiah; Micah, Zephaniah, Nahum, Habakkuk, Obadiah, Joel]*

*Andrew Baird, "'The Day of Jahve' in the Old Testament Prophets," *GUOST* 4 (1913-22) 35-37.

*G. A. Cooke, "The Prophets and War," *Exp, 8th Ser.*, 10 (1915) 214-223.

W. B. Selbie, "The Prophets of the Restoration," *ICMM* 13 (1916-17) 128-133.

Theodore H. Robinson, "Prolegomena to the Study of the Prophets," *ICMM* 13 (1916-17) 137-145.

*W. Emery Barnes, "The Task of the Prophets,"*ICMM* 16 (1919-20) 187-199.

*Phillip Wendell Carnnell, "The Prophets and the Cultus," *R&E* 17 (1920) 137-157.

Anonymous, "The Social Message of the Prophets," *MR* 104 (1921) 800-808.

Henry S. Gehman, "The Prophets and Their Message for To-day," *RChR, 5th Ser.*, 4 (1925) 341-366.

T. E. Robinson, "The Seventh Century Prophets," *CQR* 104 (1927) 324-353.

*L[ewis] B[ayles] Paton, "The Problem of Suffering in the Pre-Exilic Prophets," *JBL* 46 (1927) 111-131.

T[heodore] H. Robinson, "The Hebrew Prophets and Their Modern Interpretation,"·*ET* 40 (1928-29) 296-300.

Theodore H. Robinson, "The Prophetic Literature in Recent Criticism," *JR* 10 (1930) 200-221.

*Sigmund Mowinckel, "'The Spirit' and the 'Word' in the Pre-Exilic Reforming Prophets," *JBL* 53 (1934) 199-227.

*Alexander Moffatt, "The Prophet as Orator, with Illustrations from Micah and Isaiah of Jerusalem," *GUOST* 8 (1936-37) 32-33.

*Sigmund Mowinckel, "A Postscript to the Paper 'The Spirit and the Word in the Preexilic Reform-Prophets in *JBL,* LII, 799ff.*[sic]*," *JBL* 56 (1937) 261-265.

G. R. Berry, "The Future in the Later Prophets," *JBL* 57 (1938) vii.

T[heodore] H. Robinson, "After Fifty Years. IV. Higher Criticism and the Prophetic Literature," *ET* 50 (1938-39) 198-202.

W[illiam] F[oxwell] Albright, "The Archaeological Background of the Hebrew Prophets of the Eighth Century," *JAAR* 8 (1940) 131-136.

*J. S. MacArthur, "The Pre-Exilic Prophets and Pacifism," *ET* 52 (1940-41) 97-100.

Joh. Lindblom, "The Character of the Prophetic Literature," *ET* 52 (1940-41) 126-131.

Ovid R. Sellers, "The Message of the Eighth-Century Prophets for Today," *JAAR* 11 (1943) 88-92.

J. Philip Hyatt, "The Message of the Seventh-Century Prophets for Today," *JAAR* 11 (1943) 93-97.

William A. Irwin, "The Message of the Exilic Prophets for Our Day," *JAAR* 11 (1943) 98-103.

Otto J. Baab, "The Message of the Post-Exilic Prophets for Our Day," *JAAR* 11 (1943) 104-106.

*LeRoy Waterman, "The Ethical Clarity of the Prophets," *JBL* 64 (1945) 297-307.

R. B. Y. Scott, "Oracles of God. The Prophetic Literature as a Medium of Revelation," *Interp* 2 (1948) 131-142.

*J. M. Myers, "The Message of the Prophets," *LCQ* 21 (1948) 351-368. [I. The Holiness of God; II. God's Demands; III. The Prophets and Principles; IV. The Prophetic Principles of Life; V. The Prophetic Conception of the World; VI. The Prophetic Doctrine of Sin; VII. The Prophets as God's Men]

Clyde T. Francisco, "The Moral Message of the Hebrew Prophets," *R&E* 45 (1948) 435-444.

*H. F. D. Sparks, "The Witness of the Prophets to Hebrew Tradition," *JTS* 50 (1949) 129-141.

J. Hardee Kennedy, "The Pertinence of the Prophets," *R&E* 46 (1949) 307-323.

*A. S. Kapelrud, "Cult and Prophetic Word," *ST* 4 (1950) 5-12.

*William J. Ahern, "Social Justice in the Prophets of the Old Testament," *MH* 9 (Spring, 1953) 19-25.

*D[avid] N[oel] Freedman, "Messianic Passages in the Prophets," *JBL* 72 (1953) xx.

Conald Foust, "The Covenant Message of the Prophets," *Scotist* [9] (1953) 42-59.

*Johannes Lindblom, "Wisdom in the Old Testament prophets," *VTS* 3 (1955) 192-204.

*Sheldon H. Blank, "The Relevance of Prophetic Thought for the American Rabbi," *YCCAR* 65 (1955) 163-177.

L. Janetzki, "The Historical Setting of the Prophets," *AusTR* 28 (1957) 63-71.

*Herbert B. Huffmon, "The Covenant Lawsuit in the Prophets," *JBL* 78 (1959) 285-295.

*E. Hammershaimb, "On the ethics of the Old Testament prophets," *VTS* 7 (1960) 75-101.

*Lionel A. Whiston Jr., "The Unity of Scripture and the Post-Exilic Literature," *JAAR* 29 (1961) 290-298.

Erhard Gerstenberger, "The Woe-Oracles of the Prophets," *JBL* 81 (1962) 249-263.

Richard Kugelman, "The Prophets," *CTSP* 19 (1964) 139-141. *(Review)*

Paul J. Duffy, "The Relevance of the Prophetic Word," *Focus* 3 (1966-67) #2, 18-26.

James G. Williams, "The Alas-Oracles of the Eighth Century Prophets," *HUCA* 38 (1967) 75-91.

F. N. Jasper, "Reflections on the Moral Teaching of the Prophets," *SJT* 21 (1968) 462-476.

*James Limburg, "The Root ריב and the Prophetic Lawsuit Speeches," *JBL* 88 (1969) 291-304.

§345 *3.2.10.4.1 Literary Criticism of the Major Prophets - General Studies*

[Frédéric] Godet, "The Four Greater Prophets," *ONTS* 4 (1884-85) 179-180.

Earle Bennett Cross, "Three Who Answered the Voice," *CRDSB* 19 (1946-47) 45-56.

Norman H. Snaith, "The Prophets of the Exile," *RL* 19 (1950) 83-91.

*Theodore Woods Noon, "The Idea of Individualism in Jeremiah and Ezekiel," *MQR, 3rd Ser.,* 52 (1926) 659-665.

§346 *3.2.10.4.1.1 Literary Criticism of Isaiah - General Studies*

†Anonymous, "Bishop Stock's Isaiah," *BCQTR* 28 (1806) 465-479, 608-619; 29 (1807) 134-147. *(Review)*

Anonymous, "Alexander on the Earlier Prophecies of Isaiah," *BRCM* 2 (1846) 321-333. *(Review)*

†Anonymous, "Alexander's Isaiah," *SPR* 1 (1847-48) 129-154. *(Review)*

†[David N. Lord], "Alexander's Earlier and Later Prophecies of Isaiah," *TLJ* 1 (1848-49) 544-603. *(Review)*

A. P. P., "Alexander's Isaiah," *CE* 46 (1849) 48-58. *(Review)*

Anonymous, "The Prophecies of Isaiah," *JSL, 1st Ser.,* 4 (1849) 356-370. *(Review)*

P. F., "Literal Interpretation of Prophecy," *JSL, 1st Ser.,* 6 (1850) 389-402. *(Review) [Isaiah]*

*G. B., "The Dial of Ahaz and the Embassy from Merodach Baladan," *JSL, 3rd Ser.,* 2 (1855-56) 163-179.

George Vance Smith, "The Prophet Isaiah," *TRL* 3 (1866) 1-21.

Thos. D. Anderson Jr., "An Introduction to the Book of Isaiah," *BQR* 1 (1879) 335-354.

J. Estlin Carpenter, "The Prophecies of Isaiah," *ModR* 2 (1881) 1-25, 225-251. *(Review)*

C. N. Patterson, "Isaiah and the New Criticism," *ONTS* 3 (1883-84) 11-14.

*T. K. Cheyne, "The Land of Sinim in Isaiah," *BOR* 1 (1886-87) 182.

G[eorge] Rawlinson, "Introduction to the Book of Isaiah," *MI* 3 (1886-87) 321-337, 401-426.

*Archibald Duff, "Isaiah and Zion; or, the Development of Thought in Isaiah. A Study in the History of Hebrew Religion," *AR* 9 (1888) 426-431; 528-547.

James Orr, "Isaiah and the Spirit of Prophecy," *TML* 1 (1889) 361-378. *(Review)*

James Strong, "The Prophecy of Isaiah," *MR* 72 (1890) 169-183.

Anonymous, "The Critical Problem of Isaiah," *LQHR* 76 (1891) 137-162.

George C. M. Douglas, "Mr. George Adam Smith's Isaiah," *PRR* 2 (1891) 424-442. *(Review)*

T. K. Cheyne, "Critical Analysis of the First Part of Isaiah," *JQR* 4 (1891-92) 562-570.

George Adam Smith, "Duhm's Isaiah, and the New Commentary to the Old Testament," *Exp, 4th Ser.,* 6 (1892) 312-318. *(Review)*

F. W. C. Meyer, "A Sermon of the Eighth Century Before Christ," *ONTS* 14 (1892) 224-227. *[An Early Sermon of Isaiah]*

*Charles F. Kent, "The Social Philosophy of the Royal Prophet Isaiah," *BW* 1 (1893) 248-262.

A. B. Davidson, "The Earlier Ideas of Isaiah," *Exp, 4th Ser.,* 7 (1893) 241-255.

W. W. Elwang, "Isaiah versus the Divisive Critics," *USR* 5 (1893-94) 179-188.

G. Buchanan Gray, "Isaiah's Anticipations of the Future: Some Recent Theories," *Exp, 4th Ser.,* 10 (1894) 330-342.

*W. A. Shedd, "The Relation of the Messianic Teaching of Isaiah to Contemporary Events," *PRR* 5 (1894) 575-591.

Frank Grether, "Isaiah," *RCM* 2 (1894-95) #5, 33-35.

Theo. G. Soares, "A Chronological Discussion of the Virgin Oracle of Isaiah," *BW* 6 (1895) 58-61.

T. K. Cheyne, "Problems of the Prophetic Literature: Isaiah," *Exp, 5th Ser.,* 1 (1895) 81-93.

F. C. Porter, "A Suggestion Regarding Isaiah's Immanuel," *JBL* 14 (1895) 19-36.

C[arl] H[einrich] Cornill, "Isaiah," *OC* 9 (1895) 4488-4491.

*William R. Harper, "Outline Topics in the History of Old Testament Prophecy VII. Prophecy of Isaiah and His Contemporaries," *BW* 8 (1896) 221-228.

William R. Harper, "The Child Prophecies of Isaiah," *BW* 8 (1896) 417-422.

T. K. Cheyne, "Recent study of Isaiah," *JBL* 16 (1897) 131-135.

T. J. Ramsdell, "The Missionary Future in the Book of Isaiah," *BW* 10 (1897) 190-197.

J. Hoeness, "A Penpicture of Christ Drawn from the Prophet Isaiah," *TQ* 3 (1899) 452-471; 4 (1900) 42-67, 157-173.

Cunningham Geikie, "Isaiah of Jerusalem as a Preacher of Moral and Religious Reform," *HR* 39 (1900) 309-314

Cunningham Geikie, "Isaiah of Jerusalem as a Preacher of National Righteousness," *HR* 40 (1900) 106-111.

Adolf Kamphausen, "Isaiah's Prophecy Concerning the Major-Domo of King Hezekiah," *AJT* 5 (1901) 43-74.

G[eorge] H. Schodde, "The Book of Isaiah," *ColTM* 21 (1901) 285-291.

William Henry Cobb, "On integrating the book of Isaiah," *JBL* 20 (1901) 77-100.

A. H. Sayce, "Light from the Monuments of the Times of Isaiah," *HR* 44 (1902) 195-200.

Paul Haupt, "Isaiah's Parable of the Vineyard," *AJSL* 19 (1902-03) 193-202.

Theodore G. Soares, "The Virgin Birth of the Son Immanuel," *BW* 23 (1904) 417-421.

J. W. McGarvey, "Should Isaiah be Sawn Asunder?" *CFL, 3rd Ser.,* 2 (1905) 60-63.

*G. G. Findlay, "The Messianic Teaching of Isaiah," *ET* 17 (1905-06) 200-205.

*G. Buchanan Gray, "The Heavenly Temple and the Heavenly Altar: Some Babylonian and Jewish Conceptions," *OSHTP* (1907-08) 65-67.

Anonymous, "The Fifth Decree of the Biblical Commission," *AER* 39 (1908) 575-582.

*G. Buchanan Gray, "The Heavenly Temple and the Heavenly Altar," *Exp, 7th Ser.,* 5 (1908) 385-402, 530-546.

*Anonymous, "Isaiah's Knowledge of the Sudan," *CFL, 3rd Ser.,* 11 (1909) 200.

*Anonymous, "Isaiah's Knowledge of the Sudan," *RP* 8 (1909) 218-219.

William F. McCauley, "Two Virgin Births—One in the New Testament, One in the Old," *CFL, 3rd Ser.,* 14 (1911-12) 71-73.

*Hewlett Johnson, "Editor's Notes," *ICMM* 8 (1911-12) 8-20. ["Isaiah" as a Center of Interest and Dispute; Canon Kennett's Schweich Lectures; The Date of "Isaiah"; Did Isaiah write his Oracles? Why a mere Fragment of Isaiah's Oracles Remain; The Babylonian and Persian Streams of Prophecy; Maccabean Influence on "Isaiah"; Maccabean Authorship of Is. liii; The Value of this Contention, if True; Dr. Wade's Commentary on "Isaiah"; Why one name embraces many Oracles; The Nature of Prophecy; Another Commentary on Isaiah] *[Editorial]*

*Harold M. Wiener, "Two New Volumes of the International Critical Commentary," *BS* 69 (1912) 464-491. *[Isaiah]*

T. K. Cheyne, "Dr. Gray's New Book on Isaiah," *Exp, 8th Ser.,* 3 (1912) 545-556. *(Review)*

*C. F. Burney, "The Book of Isaiah: A New Theory," *CQR* 74 (1912) 99-123.

*C. F. Burney, "The Book of Isaiah: A New Theory, II," *CQR* 75 (1912-13) 99-139.

W. Manning, "The Message of Isaiah," *MC* 2 (1912-13) 51-57.

Kemper Fullerton, "The Book of Isaiah: Critical Problems and a New Commentary," *HTR* 6 (1913) 478-520. *(Review)*

*G. A. Cooke, "The Prophets and War," *Exp, 8th Ser.,* 10 (1915) 214-223.

*J. S. Ross, "Methodist Higher Criticism Arm-in-Arm with Infidelity. Paper No. II.," *CFL, 3rd Ser.,* 21 (1916) 161-163. [VIII. Isaiah, p. 163]

*J. E. McFadyen, "Isaiah and War," *Exp, 8th Ser.,* 11 (1916) 161-175.

Kemper Fullerton, "Isaiah's Earliest Prophecy Against Ephraim," *AJSL* 33 (1916-17) 9-39.

Kemper Fullerton, "Immanuel," *AJSL* 34 (1917-18) 256-283.

*L. P. Smith, "The Messianic Ideal of Isaiah," *JBL* 36 (1917) 158-212.

Hinckley G. Mitchell, "Isaiah on the Fate of His People and Their Capital," *JBL* 37 (1918) 149-162.

H. C. Ackerman, "The Immanuel Sign and Its Meaning," *AJSL* 35 (1918-19) 205-214.

*John Gamble, "The Messiahs of Virgil and Isaiah," *MC* 8 (1918-19) 386-389. *(Review)*

Kemper Fullerton, "The Problem of Isaiah," *JR* 1 (1921) 307-309.

Kemper Fullerton, "Viewpoints in the Discussion of Isaiah's Hopes for the Future," *JBL* 41 (1922) 1-101.

*Douglas Hilary Corley, "Messianic Prophecy in First Isaiah," *AJSL* 39 (1922-23) 200-224.

Benjamin Reno Downer, "The Added Years of Hezekiah's Life. An Inquiry into the Significance of this Period for Isaiah Criticism," *BS* 80 (1923) 360-391.

J. M. Powis Smith, "Isaiah and the Future," *AJSL* 40 (1923-24) 252-258.

Paul Haupt, "Philological Notes. 8. The Poems of Isaiah," *AJP* 45 (1924) 59-61.

William Popper, "A Suggestion as to the Sequence of Some Prophecies in the First Isaiah," *HUCA* 1 (1924) 79-96.

P[hilip] M[auro], "A Sign—The Woman's Seed," *CFL, 3rd Ser.*, 32 (1926) 122-126.

*Harold M. Wiener, "The Relation of Egypt and Israel and Judah in the Age of Isaiah," *AEE* 11 (1926) 51-53, 70-72.

*Anonymous, "The Virgin Birth in Isaiah," *MR* 110 (1927) 137-138.

E. W. Hammer, "Koenig's Commentary on Isaiah," *CFL, 3rd Ser.*, 33 (1927) 177-178. *(Review)*

*[Jay Benson Hamilton], "International Sunday School Lessons for 1917: Studies in Isaiah and Daniel," *CFL, 3rd Ser.*, 23 (1927) 266-267.

Harold M. Wiener, "Isaiah and the Siege of Jerusalem," *JSOR* 11 (1927) 195-209.

*T. O. Rorie, "Isaiah's Conception of God," *MQR, 3rd Ser.*, 53 (1927) 130-132.

John E. McFadyen, "The Revised Edition of Sir George Adam Smith's Exposition of the Book of Isaiah," *ET* 39 (1927-28) 225-230. *(Review)*

L. O. Lineberger, "Isaiah: The Prophet of the High Vision," *MQR, 3rd Ser.*, 54 (1928) 99-105.

James A. Kelso, "The Prophecy of Isaiah," *BWTS* 21 (1928-29) 202-210.

*Gerson S. Englemen, "The Ethics of Isaiah," *CTSQ* 7 (1929-30) #3, 2-6.

*Robert S. Mathes, "'The Prophet Isaiah and the Growth of the Hebrew Religion'," *CTSQ* 7 (1929-30) #3, 6-10.

William H. McClellan, "Rediscovering a Prophet," *TFUQ* 6 (1931-32) 70-87.

*Annie E. Skemp, "'Immanuel' and 'The Suffering Servant of Jahweh': A Suggestion," *ET* 44 (1932-33) 94-95.

William C. Graham, "Isaiah's Part in the Syro-Ephraimitic Crisis," *AJSL* 50 (1933-34) 201-216.

Charles Lee Feinberg, "The Place that Isaiah Holds in Prophetic Truth," *BS* 93 (1936) 450-455.

William A. Irwin, "The Attitude of Isaiah in the Crisis of 701," *JR* 16 (1936) 406-418.

Charles C. Torrey, "Some Important Editorial Operations in the Book of Isaiah," *JBL* 57 (1938) 109-140.

*Patrick Skehan, "Isaias and the Teaching of the Book of Wisdom," *CBQ* 2 (1940) 289-299.

*Aapeli Saarisalo, "The Book of Isaiah," *JTALC* 5 (1940) 885-893. [1. The Unity of Isaiah; 2. The Central Theme of Isaiah] *(Trans. by Carl Tomminen)*

E. C. Blackman, "The Relevance of the Old Testament Prophets: Isaiah," *ET* 52 (1940-41) 64-67.

Edward J. Young, "The Study of Isaiah Since the Time of Joseph Addison Alexander—I.," *WTJ* 9 (1946-47) 1-30.

Edward J. Young, "The Study of Isaiah Since the Time of Joseph Addison Alexander—II.," *WTJ* 10 (1947-48) 23-56.

Edward J. Young, "The Study of Isaiah Since the Time of Joseph Addison Alexander—III.," *WTJ* 10 (1947-48) 139-167.

Sheldon H. Blank, "The Current Misinterpretation of Isaiah's *Shear Yashub*," *JBL* 67 (1948) vi.

Sheldon H. Blank, "The Current Misinterpretation of Isaiah's *She'ar Yashub*," *JBL* 67 (1948) 211-215.

Frederick Bronkema, "Isaiah, the Evangelist of the Old Testament, preaches Christ," *CCQ* 6 (1948-49) #3/4, 17-23.

E. Hammershaimb, "The Immanuel Sign," *ST* 3 (1949) 124-142.

Roman Halas, "The Universalism of Isaiah," *CBQ* 12 (1950) 162-170.

Annie S. D. Maunder, "The Shadow Returning on the Dial of Ahaz," *JASA* 3 (1951) #3, 21-26. (Discussion, Written Communications, and Lecturer's reply, pp. 26-32)

*L. H. Brockington, "The Greek Translator of Isaiah and his interest in *ΔΟΞΑ*," *VT* 1 (1951) 23-32.

James Siefkes, "A Look Into Isaiah," *Amb* 1 (1952-53) #4, 5, 9.

Anton T. Pearson, "Messianic Conceptions in the Book of Isaiah," *BSQ* 1 (1952-53) #1, 22-37.

C. Lattey, "The Book of Isaiah the Prophet," *Scrip* 5 (1952-53) 2-7.

R. B. Y. Scott, "Studia Biblica. XXIII. Isaiah 1-39," *Interp* 7 (1953) 453-465.

*Harry M. Orlinsky, "The Treatment of Anthropomorphisms and Anthropopathisms in the LXX of Isaiah," *EI* 3 (1954) IX-X.

Douglas Jones, "The Traditio of the Oracles of Isaiah of Jerusalem," *ZAW* 67 (1955) 226-246.

*Leon J. Liebreich, "The Compilation of the Book of Isaiah," *JQR, N.S.,* 46 (1955-56) 259-277. [I. The Divisions of the Book, The Three Super-scriptions, Chaps. 1-39, Division I, Division II, Division III, Division IV; Chaps. 40-66]

Sheldon H. Blank, "Traces of Prophetic Agony in Isaiah," *HUCA* 27 (1956) 81-92.

*Harry M. Orlinsky, "The Treatment of Anthropomorphisms and Anthropopathisms in the Septuagint of Isaiah," *HUCA* 27 (1956) 193-200.

*Leon J. Liebreich, "The Compilation of the Book of Isaiah," *JQR, N.S.,* 47 (1956-57) 114-138. [II. The Connections Between the Chapters, Division I, Division II, Division III, Division IV, Chaps. 40-66; III. The Delimitation of Units of Thought]

*Richard L. Twomey, "Imagery in Isaiah and the Apocalypse," *MH* 12 (1956-57) #3, 13-21.

*Samuel Iwry, "The Qumran Isaiah and the End of the Dial of Ahaz," *BASOR* #147 (1957) 27-33.

Frederick L. Moriarty, "The Emmanuel Prophecies," *CBQ* 19 (1957) 226-233. [cf. p. 15]

Thomas O. Hall Jr., "Introduction to Isaiah," *R&E* 54 (1957) 501-509.

N. K. Gottwald, "Immanuel as the Prophet's Son," *VT* 8 (1958) 36-47.

J. H. Eaton, "The Origin of the Book of Isaiah," *VT* 9 (1959) 138-157.

Charles B. Kopher, "Isaiah and the Inviolability of Zion," *Center* 1 (1960) #2, 1-7.

*Robert A. Kraft, "Barnabas' Isaiah Text and the 'Testimony Book' Hypothesis," *JBL* 79 (1960) 336-350.

Edward J. Young, "Isaiah's Majestic Prophecy," *SR* 8 (1961-62) 3-25.

Edward J. Young, "The Promise of a Saviour-King," *SR* 8 (1961-62) 26-49.

G. W. Anderson, "Old Testament Books," *PQL* 8 (1962) 182-187, 267-271; 9 (1963) 6-12. [IV-VI Isaiah]

Menashe Harel, "Desert Landscapes in Isaiah's Prophecy," *Interp* 17 (1963) 319-323.

J. Milgrom, "Did Isaiah Prophesy During the Reign of Uzziah?" *VT* 14 (1964) 164-182.

B. D. Napier, "Isaiah and the Isaian," *VTS* 15 (1965) 240-251.

James M. Reese, "The Gifts of Immanuel," *BibT* #27 (1966) 1880-1885.

*Julian Morgenstern, "Further Light from the Book of Isaiah upon the Catastrophe of 485 B.C.," *HUCA* 37 (1966) 1-28.

Karen Randolph Joines, "Winged Serpents in Isaiah's Inaugural Vision," *JBL* 86 (1967) 410-415.

H. L. Ginsberg, "Isaiah in the Light of History," *CJ* 22 (1967-68) #1, 1-18.

*H. L. Ginsberg, "Reflexes of Sargon in Isaiah after 715 B.C.E.," *JAOS* 88 (1968) 47-53.

Joseph A. Callaway, "Isaiah and Modern Scholarship," *R&E* 65 (1968) 397-408.

Marvin E. Tate, "King and Messiah in Isaiah of Jerusalem," *R&E* 65 (1968) 409-422.

Roy L. Honeycutt Jr., "Introducing Isaiah," *SWJT, N.S.,* 11 (1968-69) #1, 9-28.

Edward E. Hindson, "Isaiah's Immanuel," *GJ* 10 (1969) #3, 3-15.

§347　*3.2.10.4.1.2　Literary Criticism of Deutero-Isaiah (Includes Studies on the Servant of the Lord)*

M. N., "Alexander on the Later Prophecies of Isaiah," *BRIM* 4 (1847-48) 441-465. *(Review)*

Anonymous, "The Later Prophecies of Isaiah," *CR* 1 (1848-49) 29-47. *(Review)*

George Vance Smith, "The Later Isaiah," *TRL* 3 (1866) 541-564.

A. B. Davidson, "The Servant of the Lord in Isaiah," *BFER* 21 (1872) 617-640.

*John Forbes, "The Servant of the Lord in Isaiah," *BFER* 22 (1873) 638-671.

†Anonymous, "Reuss and Urwick on the Later Isaiah," *LQHR* 48 (1877) 153-181. *(Review)*

*D. G. Lyon, "The Cyrus cylinder," *JBL* 6 (1886) part 1, 139.

T. K. Cheyne, "Critical Problems of the Second Part of Isaiah—I," *JQR* 3 (1890-91) 587-603.

T. K. Cheyne, "Critical Problems of the Second Part of Isaiah—II," *JQR* 4 (1891-92) 102-128.

William Henry Green, "Genuineness of Isaiah XL-LXVI," *PRR* 3 (1892) 229-245.

T. S. Potwin, "The 'Sufficient Reason' for Isaiah XL-LXVI," *BW* 3 (1894) 435-439.

*Milton S. Terry, "What Higher Criticism is Not," *BW* 6 (1895) 22-25.

C[arl] H[einrich] Cornill, "Deutero-Isaiah," *OC* 9 (1895) 4576-4580.

W. E[mery] Barnes, "The Two Servants of Jehovah, the Conqueror and the Sufferer, in Deutero-Isaiah," *ET* 8 (1896-97) 28-31.

*J. A. Selbie, "Cyrus and Deutero-Isaiah," *ET* 9 (1897-98) 407-408.

*J. A. Selbie, "The 'Servant of the Lord' Passages," *ET* 12 (1900-01) 170.

George H. Schodde, "Some Leading Biblical Problems," *ColTM* 23 (1903) 79-85. *[Deutero-Isaiah]*

Richard B. de Bary, "Deutero-Isaiah and the Empire of the Servant," *HR* 47 (1904) 361-362.

Benjamin W. Robinson, "Some Elements of Forcefulness in Jesus' Comparisons," *JBL* 23 (1904) 106-179. [Section IV. Two Tables Comparing Deutero-Isaiah, Jesus, and Paul, pp. 114-140]

J. W. McGarvey, "The Disputed Chapters in Isaiah: Their Real Value," *CFL, 3rd Ser.*, 2 (1905) 214-220.

R. W. Lowe, "The Problem of a Second Isaiah in Its Relation to Certain Critical Methods," *CFL, 3rd Ser.*, 4 (1906) 266-275.

*E. Cutler Shedd, "The Servant of Jehovah in the Light of the Inscriptions. A World Empire, A World Religion," *BW* 30 (1907) 464-468.

S. R. Driver, "A Light to the Gentiles," *ICMM* 4 (1907-08) 245-252. *[Servant of the Lord]*

R. G. Martin, "'The Servant of Jehovah.'," *MQR, 3rd Ser.*, 35 (1909) 303-312.

A. W. F. Blunt, "The 'Servant' Passages in Deutero-Isaiah," *ICMM* 8 (1911-12) 184-191.

James Strong, "Not Two Isaiahs," *CFL, 3rd Ser.*, 18 (1914) 159-161.

A. H. Tuttle, "The Deutero-Isaiah," *CFL, 3rd Ser.*, 18 (1914) 161-162.

F. R. Montgomery Hitchcock, "The 'Servant' in Isaiah and the New Testament," *Exp, 8th Ser.*, 14 (1917) 309-320.

J. A. Maynard, "The Home of Deutero-Isaiah," *JBL* 36 (1917) 213-224.

A. Haire Forster, "The Servant of Isaiah and the Second Coming of Christ: A Parallel," *BW* 52 (1918) 194-195.

M. Buttenwieser, "Where did Deutero-Isaiah Live?" *JBL* 38 (1919) 94-112.

Charles Roads, "'Deutero-Isaiah'," *CFL, 3rd Ser.*, 26 (1920) 66-67.

C. Theodore Benze, "Isaiah II," *LCR* 39 (1920) 176-184.

*John E. McFadyen, "A New View of the Servant of the Lord," *ET* 34 (1922-23) 294-296.

*Stanley A. Cook, "The Servant of the Lord," *ET* 34 (1922-23) 440-442.

E. Herman, "The 'Servant of Jahweh' Passages in Deutero-Isaiah: A New Interpretation," *HR* 86 (1923) 110.

Owen C. Whitehouse, "The Historical Background of the Deutero-Isaiah," *Exp, 8th Ser.*, 25 (1923) 241-259, 321-344, 405-426; 26 (1923) 108-129.

A[lfred] Guillaume, "The Servant Poems in Deutero-Isaiah," *Theo* 11 (1925) 254-263, 309-319.

Kemper Fullerton, "Isaiah's Attitude in the Sennacherib Campaign," *AJSL* 42 (1925-26) 1-25.

Alfred Guillaume, "The Servant Poems in Deutero-Isaiah," *Theo* 12 (1926) 2-10, 63-72.

*F. A. Farley, "Jeremiah and 'The Suffering Servant of Jehovah' in Deutero-Isaiah," *ET* 38 (1926-27) 521-524.

*Robert H. Pfeiffer, "The Dual Origin of Hebrew Monotheism," *JBL* 46 (1927) 193-206. [III. Second Isaiah's synthesis of the two conceptions, pp. 200-202]

E. L. Peerman, "The Servant Poems of Isaiah," *MQR, 3rd Ser.*, 53 (1927) 285-289.

W. Rolfe Brown, "More Concerning Isaiah's Servant of Yahweh," *MQR, 3rd Ser.*, 54 (1928) 105-107.

*C[harles] C. Torrey, "The Influence of Second Isaiah in the Gospels and Acts," *JBL* 48 (1929) 24-36.

*J. H. Ropes, "The Influence of Second Isaiah on the Epistles," *JBL* 48 (1929) 37-39.

G. Dahl, "Some Recent Interpretations of Second Isaiah," *JBL* 48 (1929) 362-377.

William Creighton Graham, "The Second Rescue of the Second Isaiah," *JR* 9 (1929) 66-84.

*Annie E. Skemp, "'Immanuel' and 'The Suffering Servant of Jahweh': A Suggestion," *ET* 44 (1932-33) 94-95.

*R. B. Y. Scott, "The Relation of Isaiah, Chapter 35, to Deutero-Isaiah," *AJSL* 52 (1935-36) 178-191.

*A. T. Olmstead, "II Isaiah and Isaiah, Chapter 35," *AJSL* 53 (1936-37) 251-253.

W. B. Stevenson, "Successive Phases in the Career of the Babylonian Isaiah," *GUOST* 8 (1936-37) 26-28.

*Carroll E. Simcox, "The *Rôle* of Cyrus in Deutero-Isaiah," *JAOS* 57 (1937) 158-171.

R[obert] Gordis, "The *Ebed Yahveh*," *JBL* 57 (1938) xii.

Sheldon H. Blank, "Studies in Deutero-Isaiah," *HUCA* 15 (1940) 1-46.

*Julian Morgenstern, "Deutero-Isaiah's Terminology for 'Universal God'," *JBL* 62 (1943) 269-280.

*Norman H. Snaith, "The So-Called Servant Songs," *ET* 66 (1944-45) 79-81.

Richard T. Murphy, "Second Isaias: the Literary Problem," *CBQ* 9 (1947) 170-178.

Richard T. Murphy, "Second Isaias: The Servant of the Lord," *CBQ* 9 (1947) 262-274.

W. F. Lofthouse, "Some Reflections on the 'Servant Songs'," *JTS* 48 (1947) 169-176.

Aage Bentzen, "On the Idea of 'the old' and 'the new' in Deutero-Isaiah," *ST* 1 (1947) 183-187.

Ivan Engnell, "The 'ebed Yahweh Songs and the Suffering Messiah in 'Deutero-Isaiah'," *BJRL* 31 (1948) 54-95.

Julian Morgenstern, "Some Findings of a Seminar of Isaiah 40-66," *JBL* 67 (1948) vii.

James P. Berkeley, "One God, One World, One Destiny: The Message of Second Isaiah," *ANQ* 41 (1948-49) #3, 9-20.

Joh. Lindblom, "The servant songs in Deutero-Isaiah. A new attempt to solve an old problem," *AULLUÅ, N.S., 47* (1951) #5, 1-114.

John Bright, "Faith and Destiny. The Meaning of History in Deutero-Isaiah," *Interp* 5 (1951) 3-26.

J. A. Hutchinson, "A 'Via Analogia' in Second Isaiah," *JBL* 70 (1951) xiii-xiv.

J[ulian] Morgenstern, "The Evolution of the Message of Deutero-Isaiah," *JBL* 71 (1952) xi.

*F[rank] M[oore] Cross Jr., "The Council of Yahweh in Second Isaiah," *JBL* 71 (1952) xi.

*Frank M[oore] Cross Jr., "The Council of Yahweh in Second Isaiah," *JNES* 12 (1953) 274-277.

*David R. Griffiths, "Deutero-Isaiah and the Fourth Gospel: Some Points of Comparison," *ET* 65 (1953-54) 355-360.

H. H. Rowley, "The Servant Mission. *The Servant Songs and Evangelism,*" *Interp* 8 (1954) 259-272.

Herbert G[ordon] May, "The Righteous Servant in the Second Isaiah's Songs," *ZAW* 66 (1954) 236-244.

Christopher R. North, "The Interpretation of Deutero-Isaiah," *NTTO* 56 (1955) 133-145.

*Curt Lindhagen, "Important Hypotheses Reconsidered. IX. The Servant of the Lord," *ET* 67 (1955-56) 179-283, 300-302.

P. A. H. de Boer, "Second-Isaiah's Message," *OTS* 11 (1956) 1-121.

*Martin J. Wyngaarden, "The Servant of Jehovah in Isaiah and the Dead Sea Scrolls," *BETS* 1 (1958) #3, 20-24.

Julian Morgenstern, "The Message of Deutero-Isaiah in its Sequential Unfolding," *HUCA* 29 (1958) 1-67; 30 (1959) 1-102.

P. Saydon, "The Use of Tenses in Deutero-Isaiah," *B* 40 (1959) 290-301.

*J. Benjamin Bedenbaugh, "The Doctrine of God in Deutero-Isaiah," *LQ*, *N.S.*, 11 (1959) 154-158.

*P. Saydon, "The use of tenses in Deutero-Isaiah," *SBO* 1 (1959) 156-167.

*David Noel Freedman, "The Slave of Yahweh," *WW* 10 (1959) #1, 1-19.

*Reidar B. Bjornard, "The Servant of God," *Found* 3 (1960) 259-261.

John Hamlin, "The Nations in Second Isaiah," *SEAJT* 2 (1960-61) #2, 37-48.

J[ulian] Morgenstern, "The Suffering Servant—A New Solution (I)," *VT* 11 (1961) 292-320.

J[ulian] Morgenstern, "The Suffering Servant—A New Solution (II)," *VT* 11 (1961) 406-431.

Edward J. Young, "The Suffering Servant of the Lord," *SR* 8 (1961-62) 53-74.

J. Blenkinsopp, "The Unknown Prophet of the Exile—I," *Scrip* 14 (1962) 81-90.

J. Blenkinsopp, "The Unknown Prophet of the Exile—II," *Scrip* 14 (1962) 109-118.

Morton Smith, "II Isaiah and the Persians," *JAOS* 83 (1963) 415-421.

Robert Davidson, "Universalism in Second Isaiah," *SJT* 16 (1963) 166-185.

J[ulian] Morgenstern, "Two Additional notes to 'The Suffering Servant—a new solution'," *VT* 13 (1963) 321-332.

*F. Charles Fensham, "Common Trends in the Curses of Near Eastern Treaties and *Kudurr*—Inscriptions Compared with the Maledictions of Amos and Isaiah," *ZAW* 75 (1963) 155-175.

Allan A. MacRae, "The Servant of the Lord in Isaiah," *BS* 121 (1964) 125-132, 218-227.

A. Gelston, "The Missionary Message of Second Isaiah," *SJT* 18 (1965) 308-318.

*Joseph L. Mihelic, "The Concept of God in Deutero-Isaiah," *BRes* 11 (1966) 29-41.

Carroll Stuhlmueller, "The Paschal Mystery in Deutero-Isaiah," *BibT* #23 (1966) 1504-1510.

Morris S. Seale, "'The Servant'," *NEST* 13 (1966) #4, 3-4; 14 (1967) #1, 5-6; #2/3, 3-5; #4, 3-6. *(Editorial)*

Nieves Alonso, "The Problem of the Servant Songs," *Scrip* 18 (1966) 18-26.

August Piper, "The Criticism of Isaiah II (From Jesaias II by August Piper, Introduction, pp. XX-XLII, Translated by Reinhart J. Pope)," *WLQ* 63 (1966) 170-184, 234-244.

J. Barton Payne, "Eighth Century Israelitish Background of Isaiah 40-66—I," *WTJ* 29 (1966-67) 136-178.

Carroll Stuhlmueller, "'First and Last' and 'Yahweh-Creator' in Deutero-Isaiah," *CBQ* 29 (1967) 495-511.

*W. R. Hanford, "Deutero-Isaiah and Luke-Acts: Straightforward Universalism?" *CQR* 168 (1967) 141-152.

D. F. Payne, "Characteristic Word-play in 'Second Isaiah': A Reappraisal," *JSS* 12 (1967) 207-229.

*Ph. B. Harner, "Creation Faith in Deutero-Isaiah," *VT* 17 (1967) 298-306.

Harry M. Orlinsky, "The so-called 'Servant of the Lord' and 'Suffering Servant' in Second Isaiah," *VTS* 14 (1967) 1-133. (Reprinted with Additions and Corrections in 1977)

*Moshe Weinfeld, "God the Creator in Gen. I and in the Prophecy of Second Isaiah," *Tarbiz* 37 (1967-68) #2, I-II.

J. Barton Payne, "Eighth Century Israelitish Background of Isaiah 40-66—II," *WTJ* 30 (1967-68) 50-58.

J. Barton Payne, "Eighth Century Israelitish Background of Isaiah 40-66—III," *WTJ* 30 (1967-68) 185-203.

H. Eberhard von Waldo, "The Message of Deutero-Isaiah," *Interp* 22 (1968) 259-287.

Shalom M. Paul, "Deutero-Isaiah and Cuneiform Royal Inscriptions," *JAOS* 88 (1968) 180-186.

Donald L. Williams, "The Message of the Exilic Isaiah," *R&E* 65 (1968) 423-432.

James M. Ward, "The Servant Songs in Isaiah," *R&E* 65 (1968) 433-446.

Walter Brueggemann, "The Kerygma of the Deuteronomistic Historian. *Gospel for Exiles," Interp* 22 (1968) 387-402.

*Chayim Cohen, "The Idiom קרא בשם in Second Isaiah," *JANES* 1 (1968-69) #1, 32-34.

Philip B. Harner, "The Salvation Oracle in Second Isaiah," *JBL* 88 (1969) 418-434.

§348 *3.2.10.4.1.3 Literary Criticism of Trito-Isaiah*

J. A. Selbie, "Among the Periodicals. Trito-Isaiah," *ET* 8 (1896-97) 232-233.

Hugo Odeberg, "Trito-Isaiah (Isaiah 56-66). A literary and linguistic analysis," *UUÅ* (1931), Telologi 1, 1-285.

Bruce C. Cresson, "Isaiah and the Restoration Community," *R&E* 65 (1968) 447-458.

§349 **3.2.10.4.1.4 *Studies concerning Date, Authorship, Sources, Authenticity, and Unity of Isaiah***

[Johann] Jahn, "On the Genuineness of Isaiah's Prophecies; Extracted from Jahn's Einleitung ins Alte Testament," *BibR* 2 (1826) 153-162.

[Ernst Wilhelm] Hengstenberg, "Genuiness of Isaiah, Chap. XL.—LXVI.," *BRCR* 1 (1831) 700-733. *(Trans. by Edward Robinson)*

Henry Cowels, "On the Authorship of Isaiah XL—LXVI," *BS* 30 (1873) 521-533.

William Henry Cobb, "Two Isaiahs, or One?" *BS* 38 (1881) 230-253.

W[illiam] Henry Cobb, "The Integrity of the Book of Isaiah," *BS* 39 (1882) 519-554.

Wm. Henry Cobb, "The Integrity of the Book of Isaiah," *DTQ, N.S.,* 1 (1882) 509-519.

Wm. Henry Cobb, "The Genuineness of Isaiah's Prophecies," *ONTS* 2 (1882-83) 77-81.

George C. M. Douglas, "The Two Isaiahs, the Real and the Imaginary," *PR* 9 (1888) 602-637.

Francis Brown, "The Date of Isa. 12," *JBL* 9 (1890) 128-131.

F. W. Stellhorn, "Who is the Author of Isaiah xl-xlvi?" *ColTM* 11 (1891) 220-229.

Sylvester Burnham, "The Authorship of Isaiah XL—LXVI," *SJH* 1 (1892) 200-210.

*D. A. Murray, "The Authorship of Isaiah xl. 66," *HR* 27 (1894) 168-176.

W[illiam] M. McPheeters, "Dr. Driver on the Authorship of Isaiah XIII. and XIV.," *PQ* 8 (1894) 187-208, 489-511.

C. Caverno, "The Isaiah Controversy," *BS* 52 (1895) 347-351. *[Authorship]*

W. H. Johnson, "The Authorship of Isaiah XL.—LXVI.," *CFL, N.S.,* 2 (1900) 42-44.

D. S. Margoliouth, "Lines of Defence of the Biblical Revelation. 3. Unity Against Plurality," *Exp, 6th Ser.,* 1 (1900) 241-262, 321-346, 422-435; 2 (1900) 25-36. *[Unity of Isaiah]*

Howard Osgood, "Isaiah the Myth and Isaiah the Prophet," *BS* 58 (1901) 68-87.

Ed[uard] König, "The Question of the Unity of Isaiah," *ET* 13 (1901-02) 90-94, 132-135.

William H[enry] Cobb, "On Certain Isaian Questions," *ET* 13 (1901-02) 285-287.

Francis E. Gigot, "The Authorship of Isaias, XL—LXVI. *I. Arguments in Favor of the Traditional View,* " *NYR* 1 (1905-06) 151-168.

Francis E. Gigot, "The Authorship of Isaias, XL.—LXVI. II. Arguments Against the Isaianic Authorship," *NYR* 1 (1905-06) 277-296.

F. Hugh Pope, "The Integrity of the Book of Isaias," *ITQ* 1 (1906) 447-457.

Parke P. Flournoy, "The Unity of Isaiah," *USR* 18 (1906-07) 149-154.

William H. Cobb, "Where was Isaiah xl-lxvi Written?" *JBL* 27 (1908) 48-64.

Eduard König, "Professor Eduard König's Reply to Dr. Cobb's 'Where was Isaiah 40-66 Written?'," *JBL* 28 (1909) 100-102.

G. Margoliouth, "Isaiah and Isaianic," *Exp, 7th Ser.,* 9 (1910) 525-529.

*C. F. Burney, "The Book of Isaiah: A New Theory," *CQR* 74 (1912) 99-123.

*C. F. Burney, "The Book of Isaiah: A New Theory, II," *CQR* 75 (1912-13) 99-139.

G. H. Box, "Is the Book of Isaiah mainly a Maccabean work?" *IJA* #30 (1912) 53-55. *(Review)*

G. Frederick Wright, "Who is Deutero-Isaiah?" *CFL, 3rd Ser.,* 18 (1914) 178. *(Editorial)*

D. S. Margoliouth, "The Unity of Isaiah," *TZTM* 4 (1914) 437-477.

J. J. Lias, "The Unity of Isaiah," *BS* 72 (1915) 560-591.

J. J. Lias, "The Unity of Isaiah," *JTVI* 48 (1916) 65-80, 83-84. (Discussion, pp. 80-83)

G. Frederick Wright, "The Unity of Isaiah," *CFL, 3rd Ser.,* 23 (1917) 268-269.

J. J. Lias, "The Unity of Isaiah," *BS* 75 (1918) 267-274.

I. O. Nothstein, "Still Guessing About Isaiah," *AQ* 7 (1928) 47.

*Aapeli Saarisalo, "The Book of Isaiah," *JTALC* 5 (1940) 885-893. [1. The Unity of Isaiah; 2. The Central Theme of Isaiah] *(Trans. by Carl Tomminen)*

W. A. Wordsworth, "The Unity of Isaiah," *JTVI* 72 (1940) 180-190, 200-201. [(Discussion, pp. 190-195) (Communications by H. S. Curr, pp. 195-196; Miss A. M. Hodgkin, pp. 196-197; F. C. Molesworth p. 198; A. H. van Straubenzee, pp. 198-199)]

Edward J. Young, "Who Wrote Isaiah?" *CO* 3 (1945-46) 56-59.

Helen Genevieve Jefferson, "Notes on the Authorship of Isaiah 65 and 66," *JBL* 68 (1949) 225-230.

*Theophile J. Meek, "Some Passages Bearing on the Date of Second Isaiah," *HUCA* 23 (1950-51) Part 1, 173-184.

P. P. Saydon, "The Authorship of the Book of Isaiah. Value of the Scriptural Evidence," *Scrip* 5 (1952-53) 55-59.

H. W. F. Saggs, "A Lexical Consideration for the Date of Deutero-Isaiah," *JTS, N.S.,* 10 (1959) 84-87.

*Robert J. Marshall, "The Unity of Isaiah 1-12," *LQ, N.S.,* 14 (1962) 21-38.

*A. H. van Zyl, "Isaiah 24-27: Their Date of Origin," *OTW* 5 (1962) 44-57.

J. Barton Payne, "The Unity of Isaiah: Evidence from Chapters 36-39," *BETS* 6 (1963) 50-56.

J. Harold Thomas, "The Authorship of the Book of Isaiah," *RestQ* 10 (1967) 46-55.

Edward J. Young, "The Authorship of Isaiah," *Them* 4 (1967) #3, 11-16.

§350 *3.2.10.4.1.5 Literary Criticism of Jeremiah - General Studies*

*George R. Entler, "A Comparative View of the Language of Deuteronomy and Jeremiah," *PAPA* 7 (1875) 9-10. *[Bound with Transactions, but paged separately]*

*R. Payne Smith, "Short Papers upon the Prophet Jeremiah. No. 1. —Jeremiah's Call," *Exp, 1st Ser.,* 7 (1878) 241-248.

R. Payne Smith, "Short Papers upon the Prophet Jeremiah. No. 2.—The Opening Visions," *Exp, 1st Ser.,* 7 (1878) 358-368.

R. Payne Smith, "Short Papers upon the Prophet Jeremiah. No. 3.— Jeremiah's Labours in the First Year of Jehoiakim," *Exp, 1st Ser.,* 7 (1878) 453-465.

R. Payne Smith, "Short Papers on Jeremiah. 4. Jeremiah's Labours up to the Fourth Year of Jehoiakim," *Exp, 1st Ser.,* 8 (1878) 59-69.

R. Payne Smith, "Short Papers on Jeremiah. 5. The Linen Girdle and the Special Function of Nebuchadnezzar," *Exp, 1st Ser.,* 8 (1878) 230-240.

R. Payne Smith, "Short Papers on Jeremiah. 6. The Capture of Jerusalem, and the Flight into Egypt," *Exp, 1st Ser.,* 8 (1878) 304-315.

*J. Edwin Odgers, "Jeremiah and the Fall of Judah," *ModR* 5 (1884) 211-237.

*Henry Preserved Smith, "The Targum to Jeremiah," *AJSL* 4 (1887-88) 140-145.

S. R. Driver, "The Double Text of Jeremiah," *Exp, 3rd Ser.,* 9 (1889) 321-337. *[Comparison of the LXX and MT]*

G. H. Skipworth, "The Second Jeremiah," *JQR* 6 (1893-94) 278-298, 586.

G. H. Skipworth, "Studies in the Book of Jeremiah," *JQR* 7 (1894-95) 568-580.

Edward D. Pollard, "The Burning of Jeremiah's Roll," *BW* 6 (1895) 15-21.

C[arl] H[einrich] Cornill, "Jeremiah," *OC* 9 (1895) 4527-4531.

*William R. Harper, "Outline Topics in the History of Old Testament Prophecy. VIII. Prophecy of Jeremiah and His Contemporaries," *BW* 8 (1896) 280-288.

Nathaniel Schmidt, "The Book of Jeremiah," *NW* 9 (1900) 655-673.

*[Ernst Friedrich Max] Sellin, "Jeremiah of Anathoth. A Study of Old Testament Prophecy," *ColTM* 21 (1901) 112-123, 173-185. *(Trans. by D. M. Martens from Neue Kirchliche Zeitschrift)*

*Max L. Margolis, "Jeremiah a Protesting Witness of the Act of 621," *PAPA* 34 (1902) cvi-cviii.

*H. St. J. Thackeray, "The Greek Translators of Jeremiah," *JTS* 4 (1902-03) 245-266.

Alexander R. Gordon, "A Study in Jeremiah," *BW* 22 (1903) 98-106, 195-208.

M. Kaufmann, "Was the 'Weeping Prophet' a Pessimist?" *Exp, 6th Ser.,* 9 (1904) 186-200.

W. S. MacTavish, "Unjust to Jeremiah: Notice of Prof. Peake's Commentary," *CFL, 3rd Ser.,* 14 (1911-12) 68-69. *(Review)*

*George Aaron Barton, "The Evolution of the Religion of Israel. IV. Deuteronomy and Jeremiah," *BW* 39 (1912) 268-281.

Adam C. Welch, "Jeremiah and Northern Israel: a Study in Spiritual Religion," *Exp, 8th Ser.,* 10 (1915) 481-492.

T. H. Robinson, "The Structure of the Book of Jeremiah," *OSHTP* (1918-19) 18-20.

Adam C. Welch, "The Call and Commission of Jeremiah," *Exp, 8th Ser.,* 21 (1921) 129-147.

Adam C. Welch, "Jeremiah and the Essence of Religion," *Exp, 8th Ser.,* 21 (1921) 254-270.

Adam C. Welch, "Jeremiah and Religious Reform," *Exp, 8th Ser.,* 21 (1921) 462-472.

*Theophile James Meek, "The Poetry of Jeremiah," *JQR, N.S.,* 14 (1923-24) 281-291.

Theodore H. Robinson, "Baruch's Roll," *ZAW* 42 (1924) 209-221.

Alexander P. Kelson, "The Religious Consciousness of Jeremiah," *AJSL* 41 (1924-25) 233-242.

Oswald T. Allis, "The Modernistic View of Jeremiah," *PTR* 23 (1925) 82-132.

*F. A. Farley, "Jeremiah and Deuteronomy," *ET* 37 (1925-26) 316-318.

*F. A. Farley, "Jeremiah and 'The Suffering Servant of Jehovah' in Deutero-Isaiah," *ET* 38 (1926-27) 521-524.

*W. E[mery] Barnes, "Prophecy and the Sabbath. (A note on the teaching of Jeremiah)," *JTS* 29 (1927-28) 386-390.

Pearle Felicia Stone, "The Temple Sermons of Jeremiah," *AJSL* 50 (1933-34) 73-92.

*W[illiam] F[oxwell] Albright, "A Supplement to Jeremiah: The Lachish Ostraca," *BASOR* #61 (1936) 10-16.

J. Philip Hyatt, "The Peril from the North in Jeremiah," *JBL* 59 (1940) 499-513.

J. P[hilip] Hyatt, "*Tôrah* in the Book of Jeremiah," *JBL* 60 (1941) v-vi.

J. Philip Hyatt, "Torah in the Book of Jeremiah," *JBL* 60 (1941) 381-395.

*Eustace J. Smith, "The Decalogue in the Preaching of Jeremias," *CBQ* 4 (1942) 197-209.

H[erber]t G[ordon] May, "Suggestions for a Fresh Approach to Study of the Book of Jeremiah," *JBL* 61 (1942) iv.

*J. Philip Hyatt, "Jeremiah and Deuteronomy," *JNES* 1 (1942) 156-173.

*J. Philip Hyatt, "Jeremiah and War," *CQ* 20 (1943) 52-58.

Harry R. Baughman, "'This is the People.' Jeremiah on the State of the Nation," *LCQ* 19 (1946) 133-150.

*Sheldon H. Blank, "The Confessions of Jeremiah and the Meaning of Prayer," *HUCA* 21 (1948) 331-354.

John Curtis Crane, "A Stamina of Faith," *Interp* 2 (1948) 340-341.

*Patrick Cummins, "Jeremias, Orator," *CBQ* 11 (1949) 191-201.

Corwin C. Roach, "The Relevance of Jeremiah," *JAAR* 17 (1949) 231-235.

E. A. Leslie, "The Poetry of Jeremiah," *JBL* 70 (1951) v-vi.

*John Bright, "The Date of the Prose Sermons of Jeremiah," *JBL* 70 (1951) 15-35.

A. Malamat, "Jeremiah and the Last Two Kings of Judah," *PEQ* 83 (1951) 81-87.

H. Cunliffe-Jones, "The Word of God in Jeremiah," *IJT* 1 (1952) #1, 21-32.

L. A. Whiston, "'The Enemy from the North' in Jeremiah," *JBL* 72 (1953) xxii.

Alfred von Rohr Sauer, "Let Jeremiah Speak Today!" *CTM* 26 (1955) 842-850.

John Bright, "The Book of Jeremiah. *Its Structure, its Problems, and Their Significance for the Interpreter," Interp* 9 (1955) 259-278.

G. Herbert Livingston, "Kierkegaard and Jeremiah," *ASW* 11 (1957) #2, 46-61.

*George H. Cramer, "The Messianic Hope of Jeremiah," *BS* 115 (1958) 237-246.

Abraham Cronbach, "A Modernist Looks at Jeremiah," *CCARJ* #24 (1959) 36-39.

H. L. Ellison, "The Prophecy of Jeremiah," *EQ* 31 (1959) 143-151, 205-217. [I. In the Eighteenth Year of King Josiah; II. The Growth of the Book of Jeremiah; III. The Priests that were at Anathoth; IV. Jeremiah's Call (Ch. 1), 1. *The Background of the Call*, 2. *The Call* (1:4-10), 3. *The Prophet's Message* (1:11-16)]

H. L. Ellison, "The Prophecy of Jeremiah *(continued)*," *EQ* 32 (1960) 3-14, 107-113, 212-223. [V. The Earliest Oracles; VI. The Failure of Reform; VII. Grace and Judgment; VIII. Doom from the North]

Joseph L. Mihelic, "Dialogue with God. *A Study of Jeremiah's Confessions," Interp* 14 (1960) 43-50.

William L. Holladay, "Prototype and Copies: A New Approach to the Poetry-Prose Problem in the Book of Jeremiah," *JBL* 79 (1960) 351-367.

H. L. Ellison, "The Prophecy of Jeremiah *(continued)* ," *EQ* 33 (1961) 26-33, 148-156, 220-227. [IX. The Sin of Jerusalem; X. The Closing Years of Josiah; XI. In the Beginning of the Reign of Jehoiakim]

*David Smith, "Jeremiah in Political Context," *R&E* 58 (1961) 417-427.

*Marvin Tate, "Jeremiah and Social Reform," *R&E* 58 (1961) 438-451.

*Page H. Kelley, "Jeremiah's Concept of Individual Religion," *R&E* 58 (1961) 452-463.

*Roy Lee Honeycutt, "Jeremiah and the Cult," *R&E* 58 (1961) 464-473.

Ralph L. Smith, "The Book of Jeremiah," *SWJT, N.S.,* 4 (1961-62) #1, 11-32.

E. Leslie Carlson, "The World of Jeremiah," *SWJT, N.S.,* 4 (1961-62) #1, 57-68.

*L. Johnston, "Jeremiah and Morality," *CIR* 47 (1962) 142-147.

H. L. Ellison, "The Prophecy of Jeremiah *(Continued)* ," *EQ* 34 (1962) 16-28, 96-102, 154-162. [XII. Jeremiah and the Cultus; XIII. The Shame of Judah; XIV. "Hear the Words of this Covenant!"]

H. H. Rowley, "The Early Prophecies of Jeremiah in Their Setting," *BJRL* 45 (1962-63) 198-234.

G. W. Anderson, "Old Testament Books," *PQL* 9 (1963) 92-97, 178-183. [VII-VIII. Jeremiah]

H. L. Ellison, "The Prophecy of Jeremiah *(continued)* ," *EQ* 35 (1963) 4-14, 160-167, 196-205. [XV. The Prophet's Passion; XVI. The Prophet's Despair; XVII. In the Fourth Year of Jehoiakim]

J. Barton Payne, "The Arrangement of Jeremiah's Prophecies," *BETS* 7 (1964) 120-130.

*H. L. Ellison, "The Prophecy of Jeremiah *(Continued)* ," *EQ* 36 (1964) 3-11, 92-99, 148-156. [XVIII. The Prophet Reappears; XIX. The Book of Hope; XX. The Day of the Lord (30:4-11); XXI. The True Restoration of Israel]

*R. Davidson, "Orthodoxy and the Prophetic Word. A Study in the Relationship between Jeremiah and Deuteronomy," *VT* 14 (1964) 407-416.

*William L. Holladay, "The Background of Jeremiah's Self-Understanding: Moses, Samuel, and Psalm 22," *JBL* 83 (1964) 153-164.

William L. Holladay, "Jeremiah's vision of cosmic destruction," *NEST* 12 (1964-65) #4, 2-23.

Theodore M. Ludwig, "The Law-Gospel Tension in Jeremiah," *CTM* 36 (1965) 70-79.

H. L. Ellison, "The Prophecy of Jeremiah *(Continued)*," *EQ* 37 (1965) 21-28, 100-109, 147-167, 232-241. [XXII. The New Covenant; XXIII. The Prophet's Dichotomy; XXIV. Jeremiah and the Prophets]

William Johnstone, "The Setting of Jeremiah's Prophetic Activity," *GUOST* 21 (1965-66) 47-55.

William L. Holladay, "Jeremiah and Moses: Further Observations," *JBL* 85 (1966) 17-27.

William L. Holladay, "The Recovery of Poetic Passages of Jeremiah," *JBL* 85 (1966) 401-435.

H. L. Ellison, "The Prophecy of Jeremiah *(Continued)*," *EQ* 38 (1966) 40-51, 158-168, 233-240. [XXV. The Lull before the Storm; XXVI. The Siege of Jerusalem; XXVII. The Destruction of Jerusalem]

John Bright, "The prophetic reminiscence; its place and function in the book of Jeremiah," *OTW* 9 (1966) 11-30.

J. Philip Hyatt, "The Beginning of Jeremiah's Prophecy," *ZAW* 78 (1966) 204-214.

*Samuel Amirtham, "Prophecy and Politics in Jeremiah," *BTF* 1 (1967) #2, 1-22.

H. L. Ellison, "The Prophecy of Jeremiah *(Continued)*," *EQ* 39 (1967) 40-64, 165-172, 216-224. [XXVIII. Jeremiah in Egypt; XXIX. The Oracles Against Nations]

*Thomas W. Overholt, "King Nebuchadnezzar in the Jeremiah Tradition," *CBQ* 30 (1968) 39-48.

Theodore M. Ludwig, "The Shape of Hope: Jeremiah's Book of Consolation," *CTM* 39 (1968) 526-541.

*H. L. Ellison, "The Prophecy of Jeremiah," *EQ* 40 (1968) 34-40, 157-164. [XXX. Jeremiah's Symbolism; XXXI. Jeremiah's Message and Character]

*Peter R. Ackroyd, "Historians and Prophets," *SEÅ* 33 (1968) 18-54. [Jeremiah and the Fall of Jerusalem, pp. 37-54]

C. F. Whitley, "Charchemish and Jeremiah," *ZAW* 80 (1968) 38-49.

*Albert Plotkin, "The Nature of God According to Jeremiah," *CCARJ* 16 (1969) #1, 21-31.

*Albert Plotkin, "The Nature of Suffering in Jeremiah," *CCARJ* 16 (1969) #2, 13-19.

*George Telcs, "Jeremiah and Nebuchadnezzar, King of Justice," *CJT* 14 (1969) 122-130.

*Ziony Zevit, "The Use of עֶבֶד as a Diplomatic Term in Jeremiah," *JBL* 88 (1969) 74-77.

James G. Williams, "The Death of God on Zion," *IR* 26 (1969) #1, 25-28.

§351 *3.2.10.4.1.6 Studies Concerning Date, Authorship, Sources, and Authenticity*

T. Crouther Gordon, "A New Date for Jeremiah," *ET* 44 (1932-33) 562-565.

Herbert Gordon May, "Jeremiah's Biographer," *JAAR* 10 (1942) 195-201.

Herbert Gordon May, "Towards an Objective Approach to the Book of Jeremiah: The Biographer," *JBL* 61 (1942) 139-155.

*John Bright, "The Date of the Prose Sermons of Jeremiah," *JBL* 70 (1951) 15-35.

*M. D. Goldman, "The Authorship of Jeremiah Chap. XXXI," *ABR* 2 (1952) 108-110.

*Jacob Milgrom, "The Date of Jeremiah Chapter 2," *JNES* 14 (1955) 65-69.

*William L. Holladay, "Style, Irony, and Authenticity in Jeremiah," *JBL* 81 (1962) 44-54.

C. F. Whitley, "The Date of Jeremiah's Call," *VT* 14 (1964) 467-483.

§352 *3.2.10.4.1.7 Literary Criticism of Ezekiel - General Studies*

*H. A. Ch. Havernick, "Havernick's Introductory Remarks to His Commentary on Ezekiel," *BS* 5 (1848) 434-447. [Circumstances of the Life of Ezekiel; Personal Character of Ezekiel; Style and Method of Ezekiel; Composition of the Book] *(Trans. by Edward Robie)*

H. A. Ch. Havernick, "Commentary on the Vision of Ezekiel Introductory to His Prophecy," *BS* 5 (1848) 700-725. *(Trans. by Edward Robie)*

H. A. C. Havernick, "An Introduction to the Book of Ezekiel," *JSL, 1st Ser.*, 1 (1848) 22-42. *(Trans. by F. W. Gotch)*

(   ) Z., "The Last Vision of Ezekiel," *JSL, 2nd Ser.*, 1 (1851-52) 434-447. *(Review)*

Nelson Head, "Ezekiel and the Book of His Prophecy," *MQR* 7 (1853) 174-196. *(Review)*

J. I., "Ezekiel's Place in the Old Testament Church," *BFER* 19 (1870) 285-305.

Milton S. Terry, "Ezekiel's Vision," *MR* 53 (1871) 260-278.

M. P. L., "Morning Hours with the Bible. I. Ezekiel," *URRM* 1 (1874) 158-162.

*Frederic Gardiner, "The Relation of Ezekiel to the Levitical Law," *JBL* 1 (1881) 172-205.

*F[rederic] Gardiner, "The Relation of Ezekiel to the Levitical Law," *BFER* 32 (1883) 150-177.

*Frederic Gardiner, "The Relation of Ezekiel to the Levitical Law," *DTQ, N.S.*, 2 (1883) 17-47.

Oxonian, "Note on the 'Key to Ezekiel's Prophetic Divisions'," *PEFQS* 15 (1883) 102-105.

A. Kuenen, "Ezekiel," *ModR* 5 (1884) 617-640.

Edward G. King, "The Prince in Ezekiel," *ONTS* 5 (1884-85) 111-116.

*J. Stow, "Mount Horeb," *PEFQS* 23 (1891) 178-182. (Note by C. R. Conder, p. 182) [Correction, *PEFQS* 24 (1892) p. 47]

*E. A. Wallis Budge, "Alexander the Great and Gog and Magog," *ZA* 6 (1891) 357-358.

James Hastings, "Requests and Replies," *ET* 3 (1891-92) 207. *[Ezekiel's Temple Vision]*

S. R. Driver, "Professor A. B. Davidson on the Prophet Ezekiel," *Exp, 4th Ser., 6* (1892) 392-397. *(Review)*

*Thomas Whitelaw, "Ezekiel and the Priests' Code," *PRR* 5 (1894) 434-453.

C[arl] H[einrich] Cornill, "Ezekiel," *OC* 9 (1895) 4547-4549.

*Lewis Bayles Paton, "The Holiness Code and Ezekiel," *PRR* 7 (1896) 98-115.

George C. M. Douglas, "Ezekiel's Temple," *ET* 9 (1897-98) 365-367, 420-422, 468-470, 515-518.

Theo. G. Soares, "Ezekiel's Temple," *BW* 14 (1899) 93-103.

Edward L. Curtis, "The Messages of Ezekiel to the Human Heart," *BW* 14 (1899) 125-131.

*A. van Hoonacker, "Ezekiel's Priests and Levites—A Disclaimer," *ET* 12 (1900-01) 383.

*A. van Hoonacker, "Ezekiel's Priests and Levites," *ET* 12 (1900-01) 494-498.

Ed[uard] König, "Ezekiel Problems," *ET* 12 (1900-01) 566-567.

T. K. Cheyne, "The Image of Jealousy in Ezekiel," *ZAW* 21 (1901) 201-202.

William R. Harper, "Constructive Studies in the Literature of Worship in the Old Testament. II. The Legal Literature—Ezekiel's Contribution," *BW* 19 (1902) 199-208.

G. C. M. Douglas, "Ezekiel's Vision of the Temple," *ET* 14 (1902-03) 365-368, 424-427.

*H. St. J. Thackeray, "The Greek Translators of Ezekiel," *JTS* 4 (1902-03) 398-411.

George St. Clair, "The Throne of God in Ezekiel," *HR* 48 (1904) 277-279.

*Samuel Daiches, "Ezekiel and the Babylonian Account of the Deluge," *JQR* 17 (1904-05) 441-455.

W. H. Bennett, "Ezekiel's Message to the Community," *HR* 52 (1906) 366-367.

*Grey Hubert Skipwith, "The Lord of Heaven (The Fire of God; The Mountain Summit; The Divine Chariot; and the Vision of Ezekiel)," *JQR* 19 (1906-07) 688-703.

W. H. Bennett, "Ezekiel's Message to the Individual," *HR* 53 (1907) 50-51.

*Adolf Hult, "Ezekiel and the Levitic Code," *LCR* 26 (1907) 7-19.

*Adolf Hult, "Ezekiel and the Levitic Code. Part II," *LCR* 26 (1907) 302-314.

*R. B. Pattie, "Ezekiel's Temple," *GUOST* 3 (1907-12) 17-21.

*G. Buchanan Gray, "The Heavenly Temple and the Heavenly Altar," *Exp, 7th Ser.,* 5 (1908) 385-402, 530-546.

T. K. Cheyne, "Ezekiel's Visions of Jerusalem," *Exp, 7th Ser.,* 5 (1908) 525-530.

*James Oscar Boyd, "Ezekiel and the Modern Dating of the Pentateuch," *PTR* 6 (1908) 29-51.

*E. J. Pilcher, "A Coin of Gaza, and the Vision of Ezekiel," *SBAP* 30 (1908) 45-52.

C. A. Carus-Wilson, "Ezekiel's Vision of the Divine Glory," *JTVI* 41 (1909) 167-172.

Edward C. Baldwin, "Ezekiel's Holy State and Plato's 'Republic'," *BW* 41 (1913) 365-372.

S. H. Hooke, "Gog and Magog," *ET* 26 (1914-15) 317-319.

Edward Shillito,"Ezekiel and Reconstruction,"*Exp, 8th Ser.*,14(1917)72-80.

*Joseph Rauch, "Apocalypse in the Bible," *JJLP* 1 (1919) 163-195. [VI. Transition: Ezekiel, pp. 178-180]

William H. Bates, "The Book of Ezekiel," *CFL, 3rd Ser.*, 26 (1920) 105-107.

*William L. Baxter, "'Smooth Stone Out of the Brook'," *PTR* 19 (1921) 177-224. [Ezekiel the Sacrificial Pioneer, pp. 216-223]

*C. M. Mackay, "Ezekiel's Sanctuary and Wellhausen's Theory," *PTR* 20 (1922) 661-665.

W. F. Lofthouse, "The City and the Sanctuary," *ET* 34 (1922-23) 198-202.

C. M. Mackay, "The City and the Sanctuary," *ET* 34 (1922-23) 475-476.

C. M. Mackay, "The City of Ezekiel's Oblation," *PTR* 21 (1923) 372-388.

*W[illiam] F[oxwell] Albright, "Contributions of Biblical Archaeology and Philology," *JBL* 43 (1924) 363-393. [3. Gog and Magog, pp. 378-385]

C. M. Mackay, "Ezekiel's Division of Palestine Among the Tribes," *PTR* 22 (1924) 27-45.

R. Birch Hoyle, "Spirit in Ezekiel's Writings and Experience," *BR* 10 (1925) 46-65.

I. G. Matthews, "'The Mind of the Prophet.' A Study in Jeremiah," *CQ* 6 (1929) 447-457. [I. The Influence of Heredity and Environment; II. An Old Message Through a New Personality; III. Reaction in Favor of Reform; IV. Reaction Against Institutionalism; V. The Deepening of Spiritual Insight]

*Shalom Spiegel, "Ezekiel or Pseudo-Ezekiel?" *HTR* 24 (1931) 245-321. [1. Doubts concerning the Homogeneity and Genuineness of the Book; 2. The Babylonian Exile—Fact or Fiction? 3. Ezekiel in Rabbinic Tradition; 4. The Ancient crux interpretum: Ezekiel 1:1; 5. The Siege of Tyre and Other Dubious Passages; 6. Language and Landscape; 7. On Method]

J. Battersby Harford, "Is the Book of Ezekiel Pseudo-Epigraphic?" *ET* 43 (1931-32) 20-25.

*W[illiam] F[oxwell] Albright, "The Seal of Eliakim and the Latest Preëxilic History of Judah, with Some Observations on Ezekiel," *JBL* 51 (1932) 77-106.

Charles C. Torrey, "Ezekiel and the Exile. A Reply," *JBL* 51 (1932) 179-181.

W[illiam] F[oxwell] Albright, "The Chaldaean Conquest of Judah. A Rejoinder," *JBL* 51 (1932) 381-382.

G. A. Cooke, "New Views on Ezekiel," *Theo* 24 (1932) 63-69.

John E. McFadyen, "Ezekiel," *ET* 44 (1932-33) 471-474.

John L. Myres, "Gog and the Danger from the North, in Ezekiel," *PEFQS* 64 (1932) 213-219.

Theo. Paterson, "Ezekiel," *NZJT* 3 (1933-34) 73-77.

W. E[mery] Barnes, "The Scene of Ezekiel's Ministry and His Audience," *JTS* 35 (1934) 163-169.

*G. R. Berry, "The Glory of Yahweh and the Temple," *JBL* 56 (1937) 115-117.

*Herbert Gordon May, "The Departure of the Glory of Yahweh," *JBL* 56 (1937) 309-321.

David M. G. Stalker, "Some Present-Day Problems in Ezekiel-Criticism," *GUOST* 10 (1940-41) 31-33.

Otis R. Fischer, "Unity of Ezekiel," *JBL* 59 (1940) viii.

*Rachel Wischnitzer-Bernstein, "The Conception of the Resurrection in the Ezekiel Panel of the Dura Synagogue," *JBL* 60 (1941) 43-55.

*Theodor H. Gaster, "Ezekiel and the Mysteries," *JBL* 60 (1941) 289-310.

*Michael J. Gruenthaner, "Messianic Concepts of Ezechiel," *ThSt* 2 (1941) 1-18.

J. Skinner, "Story of God and Magog in the Colophon of a Newly Discovered Armenian MS of the 'Alexander Romance'," *JBL* 61 (1942) ix-x.

Michael J. Gruenthaner, "Recent Theories about Ezechiel," *CBQ* 7 (1945) 438-446.

Cameron Mackay, "Rainbow in Babylon," *CongQL* 24 (1946) 331-339. *[Ezekiel]*

Norman H. Snaith, "The Dates in 'Ezekiel'," *ET* 59 (1947-48) 315-316.

E. L. Allen, "Ezekiel and His Book," *LQHR* 172 (1947) 156-160.

Merrill F. Unger, "The Temple Vision of Ezekiel," *BS* 105 (1948) 418-432; 106 (1949) 48-64, 169-177.

Walter R. Roehrs, "The Inaugural Vision of Ezekiel," *CTM* 19 (1948) 721-737.

*Merrill F. Unger, "Ezekiel's Vision of Israel's Restoration," *BS* 106 (1949) 312-324, 432-445.

*Merrill F. Unger, "Ezekiel's Vision of Israel's Restoration (Concluded)," *BS* 107 (1950) 51-63.

T. Brown, "A Note on Gog," *Folk* 61 (1950) 98-103.

Jack Finegan, "The Chronology of Ezekiel," *JBL* 69 (1950) 61-66.

Max Vogelstein, "Nebuchadnezzar's Reconquest of Phoenicia and Palestine and the Oracles of Ezekiel," *HUCA* 23 (1950-51) Part 2, 197-220.

Harry M. Orlinsky, "Where did Ezekiel Receive the Call to Prophesy?" *BASOR* #122 (1951) 34-35.

H[arry] M. Orlinsky, "Where Did Ezekiel Prophesy?" *JBL* 70 (1951) vi.

G. R. Driver, "Ezekiel's Inaugural Vision," *VT* 1 (1951) 60-62.

W[illiam] A. Irwin, "Ezekiel Research since 1943," *JBL* 71 (1952) xi.

Cecil J. Mullo Weir, "Aspects of the Book of Ezekiel," *VT* 2 (1952) 97-112.

William A. Irwin, "Hashmal," *VT* 2 (1952) 169-170. *[Ezekiel's Inaugural Vision]*

William A. Irwin, "Ezekiel Research Since 1943," *VT* 3 (1953) 54-66.

H. H. Rowley, "The Book of Ezekiel in Modern Study," *BJRL* 36 (1953-54) 146-190.

David Noel Freedman, "Studia Biblica. XXVII. The Book of Ezekiel," *Interp* 8 (1954) 446-471.

John Bowman, "Ezekiel and the Zadokite Priesthood," *GUOST* 16 (1955-56) 1-14.

*Dane R. Gordon, "Two Problems in the Book of Ezekiel," *EQ* 28 (1956) 148-151. [Ezekiel's Knowledge of Jerusalem; Was Ezekiel a prophet?]

*Nigel Turner, "The Greek Translators of Ezekiel," *JTS, N.S.,* 7 (1956) 12-24.

*Matitiahu Tsevat, "The Neo-Assyrian and Neo-Babylonian Vassal Oaths and the Prophet Ezekiel," *JBL* 78 (1959) 199-204.

*Charles De Santo, "God and Gog," *RL* 30 (1960-61) 112-117.

*I. H. Eybers, "The Book of Ezekiel and the Sect of Qumran," *OTW* 4 (1961) 1-9.

J. H. Kroeze, "The Tyre-Passages in the Book of Ezekiel," *OTW* 4 (1961) 10-23.

*A. van Selms, "Literary Criticism of Ezekiel as a Theological Problem," *OTW* 4 (1961) 24-37.

A. H. van Zyl, "Solidarity and Individualism in Ezekiel," *OTW* 4 (1961) 38-52.

Simon J. de Vries, "Remembrance in Ezekiel. *A Study of an Old Testament Theme,*" *Interp* 16 (1962) 58-64.

Eamonn O'Doherty, "Ezechiel Today," *BibT* #6 (1963) 386-391.

Carl Armerding, "Russia and the King of the North," *BS* 120 (1963) 50-55.

R. S. Foster, "Study in Ezekiel," *Coll* 1 (1964-66) 1-11.

*Bruce Vawter, "Ezekiel and John," *CBQ* 26 (1964) 450-458.

H. McKeating, "Our Understanding Ezekiel," *LQHR* 190 (1965) 36-43.

B. Lindars, "Ezekiel and Individual Responsibility," *VT* 15 (1965) 452-467.

W[alther] Zimmerli, "The Special Form- and Traditio-Historical Character of Ezekiel's Prophecy," *VT* 15 (1965) 515-527.

Clive A. Thomson, "The Necessity of Blood Sacrifices in Ezekiel's Temple," *BS* 123 (1966) 237-248.

*Walther Zimmerli, "The Word of God in the Book of Ezekiel," *JTC* 4 (1967) 1-13.

Walther Zimmerli, "Form and Tradition in Ezekiel," *TD* 15 (1967) 223-227.

Jon Ruthven, "Ezekiel's Rosh and Russia: a Connection?" *BS* 125 (1968) 324-333.

M. H. Woudstra, "Edom and Israel in Ezekiel," *CJT* 3 (1968) 21-35.

Dennis J. Murphy, "Ezekiel and the New Temple," *BibT* #40 (1969) 2805-2809.

*R. D. Barnett, "Ezekiel and Tyre," *EI* 9 (1969) 6-13. *[Non-Hebrew Section]*

Walther Zimmerli, "The Message of the Prophet Ezekiel," *Interp* 23 (1969) 131-157.

Cornelius B. Houk, "בראשם Patterns as Literary Criteria in Ezekiel," *JBL* 88 (1969) 184-190.

§353 *3.2.10.4.1.8 Studies concerning Date, Authorship, Sources, and Authenticity*

Anonymous, "Concerning the Author of some Poems ascribed to Ezekiel," *MMBR* 5 (1798) 189-190.

Crawford H. Toy, "The Babylonian Element in Ezekiel," *JBL* 1 (1881) 59-66.

*George R. Berry, "The Authorship of Ezekiel 40-48," *JBL* 34 (1915) 17-40.

*G[eorge] R. Berry, "The Date of Ezekiel 45:1-8 and 47:13; 48:35," *JBL* 40 (1921) 70-75.

*G[eorge] R. Berry, "The Date of Ezekiel 38:1-39:20," *JBL* 41 (1922) 224-236.

*J. E. Dean, "The Date of Ezekiel 40-43," *AJSL* 43 (1926-27) 231-233.

Moses Buttenwieser, "The Character and Date of Ezekiel's Prophecies," *HUCA* 7 (1930) 1-18.

G[eorge] R. Berry, "Was Ezekiel in the Exile?" *JBL* 49 (1930) 83-93.

[Charles] C. Torrey, "Ezekiel and the Exile. A Reply," *JBL* 51 (1932) 179-181.

Charles C. Torrey, "Certainly Pseudo-Ezekiel," *JBL* 53 (1934) 291-320.

*Shalom Spiegel, "Toward Certainty in Ezekiel," *JBL* 54 (1935) 145-171.

George Ricker Berry, "The Composition of the Book of Ezekiel," *JBL* 58 (1939) 163-176.

§354 *3.2.10.4.2 Literary Criticism of the Minor Prophets
        - General Studies*

†Anonymous, "Henderson's Translation of the Minor Prophets," *BQRL* 4 (1846) 419-427. *(Review)*

Anonymous, "Henderson's Minor Prophets," *BRCM* 1 (1846) 249-266. *(Review)*

†Anonymous, "The Prophets of the Restoration," *BFER* 5 (1856) 641-647. *(Review)*

Anonymous, "Sketch of the Minor Prophets," *SPR* 26 (1875) 716-734.

Anonymous, "The Post-Captivity Prophets; or, The Effect of the Word of God," *BWR* 3 (1881) 251-263.

*H[enry] P[reserved] Smith, "The Law and the Prophets," *ONTS* 2 (1882-83) 315-319.

Anonymous, "Neglect of the Minor Prophets," *ONTS* 4 (1884-85) 283.

*A. S. Carrier, "The Hapax Legomena of the Minor Prophets," *AJSL* 5 (1888-89) 131-136, 209-214.

John Taylor, "Wellhausen's 'Minor Prophets'," *Exp, 4th Ser.,* 7 (1893) 108-118. *(Review)*

T. K. Cheyne, "A New German Commentary on the Minor Prophets," *Exp, 5th Ser.,* 6 (1897) 361-371. *(Review)*

John Oman, "The Text of the Minor Prophets," *PRR* 10 (1899) 441-471. *(Review)*

W[illiam] M. McPheeters, "'The Book of the Twelve Prophets, Commonly Called the Minor:' Considered as a Type," *PQ* 13 (1899) 425-452. *(Review)*

F[enton] W. Farrar, "The Minor Prophets," *Exp, 6th Ser.,* 5 (1902) 81-92, 271-286.

*Harold M. Wiener, "Two New Volumes of the International Critical Commentary," *BS* 69 (1912) 464-491. *[The Minor Prophets, Micah, Zephaniah, Nahum, Habakkuk, Obadiah and Joel; and Isaiah]*

C. J. Ritchie, "Prophets of the Seventh Century B.C.," *GUOST* 4 (1913-22) 69-71. *[Zephaniah; Nahum; Habakkuk]*

*R[olland] E[merson] Wolfe, "The Day of Yahweh Editor in the Book of the Twelve," *JBL* 54 (1935) iii.

Rolland Emerson Wolfe, "The Editing of the Book of the Twelve," *ZAW* 53 (1935) 90-129.

Richard M. Brackett, "Modern Anguish and Minor Prophets," *MH* 11 (1954-59) #4, 25-31, 41.

§355 *3.2.10.4.2.1 Literary Criticism of Hosea - General Studies*

[Samuel] Horsely, "Preface to the Translation of Hosea," *BibR* 4 (1828) 59-104.

Anonymous, "Restoration," *BWR* 3 (1881) 264-270.

George Matheson, "Studies in the Minor Prophets. 4. Hosea," *Exp, 2nd Ser.,* 4 (1883) 132-145.

Charles Elliott, "The Book of Hosea," *ONTS* 4 (1884-85) 193-202.

*W. T. Lynn, "The meaning of Jareb in Hosea," *BOR* 2 (1887-88) 127-128.

*Archibald Duff, "Isaiah and Zion; or, the Development of Thought in Isaiah. A Study in the History of Hebrew Religion," *AR* 9 (1888) 426-431; 528-547. [I. Amos and Hosea: Their Sanctuary Faith, pp. 427-431]

A. H. Sayce, "The Book of Hosea in the Light of Assyrian Research," *JQR* 1 (1888-89) 162-172.

W. G. Elmslie, "Hosea," *Exp, 4th Ser.,* 3 (1891) 63-80.

L. F. Badger, "Israel in Hosea," *ONTS* 13 (1891) 77-88.

S. P. Rose, "Hosea," *CMR* 5 (1893) 434-451.

C[arl] H[einrich] Cornill, "Hosea," *OC* 9 (1895) 4479-4481.

Lewis B[ayles] Paton, "Notes on Hosea's Marriage," *JBL* 15 (1896) 9-17.

*J. C. Calhoun Newton, "Studies in Amos and Hosea," *MQR, 3rd Ser.,* 22 (1897) 75-92.

Hugh Ross Hatch, "The Story of Hosea, the Prophet, as it Might Have Been Told in Contemporary Chronicles," *BW* 12 (1898) 257-265.

*G. Currie Martin, "Our Lord's Use of the Book of Hosea," *ET* 10 (1898-99) 281.

J. G. Tasker, "Hosea," *ET* 12 (1900-01) 108.

*Walter R. Betteridge, "The Attitude of Amos and Hosea toward the Monarchy," *BW* 20 (1902) 361-369. 457-464.

Hugh Rose Rae, "The Prophet's Domestic Scandal: An Introduction to Hosea," *HR* 44 (1902) 254-257.

William R. Harper, "The Utterances of Hosea Arranged Strophically," *BW* 24 (1904) 412-430.

Julius A. Bewer, "The Story of Hosea's Marriage," *AJSL* 22 (1905-06) 120-130.

Edward Day, "Is the Book of Hosea Exilic?" *AJSL* 26 (1909-10) 105-132.

J. M. Powis Smith, "The Marriage of Hosea," *BW* 42 (1913) 94-101.

Paul Haupt, "Hosea's Erring Spouse," *JBL* 34 (1915) 41-53.

Leroy Waterman, "The Marriage of Hosea," *AJA* 21 (1917) 83-84.

L[eroy] Waterman, "The Marriage of Hosea," *JBL* 37 (1918) 193-208.

William H. Bates, "The Book of Hosea," *CFL, 3rd Ser.,* 28 (1922) 312-313.

J. F. Springer, "The Misplacement in Hosea," *LQ* 52 (1922) 460-463.

O. R. Sellers, "Hosea's Motives," *AJSL* 41 (1924-25) 243-247.

J. G. Tasker, "Budde on Hosea's Marriage," *ET* 36 (1924-25) 522-523.

Adam C. Welch, "The Editing of the Book of Hosea," *AfO* 4 (1927) 66-70.

Hartwig Hirschfeld, "The marriages of Hosea," *JAOS* 48 (1928) 276-277.

L. W. Batten, "Hosea's Message and Marriage," *JBL* 48 (1929) 257-273.

H. Wheeler Robinson, "The Marriage of Hosea," *BQL* 5 (1930-31) 304-313.

Earle Bennett Cross, "The Trialogue in Hosea," *CRDSB* 3 (1930-31) 94-113.

*H[erbert] G[ordon] May, "The Fertility Cult in Hosea," *AJSL* 48 (1931-32) 73-98.

W. E. Crane, "The Prophecy of Hosea," *BS* 89 (1932) 480-494.

Robert Henry Miller, "Hosea and Gomer: Lovers who Discovered the Love of God," *CFL, 3rd Ser.,* 41 (1935) 65-66.

R. E. Wolfe, "Unity in the Prophecies of Hosea," *JBL* 55 (1936) xi.

J. Peritz, "Hosea's Marriage Story a Midrash," *JBL* 55 (1936) xi.

H. H. Walker, "Literary Structure in the Book of Hosea," *JBL* 55 (1936) xii.

Herbert G[ordon] May, "An Interpretation of the Names of Hosea's Children," *JBL* 55 (1936) 285-291.

Walter G. Williams, "Hosea: His Message, His Wife, and His Children," *IR* 1 (1944) 31-34.

*J. A. T. Robinson, "Hosea and the Virgin Birth," *Theo* 51 (1948) 373-375.

W. F. Stinespring, "Hosea, Prophet of Doom," *CQ* 27 (1950) 200-207.

R[obert] Gordis, "The Two Accounts of Hosea's Marriage—An Inductive Approach to the Problem," *JBL* 71 (1952) xi-xii.

R[obert] Gordis, "The Problem of Hosea's Marriage—A New Approach," *JBL* 72 (1953) xxi.

J. L. McKenzie, "Knowledge of God in Hosea," *JBL* 72 (1953) xxi.

W. A. Page, "Hosea: Poetry Transposed to Another Scale," *JBL* 72 (1953) xxi-xxii.

Robert Gordis, "Hosea's Marriage and Message: A New Approach," *HUCA* 25 (1954) 9-35.

Bernard W. Anderson, "Studia Biblica. XXVI. The Book of Hosea," *Interp* 8 (1954) 290-303.

Gunnar Östborn, "Yahweh and Baal. Studies in the book of Hosea and related documents," *AULLUÅ, N.S.,* 51 (1955) #6, 1-107.

John L. McKenzie, "Divine Passion in Osee," *CBQ* 17 (1955) 287-299.

H. H. Rowley, "The Marriage of Hosea," *BJRL* 39 (1956-57) 200-233.

Francis Sparling North, "Solution of Hosea's Marital Problems by Critical Analysis," *JNES* 16 (1957) 128-130.

G. Farr, "The concept of Grace in the book of Hosea," *ZAW* 70 (1958) 98-107.

Elizabeth R. Achtemeier, "The Content of the Book of Hosea in its Old Testament Context," *T&L* 5 (1962) 125-132.

Clyde T. Francisco, "Evil and Suffering in the Book of Hosea," *SWJT, N.S.,* 5 (1962-63) #2, 33-42.

P[eter] R. Ackroyd, "Hosea and Jacob," *VT* 13 (1963) 245-259.

J. R. B. McDonald, "The Marriage of Hosea," *Theo* 67 (1964) 149-156.

F. Charles Fensham, "The covenant-idea in the book of Hosea," *OTW* 7&8 (1964-65) 35-49.

J. J. Glück, "Some semantic complexities in the book of Hosea," *OTW* 7&8 (1964-65) 50-63.

*L. M. Muntingh, "Married life in Israel according to the book of Hosea," *OTW* 7&8 (1964-65) 77-84.

*A. van Selms, "Hosea and Canticles," *OTW* 7&8 (1964-65) 85-89.

*B. J. van der Merwe, "Echoes from the teaching of Hosea in Isaiah 40-55," *OTW* 7&8 (1964-65) 90-99.

*A. van Selms, "The Southern Kingdom in Hosea," *OTW* 7&8 (1964-65) 100-111.

*B. J. van der Merwe, "A few remarks on the religious terminology in Amos and Hosea," *OTW* 7&8 (1964-65) 143-152.

Philip B. Harner, "Nature and History in Hosea," *T&L* 9 (1966) 308-317.

E[dwin] M. Good, "Hosea and the Jacob Tradition," *VT* 16 (1966) 137-151.

*Robert A. Trabold, "Amos, Micah, and Hosea: Prophets in Crisis," *Focus* 3 (1966-67) #2, 27-37.

Charles J. Beirne, "The Prophet in Hosea and in Our Time," *BibT* #40 (1969) 2765-2772.

H. L. Ellison, "The Message of Hosea in the Light of His Marriage," *EQ* 41 (1969) 3-9.

James M. Ward, "The Message of the Prophet Hosea," *Interp* 23 (1969) 387-407.

*Martin J. Buss, "Mari Prophecy and Hosea," *JBL* 88 (1969) 338.

§356 *3.2.10.4.2.2 Studies Concerning Date, Authorship, Sources, and Authenticity*

Edwin M. Good, "The Composition of Hosea," *SEÅ* 31 (1966) 21-63.

§357 *3.2.10.4.2.3 Literary Criticism of Joel - General Studies*

George Matheson, "Studies in the Minor Prophets. 2. Joel," *Exp, 2nd Ser.,* 3 (1882) 191-203.

*Edward L. Curtis, "Some Features of Messianic Prophecy as Illustrated by the Book of Joel," *ONTS* 3 (1883-84) 97-102, 141-145.

Charles Elliott, "The Book of Joel," *ONTS* 4 (1884-85) 261-267.

R. A. Redford, "Studies in the Minor Prophets. Joel," *MI* 1 (1884-85) 130-144, 215-227, 308-320; 2 (1885) 387-400; 3 (1885-86) 308-320; 4 (1886) 332-344.

A. B. Davidson, "The Prophet Joel," *Exp, 3rd Ser.,* 7 (1888) 198-211.

*Willis J. Beecher, "The Historical situation in Joel and Obadiah," *JBL* 8 (1888) 14-40.

*Willis J. Beecher, "'The Day of Jehovah' in Joel," *HR* 18 (1889) 355-358.

Langhorne Leitch, "The Prophecy of Joel," *MQR, 3rd Ser.,* 7 (1889-90) 335-351.

*A[ngus] Crawford, "Joel, Obadiah, and Amos," *PER* 3 (1889-90) 161-170.

W. G. Elmslie, "Joel," *Exp, 4th Ser.,* 3 (1891) 161-179.

Wm. Johnston, "Joel," *CMR* 5 (1893) 217-233.

Vernon Bartlet, "Is Joel a Unity?" *ET* 5 (1893-94) 567-568.

G. Buchanan Gray, "Is Joel a Unity?" *ET* 6 (1894-95) 91.

Henry T. Fowler, "The Chronological position of Joel among the prophets," *JBL* 16 (1897) 146-154.

W. H. Marquess, "The Teaching of Joel," *BRec* 6 (1909) 261-264.

W. Lansdell Wardle, "The Book of Joel," *ICMM* 6 (1909-10) 289-297.

Adam C. Welch, "Joel and the Post-Exilic Community," *Exp, 8th Ser.,* 20 (1920) 161-180.

*Paul Haupt, "Biblical Studies," *AJP* 43 (1922) 238-249. [3. The Valley of the Gorge, pp. 240-241]

*W. W. Cannon, "'The Day of the Lord'," *CQR* 103 (1926-27) 32-63.

Ovid R. Sellers, "Stages of Locust in Joel," *AJSL* 52 (1935-36) 81-85.

R. E. Wolfe, "The Documents in the Joel Prophecies," *JBL* 57 (1938) viii.

Arvid S. Kapelrud, "Joel Studies," *UUÅ* (1948) #4, i-viii, 1-211.

John A. Thompson, "Joel's Locusts in the Light of Near Eastern Parallels," *JNES* 14 (1955) 52-54.

*C. Roth, "The Teacher of Righteousness and the Prophecy of Joel," *VT* 13 (1963) 91-95.

§358 *3.2.10.4.2.4 Studies Concerning Date, Authorship, Sources, and Authenticity*

G. Buchanan Gray, "The Parallel Passages in 'Joel' in Their Bearing on the Question of Date," *Exp, 4th Ser.,* 8 (1893) 208-225.

W[illiam] M. McPheeters, "The Date of Joel. *No. I. The Problem Stated,*" *CFL, N.S.,* 4 (1901) 33-39.

W[illiam] M. McPheeters, "The Date of Joel. *No. 2 Argument for Post-Exilic Date Examined,*" *CFL, N.S.,* 4 (1901) 101-111.

W[illiam] M. McPheeters, "The Date of Joel. *No. 3 Argument for Post-Exilic Date Further Examined,*" *CFL, N.S.,* 4 (1901) 168-175.

W[illiam] M. McPheeters, "The Date of Joel. *No. 4. Examination of Argument for Late Date Concluded,*" *CFL, N.S.,* 4 (1901) 283-295.

W[illiam] M. McPheeters, "The Significance of a Date. No. I.," *CFL, 3rd Ser.,* 1 (1904) 28-33. *[The Date of Joel]*

W[illiam] M. McPheeters, "The Significance of a Date. No. 2.," *CFL, 3rd Ser.,* 1 (1904) 298-301. *[The Date of Joel]*

V. H. Hegstrom, "The Date of the Book of Joel," *AQ* 5 (1926) 34-39.

M.   Treves,   "The   Date   of   Joel,"   *VT*   7   (1957)   149-156.

Jacob M. Myers, "Some Considerations Bearing on the Date of Joel," *ZAW* 74 (1962) 177-195.

F. R. Stephenson, "The Date of the Book of Joel," *VT* 19 (1969) 224-229.

§359   *3.2.10.4.2.5 Literary Criticism of Amos - General Studies*

Edward Wilton, "The Prophet Amos, and 'the River of the Wilderness'," *JSL, 4th Ser.,* 5 (1864) 175-180.

George Matheson, "Studies in the Minor Prophets. 3. Amos," *Exp, 2nd Ser.,* 3 (1882) 338-352.

Charles   Elliott,   "The   Words   of   Amos,"   *ONTS*   5   (1885-86)   13-17.

*Edward L. Curtis, "Some Features of Old Testament Prophecy Illustrated by the Book of Amos," *ONTS* 6 (1886-87) 136-139.

A. B. Davidson, "The Prophet Amos.—I. Jehovah, God of Israel," *Exp, 3rd Ser.,* 5 (1887) 161-179.

*Archibald Duff, "Isaiah and Zion; or, the Development of Thought in Isaiah. A Study in the History of Hebrew Religion," *AR* 9 (1888) 426-431; 528-547. [I. Amos and Hosea: Their Sanctuary Faith, pp. 427-431]

*Wm. E. Chancellor, "The Literary Study of the Bible: Its Methods and Purposes Illustrated in a Criticism of the Book of Amos," *ONTS* 8 (1888-89) 10-19.

E. E. Atkinson, "The Religious Ideas of the Book of Amos," *ONTS* 8 (1888-89) 284-290.

*A[ngus] Crawford, "Joel, Obadiah, and Amos," *PER* 3 (1889-90) 161-170.

*Willis J. Beecher, "The Doctrine of the Day of Jehovah in Obadiah and Amos," *HR* 19 (1890) 157-160.

Milton S. Terry, "The Prophecy of Amos," *MR* 72 (1890) 868-885.

*Louis M. Flocken, "Physical Evil: Its Sources and Office According to Amos," *ONTS* 12 (1891) 28-33

*John Taylor, "A Prophet's View of International Ethics," *Exp, 4th Ser.,* 8 (1893) 96-109.

Lewis B[ayles] Paton, "Did Amos Approve of the Calf Worship at Bethel?" *JBL* 13 (1894) 80-90.

C[arl] H[einrich] Cornill, "Amos," *OC* 9 (1895) 4473-4475.

*J. C. Calhoun Newton, "Studies in Amos and Hosea," *MQR, 3rd Ser.,* 22 (1897) 75-92.

Anonymous, "Amos and Criticism," *MR* 81 (1899) 815-818.

J. M. Danson, "Amos," *ET* 11 (1899-1900) 442-446.

F. C. Burkitt, "The Thunders of the Lord in Amos," *Exp, 6th Ser.,* 1 (1900) 308-311.

*A. Zimmerman, "The Ethics of Amos," *RChR, 4th Ser.,* 4 (1900) 196-212.

*W. G. Jordan, "Amos the Man and the Book in the Light of Recent Criticism," *BW* 17 (1901) 265-271.

Thomas F. Day, "The Moral Range of the Prophet Amos," *CFL, N.S.,* 4 (1901) 148-154.

Edward Day and Walter H. Chapin, "Is the Book of Amos Post-Exilic?" *AJSL* 18 (1901-02) 65-93.

Edward E. Braithwaite, "Why Did Amos Predict the Captivity?" *BS* 59 (1902) 192-197.

*Walter R. Betteridge, "The Attitude of Amos and Hosea toward the Monarchy," *BW* 20 (1902) 361-369, 457-464.

Anonymous, "'Why Did Amos Predict the Captivity?'" *HR* 43 (1902) 167-168.

G. L. Young, "A Short Study in the Book of Amos," *CFL, N.S.,* 8 (1903) 295-297.

John Taylor, "The Book of Amos," *ET* 15 (1903-04) 64-65.

*William R. Harper, "Constructive Studies in the Prophetic Element of the Old Testament. VIII. The Prophetic Message of Amos," *BW* 24 (1904) 448-462. [Amos, pp. 543-546]

*S. Lawrence Brown, "Amos: The Man and His Message," *ICMM* 3 (1906-07) 296-304.

Louis I. Newman, "Studies in Biblical Parallelism. Part I. Parallelism in Amos," *UCPSP* 1 (1907-23) 57-265.

Henry W. A. Hanson, "The Prophet Amos," *LQ* 40 (1910) 34-64.

George Stibitz, "The Message of the Book of Amos," *BS* 68 (1911) 308-342.

John B. Whitford, "The Vision of Amos," *BS* 70 (1913) 109-122.

C. Theodore Benze, "The Prophet Amos and His Times," *LCR* 37 (1918) 111-133.

John E. McFadyen, "An Old Testament Message," *Exp, 8th Ser.,* 21 (1921) 1-18. *[Amos]*

William H. Bates, "The Book of Amos," *CFL, 3rd Ser.,* 28 (1922) 362-363.

W. F. Lofthouse, "The Call of Amos," *Exp, 8th Ser.,* 24 (1922) 45-51.

L. O. Luneberger, "Amos, the Preacher of the Gospel of Law," *BS* 84 (1927) 402-410.

*D. E. Thomas, "The Experience Underlying the Social Philosophy of Amos," *JR* 7 (1927) 136-145

James Leon Kelso, "Amos: A Critical Study," *BS* 85 (1928) 53-62.

F. C. Burkitt, "The Book of Amos," *Theo* 19 (1929) 266-272.

George Brockwell King, "The Changing World of Amos' Day—and of Ours," *CJRT* 8 (1931) 397-406.

W[illiam] A. Irwin, "The Thinking of Amos," *AJSL* 49 (1932-33) 102-114.

John R. Sampey, "Notes on Amos," *R&E* 30 (1933) 284-295.

H. M. Du Bose, "The Oldest Written Prophecy," *HR* 108 (1934) 61-63. *[Amos]*

Theodor Herzl Gaster, "An Ancient Hymn in the Prophecies of Amos," *JMUEOS* #19 (1935) 23-26.

Julian Morgenstern, "Amos Studies I," *HUCA* 11 (1936) 19-140.

*Julian Morgenstern, "Amos Studies, II—The Sin of Uzziah, the Festival of Jeroboam, and the Date of Amos," *HUCA* 12&13 (1937-38) 1-53.

P. W. Miller, "Amos," *EQ* 12 (1940) 48-59.

Julian Morgenstern, "Amos Studies, Part III—The Historical Antecedents of Amos," *HUCA* 15 (1940) 59-304.

Charles W. Sandrock, "The Prophet Amos Speaks to 1942," *JTALC* 7 (1942) 684-694.

*Mary E. Andrews, "Hesiod and Amos," *JR* 23 (1943) 194-205.

John L. Riach, "The Story of Amos in Dialogue," *ET* 55 (1943-44) 191-194.

J. Philip Hyatt, "Studia Biblica. VII. The Book of Amos," *Interp* 3 (1949) 338-348.

W. S. McCullough, "Some Suggestions About the Prophet Amos," *JBL* 70 (1951) xii.

*M. B. Crook, "Did Amos & Micah Know Isaiah 9:2-7 & 11:1-9?" *JBL* 70 (1951) xiii.

W. S. McCullough, "Some Suggestions About Amos," *JBL* 72 (1953) 247-254.

*Michael Leahy, "The Popular Idea of God in Amos," *ITQ* 22 (1955) 68-73.

James L. Mays, "Words About the Words of Amos. *Recent Study in the Book of Amos," Interp* 13 (1959) 259-272.

Hector Maclean, "Amos and Israel," *RTR* 18 (1959) 1-6.

Roland Potter, "Spirituality of the Judean Desert III: Amos of Tekoa," *LofS* 14 (1959-60) 349-358.

G. Henton Davies, "Amos reconsidered," *OSHTP* (1959-60) 19-20.

Walther Lempp, "'The Nations in Amos'," *SEAJT* 1 (1959-60) #3, 20-33.

Julian Morgenstern, "Amos Studies. Part Four. The Address of Amos —Text and Commentary,"*HUCA* 32 (1961) 295-350.

*F. Charles Fensham, "Common Trends in the Curses of Near Eastern Treaties and *Kudurr*—Inscriptions Compared with the Maledictions of Amos and Isaiah," *ZAW* 75 (1963) 155-175.

*Eva Radanovsky, "Time: The Priceless Gift of God as seen by Amos," *HQ* 4 (1963-64) #4, 65-68.

*B. J. van der Merwe, "A few remarks on the religious terminology in Amos and Hosea," *OTW* 7&8 (1964-65) 143-152.

*L. M. Muntingh, "Political and international relations of Israel's neighbouring peoples according to the oracles of Amos," *OTW* 7&8 (1964-65) 134-142.

*A. van Selms, "Isaac in Amos," *OTW* 7&8 (1964-65) 157-165.

*A. van Selms, "Amos's Geographical Horizon," *OTW* 7&8 (1964-65) 166-169.

*Simon Cohen, "The Political Background of the Words of Amos," *HUCA* 36 (1965) 153-160.

*B. Alger, "The Theology and Social Ethic of Amos," *Scrip* 17 (1965) 109-116.

Arvid S. Kapelrud, "New ideas in Amos," *VTS* 15 (1965) 193-206.

W. E. Stamples, "Epic Motifs in Amos," *JNES* 25 (1966) 106-112.

*Page H. Kelley, "Contemporary Study of Amos and Prophetism," *R&E* 63 (1966) 375-386.

Roy L. Honeycutt, "Amos and Contemporary Issues," *R&E* 63 (1966) 441-458.

*Robert A. Trabold, "Amos, Micah, and Hosea: Prophets in Crisis," *Focus* 3 (1966-67) #2, 27-37.

John D. W. Watts, "Amos—The Man and His Message," *SWJT, N.S.,* 9 (1966-67) #1, 21-26.

Larry L. Walker, "The Language of Amos," *SWJT, N.S.,* 9 (1966-67) #1, 37-48.

*F. B. Huey Jr., "The Ethical Teaching of Amos, Its Content and Relevance," *SWJT, N.S.,* 9 (1966-67) #1, 57-68.

Ralph L. Lewis, "Four Preaching Aims of Amos," *ASW* 21 (1967) #2, 14-18.

J. L. Crenshaw, "The Influence of the Wise upon Amos," *ZAW* 79 (1967) 42-52.

J. L. Crenshaw, "Amos and the Theophanic Tradition," *ZAW* 80 (1968) 203-215.

Leslie C. Allen, "Amos, Prophet of Solidarity," *VE* 6 (1969) 42-53.

§360 *3.2.10.4.2.6 Studies Concerning Date, Authorship, Sources, and Authenticity*

Edward E. Braithwaite, "Is the Book of Amos Post-Exilic?" *BS* 59 (1902) 366-374.

Moses Bailey, "The Formation of the Book of Amos," *JBL* 56 (1937) ix.

*Julian Morgenstern, "Amos Studies, II—The Sin of Uzziah, the Festival of Jeroboam, and the Date of Amos," *HUCA* 12&13 (1937-38) 1-53.

Robert Gordis, "The Composition and Structure of Amos," *HTR* 33 (1940) 239-251.

R[obert] Gordis, "Composition and Structure of Amos," *JBL* 59 (1940) vii.

John D. W. Watts, "The Origin of the Book of Amos," *ET* 66 (1954-55) 109-112.

G. Farr, "The Language of Amos, Popular or Cultic?" *VT* 16 (1966) 312-324.

§361 *3.2.10.4.2.7 Literary Criticism of Obadiah - General Studies*

†Anonymous, "Caspari on Obadiah," *BFER* 2 (1853) 399-411. *(Review)*

Joseph   Horner,   "Obadiah,"   *MR*   58   (1876)   389-415.

R[evere] F. Weidner, "On Some Points connected with the Prophecy of Obadiah, with a revised Translation," *PAPA* 12 (1879-80) 16-17. *[Bound with Transactions, but paged separately]*

Revere F. Weidner, "Studies in Obadiah," *LCR* 5 (1886) 283-291; 6 (1887) 128-139, 325-332.

*Willis J. Beecher, "The Historical situation in Joel and Obadiah," *JBL* 8 (1888) 14-40.

*A[ngus] Crawford, "Joel, Obadiah, and Amos," *PER* 3 (1889-90) 161-170.

*Willis J. Beecher, "The Doctrine of the Day of Jehovah in Obadiah and Amos," *HR* 19 (1890) 157-160.

J. A. Selbie, "The Unity of Obadiah," *ET* 11 (1899-1900) 446.

C.   A.   Blomgren,   "Obadiah,"   *TTKF*   5   (1903)   101-117.

T. H. Robinson, "The Structure of the Book of Obadiah," *JTS* 17 (1915-16) 402-408.

W. W. Cannon, "Israel and Edom: The Oracle of Obadiah," *Theo* 15 (1927) 129-140, 191-200.

George Dahl, "Obadiah Problems," *JBL* 55 (1936) xi.

*Theo. F. Stern, "Introduction to the Literal and Free Translations of Obadiah, Nahum, and Haggai," *WLQ* 54 (1957) 265-289.

George H. Mennenga, "Obscure Obadiah and His Message," *RefR* 12 (1958-59) #3, 24-32.

§362 *3.2.10.4.2.8 Studies Concerning Date, Authorship, Sources, and Authenticity*

Charles Elliott, "The Date of Obadiah," *ONTS* 3 (1883-84) 321-324.

§363 *3.2.10.4.2.9 Literary Criticism of Jonah - General Studies*

†Anonymous, "Benjoin's Translation of Jonah," *BCQTR* 10 (1797) 493-506, 622-636. *(Review)*

Anonymous, "Jonah's Mission to Nineveh," *CongML* 8 (1825) 689-692.

Γαμμα, "On the Great Fish in the Prophecy of Jonah," *CongML* 20 (1837) 703-705.

George Shepard, "The Preaching of Jonah," *BRCR, 3rd Ser.,* 5 (1849) 129-136.

C. E. Stowe, "The Prophet Jonah," *BS* 10 (1853) 739-764. [I. The Prophets generally; II. The oldest Prophetic Book in the Bible; III. Age of the Prophet Jonah; IV. Reputation of the Book of Jonah; V. Testimony of Christ; VI. Oriental and Classical Traditions illustrative of the Narrative of Jonah; VII. The Fish by which Jonah's Life was Saved; VIII. Popular Objections to the Book of Jonah; IX. The great Religious Truths particularly Enforced and Illustrated by the Book of Jonah]

M. P., "The Book of Jonah: How Far is it Historical?" *JSL, 4th Ser.,* 8 (1865-66) 110-123.

Anonymous, "Thoughts on the Book of Jonah," *JSL, 5th Ser.,* 1 (1867) 437-464.

J. B. Kerschner, "The Book of Jonah," *RChR* 18 (1871) 303-321.

T. K. Cheyne, "Jonah: A Study in Jewish Folklore and Religion," *TR* 14 (1877) 211-219.

George Matheson, "Studies in the Minor Prophets. 1. Jonah," *Exp, 2nd Ser.*, 3 (1882) 35-49.

William R. Harper, "Is the Book of Jonah Historical?" *ONTS* 3 (1883-84) 33-39, 65-73, 225-234.

W. W. Martin, "A Study of the Book of Jonah. First Paper," *MQR, 3rd Ser.*, 4 (1888) 26-32.

W. W. Martin, "A Study of the Book of Jonah. Second Paper," *MQR, 3rd Ser.*, 4 (1888) 170-178.

W. W. Martin, "A Study of the Book of Jonah. Third Paper," *MQR, 3rd Ser.*, 4 (1888) 346-359.

W. W. Davies, "Is the Book of Jonah Historical?" *MR* 70 (1888) 827-844.

Charles   Elliott,   "Jonah,"   *ONTS*   10   (1890)   134-140.

H. Clay Trumbull, "Jonah in Nineveh," *BS* 49 (1892) 669-675.

R.   W.   Dale,   "Jonah,"   *Exp, 4th Ser.*,   6   (1892)   1-18.

H. Clay Trumbull, "Jonah in Nineveh," *JBL* 11 (1892) 53-60.

A[ngus] Crawford, "The Book of Jonah," *PER* 6 (1892-93) 302-309.

Wm. Hoge Marquess, "The Book of Jonah," *USR* 4 (1892-93) 249-257.

Luther Link, "The Book of Jonah," *PQ* 8 (1894) 77-93.

C[arl] H[einrich] Cornill, "Jonah," *OC* 9 (1895) 4616-4618.

W. W. Moore, "The Great Fish of Jonah," *USR* 7 (1895-96) 24-35.

*W. W. Moore, "Oannas and Dagon," *USR* 7 (1895-96) 191-197. *[Jonah]*

J. Kennedy, "The Book of Jonah," *BOR* 8 (1895-1900) 184-192.

Arthur W. Ackerman, "The Purpose of Jonah's Mission to Nineveh," *BW* 12 (1898) 190-195.

Anonymous, "Exegetical Suggestion and Opinion. 'The Purpose of Jonah's Mission to Nineveh'," *CFL, O.S.,* 2 (1898) 261-262.

T. M'William, "The Book of Jonah," *ET* 12 (1900-01) 77-80.

Charles M. Jones, "What Shall We Do with Jonah?" *HR* 44 (1902) 451-452.

Edmund B. Fairfield, "Is the Book of Jonah True History?" *HR* 45 (1903) 354-361.

Dwight Mallory Pratt, "The Book of Jonah on Its Spiritual Side," *HR* 47 (1904) 359-360.

A. S. Carrier, Henry Preserved Smith, Francis B. Denio, Benjamin W. Bacon, and James A. Kelso, "Was Jonah's Whale a Barge?" *HR* 48 (1904) 438-441.

John Urquhart, "'Is the Book of Jonah History? or Parable?'" *CFL, 3rd Ser.,* 3 (1905) 174-181.

John Taylor, "Jonah in 'Zeitschrift f. A. T. Wissenschaft'," *ET* 17 (1905-06) 16-17.

A. Lukyn Williams, "The Whale," *ET* 17 (1905-06) 429-430.

Ed[uard] König, "A Modern Jonah?" *ET* 17 (1905-06) 521.

Arthur S. Peake, "The Book of Jonah," *ICMM* 2 (1905-06) 43-50.

Francis E. Gigot, "The Book of Jonas: Arguments For and Against Its Historical Character," *NYR* 1 (1905-06) 411-424.

Leander S. Keyser, "The Book of Jonah," *LCR* 25 (1906) 217-236.

J. B. Killam, "A Modern Jonah?" *ET* 18 (1906-07) 239.

Anonymous, "Jonah's Earlier and Later Prophecies. Mr. James Bowron's Inquiry Answered," *CFL, 3rd Ser.,* 9 (1908) 105-106.

Rudolph M. Binder, "Jonah: A Sociological Study," *HR* 60 (1910) 218-220.

H. Clay Trumbull, "Is Jonah's Deliverance a Reasonable Miracle?" *LCR* 30 (1911) 293-298.

[Paul Carus], "The Jonah Story and Kindred Legends," *OC* 25 (1911) 271-285.

A. Kampmeier, "Jonah and Nineveh," *OC* 25 (1911) 383. *[Editorial Comment by Paul Carus]*

George Macloskie, "The Whale and Jonah," *CFL, 3rd Ser.,* 14 (1911-12) 320-322.

Dyson Hague, "'Jonah The Book and the Man: A Twentieth Century Message'," *CFL, 3rd Ser.,* 14 (1911-12) 355-356. *(Review)*

Luther T. Townsend, "Story of Jonah in the Light of the Highest Criticism," *CFL, 3rd Ser.,* 16 (1913) 51-67.

Francis J. Lamb, "Libel of Jonah. Tried in the Court of Public Opinion," *CFL, 3rd Ser.,* 16 (1913) 99-122.

G. Macloskie, "How to Test the Story of Jonah," *BS* 72 (1915) 334-338.

*J. S. Ross, "Methodist Higher Criticism Arm-in-Arm with Infidelity," *CFL, 3rd Ser.,* 21 (1916) 208-211. [X. Jonah, p. 208]

Philip Magnus, "The Book of Jonah," *HJ* 16 (1917-18) 429-442.

W. Emery Barnes, "The Pre-Christian Apostle to the Gentiles, (Jonah)," *ICMM* 15 (1918-19) 12-18.

H[erbert] W. Magoun, "The Story of Jonah," *CFL, 3rd Ser.,* 25 (1919) 493-499.

A. C. Hill, "Jonah—An Ancient Problem Novel," *HR* 78 (1919) 157-160. *(Sermon) [Text: Jonah 4:2]*

Helen Grace Murray, "The Historicity of the Whale," *MR* 102 (1919) 429-431.

Frederick C. Grant, "The Message of the Book of Jonah," *ACM* 6 (1919-20) 287-295.

Francis J. Lamb, "The Book of Jonah," *BS* 81 (1924) 152-169.

Francis Woodgate Mozley, "Proof of the Historical Truth of the Book of Jonah," *BS* 81 (1924) 170-200.

Anonymous, "Jonah and the Great Fish," *CFL, 3rd Ser.,* 27 (1921) 334.

Anonymous, "The Book of Jonah," *CFL, 3rd Ser.,* 28 (1922) 387-389.

*Henry S. Gehman, "A Jonah-Parallel in Buddhism," *RChR, 5th Ser.*, 2 (1923) 369-371.

E. J. Sewell, "The Historical Value of the Book of Jonah," *JTVI* 56 (1924) 41-80. (Discussion and Communications, pp. 81-96)

*Jalmar Bowden, "The Enlarging Spiritual Horizon of Judaism as Seen in the Books of Ruth and Jonah," *MQR, 3rd Ser.*, 50 (1924) 684-690.

W. A. Wright, "The Message of the Book of Jonah," *MQR, 3rd Ser.*, 52 (1926) 654-659.

*Cornelia Catlin Coulter, "The 'Great Fish' in Ancient and Medieval Story," *TAPA* 57 (1926) 32-50. [Jonah, p. 42]

Ambrose John Wilson, "The Sign of the Prophet Jonah and Its Modern Confirmations," *PTR* 25 (1927) 630-663; 26 (1928) 618-621.

M. Sheehan, "The Book of Jonas," *ACR* 6 (1929) 288-295.

James A. Burrow, "Jonah," *MQR, 3rd Ser.*, 55 (1929) 274-280.

S. D. F. Goitein, "Some Observations on Jonah," *JPOS* 17 (1937) 63-77.

J. H. Morrison, "The Missionary Prophet," *ET* 49 (1937-38) 487-489. *[Jonah]*

D. E. Hart-Davies, "The Book of Jonah in the Light of Assyrian Archaeology," *JTVI* 69 (1937) 230-245, 248-249. (Discussion, pp. 245-248)

*H[enry] S. Gehman, "A Jonah and a David-Uriah Parallel in Buddhist Literature," *JBL* 57 (1938) ix.

Rolland E. Wolfe, "The Mythological Aspects of the Jonah Story," *JBL* 65 (1946) v.

*Joseph O. Eckelkamp, "Jonas and the Will of God," *Scotist* 6 (1947) 58-63.

R. T. Daniel, "Jonah's Timeless Message," *R&E* 45 (1948) 321-325.

F. A. Rayner, "The Story of Jonah: An Easter Study," *EQ* 22 (1950) 123-125.

Gerald B. Stanton, "The Prophet Jonah and His Message," *BS* 108 (1951) 237-249, 363-376.

Benoit Trepanier, "The Story of Jonas," *CBQ* 13 (1951) 8-16.

W. M. Valk, "Jonas and the 'Whale'," *Scrip* 6 (1953-54) 46-49.

*Brevard S. Childs, "'Jonah' A Study in Old Testament Interpretation," *MHSB* 3 (1956) #1, 7-14.

E[dward] J. Young and B[revard] S. Childs, "An Exchange of Thoughts on Jonah," *MHSB* 3 (1956) #2, 23-29.

Robert Dobbie, "A Meditation on Jonah," *CJT* 4 (1958) 195-199.

*Brevard S. Childs, "Jonah: A Study in Old Testament Hermeneutics," *SJT* 11 (1958) 53-61.

Duane Priebe, "Teaching Values in the Book of Jonah," *Voice* 1 (1958) 57-63.

*M. Lawrence, "Ships, Monsters and Jonah," *AJA* 66 (1962) 289-296.

R. C. Foster, "A Ticket to Tarshish," *SR* 9 (1962-63) 73-82.

John H. Hayes, "Studies in Jonah," *TUSR* 8 (1964-67) 18-29.

R. B. Y. Scott, "The Sign of Jonah. *An Interpretation*," *Interp* 19 (1965) 16-25.

George M. Landes, "The Kerygma of the Book of Jonah. *The Contextual Interpretation of the Jonah Psalm*," *Interp* 21 (1967) 3-31.

J. H. Stek, "The Message of the Book of Jonah," *CTJ* 4 (1969) 23-50.

*J. L. Helberg, "Nahum—Jonah—Lamentations—Isaiah 51-53 (A Possibility for Establishing a Connection)," *OTW* 12 (1969) 46-55.

*T. Francis Glasson, "The Final Question—In Nahum and Jonah," *ET* 81 (1969-70) 54-55.

§364 *3.2.10.4.2.10 Studies Concerning Date, Authorship,*
Sources, and Authenticity

Robert Dick Wilson, "The Authenticity of Jonah, Article I," *PTR* 16 (1918) 280-298. [I. The Objections Stated; II. The Evidence; III. Conclusions]

Robert Dick Wilson, "The Authenticity of Jonah, Article II," *PTR* 16 (1918) 430-456. [Objections Stated; Assumptions; Discussion of the Assumptions; Conclusion]

M. D. Goldman, "Lexicographical Notes on Exegesis: Was the Book of Jonah Originally Written in Aramaic?" *ABR* 3 (1953) 49-50.

§365 *3.2.10.4.2.11 Literary Criticism of Micah - General Studies*

Anonymous, "Thoughts on Micah," *BWR* 3 (1881) 271-279.

Samuel Sellery, "The Book of Micah," *CMR* 5 (1893) 10-29.

*G. H. Skipwith, "On the Structure of the Book of Micah, and on Isaiah ii. 2-5," *JQR* 6 (1893-94) 583-586.

John Taylor, "The Message of Micah," *BW* 25 (1905) 201-214.

W. Emery Barnes, "Micah the Prophet: An Introduction," *ICMM* 5 (1908-09) 353-364.

Paul Haupt, "Micah's Capucinade," *JBL* 29 (1910) 85-112.

W. G. Gilmore, "Prophecy," *HR* 73 (1917) 484-485. *(Review)*

W. J. Young, "The Message of Micah to the Men of Today," *USR* 39 (1927-28) 235-246.

*Z. Vilnai, "The Topography of Palestine in the Prophecies of Micah," *BIES* 6 (1938-39) #3, II-III.

*M. B. Crook, "Did Amos & Micah Know Isaiah 9:2-7 & 11:1-9?" *JBL* 70 (1951) xiii.

Louise Pettibone Smith, "Studia Biblica. XVIII. The Book of Micah," *Interp* 6 (1952) 210-227.

*Robert A. Trabold, "Amos, Micah, and Hosea: Prophets in Crisis," *Focus* 3 (1966-67) #2, 27-37.

F. C[harles] Fensham, "The divine subject of the verb in the Book of Micah," *OTW* 11 (1968) 25-34.

*J. P. van der Westhuizen, "The Term *'ètnăn* in Micah," *OTW* 11 (1968) 54-61.

A. H. van Zyl, "Messianic scope in the Book of Micah," *OTW* 11 (1968) 62-72.

John T. Willis, "The Structure of the Book of Micah," *SEÅ* 34 (1969) 5-42.

A. S. van der Woude, "Micah in dispute with the pseudo-prophets," *VT* 19 (1969) 244-260.

§366 *3.2.10.4.2.12 Studies Concerning Date, Authorship, Sources, and Authenticity*

*J. Philip Hyatt, "On the Meaning and Origin of Micah 6:8," *ATR* 34 (1952) 232-239.

E. Cannawurf, "The Authenticity of Micah, iv 1-4," *VT* 13 (1963) 1-25.

§367 *3.2.10.4.2.13 Literary Criticism of Nahum - General Studies*

S. Burnham, "Isagogical Introduction to the Prophecy of Nahum," *ONTS* 2 (1882-83) 37-41.

J. J. Dillon, "Nahum: a Study," *CM, 3rd Ser.,* 4 (1892) 163-171.

*J. F. McCurdy, "Light on Scriptural Texts from Recent Discoveries. *The Book of Nahum and the Fall of Nineveh,*" *HR* 33 (1897) 408-411.

G. Buchanan Gray, "The Alphabetic Poem in Nahum," *Exp, 5th Ser.,* 8 (1898) 207-220.

T. K. Cheyne, "Note on Mr. Gray's Article, 'The Alphabetical Poem in Nahum'," *Exp, 5th Ser.,* 8 (1898) 304-305.

H. W. Mengedoht, "The Book of Nahum in the Light of Assyriology," *OC* 33 (1919) 432-440.

W. A. Maier, "Recent Archaeological Light on Nahum," *CTM* 7 (1936) 692-698.

Alfred Haldar, "Studies in the Book of Nahum," *UUÅ* (1946) #7, i-viii, 1-173.

*Joseph L. Mihelic, "The Concept of God in the Book of Nahum," *Interp* 2 (1948) 199-207.

*O[swald] T. Allis, "Nahum, Nineveh, Elkosh," *EQ* 27 (1955) 67-82. [I. The Alphabet Poem and the Massoretic Text; II. "Not an Alphabet Poem of the Ordinary Kind"; III. Repetition, Assonance, Alliteration, Paronomasia in Nahum; IV. Sudden Transitions; V. The Paronomasia in Nahum i. 2; VI. Paronomasia in the Prophets]

*Theo. F. Stern, "Introduction to the Literal and Free Translations of Obadiah, Nahum, and Haggai," *WLQ* 54 (1957) 265-289.

I. H. Eybers, "A Note concerning the date of Nahum's Prophecy," *OTW* 12 (1969) 9-12.

F. C[harles] Fensham, "Legal activities of the Lord according to Nahum," *OTW* 12 (1969) 13-20.

*J. L. Helberg, "Nahum—Jonah—Lamentations—Isaiah 51-53 (A Possibility for Establishing a Connection)," *OTW* 12 (1969) 46-55.

*J. P. J. Olivier, "The concept *day* in Nahum and Habakkuk," *OTW* 12 (1969) 71-74.

*H. W. F. Saggs, "Nahum and the Fall of Nineveh," *JTS, N.S.,* 20 (1969) 220-225.

*T. Francis Glasson, "The Final Question—In Nahum and Jonah," *ET* 81 (1969-70) 54-55.

§368 *3.2.10.4.2.14 Studies Concerning Date, Authorship, Sources, and Authenticity*

George Dahl, "Nahum Origins," *JBL* 56 (1937) ix.

§369 **3.2.10.4.2.15 Literary Criticism of Habakkuk - General Studies**

†Anonymous, "Delitzsch on Habakkuk," *BFER* 2 (1853) 590-612. *(Review)*

W. G. Elmslie, "Habakkuk," *Exp, 4th Ser.*, 3 (1891) 427-442.

A. C. Thiselton, "Homilies on the Book of the Prophet Habakkuk," *CM, 3rd Ser.*, 5 (1893) 53-58, 106-109, 225-229, 291-295, 358-362; 6 (1893) 31-35, 180-184; 7 (1894) 38-42, 232-236; 8 (1894) 40-49, 238-246, 239-301; 10 (1895) 104-108, 249-253.

*E. A. Chown, "Habakkuk—the prophet and prophecy," *CMR* 6 (1894) 34-48.

J. J. Dillon, "Habakkuk," *CM, 3rd Ser.*, 9 (1895) 303-318.

Karl Budde, "Problems of the Prophetic Literature: Habakkuk," *Exp, 5th Ser.*, 1 (1895) 372-385.

Walter R. Betteridge, "The Interpretation of the Prophecy of Habakkuk," *AJT* 7 (1903) 647-661.

Allen H. Godbey, "The Soul of Habakkuk," *MR* 86 (1904) 866-878.

E. B. Pollard, "'Is God's Moral Government Out of Order?' The Burden of Habakkuk," *R&E* 1 (1904) 45-54.

A[llen] H. Godbey, "Recent Criticism of Habakkuk—Giesebrecht and Stade," *RChR, 4th Ser.*, 9 (1904) 196-214.

T. K. Cheyne, "An Appeal for a More Complete Criticism of the Book of Habakkuk," *JQR* 20 (1907-08) 3-30.

T. Johnstone Irving, "Habakkuk," *BW* 31 (1908) 51-61.

John B. Whitford, "The Vision of Habakkuk," *MQR, 3rd Ser.*, 36 (1910) 684-696.

F. C. Burkitt, "The Psalm of Habakkuk," *JTS* 16 (1914-15) 62-66.

M. J. Gruenthaner, "Chaldaeans or Macedonians? A Recent Theory on the Prophecy of Habakkuk," *B* 8 (1927) 129-160, 257-289.

T. R. Glover, "A Minor Prophet," *MR* 110 (1927) 801-804. *[Habakkuk]*

C. V. Pilcher, "Habakkuk—A Perplexity and a Solution," *CJRT* 8 (1931) 306-313.

*Theodor H. Gaster, "The Battle of the Rain and the Sea: An Ancient Semitic Nature-Myth," *Iraq* 4 (1937) 21-32. *[Habakkuk]*

J. Ellwod Evans, "The Song of Habakkuk," *BS* 112 (1955) 62-67, 164-169; 113 (1956) 57-65.

George H. Mennenga, "The Conflict of Faith in Habakkuk," *RefR* 9 (1955-56) #4, 19-29.

*J. A. Sanders, "Habakkuk in Qumran, Paul, and the Old Testament," *JR* 39 (1959) 232-244.

*S. Coleman, "Dialogue of Habakkuk in Rabbinic Doctrine," *Abr-N* 5 (1964-65) 57-85.

Joseph D. Herzog, "Habakkuk—A New Translation," *CCARJ* 13 (1965-66) #4, 27-30.

*Donald E. Gowan, "Habakkuk and Wisdom," *PP* 9 (1968) 157-166.

*J. P. J. Olivier, "The concept of *day* in Nahum and Habakkuk," *OTW* 12 (1969) 71-74.

I. H. Eybers, "Diverse applications of the 'Oracle of Habakkuk'," *TEP* 2 (1969) 50-59.

§370 *3.2.10.4.2.16 Studies Concerning Date, Authorship, Sources, and Authenticity*

R. E. Wolfe, "The Date of Habakkuk," *JBL* 56 (1937) ix.

§371 *3.2.10.4.2.17 Literary Criticism of Zephaniah - General Studies*

Henry Ferguson, "The historical testimony of the prophet Zephaniah," *JBL* 3 (1883) 42-59.

M[ilton] S. Terry, "Zephaniah," *ONTS* 11 (1890) 262-272.

J. Philip Hyatt, "The Historical Background to Zephaniah," *JBL* 67 (1948) iii.

*J. Philip Hyatt, "The Date and Background of Zephaniah," *JNES* 7 (1948) 25-29.

§372 *3.2.10.4.2.18 Studies Concerning Date, Authorship, Sources, and Authenticity*

George Dahl, "The Date of Zephaniah," *JBL* 53 (1934) x-xi.

*J. Philip Hyatt, "The Date and Background of Zephaniah," *JNES* 7 (1948) 25-29.

Louise Pettibone Smith and Ernest R. Lachemann, "The Authorship of the Book of Zephaniah," *JNES* 9 (1950) 137-142.

Donald L. Williams, "The Date of Zephaniah," *JBL* 82 (1963) 77-88.

§373 *3.2.10.4.2.19 Literary Criticism of Haggai - General Studies*

F. B. Denio, "The Messianic Element in Haggai," *ONTS* 5 (1884-85) 399-401.

Marcus Dods, "Haggai," *Exp, 3rd Ser.,* 5 (1887) 344-354.

*George S. Goodspeed, "Haggai and Zechariah," *BW* 1 (1893) 124-133.

*[Nathaniel Burwash], "Analytical studies in the English Bible: Brief outline of Ezra, Nehemiah, Esther, with Haggai and Zechariah," *CMR* 5 (1893) 87-104.

*Thomas D. Anderson, "The Religious Teachings of Haggai and Zechariah," *BW* 14 (1899) 195-199.

E. C. Gordon, "The Prophecies of Haggai. A Biblical Study," *CFL, O.S.,* 3 (1899) 339-343.

Henry Nelson Bullard, "The Prophecy of Haggai," *CFL, 3rd Ser.,* 3 (1905) 154-156.

Julius A. Bewer, "Ancient Babylonian Parallels to the Prophecies of Haggai," *AJSL* 35 (1918-19) 128-133.

*William H. Bates, "Haggai and Zechariah," *CFL, 3rd Ser.,* 28 (1922) 420-421.

Paul F. Bloomhardt, "The Poems of Haggai," *HUCA* 5 (1928) 153-195.

*Fleming James, "Thoughts on Haggai and Zechariah," *JBL* 53 (1934) xi.

*Fleming James, "Thoughts on Haggai and Zechariah," *JBL* 53 (1934) 229-235.

*J. C. Fenton, "The Promises of Haggai and the Yea of Christ," *Theo* 49 (1946) 47-51.

Peter R. Ackroyd, "Studies in the Book of Haggai," *JJS* 2 (1950-51) 163-175; 3 (1952) 1-13. [I. The Book of Haggai; II. The Framework of the Oracles, A. Passages integral to the Prophetic Oracles, B. Introductory Notes, Editorial in Character; III. The Arrangement of the Oracles; IV. The Interpretation of the Oracles; V. The Significance of Haggai]

*Theo. F. Stern, "Introduction to the Literal and Free Translations of Obadiah, Nahum, and Haggai," *WLQ* 54 (1957) 265-289.

*Peter R. Ackroyd, "Two Old Testament Historical Problems of the Early Persian Period," *JNES* 17 (1958) 13-27. [A. The First Years of Darius I and the Chronology of Haggai, Zechariah 1-8, pp. 13-22]

I. H. Eybers, "Haggai, the mouthpiece of the Lord," *TEP* 1 (1968) 62-71.

(§374) **3.2.10.4.2.20 Studies Concerning Date, Authorship, Sources, and Authenticity**

§375 **3.2.10.4.2.21 Literary Criticism of Zechariah - General Studies**

†Anonymous, "Dr. Blayney's Version of Zechariah," *BCQTR* 13 (1799) 651-654. *(Review)*

William Burnet, "The Visions of Zechariah," *BFER* 33 (1884) 114-124.

[W. H.] Lowe, "Zechariah's Times, and the Occasion of His Mission," *ONTS* 4 (1884-85) 79-80.

Marcus Dods, "The Book of Zechariah," *Exp, 3rd Ser.,* 3 (1886) 136-146, 335-345, 445-456; 4 (1886) 119-131, 216-227, 306-316, 335-345, 453-464. [I. The First Three Visions; II. The Fourth Vision; III. Vision of the Candlestick; IV. The Flying Roll and the Ephah; V. Religious Observances; VI. The Shepherd of Israel; VII. National Revival; VIII. The Consummation]

W. G. Elmslie, "Zechariah," *Exp, 4th Ser.,* 4 (1891) 302-320.

*George S. Goodspeed, "Haggai and Zechariah," *BW* 1 (1893) 124-133.

*[Nathaniel Burwash], "Analytical studies in the English Bible: Brief outline of Ezra, Nehemiah, Esther, with Haggai and Zechariah," *CMR* 5 (1893) 87-104.

Walter R. Betteridge, "A Sketch of the History of the Book of Zechariah," *BS* 54 (1897) 634-645.

*Thomas D. Anderson, "The Religious Teachings of Haggai and Zechariah," *BW* 14 (1899) 195-199.

*F. P. Ramsay, "Textual Emendation and Higher Criticism," *USR* 13 (1901-02) 13-18.

F. Bertram Clogg, "Zechariah: His Visions and Teachings," *ICMM* 9 (1912-13) 198-209.

Adam C. Welch, "Zechariah's Vision of the Lampstand," *ET* 29 (1917-18) 239-240.

Adam C. Welch, "A Fresh Study of Zechariah's Visions," *Exp, 8th Ser.,* 15 (1918) 178-197.

*William H. Bates, "Haggai and Zechariah," *CFL, 3rd Ser.,* 28 (1922) 420-421.

Bernard T. Holden, "The Visions of Zechariah," *CJRT* 3 (1926) 291-295.

*Fleming James, "Thoughts on Haggai and Zechariah," *JBL* 53 (1934) xi.

*Fleming James, "Thoughts on Haggai and Zechariah," *JBL* 53 (1934) 229-235.

W. D. Monro, "Why Dissect Zechariah?" *EQ* 10 (1938) 45-55.

H[erbert] G[ordon] May, "A Key to the Interpretation of Zechariah's Visions," *JBL* 57 (1938) x-xi.

Herbert Gordon May, "A Key to the Interpretation of Zechariah's Visions," *JBL* 57 (1938) 173-184.

E. E. Le Bas, "Zechariah's Enigmatical Contribution to the Corner-Stone," *PEQ* 82 (1950) 102-122.

Iain Murray, "Thomas V. Moore on Zechariah," *BofT* #10 (1958) 19-22. *(Review)*

*Peter R. Ackroyd, "Two Old Testament Historical Problems of the Early Persian Period," *JNES* 17 (1958) 13-27. [A. The First Years of Darius I and the Chronology of Haggai, Zechariah 1-8, pp. 13-22]

F. F. Bruce, "The Book of Zechariah and the Passion Narrative," *BJRL* 43 (1960-61) 336-353.

J. R Porter, "Some recent work on Deutero-Zechariah," *OSHTP* (1964-66) 16-18.

*Cameron Mackay, "Zechariah in Relation to Ezekiel 40-48," *EQ* 40 (1968) 197-210.

§376 **3.2.10.4.2.22 Studies Concerning Date, Authorship, Sources, and Authenticity**

David Shanks, "The Book of Zechariah: Its Authorship," *MI* 3 (1885-86) 81-101.

[T. K.] Cheyne, "The Origin of the Book of Zechariah," *JQR* 1 (1888-89) 76-83.

*John Elsworth, "Historical Setting of the Post-Exilian Period of the Old Testament, Showing the Approximate Place of Zechariah," *ET* 6 (1894-95) 333.

*George Livingstone Robinson, "The Prophecies of Zechariah with Special Reference to the Origin and Date of Chapters 9-14," *AJSL* 12 (1895-96) 1-92.

*William Walter Cannon, "Some Notes on Zechariah c. 11," *AfO* 4 (1927) 139-146. [1. The Date of the Oracle, pp. 139-143]

*M. Treves, "Conjectures concerning the date and authorship of Zechariah IX-XIV," *VT* 13 (1963) 196-207.

§377 *3.2.10.4.2.23 Literary Criticism of Malachi - General Studies*

*Idiota, "On the Elijah foretold by Malachi," *TRep* 6 (1788) 135-175.

Anonymous, "Elijah's Coming,"*JSL, 2nd Ser.,* 2 (1852) 420-432.

Anonymous, "Elijah's Coming," *MQR* 6 (1852) 618-633.

Anonymous, "The Tishbite and the Baptist," *SPR* 18 (1867) 388-404.

Marcus Dods, "Malachi," *Exp, 3rd Ser.,* 6 (1887) 414-435.

[E. H. Dewart], "The Prophecy of Malachi," *CMR* 5 (1893) 281-301.

Charles C. Torrey, "The Prophecy of Malachi," *JBL* 17 (1898) 1-15.

Clifton D. Gray, "The Historical Background of Malachi," *BW* 14 (1899) 404-411.

Frank K. Sanders, "The Spiritual Message of Malachi," *BW* 14 (1899) 412-416.

S. Lawrence Brown, "The Book of Malachi," *ICMM* 4 (1907-08) 402-408.

*R. B. Y. Scott, "The Expectation of Elijah," *CJRT* 3 (1926) 490-502.

*J. G. Matthews, "Tammuz Worship in the Book of Malachi," *JPOS* 11 (1931) 42-50.

Albert Leonard Murray, "A Lent with Malachi," *HR* 105 (1932) 176-178.

Carl Armerding, "Will There Be Another Elijah?" *BS* 100 (1943) 89-97.

§378 *3.2.10.4.2.24 Studies Concerning Date, Authorship, Sources, and Authenticity*

*†E[duard] König, "Requests and Replies. The Massoretical note at the end of the Minor Prophets," *ET* 10 (1898-99) 255-257. [The Date of Malachi - Answer to a question posed by Eb. Nestle regarding §70 of the *Dikdûkêha-te'amîm*]

Hans H. Spoer, "Some New Considerations Towards the Dating of the Book of Malachi," *JQR* 20 (1907-08) 167-186.

(§379) **3.2.11 Literary Criticism of the Hagiographa**
          - General Studies

§380 **3.2.11.1 Literary Criticism of the Poetical Books**
          - General Studies

Anonymous, "Noyes's Hebrew Poets," *CE* 88 (1867) 175-186. *(Review)*

[Nathaniel] Burwash, "The poetical books of the Old Testament," *CMR* 1 (1889) 381-390.

[Nathaniel] Burwash, "The poetical books of the Old Testament II," *CMR* 2 (1890) 1-6.

*[Nathaniel] Burwash, "Analytical studies in the English Bible: The Books of Job and Proverbs and Ecclesiastes," *CMR* 5 (1893) 251-265.

*Anonymous, "The Word 'Torah' in Job and Proverbs," *CFL, O.S.,* 1 (1897) 191-192.

*Moncure D. Conway, "Solomonic Literature," *OC* 12 (1898) 385-410. [Solomonic Antijahvism, pp. 385-390]

*A. H. Tuttle, "The Golden Age of Hebrew Literature," *MR* 87 (1905) 888-902. [Job. Psalms, Proverbs, Ecclesiastes, Song of Solomon, Ruth]

*E. G. King, "Job and the Alphabetical Psalms," *ICMM* 14 (1917-18) 31-39.

*Joseph Qafiḥ, "The Accents of Job, Proverbs and Psalms in Yemenite Tradition," *Tarbiz* 31 (1961-62) #4, III.

§381 **3.2.11.1.1 Literary Criticism of Job - General Studies**

†Anonymous, "Garden's Version of Job," *BCQTR* 9 (1797) 168-175. *(Review)*

†Anonymous, "Bishop Stock on the Book of Job," *BCQTR* 29 (1807) 368-375, 496-508. *(Review)*

Anonymous, "The   Book   of   Job,"   *CE*   23   (1837)   29-53.

Ralph Wardlaw, "Essays on the Book of Job," *CongML* 23 (1840) 274-280, 357-363, 444-450, 525-533, 591-600, 660-666; 24 (1841) 624-632, 699-705, 760-769, 838-845.

*[Albert] Barnes, "The Patriarchal Religion, as developed in the Book of Job," *BRCR, N.S.,* 11 (1844) 163-179.

*Ludwig Hirzel, "Introduction to the Book of Job," *BS* 7 (1850) 144-162. [1. Contents of the Book; 2. Doctrine and Object of the Book; 3. Unity of the Book; 4. General Plan; 5. Subject of the Poem; 6. Time and Place of the Composition of the Book] *(Trans. by William C. Duncan)*

Anonymous, "The Book of Job," *WR* 60 (1853) 417-450. *(Review)*

Anonymous, "The Book of Job," *SPR* 9 (1855-56) 390-402.

†Anonymous, "The Book of Job," *BFER* 6 (1857) 561-600; 8 (1859) 670-706. *(Review)*

Joseph Muenscher, "The Book of Job," *CRB* 23 (1858) 75-100.

J. L. B., "The Literature of the Book of Job," *JSL, 3rd Ser.,* 8 (1858-59) 25-46.

Anonymous, "The Book of Job," *CE* 67 (1859) 254-259; 68 (1860) 201-211. *(Review)*

W. E. T., "Revised English Version of the Book of Job," *JSL, 3rd Ser.,* 9 (1859) 257-274. *(Review)*

Anonymous, "Carey's Translation of the Book of Job," *CR* 12 (1859-60) 249-262. *(Review)*

[B. F. Hayes], "The Book of Job," *FBQ* 8 (1860) 443-460. *(Review)*

*Anonymous, "Renan on Job and Canticles," *AThR* 3 (1861) 478-486. *(Review)*

[B. F. Hayes], "The Book of Job," *FBQ* 9 (1861) 72-90.

H. P., "Remarks on a New Version of the Book of Job," *JSL, 3rd Ser.,* 14 (1861-62) 454-456. (Remarks by Charles H. H. Wright, pp. 456-463)

Lic Konstantin Schlottman, "The Book of Job," *ER* 14 (1862-63) 1-33. *(Trans by Charles F. Schaeffer)*

†Anonymous, "The Book of Job," *BQRL* 46 (1867) 70-96. *(Review)*

W. G[illespie], "Job," *JSL, 5th Ser.,* 1 (1867) 338-362.

J. W. Jackson, "On Mr. Gillespie's Article, 'Job'," *JSL, 5th Ser.,* 2 (1867-68) 213-214.

[D. Waterman], "The Book of Job and its Lessons," *FBQ* 16 (1868) 402-412.

J. G. Herder, "The Book of Job Considered as an Art-Composition," *JSP* 4 (1870) 284-288. *(Trans. by A. E. Kroeger)*

W. R. French, "The Time of Job," *UQGR, N.S.,* 7 (1870) 269-277.

Thomas Whitelaw, "The Problem of Job," *BFER* 21 (1872) 742-757.

†Anonymous, "The Book of Job," *LQHR* 50 (1878) 368-391; 51 (1878-79) 52-83. *(Review)*

G. H. Zimmerman, "The Book of Job," *MQR, 2nd Ser.,* 1 (1879) 703-716.

R. Leighton Gerhart, "The Book of Job," *RChR* 26 (1879) 277-310.

N. T., "The Book of Job," *MQR, 2nd Ser.,* 2 (1880) 183-186.

*R. V. Foster, "Some Astronomy in the Book of Job," *ONTS* 4 (1884-85) 358-363.

R. V. Foster, "The Hebrew Wisdom—The Book of Job," *ONTS* 5 (1884-85) 256-261.

Samuel Dyson, "The Problem concerning the Book of Job," *CM* 23 (1886) 65-74.

*Henry M. Harman, "The Divine Names of the Book of Job," *JBL* 6 (1886) part 1, 119.

David Shanks, "The Argument of the Book of Job," *MI* 4 (1886) 269-286.

T. W. Moore, "The Book of Job—Revised Version Old Testament," *MQR, 2nd Ser.,* 8 (1886) 261-271.

*Fergus A. Ferguson, "Job on Life and Resurrection," *ERG, 9th Ser.,* 2 (1887) 20-25.

John F. Genung, "The Interpretation of the Book of Job," *AR* 10 (1888) 437-466.

[Francis Bartlett Proctor], "The Story of Job: Doctrinal and Homiletic Suggestions, with Literary Notes and Illustrations," *CM, N.S.,* 3 (1888) 48-59, 116-126, 180-185, 225-232, 356-369; 4 (1888) 23-33, 90-97, 158-166, 218-226, 291-296, 349-356.

S. G. Green, "The Book of Job: Dean Bradley's Lectures," *CongRL* 2 (1888) 884-895, 983-991. *(Review)*

[William Pope Harrison], "Christ in the Book of Job," *MQR, 3rd Ser.,* 4 (1888) 390-400. *(Editorial)*

*J. G. Lansing, "The Messianic Element in the Book of Job," *CT* 6 (1888-89) 401-430.

John S. Zelie, "The Figurative Element in Job," *ONTS* 8 (1888-89) 332-335, 368-370.

[Francis Bartlett Proctor], "The Story of Job. (Second Series)," *CM, N.S.,* 5 (1889) 48-58, 116-123, 176-181, 243-251, 310-312, 373-379.

Anonymous, "A New Reading of the Book of Job," *WR* 132 (1889) 56-73.

Wm. G. Ballantine, "The Book of Job," *BS* 47 (1890) 54-67.

W. W. Davies, "The Integrity of the Book of Job," *MR* 72 (1890) 329-346.

W. W. Davies, "The Mythological Element in Job," *ONTS* 11 (1890) 207-212.

Albert P. Brigham, "Inorganic Nature in the Poem of Job," *ONTS* 13 (1891) 98-107.

*Geo[rge] S. Goodspeed, "The Book of Job in Other Literatures," *ONTS* 15 (1892) 45-51, 105-114.

*Anson P. Atterbury, "Ethical Teaching of the Book of Job Concerning the Conduct of God Toward Man," *CT* 10 (1892-93) 123-136.

* E. L. Curtis, "Messianic Prophecy in the Book of Job," *BW* 1 (1893) 119-121.

George S. Goodspeed, "The Book of Job," *BW* 1 (1893) 288-293.

Bernhard Duhm, "The Book of Job," *NW* 3 (1894) 328-344.

Adelaide I. Locke, "Job and Faust," *HSR* 5 (1894-95) 297-306.

Hugh S. Dougall, "The Problem of Job," *CMR* 7 (1895) 1-19.

George Augustus Simcox, "On the Structure of the Book of Job," *Exp, 5th Ser.,* 2 (1895) 377-394.

*S. R. Driver, "'Sceptics of the Old Testament'," *ContR* 69 (1896) 257-269. *[Job, Koheleth, Agur (Prov. xxx)] (Review)*

K. Budde, "The Book of Job," *ET* 8 (1896-97) 111-112.

T. K. Cheyne, "Professor Budde's Job: An Explanation," *ET* 8 (1896-97) 288, 384.

*G. Buchanan Gray, "Two Notes on the Hebrew Ecclesiasticus," *OSHTP* (1896-97) 36-40. [I. The Reference to Job and the Canon in Eccles. XLIX. 8-10, pp. 36-39]

T. K. Cheyne, "The Book of Job and Its Latest Commentator," *Exp, 5th Ser.,* 5 (1897) 401-416. *(Review)*

T. K. Cheyne, "The Book of Job and Its Latest Commentator, Part II," *Exp, 5th Ser.,* 6 (1897) 22-36.

John Christian Kenner, "Job, A Prince of the East; and His Inspired Epic," *MQR, 3rd Ser.,* 22 (1897) 323-341.

William Henry Green, "The Dramatic Character and Integrity of the Book of Job," *PPR* 8 (1897) 683-701. *(Review)*

†Anonymous, "Job and 'Faust'," *QRL* 186 (1897) 213-240. *(Review)*

W. L. Lingle, "Is the Book of Job Fact or Fiction?" *USR* 9 (1897) 97-106.

C[laude] R. Conder, "Illustrations of the Book of Job," *PEFQS* 30 (1898) 254-261. [Language; Civilisation; Natural History]

Henry J. Weber, "Material for the Construction of a Grammar of the Book of Job," *AJSL* 15 (1898-99) 1-32.

*Duncan B. Macdonald, "Job and Muslim Cosmology," *AJSL* 15 (1898-99) 168-169.

*James A. Craig, "A Study of Job and the Jewish Theology of Suffering," *Monist* 9 (1898-99) 481-523.

*A[ngus] Crawford, "Exploration and Discovery," *PER* 12 (1898-99) 149-160. [The Book of Job, pp. 158-160]

Anonymous, "Current Criticism and Interpretation of the Old Testament. Job, An Appreciation," *CFL, O.S.,* 3 (1899) 307.

Charles H. Dickinson, "The Drama of Job," *BS* 57 (1900) 68-94.

*D. S. Margoliouth, "Lines of Defence of the Biblical Revelation. 3. Unity Against Plurality," *Exp, 6th Ser.,* 1 (1900) 241-262, 321-346, 422-435; 2 (1900) 25-36. *[Job]*

W. E. Smyser, "A Literary Study of the Book of Job," *MR* 82 (1900) 849-868.

*Anonymous, "Job and Prometheus," *CQR* 51 (1900-01) 325-350.

W. R. Worthington, "The Book of Job," *HR* 42 (1901) 352-353.

William Brenton Greene Jr., "Job's Philosophy of Affliction," *CFL, N.S.,* 5 (1902) 227-235.

*C. Clermont-Ganneau, "Archaeological and Epigraphic Notes on Palestine. 10. *Dannaba and Job's Country*," *PEFQS* 34 (1902) 10-15.

*Jas. C. Morris, "The Book of Job and the Revelation of the Messiah," *MQR, 3rd Ser.,* 29 (1903) 498-506.

Eduard König, "The Problem of the Poem of Job," *AJT* 8 (1904) 66-77.

Carl A. Blomgren, "A Treatise on the Book of Job," *TTKF* 7 (1905) 94-112.

Walter Lock, "The Teaching of the Book of Job," *ICMM* 2 (1905-06) 350-363.

Francis E. Gigot, "Leading Problems Concerning the Book of Job: A Brief Exposition and Discussion," *NYR* 1 (1905-06) 579-596.

John E. McFadyen, "Light upon Life's Mystery from the Book of Job," *HR* 52 (1906) 48-51.

*Morris Jastrow Jr., "A Babylonian Parallel to the Story of Job," *JBL* 25 (1906) 135-191.

*T. W. Kretschmann, "Job on the Resurrection of the Body," *LCR* 25 (1906) 570-579.

W. B. Carney, "A Literary Study of Job," *LQ* 36 (1906) 423-438.

Edward M. Merrins, "The Patience of Job," *BS* 64 (1907) 224-249. *[Discussion of Job's affliction]*

Alex R. Gordon, "Job," *Exp, 7th Ser.*, 3 (1907) 185-192, 228-245.

Gustavus E. Hiller, "A Fresh Look at the Book of Job," *MQR, 3rd Ser.*, 33 (1907) 663-671.

*F. Y. Leggatt, "Job's Contribution to the Problem of the Future State," *Exp, 7th Ser.*, 9 (1910) 326-340.

J. O. Knott, "An Interpretation of the Book of Job," *MQR, 3rd Ser.*, 36 (1910) 553-567.

*[Paul Carus], "Tabi-utul-Bel, the Pious Sufferer," *OC* 24 (1910) 505-509. *[The Babylonian "Job"]*

*Helen Halwey Nichols, "The Composition of the Elihu Speeches," *AJSL* 27 (1910-11) 97-186.

*Eb. Nestle, "David in the Book of Job," *ET* 22 (1910-11) 90-91.

F. Gilmore, "Literary Interest in the Book of Job," *ACQR* 36 (1911) 349-354.

Henry H. Howorth, "Some Unconventional Views on the Text of the Bible. IX. Job, etc.," *SBAP* 33 (1911) 26-33, 53-61.

*H. F. B. Compston, "The Accentuation of *wayyomar* in Job," *JTS* 13 (1911-12) 426-427. [וַיֹּאמַר]

George A. Barton, "The Original Home of the Story of Job," *JBL* 31 (1912) 63-68.

*H. Townsend, "Job and Buddha," *ET* 24 (1912-13) 499-501.

Andrew C. Zenos, "The Problem of Job in the Twentieth Century," *HR* 65 (1913) 373-375.

Walter Krumweide, "The Book of Job: A Critical Study," *LQ* 43 (1913) 410-417.

Camden M. Cobern, "A New Interpretation of the Book of Job," *MR* 95 (1913) 419-439.

Camden M. Cobern, "A New Egyptological Interpretation of Job," *RP* 12 (1913) 152-154. *(Review)*

A. D. Martin, "The Book of Job," *ET* 26 (1914-15) 75-81.

*T. F. Royds, "Job and the Problem of Suffering," *ICMM* 11 (1914-15) 378-387.

S. M. Provence, "The Book of Job. An Interpretation," *R&E* 13 (1916) 214-231.

Theodore Copeland, "Job—A Study," *MQR, 3rd Ser.*, 43 (1917) 461-466.

M. C. Hazard, "The Book of Job," *BW* 53 (1919) 60-64.

*Anonymous, "Job's Conception of God," *CFL, 3rd Ser.*, 25 (1919) 289.

William H. Bates, "The Book of Job," *CFL, 3rd Ser.*, 26 (1920) 194-197.

G. Buchanan Gray, "The Additions in the Ancient Greek Version of Job," *Exp, 8th Ser.*, 19 (1920) 422-438.

*Ed[uard] König, "The Problem of Suffering in the Light of the Book of Job," *ET* 32 (1920-21) 361-363.

*Edward Shillito, "The Sequel to Job. The Christian Other Alternative," *Exp, 8th Ser.*, 21 (1921) 417-424.

*J. C. Jacoby, "The Book of Job: Its Author and Its Doctrine," *LQ* 51 (1921) 182-189.

R. B. Steele, "The Book of Job," *MQR, 3rd Ser.*, 47 (1921) 523-534.

J. T. Mueller, "The Paramount Lesson of Job: God's Glory Magnified by Faith Triumphant over Tribulation," *TM* 1 (1921) 161-173.

G. Buchanan Gray, "A New Interpretation of Job," *AJSL* 38 (1921-22) 63-70. *(Review)*

A. Nairne, "Job," *CQR* 93 (1921-22) 103-122. *(Review)*

*John H. Raven, "Job's Messianic Hope," *BR* 7 (1922) 537-554.

W. Ernest Beet, "The Message of the Book of Job," *Exp, 8th Ser.,* 24 (1922) 111-120.

*R. B. Steele, "Notes on the Book of Job and Maccabees I. and II.," *MQR, 3rd Ser.,* 48 (1922) 148-150.

D[avid] E. Culey, "Recent Literature on the Book of Job," *BWTS* 15 (1922-23) 5-18.

*John H. Raven, "Job's Messianic Hope. II," *BR* 8 (1923) 35-60.

A. Nairne, "Job's Interpreters," *CQR* 97 (1923-24) 49-70. *(Review)*

Kemper Fullerton, "The Original Conclusion to the Book of Job," *ZAW* 42 (1924) 116-135.

J. P. Naish, "The Book of Job and the Early Persian Period," *Exp, 9th Ser.,* 3 (1925) 34-49, 94-104.

(Mrs.) Evelyn Baker Dodd, "The Integrity of Job's Friends," *MQR, 3rd Ser.,* 51 (1925) 127-130.

Victor L. Trumper, "Modern Science in the Book of Job," *JTVI* 58 (1926) 63-74, 84-86. (Discussion and Communications, pp. 74-84)

*Robert H. Pfeiffer, "The Dual Origin of Hebrew Monotheism," *JBL* 46 (1927) 193-206. [Critical Note: The priority of Job over Is. 40-55, pp. 202-205]

*Eduard König, "The Problem of Suffering and the Book of Job," *MR* 110 (1927) 582-586.

Earl Bennett Cross, "God's Good Man," *CRDSB* 1 (1928-29) 150-162.

George L. Hurst, "The Voice Out of the Whirlwind," *ET* 39 (1928-29) 137.

Marjory S. West, "The Book of Job and the Problem of Suffering," *ET* 40 (1928-29) 358-364.

Walter Romig, "Job—A Dramatic Debate," *SS* 3 (1929) #1, 24-29.

K[emper] Fullerton, "Double Entendre in the First Speech of Eliphaz," *JBL* 49 (1930) 320-374.

W. H. Stubbs, "The Drama of Job," *LQHR* 154 (1930) 213-219.

H. F. B. Compston, "Marginal Notes on Driver-Gray's 'Job' (I.C.C.)," *ET* 42 (1930-31) 92-93.

Milton Steinberg, "Job Answers God: Being the Religious Perplexities of an Obscure Pharisee," *JR* 12 (1932) 159-176.

H. Grady Davis, "The Message of the Book of Job for Today," *LCQ* 6 (1933) 131-146.

D. Winton Thomas, "Job's 'comforters'," *DUJ* 28 (1933-34) 276-277.

Charles Lee Feinberg, "The Book of Job," *BS* 91 (1934) 78-86.

*E. Brennecke, "The Place of Suffering in the Plan of God as Debated in the Book of Job," *LCQ* 7 (1934) 165-180.

H. J. Flowers, "The Book of Job," *R&E* 31 (1934) 158-172.

*David E. Faust, "A Prophet Attacks Profit," *JAAR* 3 (1935) #1, 29-31.

*A. P. Drucker, "The Book of Job," *OC* 49 (1935) 65-78. [The Difficulties of the Book of Job; Why has the Book of Job been Misunderstood? The Date and Composition of Job; Job as a Drama; The Purpose of the Drama]

John E. Moyle, "The Redeemer in the Book of Job," *CFL, 3rd Ser.,* 42 (1936) 149-155.

Katherine McNeill, "An Interpretation of Job," *JAAR* 4 (1936) #1, 23-24.

*Harry M. Orlinsky, "'Αποβαίνω and ἐπιβαίνω in the Septuagint of Job," *JBL* 56 (1937) 361-367.

William A. Irwin, "The Elihu Speeches in the Criticism of the Book of Job," *JR* 17 (1937) 37-47.

Wilfrid Bovey, "The Unjust God? Job's Problem and Ours," *HJ* 36 (1937-38) 353-364.

*A. W. Harrison, "The Poetry of the Book of Job," *LQHR* 163 (1938) 327-336.

*Charles Lee Feinberg, "Job and the Nation Israel. First Study: In the Hands of the Enemy," *BS* 96 (1939) 405-411.

E. E. Kellett, "'Job': An Allegory?" *ET* 51 (1939-40) 250-251.

*Charles Lee Feinberg, "Job and the Nation Israel. Second Study: At the Mercy of the Critics," *BS* 97 (1940) 27-33.

*Charles Lee Feinberg, "Job and the Nation Israel. Third Study: Face to Face With the Lord," *BS* 97 (1940) 211-216.

P. A. Spalding, "The Poem of Job," *CongQL* 18 (1940) 190-299.

*William R. Seaman, "The Book of Job and the Problem of Suffering," *LCQ* 14 (1941) 52-60.

C. E. B. Cranfield, "An Interpretation of the Book of Job," *ET* 54 (1942-43) 295-298.

J. R. Coates, "The Gospel of Job," *OSHTP* (1942-43) 27-31.

*Ralph Rogers Hawthorne, "Jobine Theology," *BS* 101 (1944) 64-75, 173-186, 290-303, 417-433; 102 (1945) 37-54.

*A. A. Jones, "The Problem of Suffering in the Book of Job," *EQ* 16 (1944) 282-293.

*S. L. Terrien, "The Babylonian Dialogue on Theodicy and the Book of Job," *JBL* 63 (1944) vi.

Henry S. Gehman, "סֵפֶר an Inscription, in the Book of Job," *JBL* 63 (1944) 303-307.

*B[enjamin] Maisler, "The Genealogy of the Sons of Nahor and the Historical Background of the Book of Job," *Zion* 11 (1945-46) #1, I.

Charles Lee Feinberg, "The Poetic Structure of Job and the Ugaritic Literature," *BS* 103 (1946) 283-292.

*Pascal P. Parente, "The Book of Job: Reflections on the Mystic Value of Human Suffering," *CBQ* 8 (1946) 213-219

W. A. Wordsworth, "Job's Murmurings," *EQ* 18 (1946) 169-172.

*Peter Katz, "Notes on the Septuagint, IV. *Ἔα δέ let alone* in Job," *JTS* 47 (1946) 168-169.

Gillis Gerleman, "Studies in the Septuagint. I. Book of Job," *AULLUÅ, N.S.*, 43 (1947) #2, 1-86.

*Titus Ludes, "Job and the Wisdom of God," *Scotist* 6 (1947) 43-48.

J. Steinmann, "The Book of Job," *LofS* 3 (1948-49) 24-31. *(Trans. by K. Pond)*

J. Steinmann, "Job, God's Witness," *LofS* 3 (1948-49) 118-124. *(Trans. by K. Pond)*

Ralph Marcus, "Job and God," *RR* 14 (1949-50) 5-29.

*William A. Irwin, "Job and Prometheus," *JR* 30 (1950) 90-108.

Otto J. Baab, "Studia Biblica. XV. The Book of Job," *Interp* 5 (1951) 329-343.

Theodore O. Wedel, "I Hate Myself," *Interp* 5 (1951) 427-431.

*R. K. Harrison, "The Problem of Suffering and the Book of Job," *EQ* 25 (1953) 18-27.

H[illel A.] Fine, "The Patient Job," *JBL* 72 (1953) vi-vii.

Donald H. Gard, "The Concept of Job's Character According to the Greek Translator of the Hebrew Text," *JBL* 72 (1953) 182-186.

Max Laseron, "Power and Justice. *Hobbs Versus Job*," *Jud* 2 (1953) 52-60.

Walter R. Roehers, "The Theme of the Book of Job," *CTM* 25 (1954) 298-302.

*Maximiliano Garcia Cordero, "Corporal Resurrection in the Book of Job," *TD* 2 (1954) 90-93.

Hillel A. Fine, "The Tradition of a Patient Job," *JBL* 74 (1955) 28-32.

Victor White, "Jung on Job," *NB* 36 (1955) 52-60.

Lester J. Kuyper, "The Repentance of Job," *RefR* 9 (1955-56) #4, 30-44.

W. S. Taylor, "Theology and Therapy in Job," *TT* 12 (1955-56) 451-462.

*David S. Shapiro, "The Problem of Evil and the Book of Job," *Jud* 5 (1956) 46-52.

Jean Danielou, "The Meaning of Job," *TD* 4 (1956) 189. *[Synopsis]*

William Lillie, "The Religious Significance of the Theophany in the Book of Job," *ET* 68 (1956-57) 355-358.

M[itchell] Dahood, "Some Northwest-Semitic Words in Job," *B* 38 (1957) 306-320.

Harry M. Orlinsky, "Studies in the Septuagint of Job," *HUCA* 28 (1957) 53-74; 29 (1958) 229-271; 30 (1959) 153-168; 32 (1961) 239-268; 33 (1962) 119-151; 35 (1964) 37-47; 36 (1965) 57-78.

Nahum M. Sarna, "Epic Substratum in the Prose of Job," *JBL* 76 (1957) 13-25.

P. Peters, "Isagogical Study of the Book of Job," *WLQ* 55 (1958) 272-295.

H. H. Rowley, "The Book of Job and Its Meaning," *BJRL* 41 (1958-59) 167-207.

Arthur Foote, "Job—Fore-Runner of Existentialism?" *UC* 14 (1958-59) #4, 5-9, 14.

R. A. F. Mackenzie, "The Purpose of the Yahweh Speeches in the Book of Job," *B* 40 (1959) 435-445.

* Mary Frances Thelen, "*J.B.*, Job, and the Biblical Doctrine of Man," *JAAR* 27 (1959) 201-205.

*Mitchell Dahood, "The Root עוב II in Job," *JBL* 78 (1959) 303-309.

R. A. F. Mackenzie, "The purpose of the Yahweh speeches in the book of Job," *SBO* 1 (1959) 301-311.

Lester J. Kuyper, "The Repentance of Job," *VT* 9 (1959) 91-94.

*James Wood, "The Idea of Life in the Book of Job," *GUOST* 18 (1959-60) 29-37.

Hugh Anderson, "Another Perspective on the Book of Job," *GUOST* 18 (1959-60) 53-56.

Kenneth Thompson Jr., "Out of the Whirlwind. *The Sense of Alienation in the Book of Job*," *Interp* 14 (1960) 51-63.

A. Piper, "The Book of Job and its Significance for Preaching and the Cure of Souls," *WLQ* 57 (1960) 50-71, 118-141, 197-219. *(Trans. by J. A. Fricke and A. Schuteze)*

Patrick W. Skehan, "Strophic Patterns in the Book of Job," *CBQ* 23 (1961) 125-142.

*S. G. F. Brandon, "The Book of Job: Its Significance for the History of Religions," *HT* 11 (1961) 547-554.

Wilhelm Vischer, "God's Truth and Man's Lie. *A Study of the Message of the Book of Job*," *Interp* 15 (1961) 131-146. *(Trans. by Donald G. Miller)*

Eugene Goodheart, "Job and the Modern World," *Jud* 10 (1961) 21-28.

Margaret B. Crook and Samuel A. Eliot, "Tracing Job's Story," *HJ* 60 (1961-62) 323-329.

*David S. Shapiro, "The Book of Job and the the Trial of Abraham," *Trad* 4 (1961-62) 210-220.

William A. Irwin, "Job's Redeemer," *JBL* 81 (1962) 217-229.

A. Guillaume, "The Unity of the Book of Job," *ALUOS* 4 (1962-63) 26-46.

A. Peters, "The Problem of the Book of Job," *AfER* 5 (1963) 55-60.

Gilmore H. Guyot, "Reflections on the Book of Job," *BibT* #7 (1963) 452-456.

*Maurice Friedman, "The Modern Job. On Melville, Dostoievsky, and Kafka," *Jud* 12 (1963) 436-455.

*Robert Hillis Goldsmith, "The Healing Scourge. *A Study in Suffering and Meaning*," *Interp* 17 (1963) 271-279.

G. W. Anderson, "Old Testament Books," *PQL* 9 (1963) 319-325. [IX. Job]

Steven Riskin, "Job," *YR* 3 (1963) 59-65.

H. Joel Laks, "The Enigma of Job: Maimonides and the Moderns," *JBL* 83 (1964) 345-364.

Robert Gordis, "The Lord out of the Whirlwind. The Climax and Meaning of Job," *Jud* 13 (1964) 48-63.

Gerald A. Laurie, "The Book of Job, on the Futility of Theological Discussion," *Person* 45 (1964) 72-79.

James K. Zink, "Impatient Job," *JBL* 84 (1965) 147-152.

Matitiahu Tsevat, "The Meaning of the Book of Job," *HUCA* 37 (1966) 73-106.

Nahum N. Glatzer, "The Book of Job and its Interpreters," *LIST* 3 (1966) 197-220.

Leonard S. Kravitz, "Maimonides and Job: An Inquiry as to the Method of the *Moreh*," *HUCA* 38 (1967) 149-158.

David Noel Freedman, "The Elihu Speeches in the Book of Job. A Hypothetical Episode in the Literary History of the Work," *HTR* 61 (1968) 51-59.

*J. Murtagh, "The Book of Job and the Book of the Dead," *ITQ* 35 (1968) 166-173.

Norman D. Hirsh, "The Architecture of the Book of Job," *CCARJ* 16 (1969) #1, 32-35.

D[avid] N[oel] Freedman, "Orthographic Peculiarities in the Book of Job," *EI* 9 (1969) 35-44. *[Non-Hebrew Section]*

H. L. Ginsberg, "Job the patient and Job the impatient," *VTS* 17 (1969) 88-111.

Daniel Jeremy Silver, "Nachmanides' Commentary of the Book of Job," *JQR, N.S.,* 60 (1969-70) 9-26.

§382 *3.2.11.1.2 Studies concerning Date, Authorship, Sources, and Authenticity*

F. G. Vaihinger, "On the Age of the Book of Job," *BRCM* 2 (1846) 93-108.

F. G. Vaihinger, "The Date of the Book of Job," *BRCR, 3rd Ser.,* 3 (1847) 174-188.

*Ludwig Hirzel, "Introduction to the Book of Job," *BS* 7 (1850) 144-162. [6. Time and Place of the Composition of the Book, pp. 159-162] *(Trans. by William C. Duncan)*

*Henry Ferguson, "The Authenticity of Job, XXXII-XXXVII," *CR* 29 (1877) 420-434.

E. J. Dillon, "The Original Poem of Job," *ContR* 64 (1893) 108-156.

Duncan B. Macdonald, "The Original form of the legend of Job," *JBL* 14 (1895) 63-71.

Duncan B. Macdonald, "Some External Evidence of the Original Form of the Legend of Job," *AJSL* 14 (1897-98) 137-164.

Helen Hawley Nichols, "The Composition of the Elihu Speeches," *AJSL* 27 (1910-11) 97-186.

*George A. Barton, "The Composition of Job 24-30," *JBL* 30 (1911) 66-77.

Gerry W. Hazelton, "The Book of Job—Who Wrote It?" *BS* 71 (1914) 573-581.

H. Beveridge, "The Date of the Book of Job," *JRAS* (1919) 234.

Victor L. Trumper, "The Date of the Book of Job," *JRAS* (1919) 586-587.

*J. C. Jacoby, "The Book of Job: Its Author and Its Doctrine," *LQ* 51 (1921) 182-189.

*G. R. Driver, "Some Recent Discoveries in Babylonian Literature. III.—The Righteous Sufferer," *Theo* 8 (1924) 123-130.

Judah J. Slotki, "The Origin of the Book of Job," *ET* 39 (1927-28) 131-134.

Charles Roads, "Abraham, Author of the Book of Job," *MR* 112 (1929) 456-458.

Elizabeth L. Foote, "Who Wrote Job?" *MR* 112 (1929) 609-610.

Charles Roads, "Abraham, Author of the Book of Job," *CFL, 3rd Ser.,* 36 (1930) 375-377.

Frank Hugh Foster, "Is the Book of Job a Translation from an Arabic Original?" *AJSL* 49 (1932-33) 21-45.

*A. P. Drucker, "The Book of Job," *OC* 49 (1935) 65-78. [The Date and Composition of Job, pp.70-72]

F. A. Aston, "Some Theories of the Date of the Book of Job," *EQ* 10 (1938) 92-112.

Walter G. Williams, "Relative Dating of Additions to Job," *IR* 17 (1960) #1, 11-14.

§383 *3.2.11.1.3 Literary Criticism of the Psalms - General Studies*

*†Anonymous, "Travell on the Psalms," *BCQTR* 6 (1795) 625-628. *(Review)*

†Anonymous, "Reeves on the Psalms," *BCQTR* 17 (1801) 341-350, 624-637. *(Review)*

†Anonymous, "Gedd's Translation of the Psalms," *BCQTR* 33 (1809) 355-358. *(Review)*

*Anonymous, "Remarks on the Curses in the Psalms," *MR* 1 (1818) 175-177.

[H. Ware(?)], "Cotton Mather's Psalms," *CD, N.S.,* 4 (1822) 325-332. *(Review)*

*†Anonymous, "The Book of Psalms," *BCQTR, N.S.,* 23 (1825) 252-255. *(Review)*

*†Anonymous, "New Translations of the Book of Psalms," *BCQTR, 4th Ser.,* 9 (1831) 404-440. *(Review)*

[Wilhelm Martin Leberecht] De Wette, "Introduction to the Psalms," *BRCR* 3 (1833) 445-518. *(Trans. by J. Torrey)*

Anonymous, "A New Translation of the Book of Psalms, with an Introduction. By George R. Noyes," *CE* 11 (1831) 99-109. *(Review)*

Anonymous, "Bush's Commentary on the Book of Psalms," *PRev* 7 (1835) 73-89. *(Review)*

*†Anonymous, "The Christian Use of the Psalms of David," *DR* 23 (1847) 27-58. *(Review)*

*†Anonymous, "Translation of the Hebrew Psalter," *ERL* 7 (1847) 71-87. *(Review)*

M. N., "Hengstenberg and Phillips on the Psalms," *BRCM* 4 (1847-48) 145-172. *(Review)*

Anonymous, "Hupfeld's Commentary on the Psalms," *AThR* 1 (1859) 688-698. *(Review)*

Anonymous, "De Burgh on the Psalms," *DUM* 55 (1860) 741-745. *(Review)*

S. P. T., "Some Modern Commentators on the Book of Psalms," *JSL, 3rd Ser.*, 11 (1860) 182-185.

*†Anonymous, "Perowne on the Psalms," *LQHR* 24 (1865) 267-315. *(Review)*

William Lee, "Alternate Versions of the Psalms," *JSL, 4th Ser.*, 10 (1866-67) 1-21.

Anonymous, "Interpretation of the Psalms," *BFER* 16 (1867) 374-383. *(Review)*

Anonymous, "The Position of the Book of Psalms in the Plan of the Old Testament," *PRev* 39 (1867) 256-287.

Anonymous, "Revised English Version of the Psalms," *DR, N.S.*, 18 (1872) 351-362. *[Revised Douay] (Original numbering as Vol. 70)*

Thomas H. Gill, "Watts in his Dealings with the Psalms," *CongL* 5 (1876) 424-439.

John Henry Hopkins, "Neale and Littledale on the Psalms," *CR* 28 (1876) 388-409. *(Review)*

*W. Gray Elmslie, "The Place of the Psalms in Modern Apologetic," *BFER* 26 (1877) 726-755.

N. S. Folsom, "The Book of Psalms," *URRM* 7 (1877) 624-639. *(Review)*

*John DeWitt, "Bible Revision and the Psalms," *PR* 1 (1880) 499-525.

*H. F. Woolrych, "The Prayer-Book and Bible Version of the Psalms," *CM* 15 (1882) 321-331.

Geo. Dana Broadman, "The Alphabetical Psalms," *ONTS* 5 (1884-85) 334-335.

C[rawford] H. Toy, "On Maccabean Psalms," *URRM* 26 (1886) 1-21.

*A. J. Maas, "The Use of Pesiq in the Psalms," *AJSL* 5 (1888-89) 121-130.

Anonymous, "The Psalms and Modern Criticism," *LQHR* 72 (1889) 1-22. *(Review)*

C. G. Montefiore, "Mystic Passages in the Psalms," *JQR* 1 (1888-89) 143-161.

*W. Pakenham Walsh, "From 'The Voices of the Psalms'," *CM, N.S.,* 8 (1890) 65-72.

Anonymous, "Delitzsch on 'The Psalms'," *EN* 2 (1890) 85-86.

L. W. Batten, "Duplicates in the Psalter," *ONTS* 13 (1891) 16-20.

C[laude] R. Conder, "Notes by Major Conder. V. Quotations of Psalms," *PEFQS* 23 (1891) 71. (Corr. p. 186)

C[laude] R. Conder, "Quotations of Psalms," *PEFQS* 23 (1891) 183-184.

A. J. Maas, "The Use of Paseq in the Psalms. II," *AJSL* 8 (1891-92) 89-97.

S. C. Bartlett, "Cheyne on the Psalter," *BS* 49 (1892) 292-312. *(Review)*

W. W. Davies, "Origin and Religious Contents of the Psalter," *MR* 74 (1892) 884-901. *(Review)*

*George H. Schodde, "Post-Exilic Legalism and Post-Exilic Literature," *ONTS* 15 (1892) 201-206.

Alex. Cumming, "On Some of the Psalms," *ET* 4 (1892-93) 322-323.

*Henry Hayman, "The Evidence of the Psalter to a Levitical System," *BS* 50 (1893) 238-260.

E. Nestle, "Pathros in the Psalms," *JAOS* 15 (1893) cviii-cix.

Howard Osgood, "The Two-Edged Sword in the Psalms," *HR* 28 (1894) 99-105.

*G. Buchanan Gray, "The References to the 'King' in the Psalter, in their Bearing on the Questions of Date and Messianic Belief," *JQR* 7 (1894-95) 658-686.

*G. Buchanan Gray, "The References to the 'King' in the Psalter, in their Bearing on (A) Questions of Date, (B) Messianic Belief," *OSHTP* (1894-95) 27-29.

H. B. Swete, "St. Jerome on the Psalms," *Exp, 5th Ser.,* 1 (1895) 424-434.

Eugene R. Hendrix, "The Throne of Praises: A Study in the Psalms," *MQR* 18 (1895) 55-66.

T. K. Cheyne, "Some Aspects of the Criticism of the Psalms," *OSHTP* (1895-96) 39-44.

G. R. Wynne, "Notes on the Collocation of the Psalms," *CM, 3rd Ser.,* 11 (1896) 166-177.

*†Anonymous, "The Psalms in History," *QRL* 185 (1897) 305-330. *(Review)*

F. H. Woods, "A New Critical and Devotional Commentary on the Psalms," *ET* 9 (1897-98) 322-326. *(Review)*

Frants Buhl, "The Aid of Criticism in the Interpretation of the Psalms," *AJT* 2 (1898) 763-775.

*T. K. Cheyne, "The New Versions of the Psalter and the Book of Judges," *Exp, 5th Ser.,* 7 (1898) 259-275.

Carl Heinrich Cornill, "The Psalms in Universal Literature," *OC* 12 (1898) 449-466. *(Trans. by W. H. Carruth)*

Anonymous, "The Psalms and the New Criticism," *CQR* 48 (1899) 31-54.

George H. Schodde, "Problems of the Psalms," *HR* 39 (1900) 164-165.

*D. S. Margoliouth, "Lines of Defence of the Biblical Revelation. 4. The Argument from Silence," *Exp, 6th Ser.,* 2 (1900) 129-154. *[Psalms]*

Parke P. Flournoy, "The Psalms Not Post-Exilic," *CFL, N.S.,* 3 (1901) 60.

E. H. Dewart, "The Psalms of David," *MQR, 3rd Ser.,* 28 (1902) 583-590.

*William T. Allison, "The Poetry of the Psalms," *BW* 22 (1903) 42-48.

E. G. King, "The Influence of the Triennial Cycle on the Psalter," *JTS* 5 (1903-04) 203-213.

Robert Cameron, "New Light on the Psalms," *BS* 61 (1904) 689-710.

Robert Cameron, "New Light on the Psalms," *CLF, 3rd Ser.,* 1 (1904) 460-470.

Henry Nelson Bullard, "An Introduction to the Study of the Psalms," *CFL, 3rd Ser.*, 2 (1905) 220-223.

*W. T. Allison, "The Nature-Poetry of the Psalms," *BW* 28 (1906) 87-93, 261-273. *[Parts I and II]*

P[atrick] V. Higgins, "On the Study of the Psalms," *IER, 4th Ser.*, 20 (1906) 127-132.

F. W. Klingensmith, "The Psalter and the New Testament. I," *LCR* 25 (1906) 457-465.

F. W. Klingensmith, "The Psalter and the New Testament. II," *LCR* 25 (1906) 711-718.

Wm. G. Seiple, "Maccabean Psalms," *RChR, 4th Ser.*, 10 (1906) 191-197.

*W. T. Allison, "The Nature-Poetry of the Psalms," *BW* 29 (1907) 208-216. *[Part III]*

*W. T. Allison, "The Nature-Poetry of the Psalms. IV. The Mountains, Sea, Trees and Flowers," *BW* 30 (1907) 111-117.

T. K. Cheyne, "Maccabaean Psalms," *IJA* #11 (1907) 3-5.

Arthur Stanley Pease, "Notes on St. Jerome's Tractates on the Psalms," *JBL* 16 (1907) 107-131.

*A. C. Baird, "Hebrew and Babylonian Psalms: A Comparison," *GUOST* 3 (1907-12) 27-30.

Crawford Howell Toy, "On Some Conceptions of the Old Testament Psalter," *AJT* 12 (1908) 1-33.

*P[atrick] V. Higgins, "David's Life a Key to the Psalms and Vice Versa," *IER, 4th Ser.*, 24 (1908) 283-289.

Kemper Fullerton, "Studies in the Psalter," *BW* 36 (1910) 176-192, 252-267, 323-328, 395-406; 37 (1911) 48-58, 128-136, 189-198.

*S. R. Driver, "The Method of Studying the Psalter. With Special Application to Some of the Messianic Psalms," *Exp, 7th Ser.*, 9 (1910) 20-41.

*John P. Peters, "Notes on Some Ritual Uses of the Psalms," *JBL* 29 (1910) 113-125.[1. Tehillim, pp. 113-114; 2. The Tehillah of the Thank Offering, pp. 114-116; 3. A Babylonian and Hebrew Ritual Phrase, pp. 116-118; 4. The Ritual of the Penitential Psalms, pp. 118-121; 5. Selah, p. 121; 6. Maskil, p. 122-125]

Frank Holmes, "The Abiding Religious Value of the Hebrew Psalter," *ICMM* 8 (1911-12) 56-67.

*E. G. King, "The Covenant of Creation in the Psalms," *ICMM* 8 (1911-12) 410-421.

George Adam Smith, "The Natural Strength of the Psalms," *Exp, 8th Ser.,* 8 (1912) 1-15.

*Kemper Fullerton, "The International Critical Commentary on Genesis, Chronicles, and the Psalms," *HTR* 5 (1912) 20-109. *(Review)*

John Muir, "The Personal Element in the Psalter," *GUOST* 4 (1913-22) 22-24.

*William Fulton, "The Temple in the Psalter," *GUOST* 4 (1913-22) 24-25.

C. J. Ritchie, "Nature in the Psalter," *GUOST* 4 (1913-22) 26-27.

*Duncan Cameron, "The Covenants in the Psalter," *GUOST* 4 (1913-22) 27-29, 84.

C. J. Ritchie, "The Personal Piety of the Psalter," *GUOST* 4 (1913-22) 29-31.

A. T. Burbridge, "The Autobiographic Element in the Psalms, *ICMM* 11 (1914-15) 95-106.

*H. St. J. Thackeray, "The Song of Hannah and Other Lessons and Psalms for the Jewish New Year's Day," *JTS* 16 (1914-15) 177-203.

J. Gregory Smith, "The Hebrew Psalter," *MC* 4 (1914-15) 246-250.

John P. Peters, "Hebrew Psalmody," *HTR* 9 (1916) 36-55. *(Review)*

J[ohn] P. Peters, "Ritual in the Psalms," *JBL* 35 (1916) 143-154.

*Oswald T. Allis, "The Bearing of Archaeology on the Higher Criticism of the Psalms," *PSB* 10 (1916) #3, 12-14.

John E. M'Fadyen, "The Psalter and the Present Distress," *ET* 28 (1916-17) 245-249, 305-307, 373-377.

*Oswald T. Allis, "The Bearing of Archaeology upon the Higher Criticism of the Psalms," *PTR* 15 (1917) 277-324.

G. C. Binyon, "The Mystical Interpretation of the Psalms," *ET* 29 (1917-18) 343-348.

A. R. Gordon, "Pioneers in the Study of Old Testament Poetry. Ley and the Metricists," *ET* 29 (1917-18) 541-547.

A. R. Howell, "The Re-Discovery of the Psalms," *ET* 29 (1917-18) 558-559.

H. J. D. Astley, "Mythology in the Psalms," *ICMM* 14 (1917-18) 305-315.

A. R. Howell, "The Re-Discovery of the Psalms. II.," *ET* 30 (1918-19) 35-36.

*C. G. Montefiore, "The Psalter: Its Contents and Date," *QRL* 230 (1918) 1-20. *(Review)*

Harris B. Stewart, "The Out of Door World in the Psalms," *ASRec* 15 (1919) 215-225.

*J. Richie Smith, "The Proverbs," *HR* 78 (1919) 318-322. *[Psalms] (Sermon)*

John P. Peters, "Notes of Locality in the Psalter," *JPOS* 1 (1920-21) 122-131.

M. R. James, "Robert Grosseteste on the Psalms," *JTS* 23 (1921-22) 181-185.

William H. Bates, "The Book of Psalms," *CFL, 3rd Ser.,* 28 (1922) 30-32.

Frederick G. Powicke, "Richard Baxter's Paraphrase of the Psalms," *ET* 35 (1923-24) 471-474.

Moses Buttenweiser, "The Importance of the Tenses for the Interpretation of the Psalms," *HUCA, Jubilee Volume* (1925) 89-112.

*F. Herbert Stead, "The Idea of God in the Psalms. I.," *ET* 37 (1925-26) 547-551.

*F. Herbert Stead, "The Idea of God in the Psalms. II.," *ET* 38 (1926-27) 18-20.

R[obert] Dick Wilson, "The Radical Criticism of the Psalter," *JTVI* 59 (1927) 256-270. [(Discussion, pp. 270-278) (Communications by J. J. B. Coles, p. 278; H. Biddulph, pp. 278-279; W. C. Edwards, pp. 279-280; Percy O. Ruoff, p. 280)]

*R[obert] Dick Wilson, "The Names of God in the Psalms," *PTR* 25 (1927) 1-39.

Theodore R. Robinson, "Recent Research in the Book of Psalms," *CQR* 106 (1928) 335-352. *(Review)*

Harris B. Stewart, "The Psalter and Modern Life," *ASRec* 24 (1928-29) 149-162.

David E. Culley, "Some Recent Studies in the Psalter," *BWTS* 21 (1928-29) 189-201.

*Henry E. Donnelly, "Nationalism in the Psalms," *SS* 3 (1929) #1, 44-49.

Dorothy Carver, "Nature in the Psalms," *R&E* 28 (1931) 410-416.

†[Gordon] Cumming, "The Religion of the Psalms," *AABTS* 6 (1931-32) #1, 2-3.

Earle Bennet Cross, "Limitations of Some Psalms," *CRDSB* 4 (1931-32) 73-86.

*W. Emery Barnes, "Hebrew Metre and the Text of the Psalms," *JTS* 33 (1931-32) 374-382.

H. J. Flowers, "The Book of Psalms," *R&E* 29 (1932) 417-435.

W. K. Lowther Clarke, "Notes. I.—Gunkel on the Psalms," *Theo* 25 (1932) 282-284.

*Algernon Ward, "Jerome's Work on the Psalter," *ET* 44 (1932-33) 87-92.

James A. Montgomery, "Recent Developments in the Study of the Psalter," *ATR* 16 (1934) 185-198.

Shalom Spiegel, "Liturgies of Departure in the Psalter," *JBL* 53 (1934) ix.

*W. Leonard, "Sionism in the Psalter," *ACR* 13 (1936) 118-134.

*Oscar N. Olson, "The Ethical Concepts of the Psalms," *AQ* 15 (1936) 348-361.

*W. Emery Barnes, "A Note on the Meaning of יעקב יעקב (אלהי יעקב) in the Psalter," *JTS* 38 (1937) 405-410. *[The God of Jacob]*

Norman H. Snaith, "After Fifty Years. V. The Background of the Psalms," *ET* 50 (1938-39) 246-249.

*Michael J. Gruenthaner, "The Future Life in the Psalms," *CBQ* 2 (1940) 57-63.

Ovid R. Sellers, "Self-Pity in the Psalms," *CQ* 18 (1941) 297-300.

E. R. Rowlands, "Inner-Syriac Corruptions in the Book of Psalms," *JTS* 42 (1941) 65-67.

John Maclean, "The Sure Mercies of David," *EQ* 14 (1942) 128-138. *[Thematic treatment]*

B. D. Eerdmans, "Sojourn in the Tent of Jahu," *OTS* 1 (1942) 1-16.

*B. D. Eerdmans, "Psalm XIV, LIII and the Elohim-Psalms," *OTS* 1 (1942) 258-267.

*David de Sola Pool, "The Constructive Use of כל in the Book of Psalms," *PAAJR* 13 (1943) 41-46.

*C. M. Cooper, "The Divine Personal Pronoun in the Psalms," *JBL* 64 (1945) iii.

William F. Lynch, "A Simpler Theory of Literature," *MH* 2 (1945-46) #1, 6-8.

*B. D. Eerdmans, "The Hebrew Book of Psalms," *OTS* 4 (1947) 1-610. [Introduction, 1; I. The so-called Hymnbook of the Second Temple, 2-6; II. The Classes of Psalms (Gattungsforschung) 6-11; III. Metric System, 11-14; IV. Collection of the Psalms, 14-27; V. Established Religion: The Enemies of the Psalms, 27-35; VI. Origin and Date of Psalms, 35-44; VII. The Singers, 45-51; VIII. Titles and Technical Terms: Oriental Music and Western Singing, 51-90 (Lammenazzeah 'al Hassheminith, 54-61; 'al 'alamoth and other Terms, 61-80; *Selah,* 80-90); Pss. I-CL, 91-610]

‡Edward P. Arbez, "Recent Publications on the Psalms," *AER* 119 (1948) 105-114, 187-195.

Charles Lee Feinberg, "The Uses of the Psalter," *BS* 105 (1948) 154-169, 463-477.

James A. Kleist, "Toward a More Rhythmical Rendering of the Psalms," *CBQ* 11 (1949) 66-75.

P. P. Saydon, "The Origin of the 'Polyglot' Arabic Psalms," *B* 31 (1950) 226-236.

N. H. Tur-Sinai, "The Literary Character of the Book of Psalms," *OTS* 8 (1950) 263-281.

A. v. R. Sauer, "The Book of Psalms," *CTM* 21 (1950) 518-520. *(Review)*

John Paterson, "A Fresh Approach to the Psalter," *DG* 20 (1950) #2/3, 9-13.

Elmer A. Leslie, "Studia Biblica IX. The Book of Psalms," *Interp* 4 (1950) 62-77.

*John Paterson, "The Psalms and the Cult," *GUOST* 14 (1950-52) 42-47.

Sigmund Mowinckel, "Traditionalism and Personality in the Psalms," *HUCA* 23 (1950-51) Part 1, 205-231.

*(Sister) St. Catherine Nestor, "Music in the Psalms," *ABenR* 2 (1951) 190-193.

J. H. Darby, "Jewish Psalms and Christian Prayers," *ClR* 35 (1951) 25-33.

G. Lacey May, "The Catholicity of the Psalter," *CQR* 152 (1951) 180-190.

Reginald Glanville, "The Psalms and the Resurrection of Jesus," *LQHR* 176 (1951) 209-215.

A. G. Matthews, "From the Margins of a Psalter," *CongQL* 30 (1952) 113-117.

R. Loewe, "Herbert of Bosham's Commentary on Jerome's Hebrew Psalter," *B* 34 (1953) 44-77, 159-192, 275-298.

*A. R. Crabtree, "The Revised Standard Version of the Psalms," *R&E* 50 (1953) 443-452.

Balthasar Fischer, "Christ in the Psalms," *TD* 1 (1953) 53-58.

*Mitchell Dahood, "The Divine Name 'Ēlî in the Psalms," *ThSt* 14 (1953) 452-457.

*Mitchell Dahood, "The Root GMR in the Psalms," *ThSt* 14 (1953) 595-597.

*John Fearon, "The Psalms and Prayer," *C&C* 7 (1955) 330-336.

*Cecil S. Emden, "The Psalmist's Emphasis on God's Kindness," *CQR* 156 (1955) 233-235.

Bernard Hall, "The Problem of Retribution in the Psalms," *Scrip* 7 (1955) 84-92.

S[igmund] Mowinckel, "Psalm Criticism between 1900 and 1935," *VT* 5 (1955) 13-33.

*S[igmund] Mowinckel, "Psalms and wisdom," *VTS* 3 (1955) 205-224.

Dom Gregory Murray, "The Psalms: A Rhythmic Restoration Leads to a Popular Revival," *DownsR* 74 (1955-56) 95-102.

*Edgar Jones, "Suffering in the Psalter: A Study of the Problem of Suffering in the Book of Psalms," *CongQL* 34 (1956) 53-63.

*Arthur Soffer, "The Treatment of Anthropomorphisms and Anthropopathisms in the Septuagint of Psalms," *HUCA* 28 (1957) 85-107.

Walter G. Williams, "Liturgical Aspects in Enthronement Psalms," *JAAR* 25 (1957) 118-122.

John M. Stensvaag, "Recent Approaches to the Psalms," *LQ, N.S.,* 9 (1957) 195-212.

*William Green, "Ancient Comment on Instrumental Music in the Psalms," *RestQ* 1 (1957) 3-8.

Joseph Bourke, "Supplication in the Psalms," *NB* 39 (1958) 16-22.

*S. B. Frost, "Asseveration by Thanksgiving,"*VT* 8 (1958) 380-390.

Edmund Hill, "The Psalms and Everyday Life," *LofS* 13 (1958-59) 99-105.

Martin Luther, "Martin Luther's Preface to the Book of Psalms," *BofT* #17 (1959) 27-30.

S. B. Frost, "The Christian Interpretation of the Psalms," *CJT* 5 (1959) 25-34.

Roland E. Murphy, "A New Classification of Literary Forms in the Psalms," *CBQ* 21 (1959) 83-87.

Robert G. Boling, "'Synonymous' Parallelism in the Psalms," *JSS* 5 (1960) 221-255.

Bernard Jones, "A Version of the Psalms," *LQHR* 185 (1960) 216-220. *[William Barnes 'Version']*

*Prosper Grech, "The Experience of Sin in the Psalms," *Scrip* 12 (1960) 106-112.

Svend Holm-Nielsen, "The Importance of Late Jewish Psalmody for the Understanding of Old Testament Psalmodic Tradition," *ST* 14 (1960) 1-53.

*N. E. Wagner, "רִנָּה" in the Psalter," *VT* 10 (1960) 435-442.

*O. Linton, "Interpretation of the Psalms in the Early Church," *StP* 4 (1961) 143-156.

*R. E. Clements, "Temple and Land: A Significant Aspect of Israel's Worship," *GUOST* 19 (1961-62) 16-28.

*Helmer Ringgren, "Enthronement Festival or Covenant Renewal?" *BRes* 7 (1962) 45-48.

*C. J. Labuschagne, "Some Remarks on the Translation and Meaning of ʾāmartî in the Psalms," *OTW* 5 (1962) 27-33.

Martin J. Buss, "The Psalms of Asapha and Korah," *JBL* 82 (1963) 382-392.

*Chr. Brekelmans, "Pronominal suffixes in the Hebrew Book of Psalms," *JEOL* #17 (1963) 202-206.

*Nic. N. Ridderbos, "The Psalms: Style-Figures and Structures (certain considerations, with special reference to Pss. xxii, xxv, and xlv)," *OTS* 13 (1963) 43-97.

S. du Toit, "The Psalms and History," *OTW* 6 (1963) 18-29.

J. J. Glueck, "Some Remarks On the Introductory Notes of The Psalms," *OTW* 6 (1963) 30-39.

J. H. Kroeze, "Some Remarks On Recent Trends in The Exegesis Of The Psalms," *OTW* 6 (1963) 40-47.

*L. M. Muntingh, "A Few Social Concepts In The Psalms And Their Relation To The Canaanite Residential Area," *OTW* 6 (1963) 48-57.

*I. H. Eybers, "The Stem S-P-T in The Psalms," *OTW* 6 (1963) 58-63.

*Roland E. Murphy, "A consideration of the classification 'Wisdom Psalms'," *VTS* 9 (1963) 156-167.

Gregory Murray and Daniel Rees, "A New Translation of the Psalms," *DownsR* 82 (1964) 36-46. [Part I - Its Origin and Purpose, by Gregory Murray, pp. 36-41; Part II - The Translation Examined, by Daniel Rees, pp. 41-46]

Julian Morgenstern, "The Cultic Setting of the 'Enthronement Psalms'," *HUCA* 35 (1964) 1-42.

Gerald J. Blidstein, "Nature in the 'Psalms'," *Jud* 13 (1964) 29-36.

Wallace I. Wolverton, "The Meaning of the Psalms," *ATR* 47 (1965) 16-33.

A. Kapelrud, "Scandinavian Research in the Psalms after Mowinckel," *ASTI* 4 (1965) 74-90.

Fr. Luke, "The Songs of Zion as a Literary Category of the Psalter," *IJT* 14 (1965) 72-90.

A. S. Herbert, "Our Present Understanding of the Psalms," *LQHR* 190 (1965) 25-29.

*Henry McKeating, "Divine Forgiveness in the Psalms," *SJT* 18 (1965) 69-83.

George W. Anderson, "Enemies and Evildoers in the Book of Psalms," *BJRL* 48 (1965-66) 18-29.

*J. A. Sanders, "The Psalter at the Time of Christ," *BibT* #22 (1966) 1462-1469.

*Peter R. Ackroyd and Michael A Knibb, "Translating the Psalms," *BTr* 17 (1966) 110.

I. D. L. Clark and B. A. Mastin, "Venite, Exultemus Domino: Some Reflections on the Interpretation of the Psalter," *CQR* 167 (1966) 413-424.

*D. R. Ap-Thomas, "An Appreciation of Sigmund Mowinckel's Contribution to Biblical Studies," *JBL* 85 (1966) 315-325. *[Psalm Criticism]*

*E. Reim, "Seasonal Psalms and Prophecy," *JTLC* 6 (1966) #5, 1-5.

*J. Shunary, "Avoidance of Anthropomorphism in the Targum of Psalms," *Text* 5 (1966) 133-144.

*Basil De Pinto, "The Torah and the Psalms," *JBL* 86 (1967) 154-174.

*Charles M. Cooper, "The Revised Standard Version of Psalms," *JQR, 75th* (1967) 137-148.

*D. J. A. Clines, "Psalm Research Since 1955: I. The Psalms and the Cult," *TB* #18 (1967) 103-126.

F. N. Jasper, "Early Israelite Traditions and the Psalter," *VT* 17 (1967) 50-59.

Khone Shmeruk, "Mendele's Translation of the Book of Psalms into Yiddish," *HS* 1 (1968-69) 448. *[English Summary]*

*N. A. van Uchelen, "אנשי דמים in the Psalms," *OTS* 15 (1969) 205-212.

*D. J. A. Clines, "Psalm Research Since 1955: II. The Literary Genres," *TB* #20 (1969) 105-125.

*Bezalel Safran, "The Problem of Theodicy in the Book of Psalms," *YR* 7 (1969) 63-68.

Arnold A. Anderson, "Psalm Study Between 1955 and 1969," *BQL* 23 (1969-70) 155-164.

§384 ***3.2.11.1.3.1 Studies concerning the Imprecatory Psalms***

*Anonymous, "Remarks on the Curses in the Psalms," *MR* 1 (1818) 175-177.

*W. C., "On the Imprecations of David. In what matter shall the imprecations of David in Ps. V. 10, and in other places, be reconciled with the spirit of piety, and the inspiration of the Psalms?" *QCS* 1 (1819) 613-616.

F. B., "The Interpretation of the Imprecatory Passages in the Psalms," *BRCM* 3 (1847) 199-210.

John J. Owen, "The Imprecatory Psalms," *BS* 13 (1856) 551-563.

Anonymous, "The Imprecatory Psalms," *PQR* 9 (1860-61) 575-588.

Edwards A. Park, "The Imprecatory Psalms, viewed in the light of the Southern Rebellion," *BS* 19 (1862) 165-210.

Anonymous, "The Imprecatory Psalms," *BFER* 13 (1864) 496-515.

Anonymous, "The Imprecatory Psalms," *TE* 2 (1865) 121-142.

Anonymous, "Interpretation of the Psalms," *BFER* 16 (1867) 374-383. *(Review)*

Joseph Hammond, "The Vindictive Psalms Vindicated," *Exp, 1s Ser.,* 3 (1876) 27-47, 101-118, 185-203, 452-471; 4 (1876) 56-70, 212-240.

Anonymous, "The Vindictive Psalms," *ERG, 8th Ser.,* 2 (1883-84) 246-254.

H. N. Bernard, "The Vindictive Psalms," *Exp, 2nd Ser.,* 7 (1884) 131-144.

A. S. Aglen, "The Vindictive Psalms," *Exp, 2nd Ser.,* 7 (1884) 357-365.

W. W. Davies, "The Imprecatory Psalms," *ONTS* 14 (1892) 154-159.

J. W. Beardslee, "The Imprecatory Psalms," *PRR* 8 (1897) 490-505.

J. A. DeBaun, "The Imprecatory Psalms," *PQ* 12 (1898) 45-56.

W. R. Worthington, "The Minatory Psalms," *HR* 39 (1900) 67.

John Hedley, "The Imprecatory Psalms," *ET* 15 (1903-04) 383.

Chalmers Martin, "The Imprecations in the Psalms," *PTR* 1 (1903) 537-553.

Edward Pfeiffer, "How Can the Imprecatory Psalms be Reconciled with the Spirit of the Gospel?" *ColTM* 27 (1907) 130-158.

T. K. Cheyne, "Maccabaean Psalms," *IJA* #11 (1907) 3-5.

Arthur Stanley Pease, "Notes on St. Jerome's Tractates on the Psalms," *JBL* 16 (1907) 107-131.

T. Barns, "The Psalms of Vengeance," *ET* 19 (1907-08) 185-187.

W. A. Jarrel, "The Hun and the Imprecatory Psalms," *BS* 76 (1919) 228-232.

W. A. Jarrel, "The Imprecatory Psalms," *R&E* 19 (1922) 460-464.

Edwin F. Keever, "The Imprecatory Psalms," *LCQ* 13 (1940) 131-142.

Johannes G. Vos, "The Ethical Problem of the Imprecatory Psalms," *WTJ* 4 (1941-42) 123-138.

*Thomas Smith, "Cursing Psalms: can we still pray them?" *AfER* 8 (1966) 324-328.

Joseph Rwampigi, "Cursing Psalms are Inspired, So What?" *AfER* 10 (1968) 68-70.

§385 **3.2.11.1.3.2 *Studies concerning the Songs of Degrees;
Songs of Ascent; Songs of Return***

(   ) M., "The Songs of Degrees," *JSL, 2nd Ser.,* 7 (1854-55) 39-53; *3rd
Ser.,* 1 (1855) 56-74. *[Psa. 120-134]*

W. W. Davis, "'The Songs of Degrees.'," *HR* 18 (1889) 66-68.

*John P. Peters, "Notes on the Pilgrim Psalter," *JBL* 13 (1894) 31-39.

Daniel Gurden Stevens Jr., "A Critical Commentary on the Songs of the
Return with a Historical Introduction and Indexes. Part I," *AJSL* 11
(1894-95) 1-100.

Daniel Gurden Stevens Jr., "A Critical Commentary on the Songs of the
Return with a Historical Introduction and Indexes. Part II," *AJSL* 11
(1894-95) 119-173.

Eneas B. Goodwin, "The Gradual Psalms," *AER* 14 (1896) 385-395.

J[ohn] P. Peters, "A Jerusalem Processional," *JBL* 39 (1920) 52-59.

J[ohn] P. Peters, "A Jerusalem Processional," *JPOS* 1 (1920) 36-41.

Herbert H. Gowen, "The Egyptian Hallel," *ATR* 9 (1926-27) 21-41. *[Psalms
111-117]*

W. R. Siegart, "A Study of the Pilgrim Psalms," *LCQ* 3 (1930) 397-413.

T. Torrance, "The Last of the Hallel Psalms," *EQ* 28 (1956) 101-128.
[Psalms 113-118]

Carl H. Lundquist, "Moods of Worship in the Songs of Degrees," *BSQ* 5
(1956-57) #2, 4-9. *[Psalms 120-134]*

§386 **3.2.11.1.3.3 *Studies concerning the "Messianic" Psalms***

Anonymous, "Tholuck on the Messianic Psalms," *BRCM* 5 (1848-49) 25-38.

John Page Hopps, "'The Witness of the Psalms to Christ and Christianity',"
URRM 17 (1882) 97-116. *(Review)*

T. K. Cheyne, "The Messianic Element in the Psalms," *ONTS* 3 (1883-84) 196-200.

*G. Buchanan Gray, "The References to the 'King' in the Psalter, in their Bearing on the Questions of Date and Messianic Belief," *JQR* 7 (1894-95) 658-686.

*G. B[uchanan] Gray, "The References to the 'King' in the Psalter, in their Bearing on (A) Questions of Date, (B) Messianic Belief," *OSHTP* (1894-95) 27-29.

*George Dahl, "The Messianic Expectation in the Psalter," *JBL* 57 (1938) 1-12.

*W. M. Mackay, "Messiah in the Psalms," *EQ* 11 (1939) 153-164.

Norbert J. McCarthy, "There Is a Picture in the Psalms," *SS* 15 (Jan., 1946) 50-59. *[The Messiah in the Psalms]*

*D. Paech, "Is Psalm 8 Messianic?" *AusTR* 27 (1956) 109-128.

S. H. Russell, "Calvin and the Messianic Interpretation of the Psalms," *SJT* 21 (1968) 37-47.

§387 *3.2.11.1.3.4 Studies concerning Titles and Divisions of the Psalms*

Anonymous, "The Titles of the Psalms," *CQR* 7 (1878-79) 370-392.

William Henry Green, "The Titles of the Psalms," *MR* 72 (1890) 489-506.

W[illiam] Henry Green, "The Title of the Psalms," *ONTS* 11 (1890) 153-167.

*Ad. Neubauer, "The Authorship and Titles of the Psalms according to early Jewish authorities," *SBE* 2 (1890) 1-58.

*Willis J. Beecher, "Hebrew Word Studies. The Word Maschil in the Psalm Titles," *HR* 33 (1897) 262.

Chalmers Martin, "The Inscriptions of the Psalms," *PRR* 11 (1900) 638-653.

*Ivan Panin, "The Titles of the Psalms," *BN* 1 (1904) #6, 178-184.

Robert Cameron, "'The New Key to the Psalm Titles'," *CFL, 3rd Ser.*, 1 (1904) 366-368.

Llewellyn L. Henson, "The Musical Titles of the Psalms," *R&E* 3 (1906) 562-570.

Eb. Nestle, "'The Titles of the Psalms'," *ET* 23 (1911-12) 383-384.

George R. Berry, "The Titles of the Psalms," *JBL* 33 (1914) 198-200.

T. Herbert Bindley, "The Titles of the Psalms," *ICMM* 13 (1916-17) 43-49.

*John P. Peters, "Notes on Some Ritual Uses of the Psalms," *JBL* 29 (1910) 113-125.[1. Tehillim, pp. 113-114; 2. The Tehillah of the Thank Offering, pp. 114-116; 6. Maskil, p. 122-125]

R[obert] D[ick] Wilson, "The Headings of the Psalms," *PTR* 24 (1926) 1-37, 353-395. [Proper Names in the Psalms, A. Simple Names for God, B. Composite Names for God, Words Alleged to be Late; Table of Hebrew Words; Headings of the Psalms, I. Kinds of Headings, II. Vocabulary of Headings, III. The Text of the Headings; Conclusions]

James Wm. Thistle, "Notes on the Titles of the Psalms," *CTSQ* 6 (1928-29) #1, 8-10.

Herbert Gordon May, "'Al....' in the Superscriptions of the Psalms," *AJSL* 58 (1941) 70-83.

*W. Wilson, "The Annotations to the Psalms: A New Theory," *Theo* 51 (1948) 52-59.

[Aurelius] Augustine, "A Sermon of St Augustine on the Title of Psalm 33: I," *LofS* 12 (1957-58) 29-34. *(Trans. by Edmund Hill)*

[Aurelius] Augustine, "A Sermon of St Augustine on the Title of Psalm 33: II," *LofS* 12 (1957-58) 79-82. *(Trans. by Edmund Hill)*

John F. A. Sayner, "An Analysis of the Context and Meaning of the Psalm-Headings," *GUOST* 22 (1967-68) 26-38.

I. Yevin, "The Division into Sections in the Book of Psalms," *Text* 7 (1969) 76-102.

§388　*3.2.11.1.3.5 Studies concerning "Selah"*

Anonymous, "The Meaning and Use of Selah," *DQR* 4 (1864) 214-247.

*†Anonymous, "Perowne on the Psalms," *LQHR* 24 (1865) 267-315. [Selah, pp. 303-305] *(Review)*

Anonymous, "The Meaning of the Word Selah," *ER* 20 (1869) 217-221.

C[harle]s A[ugustus] Briggs, "An Inductive Study of Selah," *JBL* 18 (1899) 132-143.

*John P. Peters, "Notes on Some Ritual Uses of the Psalms," *JBL* 29 (1910) 113-125. [5. Selah, p. 121]

Paul Haupt, "Selah as 'Reverential Prostration'," *ET* 22 (1910-11) 374-377.

F.　C.　Burkitt,　"Selah,"　*ICMM*　8　(1911-12)　98-99.

W. E[mery] Barnes, "Selah—Some Facts and a Suggestion," *JTS* 18 (1916-17) 263-273.

*I. W. Slotki, "A Lost Selah, and Psalm LXXV 9 [8]," *JTS* 20 (1918-19) 250-251.

E.　E.　Vernon,　"'Selah',"　*MR*　113　(1930)　446-447.

Norman　[H.]　Snaith,　"Selah,"　*VT*　2　(1952)　43-56.

§389　*3.2.11.1.3.6 Studies on the "Psalter"*

†Anonymous, "Versions of the Psalms," *BCQTR, 4th Ser.,* 15 (1834) 153-161. *(Review)*

†Anonymous, "Oxford Psalter in English Verse," *BCQTR, 4th Ser.,* 27 (1840) 1-23. *(Review)*

†Anonymous, "The Psalter, or Psalms of David, pointed for Chanting," *BCQTR, 4th Ser.,* 28 (1840) 371-390. *(Review)*

Anonymous, "Sacred Poetry," *CTPR, 3rd Ser.,* 3 (1847) 70-104. *(Review)*

†Anonymous, "Church Music," *ERCJ* 95 (1852) 123-145.   [Metrical Versions of the Psalms, pp. 133-139] *(Review)*

Frederic Vinton, "The Utrecht Psalter and the Athanasian Creed," *PQPR* 5 (1876) 160-170.

M. M. Ripley, "The Jewish Psalter," *UQGR, N.S.,* 13 (1876) 292-308. *[pp. misnumbered 192-208]*

J. Stewart Wilson, "The Story of the Scottish Metrical Version of the Psalms," *BFER* 28 (1879) 54-67.

*H. F. Woolrych, "The Prayer-Book and Bible Version of the Psalms," *CM* 15 (1882) 321-331.

C. Kegan Paul, "The Psalter," *BQRL* 81 (1885) 95-111.

Anonymous, "Hampole's Psalter," *SRL* 5 (1885) 264-284. *(Review)*

J. Cuthbert Hadden, "The Literary Materials of the First Scottish Psalter," *SRL* 17 (1891) 1-32.

E. D. Stone, "The Psalter," *MC* 2 (1912-13) 375-377.

G. W. Wade, "The Revision of the Psalter," *MC* 3 (1913-14) 192-197.

W. Emery Barnes, "Revision of the Prayer Book Psalter. Being the Report of a Committee appointed by the Archbishop of Canterbury. S. P. C. K. 1916," *JTS* 18 (1916-17) 61-67.

N. D. Coleman, "The English Psalter and its sources," *DUJ* 29 (1934-35) 19-26.

L. B. Towner, "Versions of the Psalter," *Theo* 31 (1935) 32.

Henry Wilder Foote, "The Bay Psalm Book and Harvard Hymnody," *HTR* 33 (1940) 225-237.

*Eric Werner, "Notes on the Attitude of the Early Church Fathers Towards Hebrew Psalmody,"*RR* 7 (1942-43) 339-352.

*Louis I. Rabinowitz, "The Psalms in Jewish Liturgy," *HJud* 6 (1944) 109-122.

W. Leonard, "The New Latin Psalter," *ACR* 22 (1945) 189-193.

Edward P. Arbez, "The New Psalter," *AER* 113 (1945) 16-26.

P. Boylan, "New Official Latin Version of the Breviary Psalter," *IER, 5th Ser.,* 66 (1945) 73-80.

F. L. Moriarty, "The New Translation of the Psalms," *MH* 2 (1945-46) #1, 9-10.

*Augustine Bea, "The New Psalter: Its Origin and Spirit," *CBQ* 8 (1946) 4-35. *(Trans. by Augustine Wand)*

Dom Aelred Watkin, "The New Psalter," *DownsR* 64 (1946) 266-276.

James Kulp, "The Old Psalter and the New," *SS* 16 (June, 1946) 18-22.

E. C. Messenger, "The New Psalter: Some Notes and Queries," *ClR* 27 (1947) 174-178.

Henry de Kandole, "The Use of the Psalms To-day," *Theo* 50 (1947) 172-178, 215-220.

Richard Rolle, "The English Psalter," *LofS* 2 (1947-48) 547-551. *(Trans. by Hilary Froomberg, with note, pp. 551-552)*

F. J. Pinkman, "The New Latin Psalter," *IER, 5th Ser.,* 70 (1948) 193-205.

Dom Aelred Watkin, "A Note on Father Pinkman's Article on the Psalter," *IER, 5th Ser.,* 70 (1948) 524-530.

C. M. Cooper, "Jerome's 'Hebrew Psalter' and the New Latin Version," *JBL* 68 (1949) v-vi.

Christine Mohrmann, "The New Latin Psalter: Its Diction and Style," *ABenR* 4 (1953) 7-33. *(Trans. from the Dutch by Abbot Justine McCann)*

Luanne Meagher, "The New Latin Psalter," *ABenR* 5 (1954) 215-232.

Eric Werner, "The Origin of Psalmody," *HUCA* 25 (1954) 327-345.

Sebastian Bullough, "The Psalms for Sunday Vespers," *LofS* 10 (1955-56) 457-461. *[Ps. 109-113]*

Hugh Casson, "The Revision of the Psalter," *Theo* 59 (1956) 46-53.

Cyril V. Taylor, "Psalter Revision," *Theo* 59 (1956) 234-240.

(Miss) E. M. Bullock, "The Revised Psalter," *Theo* 59 (1956) 379.

Sebastian Bullough, "The Psalms for Sunday Vespers," *LofS* 11 (1956-57) 38-40. *[Ps. 4; 90 (Hebrew 91); 133 (Hebrew 134)]*

L. Johnston, "The New Latin Psalter," *ClR* 42 (1957) 98-103.

Meyer Schapiro, "An Illuminated English Psalter of the Early Thirteenth Century," *JWCI* 23 (1960) 179-189.

J. R. Poerter, "The Revised Psalter," *Theo* 66 (1963) 359-366.

D. Winton Thomas, "The Revised Psalter," *Theo* 66 (1963) 504-507.

Leslie S. Hunter, "Reflections on the Revised Psalter," *CQR* 165 (1964) 164-170.

D. H. Turner, "The Evesham Psalter," *JWCI* 27 (1964) 23-41.

§390 *3.2.11.1.4 Studies concerning Date, Authorship, Sources, and Authenticity*

*G. M. Bell, "Thoughts on the Literary Character of David," *JSL, 1st Ser.*, 4 (1849) 335-342.

T. B., "The Authorship of the Imprecatory Psalms," *CE* 52 (1852) 244-253.

*Samuel Cox, "The First Psalm," *Exp, 2nd Ser.*, 1 (1881) 81-103. [1. The Author of the Psalm, pp. 81-90]

P. A. Nordell, "The Authorship of the Fifty-First Psalm," *ONTS* 2 (1882-83) 257-263.

Crawford H. Toy, "The Date of the Korah Psalms," *JBL* 4 (1884) 80-92.

Crawford H. Toy, "The Rise of Hebrew Psalm Writing," *JBL* 7 (1887) Part 1, 47-60.

Anonymous, "The Maccabaean Psalms," *ONTS* 10 (1890) 380.

*Ad. Neubauer, "The Authorship and Titles of the Psalms according to early Jewish authorities," *SBE* 2 (1890) 1-58.

P. H. Steenstra, "Can there be no Davidic Psalms in the Psalter?" *AR* 15 (1891) 662-675.

T. K. Cheyne, "Psalms of Solomon," *Exp, 4th Ser.*, 3 (1891) 398-400.

Anonymous, "The Origin of the Psalter," *LQHR* 78 (1892) 26-48.

Harlan Creelman, "Are There Maccabean Psalms? I," *ONTS* 15 (1892) 94-104.

Harlan Creelman, "Are There Maccabean Psalms? II," *ONTS* 15 (1892) 192-201.

John Taylor, "Canon Cheyne on King David and the Psalter," *Exp, 4th Ser.*, 6 (1892) 255-272.

John P. Peters, "The Development of the Psalter," *NW* 2 (1893) 285-311.

Anonymous, "David as a Psalmist," *MR* 77 (1895) 811-814.

W. T. Davidson, "Requests and Replies," *ET* 7 (1895-96) 460-461. *[The Authorship of Psalm 110]*

*T. K. Cheyne, "The Witness of Amos to David as a Psalmist (Amos VI. 5)," *ET* 9 (1897-98) 334.

George A. Barton, "The Bearing of the Composition of the Psalter on the Date of the Forty-Fourth Psalm," *AJT* 3 (1899) 740-746.

J. A. Howlett, "Age and Authorship of the Psalter," *DR* 128 (1901) 324-350.

*William C. Wilkinson, "Questions of Authorship: Psalm CX," *HR* 43 (1902) 308-311.

*C. F. Burney, "David as a Poet," *ICMM* 6 (1909-10) 49-65.

*Kemper Fullerton, "Studies in the Psalter," *BW* 37 (1911) 48-58. *[Title from the Table of Contents: "The Testimony of Ecclesiasticus as to the Psalter"]*

*A. T. Burbridge, "The Date and Interpretation of the XXIII. Psalm," *ICMM* 9 (1912-13) 71-78.

W. S. Pratt, "The Diction of the Psalter as a Clue to Its Development," *JTS* 14 (1912-13) 220-241.

John H. Raven, "The Psalms of David," *CFL, 3rd Ser.*, 21 (1916) 71-75, 170-174.

Moses Buttenwieser, "Are There Any Maccabaean Psalms?" *JBL* 36 (1917) 225-248.

*C. G. Montefiore, "The Psalter: Its Contents and Date," *QRL* 230 (1918) 1-20. *(Review)*

Edward Day, "The Reminiscences of the Psalter," *AJSL* 37 (1920-21) 263-299.

*M. Meyer, "The Author of Psalm 118," *AER* 76 (1927) 19-27.

*H. L. Ginsberg, "Canaanite Vestiges in the Psalter," *JBL* 56 (1937) iv.

E. R. Hardy Jr., "The Date of Psalm 110," *JBL* 63 (1944) iv.

B. J. Bamberger, "Authorship of the 'Psalms of Ascent'," *JBL* 64 (1945) iii.

E. R. Hardy Jr., "The Date of Psalm 110," *JBL* 64 (1945) 385-390.

Robert J. Handley, "The Davidic Authorship of the Psalms," *SS* 15 (Jan., 1946) 37-44.

Charles Lee Feinberg, "Parallels to the Psalms in Near Eastern Literature," *BS* 104 (1947) 290-297.

Charles Lee Feinberg, "The Date of the Psalms," *BS* 104 (1947) 426-440.

Charles Lee Feinberg, "Are There Maccabean Psalms in the Psalter?" *BS* 105 (1948) 44-55.

H. Torczyner, "A Psalm by the Sons of Heman," *JBL* 68 (1949) 247-249.

H. Heinemann, "The Date of Psalm 80," *JQR, N.S.,* 40 (1949-50) 297-302.

*Folker Willensen, "The Cultic Situation of Psalm LXXIV," *VT* 2 (1952) 289-306.

Roger T. O'Callaghan, "Echoes of Canaanite Literature in the Psalms," *VT* 4 (1954) 162-176.

*Helen Genevieve Jefferson, "Canaanite Literature and the Psalms," *Person* 39 (1958) 356-360.

M. Treves, "The Date of Psalm XXIV," *VT* 10 (1960) 428-434.

H. G. Jefferson, "The Date of Psalm LXVII," *VT* 12 (1962) 201-205.

Walter Brueggemann, "The Trusted Creature," *CBQ* 31 (1969) 484-498. *[Psalm Authorship]*

§391 *3.2.11.1.5 Literary Criticism of Proverbs - General Studies*

Tayler Lewis, "The Book of Proverbs," *BRCR, 3rd Ser.,* 6 (1850) 339-361.

*E. P. Barrows, "Wisdom as a Person in the Book of Proverbs," *BS* 15 (1858) 353-381.

*E. P. Barrows, "Wisdom as a Person in the Book of Proverbs," *JSL, 3rd Ser.,* 7 (1858) 346-368.

J. A. Bauman, "Pedagogical Value of the Book of Proverbs," *RChR* 28 (1881) 5-26.

O. O. Fletcher, "Errata in the Baer-Delitzsch Edition of Proverbs," *AJSL* 1 (1884-85) 252-253.

*R. F. Horton, "Christ's Use of the Book of Proverbs," *Exp, 3rd Ser.,* 7 (1888) 105-123.

*J. Monro Gibson, "Wisdom Personified, and Love Incarnate," *Exp, 3rd Ser.,* 8 (1888) 193-202.

J. Rawson Lumby, "Some Thoughts on the Structure of the Book of Proverbs," *Exp, 4th Ser.,* 1 (1890) 452-465.

*Edward Tallmage Root, "'Neither Poverty nor Riches:' or the Teachings of Proverbs Regarding Property," *ONTS* 11 (1890) 223-230.

Kichiro Yuasa, "A Classification of the Solomonic Proverbs," *ONTS* 13 (1891) 147-153.

George S. Goodspeed, "The Proverbs of the Bible and other Proverbs," *ONTS* 13 (1891) 344-348.

George S. Goodspeed, "The Book of Proverbs," *BW* 1 (1893) 365-370.

Charles F. Kent, "The Duties of Man as Taught by the Book of Proverbs," *BW* 3 (1894) 189-197.

*Moncure D. Conway, "Solomonic Literature," *OC* 12 (1898) 385-410. [Wisdom in the Book of Proverbs, and the Avesta, pp. 390-410]

J. A. Selbie, "The International Critical Commentary on 'Proverbs'," *ET* 11 (1899-1900) 383-384. *(Review)*

*W. Brenton Green Jr., "The Ethics of the Book of Proverbs," *CFL, N.S.,* 4 (1901) 136-141.

E. B. Pollard, "Self-Control in the Book of Proverbs," *CFL, N.S.,* 8 (1903) 325-329.

Henry Nelson Bullard, "An Introduction to the Study of the Proverbs," *CFL, 3rd Ser.,* 3 (1905) 393-396.

Arnold V. C. P. Huizinga, "Is Proverbs 'Utilitarian'?" *BS* 64 (1907) 66-75.

*H. St. J. Thackeray, "The Poetry of the Greek Book of Proverbs," *JTS* 13 (1911-12) 46-66.

W. Watson, "Illustrations from Egyptian Ethics of Texts in 'Proverbs'," *ET* 24 (1912-13) 474-475.

*J. Richie Smith, "The Proverbs," *HR* 78 (1919) 318-322. *(Sermon)*

William H. Bates, "The Book of Proverbs," *CFL, 3rd Ser.,* 28 (1922) 77-81.

*Anonymous, "Egyptian and Hebrew Prophets," *MR* 109 (1926) 462-464. *[Egyptian Texts and Proverbs]*

*W. O. E. Oesterley, "The 'Teaching of Amen-em-ope' and the Old Testament," *ZAW* 45 (1927) 9-23.

E. J. Harris, "Some Psychological Terms of the Book of Proverbs," *GUOST* 6 (1929-33) 22.

*C. H. Gordon, "Rabbinic Exegesis in the Vulgate of Proverbs," *JBL* 49 (1930) 384-416.

*Robert Oliver Kevin, "The Wisdom of Amen-em-apt and its possible dependence upon the Hebrew Book of Proverbs," *JSOR* 14 (1930) 115-157.

F. James, "Some Aspects of the Religion of Proverbs," *JBL* 51 (1932) 31-39.

H. J. Flowers, "The Humour of the Book of Proverbs," *BQL* 6 (1932-33) 312-317.

*Elizabeth G. K. Hewat, "Hebrew and Chinese Wisdom: A Comparative Study of the Book of Proverbs and the Analects of Confucius," *IRM* 24 (1935) 506-514.

R. H. Pfeiffer, "Secular and Deuteronomic Wisdom in the Book of Proverbs," *JBL* 54 (1935) iii.

John Oman, "The Book of Proverbs," *RL* 4 (1935) 330-336.

Maurice A. Canney, "'Healing' in the Book of Proverbs," *ET* 49 (1937-38) 237-238.

*Ralph Marcus, "The Tree of Life in Proverbs," *JBL* 62 (1943) 117-120.

John Kennedy, "Riches, Poverty, and Adversity in the Book of Proverbs," *GUOST* 12 (1944-46) 18-22.

*R. E. Wolfe, "Continuity of Thought between Proverbs and the Fourth Gospel as Regards *Logos,* " *JBL* 64 (1945) x.

Cullen I. K. Story, "The Book of Proverbs and Northwestern Semitic Literature," *JBL* 64 (1945) 319-337.

Balmer H. Kelly, "Studia Biblica. III. The Book of Proverbs," *Interp* 2 (1948) 342-355.

C[harles] T. Fritsch, "Doublets in the Greek Text of Proverbs," *JBL* 67 (1948) xii.

G. Gerleman, "The Septuagint Proverbs as a Hellenistic Document," *OTS* 8 (1950) 15-27.

*Charles T. Fritsch, "The Gospel in the Book of Proverbs," *TT* 7 (1950-51) 169-183.

Charles T. Fritsch, "The Treatment of the Hexaplaric Signs in the Syro-Hexaplar of Proverbs," *JBL* 72 (1953) 169-181.

Meir Ruttenberg, "Proverb Clusters in the Book of Proverbs," *Tarbiz* 26 (1956-57) #3, IX.

Gillis Gerleman, "Studies in the Septuagint. III. Proverbs," *AULLUÅ, N.S.,* 52 (1956) #3, 1-63.

F. D. Kidner, "The Relationship Between God and Man in Proverbs," *TB* #7&8 (1961) 4-9.

*Song Nai Rhee, "'Fear God' and 'Honor Your Father and Mother'. Two Injunctions in the Book of Proverbs and the Confuscian Classics," *SQ/E* 26 (1965) 207-214.

Roland E. Murphy, "The Kerygma of the Book of Proverbs," *Interp* 20 (1966) 3-14.

Patrick W. Skehan, "Wisdom's House," *CBQ* 29 (1967) 468-486.

Michael V. Fox, "Aspects of the Religion of the Book of Proverbs," *HUCA* 39 (1968) 55-69.

P. [H. de v.] Uys, "Justice and Righteousness towards the less Privileged in the Book of Proverbs," *NGTT* 9 (1968) 183-185.

*P. H. de v. Uys, "The term gᵉbîrâ in the Book of Proverbs," *OTW* 11 (1968) 82-85.

§392 *3.2.11.1.6 Studies concerning Date, Authorship, Sources, and Authenticity*

C. G. Montefiore, "Notes Upon the Date and Religious Value of the Book of Proverbs," *JQR* 2 (1889-90) 430-453.

Marion Hiller Dunsmore, "An Egyptian Contribution to the Book of Proverbs," *JR* 5 (1925) 300-308.

*Samuel A. B. Mercer, "A New-Found Book of Proverbs," *ATR* 8 (1925-26) 237-244.

*D. C. Simpson, "The Hebrew Book of Proverbs and the Teaching of Amenophis," *JEA* 12 (1926) 232-239.

*Ludwig Keimer, "The Wisdom of Amen-em-ope and the Proverbs of Solomon," *AJSL* 43 (1926-27) 8-21. [The Teaching of Amen-em-ope; The Teaching of Amen-em-ope and Prov. 22:17-23:17; The Limits of the Relationship of Dependence]

Henry J. Cadbury, "Egyptian Influence in the Book of Proverbs," *JR* 9 (1929) 99-108.

*Samuel A. B. Mercer, "The Wisdom of Amenemope and his Religious Ideas," *EgR* 2 (1934) 27-69. [IV. The Wisdom of Amenemope and the Book of Proverbs, pp. 56-65]

Patrick W. Skehan, "A Single Editor for the Whole Book of Proverbs," *CBQ* 10 (1948) 115-130.

§393 *3.2.11.2 Literary Criticism of the Megilloth*
- General Studies

*A. H. Tuttle, "The Golden Age of Hebrew Literature," *MR* 87 (1905) 888-902. *[Job, Psalms, Proverbs, Ecclesiastes, Song of Solomon, Ruth]*

§394 *3.2.11.2.1 Literary Criticism of the Song of Solomon*
(Canticles) - General Studies

Anonymous, "On the Song of Solomon," *BibR* 4 (1828) 495-507.

C. E. Stowe, "Solomon's Song," *BRCR, 3rd Ser.,* 3 (1847) 255-272.

Asa Mahan, "Solomon's Song," *OQR* 3 (1847-48) 311-320.

C. E. Stowe, "Solomon's Song," *JSL, 2nd Ser.,* 1 (1851-52) 320-339.

†Anonymous, "The Song of Solomon," *ER* 5 (1853-54) 578-586. *(Review)*

J. Forsyth Jr., "Hengstenberg on the Song of Solomon," *TLJ* 6 (1853-54) 493-507. *(Review)*

Christian D. Ginsburg, "The Literature of the Song of Songs," *JSL, 3rd Ser.,* 7 (1858) 1-34.

*Anonymous, "Renan on Job and Canticles," *AThR* 3 (1861) 478-486. *(Review)*

J. A. W., "'The Song of Songs'—A New Reading of its Plot," *BFER* 18 (1869) 773-796.

Anonymous, "The Song of Songs,"*WR* 101 (1874) 342-354. *(Review)*

William B. Clarke, "The Song of Solomon," *AR* 3 (1885) 572-582.

J. Barmby, "The Song of Solomon," *MI* 2 (1885) 408-421.

R. A. Redford, "The Song of Solomon," *MI* 4 (1886) 401-438.

H. P. Laird, "Analysis of the Song of Songs which is Solomon's; or, 'Dance of Mahanaim'," *RChR* 35 (1888) 5-23.

(   ) Ilfracombe, "The Song of Songs," *CR* 63 (1891) 145-172.

Anonymous, "The Song of Songs," *ONTS* 13 (1891) 121.

Russell Martineu, "The Song of Songs," *OSHTP* (1891-92) 29-31.

Russell Martineu, "The Song of Songs," *AJP* 13 (1892) 307-328.

Karl Budde, "The Song of Solomon," *NW* 3 (1892) 56-77.

A. S. Carrier, "A Study of the Form and Contents of the Song of Songs," *BW* 2 (1893) 247-258.

M. Friedlander, "The Plot of the Song of Songs," *JQR* 6 (1893-94) 648-655.

*S. Schechter, "Agadath Shir Hashirim," *JQR* 6 (1893-94) 672-697. *[Midrash on the Song of Songs]*

Russell Martineu, "The Song of Songs Again," *AJP* 16 (1895) 435-443.

W. W. Martin, "The Song of Songs—A Study of Its Plan and Purport," *MR* 77 (1895) 775-786.

T. A. Goodwin, "The Song of Songs. Part 1: The History of the Book," *OC* 9 (1895) #42, 4671-4673.

T. A. Goodwin, "The Song of Songs. Part II: The Character of the Poem," *OC* 9 (1895) #44, 4688-4691.

T. A. Goodwin, "The Song of Songs. Part III: Lovers Three Thousand Years Ago," *OC* 9 (1895) #45, 4695-4700.

Angus Crawford, "The Song of Songs," *PER* 10 (1896-97) 41-51.

Samuel Ives Curtiss, "Does a Literal Interpretation of the Song of Songs Remove Its Character as Scripture," *BS* 55 (1898) 53-91.

C[arl] H[einrich] Cornill, "The Song of Songs," *OC* 12 (1898) 371-374.

*Moncure D. Conway, "Solomonic Literature," *OC* 12 (1898) 321-335. [The Song of Songs, pp. 325-335]

Dallas Lore Sharp, "The Old Song of Solomon: The New Song of Songs," *MQR, 3rd Ser.,* 25 (1899) 837-844.

M. Kaufmann, "Is the 'Song of Songs' a Mystical Poem?" *Exp, 6th Ser.,* 2 (1900) 241-251.

G. W. Robinson, "An Outline for Studying the Song of Songs," *BW* 20 (1902) 191-195.

Paul Haupt, "Biblical Love-Ditties," *OC* 16 (1902) 291-299. *[Song of Solomon]*

Wm. G. Seiple, "Theocritean Parallels to the Song of Songs," *AJSL* 19 (1902-03) 108-115.

*C. F. Burney, "Old Testament Notes. II. Rhyme in the Song of Songs," *JTS* 10 (1908-09) 584-587.

George Holley Gilbert, "How Men Have Read the Song of Songs," *BW* 33 (1909) 171-181.

Joseph D. Ibbotson Jr., "The Song of Songs—A Secular Poem," *BW* 41 (1913) 314-321.

*Leroy Waterman, "דודי in the Song of Songs," *AJSL* 35 (1918-19) 101-110.

St. H. Stephan, "Modern Palestinian Parallels to the Song of Songs," *JPOS* 2 (1922) 199-278.

*Theophile James Meek, "Canticles and the Tammuz Cult," *AJSL* 39 (1922-23) 1-14.

J. H. Power, "The Literal Interpretation of the Canticle of Canticles," *IER*, 5th Ser., 22 (1923) 261-270.

L[eroy] Waterman, "The Role of Solomon in the Song of Songs," *JBL* 44 (1925) 171-187.

Nathaniel Schmidt, "Is Canticles an Adonis Litany?" *JAOS* 46 (1926) 156-164.

Norman H. Snaith, "The Song of Songs: The Dances of the Virgins," *AJSL* 50 (1933-34) 129-142.

H. H. Rowley, "The Riddle of the Song of Songs," *BQL* 8 (1936-37) 411-416.

H. H. Rowley, "The Interpretation of the Song of Songs," *JTS* 38 (1937) 337-363.

H. H. Rowley, "The Song of Songs: an Examination of Recent Theory," *JRAS* (1938) 251-276.

Samuel Krauss, "The Archaeological Background of Some Passages in the Song of Songs," *JQR, N.S.*, 32 (1941-42) 115-137; 33 (1942-43) 17-27; 35 (1944-45) 59-78.

Robert Gordis, "A Wedding Song for Solomon," *JBL* 63 (1944) vi.

R[obert] Gordis, "A Wedding Song for Solomon," *JBL* 63 (1944) 263-270.

Solomon B. Freehof, "The Song of Songs," *JQR, N.S.*, 39 (1948-49) 397-402.

Roland E. Murphy, "The Structure of the Canticle of Canticles," *CBQ* 11 (1949) 381-391.

Richard Kehoe, "The Song of Songs," *LofS* 6 (1951-52) 337-343.

Anonymous, "The Song of Love—II. A Modern Commentary on the Song of Songs," *LofS* 8 (1953-54) 96-101.

Roland E. Murphy, "The Canticle of Canticles and the Virgin Mary," *Carm* 1 (1954) 18-28.

Jean-Paul Audet, "The Meaning of the Canticle of Canticles," *TD* 5 (1957) 88-92.

Roland Potter, "Fairest of Songs," *LofS* 15 (1960-61) 358-362.

Edwin Yamauchi, "Cultic Clues in Canticles?" *BETS* 4 (1961) 80-88.

*Albert Wifstrand, "The New Edition of Gregory of Nyssa's Commentary on the Song of Solomon," *JTS, N.S.*, 12 (1961) 291-298.

D. Broadribb, "Thoughts on the Song of Solomon," *Abr-N* 3 (1961-62) 11-36.

M. H. Segal, "The Song of Songs," *VT* 12 (1962) 470-490.

*Samuel Noah Kramer, "The Biblical 'Song of Songs' and the Sumerian Love Songs," *Exped* 5 (1962-63) #1, 25-31.

*Leo Schwartz, "On Translating the 'Song of Songs'," *Jud* 13 (1964) 64-76.

Laurence Cantwell, "The Allegory of the Canticle of Canticles," *Scrip* 16 (1964) 76-93.

Samuel Tobias Lachs, "Prolegomena to Canticles Rabba," *JQR, N.S.*, 55 (1964-65) 235-255.

*A. van Selms, "Hosea and Canticles," *OTW* 7&8 (1964-65) 85-89.

J. Coert Rylaarsdam, "The Song of Songs and Biblical Faith," *BRes* 10 (1965) 7-18.

Thomas E. Fountain, "A Parabolic View of the Song of Solomon," *BETS* 9 (1966) 97-101.

*Raphael J. Loewe, "Apologetic Motifs in the Targum to the Song of Songs," *LIST* 3 (1966) 159-196.

Eric F. F. Bishop, "Palestiniana in Canticulis," *CBQ* 29 (1967) 20-30.

*Richard N. Soulen, "The *waṣfs* of the Song of Songs and Hermeneutic," *JBL* 86 (1967) 183-190.

Robert Gordis, "The Root דגל in the Song of Songs," *JBL* 88 (1969) 203-204.

*Samuel Noah Kramer, "Sumerian Sacred Marriage Songs and the Biblical 'Song of Songs'," *MIO* 15 (1969) 262-274.

§395 *3.2.11.2.2 Studies Concerning Date, Authorship, Sources, and Authenticity*

(   ) Nemo, "The Divine Authority of Solomon's Song Vindicated, with answers to some objections in the new edition of Dr. J. P. Smith's 'Testimony to the Messiah'," *CongML* 13 (1830) 232-236, 294-299.

J. Pye Smith, "Dr. J. P. Smith on the Authority of Solomon's Song," *CongML* 20 (1837) 413-429.

James Bennett, "Dr. Bennett on the Inspiration and Spiritual Sense of the Song of Solomon," *CongML* 20 (1837) 610-615.

J. Pye Smith, "Dr. Pye Smith's Reply to Dr. Bennett's Letter," *CongML* 20 (1837) 694-702.

J. Pye Smith, "Sequel to Dr. Pye Smith's Reply to Dr. Bennett," *CongML* 20 (1837) 784-786.

James Bennett, "Dr. Bennett's Reply to the First Part of Dr. Smith's Answer," *CongML* 21 (1838) 20-29.

James Bennett, "Dr. Bennett's Reply to Dr. Smith on Solomon's Song," *CongML* 21 (1838) 82-98, 142-154.

B. R., "On the Divine Authority of Solomon's Song," *CongML* 21 (1838)197-208.

James Bennett, "Dr. Bennett's Final Communication on Solomon's Song," *CongML* 21 (1838) 636.

T[heophile] J. Meek, "Babylonian Parallels to the Song of Songs," *JBL* 43 (1924) 245-252.

James Cannon III, "The Linguistic Argument for the Late Date of Canticles," *MQR, 3rd Ser.,* 51 (1925) 337-338.

E. E. Pierce, "The Sufis and the Song of Songs," *JBL* 53 (1934) xi-xii.

§396 *3.2.11.2.3 Literary Criticism of the Book of Ruth - General Studies*

J. C. H., "The Story of Ruth. A Modern Version," *DUM* 76 (1870) 289-296.

C. E. Crandall, "The Book of Ruth Considered Statistically," *ONTS* 2 (1882-83) 18-21.

Newell Woolsey Wells, "Ruth and the New Criticism," *ONTS* 3 (1883-84) 86-90.

*Anonymous, "Judges and Ruth," *CongRL* 4 (1890) 301-303. *(Review)*

Eneas B. Goodwin, "The Book of Ruth.—A Hebrew Idyl," *AER* 16 (1897) 382-392.

Armstrong Black, "Ruth: A Hebrew Idyl," *Exp, 6th Ser.,* 5 (1902) 360-366.

*Julius A. Bewer, "The Ge'ullāh in the Book of Ruth," *AJSL* 19 (1902-03) 143-148.

*Willis J. Beecher, "The International Lessons in Their Setting. I.," *CFL, N.S.*, 8 (1903) 17-25. [Judges and Ruth and Samuel Form one Book, p. 17]

W. S. Currell, "Ruth: A Study in the Short Story," *CFL, N.S.*, 8 (1903) 283-288.

W. A. Quayle, "The Book of Ruth," *MR* 90 (1908) 345-359.

*Louis B. Wolfenson, "The Character, Contents, and Date of Ruth," *AJSL* 27 (1910-11) 285-300.

Louis B. Wolfenson, "The Purpose of the Book of Ruth," *BS* 69 (1912) 329-344.

J. J. Blythe, "The Book of Ruth," *CFL, 3rd Ser.*, 19 (1915) 167-168.

Milton S. Terry, "A Romantic Hebrew Idyl," *CFL, 3rd Ser.*, 19 (1915) 169-170.

J. Gray McAllister, "The Book of Ruth," *USR* 33 (1921-22) 193-209.

Jacob Philip Rudin, "'Higher Criticism' of Ruth," *JIQ* 1 (1924-25) 105-109.

L[ouis] B. Wolfenson, "Implications of the Place of the Book of Ruth in Editions, Manuscripts, and Canon of the Old Testament," *HUCA* 1 (1924) 151-178.

*Jalmar Bowden, "The Enlarging Spiritual Horizon of Judaism as Seen in the Books of Ruth and Jonah," *MQR, 3rd Ser.*, 50 (1924) 684-690.

Charles Edward Smith, "The Book of Ruth," *BS* 82 (1925) 177-184.

*John C. Montgomery, "The Sin and Salvation of Israel: A Study of Judges and Ruth," *MQR, 3rd Ser.*, 51 (1925) 199-127.

W. W. Cannon, "The Book of Ruth," *Theo* 16 (1928) 310-319.

A. Q. Bailey, "The Book of Ruth," *ACM* 30 (1931) 58-60.

W. E. Staples, "The Book of Ruth," *AJSL* 53 (1936-37) 145-157.

Millar Burrows, "The Marriage of Boaz and Ruth," *JBL* 59 (1940) 445-454.

Margaret B. Crook, "The Book of Ruth. A New Solution," *JAAR* 16 (1948) 155-160.

Margaret B. Crook, "The Book of Ruth—A New Solution," *JBL* 67 (1948) xi.

*Leon Nemoy, "Did Salomon ben Jeroham Compose a Commentary on Ruth?" *JQR, N.S.,* 39 (1948-49) 215-216.

E. Robertson, "The Plot of the Book of Ruth," *BJRL* 32 (1949-50) 207-228.

S. B. Gurewicz, "Some Reflections on the Book of Ruth," *ABR* 5 (1956) 42-57.

Oswald Loretz, "The Theme of the Ruth Story," *CBQ* 22 (1960) 391-399.

*William McKane, "Ruth and Boaz," *GUOST* 19 (1961-62) 29-40.

William L. Reed, "Translation Problems in the Book of Ruth," *CollBQ* 41 (1964) #2, 1-18.

G. W. Anderson, "Old Testament Books," *PQL* 10 (1964) 147-151. [X. Ruth]

D. R. Ap-Thomas, "The Book of Ruth," *ET* 79 (1967-68) 369-373.

*Thomas Thompson and Dorothy Thompson, "Some Legal Problems in the Book of Ruth," *VT* 18 (1968) 79-99.

*Susan Lee Sherman and John Briggs Curtis, "Divine-Human Conflicts in the Old Testament," *JNES* 28 (1969) 231-242. [The Book of Ruth, pp. 235-240]

§397 *3.2.11.2.4 Studies Concerning Date, Authorship, Sources, and Authenticity*

*Louis B. Wolfenson, "The Character, Contents, and Date of Ruth," *AJSL* 27 (1910-11) 285-300.

M. David, "The Date of the Book of Ruth," *OTS* 1 (1942) 54-63.

George S. Glanzman, "The Origin and the Date of the Book of Ruth," *CBQ* 21 (1959) 201-207.

§398 *3.2.11.2.5 Literary Criticism of Lamentations - General Studies*

C. J. Ball, "The Metrical Structure of Qinoth. The Book of Lamentations arranged according to the Original Measures," *SBAP* 9 (1886-87) 131-153.

James Stalker, "The Book of Lamentations," *Exp, 4th Ser.,* 5 (1892) 65-75.

Emil Lund, "The Lamentations," *TTKF* 8 (1906) 38-44, 104-121, 168-179, 231-240.

H. J. Flowers, "The Book of Lamentations," *R&E* 31 (1934) 452-460.

Norman K. Gottwald, "Studia Biblica. XXX. Lamentations," *Interp* 9 (1955) 320-338.

Bernard [P.] Robinson, "The Book of Lamentations," *LofS* 16 (1961-62) 142-148.

T. F. McDaniel, "Philological Studies in Lamentations," *B* 49 (1968) 27-53, 199-200. [Index of Scripture References, pp. 217-219; Index of Hebrew Words, pp. 219-220]

*J. L. Helberg, "Nahum—Jonah—Lamentations—Isaiah 51-53 (A Possibility of Establishing a Connection)," *OTW* 12 (1969) 46-55.

§399 *3.2.11.2.6 Studies concerning Date, Authorship, Sources, and Authenticity*

Archibald Duff, "The Date of the Book of Lamentations," *ICMM* 12 (1915-16) 284-297.

William Walter Cannon, "The Authorship of Lamentations," *BS* 81 (1924) 42-58.

*Samuel Tobias Lachs, "The Date of Lamentations," *JQR, N.S.,* 57 (1966-67) 46-56.

Th. F. McDaniel, "The Alleged Sumerian Influence upon Lamentations," *VT* 18 (1968) 198-209.

§400 *3.2.11.2.7 Literary Criticism of Ecclesiastes (Qoheleth) - General Studies*

*Anonymous, "An Attempt to Explain the Discrepancies Between the Book of Ecclesiastes and the Pentateuch," *CongML* 5 (1822) 686-689.

†B., G., "Remarks on the Design and Character, of the Book of Ecclesiastes," *QCS* 4 (1822) 524-525. [Anonymous reply, pp. 525-530]

[Isaac(?)] Nordheimer, "The Philosophy of Ecclesiastes," *BRCR* 12 (1838) 197-219. *(Trans. by Wm. W. Turner)*

Anonymous, "The Philosophy of Ecclesiastes," *BRCM* 1 (1846) 433-442.

James M. Macdonald, "An Analysis of Ecclesiastes," *BRCR, 3rd Ser.,* 5 (1849) 145-174.

[J. G.] Vaihinger, "Plan and Structure of the Book of Ecclesiastes," *MR* 31 (1849) 173-185, 417-429. *[Modified from the German of Vaihinger in the* Theologische Studien and Kritiken *for July, 1848]*

Anonymous, "The Scope and Plan of the Book of Ecclesiastes," *PRev* 29 (1857) 419-440.

Anonymous, "Hengstenberg's Commentary on Ecclesiastes," *AThR* 1 (1859) 260-275. *(Review)*

W. K., "Ecclesiastes," *JSL, 3rd Ser.,* 14 (1861-62) 100-119.

Anonymous, "Commentary on Ecclesiastes, by Moses Stuart, late professor of Sacred Literature in the Theological Seminary at Andover. Edited and Revised by R. D. C. Robbins, professor in Middlebury College," *DQR* 3 (1863) 38-61. *(Review)*

Anonymous, "The Problem of Life—The Book of Ecclesiastes," *MQR, 2nd Ser.,* 2 (1880) 83-94.

Thomas Tyler, "Ecclesiastes," *ModR* 3 (1882) 225-256. *(Review)*

T. K. Cheyne, "Notes on Ecclesiastes," *Exp, 3rd Ser.,* 1 (1885) 319.

Milton S. Terry, "Studies in Koheleth," *MR* 70 (1888) 365-375.

M. Friedlander, "The Design and Contents of Ecclesiastes," *JQR* 1 (1888-89) 29-41.

Edward T. Root, "Ecclesiastes Considered Psychologically," *ONTS* 9 (1889) 138-142.

C. Taylor, "The Dirge of Coheleth," *JQR* 4 (1891-92) 533-549.

F. B. Denio, "The Book of Ecclesiastes," *ONTS* 14 (1892) 98-105.

C. Taylor, "The Dirge of Coheleth, II.," *JQR* 5 (1892-93) 5-17.

George S. Goodspeed, "The Book of Ecclesiastes," *BW* 1 (1893) 453-460.

*[Nathaniel Burwash], "Analytical studies in the English Bible: The Books of Job and Proverbs and Ecclesiastes," *CMR* 5 (1893) 251-265.

F. B. Denio, "The Course of Thought in Ecclesiastes," *BW* 4 (1894) 326-330.

E. J. Dillon, "Ecclesiastes and Buddhism," *ContR* 65 (1894) 153-176.

*J. Cheston Morris, "The Ethics of Solomon," *PAPS* 33 (1894) 310-332. *[Ecclesiastes]*

S. R. Driver, "Sceptics of the Old Testament," *ContR* 69 (1896) 257-269. *[Koheleth] (Review)*

Winfred Chesney Rhoades, "Qohéleth and Omar Khayyám, Two Ancient Critics of Life," *HSR* 8 (1897-98) 40-48.

A. J. Maas, "The Problem of Happiness in the Light of Ecclesiastes," *ACQR* 23 (1898) 576-597.

*Moncure D. Conway, "Solomonic Literature," *OC* 12 (1898) 556-564. [Koheleth (Ecclesiastes), pp. 556-560]

Anonymous, "Current Criticism and Interpretation of the Old Testament. Ecclesiastes," *CFL, O.S.,* 3 (1899) 266-267.

M. Kaufmann, "Was Koheleth a Sceptic?" *Exp, 5th Ser.,* 9 (1899) 389-400.

W. D. Kerswill, "The Scepticism of Ecclesiastes," *CFL, N.S.,* 2 (1900) 72-78.

W. D. Kerswill, "The Scepticism of Ecclesiastes," *CFL, N.S.,* 2 (1900) 72-78.

Joseph Bruneau, "Some Recent Views of the Book of Ecclesiastes," *CUB* 6 (1900) 498-509.

Bernard Pick, "Ecclesiastes or the Sphinx of Hebrew Literature," *OC* 17 (1903) 361-371.

William Byron Forbush, "Ecclesiastes and the Rubaiyat," *BW* 26 (1905) 355-363.

Henry Nelson Bullard, "An Introduction to the Study of Ecclesiastes," *CFL, 3rd Ser.,* 5 (1906) 151-152.

Bernard Pick, "Koheleth," *HR* 51 (1906) 363-364.

Adolph Lehmann, "Ecclesiastes—an Interpretation," *CFL, 3rd Ser.,* 6 (1907) 16-21.

*D. S. Margoliouth, "Ecclesiastes and Ecclesiasticus," *Exp, 7th Ser.,* 5 (1908) 118-126.

James Allen Geissinger, "The Worst-Understood Book," *MR* 91 (1909) 734-741. *[Ecclesiastes]*

A. H. Godbey, "The Greek Influence in Ecclesiastes," *Monist* 20 (1910) 174-194.

D. S. Margoliouth, "The Prologue of Ecclesiastes," *Exp, 8th Ser.,* 2 (1911) 463-470.

Hinckley G. Mitchell, "'Work' in Ecclesiastes," *JBL* 32 (1913) 123-138.

H. C. Ackerman, "The Problem of Ecclesiastes," *BW* 48 (1916) 82-88.

J. M. Hantz, "Man's Pre-eminence Among Creatures," *LQ* 46 (1916) 196-211.

George Ricker Berry, "The Purpose of the Book of Ecclesiastes," *R&E* 13 (1916) 88-98.

H. Ranston, "Ecclesiastes and Theognis," *AJSL* 34 (1917-18) 99-122.

J. Ritchie Smith, "Ecclesiastes," *PTR* 16 (1918) 262-279.

N. Liebschutz, "The Cynic in the Bible," *MQR, 3rd Ser.*, 46 (1920) 731-741. *[Koheleth]*

R. M. Gwynn, "Notes on the Vocabulary of *Ecclesiastes* in Greek," *Herm* 19 (1920-22) 115-122.

F. C. Burkitt, "Is Ecclesiastes a Translation?" *JTS* 23 (1921-22) 22-26.

H. Ranston, "Koheleth and the Early Greeks," *JTS* 24 (1922-23) 160-169.

Carl S. Knopf, "The Reinstatement of Ecclesiastes," *Person* 6 (1925) 191-195.

M[illar] Burrows, "Kuhn and Koheleth," *JBL* 66 (1927) 90-97.

Avary H. Forbes, "Science in the Book of Ecclesiastes," *JTVI* 60 (1928) 175-188, 192-193. (Discussion, pp. 188-192)

C. S. Knoff, "The Optimism of Koheleth," *JBL* 49 (1930) 195-199.

R[obert] H. Pfeiffer, "The Peculiar Skepticism of Ecclesiastes," *JBL* 53 (1934) iii.

Robert H. Pfeiffer, "The Peculiar Skepticism of Ecclesiastes," *JBL* 53 (1934) 100-109.

*J. B. Rowell, "Immortality," *BS* 92 (1935) 154-169. [A Brief Study in Ecclesiastes, pp. 163-165]

*David E. Faust, "A Prophet Attacks Profit," *JAAR* 3 (1935) #1, 29-31.

E. J. Prince, "*Koheleth* and the Modern Mood," *CongQL* 14 (1936) 410-423.

Robert Gordis, "The Personality of Koheleth," *JBL* 56 (1937) x.

Elizabeth Stone, "Old Man Koheleth," *JAAR* 10 (1942) 98-102.

J. J. Murray, "Koheleth and Omar Khayyam," *RL* 11 (1942) 213-222.

W. E. Staples, "The 'Vanity' of Ecclesiastes," *JNES* 2 (1943) 95-104.

Michael Leahy, "The Book of Ecclesiastes," *IER, 5th Ser.*, 64 (1944) 84-93.

William R. Seaman, "Life May Be Like That: A Study in the Book of Ecclesiastes," *LCQ* 17 (1944) 115-123.

W. E. Staples, "'Profit' in Ecclesiastes," *JNES* 4 (1945) 87-96.

Frank Zimmermann, "The Aramaic Provenance of Qohelet," *JQR, N.S.,* 36 (1945-46) 17-45.

J. Stafford Wright, "The Interpretation of Ecclesiastes," *EQ* 18 (1946) 18-34.

Robert Gordis, "The Original Language of Koheleth," *JBL* 65 (1946) vi.

Robert Gordis, "The Original Language of Qoheleth," *JQR, N.S.,* 37 (1946-47) 67-84.

Charles C. Torrey, "The Question of the Original Language of Qoheleth," *JQR, N.S.,* 39 (1948-49) 151-160.

Frank Zimmermann, "The Question of Hebrew in Qoheleth," *JQR, N.S.,* 40 (1949-50) 79-102.

Robert Gordis, "The Translation-Theory of Qohelet Re-Examined," *JQR, N.S.,* 40 (1949-50) 103-116.

Thomas M. Durant, "Geriatrics and the Book of Ecclesiastes," *JASA* 2 (1950) #3, 10-13.

Frederick W. Danker, "The Pessimism of Ecclesiastes," *CTM* 22 (1951) 9-32.

Mitchell [J.] Dahood, "The Language of Qoheleth," *CBQ* 14 (1952) 227-232.

H. L. Ginsberg, "Supplementary Studies in Koheleth," *PAAJR* 21 (1952) 35-62. [I. 'ml in the Sense of 'Earning' and Related Matters; II. Koheleth's Second Main Division: Predestination and What to Do About it: 3:1-4:3; III. Koheleth's Third Main Division, a Pendant to the First: 4:4-6:9; IV. Koheleth's Fourth Main Division, a Pendent to the Second: 6:10-9:18; V. Conclusion; Appendices, 1. Errors of Critics, 2. The Word (haq) qohelet; 3. The Alleged Bearing of Paronomasia and Meter on the Translation Theory]

Mitchell J. Dahood, "The Geographical Allusions in Ecclesiastes," *MH* 9 (Winter, 1953) 6-9.

Ch. W. Reines, "Koheleth on Wisdom and Wealth," *JJS* 5 (1954) 80-84.

Roland E. Murphy, "The *Pensees* of Coheleth," *CBQ* 17 (1955) 304-314.

Ch. W. Reines, "Koheleth on Wisdom and Wealth," *JJS* 5 (1954) 80-84.

Roland E. Murphy, "The *Pensees* of Coheleth," *CBQ* 17 (1955) 304-314.

W. E. Staples, "Vanity of Vanities," *CJT* 1 (1955) 141-156. *[Ecclesiastes]*

*Robert Gordis, "Was Koheleth a Phoenician?" *JBL* 74 (1955) 103-114.

H. L. Ginsberg, "The structure and contents of the Book of Koheleth," *VTS* 3 (1955) 138-149.

M[itchell J.] Dahood, "Qoheleth and Recent Discoveries," *B* 39 (1958) 302-318.

C[harles] C. Forman, "The Pessimism of Ecclesiastes," *JSS* 3 (1958) 336-343.

H. McKeating, "...and a Time to Doubt?" *PQL* 5 (1959) 156-160.

Dan Vogel, "Koheleth and the Modern Temper," *Trad* 2 (1959-60) 82-92.

*Charles C. Forman, "Koheleth's Use of Genesis," *JSS* 5 (1960) 256-263.

Frederick Neumann, "Ecclesiastes—Philosopher Without Propositions," *HQ* 1 (1960-61) #3, 35-49.

Suzanne Billitzer, "Camus and Koheleth: Existentialism and Ecclesiastes," *YR* 1 (1961) 3-9.

Frank Zimmermann, "Qohelet," *JQR, N.S.,* 52 (1961-62) 273-278. *(Review)*

*M[itchell J.] Dahood, "Qoheleth and Northwest Semitic Philology," *B* 43 (1962) 349-365.

*J. Edgar Bruns, "Some Reflections on Coheleth and John," *CBQ* 25 (1963) 414-416.

*Arthur Maltby, "The Book of Ecclesiastes and the After-Life," *EQ* 35 (1963) 39-44.

H. L. Ginsberg, "The Quintessence of Koheleth," *LIST* 1 (1963) 47-59.

A[nson] F. Rainey, "The Study of Ecclesiastes," *CTM* 35 (1964) 148-157.

*Anson F. Rainey, "A Second Look at Amal in Qoheleth," *CTM* 36 (1965) 805.

*W. E. Staples, "The Meaning of *ḥēpeṣ* in Ecclesiastes," *JNES* 24 (1965) 110-112.

M[itchell J.] Dahood, "The Phoenician Background of Qoheleth," *B* 47 (1966) 264-282.

Lionel Swain, "The Bible and the People. The Message of Ecclesiastes," *ClR* 51 (1966) 862-868.

Judah Goldin, "The End of Ecclesiastes: Literal Exegesis and its Transformation," *LIST* 3 (1966) 135-158.

George R. Castellino, "Qohelet and His Wisdom," *CBQ* 30 (1968) 15-28.

Addison G. Wright, "The Riddle of the Sphinx: The Structure of the Book of Qoheleth," *CBQ* 30 (1968) 313-334.

Eric F. F. Bishop, "A Pessimist in Palestine (B.C.)," *PEQ* 100 (1968) 33-41.

Lawrence B. Porter, "Bankruptcy: The words of Qoheleth, Son of David, King in Jerusalem," *BibT* #44 (1969) 3041-3046.

§401 *3.2.11.2.8 Studies Concerning Date, Authorship, Sources, and Authenticity*

[Elias] Riggs, "Did Solomon Write the Book of Ecclesiastes," *BFER* 1 (1852) 170-180.

[Elias Riggs], "Did Solomon Write the Book of Ecclesiastes," *PRev* 24 (1852) 79-91.

E. H. Plumptre, "The Author of Ecclesiastes. An Ideal Biography," *Exp, 1st Ser.*, 11 (1880) 401-430.

E. H. Plumptre, "Note on 'The Author of Ecclesiastes'," *Exp, 1st Ser.*, 12 (1880) 88.

W. W. Davies, "Authorship of Ecclesiastes," *MR* 66 (1884) 482-502.

M. Friedlander, "The Age and Authorship of Ecclesiastes," *JQR* 1 (1888-89) 359-375.

James Robinson, "Requests and Replies. Professor Margoliouth on the Date of Ecclesiastes," *ET* 5 (1893-94) 239.

F. Zimmerman*[sic]*, "Aramaic Origin of Qoheleth," *JBL* 64 (1945) vii.

Robert Gordis, "Koheleth—Hebrew or Aramaic," *JBL* 70 (1951) xiii.

Robert Gordis, "Koheleth—Hebrew or Aramaic," *JBL* 71 (1952) 93-109.

M[itchell] J. Dahood, "Canaanite-Phoenician Influence in Qoheleth," *B* 33 (1952) 30-52, 191-221.

*Robert Gordis, "Was Koheleth a Phoenician?" *JBL* 74 (1955) 103-114.

G. L. Archer, "The Linguistic Evidence for the Date of 'Ecclesiastes'," *BETS* 12 (1969) 167-182.

§402 *3.2.11.2.9 Literary Criticism of the Book of Esther - General Studies*

†Anonymous, "More Comments on the Book of Esther," *MMBR* 9 (1800) 454-455.

[Heinrich Andreas Christoph] Hävernick, "The Book of Esther. *Translated chiefly from the German of Hävernick*," *CRB* 13 (1848) 365-401.

(   ) G., "Remarks on the Book of Esther," *JSL, 3rd Ser.,* 11 (1860) 112-142.

Anonymous, "The Book of Esther," *JSL, 3rd Ser.,* 11 (1860) 204-205.

*J. W. Bosanquet, "Chronological Remarks on the History of Esther and Ahasuerus, or "Atossa and Tanu-Axares," *SBAT* 5 (1876-77) 225-292.

J. L. Leucht, "The Mysteries of the Book of Esther," *SPR* 34 (1883) 588-604.

*M. Dieulafoy, "The Book of Esther and the Palace of Ahasuerus," *BS* 46 (1889) 626-653. *(Trans. by Florence Osgood)*

*J. A. MacDonald, "The name of Jehovah in the Book of Esther," *CMR* 2 (1890) 174-181.

Arthur T. Pierson, "The Hiding of God in the Book of Esther," *HR* 22 (1891) 123-127.

[Nathaniel Burwash], "Analytical studies in the English Bible: Brief outline of Ezra, Nehemiah, Esther, with Haggai and Zechariah," *CMR* 5 (1893) 87-104.

George S. Burroughs, "A Syllabus on the Book of Esther," *CMR* 5 (1893) 105-107.

A. H. Huizinga, "The Book of Esther," *PQ* 7 (1893) 395-409.

E. W. Cook, "The Book of Esther," *HR* 43 (1902) 163-166.

*James Oscar Boyd, "Esther and Anti-Semitism," *CFL, N.S.*, 8 (1903) 298-300.

John Urquhart, "The Book of Esther," *CFL, 3rd Ser.*, 2 (1905) 430-441.

F. Hugh Pope, "Why Does the Protestant Church Read the Book of Esther?" *DR* 137 (1905) 77-98.

J. A. Selbie, "The International Critical Commentary on 'Esther'," *ET* 20 (1908-09) 225-226. *(Review)*

Alfred Chipman, "Professor Lewis B. Paton's View of the Book of Esther," *CFL, 3rd Ser.*, 10 (1909) 87-88. *[ICC] (Review)*

*Henry H. Howorth, "Some Unconventional Views on the Text of the Bible. VIII. *The Prayer of Manasses and the Book of Esther*," *SBAP* 31 (1909) 89-99, 156-168.

George O. Little, "Addition to the Sum of Revelation, Found in the Book of Esther," *BS* 71 (1914) 19-37.

Aaron P. Drucker, "The Book of Esther," *OC* 28 (1914) 232-243.

A. G. Jayne, "The Book of Esther," *ICMM* 11 (1914-15) 50-64.

*W. Ernest Beet, "The Humorous Element in the Old Testament," *Exp, 8th Ser.*, 22 (1921) 59-68. *[The Book of Esther]*

W. Ernest Beet, "The Message of the Book of Esther," *Exp, 8th Ser.*, 22 (1921) 291-300.

William H. Bates, "The Book of Esther," *CFL, 3rd Ser.*, 28 (1922) 207-208.

John P. Naish, "Fresh Light on the Book of Esther," *Exp, 8th Ser.*, 25 (1923) 56-66.

H[enry] S. Gehman, "Notes on the Persian Words in the Book of Esther," *JBL* 43 (1924) 321-328.

Charles Edward Smith, "The Book of Esther," *BS* 82 (1925) 397-402.

Paul Haupt, "The Story of Esther," *OOR* 1 (1926) #1, 1-2.

A. E. Morris, "The Purpose of the Book of Esther," *ET* 42 (1930-31) 124-128.

William Vischer, "The Book of Esther," *EQ* 11 (1939) 3-21.

H. Hamann, "The Absence of the Name of God in Esther," *AusTR* 13 (1942) 69-70.

*T. E. N. Pennell, "Esther and Antisemitism," *ET* 55 (1943-44) 237-240.

E[lias J.] Bickerman, "The Colophon of the Greek Book of Esther," *JBL* 63 (1944) 339-362.

Bernard W. Anderson, "The Place of the Book of Esther in the Christian Bible," *JR* 30 (1950) 32-43.

*A. D. H. Fishlock, "The Rabbinic Material in the *Ester [sic]* of Pinto Delgardo," *JJS* 2 (1950-51) 37-50.

Elias J. Bickerman, "Notes on the Greek Book of Esther," *PAAJR* 20 (1951) 101-133.

Frederick Neumann, "The Weapon and Comfort of Humor. A Vindication of the Book of Esther," *HQ* 2 (1961-62) #4, 57-70.

*Moshe Gan, "The Book of Esther in the Light of the Story of Joseph in Egypt," *Tarbiz* 31 (1961-62) #2, I-II.

*B. Schneider, "Esther Revised According to the Maccabees," *SBFLA* 13 (1962-63) 190-218.

*S. Talmon, "'Wisdom' in the Book of Esther," *VT* 13 (1963) 419-455.

K. A. M., "Your Questions Answered. Book of Esther," *BH* 5 (1969) 62. *[Book not found at Qumran]*

§403 *3.2.11.2.10 Studies Concerning Date, Authorship, Sources, and Authenticity*

W. Scott Watson, "The Authenticity and Genuineness of the Book of Esther," *PTR* 1 (1903) 62-74.

C[harles] C. Torrey, "The Older Book of Esther," *HTR* 37 (1944) 1-40.

§404 *3.2.11.3 Literary Criticism of the Historical Books - General Studies*

C[harles] C. Torrey, "The Greek Versions of Chronicles, Ezra, and Nehemiah," *SBAP* 25 (1903) 139-140.

Henry H. Howorth, "Some Unconventional Views on the Text of the Bible. VII. *Daniel and Chronicles,*" *SBAP* 29 (1907) 31-38, 61-69.

*Robert Dick Wilson, "The Title 'King of Persia' in the Scriptures," *PTR* 15 (1917) 90-145.

*S. Japhet, "A Supposed Common Authorship of Chron. and Ezra-Neh. investigated Anew," *VT* 18 (1968) 330-371.

§405 *3.2.11.3.1 Literary Criticism of the Book of Daniel - General Studies*

*Anonymous, "Chronological Remarks on the Time of Daniel," *MMBR* 4 (1797) 258-259.

Anonymous, "On the Watchers and Holy Ones, Mentioned in the Book of Daniel," *CongML* 1 (1818) 581-582.

Anonymous, "Hengstenberg's Vindication of the Book of Daniel," *PRev* 4 (1832) 48-71. *(Review)*

Anonymous, "Remarks on the Book of Daniel," *CRB* 7 (1842) 1-46. [The Four Kingdoms; especially the Fourth; Objections considered, which have been urged against the preceding view; the "Two Thousand and Three Hundred Days" The Seventy Weeks; The Events predicted in the last three Chapters]

W. P. L., "Belshazzar's Feast," *CE* 37 (1844) 49-57.

Anonymous, "The Times of Daniel," *DUM* 25 (1845) 612-615. *(Review)*

*Anonymous, "Who was Darius the Median in the Book of Daniel?" *BRCM* 1 (1846) 25-38.

Anonymous, "The Times of Daniel, etc.," *DUM* 27 (1846) 497-506. *(Review)*

[David N. Lord], "Professor Stuart's Commentary on Daniel," *TLJ* 3 (1850-51) 353-383. *(Review)*

R. P. S., "Stuart's Commentary on Daniel," *CE* 51 (1851) 368-376. *(Review)*

Anonymous, "Introduction to the Book of Daniel," *PQR* 1 (1852-53) 32-83, 208-259. [1. The Life of Daniel; 2. Genuineness and Authenticity of the Book—Negative Proofs; 3. Genuineness and Authenticity of the Book—Positive Proofs; 4. Nature, Design, and General Character; 5. Apocryphal Additions; 6. Ancient Versions; 7. Exegetical Helps]

*H. M. G., "The Identity of Cyrus and the Times of Daniel," *JSL, 2nd Ser.,* 6 (1854) 435-465; 7 (1854-55) 364-381.

G. J., "Confirmation of Daniel's Narrative," *JSL, 2nd Ser.,* 6 (1854) 521.

H. M. Harman, "The Genuineness of Daniel," *MR* 36 (1854) 553-578. *(Review)*

Anonymous, "The Duke of Manchester on 'The Times of Daniel'," *JSL, 2nd Ser.,* 7 (1854-55) 451-460.

*G. B., "On Daniel and Ezra, Compared with the Inscription at Behistun," *JSL, 3rd Ser.,* 5 (1857) 170-172.

G. B., "Xenophon's 'Cyropaedia'," *JSL, 3rd Ser.,* 7 (1858) 466-474. *[Daniel]*

*G. J. M'., "The Chaldee of Daniel and Ezra," *JSL, 3rd Ser.,* 12 (1860-61) 373-391.

[S. D. Church], "The Prophetical Days of Daniel," *FBQ* 11 (1863) 267-279. ["Seven Times"; A Time and Times and a Dividing of Times; Two Thousand Three Hundred Days]

*Anonymous, "The Book of Daniel: as viewed by Hippolytus, Porphyry and others," *JSL, 4th Ser.,* 4 (1863-64) 257-285.

Franke Parker, "'Daniel the Prophet,' by Dr. Pusey," *JSL, 4th Ser.,* 7 (1865) 345-359. *(Review)*

Anonymous, "Doctor Pusey's Lectures on Daniel," *DR, N.S.,* 5 (1865) 189-205. *(Review) [Original numbering as Volume 57]*

R. M., "The Book of Daniel," *TR* 2 (1865) 172-201, 477-505.

T. A., Dr. Pusey's Daniel," *JSL, 4th Ser.,* 8 (1865-66) 202-203.

E. Greenwald, "Daniel's Seventy Weeks," *ER* 18 (1867) 204-216.

Josiah Pratt, "The Seventy-Weeks Prophecy in Daniel," *JSL, 5th Ser.,* 2 (1867-68) 210-213.

J. W. Bosanquet, "'Messiah the Prince'," *JSL, 5th Ser.,* 2 (1867-68) 428-438.

*[S. D. Church], "Cowles's Exposition of Daniel," *FBQ* 16 (1868) 178-193. *(Review)*

J. A. Seiss, "Daniel and his Prophecies," *ER* 20 (1869) 579-596.

H. Fox Talbot, "Illustrations of the Prophet Daniel from the Assyrian Writings," *SBAT* 2 (1873) 360-364.

†Anonymous, "Daniel the Prophet," *LQHR* 43 (1874-75) 292-328. *(Review)*

Anonymous, "'The King' in Daniel," *BWR* 1 (1877) 322.

*Howard Crosby, "Light on Important Texts. No. XVIII," *HR* 6 (1881-82) 472. *[Daniel and the Lion's Den]*

Wilbur F. Tillett, "The Genuineness of the Book of Daniel," *MQR, 2nd Ser.,* 4 (1882) 441-470.

William Hayes Ward, "The Historical Chapters of Daniel Attested by Contemporary Records," *JCP* 3 (1883-84) 116-139.

W. G. Moorehead, "'Daniel and the First Resurrection'," *ONTS* 3 (1883-84) 308-310.

William Hayes Ward, "The Historical Chapters of Daniel Attested by Contemporary Records," *JLTQ* 1 (1884) 431-452.

J. M. Fuller, "The Book of Daniel in the Light of Recent Research and Discovery," *Exp, 3rd Ser.*, 1 (1885) 217-225, 431-438. *[Parts I and II]*

J. M. Fuller, "The Book of Daniel in the Light of Recent Research and Discovery. III. Cyrus," *Exp, 3rd Ser.*, 2 (1885) 437-447.

M. Clermont-Ganneau, "Mene, Tekel, Peres, and the Feast of Belshazzar," *AJSL* 3 (1886-87) 87-102. *(Trans. by Robert W. Rogers)*

*George Bertin, "'The Burning Fiery Furnace'," *BOR* 1 (1886-87) 17-21.

Hartwig Derenbourg, "The Greek Words in the Book of Daniel," *AJSL* 4 (1887-88) 7-13.

Anonymous, "The Book of Daniel: Outlines for a Course of Advent Lectures," *CM, N.S.*, 4 (1888) 232-246, 307-313.

Josiah Gilbert, "The Image and the Stone," *Exp, 3rd Ser.*, 9 (1889) 449-460.

Howard Crosby, "The Book of Daniel," *HR* 18 (1889) 540-541.

Wm. Schmidt, "Nebuchadnezzar's Dream. First Article," *ColTM* 10 (1890) 146-166.

Wm. Schmidt, "Nebuchadnezzar's Dream. Second Article," *ColTM* 10 (1890) 212-229.

(   ) Tyler, "'The Ancient of Days'," *EN* 2 (1890) 497-499.

John Poucher, "Is the Book of Daniel a Prophecy?" *MR* 72 (1890) 649-666.

James H. Breasted, "The Order of the Sentences in the Hebrew Portions of Daniel," *AJSL* 7 (1890-91) 245-252.

*H. B. Swete, "Requests and Replies," *ET* 3 (1891-92) 300. *[Alexander's visit to Jerusalem in Josephus and the Prophecies of Daniel]*

H. M. Jackson, "The Article 'Daniel' in the Encyclopedia Britannica," *PER* 5 (1891-92) 149-159.

William Hayes Ward, "Light on Scriptural Texts from Recent Discoveries. X. 'Mene, Mene, Tekel, Upharsin'," *HR* 26 (1893) 411-412.

*Buchanan Blake, "Darius the Mede, and the Seventy Weeks of Daniel," *ET* 5 (1893-94) 479.

G. H. Rouse, "Chaldeans," *ET* 6 (1894-95) 566. *[As referred to by Daniel]*

Ira M. Price, "Some Queries About the Book of Daniel," *BW* 6 (1895) 264-269.

J. A. Howlett, "The Book of Daniel," *DR* 117 (1895) 27-40.

J. E. H. Thomson, "Chaldeans," *ET* 7 (1895-96) 46-47. *[As referred to by Daniel]*

D. K. Auchterlonie, "Chaldeans,"*ET* 7 (1895-96) 94. *[As referred to by Daniel]*

*John P. Peters, "Notes on the Old Testament," *JBL* 15 (1896) 106-117. [3. The Nebuchadnezzars of Daniel, pp. 111-114]

J. A. Selbie, "The Four Empires of Daniel," *ET* 8 (1896-97) 32-33.

Anonymous, "Exegetical Suggestion and Opinion. Greek Words in Daniel," *CFL, O.S.,* 2 (1898) 212-213.

Edward Mack, "Problems in the Historical Section of the Book of Daniel," *USR* 10 (1898) 250-259.

Anonymous, "The Book of Daniel and the Monuments," *MR* 81 (1899) 636-640.

Anonymous, "Current Criticism and Interpretation of the Old Testament. The Greek Words in Daniel," *CFL, O.S.,* 3 (1899) 268-269.

M. B. Chapman, "The Book of Daniel," *MQR, 3rd Ser.,* 25 (1899) 561-568.

Ira M. Price, "The Book of Daniel," *BW* 14 (1899) 27-35.

Milton S. Terry, "Religious Lessons in the Book of Daniel," *BW* 14 (1899) 50-53.

William M. McPheeters, "Current Criticism and Interpretation of the Old Testament," *CFL, O.S.,* 3 (1899) 391-394. [Daniel in the Sabbath School; Specimens; The Difficulties of Daniel]

William M. McPheeters, "Bible Study," *CFL, O.S.,* 3 (1899) 425-431. [The Difficulties of the Bible; How Shall We Deal With Them? The Difficulties in Daniel; Darius the Mede; Our Primary Sources of Information; Prediction and Fulfillment—A Curious Question]

*George A. Barton, "The Story of Aḥiḳar and the Book of Daniel," *AJSL* 16 (1899-1900) 242-247.

J. Moore Lister, "'Mene, Mene, Tekel, Upharsin'," *ET* 11 (1899-1900) 234.

*Nathaniel Schmidt, "'Son of Man' in the Book of Daniel," *JBL* 19 (1900) 22-28.

S. R. Driver, "A Correction," *ET* 12 (1900-01) 187. *[Ref. Driver's Commentary on Daniel, p. 69]*

D. S. Margoliouth, "The Greek Words in Daniel," *ET* 12 (1900-01) 237-238.

A. van Hoonacker, "The Four Empires of the Book of Daniel," *ET* 13 (1901-02) 420-423.

J. A. Selbie, "The Book of Daniel," *ET* 13 (1901-02) 457.

Ed. König, "The 'Weeks' of Daniel," *ET* 13 (1901-02) 468-470.

William C. Wilkinson, "Those Famous Three Greek Words in the Book of Daniel," *HR* 44 (1902) 305-308.

Anonymous, "The Book of Daniel," *MR* 84 (1902) 128-130.

George C. M. Douglas, "The Book of Daniel," *PRR* 13 (1902) 224-253.

Camden M. Cobern, "The Modern Critical View of the Book of Daniel. From the Critic's Point of View," *HR* 46 (1903) 3-8.

Robert Anderson, "The Modern Critical Views of Daniel. From the Judge's Point of View," *HR* 46 (1903) 9-15.

Theo. Graebner, "A Last Word on the Seventy Weeks of Daniel," *TTD* 6 (1904) 14-19.

*T[heophilus] G. P[inches], "The Chaldeans of the Book of Daniel," *JRAS* (1904) 368-369.

*Edward M. Merrins, "The Abasement of Nebuchadnezzar," *BS* 62 (1905) 601-625.

John Urquhart, "'The Book of Daniel—The Critic and the Archæologist'," *CFL, 3rd Ser.,* 3 (1905) 104-120.

Joseph D. Wilson, "The Possibility of Self-deception," *CFL, 3rd Ser.*, 6 (1907) 34-39.

Joseph D. Wilson, "'The Third Year of Jehoiakim'," *CFL, 3rd Ser.*, 9 (1908) 94-97. *(Editorial Note)*

Joseph D. Wilson, "Professor Sayce of Daniel: A Correction," *CFL, 3rd Ser.*, 8 (1908) 427-430.

Margaret D. Gibson, "Mene, Tekel, Upharsin," *ET* 20 (1908-09) 562-563.

Joseph D. Wilson, "The 'Standard Bible Dictionary' on 'Daniel'," *CFL, 3rd Ser.*, 10 (1909) 220-224. *(Review)*

C. R. Vaughan, "The Little Horn," *USR* 21 (1909-10) 183-203.

Rayner Winterbotham, "The Four Empires of Daniel," *Exp, 7th Ser.*, 10 (1910) 428-439.

Rayner Winterbotham, "The Angel-Princes of Daniel," *Exp, 8th Ser.*, 1 (1911) 50-58.

*Joseph D. Wilson, "The Seventy Weeks of Daniel in the Hands of a Septuagint Translator," *CFL, 3rd Ser.*, 14 (1911-12) 351-352.

Anonymous, "Outline View of the Book of Daniel," *CFL, 3rd Ser.*, 14 (1911-12) 352-354.

*[Daniel S. Gregory], "The International Lessons in Their Historical Setting," *CFL, 3rd Ser.*, 14 (1911-12) 357-371. [Daniel, pp. 357-359]

Margaret D. Gibson, "Belshazzar's Feast," *ET* 23 (1911-12) 181.

George Buchanan Gray, "The Title 'King of Persia'," *ET* 25 (1913-14) 245-251.

Theophilus G. Pinches, "Fresh Light on the Book of Daniel," *ET* 26 (1914-15) 297-299.

*J. S. Ross, "Methodist Higher Criticism Arm-in-Arm with Infidelity. Paper No. II.," *CFL, 3rd Ser.*, 21 (1916) 161-163. [IX. Daniel, p. 163]

Anonymous, "The Spade, History, and the Bible," *HR* 71 (1916) 488. *(Review)*

Joseph Offord, "The Warning on the Wall of Belshazzar's Banquet," *PEFQS* 48 (1916) 196-201.

Anonymous, "Prof. R. D. Wilson's Volume on Daniel," *PSB* 10 (1916) #3, 23-27. *(Review)*

*Theo[philus] G. Pinches, "Two Late Tablets of Historical Interest," *SBAP* 38 (1916) 27-34. *[Background on Daniel]*

G. Frederick Wright, "The Historical Character of Daniel Vindicated," *CFL, 3rd Ser.*, 23 (1917) 320-321.

Robert Dick Wilson, "The Present State of the Daniel Controversy," *BR* 4 (1919) 226-246.

*Joseph Rauch, "Apocalypse in the Bible," *JJLP* 1 (1919) 163-195. [IX. Contribution of Apocalypse to the Religion of Israel. The Book of Daniel, pp. 188-195]

C. J. Ball, "Daniel and Babylon," *Exp, 8th Ser.*, 19 (1920) 235-240.

*W. St. Clair Tisdall, "Egypt and the Book of Daniel; or, What say the Papyri?" *Exp, 8th Ser.*, 22 (1921) 340-357.

*James A. Montgomery, "The Survival of the Tetragrammaton in Daniel," *JBL* 40 (1921) 86.

Edward J. Kissane, "Daniel and the Modern Critics," *ITQ* 17 (1922) 70-73.

Robert Dick Wilson, "Daniel Not Quoted," *PTR* 20 (1922) 57-68.

*Robert Dick Wilson, "Darius the Mede," *PTR* 20 (1922) 177-211.

[Robert Dick Wilson], "*The Continent* Attacks the Book of Daniel—Dr. Robert Dick Wilson Answers," *CFL, 3rd Ser.*, 29 (1923) 221-223.

R[obert] D[ick] Wilson, "The Influence of Daniel," *PTR* 21 (1923) 337-371, 541-584. [Objections of the Critics; Assumptions; Answers to Assumptions; I. The Argument from Silence; II. Traces of Daniel's Influence on Hebrew Literature up to 200 B.C.; III. Traces of Daniel's influence from 200 B.C. to 135 A.D.; IV. A Comparative Study of Daniel's Influence; Conclusions; The Approximation of Daniel and Enoch]

W. J. Erdman, "When did the Stone Strike?" *CFL, 3rd Ser.*, 30 (1924) 519-520.

William H. Bates, "The Book of Daniel," *CFL, 3rd Ser.*, 30 (1924) 520-522, 584-587.

*H. H. Rowley, "The Belshazzar of Daniel and of History," *Exp, 9th Ser.*, 2 (1924) 182-195, 255-272.

R[obert] D[ick] Wilson, "The Background of Daniel," *PTR* 22 (1924) 1-26.

R[obert] D[ick] Wilson, "The Prophecies of Daniel," *PTR* 22 (1924) 377-401. [The Fourth Kingdom; Darkness and Light in Daniel's Predictions; The Importance of Antiochus Epiphanes]

George Wilson Brent, "The Image of Nebuchadnezzar's Dream: A New Interpretation," *CFL, 3rd Ser.*, 31 (1925) 90-91.

Nathaniel Schmidt, "Daniel and Androcles," *JAOS* 46 (1926) 1-7.

H. H. Rowley, "The 'Chaldeans' in the Book of Daniel," *ET* 38 (1926-27) 423-428.

*[Jay Benson Hamilton], "International Sunday School Lessons for 1917: Studies in Isaiah and Daniel," *CFL, 3rd Ser.*, 23 (1927) 266-267.

R[obert] D[ick] Wilson, "On the Hebrew of Daniel," *PTR* 25 (1927) 177-199.

Geo. B. Michell, "'The Chaldeans'," *ET* 39 (1927-28) 45-46. *[In Daniel]*

H. H. Rowley, "'The Chaldeans'," *ET* 39 (1927-28) 188-189. *[In Daniel]*

W. R. Taylor, "Modern Criticism and the Book of Daniel," *CJRT* 5 (1928) 426-437.

W. O. E. Oesterley, "The Book of Daniel," *CQR* 110 (1930) 120-129. *(Review)*

*G. Ch. Aalders, "The Book of Daniel: Its Historical Trustworthiness and Prophetical Character," *EQ* 2 (1930) 242-254.

Henry S. Gehman, "The Armenian Version of the Book of Daniel and Its Affinities," *ZAW* 48 (1930) 82-99.

*P. E. Kretzmann, "Nabonidus—Belshazzar," *CTM* 3 (1932) 215.

Bruce M. Metzger, "The Book of Daniel," *CFL, 3rd Ser.*, 40 (1934) 218-220.

W. B. Stevenson, "The Identification of the Four Kingdoms of the Book of Daniel," *GUOST* 7 (1934-35) 4-8.

William Bell Dawson, "Prophetical Numbers in Daniel, in Relation to Celestial Cycles," *JTVI* 67 (1935) 129-149, 154-156. (Discussion, pp. 149-154)

H. H. Rowley, "Some Outstanding Old Testament Problems. IV. Some Problems in the Book of Daniel," *ET* 47 (1935-36) 216-220.

George S. Mellor, "The Time Element in Daniel's Prophecy of the Seventy Weeks," *CFL, 3rd Ser.,* 42 (1936) 221-228.

James H. Maxwell, "The Prophecy of Daniel," *CRP* 5 (1936) 109-120.

*Elias Newman, "Is the Time of Jacob's Trouble Past or Future? *A Study in the Misleading Conceptions of Present-Day Millennialists,*" *JTALC* 1 (1936) #2, 11-30.

*J. B. Orchard, "St Paul and the Book of Daniel," *B* 20 (1939) 172-179.

Michael J. Gruenthaner, "The Seventy Weeks," *CBQ* 1 (1939) 44-54.

Frank Zimmermann, "Some Verses in Daniel in the Light of a Translation Hypothesis," *JBL* 58 (1939) 349-355.

[W.(?)] A[rndt], "The Four Monarchies in Ancient Literature," *CTM* 11 (1940) 206-207.

H. C. Leupold, "Studies in Daniel," *JTALC* 5 (1940) 241-248, 320-327, 402-409, 481-487, 574-582, 642-649, 732-739, 823-831; 6 (1941) 177-184.

Ambrose Fleming, "The Visions of Nebuchadnezzar and Daniel, and the Seventy Weeks Prophecy," *JTVI* 73 (1941) 1-11, 26-28. (Discussions and communications, pp. 11-26)

John F. Walvoord, "Is the Seventieth Week of Daniel Future?" *BS* 101 (1944) 30-49.

E. G. Kraeling, "The Handwriting on the Wall," *JBL* 63 (1944) 11-18.

Edward J. Young, "The Accuracy of Daniel," *CO* 2 (1944-45) 105-108.

*Louis E. Knowles, "The Interpretation of the Seventy Weeks of Daniel in the Early Fathers," *WTJ* 7 (1944-45) 136-160.

Michael J. Gruenthaner, "The Four Empires of Daniel," *CBQ* 8 (1946) 72-82, 201-212.

*Charles C. Torrey, "'Medes and Persians'," *JAOS* 66 (1946) 1-15.

G. R. Beasley-Murray, "A Conservative Thinks Again about Daniel," *BQL* 12 (1946-48) 341-346, 366-370.

S[olomon] Zeitlin, "The Cryptic Numbers in Daniel," *JQR, N.S.*, 39 (1948-49) 321-324.

* Michael J. Gruenthaner, "The Last Kingdom of Babylon," *CBQ* 11 (1949) 406-427.

John B. Alexander, "New Light on the Fiery Furnace," *JBL* 69 (1950) 375-376.

H. H. Rowley, "The Unity of the Book of Daniel," *HUCA* 23 (1950-51) Part 1, 233-273.

Arnold Black Rhodes, "Studia Biblica. XX. The Book of Daniel," *Interp* 6 (1952) 436-450.

B. G. Sanders, "The Burning Fiery Furnace," *Theo* 58 (1955) 340-345.

Achille Brunet, "The Book of Daniel," *TD* 5 (1957) 58-63.

*James Muilenburg, "The Son of Man in Daniel and the Ethiopic Apocalypse of Enoch," *JBL* 79 (1960) 197-209.

Clyde T. Francisco, "The Seventy Weeks of Daniel," *R&E* 57 (1960) 126-137.

Frank Zimmermann, "Hebrew Translation in Daniel," *JQR, N.S.*, 51 (1960-61) 198-208.

H. H. Rowley, "The Meaning of Daniel for Today. *A Study of Leading Themes*," *Interp* 15 (1961) 387-397.

E. Schaller, "Meditation in the Book of Daniel," *JTLC* 4 (1964) #3, 19-26; #4, 23-29; #5, 1-18; 5 (1965) #1, 21-31.

*F. F. Bruce, "Josephus and Daniel," *ASTI* 4 (1965) 148-162.

Sidney Allen, "On Schedl's Attempt to Count the Days of Daniel," *AUSS* 4 (1966) 105-106

Anonymous, "Notes on Some Problems in the Book of Daniel," *BH* 2 (1965) #3, 15, 24. *(Review)*

*Werner E. Lemke, "'Nebuchadrezzar, My Servant'," *CBQ* 28 (1966) 45-50.

*David F. Payne, "The Place of Daniel in the Old Testament Eschatology," *Them* 4 (1967) #1, 33-40.

§406 *3.2.11.3.2 Studies Concerning the Aramaic Sections of Daniel*

*G. J. M'., "The Chaldee of Daniel and Ezra," *JSL, 3rd Ser.*, 12 (1860-61) 373-391.

William H[ayes] Ward, "The Aramaean Portion of Daniel, a Translation," *ONTS* 3 (1883-84) 90-91.

J. E. H. Thomson, "Was the Aramaic of Daniel Originally Eastern or Western?" *GUOST* 2 (1901-07) 52-54.

Charles C. Torrey, "Notes on the Aramaic Part of Daniel," *CAAST* 15 (1909) 239-282.

*Charles C. Torrey, "Stray Notes on the Aramaic of Daniel and Ezra," *JAOS* 43 (1923) 229-238. [Daniel, pp. 229-234]

G. R. Driver, "The Aramaic of the Book of Daniel," *JBL* 45 (1926) 110-119. *(Correction p. 325)*

H. H. Rowley, "The bilingual problem of Daniel," *ZAW* 50 (1932) 256-268.

H. H. Rowley, "Early Aramaic Dialects and the Book of Daniel," *JRAS* (1933) 777-805.

*Frank Zimmermann, "The Aramaic Original of Daniel 8-12," *JBL* 57 (1938) 255-272.

H. B. Rosen, "On the Use of the Tenses in the Aramaic of Daniel," *JSS* 6 (1961) 183-203.

§407 *3.2.11.3.3 Daniel as an Apocalyptic Writing*

*Joseph Rauch, "Apocalypse in the Bible," *JJLP* 1 (1919) 163-195. [IX. Contribution of Apocalypse to the Religion of Israel. The Book of Daniel, pp. 188-195]

R. B. Y. Scott, "I Daniel, the Original Apocalypse," *AJSL* 47 (1930-31) 289-296.

*E. W. Heaton, "The Affiliation of the Book of Daniel," *OSHTP* (1954-55) 23-24.

*David Noel Freedman, "The Flowering of Apocalyptic," *JTC* 6 (1969) 166-174. [II. The Book of Daniel, pp. 168-170]

§408 *3.2.11.3.4 Daniel and Revelation Compared*

†Anonymous, "Maitland—On the Prophetic Period of Daniel and St. John," *BCQTR, 4th Ser.*, 2 (1827) 497-498. *(Review)*

William Allen, "On the Designations of Time in Daniel and John:—The 1260 Days of Daniel and John, and the 1000 Years of John," *BRCR, N.S.*, 4 (1840) 35-53.

†Anonymous, "The Prophecies of Daniel and the Revelation of St. John," *TLJ* 9 (1856-57) 314-333, 484-500. *(Review)*

Anonymous, "The Prophetic Periods of the Apocalypse and Daniel," *TLJ* 11 (1858-59) 53-70.

P. S. D., "Analogy Between the Apocalypse of the Old Testament and that of the New," *JSL, 4th Ser.*, 6 (1864-65) 76-90.

W. Webster, "An Analogy of the Apocalypse of the Old and New Testaments," *JSL, 4th Ser.*, 6 (1864-65) 462-464.

*Lawrence Heyworth Mills, "Avesta Eschatology Compared with the Books of Daniel and Revelation," *Monist* 17 (1907) 321-346, 583-609.

Arthur Chase, "Apocalyptic Literature in the Bible," *ACM* 6 (1919-20) 62-71.

§409 *3.2.11.3.5 Studies Concerning Date, Authorship,*
Sources, and Authenticity

J. A. Paine, "As to the Age of Daniel," *BS* 46 (1889) 371-374. *[Study on Authenticity]*

T. K. Cheyne, "The Book of Daniel," *Exp, 4th Ser.*, 4 (1891) 399-400. *[Date of Daniel, Chapter 7]*

J. Dyneley Prince, "Professor Kamphausen on the Book of Daniel," *BW* 1 (1893) 355-358. *(Review)*

Joseph J. Lampe, "The Authenticity and Genuineness of Daniel," *PRR* 6 (1895) 440-480.

George A. Barton, "The Composition of the Book of Daniel," *JBL* 17 (1898) 62-86.

*D. S. Margoliouth, "Line of Defence of the Biblical Revelation. 4. The Argument from Silence," *Exp, 6th Ser.*, 2 (1900) 129-154. *[Evidence in Ecclesiasticus for Daniel in the Canon]*

William C. Wilkinson, "Questions of Authorship: The Book of Daniel," *HR* 43 (1902) 208-212.

Nathan Soderblom, "The Morals of Pseudepigraphy," *ET* 17 (1905-06) 45. *[Authorship of Daniel]*

R. E. Golladay, "The Authorship of the Book of Daniel," *ColTM* 26 (1906) 361-378; 27 (1907) 20-39, 74-102.

H. T. F. Duckworth, "The Origin of the Book of Daniel," *Exp, 7th Ser.*, 2 (1906) 224-233.

Anonymous, "Appendix to 'Did Daniel Write Daniel?'," *CFL, 3rd Ser.*, 15 (1912) 42.

*Robert Dick Wilson, "The Book of Daniel and the Canon," *PTR* 13 (1915) 352-408. [The Charge; Assumptions; Admissions of the Critics; Evidence, 1. Divisions, Number and Order, 2. The Use; Discussion; Conclusions]

*Robert Dick Wilson, "The Silence of Ecclesiasticus Concerning Daniel," *PTR* 14 (1916) 448-474.

W. St. Clair Tisdall, "The Book of Daniel: Some Linguistic Evidence Regarding its Date," *JTVI* 53 (1921) 206-245, 255. (Discussion, pp. 246-254)

R[obert] D[ick] Wilson, "Apocalypses and the Date of Daniel," *PTR* 19 (1921) 529-545.

R[obert] D[ick] Wilson, "The Origin of the Ideas in Daniel," *PTR* 21 (1923) 161-201. [Objections of the Critics; Assumptions; Answers to Objections; I. The Antiquity of the Ideas of Daniel; II. Daniel and Enoch; Special Conclusions; General Conclusions]

H[enry] S. Gehman, "The Hesychian Influence in the Versions of Daniel," *JBL* 48 (1929) 329-332.

*G. Ch. Aalders, "The Book of Daniel: Its Historical Trustworthiness and Prophetical Character," *EQ* 2 (1930) 242-254.

H. L. Ginsberg, "The Composition of the Book of Daniel," *VT* 4 (1954) 246-275.

H. H. Rowley, "The Composition of the Book of Daniel," *VT* 5 (1955) 272-276.

C[lifford] A. Wilson and M. E. M., "Where was the Book of Daniel Written?" *BH* 5 (1969) 90-94.

Stephen M. Clinton, "S. R. Driver and the Date of Daniel," *JC&S* 5 (1969) #2, 30-41.

§410 *3.2.11.3.6 Literary Criticism of the Books of Nehemiah and Ezra (Includes Studies on Ezra-Nehemiah Synthesis)*

Anonymous, "Sir Isaac Newton on Ezra and Nehemiah," *JSL, 4th Ser.,* 1 (1862) 456-468; 2 (1862-63) 143-162.

I.*[sic]* W. Bosanquet, "The Newtonian Theory of the Books of Ezra and Nehemiah," *JSL, 4th Ser.,* 2 (1862-63) 421-431.

Daniel Henry Haigh, "Coincidence of the History of Ezra with the First Part of the History of Nehemiah," *SBAT* 2 (1873) 110-113.

*Joseph Jacobs, "The Nethinim," *BOR* 2 (1887-88) 66-71, 100-104.

George S. Goodspeed, "Ezra and Nehemiah," *BW* 1 (1893) 208-219.

*[Nathaniel] Burwash, "Analytical studies in the English Bible: Brief outline of Ezra, Nehemiah, Esther, with Haggai and Zechariah," *CMR* 5 (1893) 87-104.

J. A. Selbie, "Ezra-Nehemiah," *ET* 8 (1896-97) 509-511.

T. K. Cheyne, "The Times of Nehemiah and Ezra," *BW* 14 (1899) 238-250.

Robert Dick Wilson, "Royal Titles in Antiquity: An Essay in Criticism," *PTR* 2 (1904) 257-282.

Robert Dick Wilson, "Royal Titles in Antiquity: An Essay in Criticism, Article Two," *PTR* 2 (1904) 465-497.

Robert Dick Wilson, "Royal Titles in Antiquity: An Essay in Criticism, Article Three," *PTR* 2 (1904) 618-664.

Robert Dick Wilson, "Royal Titles in Antiquity: An Essay in Criticism, Article Three, Part II," *PTR* 3 (1905) 55-80.

Robert Dick Wilson, "Royal Titles in Antiquity: An Essay in Criticism, Article Four," *PTR* 3 (1905) 238-267.

Robert Dick Wilson, "Royal Titles in Antiquity: An Essay in Criticism, Article Five," *PTR* 3 (1905) 422-440.

Robert Dick Wilson, "Royal Titles in Antiquity: An Essay in Criticism, Article Six," *PTR* 3 (1905) 558-572.

[George] A[dam] Smith, "Ezra and Nehemiah," *Exp, 7th Ser.*, 2 (1906) 1-18.

E. L. Curtis, "Ezra Studies. An Appreciation," *YDQ* 7 (1911-12) 127-129. *[Ezra-Nehemiah] (Review)*

*Edward J. Kissane, "The Historical Value of Esdras I.-III.," *ITQ* 15 (1920) 126-138.

Edward J. Kissane, "The Mission of Esdras," *ITQ* 17 (1922) 219-230. *[Ezra-Nehemiah]*

Harry Pressfield, "Ezra and Nehemiah—Contemporaries or Successors?" *MQR, 3rd Ser.*, 48 (1922) 336-339.

M. Bailey, "Levitical Legend from the Persian Period," *JBL* 46 (1927) 132-138.

Andrew Thomson, "An Inquiry Concerning the Books of Ezra and Nehemiah," *AJSL* 48 (1931-32) 99-132.

P. Romanoff, "An Unrecorded Religious Revolution in Bible Times," *JBL* 56 (1937) ix-x.

J. Stafford Wright, "Ezra and Nehemiah," *EQ* 12 (1940) 35-47.

C. C. Keet, "Some Problems in Ezra Nehemiah," *OSHTP* (1943-44) 35-39.

W. M. F. Scott, "Nehemiah—Ezra?" *ET* 58 (1946-47) 263-267.

C[harles] C. Torrey, "The 'Books' of Ezra and Nehemiah," *JBL* 66 (1947) iv.

C. T. Wood, "Nehemiah—Ezra," *ET* 59 (1947-48) 53-54.

Sidney Jellicoe, "Nehemiah—Ezra: A Reconstruction," *ET* 59 (1947-48) 54.

Martin W. Leesberg, "Ezra and Nehemiah: A Review of the Return and Reform," *CTM* 33 (1962) 79-90.

J[ulian] Morgenstern, "The Dates of Ezra and Nehemiah," *JSS* 7 (1962) 1-11.

*Ralph Walter Klein, "Old Readings in I Esdras: The List of Returnees from Babylon (Ezra //Nehemiah 7)," *HTR* 62 (1969) 99-107.

§411 *3.2.11.3.6.1 Literary Criticism of the Book of Ezra - General Studies*

*Anonymous, "Chronological Remarks on the Book of Ezra," *MMBR* 4 (1797) 334-335.

*G. B., "On Daniel and Ezra, Compared with the Inscription at Behistun," *JSL, 3rd Ser.,* 5 (1857) 170-172.

*G. J. M'., "The Chaldee of Daniel and Ezra," *JSL, 3rd Ser.,* 12 (1860-61) 373-391.

*Arthur C. Hervey, "The Chronology of Ezra II and IV. 6-23," *Exp, 4th Ser.,* 7 (1893) 431-443.

*Arthur C. Hervey, "The Chronology of Ezra IV. 6-23," *Exp, 4th Ser.*, 8 (1893) 50-63.

James Oscar Boyd, "The Documents of the Book of Ezra," *PRR* 11 (1900) 414-437.

James Oscar Boyd, "The Historicity of Ezra," *PRR* 11 (1900) 569-607.

*Henry H. Howorth, "Some Unconventional Views on the Text of the Bible. II. *The Chronology and Order of Events in Esdras A, compared with and preferred to those in the Canonical Ezra,*" *SBAP* 23 (1901) 305-325, 328-330. (Remarks by R. B. Girdlestone, Paul Ruben, and M. Gaster, 325-328)

R. B. Girdlestone, "Notes on the Comparative Value of the two Recensions of Ezra," *SBAP* 24 (1902) 14-16. (Reply by H[enry] H. Howorth, pp. 16-20)

*C[harles] C. Torrey, "The First Chapter of Ezra in Its original Form and Setting," *AJSL* 24 (1907-08) 7-33.

C[harles] C. Torrey, "The Aramaic Portions of Ezra," *AJSL* 24 (1907-08) 209-281.

C[harles] C. Torrey, "The Ezra Story in Its Original Sequence," *AJSL* 25 (1908-09) 276-311.

William H. Bates, "The Book of Ezra," *CFL, 3rd Ser.*, 28 (1922) 129-130.

*Charles C. Torrey, "Stray Notes on the Aramaic of Daniel and Ezra," *JAOS* 43 (1923) 229-238. [Ezra, pp. 234-238]

*William R. Eichhorst, "Ezra's Ethics on Intermarriage and Divorce," *GJ* 10 (1969) #3, 16-28.

§412 3.2.11.3.6.2 Studies concerning Date, Authorship, Sources, and Authenticity

James Oscar Boyd, "The Composition of the Book of Ezra," *PRR* 11 (1900) 261-297.

*Harold M. Wiener, "The Relative Dates of Ezra and Nehemiah," *JPOS* 7 (1927) 145-158.

*S. Japhet, "A Supposed Common Authorship of Chron. and Ezra-Neh. investigated Anew," *VT* 18 (1968) 330-371.

§413 *3.2.11.3.6.3 Literary Criticism of the Book of Nehemiah - General Studies*

†Anonymous, "The Devotion of Nehemiah," *LQHR* 55 (1880-81) 149-170. *(Review)*

*George St. Clair, "Nehemiah's South Wall, and the Locality of the Royal Sepulchres," *PEFQS* 21 (1889) 90-102. [Nehemiah's Night-ride; The Rebuilding of the Walls and Gates; The Route of the Processionists; Incidents of the History; The 'Broad Wall' at Jerusalem; Twin Sacred Mounts at Jerusalem]

Howard Crosby, "Nehemiah Spiritualized," *HR* 17 (1899) 82-83.

*Hinckley G. Mitchell, "The Wall of Jerusalem according to the Book of Nehemiah," *JBL* 22 (1903) 85-163.

*H[enry] H. Howorth, "Some Unconventional Views on the Text of the Bible. V. *The Genealogies and Lists in Nehemiah*," *SBAP* 26 (1906) 25-31, 63-69, 94-100.

William H. Bates, "The Book of Nehemiah," *CFL, 3rd Ser.*, 28 (1922) 254-255.

J. A. Bewer, "Josephus' Account of Nehemiah," *JBL* 43 (1924) 224-226.

Harold H. Rowley, "Nehemiah's Mission and its Background," *BJRL* 37 (1954-55) 528-561.

*H[arold] H. Rowley, "Sanballat and the Samaritan Temple," *BJRL* 38 (1955-56) 166-198.

*Anonymous, "Nehemiah and Sanballat. Papyri Discoveries in Egypt and Palestine help to clarify and confirm the Biblical record of the days following the Exile," *BH* 1 (1964) #4, 3-7, 13.

§414 *3.2.11.3.6.4 Studies concerning Date, Authorship, Sources, and Authenticity*

*Harold M. Wiener, "The Relative Dates of Ezra and Nehemiah," *JPOS* 7 (1927) 145-158.

*S. Japhet, "A Supposed Common Authorship of Chron. and Ezra-Neh. investigated Anew," *VT* 18 (1968) 330-371.

§415   *3.2.11.3.7 Literary Criticism of the Books of 1 and 2 Chronicles - General Studies*

C. H. Mead, "Criticism on the Book of Chronicles," *DTQ, N.S.,* 2 (1883) 123-125.

*Francis Brown, "The Books of Chronicles, with especial reference to the Books of Samuel," *AR* 1 (1884) 405-426.

*J. F. McCurdy, "Uzziah and the Philistines," *Exp, 4th Ser.,* 4 (1891) 388-396.

S. R. Driver, "The Speeches in Chronicles," *Exp, 5th Ser.,* 1 (1895) 241-256; 2 (1895) 286-308.

Valpy French, "The Speeches in Chronicles: A Reply," *Exp, 5th Ser.,* 2 (1895) 140-152.

W. E[mery] Barnes, "The Midrashic Element in Chronicles," *Exp, 5th Ser.,* 4 (1896) 426-439.

W. E[mery] Barnes, "The Religious Standpoint of the Chronicler," *AJSL* 13 (1896-97) 14-20.

W. E[mery] Barnes, "Chronicles a Targum," *ET* 8 (1896-97) 316-319.

W. E[mery] Barnes, "Requests and Replies," *ET* 9 (1897-98) 464. *['The Chronicles a Targum']*

W. E[mery] Barnes, "Errors in Chronicles," *ET* 9 (1897-98) 521.

Theodore G. Soares, "The Import of the Chronicles as a Piece of Religio-Historical Literature," *AJT* 3 (1899) 251-274.

Willis J. Beecher, "Is the Chronicler a Veracious Historian for the Post-Exilian Period?" *CFL, O.S.,* 3 (1899) 385-390.

*Eb. Nestle, "The Genealogy in St. Matthew and the Septuagint of Chronicles," *ET* 11 (1899-1900) 191.

Willis J. Beecher, "Is the Chronicler a Veracious Historian for the Post-Exilian Period? II.," *CFL, N.S.,* 1 (1900) 20-25.

Willis J. Beecher, "Is the Chronicler a Veracious Historian for the Post-Exilian Period? III.," *CFL, N.S.,* 1 (1900) 77-84.

Kerr D. Macmillan, "The Latest 'Criticism' of The Chronicler," *CFL, N.S.,* 1 (1900) 172-173.

J. A. Howlett, "Wellhausen and the Chronicler," *DR* 126 (1900) 391-411.

*Willis J. Beecher, "The International Lessons in Their Literary Setting. III.," *CFL., N.S.,* 8 (1903) 128-133. [Variant Delimitations of the Historical Narratives; The Narrative of Saul's Last Battle; Duplications of Samuel in Chronicles; The Credibility of Chronicles; The Narrative of the Accession of David in Hebron; The Narrative of the Kingdoms of David and Ishbosheth; The Narrative of David's Becoming King of Israel]

*Willis J. Beecher, "The International Lessons in Their Literary Setting. V.," *CFL., N.S.,* 8 (1903) 252-259. [Outline of the Reign of David; The Temple Narratives in 1 Chronicles; The Fortieth Year of David; The Rebellions of Absalom and Sheba; The Events in their Order]

*Daniel S. Gregory, "International Lessons in Their Historical Setting,"*CFL, N.S.,* 1 (1904) 412-424. *[Chronicles]*

Henry H. Howorth, "Some Unconventional Views on the Text of the Bible. VI. *Chronicles*," *SBAP* 27 (1905) 267-278.

Grainger Tandy, "The Books of the Chronicles: An Elementary Study in Biblical Criticism," *ICMM* 3 (1906-07) 79-91.

*William H. Bates, "David's Purchase of the Temple Site from Araunah," *CFL, 3rd Ser.,* 9 (1908) 159-161.

W. Harvey-Jellie, "The Problem of the Hebrew Chronicler," *HR* 56 (1908) 134-136.

*Kemper Fullerton, "The International Critical Commentary on Genesis, Chronicles, and the Psalms," *HTR* 5 (1912) 20-109. *(Review)*

[Jay Benson Hamilton], "International Sunday School Lessons for 1917: Studies in the Book of Chronicles," *CFL, 3rd Ser.,* 23 (1917) 219-221.

Charles C. Torrey, "The Chronicler's History of the Return Under Cyrus," *AJSL* 37 (1920-21) 81-100.

*A[dam] C. Welch, "The Significance for Old Testament History of a New Tablet," *ET* 35 (1923-24) 170-172. [BM 21,901]

*Leroy Waterman, "Some Repercussions from Late Levitical Genealogical Accretions in P and the Chronicler," *AJSL* 58 (1941) 49-56.

Frank Zimmermann, "Chronicles as a Translated Book," *JBL* 63 (1944) vi.

*Charles C[utler] Torrey, "'Medes and Persians'," *JAOS* 66 (1946) 1-15.

Gillis Gerleman, "Studies in the Septuagint. II. Chronicles," *AULLUÅ, N.S.*, 43 (1947) #3, 1-46.

Frank Zimmermann, "Chronicles as a Partially Translated Book," *JQR, N.S.*, 42 (1951-52) 265-282, 387-412.

Charles C. Torrey, "An Edition of the Chronicler's History," *JBL* 72 (1953) viii.

W. Rudolph, "Problems of the Books of Chronicles," *VT* 4 (1954) 401-409.

David N[oel] Freedman, "The Chronicler's Purpose," *CBQ* 23 (1961) 436-442.

Robert D. Culver, "Peculiarities and Problems of Chronological Method and Text in the Book of Chronicles," *BETS* 5 (1962) 35-41.

Frederick L. Moriarty, "The Chronicler's Account of Hezekiah's Reform," *CBQ* 27 (1965) 399-406.

*Werner E. Lemke, "The Synoptic Problem in the Chronicler's History," *HTR* 58 (1965) 349-363.

Jacob M. Myers, "The Kerygma of the Chronicler. *History and Theology in the Service of Religion*," *Interp* 20 (1966) 259-273.

S. Japhet, "Interchanges of Verbal Roots in Parallel Texts in Chronicles," *Léš* 31 (1966-67) #3, n.p.n.; #4, n.p.n.

*Peter R. Ackroyd, "History and Theology in the Writings of the Chronicler," *CTM* 38 (1967) 501-515.

*Ralph W. Klein, "New Evidence for an Old Recension of Reigns," *HTR* 60 (1967) 93-105.

*Leslie C. Allen, "Further Thoughts on an Old Recension of Reigns in Paralipomena," *HTR* 61 (1968) 483-491.

Ralph W. Klein, "Supplements in the Paralipomena: A Rejoinder," *HTR* 61 (1968) 492-495.

James Donald Shenkel, "A Comparative Study of the Synoptic Parallels in I Paraleipomena[sic]* and I-II Reigns," *HTR* 62 (1969) 63-85.

§416   *3.2.11.3.8 Studies Concerning Date, Authorship, Sources, and Authenticity*

Anonymous, "Date of the Books of Chronicles," *BFER* 12 (1863) 783-801.

W[illiam] H[enry] Green, "Date of the Books of Chronicles," *PRev* 35 (1863) 499-520.

[Samuel Ives] Curtiss [Jr.], "Sources of the Chronicler," *ONTS* 3 (1883-84) 158-160.

Kerr D. Macmillan, "Concerning the Date of Chronicles," *PRR* 11 (1900) 507-511.

*Willis J. Beecher, "The International Lessons in Their Literary Setting. III," *CFL., N.S.,* 8 (1903) 128-133. [Duplications of Samuel in Chronicles; The Credibility of Chronicles, pp. 129-130]

C[harles] C. Torrey, "The Chronicler as Editor and as Independent Narrator," *AJSL* 25 (1908-09) 157-173, 188-217.

W[illiam] F[oxwell] Albright, "The Date and Personality of the Chronicler," *JBL* 40 (1921) 104-124.

H. Neil Richardson, "The Historical Reliability of the Chronicles," *JAAR* 26 (1958) 9-12.

David F. Payne, "The Purpose and Methods of the Chronicler," *F&T* 93 (1963-64) 64-73.